A HISTORY

OF THE

INDIAN VILLAGES AND PLACE NAMES

IN PENNSYLVANIA

WITH NUMEROUS HISTORICAL NOTES AND REFERENCES

By DR. GEORGE P. DONEHOO

Author of "Pennsylvania—A History," "History of Harrisburg and Dauphin County," "Harrisburg, The City Beautiful, Romantic and Historic," and Numerous Special Articles on Archaeology, History and Ethnology; Collaborator of the Bureau of American Ethnology, Smithsonian Institution, Handbook of American Indians. Former Secretary of the Pennsylvania Historical Commission, Former State Librarian; Member of the Pennsylvania Historical Society and Many Other Historical and Scientific Societies.

With an Introduction by the Hon. Warren K. Moorehead, United States Board of Indian Commissioners; Curator of the Department of American Archaeology, Phillips Academy, Andover, Mass., Author of The Stone Age in North America, The American Indian, and many other books relating to the American Indian.

HISTORY
OF THE
INDIAN PLACE NAMES
OF
PENNSYLVANIA

INTRODUCTION

T AFFORDS me great pleasure to write a few words in preface to Dr. Donehoo's important contribution with reference to Indian Place Names and their meanings. The work by Dr. Douglas Lithgow in New England and Mr. William Wallace Tooker, along similar lines in the lower Hudson region, together with a few other publications, are all that we have of consequence in this important field.

Pennsylvania occupied a unique position in ancient times, there being, we are sure, several cultures in the pre-Colonial period.

Our Colonial documents, historical works and the narratives of early travelers indicate considerable variation in language and custom throughout the extent of Pennsylvania. The archaeological researches of Dr. Arthur C. Parker, Dr. Donehoo himself and others indicate a very wide range in primitive arts. One observes marked differences between Monongahela Valley, Susquehanna, West Branch and Schuylkill forms of artifacts. Whether the same tribes found by the first Europeans occupied these territories in pre-historic times has not yet been determined.

Dr. Donehoo's title indicates that his observations are confined to the historic period. In future years, when funds are available for extensive archaeological research throughout Pennsylvania, we shall be able to more accurately answer some of the important questions which arise.

Was there common origin of the Algonkin and Iroquoian stocks? Was there archaic Algonkin and also archaic Iroquoian? Dr. Parker has found very old and primitive burials in northeastern New York state. The people who made these interments had passed away before the advent of the White Race. No one has attempted to set dates, but the field men, acting independently of the language students, believe that the occupation of certain Pennsylvania valleys began in early times. Whether this should be set down as 2,000, 3,000, or even 5,000 years, nobody knows.

There is a tendency now among both archaeologists and ethnologists to be rather conservative. What we need above everything else is more thorough explorations and a careful study of all the objects found in one site and their comparison in the *ensemble* with those of another site.

The important historical research, presented by Dr. Donehoo in this volume, will be of great benefit to future students. It seems to me that this is the proper method; to begin with our known historic period and work backwards—archaeology taking the place of history as soon as we pass the period where the first French came in contact with the Indians.

To make my meaning clear, permit me to offer this illustration. Let us take a known site on one of the rivers. It occupies a pleasant location, as did practically all the Indian towns. The first readers, or travelers, find at this place Indians of the Andaste. The records made at the time—brief or lengthy, as the case may be, cover the facts so far as history is concerned. Yet some of us have assumed that because the Andaste were found there in 1640, therefore the site was always Andaste. Is this correct? Digging in the site may indicate that there are two cultures, the upper one being Andaste and the lower something else. This has already been indicated in the Southwest and the Ohio Valley. It may hold true in the river valleys of Pennsylvania. It seems to me, therefore, that students of Indian occupation have a most important field in that territory lying between the Ohio and the Delaware.

It was in the Delaware Valley that a most patient worker, Earnest Volk, found very primitive implements in the Trenton sands. And yet on the surface lived the Delaware Indians—whose culture was quite different from that of the people represented by the crude artifacts dug up by Mr. Volk during 35 years of thorough research.

Dr. Donehoo has done us all a very great service in perpetuating the Indian Place Names and I commend his volume to the public. He should now work back into the strictly pre-historic epoch—a most interesting, important and fascinating field as yet untouched.

WARREN K. MOOREHEAD.

PREFACE

HE author of this work was first impressed with the great number of Indian place names in Pennsylvania, and also with their historical importance, while engaged in the work of gathering material for a series of articles for the Handbook of American Indians, since published by the Bureau of American Ethnology, of the Smithsonian Institution.

No state in the entire Nation is richer in Indian names, or in fact, in Indian history. These Indian names are full of music, but, of far greater importance, they are full of history.

As the great Algonkian tribes, the Delaware and Shawnee, migrated westward across the mountain ridges from the Delaware and Susquehanna to the Ohio, and to the setting sun, they left behind them a trail sprinkled with blood, as they retreated before the advancing tide of Anglo-Saxon civilization. Time has kindly blotted out the trail of blood, and in its place has put a trail of beautiful names, marking the pathway along which they built their villages, lived, loved, hunted, fought—and then vanished forever into the shadows of the western hills. Their wigwams no longer dot the beautiful Valley of Wyoming, their canoes have glided down the waters of the "Beautiful River" into the "Land of the Lost Ones," but they have left behind them the names, which linger like sweet melodies, over the mountains and valleys and streams of the land which they loved.

> "Ye say they have all passed away,
> That noble race and brave;
> That their light canoes have vanished
> From off the crystal wave;
> That 'mid the forest where they roamed,
> There rings no hunter's shout;
> But their name is on your waters,
> And ye cannot wash it out."

And, what a blessing it is, that we "cannot wash them out." The Red Man gave names, which meant something, to the mountains, rivers and creeks. The good American custom of making a place name a means of personal immortality was unknown to the Indian. The great ridges of cloud enshrouded mountains, the sweeping rivers, the sparkling little creeks were given names, worthy of what they were, rather than of what some man imagined he was worthy of. "What's in a name?" A whole world of melody, sentiment and of history. That which we call a rose, by any other name would smell as sweet—but, not so when the name is a NAME.

> "Who hath not owned, with rapture-smitten frame,
> The power of grace, the magic of a name?"

▼

Substitute for such names as Kittatinny, Allegheny, Susquehanna, Juniata, Ohio, Wyoming, Shenandoah, any of our modern place names—such as Smith's River, Harrighan's Fields, Frick's Run—and then say that they would "smell as sweet."

Various attempts have been made to "improve" upon the historic Indian place names, with sad results. The invasion of Pennsylvania and Western New York, by the School Teacher, of Classical training, was about as disastrous to the Indian names in the region invaded, as was the invasion of the Scotch-Irish disastrous to the Indian himself. The "Trail of the School Teacher" of the early days, can be traced as clearly as the "Trail of the Iroquois." The Iroquois left behind him a trail of wrecked and ruined wigwams and cabins. The Classic School Teacher left behind him a trail of wrecked and ruined place names, over which sprang up a series of such monuments as, Athens, Sparta, Rome, Troy, Utica, Virgil, Ovid, Homer, Carthage, etc. The Connecticut Company caused more disaster than the mere Pennamite War. The historic Indian name of Tioga had to don the Cap and Gown and become Athens. When the good, and simple-hearted Mary becomes Maryie, clad in silks and laces, an act of foolish snobbery has been committed. But when historic Tioga becomes Athens, a crime against history has been done.

It is to be hoped, for the sake of history, as well as in the interest of mere sentiment, that no attempts will be made in the future to improve upon historic place names, Indian or otherwise. The author hopes that the entire matter of giving, or changing, place names in the State of Pennsylvania, will be rendered impossible by an Act of the Legislature, which shall put such matters in charge of a Historical Commission. Vandalism of any sort should be prevented by law.

No one can realize more fully than does the author, the difficulty in attempting to trace Indian place names back to their correct form. Many of the names of Indian tribes and villages were first recorded by traders and explorers who had no correct knowledge of the Indian languages. These early scribes, of different races, wrote the Indian name as it sounded to their ears—Dutch, Swedish, French, Irish, English, as the case might be. As a consequence the German form of the name of an Indian tribe or village, bears little resemblance to the form recorded by a French or Irish writer. Consequently the various forms, being so entirely different, have been taken as belonging to different tribes, or villages, when they were all names of the same tribe or place. This led to the multiplication, not only of villages, but also of tribes, when but one was referred to. When a name had to pass from an Indian to an Irish trader, then to a French soldier, and then to a German missionary before it was finally recorded—the result can be imagined.

Another difficulty is due to the great changes which have taken place since the time when the name was given. The landscape, topography and other natural features have changed entirely. As Indian place names are usually descriptive, being given because of some natural feature, such as a mountain or river had to the eyes of the beholder, these names do not seem to fit the place as it looks now. Such a name as "Beautiful Meadows" may now belong to a place which is covered

vi

with cinder heaps, or "The Grove of Pine Trees" may belong to a place which is now destitute of trees, but covered with banks and stores.

Again, some names were given because of incidents which happened at or near the place to which they were given. The incident is now forgotten, and as a consequence the meaning of the Indian name is impossible to trace.

But, great as these difficulties now are, they will never be less. Many clues, as to the correct meaning of names, can be found in the Traders' Journals, on old maps, in early land grants, in the records and letters of the early missionaries, and sometimes the clue can be found in the study of a place as it once looked, when covered with trees or sweeping meadows, or waving cornfields.

The author has not only gone over every available source of information for the place names in this State, but has also walked over nearly every Indian trail from the Delaware to the Ohio, over the exact course as given in the Traders' Journals, with the earliest maps as guides. A list of the authorities used is given with each article, and a general Bibliography follows at the conclusion of the work. The various writings of Heckewelder, Zeisberger, Post, Gist, Croghan, Weiser and others who explored the region in the early days, have been of great value, not only in fixing the location, but also in getting the various forms of the Indian names.

The only books dealing with the Indian Place Names in Pennsylvania are the two small publications of Heckewelder and Boyd. The former's work was edited by William C. Reichel, a most thorough student, and a well informed historian; the latter work by S. G. Boyd is limited in the extent of its information. Neither of these works made any attempt to include the names of the historic Indian villages which have passed away, leaving not even their name behind, in the place where they were situated.

The author has attempted to find every Indian place name in the entire State. When possible, the meaning is given. The more important names, such as Allegheny, Ohio, Shamokin, Susquehanna, Juniata, etc., are given more space because around them clusters the Indian history of the State. At the end of each article is given a list of synonyms, for the use of students who wish to give a more exhaustive study to any particular name. The author fully realizes the defects and limitations of this book. It would not be possible to give within the limits fixed, a full history of each place and at the same time cover all of the Indian place names in the State. A few of the names do not belong to this State, but are included because the place was very closely associated with the development of history in Pennsylvania.

While the work is intended for the use of more critical students of the Indian history of Pennsylvania, it is at the same time, intended for the use of the pupils in the Public Schools, who now have no book whatever in which they may gather material concerning the Indian villages and place names of the State. The work will also be of value to students of other states, as many of the Indian names in this State have been spread over many of the states to which the Delaware and Shawnee migrated, after they had forever left the region east of the Ohio.

In addition to all of the Indian names, mentioned in the Archives and Records, in the Journals of traders and explorers, noted on the early maps and mentioned in letters, the various places of importance on Indian and Traders' trails, which do not have an Indian origin, but which are very closely associated with Indian history, are also included. Among these place names are: Edmund's Swamp, Dunning's Sleeping Place, Jack's Narrows, Black Log, etc.

The author has, no doubt, missed some names which should be included. For any information concerning such names, the author will be thankful. The names of famous Indian chiefs are not included, unless their name was given to some place. The author hopes in the future to publish a work dealing with Persons, as this work deals with Places.

The list of Indian place names in use at present is given simply for the use of any who may be interested. Many of these names are not historic, and are of doubtful Indian origin. Some of them are made up of Indian sounds, rather than Indian words. Names which do not belong in the State are given to places which might well have been given names of real historic significance.

In the Geographic America of Peter Lindestrom, published by the Swedish Colonial Society in 1925, the translator, Amandus Johnson, adds an Appendix on "Indian Geographical Names" (pages 299-408). This very fine list should be studied in conjunction with the notes in this book.

The author is indebted to many friends for assistance in collecting these notes. He is under special obligation to C. Hale Sipe, the author of "The Indian Chiefs of Pennsylvania," for his careful reading of the proofs, and making many suggestions and corrections.

Notwithstanding the care used in copying the many Indian names used in the book, no doubt many errors will be found. Blank pages are inserted for the use of students who may desire to add additional notes and references, and for recording any errors which may be discovered.

THE AUTHOR'S INTRODUCTION

HILE it is not the purpose of the author of this Handbook to give a history of the American Indian, nor of the tribes which inhabited Pennsylvania, it is, nevertheless, necessary that a few facts bearing on the history of the Indian race be understood, in order that the various events in the history, as given under the various titles in this book, be correctly apprehended.

It is essential to a right understanding of any people that we know something of the early history of that people. During the first few centuries after the discovery of the American continent, the view generally accepted, was, that the Indians had sprung from some of the European races, within comparatively recent times. Nor has this once popular fallacy entirely disappeared, however much it is opposed to the real facts in the case.

When the continent was first discovered it was inhabited by a people divided into linguistic groups having no relation whatever to each other. Differing, not only in language, but also in customs, religion and in every element which enters into the life of human beings. Such a radical difference could not possibly have been produced save after many centuries of separation of these tribes from each other, and from the parent stock from which they sprang. It must ever be borne in mind that when the first Europeans landed on the shores of the New World that the Delaware and Iroquois were as widely separated, by language and customs, as the Chinaman and American of today. It took many, many centuries to produce such a separation.

The name Indian was bestowed upon the aboriginal inhabitants of this continent by Christopher Columbus, in a letter written in February, 1493, in which he speaks of the "Indios" he had with him. It was the belief of Columbus that he had reached the shores of India, in his voyage across the Atlantic, hence the name. This name, however, unsatisfactory it may be, has always been, and no doubt always will be, the common designation of the race of aboriginal inhabitants of the New World—which after all may be the Old World.

Various names have been suggested to take the place of this common name, but none of these have been found which are satisfactory. The one which has perhaps had the widest use is, Amerind—a word composed of the first syllables of the words, American Indian. This name has been used by several authorities, but it has never come into popular use. On account of the widespread use of the term Indian, in literature, as well as in geographical and botanical names, it is likely to remain as the permanent name of the American Indian.

Owing to the lack of critical knowledge of the Indian and of the various Indian languages, many curious errors resulted on the part of the early explorers and settlers, in their attempts to record the names of the various tribes with which they came in contact, or of which they heard. Sometimes a tribe was known by a name of reproach, or ridicule, which was bestowed upon it by its enemies. The name Sioux is derived from an Algonkian word which means "snake-like," and was a term of reproach. The tribe known as Sioux by the Algonkian tribes, had as its real name "Dakota," which means "friend," or "ally." And again, the name of a tribe or village was recorded as it sounded to the ears of a Frenchman, a Dutchman, an Englishman or a German. As a result the various recorded names bore no resemblance whatever to each other, and were often made to apply to entirely different tribes or places, where but one was really mentioned. There are, for example, about 53 different names for the tribe known as the Catawba.

The first careful students of the life, language and customs and character of the Indian were the French Jesuit and Sulpician missionaries. The story of the self-sacrifice, the devotion, the true heroism of these noble men is one of the most interesting chapters of American history. The missionaries of France followed the soldier wherever he went. Into the wilds of Canada, along the shores of the northern lakes, across the trackless prairies, down the waters of the Mississippi and along the Gulf of Mexico these soldiers of the Cross followed the Lilies of France. These faithful men looked at the Indian through the eyes of the student, as well as through the eyes of the spiritual teacher. They were most careful in their observations of the language, the manners and customs and the religion of the people among whom they labored. Father Sebastian Rale, who worked among the Abnaki on the Kennebec River, gave up his life among the people, whom he had faithfully served for thirty years, in 1724, when his mission was destroyed by the New Englanders. He left behind him a Dictionary of the Abnaki language, in the preparation of which he had spent years of patient toil. James Mooney says of this Dictionary, "It ranks as one of the greatest monuments of our aboriginal languages."

The missionaries of the Protestant churches were none the less heroic as spiritual teachers, or recorders of careful observations concerning the Indians among whom they labored. Roger Williams, Thomas Mayhew, John Elliott, Samuel Danforth, John Cotton, David Brainerd, John Heckewelder, David Zeisberger, C. F. Post and many others, made up an army of devoted men who not only sought to lead the Red Men of the mountains and forests to the light of spiritual truth, but who rendered an invaluable service to the student of history by leaving behind them the records of the manners and customs, the life and character, the language and religion of the various tribes among which they labored. No higher tribute has been paid to these men than is paid in the statement of James Mooney, who says, "In the four Centuries of American history there is no more inspiring chapter of heroism, self-sacrifice and devotion to higher ideals than is afforded by the Indian Missionaries. To the student, who knows what infinite forms of cruelty, brutishness and filthiness belonged to savagery, from Florida to Alaska, it is beyond question, that, in spite of sectarian limitations and the shortcomings of individuals, the Missionaries have fought a good fight" (Handbook of American Indians, Part 1, 908.) This tribute is that of a critical student, of the Bureau of Ethnology, and not the opinion of a religious enthusiast.

It may be safely said, in addition to this statement which bears on the value of the spiritual mission of the Indian Missionary, that if the records and various literary works of these Missionaries were blotted out there would be absolutely nothing of real authoritative value left for the student of the American Indian of the early centuries after the settlement of the country.

In striking contrast to this picture of unselfish devotion and scholarly labor of Catholic and Protestant Missionary, is the picture of the selfishness and cruelty of the great majority of the early traders and settlers with whom the Indians were brought in contact. To the vast majority of these the Indian was a barbarian and a savage, to be used only as instruments in the mad lust for gold. These knew nothing and cared nothing about the Indian as a social, or even as a human being. The Indians were looked upon by the first settlers at Jamestown in the light of the barbaric dreams of India's oriental splendor. William Penn was one of the first Englishmen to realize that this new race of men were not wild barbarians, but social human beings, who were to be dealt with as such.

To the great majority of the traders and settlers of Pennsylvania, Virginia and Maryland, the Indian was—an Indian. To the great majority of the settlers who swept over the mountain ridges at the commencement of the XVIII Century an Indian was simply a member of one of the Heathen tribes which occupied the Promised Land, and as such it was the duty of the Elect to blot them from the face of the earth, as Joshua of old had blotted out the Hivites and the Jebusites. As a consequence of this attitude the writings and observations left by these early settlers is of little real historic value. The entire period of the white invasion of the Indian lands of Pennsylvania is simply a monotonous record of debauchery of the Indian by the Trader, and stealing of Indian land by the settler. Every so-called Indian massacre, or uprising, from the first landing on the Delaware to the last landing on the Yukon has been caused by one of these two causes. Ignorance of the Indian and the traffic in rum has drenched the American continent with blood.

The method of classifying the various Indian tribes, as now adopted by all authorities, is that of similarity of language. The term Linguistic Family, or Group, is used to designate a group of cognate languages, which are languages descended from a common ancestral speech. All of these groups or families are given names ending in "ian," or "an." The tribal name, for example, is Algonkin, Algonquin, while the family name of the group to which this tribe belongs is Algonkian, or Algonquian; Iroquois is the name of the Confederation of tribes belonging to the Iroquoian family or group. By this method of classification there were on the continent of North America Fifty-six linguistic groups of Indians. It must be distinctly understood that these 56 groups of languages are not 56 dialects of a common language, but 56 entirely different languages which bear no relation whatever to each other. Fifty-six linguistic groups as totally different as English and Chinese. A Dakota could no more easily understand a Delaware than an Irishman could understand a Russian, or a Chinaman. The two languages have absolutely nothing in common.

In the history of Pennsylvania but three of these Linguistic Groups are met with, the Algonkian, the Iroquoian and the Siouan (the family to which the Sioux of the west belong), and the latter only through the Catawba and Tutelo. All of the tribes having any connection with the development of the early history of the State belonged to the Iroquoian and the Algonkian linguistic groups. Among the former were the Six Nations of the Iroquois Confederation, the Erie, the Andaste (or Conestoga), the Cherokee, the Neuter, and the Wyandot, and among the latter the Delaware, Shawnee, Miami and a few of the other Algonkian tribes, which had very slight relations to the affairs of the Province. The Miami are nearly always referred to in the records of Pennsylvania as Twightwees. Of the actual inhabitants of the territory now included by Pennsylvania may be mentioned the Conestoga (or Susquehannock, or Andaste), the Delaware (or Lenni Lenape, or Loups), the Erie (or Cat, or Panther Nation), the Cherokee (or Talligewe), the Neuter, the Shawnee, the Seneca, the Conoy, the Nanticoke, and in later times (after the French and Indian War and during the Revolution), the various tribes of the Iroquois, popularly known as "Mingo," without regard to tribal connection. All of these are noted under their names in the body of this book.

Many of the early writers, and a few writers of today, speak of the Indian as being nomadic, with no fixed habitation. Such was not the condition of the Indian before the coming of the white man. The Indian tribes were sedentary, occupying the same territory for many years, and spreading out from their native habitat as the tribe increased in numbers. Migration of tribes from the main body to which they belonged was most uncommon. The Siouan family, whose main body was west of the Mississippi, had small tribes which had become widely separated from the parent stock. The Catawba were in the Carolinas, the Tutelo in Virginia and the Biloxi in Mississippi. But such separation was very unusual.

The various tribes, or village inhabitants, did not spend all seasons of the year in the same place. They would be far away from their regular village during the hunting season, and at another place during the fishing season. The Delawares went to the Ohio to hunt and to fish, and would be gone for perhaps a whole year, and then would return, to their village on the Susquehanna, or on the Delaware. Because of this seasonal migration many of the early explorers imagined that the Indians were nomadic. But these people would invariably return to the place from which they had gone to hunt, or fish, or make salt or maple sugar, after the season was over. They were nomadic in the same sense that the American of today is nomadic, in spending the winter in Florida and the summer in the Adirondacks, or in making the various temporary migrations which man has always made and always will make. As a consequence of this change of place of residence, by tribes as well as by village inhabitants, the various early travellers and explorers, would count and give different names to the same tribe or village, as it was found at various reasons at different places. The same Indians were seen on the Delaware during the shell-fish season, by one traveller and a name given to the tribe or village, the number of inhabitants estimated, and the same group of Indians would be found in the Susquehanna region during the hunting season, as they lived in their temporary quarters, and would be given another name by another explorer, and so on during the various other changes of residence of exactly the same tribe. As a consequence the number of Indian villages during a certain period would be four or five times greater than it was in reality, and the Indian population would be four or five times larger than it actually was, by thus counting the same Indians over and over again. As a result of this method of estimating the Indian population the number of Indians living in Pennsylvania, and elsewhere, was very greatly exaggerated. There were vast expanses of territory in Pennsylvania in which there was not a single permanent Indian village, and in which there never had been one.

The two factors which drove the Indian from his habitation were the introduction of fire-arms and the use of the horse. These two instruments of war and travel made changes in the condition of the Indian which we can little realize. The settlements along the seaboard drove the tribes of this region into the interior of the continent, and brought about a series of inter-tribal wars which had been unthought of before the coming of the white man, and the consequent use of the horse and fire-arms. Previous to the changes which were thus brought about the various tribes of Indians which were first met with by the Europeans had occupied the region in which they were then living for countless generations. In fact it is now the accepted belief of nearly all ethnologists and archaeologists, that the various earth-works, called Indian mounds, were made by the ancestors of the Indians who occupied the region in which they are situated within historic times. Nothing has ever been found in any of these mounds which was not in use by the Indians living in the region when the Europeans were first brought into contact with them. The Cherokee and Shawnee were "mound builders" even after the discovery of the continent.

The false idea of the size of the Indian population on the continent, when it was first discovered, has been referred to. The Indian population, in comparison with the extent of the territory occupied, was never very great. The first discoverers were led into false beliefs as to the extent of the population of the interior, by finding great bodies of Indians along the sea-shore, or at the entrance of the large rivers, where the Indians from many places had come to fish, or to make salt, or for some other purpose. The early colonists imagined that the interior was as thickly populated as were these gathering places. But, this was not the case Bancroft in his History of the United States gives the estimate of the population of the continent before its occupation by the Europeans as, 90,000 Algonkian; 17,000 Iroquois; 3,000 Catawba; 12,000 Cherokee; 3,000 eastern Dakota; 50,000 Mobilian Confederacy; Uchee 1,000; Natchez 4,000, or "in all not more than one hundred and eighty thousand souls." This simply for the region east of the Mississippi. In 1765, George Croghan gave a list of the fighting men of the different tribes in North America, as follows, "Mohawks 160; Oneidos 300; Tuscaroras 200; Onondagas 260; Cayugas 200; Senecas 1,000;—making 2,120 warriors of the Six Nations. Delawares on the

Susquehanna, 600; Delawares on the Ohio and its tributaries, 600; Shawnee, on the Scioto, 300; Chippewas, 800; Ottawas, 550; Illinois, 300; Wyandots, 250, and then gives an estimate of the Sioux as 10,000'' (Early Western Travels, I. 166).

In 1748, Conrad Weiser, at Logstown, requested the deputies of the various tribes present to give him a list of the fighting men of the various tribes settled on the Ohio, with the following result: ''The Senecas, 163; Shawonese, 162; Owendaets, 100; Tishgechroanu, 40; Mohawks, 74; Mohickons, 15; Onodagers, 35; Cajukas, 20; Oneidos, 15; Delawares, 165; in all 789.'' None of the other estimates given by men who had actual knowledge of the various Indian tribes are larger than these figures, and yet many people have the idea, due in a great measure to the false statements of unauthoritative writers, that the Ohio and Susquehanna Rivers were swarming with Indians during this period. A body of 100 Indian warriors, because of their open method of fighting and their rapid change of position, gave to the white troops, who came in contact with them, the impression of many times that number. Hence in some conflicts where the number of Indians taking part was estimated at 1,500, there were probably 200 or 300 Indians taking part. And often when the number of Indian dead found on the field was but a few, the awful slaughter which was reported was accounted for by saying that the Indians carried nearly all of their dead from the field, when, perhaps they left every body where it had been slain. Raiding parties of 20 or 30 Indians were large. Many of the war parties consisted of four or five warriors, who would cross the entire states of Pennsylvania and Virginia on their war expeditions to the Catawba country in the Carolinas.

These few introductory statements may enable the reader to more clearly understand some of the statements made in the historical notes which follow, in the various articles. The author hopes at some future time to write a history of the Indians who occupied the territory now embraced by the State of Pennsylvania. The purpose of this work is to give a history of the Place Names, which are of Indian origin, rather than to give a systematic history of the people who have left these monuments which are more enduring than those of bronze or marble.

INDIAN VILLAGES AND PLACE NAMES

ACHSINNING, ASSINSING, see *Standing Stone.*

ACTAGOUCHE. The name of a former Indian village, mentioned in the "Deposition of Stephen Coffen," in 1747. "An Indian village, 15 miles west of Chebucta" (Col. Rec. Pa., VI, 9, 1851). The location of this village is not known.

ADEEKY, also **ADIGA, ATIGA, ATIGUE, ATTIQUE,** etc. See *Kittanning.*

ADJOUQUAY. A former Indian village on the North Branch of the Susquehanna, at the mouth of the Lackawanna, "14 miles above Wyoming" (now Wilkes-Barre). The village probably stood on the south shore of the Lackawanna, near Pittston. The Iroquois requested the Provincial Council to build a fort at this point, during the Indian hostility following Braddock's defeat, in 1755. The Council, after giving the matter serious consideration, decided that the fort which had been built at Shamokin (now Sunbury) was sufficient protection for all of that region. Fort Augusta, which had been built on the site of the old Indian town of Shamokin, was easily reached from all points on the North Branch, consequently no fort was built at "Adjouquay" at this time. Some time in 1772 a fort was built on the east bank of the Susquehanna, called "Pittston Fort," and another one was built in West Pittston, which was called "Jenkins' Fort." Both of these forts occupied prominent places in the Indian hostility of the Revolutionary period. The army of General Sullivan passed through this place Aug. 1, 1779, and encamped about a mile above the mouth of the Lackawanna. See *Lackawanna.* Consult: Col. Rec. Pa., VII, 157, 159, 182, 184, 1851; Frontier Forts of Pa., I, 445, 1896.

AKANSEA, see *Allegheny.*

ALGONKIN, or **ALGONQUIN.** The word has various interpretations. Hewitt suggests that it is probably from the Micmac algoomeaking, or algoomaking, "at the place of spearing fish and eels," that is, from the bow of a canoe. The term was first used in reference to a small Algonkian tribe living on the Gatineau River, east of the present city of Ottawa, Quebec. Later the term included a number of other tribes in the region. From the commencement of the settlement of the continent, the Algonkian tribes were friendly towards the French. The Iroquois, by the use of firearms, drove the Algonkins from the St. Lawrence. Many of the bands along the Ottawa River fled westward to Mackinaw and Michigan, where they became known in later history as Ottawas. The great Algonkian family, to which belong the Delaware, Shawnee, Conoy, Nanticoke, Powhatan, Sauk, Fox, Illinois, Wea, etc., occupied a very large area on the continent. Their territory extended from the shores of the Atlantic to the Rocky Mountains, and from Newfoundland to the region of Pamlico Sound. The tribes of this great linguistic group were the first to be met with by all of the early settlers on the Atlantic seaboard. The great majority of the place names in Pennsylvania, of Indian derivation, are of Algonkian origin. The same is true of nearly all of the Indian names in the Eastern and Middle Western States. Consult: Bibliography of the Algonquian Languages, Pilling, 1891; History of the U. S., Bancroft, II, 86, 1888; Handbook of American Indians, II, 38, 1907.

ALLAQUIPPA. The name is probably derived from alloquepi, "a hat." The form given by Denny is alluquep. The name of a woman chief, to whom the title of "Queen" was given by the early explorers and traders. There is no evidence whatever that this very much talked of Indian woman ever held such a position as "Queen" of the Indians on the Ohio, or anywhere else. While her name is of Delaware origin, she is spoken of as being a Seneca by Conrad Weiser, who no doubt knew the difference between a Seneca and a Delaware. He had no trouble in deciding who were Iroquois and who were Delawares at any of the Indian Councils later on in the Indian policy of Colonial Pennsylvania. From the number of places credited as being former villages of this famous woman, she must have spent most of her time in travel—having as its motive the naming of various mountains, streams, islands and villages. She is first mentioned in 1748 by Conrad Weiser, in the Journal of his mission to the western Indians. "We dined in a Seneka Town where an old Seneka Woman Reigns with great Authority" (Col. Rec. Pa., V, 349, 1851). The following year Celoron de Bienville mentioned the village and its woman ruler. He says, "She regards herself as a Sovereign, and is entirely devoted to the English" (Jes. Rel., LXIX, 175, 1902). The situation of this village was probably at the mouth of Chartiers Creek, where the Borough of McKees Rocks is now situated. There is some reason, however, for thinking that she was living at, or near, "the Forks," near the spot where Fort Duquesne was afterwards built, just before the coming of the French to the Ohio. When the English were driven away from the fort, which was building by Edward Ward, Allaquippa removed to the mouth of the Youghiogheny, at McKeesport, where she was living when Washington and Gist passed through, on their way to the French forts, in 1753. At that time she said, "She would never go down to the river Allegheny to live, except the English built a fort" (Darlington's Gist, 86, 1903). Upon his return from the French forts at Venango and LeBoeuf, Washington stopped to see her, and made her a present of "a watch (match) coat and a bottle of rum, which latter was thought much the better present of the two" (Washington's Jour. of 1753). When Washington was encamped at the Great Meadows in 1754, "Queen Aliquipa" and the

Half King, with about 25 or 30 families of Indians joined him. Just before the battle at Fort Necessity, July 3, 1754, Allaquippa and the Half King, Tanachharison, with nearly all of the Indians, left Washington's camp and went to Aughwick, the home of George Croghan. Here Allaquippa died near the close of 1754, as George Croghan says in a letter, written Dec. 23, "Alequeapy ye old quine is Dead and Left Several Children" (Arch. Pa., II, 218, 1852). Allaquippa is often confused with Allaguipas, the father of Kanuksusy (Capt. New Castle), whose widow lived near the town of Bedford in 1755—after the date of Allaquippa's death (Col. Rec. Pa. VI, 588, 1851). The mother of New Castle could not have been Allaquippa, as Croghan and others mention her death at Aughwick in the fall of 1754. The Allaguipas' Gap, near Bedford, and the ridge of mountains in the same region, were not named for Allaquippa but for Allaguipas. There is no record that Allaquippa ever lived in the region of Bedford, or Ray's Town, as it was first known. The island in the Ohio River, just below Pittsburgh, was once known as Allaquippa's Island. The creek, now known as Chartiers Creek, was also once named for this Indian woman, who had a village at its mouth. There is now a Borough in Beaver County, with the spelling "Aliquippa," which perpetuates this name in the Ohio region.

Allaquippa's Town.—Fry and Jefferson, map, 1755. **Allequippas.**—Traders map, 1753. **Aliquippa.** — Darlington's Gist (1753), 86, 1893. **Queen Aliguippa's.**—Gist's map, 1753.

ALLEGHENY. The name is probably a corruption of Alligewi-hanna, "stream of the Alligewi." Some authorities give Alligewi-sipu, "River of the Alligewi." Others give the name a meaning similar to that of Ohio, "fair, or beautiful, river," but the former derivation has more historic authority. The Alligewi, or more correctly, Talligewi, was a tribe which, according to the traditions of the Delaware, once occupied the region east of the Mississippi drained by the Ohio River and its various tributaries. Heckewelder mentions this tradition, and gives an extensive notice to the wars between the Lenape (Delaware) and the

Mengwe (Iroquois) with the Talligewi. According to this tradition, the Lenape lived in the western part of the continent. For some unknown reason they decided to migrate eastward. After a very long journey of "many nights encampment," which may mean many years, they at last reached the "Namaesi-sipu," or "River of Fish," which has been identified with the Mississippi. Modern students, however, identify it with the Detroit River. The Lenape here met the Mengwe, who were also migrating eastward. The spies which the Lenape had sent into the unknown country returned with the report that the region to the eastward was occupied by a powerful tribe, which had many fortified villages along the great rivers and lakes. The people were called the Alligewi, and were very fierce and warlike. The warriors were strong, very tall and possessed great bravery. The Lenape then sent messengers forward to the Alligewi, asking permission to settle in their country, which was called Alligewining. (Loskiel gives the form Alligewinengk, and the meaning, "a land into which they came from distant parts." See Loskiel, Moravian Missions, I, 127, 1794). This request was refused, but they were given permission to pass through the country of the Alligewi, in order to reach the region to the eastward. When the Lenape began to cross the "River of Fish," their great numbers alarmed the Alligewi, who made an attack upon them, driving them back over the river with great loss of life. The Lenape then considered what was best for them to do. The Mengwe, who had been spectators of the conflict with the Alligewi, offered to help the Lenape in their struggle, if, after the country was conquered, they would be allowed to share it with the Lenape. This offer was accepted, and the united forces began the fight for conquest. The fortified places along the rivers fell one by one and, after many years of severe fighting, the Alligewi were driven southward. The Mengwe (Iroquois), in accordance with the agreement, took the lands to the north, in the vicinity of the Geat Lakes, and the Lenape (Delaware) took the lands to the south of that chosen by the Mengwe.

At a later period the Lenape again divided, some crossing the mountains and settling along the lower Susquehanna and Potomac, and others going eastward to the river whose English name, given many years afterwards, they were to bear. See *Delaware*. It is now generally accepted by many of the leading authorities on American Ethnology that the Alligewi, or Talligewi, were the Cherokee of historic times. The ancestors of the Cherokee inhabited the Ohio region, and were the builders of the mounds found along the Ohio and its tributaries. They were driven southward by the Iroquois, a kindred Iroquoian group of tribes. Consult: Heckewelder, Indian Nations, 46, 1876; Cyrus Thomas, The Problem of the Ohio Mounds, 1889; Handbook of American Indians, Part I, 246, 1907.

Possibly no river on the American Continent has seen as many changes in the races of Red Men living along its shores as has this most historic stream. In the Jesuit Relation for 1635 (33, 1858) the "Rhiierrhonons," identified as the Erie, and the "Ahouenrochrhonons," identified as the Wenro, are mentioned as living south of Lake Erie and the Iroquois domain. This would place them on the upper waters of the Allegheny. There is no doubt but that the Erie, or Panther Nation, spread over the region southward from Lake Erie to the Ohio. According to Herrman's map of 1670, the "Black Minquaas" are placed in the region west of the Allegheny Mountains, and on the Ohio or "Black Minquaas River." According to the Jesuit Relation, both of these peoples, the Wenro and the Black Minquas, traded with the people upon the upper Delaware, going back and forth by the trail to the waters of the West Branch, down to Shamokin (now Sunbury), then up to Wyoming (now Wilkes-Barre) and across to the Delaware Water Gap, near the present city of Easton. The legend on Herrman's map reads, "A very great river called the Black Minquaas River—where formerly those Black Minquaas came over the Susquehanna—as far as Delaware to trade, but the Sasquahana and the Sinnicus Indians went over and destroyed that very great Nation." See also, Handbook of American Indians, Part 2, 659, 944, 1907.

There is also reason for thinking that the upper Ohio was also inhabited by one of the Siouan tribes. The stream was called the "River of the Akansea," because the Akensea had formerly lived upon it. The Akansea, Arkansas, or Kwapa, was a Siouan tribe. Those who went down the Mississippi were given the name Kwapa, or "people living down the river," while those who ascended the Mississippi were called Omaha, or "people living up the river." See, "Siouan Tribes of the East," James Mooney, 1894.

The Iroquois name, "O-hee-yo," or "O-hee-yee," which has been given the meaning of "Fair" or "Beautiful River," was translated by the French into "La Belle Riviere," by which name it is always mentioned in the French documents and writings of the early period. This meaning of the Iroquois name has been disputed by several authorities. See *Ohio*. It is well to remember that the stream now known as the Allegheny was considered by all of the early writers and explorers as being the main stream, of which the present Ohio was the continuation. The Monongahela was looked at as being a tributary of this stream, and not as being an independent river. As a consequence, the various names apply to the present Allegheny and Ohio, as being one continuous river. On the map of Cornelli, published in Venice in 1690, the river is noted as, "R Ohio or la Belle Riviere, said by savages to have its source near Lake Frontenac." In the "Proces Verbal," of the taking of possession of Louisiana by Seur de la Salle, April 9, 1862. The names "Ohio" and "Alighin" are both given to the same stream. In the account of Father Anastasius Douay, the priest who was with la Salle on his last expedition down the Mississippi River, it is stated that they passed the mouth of the "Quabache," meaning the Ohio, on the 26th of Aug., 1688. He also says, "The Akansas were formerly stationed on the upper part of one of those rivers, but the Iroquois drove them out by cruel wars some years ago" (Wilderness Trail, Hanna, Vol. II, 99, 1911).

On the map of Lewis Evans, 1755, the Shawnee name "Palawa-Thepiki"

is noted. The Journal of Rev. David Jones states that "the Shawnees call it Pellewa Theepee, i. e., Turkey River" (Hanna, Wilderness Trail, II, 98, 1911). While the name "Palawa-Thepiki" can be translated "Turkey River," the name can also be from the Delaware, Palliwi, "different," and thuppeek, "cool water," the meaning being different cool water." To an Indian passing from the waters of the Ohio to those of the Allegheny this name would be a significant one. It would be just as significant in passing from the Mississippi to the Ohio. Johnson states in his Shawnee vocabulary that the Shawnee name for the Ohio means "Eagle River." This cannot be, as the Shawnee name for eagle is Wapalaneathy (see Archives of W. Va., 258. 1906). The Delawares called the river, after their migration from the Susquehanna in about 1720-27, "Kit-hanne," or "Kittan," meaning "great stream," hence the name of their village "Kittaning," "on the great stream." See *Kittanning*.

The name Allegheny has various forms. On the map of Lewis Evans it is "Allegeny"; Scull's map, 1770, "Allegany," which form is still used in various places in northwestern Penna., as Port Allegany; Pownall's map, 1776, following the map of Evans, gives "Allegeny"; Gist's map, 1753, gives the name of the river as "Allegheny," and the name of the mountains as "Aligany"; Howell's map, 1793, gives "Allegeny" for both the river and the mountains.

Other forms now used are: Allegan, a county and village in Michigan; Allegany, a county in Maryland and a county and town in New York; Port Allegany, a town in Pennsylvania; Alleghany, counties in North Carolina and Virginia; Alleghany, a mining camp in California, established by settlers from western Pennsylvania. The official form of the name, as used by the U. S. Geological Survey, for the river, mountains and county in Pennsylvania is that given at the head of this article—ALLEGHENY.

For reference, consult, under various names given: Darlington's Gist, Pittsburgh, 1893; Hanna, Wilderness Trail, New York, 1911; Heckewelder, Indian Nations, Philadelphia, 1876; Colonial Records and Archives of

Penna.—chiefly the First Series; the various maps in Appendix I-X, Third Series.

Alleghany is the name of a creek which enters the Schuylkill River from the west in' Berks County, below Reading. This creek is noted on Scull's maps of 1758 and 1770 as "Allegany."

ALLEGHENY. The name given in the early years of the 18th Century to the entire region drained by the Ohio River and its various tributaries, west of the mountains. Before this region had been explored by the English it was designated by the general term, "at Allegheny," or "at Ohio." The French documents and letters always refer to the region as "at Ohio" or "La Belle Riviere." **Alleegaeening.**—Cartlidge (1730), Arch. Pa., I. 254, 1852. **Alleeganeeing.**—Cartlidge (1730), Arch. Pa., I., 261, 1852. **Alleghening.**—Gordon (1731), Arch. Pa., I., 302, 1852. **Allegheny.**—Gordon (1729), Arch. Pa., I., 243, 1852. **Alligewinengk.**—Loskiel (1794), Hist. Mor. Miss., I., 127, 1794. **Alligewinenk.**—Zeis., Hist. Ind., N. A., 33.

ALLEGHENY INDIANS. A popular designation of a geographical group of Indians, comprising the Delaware, Shawnee, Iroquois and other tribes living within the region noted above. The term applied to all of the Indians living west of the waters of the Susquehanna, within the region drained by the Ohio. That the term did not refer simply to the Indians living on the Allegheny River is shown by its use in reference to those living on the Conemaugh, Allegheny, Ohio, Beaver and other streams west of the mountains. The term is first used by James LeTort and James Logan in 1729 (Arch. Pa., 245, 1852). For other references, consult: Col. Rec. Pa., V, 434, 608, 627, 663; Arch. Pa., I, 262, 299, etc.

ALLEGHENY MOUNTAINS. This name is often applied to the entire Appalachian mountain system, which runs along the eastern part of the continent. The name, however, as used by all of the early explorers and traders, applied to the chief range of the Appalachian system. This range, which is the most lofty and the hardest to cross, is the third range from the Ohio Valley, the first range being the Chestnut and the second the Laurel. All of the early

maps and explorers' journals so note these three ridges. The Allegheny Mountain crosses the State about ten miles west of Bedford, Schellberg being near the foot of the eastern slope, and is the range through which the P. R. R. passes at Kittanning Point, at the "Horseshoe Bend." The Allegheny Mountain presented the greatest difficulties in the way of all of the early traders, road makers and railroad builders in reaching the Ohio from the East. Washington, Gist, Braddock, Post, Forbes and all others found this great mountain barrier the one supreme difficulty in the path to the Ohio region. The French, who had reached the Ohio by way of the Allegheny, from the North, thought that it was impossible for the English to send an army over the lofty summits of the "impassable Alleghenies." There are but three natural "gaps" through this grand mountain range within the State of Pennsylvania—that cut by the Youghiogheny, by the Conemaugh, and, far to the northward, by the West Branch and the Allegheny. The Indians took this northern course long before the coming of the white race to the continent. According to the Jesuit Relation, the "Black Minquaas" and the Wenro traded on the upper waters of the Delaware long before the coming of the traders to the Ohio. The course followed by these prehistoric travelers was from the upper Allegheny to the West Branch, to Shamokin (now Sunbury), up to Wyoming (now Wilkes-Barre) and across to the Water Gap on the Delaware, near Easton. This was, beyond doubt, the earliest path through the Allegheny Mountains. Zeisberger followed it in part in 1767, when he went to the mouth of the Tionesta. The next path, southward, was across from Kittanning to the West Branch, at Clearfield, or to the Juniata, over Kittanning Point, and down to the Susquehanna. South of this path was the "main road to Allegheny" of the traders and Indians after the migration of the Delaware and Shawnee to the Ohio, early in the 18th Century. The course of this path was from Harrisburg, by various "gaps" in the Blue Mountains, to Bedford and then by way of Ligonier and the Kiskiminetas Valley to Kittanning, or Shannopin's Town (now Pittsburgh). The southern trail ran from Cumberland, Md., over the mountains to Mount Braddock, Connellsville, Mount Pleasant and on to Pittsburgh. This was the course followed by General Braddock in 1755, General Forbes taking the middle path, by way of Bedford and Ligonier.

Aligany.—Gist (1753) map, in Darlington's Gist. **Allegany.**—Croghan (1749) Arch. Pa., II. 31, 1852. **Allegene.**—Post (1762) Arch. Pa., IV. 95, 1853. **Allegeni.**—Louis Evans, map, 1755. **Allegeny.**—Louis Evans, map, 1749. **Allegheny.**—Conrad Weiser (1748) Arch. Pa. II. 13, 1852.

ALLEGUIPPAS, or ALLAGUIPAS.

Allaguippas was an Iroquois chief, whose son, Cashiowaya, or Kanuksusy, rendered efficient service to the English during the French and Indian War. When this son was a small child, his parents had presented him to William Penn, at New Castle, Del., in 1701. On the 22nd of August, 1755, Governor Morris, at a Council with the Indians, at Philadelphia, formally adopted him, with these words, "In token of our Affection for your parents & in expectation of Your being a useful man in these Perilous Times, I do in the most solemn manner adopt you by the name of Newcastle, and order you to be called hereafter by that name which I have given you, because in 1701, I am informed that your parents presented you to the late Mr. William Penn at Newcastle" (Col. Rec. Pa., VI, 589, 1851). Captain New Castle, as he was afterwards called, served the Province in many important missions during the period of Indian hostility, both as a messenger and as an interpreter. The gap in the mountains east of Bedford was named for the father of New Castle, and not for Allaquippa, as has been stated from the earliest period of white settlement of the region west of the Susquehanna. At the time when Gov. Morris gave Cashiowaya the name of Newcastle, it is stated "The Governor addressed himself to Kanuksusy (New Castle), the son of ol. Allaguipas, whose Mother was now alive and living near Ray's Town (Bedford)." Allaquippa was at that time dead, having been buried nearly a year previously at Aughwick. (See Allaquippa). Such being the case, she could not have been the mother

of New Castle. The similarity in the names of Allaquippa and Alleguippas caused this error to the early map makers. The mountain noted on Scull's map of 1770 as "Alleguippy Ridge," which is a continuation of the Warriors Ridge north of Bloody Run, and the gap noted as "Allaguippy's Gap" were named, no doubt, for Allaguippas, the Iroquois chief, who lived near Ray's Town (Bedford). There is no mention of Allaquippa ever having lived at this place. The place of residence of Allaquippa can be traced in the Colonial Records from her first notice in 1748 until her death in 1754. When she died at Aughwick, she left several small children for George Croghan to look after. Captain New Castle died in 1756, at which time he was spoken of, in the Bethlehem Diary, as "the faithful old chief" (Mem. Mor. Church, I, 234, 1870). It is not possible for him to have been the son of Allaquippa.

Allegrippus, a station on the P. R. R. in Blair County, is a more correct form of the name of Alleguippas than that now given to the mountain near Bedford.

ANALOMINK. A creek in Monroe County, flowing into the Delaware from the West. Since 1737 it has been known as Brodhead's Creek—so named from Daniel Brodhead, who settled upon it at that time. The origin of the Indian name is not known.

Analoming.—Del. Water Gap, Brodhead, 242, 1872. **Analomink.**—Minute Book, "K" (1735), Arch. Pa., Third Ser., I, 56, 1894. **Anatoming.**—Hist. map of Pa., 1875. (an error.) **Broadhead's.**—Louis Evans, map, 1749, and 1759. **Broadheads Creek.**—State map, 1912.

ANTIETAM. A creek which has its source in Franklin County. Flows southward into the Potomac. Meaning unknown.

Andiatom.—Minute Book "K" (1734), Arch. Pa., Third Ser., I, 39, 1894. **Anteetem.**—Arch. Pa. Third Ser. I, 402, (1762), 1894. **Antietam.**—Howell, map, 1792. **Antietiun.**—Louis Evans, map, 1749.

ANTIGOE. A creek mentioned by Post in 1758. Was evidently on the western side of the Allegheny River. May have been Sandy Creek. Arch. Pa., III, 541, 1854.

APPALACHIAN. The name given to the mountain system along the eastern part of the continent. Probably derived from the Choctaw a'palachi, "people on the other side." Apalachee was one of the native tribes of Florida. They were visited by Narvaez in 1528 and by DeSoto in 1539.

While they were agricultural and very industrious, they were noted as great fighters. They resisted the Spanish until after 1600, when they were conquered. The name Appalachian is sometimes used as being synonymous with Allegheny, in reference to the mountain system. This is an error. Appalachian is the general designation of the entire system of mountains; Allegheny is the name of one of the main ridges of this system.

Governor Hamilton said in 1750, in a letter to the Board of Trade, "The Apalaccian Mountains—would make a good boundary between the English and French Dominions in North America" (Arch. Pa., II, 62, 1852).

Apalaccian Mountains. — Hamilton (1751), Arch. Pa., II, 63, 1852. **Appalaccin Hills.**—Easton Council (1758), Col. Rec. Pa., VIII, 204, 1852. **Montagnes des Apalaches.**—Bellin's map, 1744. **Mont. d' Apalaches.**—VanKeulen's map, 1720.

Franquelin's map of La Salle's discoveries, 1684, notes the "Apalatche" village, in Florida, but does not note the mountain system.

APOLACON. A creek, whose source is in Susquehanna County and which enters the North Branch, near Apalachin, Tioga County, N. Y. Heckewelder gives the derivation of the name from Apelogacan, "whence the messenger returned." Zeisberger gives Allogacan as the word for "messenger." According to Brinton, Allogalan signifies "to send somebody." The name may have the same significance as Appalachian, as the early forms of both names are much alike in formation.

Auelacunng.—Adlum, map, 1790. **Appolacunck.**—Howell, map, 1792. **Apollacan.**—Morris (1848), State map.

The Penna. State map, 1912, has the form Apalachin.

The town in Tioga County, N. Y., gives this form of the name, while the township in Susquehanna County, Pa., uses the form Apolacon.

AQUAGO, see *Owego.*

Achquoanschicola, "where we fish with the bush-net," according to Heckewelder. Zeisberger gives Achquoanican, "a bush-net;" Achquoneman, "to fish with a bush-net." The valley through which this stream flows was evidently occupied by the Indians long before the period known to history, as many relics have been found in the region which were not in use by the Delawares who occupied the valley when the first white settlers entered it. Consult: Heckewelder, "Indian Names," note on p. 239, 1872. The Indian village of Meniolagomeka (q. v.) stood on the north bank of the creek, about 8 miles west of the Wind Gap, Eldred Tp., Monroe County. It was visited by Zinzendorf in July 1742, and by various missionaries of the Moravian Church from Bethlehem, until the Delawares left the region. Consult; Mem. Mor. Church, I, 33, 1870.

Aquachecola.—Adlum, map, 1790. **Aquanghekalo.**—Deed (1749) A. II, 33, 1852. **Aquanshichola.**—Scull, maps 1759 and 1770. **Aquanshicola.**—Louis Evans, map, 1749. **Aquashicola.**—State Map, 1912. **Aquashikola.**—Scull, map (small) 1770.

AQUANSHICOLA. The name of a creek which drains the first narrow valley north of the Blue Mountains.

AQUETONG. A Post Office in Bucks County. The name, which is not a historic one, is probably derived from Aquetn-ong, "at an island."

ARAMINGO. A corruption of Tumanaraming, which according to a deed of 1689, means "Wolf Walk." The Delaware word for wolf is, "Tummaa," according to Maj. Denny. Brinton gives the form, "Timmeu." This was an appropriate name for the run, as it was infested with wolves when the region was first settled by the English. The run, which enters the Delaware within the city of Philadelphia, is now known as Gunner's Run. The latter name was given soon after the settlement of the region, in honor of Gunner Rambo, a son-in-law of the famous Peter Cock, to whom was given a grant of land upon this stream. In 1689 a deed was made out to Thomas Fairman for lands on "Tumanaramanings Creek (i. e. Wolf's Walk)." In 1761 Peter Cock granted to Gunner Rambo 100 acres of land, a part of the grant which had been made to him by Gov. Lovelace in 1671, in the Shackamaxon tract. According

It enters the Lehigh river near the Gap. The name is corrupted from to Reed's map (1777) Peter Nelson is noted as being one of the first purchasers of land in the Penn Grant. His tract, which is shown on Reed's map, is described as being "in the Fork of Tumanaromaming's" (Arch. Pa., Third Ser., III, 345, 1893). A purchase of Robert Furman in the same place is noted (see same ref.). **Aramingo.**—Egle, Hist. of Pa.,1019, 1883. **Gunner's Run.**—Scull, map, 1759. **Tumanaramanings Creek**—Deed (1689) in Arch. Pa. Second Ser. XIX, 287, 1893. **Tumanaromaming.** — First Purchase (1769) Arch. Pa. Third Ser. III, 345 1896. **Tumanaroamings.**—Reed, map. 1774.

ARRONEMINK. The name given to a tract of land on Mill Creek, near its entrance into the Schuylkill River, not far from the region of Woodlands Cemetery, Philadelphia. There evidently had been an Indian village of this name near the mouth of Mill Creek. In the "Record of Upland Court" this stream is called "Captn. hans moens faalls." In the survey of the land for Moensen, the tract is called "Oronnmink" and in other documents "Arronemink" (See note, "Upland Court Records," 115, 1860). In a letter of William Beekman to Director Stuyvesant, 1660, this place is referred to as "Aroenemeck" (Arch. Pa., Second Ser., VII, 628, 1878. Arrowmink, present maps.

Aroenemeck—Beekman (1660), Arch. Pa., Second Ser. 628, 1878. **Arronemink.**—Records of Upland Court, note, 115, 1860. **Arromink.**—Deed (1681), Watson Annals, II, 476, 1850.

ASSARUGHNEY. A former Delaware village, about two miles north of the mouth of the Lackawanna River, near the present Ransom, Luzerne County. A number of the Delawares settled at this place soon after they had been commanded to leave the lands on the 'Walking Purchase" by the Iroquois. After the commencement of the French and Indian War, the Delawares at Shamokin and Nescopeck moved higher up the Susquehanna to the rocky mountain ridges above the mouth of the Lackawanna. In 1756, Conrad Weiser gave to the Provincial Council a statement of the information which he had received from John Shikellamy (Tachneckdorus) concerning the removal of the Indians from Shamokin to this place. Later in the same year, Scarouady and Andrew Montour made a report

of their journey to the Iroquois Council the previous December. On this journey they passed through this village, which was then occupied by about twenty Delaware warriors. The army of General Sullivan passed through this place on Aug. 1, 1779. The town noted on the map of Louis Evans, 1755, as "Iotocka" and on Pownall's map, 1776, as "Solocka" was near this place.

Assarockney.—Weiser (1756), Col. Rec. Pa., VII, 52, 1851. **Asserughney.**—Scarouady (1756), the same vol., 66. The Hist. map of Penna. (1875) gives the form "Assannghney," which is evidently an error.

ASSUNEPACHLA. Probably a corruption of Achsun, or Asun, "stone," and pachsajeek, "valley." A former Delaware village, near the present Hollidaysburg, Blair County. It is mentioned in the examination of James Le Tort in 1731 "Assunnepachla upon Choniata (Juniata) distant about 100 miles by water and 50 by land from Ohesson (near Lewistown) Delawares; 12 families, 36 men." This village was afterwards called Frank's Town. See *Frankstown.*

Assunnepachla.—Le Tort (1731), Arch. Pa., I, 302, 1852.

ATIGA. See *Kittanning.*

AUGHWICK. Corrupted from Achweek, 'brushy," "overgrown with brush." The name of a former Indian village, which was situated at the mouth of Aughwick Creek, near the present Shirleysburg. The creek, which has its source in Fulton County, enters the Juniata from the south, in Huntingdon County. The Indian village was settled before the westward migration of the Delaware and Shawnee, and was probably a Tuscarora settlement. There were no Indians living at the place when George Croghan moved to it, from the Cumberland Valley, in 1753. From this time until after the evacuation of Fort Shirley, in 1756, Aughwick became quite a prominent place in the Indian affairs of the Province. At the time of Washington's defeat at Fort Necessity, July, 1754, Tanachharison (the Half-King), Scarouady, "Queen Allaquippa" and other Indians went to Aughwick, which then became their headquarters for several years. In the fall of that year a Council was held with the Indians at this place, by the Provincial authorities. Conrad Weiser, George Croghan, Andrew Montour, Scarouady, Beaver and others took part in the discussion of the situation. An account of this Council, by Weiser, is found in Col. Rec. Pa., VI, 150-160, 1851. During the preparations for Braddock's expedition, George Croghan was' asked to collect what Indians he could gather together at Aughwick, and join Braddock's army at Fort Cumberland. Andrew Montour and Scarouady and about forty Indians went to Fort Cumberland with Croghan, in 1755. For various reasons, chiefly because of the relations of the British officers and soldiers with the Indian women, all but seven of these Indians returned to Aughwick. When Braddock's army reached the Little Meadows, there were but seven Indians with the force of British soldiers and Virginia and Pennsylvania frontiersmen. After Braddock's defeat, 1755, all of the Indians friendly to the English cause made Aughwick their place of refuge. In 1754, Richard Peters had advised Croghan to see that a fort was built at Aughwick for the protection of the frontiers. During the Indian raids, which followed Braddock's defeat, Croghan built a stockade fort, which is referred to as "Croghan's Fort". in the Colonial Records. In the fall of 1755, Gov. Morris erected a fort at this place, which was to be one of the points in a series of frontier forts. The fort built at Aughwick stood near the banks of Aughwick Creek, about 20 miles due north of Fort Lyttleton, in the present town of Shirleysburg. It was called Fort Shirley, in honor of General Shirley. Gov. Morris, in a letter to Gen. Shirley, says, in speaking of the fort, "This stands near the great path used by the Indians and the Indian traders, to and from the Ohio, and consequently the easiest way of access for the Indians into the Province." Aughwick was one of the prominent places on the great trail leading from the Susquehanna to the Ohio, and is frequently mentioned in the various traders' and explorers' journals. The line of Frontier Forts was completed early in 1756. In July, 1756, the hostile Indians, under Shingas and Jacobs,

captured and burned Fort Granville, about a mile west of the present Lewistown, Mifflin County, and made plans for making an attack upon Fort Shirley. In August, Col. John Armstrong made Fort Shirley the rendezvous for his expedition against Kittanning. His army left this place on Aug. 30th. See *Kittanning*. In the fall of 1756, on account of the almost entirely deserted condition of the frontiers by the settlers, and because of the remote situation, Fort Shirley was evacuated by the order of Gov. Denny.

AUGHWICK VALLEY. This valley is in the southern part of Huntingdon County. Through almost its entire course ran the famous "Great Trail" from the Susquehanna to the Ohio. To the northwest of Aughwick (Shirleysburg) this trail passed through the famous and beautiful "Jack's Narrows" to Standingstone (Huntingdon), and from there to Frankstown and then on over the mountains at Kittanning Point (near Horse-shoe Bend), to Kittanning. The first attempt made by the white settlers to take possesion of this beautiful valley was in 1749. As the lands in this region had not been purchased from the Indians, the "squatters" were ordered to remove before November, 1749. As no attention was paid to this Proclamation of Gov. Hamilton, by the settlers, Richard Peters, Conrad Weiser and the Magistrates of the Cumberland Valley were ordered by the Governor to remove these settlers by force and burn their cabins. In the spring of 1750 this order was carried out. At Aughwick, four settlers were removed. These were Peter Falconer, Nicholas DeLong, Samuel Perry and John Carleton. The removal of these settlers caused a great deal of discussion and angry feelings among the people along the frontiers, but the Provincial authorities were obliged to do what was done, in order to prevent an Indian war. The Iroquois, through Canassatego, demanded that the settlers be removed from the lands which had not been purchased from the Indians. Consult: Col. Rec. Pa., V, 436, etc., 1851; Walton, "Conrad Weiser," 199-215, 1900.

See *Burnt Cabins.*

Aokweek.—Weiser (1755) Col. Rec. Pa., VI, 494, 1851. Aghwich.—Armstrong (1755) Arch. Pa., II, 252, 1852. Aghwick.—Braddock (1755) Arch. Pa., II. 299, 1852. Auchwick.—Weiser (1755) Col. Rec. Pa., 667, 1851. Auckquick.—Ex. Council (1754) Arch. Pa., II, 194. Auckquick.—Ex. Co. (1754) Col. Rec. Pa., VI, 143. Aucquick.—Montour (1754) The same, 130. Aughick old Town.—Croghan (1754) Arch. Pa., II, 211. Aukhick.—Croghan (1753) Arch. Pa., II, 118. Aughquick.—Ex. Coun. (1754) Col. Rec. Pa., VI, 169. Aughweck.—Weiser (1754) Arch. Pa., II, 194. Aughweek.—Cluggage (1780) Arch. Pa., VIII, 278, 1853. Aughwick Falls.—Ross (1789) Col. Rec. Pa., XVI, 208, 1853. Aughwick Old Town.—Croghan (1754) Col. Rec. Pa., VI, 180. Aukwick.—Morris (1754) Arch. Pa., II, 187. Auwick.—Hoops (1755) Arch. Pa., II, 462. Awkwick.—Shippen (1755) Col. Rec. Pa., VI, 460. Oohwick.—Evans, map, 1755. Oughwhick.—Harris (1754) Arch. Pa., II. 230.

BALD EAGLE CREEK. Named for a famous Munsee chief, called Woapalanne, "Bald Eagle." His village, at the site of Milesburg, Centre County, was called Wapalanewachschiechey, "Bald Eagle's Nest." According to Zeisberger, Woap-a-lanne means "bald eagle"; wachschiechey, "nest." The name of the stream was formed by the addition of hanne, 'stream." Bald Eagle Creek enters the West Branch at Lock Haven, Clinton County. The valley through which it runs is called "Bald Eagle Valley," and the mountain ridge along the eastern side is called "Bald Eagle Mountain." The "Bald Eagles Nest" was situated on the flat at the junction of Spring Creek and Bald Eagle Creek, at the site of the present Milesburg. "The Bald Eagle" was the leader of many of the Indian raids upon the white settlements during the Revolution. On August 8, 1779, he led the Indians who made an attack upon a party of American soldiers upon Loyal Sock Creek, when James Brady was killed. On April 11, 1779, when Capt. John Brady was taking supplies from Fort Wallis to Fort Muncy, he was killed by three Indians. Capt. Samuel Brady, his son, charged the Bald Eagle with both of these acts. In the spring of 1779 many Indian raids were made by the Munsee and Seneca upon the settlements in Westmoreland County. Capt. Sam Brady went up the Allegheny River to head off one of these parties. He discovered a band of Indians at the mouth of Red Bank Creek, 15 miles above

Kittanning, at a place called at present "Brady's Bend." The chief of this party was killed by Brady. According to the traditions of the Brady family, this chief was "The Bald Eagle." The Bald Eagle's Nest, at Milesburg, was a place of resort for the Indians after the War of the Revolution had ended. Shawnee John and Job Chilloway, a Delaware interpreter, made it their place of residence. The latter was a faithful Moravian convert. He followed Zeisberger to the Allegheny, and then to the Muskingum, and was with the "Moravian Indians" in all of their migrations. He died in the fall of 1791. Shawnee John died at "the Nest" many years after the Revolution.

Milesburg was laid out by Col. Samuel Miles in 1793, upon the tract of land known as "The Bald Eagle's Nest."

Bald Eagle.—Evans, map, 1755. Bald Eagle Creek.—Scull, map, 1759. Bald Eagle's Nest.—Scull, map, 1770. Opilleyneyshagen.—Scull, map, 1759.

BEAVER. The name of a river, creek, county and town in western Pennsylvania. According to Zeisberger, the Delaware name for beaver is 'amochk." Brinton gives the form, "Ktemaque." The Beaver River was called, Amahkhanne, "beaver stream," or Amahkwi-sipu, "beaver river." The Little Beaver Creek was called Tankamahkhanne, "little beaver stream." Heckewelder states that the Beaver River was known to the Indians as Kaskaskie-sipu (Kuskuski-sipu), from the town of Kaskaskie (Kuskuski) upon its banks. Tamaque, or "King Beaver," was the leading chief of the Unalachtigo tribe of the Delaware, and a brother of the no less famous Shingas. His place of residence was at "Shingas Town," which was later known as "The Beaver's Town," at the site of the present town of Beaver. He also spent a part of his time at Kuskuski (New Castle) and at Kittanning, at both of which places he had "houses." He was a friend of the English until after Braddock's defeat, 1755, when both he and Shingas became allied with the French. After that time, both of these Delaware chiefs led many of the raids into the English settlements along the Susquehanna and in the Cumberland Valley. In 1758, when Christian F. Post went on his mission of peace to the western Indians, in advance of the army of General Forbes, "King Beaver" was living at Kuskuski and was one of the chief speakers at the various councils held by Post. Consult: Arch. Pa., III, 520, 1853. Tamaque was present at the Council held at Fort Pitt, by General Stanwix, in 1759. He never was very friendly to the English during this period, and during the "Conspiracy of Pontiac" he led various war parties against the white settlers. He moved to the Tuscarawas, after the British occupation of the Ohio, where his village was called "The Beaver's Town." In his later years he came under the influence of the Moravian missionaries, was baptized and became a zealous Christian. Just before his death, about 1770, he urged the Delawares to become Christians. Consult: De Schweinitz, "Life and Times of David Zeisberger," 349, 380, 1870; Heckewelder, "Narrative," 61, 1820; Heckewelder, "Indian Nations," 269, 1876; Arch. Pa., III, 573, 711, 745, 1853; Arch. Pa., IV, 92, 100, 106, 1853. In the autumn of 1778, General McIntosh built a fort at the site of Shinga's Town (now Beaver), which was called Fort McIntosh. This fort was made the headquarters for the Western Department early in October, 1778, and at it there was collected the largest military force which was assembled west of the mountains during the Revolution. The fort stood on the trail leading westward to the Muskingum region. When General Brodhead took command of the Western Department, April, 1779, he immediately returned the headquarters to Fort Pitt. On September 23, 1783, General William B. Irvine gave instructions for the taking possession of the fort, and the military reservation, by the State of Pennsylvania. In 1784, the United States again had to occupy the post, when the Treaty with the western Indians was held. The Commissioners appointed by the U. S. were George R. Clark, R. Butler and Arthur Lee, and those for Penna. were Col. S. J. Atlee and Col. Francis Johnston. According to the terms of the treaty, a deed,

signed Jan. 21st, 1785, by the Delaware and Wyandot, conveyed the title of the Indian lands which had been granted by the Iroquois at the treaty at Fort Stanwix, Oct. 23rd, 1784. On Oct. 2nd, 1788, Fort McIntosh was dismantled by order of the War Department. Consult: Frontier Forts of Penna., II, 485-509, 1896; Col. Rec. Pa., XIV, 73, 448, 1853; XVI, 340, 1853; Arch. Pa., IX, 39, 648, 1854; X, 109, 391, 406, 1854; Appendix, 108, 110, 248, 250, 400-404, 1856. The Indian village known as Sawcunk was situated near the site of 'Shingoe's Town." See *Sawcunk.*

Beaver Creek.—Weiser (1748) Col. Rec. Pa., V, 349, 1851. **Bever C.**—Evans, map, 1755. **Great Beaver Creek.**—Gist (1750) in Darlington's Gist, 81, 1893. **R. au Castor.**—Pouchot, map, 1758. **Riviere Chininque.**—De Lery (1755) Hanna, II, 180, 1911. **King Beaver.**—Post (1758) Arch. Pa., III, 523, 1853. **Tamaque.**—Heckewelder (1762) Heck. "Narrative," 61, 1820. **The Beaver.**—Col. Rec. Pa., V, 536, 1851, Croghan (1751).

See *Shingas*; *Sawcunk.*

BEAVER DAMS. According to Heckewelder, a branch of the Kiskiminetas, in Westmoreland County, which was called by the Delawares "Amochkapahasink," where the beaver has shut up the stream." The "Beaver Dam" was a point on the branch of the Indian trail, which forked on the Kiskiminetas River, probably near Apollo, and ran along the "divide" to Shannopin's Town (Pittsburgh). There has always been some doubt as to exactly where the Indian trail down the Loyalhanna "forked." Mr. Hanna seems to think the "fork" was made near the Unity Presbyterian Church. The author has been over this trail a number of times and is not certain as to just where the "fork of the road" was. It seems probable that it was on the bottom land in the region of Latrobe. There was also another "fork" near Saltsburg. Harris, no doubt, followed the trail, which later was the course of the army of General Forbes. But the exact course of the "Forbes Road" through this region is very hard to determine. The "Beaver Dam" was situated on one of the branches of Beaver Run, not far from the present town of Delmont. Mr. Hanna (Vol. I, 286) places the "Beaver Dam" on the headwaters of Jack's

Run, near Hannastown, as does also Dallas Albert.

Beaver Damms.—Harris (1754) Arch. Pa., II, 135, 1852.

BEECH CREEK. A branch of the Bald Eagle Creek, in Centre County. The Indian name given by Heckewelder is Schauweminsch-hanne, "beech stream." Schau-we-min-schi, "the red beech tree" (Zeisberger). Tanikaniminschi, "the white beech tree" (Brinton). One of the earliest Indian trails to the Ohio, from Shamokin, left the Bald Eagle at Beech Creek and ran along the northern bank of the latter stream to the present Clearfield, and then on to the Allegheny. This was the course followed by C. F. Post in 1758 (Arch. Pa., III, 520, 1853), and by John Ettwein in 1772, when he was leading the Moravian Indians from Wyalusing to the Beaver in 1772 ("Life and Times of David Zeisberger," 376, 1870; Hanna, "Wilderness Trail," I, 214, 1911). This trail was one of the most used paths of the Indians before the French and Indian War, and it may have been one of the routes of the "Black Minquaas" and the Wenro, as they went to the upper Delaware to trade long before the Delaware and Shawnee moved westward to the Ohio. It was a frequently used pathway by the Delaware and Shawnee who went from Shamokin and the "Big Island" to the Ohio.

Beech Creek.—Scull, map, 1770. **Schauweminsch-hanne.**—Heckewelder, "Indian Names," 241, 1872.

BIG ISLAND. There were several islands in the Susquehanna to which this name was given, the chief one, however, was the island at the site of the present Lock Haven. Heckewelder gives the Indian name as Mechek-menatey, "great island." On the map of Lewis Evans, 1755, the name given is Cawichnowane, which name is given by Scull, 1770, to the "Long Island," near the mouth of Pine Creek, near the site of Jersey Shore. This name is of Iroquois origin, having the same significance. See *Cowanesque*. Morgan gives, Gwanasegeh as "Long Island." This island, which contains about 300 acres, was a favorite gathering place for the Indians from a very early time. Being directly on the line of the trails leading into the Seneca domain, as well as on the trail from Shamokin and Wyoming to the Ohio, it was used as a stopping place and a meeting place by Delaware, Shawnee and Iroquois. The shortest course from the Genesee Valley was over the "divide," down the Pine Creek Valley to the West Branch, and then on down the Susquehanna. There evidently was a very extensive burying ground on the island, long before the coming of the historic Indian, according to the statements of the first settlers in the region. When the Delaware and Shawnee began to move westward to the Ohio, from the upper Susquehanna, the "Big Island" was one of the places at which they had a settlement for a short time. At the commencement of the Indian hostility, during the French and Indian War, the "Big Island" was the last stopping place within reach of the English settlements. At that time the Indians had no permanent village on the island, those in sympathy with the French having gone to the Ohio, and those friendly to the English having gone to Shamokin or to Aughwick. When Post passed through on his way to the Ohio in 1758, the place was deserted. After the erection of Fort Augusta, at the present Sunbury, in 1756, Col. Clapham was frequently obliged to send scouting parties up the West Branch to the island, as there was a fear that the French would make an effort to reach the Susquehanna by way of the West Branch. In 1765, Sir William Johnson warned Gov. Penn of the consequences which would follow should white settlers attempt to occupy the lands at the Great Island (Arch. Pa., IV, 227, 1853). In Dec., 1773, William Cooke informed James Tilghman that he had warned the settlers to leave the unpurchased lands on the West Branch, and that he had found William Dunn living on the Great Island. Dunn told him that he was paying rent for his land to the Indians. At that time, according to Cooke, there were "about fourty Improvements made Between Licoming and the Great Island. Some has small Cabens and some a Litel piece of Land cleared" (Arch. Pa., XII, 286-7, 1856). In 1776, John Harris informed Owen Biddle that two Senecas had visited the Great Island, and that the next day all of the Indians in the region had moved away (Arch. Pa., IV, 789, 1853). The island is mentioned quite frequently in the Colonial Records and in the Archives of Penna. See *Long Island*.

Big Island.—Weiser (1754) Col. Rec. Pa., VI, 37, 1851. **Cawichnawane.**—Evans, map, 1755. **Cawichnowane.**—Scull, map, 1770, (for Long Island), French map. **Great I.**—Scull, map, 1759. **Great Island.**—Ex. Council (1739) Col. Rec. Pa., IV, 342, 1851. **Mecheek-Menatey.**—Heckewelder, "Indian Names," 253, 1872.

BIG LICK. A point on the Indian path from the Susquehanna to the Ohio. Probably the place now known as "Flowing Spring," on the Juniata River, near Canoe Creek post-office, Blair County. There was another "big Lick," three miles beyond the "parting of the Roads," mentioned by John Harris (Arch. Pa., II, 135, 1852). This would place this "lick" about three miles west of Latrobe, Westmoreland County. There were so many so-called "licks" along the course of the Conemaugh and the Kiskiminetas, in both Indiana and Westmoreland Counties, that it is difficult to locate any special "lick" as a point on the Indian trail Gist passed over about the same course, from Ligonier, in 1750, as did Harris in 1754 (Dar. Gist, 92, 1893). Hanna places this lick as one of the head springs of Fourteen Mile Run (Vol. I, 286).

Big Lick.—Harris (1754), Arch. Pa., II 135, 1852.

BLACK LEGS CREEK. A creek which enters the north side of the Kiskiminetas, in Indiana County, a short distance below Saltsburgh. There was a former Delaware village on the right bank of the river, opposite the mouth of the Loyalhanna, at the site of Saltsburg. This village, which was known as Black Legs Town, was evidently on both sides of Black Legs Creek. On the opposite side of the Kiskiminetas River, just below the mouth of the Loyalhanna, was the site of the Indian village called Kickenapaw-lings. The trail down the Loyalhanna, from Ligonier, connected with the Frankstown trail near the present town of Apollo. C. F. Post followed this trail from Ligonier in 1758, when upon his second

journey to the western Indians. (Thwaites, Early Western Travels, I, 245, 1904). He says, 'We started early, and came to the old Shawanese town called Keekkenepolin." Many local historians, who have followed the error made in Day's "Historical Collections," have placed this village at the site of Johnstown, Cambria County. It was impossible for Post to have taken such a course from Ligonier. See *Kickenapawlings*.

Black Legs Creek.—Howell, map, 1792. **Black Leggs Town.**—Board of Property (1770) Arch. Pa., Third Ser., I, 287. **Black Legs Town.**—Scull, map, 1770. **Blackleigs Creek.**—Lochrey (177) Arch. Pa., V, 741, 1853.

BLACK LICK. A creek in Indiana County, which enters the Conemaugh from the north. Heckewelder gives the Indian name as Naeska-honi, "Black lick." Nees-ki-u, "black"; mahony, "a lick" (Zeisberger). There is a post-office in Inidana called Black Lick. See *Nesquehoning*.

BLACK LOG. A landmark on the Frankstown Trail, in the gap in the Black Log Mountain, near the present town of Orbisonia, Huntingdon County. According to John Harris, the Black Log was 3 miles from the "Shadow of Death," now Shade Gap, and 6 miles from Aughwick, now Shirleysburg. This point was a "sleeping place" on the trail to the Ohio. Conrad Weiser mentions it in his journal of 1748. Robert H. Morris says in a letter to Sir John St. Clair, "The black Log is not laid down upon this map, or the new one of Evans, but is nigh the Place called Croghan's, and considerably distant from the Turkey Foot" (Col. Rec. Pa., VI, 301, 1851).

Black Log.—Weiser (1748) Col. Rec. Pa., V, 348, 1851. Evans, map, 1749. **Black Log Mountain.**—Howell, map, 1792. **Black Log Ridge.**—Scull, map, 1770. **Black Log Valley.**—Howell, map, 1792.

BLOODY RUN. A branch of the Raystown Branch of the Juniata, which it enters from the north, about 8 miles east of Bedford, at Everett, Bedford County. Christopher Gist turned westward at this point in 1750, on his way to the Ohio. The Warriors Path, running northward from the Potomac, and the Raystown Path, from the Susquehanna to the Ohio, crossed near the mouth of Bloody Run. Various traditions have been related as to the origin of the name. During, and just after, Pontiac's Conspiracy, various attacks were made upon the traders who were carrying supplies to Fort Pitt, near Bloody Run. These attacks were ascribed to the Indians, but in all probability they were committed by the "Black Boys," an organization of white settlers, commanded by Col. James Smith, which sought to prevent the carrying of supplies to the western Indians. Consult: Hanna, Vol. I, 178, 277; II, 32, 1911. Doctor John Ewing says in his journal of 1784, "John Paxton keeps ye Tavern at ye Warrior's Mn. or Bloody Run; so called from the murder of a number of People sent to escort Provisions to Mr. Buchanan who was surveying ye Roads to Bedford in ye year 1755" (Arch. Pa., Sixth Ser., XIV, 7, 1907).

Bloody Run.—Scull, map, 1770.

BRANDT. A post-office in Susquehanna County. Probably named for the famous Mohawk chief, Thayendanegea, more popularly known as Joseph Brandt. This famous enemy of the Americans during the Revolution was born in Ohio, when his parents were on a hunting expedition, in 1742. The home of his parents was near Canajoharie, N. Y. His father died when he was a child, and his mother married an Indian known as Brandt. The sister of Joseph Brandt, Molly, married Sir William Johnson, according to the Indian rites. As Johnson sided with the British during the Revolution, Brandt went with him. He took part in many of the important engagements during the war, but was not present during the "Massacre of Wyoming," as has often been stated. He died Nov. 24, 1807.

BROKENSTRAW CREEK. A tributary of the Allegheny River, which it enters from the north, at the site of Irvineton, Warren County. It is first mentioned in Bonnecamp's Relation, and is noted on his map of Celoron's Expedition to the Ohio, in 1749, as "La Paille Coupee," which has been translated into English, giving the stream its present name. At the time of Bonnecamp's visit, there was an Indian village of the same name at the site of Irvine-

ton. Of this he says, "La Paille Coupee is a very insignificant village composed of Iroquois and some loups" (Jesuit Rel. LXIX, 167, 1900).

The name given to this village by the early English traders on the Allegheny was Buckaloon, which may be a corruption of the Delaware name, as it sounded to them—Poquihhilleu being the Delaware word for "broken," and a part of the name of the stream. The name Koshanuadeago is the Iroquois name, as given by Ellicott and Howell. Beauchamp gives the name Casyonding. The village of Buckaloon and that of Conewango, at the site of Warren, are frequently mentioned as being at the same place ("Aboriginal Place Names in New York," 260, 1907). This error is due to the ignorance of the early writers of the region. Both of these places are mentioned as being at the "headwaters of the Ohio"—which to the early writers was an almost unknown land. See *Buckaloon; Conewango.*

Brokenstraw Creek.—Gen. Irvine (1785) Arch. Pa., XI, 517, 1855. **Casyonding.**—Beauchamp, "Aboriginal Place Names," 260, 1907. **Kasanotiayogo.**—the same, 41. **Koshanuadeago.**—Howell's map, 1792. **Koshhanuadeago.**—Ellicott's map, 1787. **La Paille Coupee.**—Bonnecamp's map, 1749.

BRUSHY CREEK. A branch of the Connoquenessing, in Beaver County; also a branch of Turtle Creek, having its headwaters in Westmoreland County. The Delaware name was, according to Heckewelder, Achweek, "brushy, or overgrown with brush." The latter stream is frequently mentioned in the early records of the State, but more frequent mention is made of a branch of this stream, called *Bushy Run*, in Westmoreland County. James Dunning's Sleeping Place, which is mentioned as one of the points on the Indian Trail, and Cock-eyes Cabin, mentioned in several of the early journals, were not far from the site of Harrison City. At a very early day, soon after the capture of Fort Duquesne, in 1758, Andrew Byerly settled with his family at the place where the Forbes Road crossed Bushy Run. He must have taken the place which had been occupied by Cock-Eyes Cabin, at the crossing of Bushy Run, at Harrison City. Byerley's, as the place was known, became a stopping place for the soldiers and travelers from Ligonier to Fort Pitt. In 1760, when Col. Bouquet had a census of the region of Fort Pitt taken, Andrew Byerly (or Biarly) was among the number. C. F. Post mentions stopping at Byerly's in 1762, where he bought a young steer for the Indians he was leading to Lancaster. (Arch. Pa., IV, 95, 1853). In May, 1763, at the outbreak of the Indian hostility during the Conspiracy of Pontiac, Byerly was warned to leave within a few days. As his wife had just given birth to a child, Byerly could not leave his home. A few nights after he had received this warning, while he was away from home, a friendly Indian warned his wife that if they did not leave before morning they would be killed. She left a note for her husband and, taking her three-day-old baby, she saddled a horse, tying another small child behind her and, with her two young sons walking beside her, made the long journey to Fort Ligonier through the almost deserted wilderness. In a petition, in 1764, made to the Commissioners at Carlisle, Byerly made application for relief for having been driven from his home in 1763. "Byerley's Station" was near the site of the Battle of Bushy Run, one of the most historic conflicts in American history. The battle-field was situated in what was afterwards known as the Penn Manor of Denmark, about 2 miles north of the present Penn Station on the P. R. R., and about the same distance east of the present Harrison City.

The battle was fought on August 5th and 6th, between the force of about 500 men, chiefly Scotch Highlanders, commanded by Col. Henry Bouquet, who were marching to the relief of Fort Pitt, and a slightly smaller force of Seneca and Wyandot Indians, under the leadership of Guyasuta (more correctly, Kiasutha). The soldiers were marching along the winding road, which turned over the summit of a steep hill, when suddenly the advance guard was attacked by a force of Indians. The battle lasted until nightfall, when the Indians retired to the heavy woods near by. The soldiers of Bouquet, worn out by the heat of the

August day and by the severe fighting, went to such rest as they could get on the hill top, where they had fought the battle. The Indians made the dense forests ring with their yells the whole night through. Bouquet had small hope for the outcome of the coming day, as his letters show. The battle was resumed at daybreak. Bouquet, by a strategic movement, overwhelmed the Indians with fear and drove them from the field. Consult: Parkman, "Conspiracy of Pontiac," any edition; Frontier Forts of Penna., II, 509-636, 1896; Boucher, History of Westmoreland County, I, 24-32, 1906; Cort, Bouquet and His Campaigns, 1883; Darlington, Fort Pitt and Letters from the Frontier, 84-199, 1892; Smith, Historical Account of Bouquet's Expedition, 1765, or reprint of 1868. Also Col. Rec. Pa. and Arch. Pa., under title, Bouquet Letters.

It has long been the intention of the Historical Society of Western Pennsylvania to mark this battle field by a suitable monument, but this work of real historic interest and value has not yet been done.

See *Dunning's Sleeping Place*; *Cock Eye's Cabin*.

BUCKALOON. A former Iroquois village, at the mouth of Brokenstraw Creek, at the site of the present Irvineton, Warren County. The name is possibly a corruption of the Delaware word Poquihhilleu, "broken," which was likely a contraction of the name given to the place by the French, La Paille Coupee (broken straw). It is easy to see how the Irish traders make Buckaloon out of Poquihhilleu. This village was a short distance from Connewango, at the site of Warren, and was often confused with, or made to be the same place, by the early records of Penna. In the Colonial Records, the Indian deputies who went to Philadelphia, in 1759, are mentioned as coming from "Canawago, or Boucaloonce" (Col. Rec. Pa., VIII, 270, 1852). In 1753, Gov. Hamilton, in a letter to Gov. Dinwiddie, of Virginia, said that the French were building a fort at this place, evidently meaning the fort which was built at Le Boeuf (Col. Rec. Pa., V, 634, 1851). When Gen. Brodhead led the expedition up the Allegheny in 1779, both of the Seneca villages of Buckaloon and Connewango were deserted. He left his supplies at the former place and marched rapidly forward to Connewango, hoping to surprise the Indians there, but found that they had fled. His troops destroyed the log huts and the great corn fields along the Allegheny River at both places. Gen. Brodhead estimated that 500 acres of corn were under cultivation along the upper Allegheny at this time (Col. Rec. VIII, 263, 264, 1852; Arch. Pa., XII, 155, 158, 1856). Gen. W. B. Irvine visited the sites of all of these Indian villages in 1785 (Arch. Pa., XI, 517, 1855).

All of the names of Brokenstraw Creek and Buckaloon are attempts to translate or pronounce the Seneca name of the village, which was Kachuidagon, meaning "broken reed" (See Magazine of American History, II, 139). The Delaware Poquihhilleu, "broken," was the translation, made by the Delawares, which gave the traders the name of Buckaloon, and its various corruption. See *Brokenstraw* and *Connewango*.

Bacoaloons.—Gussefeld map, 1784. **Bacoatoons.**—Esnault and Rap. map, 1777. **Baccatous.**—Lattre map, 1784. **Bachaloons.**—Col. Bird (1757) Arch. Pa., Second Ser., II, 658, 1890. **Boccalunnce.**—Gov. Hamilton (1753) Col. Rec. Pa., V, 634, 1851. **Bookaloons.**—Gen. Irvine (1785) Arch. Pa., XI, 517, 1855. **Bouclones.**—Ex. Council (1759) Col. Rec. Pa., VIII, 264, 1852. **Bowclunce.**—the same. 263. **Bucaloons.**—Scull map, 1770. **Buchaloons.**—Lewis Evans map, 1755. **Buchloons.**—Gen. Brodhead (1779) Arch. Pa., XII, 1856. **Buckaloon.**—Day, Hist. Pa., 653, 1843. **Buckaloons.**—Butterfield, Washington-Irvine Cor., 43, 1882. **Buffaloons.**—Lotter map, 1770. **Gachimantiagon.**—Bellin map, 1755. **Kachuidagon.**—Magazine Amer. Hist., II, 139. **Kachiriodagon.**—Joncaire (1749) Margry. Dec. VI, 675, 1886. **La Paille Coupee.**—Bonnecamp map, 1749.

For other synonyms see *Brokenstraw*.

BUFFALO CREEK. A branch of the Allegheny in Armstrong County, also the name of several other creeks and runs. In Delaware, Sisiliehanna, "buffalo-stream," according to Heckewelder. The word for buffalo, given by Brinton and Anthony, is Sisilija, which signifies "an animal that butts against and breaks in pieces" (Anthony). The verb, Sillikakhammen, means "to press."

BURNT CABINS. The name of a village in Fulton County, near the headwaters of Little Aughwick Creek. It is derived from the incident of the burning of the log houses of the settlers, who had taken up lands upon the unpurchased Indian land west of the Susquehanna, in 1750. These "squatters" upon the Indian lands had been the cause of much trouble to the Provincial authorities for many years previous. The Iroquois, who claimed the land, demanded again and again that these settlers be removed. Various proclamations had been issued by the Governors of the Province, demanding that all white settlers remove from these lands, but no attention was paid to these orders by any of the people living beyond the Blue Mountains. Complaint had been made by the Iroquois as early as 1740. At the Council of the Iroquois with the Governor, Hamilton, in Philadelphia, in 1749, the Indian deputies demanded that these settlers be removed. After much discussion, Gov. Hamilton commissioned Richard Peters and Conrad Weiser to see to the carrying out of the order for the removal of all of these "squatters" upon the Indian lands. These two, with the assistance of the Magistrates of Cumberland County, went to all of the places where these settlers had built their cabins, ordered the inhabitants to leave and burnt the cabins. This order was carried out at the settlements on the Juniata, on Sherman's Creek, at Big Cove, Little Cove, and other places. Among those removed from Sherman's Creek was Simon Girty, who ever afterwards was an enemy of the white man and of every form of government. Consult: Col. Rec. Pa., V, 389, 396, 399, 401, 436, 443, 1851; XV, 121, 1853; Arch. Pa., XI, 70, 91, 158, 1855; Walton, Conrad Weiser, 211-215, 1900.

CALLAPOOSE. A post-office in Wayne County. Origin of name not known. May possibly be a corruption of Capouse (q. v.).

CALLAPATSCINK. Heckewelder gives the form, Callapatschink, "where it returns," having reference to a point where the course of the creek bends, or to the frequent bends in the stream. The name of a creek in Cumberland County, having its headwaters in the South Mountain and flowing northeast into the Susquehanna River, which it enters at the present New Cumberland. The creek has been known by the name of Yellow Breeches Creek, since the region was first settled by the white race. This name may be a corruption of Yellow Beeches, there being many such trees along the stream. The stream was also called Shawnee Creek in some of the early letters and records. Soon after the Shawnee began to settle along the Susquehanna (1698), they commenced to move northward from the mouth of Pequea Creek to various points along the river to the northward. A village was established at a very early date at the mouth of Yellow Breeches Creek. Peter Chartier, the half-breed Indian trader, made this his place of residence for some years previous to 1730. For several years previous to 1730 the Shawnee had commenced to move westward to the Ohio, chiefly on account of the abuses in the rum traffic. Here they came under the influence of the French. Every effort was made by the authorities of the Province to bring them back to the Susquehanna region. They were promised, through Peter Chartier, that if they would come back a tract of land would be laid out for them, "between Conegogwainet & The Shaawna Creeks five or six miles Back from the River, in order to Accommodate the Shaawna Indians or such others as may think fit to settle there, To Defend them from Incroachments, And we have also orders to Dispossess all Persons Settled on that side the River, That Those woods may Remain free to ye Indians for Planting & Hunting, And We Desire thee to Communicate this to the Indians who Live About Allegening" (Letter to Peter Chartier, Arch. Pa., I, 299, 1852). This letter was dated Nov. 19, 1731. At that time, according to the statement of Jonah Davenport, there were upon the Ohio "two hundred & sixty Shawanese, one hundred Asswekalaes (a Shawnee tribe), & some Mingoes" (the same ref.). In 1732 the Shawnee upon the Ohio sent a letter to Gov. Gordon, in which they informed him why they had moved to the

Ohio (Arch. Pa., I, 329, 1852). This letter was signed by James LeTort and Peter Chartier, both former residents of the "Shaawna Creeks," which include the Yellow Breeches and Le Tort's Spring. All of the efforts of the authorities of the Province to bring back the Shawnee from the Ohio were unavailing. The Iroquois were appealed to and were requested to try to induce them to return to the Susquehanna, but the Shawnee replied that the "place was more commodious for them," and absolutely refused to leave the Ohio. When one of the Iroquois deputies, who had been sent on the mission, attempted to argue the matter with the Shawnee, they killed him (Col. Rec., III, 608, 1852). The Shawnee from the region of New Cumberland and Le Tort's (near Bonny Brook) moved westward over the Indian trail, by way of Bedford, to Chartier's Town, on the Allegheny River. Consult: Walton, Conrad Weiser, 21, 22, 1900; J. R. Miller, The Yellow Breeches Creek, 1909. See *Shawnee, Chartier's Town, Conedogwinet.*

Callapatschink. — Heckewelder, Indian Names, 273, 1872. **Callapatscink.**—Miller, Yellow Breeches Creek, 1909. **Shaawna Creeks.**—Wright (1731) Arch. Pa., I, 299, 1852. **Yellow Breeches Cr.**—Louis Evans, map, 1749.

CALUMET. A post-office in Westmoreland County. A word which is oftentimes spoken of as having an Indian origin, but which is from the French, Chalumet, "a reed, pipe, or flute"; from the Latin Calamus, "a reed." In Indian usage, the term applied to the two symbolic shafts of reed, representing male and female. Later, pipe was added, representing an altar upon which tobacco was offered. By the addition of decorations of colors, ribbons, etc., various dominant gods were represented. The calumet was the most significant symbol used by the Indians. It was used on all official missions of grave import, at treaties, to attest contracts and for many other purposes. Consult the splendid article by J. N. B. Hewitt, Handbook of American Indians, Part I, 191-195, 1907.

C A N A C O S H I C K. See *Conococheague.*

CANADOHTA. The name of a lake and also of a village in Crawford County. The village is called "Canadohta, or Lakeville," on the State map of 1911. The lake is called "Oil Lake" on the Morris map of 1848. The map of Howell of 1792 does not mark the lake.

CANASERAGE. A former Shawnee village at the site of the present Muncy, Lycoming County. Was also the name of the creek now known as Muncy Creek, at the mouth of which was situated the Indian village. There was also a village and a creek of the same name in New York, the Tuscarora village being situated at the mouth of the creek, at the site of Sullivan, N. Y. The village in Penna. was visited by Conrad Weiser and John Shikellamy in 1755, at which time its population consisted of Shawnee and Chickasaw. Weiser had visited the Tuscarora village in New York in 1750. His form for the names of the two villages is the same (Col. Rec. Pa., V, 478, 1852). In 1754, Weiser wrote that the Iroquois demanded that the line of the last purchase should not take in the lands on the West Branch, or include the Big Island, but that he himself was confident that this line would cross the "Zinachsa River (the West Branch) about Canasorga" (MS. letter of Weiser in Hist. Soc. of Penna., quoted by Walton, Conrad Weiser, 296, 1900). Weiser was told that if this line was run the Indians would kill the cattle of the white settlers, and then kill the settlers themselves, if they did not remove. The failure of the white "squatters" to remove from these lands caused much trouble, and later much bloodshed. See *Muncy Creek*.

Various meanings have been given for the Indian name. Morgan gives, "among the milkweeds"; Hewitt, "at the place of mandrakes"; other meanings are given by Beauchamp, Aboriginal Place Names of New York, 25, 102, 105, 107, 110, 113, 1907. The form given by Hewitt, for the village in N. Y. is Ganasarage (Handbook of Ame. Ind., Part I, 186, 1907).

Canascoragu.—Louis Evans map, 1749. **Canaserage.**—Louis Evans map, 1755. **Canasserago.**—Scull map, 1770. **Canasoragy.**—Weiser (1755) Col. Rec. Pa., VI, 443, 1851. **Canasovagy.**—Hist. map of Penna., 1875, (an error). **Canasserago.** —Scull map, 1770-French map. The

form given in Weiser's MS. letter is Canasoragu.

CANDOWSA. A former Munsee village, on the east shore of the Susquehanna, above the mouth of the Lackawanna, not far from the boundary line of Lackawanna and Wyoming Counties. The site of the Indian village, called Quilutimack, where General Sullivan's army encamped on Aug. 1st, 1779, must have been upon the site of the village of Candowsa, noted upon Evans' map, 1755. This village and the one of Asserughney could not have been the same place, nor could it have been at the mouth of the Lackawanna, as is stated by Mr. Harvey in his "History of Wilkes-Barre." The map of Evans shows that this town was about 7 miles above the mouth of the Lackawanna, and not at the mouth. Quilutimack was, according to all of the Journals of Sullivan's expedition, 7 miles above the Lackawanna. Ransom would be much nearer to both of these villages, according to the various maps, than would the mouth of the Lackawanna. See *Quilutimack*. The name of the village may be derived from that of the chief mentioned in the Colonial Records, III, 326, as "Kindassowa," who lived, in 1728, at "the Forks of the Sasquehannah above Meehayomy" (Wyoming, now Wilkes-Barre). The "Forks" was the name of the region where Athens, Bradford County, is now situated, and also of the junction of the Lackawanna with the Susquehanna.

CANOE PLACE. There were a number of places at the headwaters of various rivers, and their branches, which were noted on the early map as "Canoe Place." These places marked the points to which canoe navigation was possible. Here the Indians hid their canoes, or carried them across the "portage" to the next "canoe place," over the divide between the waters of the two streams. On the way to the Ohio, from the West Branch, such a "Canoe Place" was situated in the northwest corner of the present Cambria County, at Cherry Tree, or Grant post-office, Indiana County. From here the trail led directly to Kittanning. Another such "Canoe Place" was upon the West Branch, near Emporium, Cameron County. Here a portage of about 20 miles over the "divide" was necessary in order to reach the headwaters of the Allegheny, at another "Canoe Place," now Port Allegany, in McKean County. By this short portage a canoe can be taken from the Atlantic Ocean to the Gulf of Mexico. At the headwaters of the Tioga River, near Knoxville, Tioga County, was another "Canoe Place." From here the portage over the divide led to the headwaters of the Allegheny, above Coudersport, Potter County, or to the headwaters of the Genesee, or to the headwaters of the West Branch, by way of Pine Creek. On the "divide," near Gold (Potter County), are the sources of the Allegheny, Genesee and Susquehanna. These various canoe places are noted on the early maps of Penna. See Reading Howell's map, 1792.

CAPOUSE. The name of a mountain range in Luzerne County, named for a Munsee chief. A town in Lackawanna County called *Capoosa* is another form of the name, as also is Callapoose, a post-office in Wayne County. The name for the mountain range as noted on Morris' map of 1848 is Capous.

CARANTOUAN. A word meaning "it is a big tree"; the name of a Susquehanna, Conestoga, village of 1615, situated at the place known as "Spanish Hill," Bradford County, near Waverly, New York, on the Chemung River, above Tioga Point. Parkman identified the Carantouannais with the Erie, which is evidently an error. Champlain said that the "Carantouanais is a Nation south of the Antouhonorons (Seneca), in a very beautiful and rich country, where they are strongly lodged." In 1615 Champlain sent one of his interpreters, Estienne Brule, three short days' journey from the region of the western Iroquois tribes, to the Carantouannais, who were allies of the Hurons, to get 500 warriors to assist him in his campaign. Before Brule returned, Champlain was obliged to leave the country, and did not hear from Brule until after his return from France in 1618, when he met him at Three Rivers.

From him he then learned that the chief town of these Huron allies was defended by 800 warriors. Brule had gone to Carantouan, had a council with the chiefs, who promised to send the 500 warriors to help Champlain, but, because of various delays, these did not reach the place where Champlain was waiting until after his departure. Brule then returned to Carantouan, where he spent the fall and winter, as he could not get an escort to take him back to his home. During his stay at Carantouan he made a trip down the Susquehanna to the ocean. On his return to Carantouan from this trip, he was given an escort to accompany him home. This village was evidently situated on the place called "Spanish Hill." Rochefoucauld, who was on a visit to the French settlement at Asylum, Bradford County, in 1795, visited this hill. He said, "These the inhabitants call the "Spanish Ramparts; but I rather judge them to have been thrown up against the Indians in the time of M. de Nonville." Consult: Handbook of Amer. Ind., II, 657; Jour. Mil. Exped. Sull., 124; Hanna, Wild. Trail, I, 31-32. See *Susquehanna, Towanda*, etc.

CARKOEN CREEK. Possibly a corruption of the Indian name, Kakarikonk, "place of wild geese." Seemingly this name was given to the stream now known as Darby Creek, Delaware County, from the junction of the present Cobbs Creek and Darby Creek to the river. This was the first place settled by the white race within the State of Penna. The creek was also called Amesland Creek by the Swedes. The mill built upon this stream by Gov. Printz, in 1643, was the first watermill built in the Delaware region. Aerelius gives the following origin of the Swedish name, "Ames-land, it was formerly called the country of the nurse, one having lived there formerly, where Archard's place now is, for that reason this farm and afterwards the whole region was given the name of the country of the nurses, and now Amas-land" (See note, Record of Upland Court, 65, 1860).

CARKOENS HOOK. This name was applied to the land between the east side of Cobbs and Darby Creeks and the western boundary of the Tacony district, according to the Editor of "Records of Upland Court." (See note, in work cited, 197). Consult: Records of Upland Court, 1860; Arch. Pa., Second Ser., VII, (Papers Relating to the Dutch and Swedish Settlements on the Delaware) 459-820, 1878; XVI, (Papers Relating to the Boundary Dispute), 1890; XIX, (Various entries in Minute Books, F, G, H, etc., 1893. See *Darby Creek*, *Naamans Creek*, *Delaware.*

Carkoen Creeke.—The same ref. p. 88. **Carcoons Hook.**—Arch. Pa. Second Ser., V, 626, (1671), 1890. **Carkoenhoeck.**—Records of Upland (1678), 119, 1860. **Kakaricon.**—Arch. Pa., Second Ser., XVI, 238 (1648), 1890.

(The synonyms which apply to Darby, under *Darby Creek.*)

CATASAUQUA. The name of a creek and town in Lehigh County. The creek enters the Lehigh River from the northeast at Catasauqua. The name is a corruption of Gattoshacki, "thirsty earth." According to Reichel, the name was found in early deeds as Calisuk and Caladaqua. The Scull map (1770) and the Howell map (1792) give the name of the stream as Mill Creek. The very fine map of Morris (1848) gives the name as Calesoque.

CATAWBA TRAIL. The name given to an Indian trail which entered Penna. near the mouth of Grassy Run, crossing the present Fayette County, through Uniontown, Mount Braddock, Connellsville (See *Stewart's Crossings*), near Mount Pleasant, and over Westmoreland County to the Allegheny River. This trail was used by the Seneca, as they went southward into the Carolinas, against the Cherokee and Catawba. The chief Iroquois trail southward ran along the eastern foot of the Warrior's Ridge, striking the Allegheny Path east of Bedford, at Bloody Run, and running on southward to the Potomac, near Old Town, Maryland. The so-called Catawba Trail, west of the mountains, was never so prominent as was this eastern trail. The main body of the Iroquois population was

much nearer to the headwaters of the Susquehanna, and the large war parties southward to the Catawba and Cherokee country, went by way of the "Warrior's Path," which was frequently mentioned in the Indian Councils. See *Warrior's Path.* The Catawba Trail, from Gist's Plantation (now Mount Braddock), to Stewart's Crossings (now Connellsville), to Mount Pleasant, and on to the "divide" above Turtle Creek, was the course followed by the army of General Braddock, in 1755. The same course was followed by Washington and Gist in 1752. Near Mount Braddock, near the Meason farm, the Nemacolin Trail, to Redstone Creek, joined the Catawba Trail. This trail ran eastward, over the mountains to Cumberland, Maryland, and was the course followed by Washington in 1752 and 1754, and by Braddock in 1755. See *Nemacolin Trail.*

The Cherokee and Catawba had been at war with the Iroquois for many years before the settlement of Penna. The Delaware and Shawnee had also been enemies of these southern Indians. When Braddock's Road was opened over the mountains, from the Potomac to the Ohio, the French made the Indians on the Ohio believe that the English had opened this road as a pathway for the southern Indians to reach their villages along the Ohio. C. F. Post had to try to convince the Ohio Indians of the falseness of this story, when he went to Kuskuski, in advance of the army of General Forbes, in 1758.

These wars between the northern and the southern Indians was the cause of many difficult problems which the Province of Pennsylvania had to try to solve before there could be any hope of driving the French from Fort Duquesne. Braddock had failed to get any Indians from the south, even though Gist had made the attempt to get them by a personal visit. The Catawba and the Cherokee did not dare show themselves within the region through which Braddock's army would pass. Even after all of the efforts of Conrad Weiser at Onondaga (Col. Rec. Pa. V., 471, 1851) to get a peace patched up between the Iroquois and the Catawba and Cherokee, in preparation for the advance of the army of

General Forbes, the appearance of the Cherokee warriors with Forbes' army threatened to alienate the Iroquois at the very time when they were most to be feared. The efforts of Weiser, Post, and Tedyuskung were all required to make the Iroquois, Shawnee and Delaware come to terms of peace with the southern Indians. The Indian problem which Pennsylvania had on its hands in 1755 and 1758 had to be solved before British success upon the expeditions against Fort Duquesne could be hoped for. With the Delaware and Shawnee under French influence on the Ohio, and alienated from the English; with the Iroquois trying to keep their hands out of the conflict, and yet sorely tempted by the French to an alliance with them, and with the Iroquois, Delaware and Shawnee at war with the southern Indians—the outlook was not of the brightest. But, the Iroquois were urged to make peace with the Catawba and Cherokee, and Tedyuskung and Post were able to keep the Delaware and Shawnee away from Fort Duquesne, and so General Forbes marched into the deserted French fort. Consult; Col. Rec. Pa., IV., 245, 345, 718, 721, 776, 668, 1851; V., 137, 402, 473, 626, 630, 688, 1851; VI., 6, 142, 162, 183, 1851; VII., 31, 289, 502, 1851; Walton, Conrad Weiser, 216-219, 1900: Handbook of Amer. Ind.; Part I, 213-215, 1907.

CATAWISSA. The name of a creek and town in Columbia County. The creek enters the Susquehanna from the east at Catawissa. From Gatawisi, "Growing fat" (Heckewelder). Reichel says, "Catawissa is regarded by some, as a corruption of Ganawese, and as designating the region to which the Conoys retired, on withdrawing from the limits of Lancaster county" (Heckewelder, Indian Names, 242, 1870). Before 1756 an Indian village, called Lapachpeton's Town, was situated at the mouth of the creek. The town was named for Lapachpeton, a famous Delaware chief, who had much influence among his people. Conrad Weiser visited him several times. There had been a village, called Oskohary, at the same situation, previous to the occupation of the upper Susquehanna by the Delaware. An Indian trail crossed the river at this point, coming down the northern shore of the creek, and passing through the hills

opposite, and leading to the upper waters of the West Branch. This was one of the branches of the path to Wyoming, from Muncy, and doubtless had been used by the Seneca from a very early time. It was a short cut to the Bald Eagle valley, and so to the Ohio, from the Wyoming region. The earliest recorded name of the village is that used by James Le Tort, who wrote a letter from "Catawasse," concerning the trouble between the Shawnee and the English, in 1728. At that time the village was occupied by the Conoy and Delaware. It is possible that Reichel is correct in Catawissa being a corruption of Ganawese, another name of the Conoy. The Conoy, or Ganawese, first appeared at a Council in Philadelphia in 1701, when they were given permission to settle upon any part "of Patowmeek River within the bounds of this Province" (Col. Rec. Pa., 11, 17, 1852). In 1705 they were given permission to settle near Tulpehocken (same vol. 191). In 1706 they had settled on the Susquehanna, near Bain bridge, at a village called Conejohela (q. v.). In 1744 they had moved up the river, and by 1749 they were at the mouth of the Juniata (Col. Rec. Pa., IV., 747, 1851; V., 389, 1851). From that time until the French and Indian War they kept constantly following the few members of the tribe who had gone northward to the region about Catawissa, when they all moved higher up the river to Wyoming and Chenango. Soon after 1765 they lost their identity in the Delaware and Mahican.

Catawasse.—Le Tort (1728), Arch. Pa., I, 216, 1852. **Catawessy.**—Howell map, 1792. **Catawesy.**—Scull map, 1759. **Catawissey.**—Arch. Pa., Third Ser. III, 408 (1793), 1896. **Catawissey Town.**—The same ref. **Labach Peters.**—Horsfield (1755), Col. Rec. Pa., II, 492, 1852. **Lapach Peetos.**—Burd (1756), Arch. Pa., Second Ser. II, 795, 1876. **Lapackpitton.**—Weiser (1754), Col. Rec. Pa., VI, 35, 1851, (the chief). **Lappachpeton.**—Weiser (1757), Col. Rec. Pa., III, 257, 1853. **Lawpaughpeton's T.**—Scull map, 1759.

CATFISH CAMP. The name of a hunting and fishing camp at the site of Washington, Pa. One of the messengers at the Council in Philadelphia in 1759, was called, "Tangoocqua, or Catfish." He had evidently been present at the councils held by C. F. Post, at Kuskuski in 1758, when the western Indians were told of the peace which the Province was making with the

Delaware, through the efforts of Tedyuskung and himself. At that time Tangoocqua was living at Kuskuski (New Castle). Mr. Boyd Crumrine states that the name "Wissameking," is found on a French map of 1757. The name Wissameking means "catfish place," or, "where there are catfish." Wisameek, "Catfish," is compounded of wisu, "fat," and Namees, "fish." (Heckewelder and Zeisberger). Catfish Camp became the site for the County-seat of the district of West Augusta (Virginia) in 1776, when it became known as Augusta Town. Here was held the first Court, by the English-speaking race, west of the Monongahela River (See, Crumrine, The Old Virginia Court House at Augusta Town, 1905). In 1781, upon the organization of Washington County, Catfish Camp became known as Washington, but even after that time the place often was spoken of by its old name.

Catfish.—Meason (1777), Arch. Pa., V, 445, 1853. **Cat Fish Camp.**—Brodhead (1785), Col. Rec. Pa., XVI, 223, 1863. **Cat fish Camp.**—Hughes (1782), Arch Pa., IX, 553, 1854. **Town of Washington, late Cat Fish Camp.**—Brodhead (1789), Arch. Pa., XI, 641, 1854. **Tangoocqua, or Catfish.**—Ex. Council (1759), Col. Rec. Pa., VIII, 415, 1852. **Tingoocqua, alias Catfish.**—The same Vol., 417. **Tingoocqua.**—Crumrine, Court House at Augusta Town, 39, 1905. **Wisameking.**—Heckewelder, Indian Names, 242, 1872. **Wissameking.**—Crumrine, work cited, 37.

CAWWANSHEE FLATS. See *Cowanesque*.

CHARTIER'S CREEK. A creek which enters the Ohio River from the south, a few miles below Pittsburgh, at McKees Rocks. Named for Peter Chartier, the famous half-breed Shawnee. Martin Chartier, his father, was a prominent Indian trader, of French parentage, and who had lived in Canada until he had moved to the French trading points on the Mississippi. He is first mentioned, in his relation to the affairs of the English, in the proceedings of the Council of Maryland in 1693, as "Martin Shortive." He was married to an Indian woman (two, according to some accounts), who belonged to the Shawnee tribe. He was possibly with the Shawnee when they settled along the Potomac river, near Old Town Md., and moved to the mouth of Pequea Creek, in 1798, when the Shawnee first entered the Province of Penn. He afterwards had a trading house at

Conestoga, the location of which is shown on the map of Conestoga Manor of 1717. He died in 1718. His son, Peter Chartier, was granted a tract of 300 acres of land on the Susquehanna, where his father had lived. (Arch. Pa., Sec. Ser., XIX., 625, 681, 749, 1893). He had trading stations at various places along the Susquehanna, at Paxtang, at the mouth of Yellow Breeches Creek, and later on the Conedogwinet, in the region of Carlisle—possibly at Bonny Brook. Some time soon after 1734 he removed westward to the Allegheny River, where he had been trading for some years. Like his father he had married a Shawnee woman, and his life became associated with the wanderings of this people with whom he was related by a double tie. When the Shawnee left the Susquehanna, to move westward to the Allegheny, he became a leader among them. While he had traded on the Allegheny and Ohio for some years, it is evident that he did not move westward until about 1734. In about 1744 the Shawnee on the upper Ohio commenced to move on down the river to the mouth of the Scioto. In 1745 Chartier had gone to join these people, after having committed a number of robberies upon the English traders. At this time it was said that he had accepted a military commission under the French King (Col. Rec. Pa., IV., 757, 1851). At this time he had persuaded the Shawnee to leave the village at Chartier's Town, in order to be with him. His influence with the Shawnee was very great and many of them joined him in his alliance with the French. The Iroquois tried to prevent the Shawnee from going with Chartier. Scarouady, who had control of the Iroquois affairs with the Shawnee, brought back many of these people "who had been seduced by Peter Chartiers," under the control of the Iroquois. By 1749 many of them had returned to the upper Ohio and at the Treaty at Lancaster in that year they asked to be taken back into the friendship with the English (Col. Rec. Pa., V., 311, 315, 316, 1851). For other references consult; Col. Rec. Pa., II., 182; IV., 757, 780; V., 1, 5, 24, 167, 293, 300, 533; VI., 678: Arch. Pa., I, 213, 299, 328, 330, 394, 425, 549; II., 61; IV., 484; IX., 49; Eagle, Hist. Penna., 847, 1883; Walton, Conrad Weiser, 127, 1900; Hanna, Wilderness

Trail, (Index), 1911. The name of Chartiers Creek has been given such a variety of spelling that a synonomy of the various forms of this word is without any value, all of the forms being different in orthography only and having no historical value. The only one which has given any trouble to the historical student is the form Shertee, upon which is founded many purely fanciful accounts of the origin of the name. A very interesting story, "The Legend of the 'Shertee,'" is contained in Judge Parke's Recollections of Seventy Years, 41 etc., 1886. The creek was sometimes called Allaquippa's Creek, as was also the island known as Nevilles Island, given the name of this woman.

Alloquepy (river).—Le Roy (1755), in Arch. Pa., Sec. Ser., VII, 409, 1878. **Chartiers Creek.**—Petition of Ohio Co. (1752), in Dar. Gist, 230, 1893. **Shurtees Creek.**—Ohio Co. (1753), the same, 236.

The various forms given in the Virginia Land Grants are; Chartiers Chertiers, Chertie, Shertiers, Shirtie and Shirtiers. The form "Shirtie" seemed to be the favorite one (Arch. Pa., Third Ser., III, 505 etc., 1896.)

It was the intention of the Ohio Company to build the fort, which Edward Ward commenced afterwards at the site of Fort Duquesne, at the mouth of Chartiers Creek. The other one was to be at the mouth of the Kanhawha. In 1781, Gen. W. B. Irvine, in a letter to Washington, advised the demolishing of Fort Pitt and Fort McIntosh and building one at the mouth of Chartiers Creek—on the high ground of McKees Rocks — which should be made the chief post on the Ohio. This plan was not carried out. Consult: Craig's "Olden Time," II., 264, etc. The "Chartiers Settlement," often noted, had reference to all of the white settlements along the creek, from its mouth to Washington, Pa. Shingas, a brother of "The Beaver," lived for a time at the mouth of Chartiers Creek, as did also Allaquippa. See *Beaver, Allaquippa, Chartiers Old Town.* The village noted in the previous article to which Peter Chartier moved from the Susquehanna with a company of Shawnee in 1734. It was situated on the northern shore of the Allegheny River, at the site of the present Tarentum. The Indian trail crossed the river from the mouth of Chartiers Run to the mouth of Bull Creek. The fording place is marked on Evans map of 1755. After the Shawnee went southward from this point the village which they had occupied became known as Chartiers Old Town. Conrad Weiser passed through this place on his way to Logstown in 1748. He mentions it as "the old Shawones Town, commonly called Chartier's Town" (Col. Rec. Pa., V, 349, 1851). It was near this place that Celoron met the six traders, with fifty horses laden with peltries, in 1749, by whom he sent the message to the Governor of Pennsylvania, warning him to keep the English traders from French possessions. The extent of the English trade with the Ohio Indians, even at this early date, is shown by the number of peltry laden horses in this train.

Chartier's Town.—Weiser (1748), Col. Rec. Pa., 349, 1851. **Chartier's old Town.** —the same ref. **Chartiers old T.**—Louis Evans map, 1755. **Old Village of Chaouanons.**—Bonnecamp Rel. (1749), Jes. Rel. LXIX, 170, 1900. **Chartiers Run (Westmoreland Co.)**—Howell's map, 1792.

CHEMUNG. The name of a former Indian village at the site of the present Chemung, New York; also the name of the branch of the Susquehanna, which unites with the North Branch at Tioga Point, Bradford County. The name means "a horn," or "antlers." The Delaware Wilawan has the same significance. The two towns of Chemung and Wilawanna, which are opposite each other on the Chemung, are simply the corruptions of the Iroquois and Delaware words for "horn," or "head-gear." The river now known as the Chemung was formerly called the Cayuga Branch, and also the Tioga. By the French it was called "R. de Kanestio," or River Canestio." This name was applied to the river to its junction with the West Branch by some of the French writers. The name Chemung has been accounted for by the finding of several large tusks, probably of the mammoth, at various places along the river, but it is possible that the name was given because of the resemblance of the various streams, which fork near the place, to the antlers of an elk or deer. The Delaware word, Wilawan, is derived from Wil, "a head," and means "head-gear." Wilawi means "rich," and also "superior." The Iroquois word also has the same derived significance of "chief," or "superior," and as such Chemung could have the significance of "chief," or "principal," and as the name of the village signify the "principal village." The "horn," or "antler" to the Indian, as, in fact, to all primitive people from the Hebrew, was an emblem of exaltation or royalty. Such a significance may also be possible in the name Chemung, or Wilawan. The name Cayuga Branch was the most commonly used name in the early Pennsylvania archives for this river, and the name Tioga River was the name used on the Boundary Survey map of Ellicott, 1787. It is also the name used on the Morris map (official) of 1848. The Indian village of Chemung was a gathering place for the Indians and Tories in 1778-1779. Col. Hartley made an expedition up the Chemung a short distance in 1778, but did not reach this village. His troops were attacked beyond Wyalusing by the Indians and Tories and drove them back. They probably retreated to Chemung (Archives, VI. 773; VII. 3-4). There were several villages along the river at this site—Chemung, a village of 50 or 60 houses, in 1779, three miles above the present Chemung; Old Chemung, a village which had been abandoned, save for about a few houses, in 1779. situated half a mile above the present Chemung. This town was destroyed by Sullivan's army on Aug. 13, 1779. The army marched on to the main town, which contained between 50 and 60 houses, and found that the Indians had fled. About a mile beyond this village was a small settlement, called Newtown, where the Indian fires were still burning. Col. Hibley's regiment moved on up the path about a mile, when it was fired upon, killing 6 and wounding 12. (Consult: Jour. Mil. Exped. Gen. Sullivan, 125-126; Hubley's Jour., Dr. Jordan, Ed., 1920; Archives, VII. 67). The army returned to Tioga, where it remained until Aug. 26th, when the march up the river was commenced. Chemung was reached on Aug. 28, where the army encamped until the 29th. Col. Hubley says in his Journal for this date, "From the great quantities of Corn & other vegetables here and in the neighborhood, it is supposed the (they) intended to establish their principal Magazine at this place, wh (which) seems to be their chief randevouze, when ever they intend to go to War, * * * The Corn already destroyed bu our Army is not less than 5000 Bushels, upon a moderate calculation" (Hubley's Jour. op. cit., 27). Chemung was a gathering place

for the Munsee and the hostile Iroquois during the French and Indian War. Many prisoners were taken to this place and from here sent to other villages along the Chemung, Tioga and Cowanesque (Col. Rec., VII. 223; VIII. 345, 416, 423, 669; Archives, IV. 46).

Chemong.—Blake (1779), Jour. Sull. Exped., 39. **Chemung.**—Hartley (1778), Archives, VII. 3. **Chimung.** — Grant (1779), same ref., Sull. Exped., 139. **Shamong.**—Barton (1779), same ref., Sull Exped., 6. **Shamung.** — Beatty (1779), same ref., Sull. Exped., 24; Hunter, (1778), Archives, VI. 773. **Shemung.**—Burton (1779), same ref., Sull. Exped., 44. **Shemoung.**—Roberts (1779), Sull. Exped., 242. **Old Shemung.**—Nukerck (1779), Sull. Exped., 219. **New Shemung.**—Nukerck (1779), Sull. Exped., 219. The river is noted as follows. **Cayuga Branch.**—Evans map, 1749. **Cayuga or Tyoga.**—Howell map, 1792. **R. de Kanestio.**—Pouchot map, 1758. **Tioga River.**—Ellicott map, 1787; Morris map, 1848. **River Canestio.**—Archives, Sec. Ser., VI 404 (1758).

CHENASTRYS. See *Otzinachson.*

CHEROKEE. The Cherokee belonged to the Iroquoian linguistic group. They occupied the whole mountain region in southwest Virginia, west North Carolina, South Carolina, and parts of Georgia, Tennessee, Alabama and evidently at one time they occupied the region at the headwaters of the Ohio. They are now identified with the Alligewi, or Talligewi, of tradition, who were driven from the Ohio by the united forces of the Delaware and Iroquois. (See *Allegheny.*) They were living in the southern mountain region, noted above, when they were first met by De Soto in 1540. (For general history, consult Handbook of American Indians, Part I, 245, 1907.) The tradition of their expulsion from the Ohio region is now accepted as an almost proven historical fact. (Consult: Cyrus Thomas, The Problem of the Ohio Mounds, 8 38-50, 1889.) The Iroquois, while belonging to the same family, waged a relentless war against the Cherokee. This warfare was the cause of their appearance in the history of Pennsylvania. Every year the war parties of the Iroquois went southward over the Warriors Path, crossing Virginia and going into the country of the Catawba and Cherokee for scalps. These wars were disastrous to the southern Indians and also to the settlers who were scattered along the frontiers of Virginia. The Iroquois warriors as they went southward often killed the cattle of these frontier settlements, in order to get food. In the fall of 1736, Gov. Gooch, of Virginia, wrote a letter to Gov. Logan, of Pennsylvania, concerning a settlement of this war between the Iroquois and the Cherokee and Catawba. It was, therefore, proposed that the Iroquois send deputies to Williamsburg to meet with the deputies of these southern tribes, in order to come to terms of peace. (Consult: Col. Rec. Pa., IV. 203, 1851.) It was decided to send Conrad Weiser to Onondaga on a mission to the Iroquois, telling them of this plan. Weiser started on this journey on the 27th of February, 1737, crossing the mountains, which were covered with snow, and undergoing fearful hardships and almost starvation before he reached Onondaga. According to his report, the Iroquois were willing to treat with the southern Indians, but declined to go to Williamsburg, and proposed Albany as a meeting place. In the meanwhile, they would agree to a cessation of arms for a year. (Consult: Walton, Conrad Weiser, 33-43, 1900.) In the fall of 1737 a party of Iroquois fell upon a party of Catawba, killing three of them, at the very time when the messengers from the Governor of Virginia were telling the southern Indians of the peace with the Iroquois. This put an end to all talk of peace with the Catawba, but the Cherokees were still willing to make peace, and would send deputies to the Iroquois with such proposals. (Col. Rec. Pa., IV, 245-246, 1851.) For several years very little was done by the Province of Pennsylvania in bringing about any sort of an understanding between the northern and the southern Indians. In 1743, Governor Thomas, of Pennsylvania, who had been seeking to bring about a reconciliation, reported to the Assembly that these differences might be settled at a treaty the next spring, and that both sides had promised to commit no acts of hostility in the meanwhile (Col. Rec. Pa., IV, 658). In August, 1743, Weiser's report of his mission to Onondaga was presented to the Council. At the conference at Onondaga, Weiser had presented all of the peace proposals of the southern Indians, and a sort of peace was patched up with the Cherokees. One of the Iroquois speakers had said, 'We are ingaged in a Warr with the Catawbas which will last to the End of the World, for they molest Us and speak Contemptu-

ously of Us, which our Warriors will not bear, and they will soon go to War against them again; it will be in vain for Us to diswade them from it." (Col Rec. Pa., IV, 668, 1851.) This condition of constant warfare between the northern Indians and those of the South continued, notwithstanding all of the efforts of the Province of Pennsylvania and the Colony of Virginia to bring about a lasting peace, until the commencement of the struggle of the French and the British for the possession of the Ohio. The frequent change of Governors in both of these English colonies did not help matters, and the absolute ignorance of the royal authorities in England concerning Indian affairs simply made matters worse. The British authorities advised the Governors of these two colonial governments to let Indian affairs alone, when they could no more keep out of them in the impending conflict than they could keep out of that conflict itself. The Indian was not a puppet on the stage of action, but one of the leading actors. In fact, he held the key to the entire situation. Iroquois hostility at this juncture meant the blotting out of the English settlements west of the seaboard cities, and the sure possession of the Ohio by the French. And yet, that was just the thing which the blundering of the British authorities and the ignorance of conditions on the part of Colonial Councils threatened to accomplish. Gov. Dinwiddie, of Virginia, wrote to Gov. Hamilton, in 1753, "I have sent to the Cherokees and the Catawbas—the Former offer a Thousand Men, and the Latter say they will all march to defend their Hunting Ground on the Ohio, but I will wait for Orders from Home and more explicit Account of the French Transactions." (Col. Rec. Pa., V, 668, 1851.) Had this help been given by the Cherokee and Catawba at this juncture, the Iroquois would have joined the French on the Ohio and blotted out every English settlement in the frontiers of Pennsylvania. As a matter of history, the attempt to get the help of these southern Indians had much to do with the complete alienation of the Indians on the Ohio, who would all alike—Delaware, Shawnee and Iroquois—fight against any army having these southern Indians as allies. An alliance with the Cherokee and Catawba, by the British, and the friendship of the Iroquois at the same time was utterly impossible. The defeat of General Braddock's expedition was due primarily to the French telling the Indians on the Ohio that Braddock was opening a road to let in the Cherokee and Catawba from Virginia. The Indians on the Ohio believed this story until Christian F. Post made them think otherwise in 1758. In 1756, when preparations were being made for another expedition to the Ohio, efforts of peace were again made, but these had little influence. After Washington's defeat at Fort Necessity, in 1754, the Half-King and other Indians, friendly to the English, went to Aughwick. Capt. Stobo, in his letter from Fort Duquesne, where he was held as a hostage, said, "Tis now reported for certain that the Half King, &c., are killed and their Wives and Children given up to the Barbarity of the Cherokees and Catawbas, of whom they say there are 300 at the New Store" (that is, at Fort Cumberland). (Col. Rec. Pa., VI, 161, 1851.) This report, according to Stobo, greatly alarmed them, and had it not been for that report I believe a great many Indians of several Nations would have been with you." In 1756, John A. Long, who had been captured and taken up the Allegheny River. reported to Gov. Dinwiddie, after his escape, that he had been carried to Buckaloon (q. v.) where the "Mingos" heard a report that the English had joined with the Cherokee and Catawba and were going against the Ohio Indians (Col. Rec. Pa., VII, 289, 1851). In the meanwhile, the British authorities went on trying to collect Cherokees for the Expedition of General Forbes, through the efforts of Mr. Atkins. Sir William Johnson, who did understand the Iroquois. wrote to Mr. Atkin that he expected this effort of an alliance with these Indians to end in a general Indian war between the northern and the southern Indians (Col. Rec. Pa., VII, 626-727, 1851). A small number of the Cherokee were finally persuaded, by many presents, to join in the expedition of General Forbes. Gov. Denny, in a letter to Col. Washington (1758), says, "I have reason to believe that the Cherokees hate the Delawares and Shawnenese, and do not desire that they should become our Friends, but would have them all destroyed, having Long born them great Enmity" (Col. Rec. Pa., VII, 56-57, 1852). In the

peace efforts which Tedyuskung was carrying on with the Delaware, with the assistance of C. F. Post his hopes of success, which seemed bright, suddenly became darkened. A general Indian war seemed imminent. When the reason for this was sought it was found that the presence of the Cherokee with the army of General Forbes was the real cause for the sudden disaffection of the Delaware. General Forbes and Gov. Denny both realized the situation. Charles Thompson and C. F. Post were sent to Wyoming to consult with Tedyuskung and gave him the messages of peace from the Cherokee. Then, after their return, Post was sent to the Indians on the Ohio with the peace proposals which had been made to the Delaware, and to carry the messages of General Forbes and Gov. Denny concerning the reason why the Cherokee warriors were with the army which was advancing towards Fort Duquesne. Even then all of the Indians on the Ohio thought that the Cherokees were being taken into their country in order to blot them out. The army of General Forbes entered the deserted ruins of the French fort, not because it was in any way superior to that of General Braddock, but because the Indians kept away from the place. The Delaware had been won back to friendship, and the Indians on the Ohio were made to believe that the southern Indians were not going to be led in, to blot them out. But, there was no peace between the northern and the southern Indians. In 1762, at the Council at Lancaster, Thomas King an Oneida Chief, said, "I never had occasion to go to war with the English Nation; the people I had occasion to go to war with, live to the Southward; it has been so from all ages and we have always gone to war against the Southern Indians." (Col. Rec. Pa., VIII, 744, 1852). About 150 Cherokees were collected for the Forbes expedition but by the time the army had reached Bedford there were only 25 with it.

The history of the relation of the Cherokee to the Indian affairs of Pennsylvania is one of the most interesting chapters in the history of the State. Consult, under the title *Cherokee*, any of the vols. in the Colonial Records and the First Series of the Archives of Penna.; Weiser, Journal to Onodaga, in Col. Rec. Pa., IV, 660-669, 1851; Post, Journal to Ohio, in Arch. Pa., III, 520, 1853; Post, Journal to Wyoming, Col. Rec. Pa., VIII. 142, 1852; Arch. Pa., III 412, 1853.

CHESTER CREEK. Enters the Delaware from the west at Chester, Delaware County. The Indian name was Macopanackhan, probably a corruption of Meechoppenackhan, signifying "large potato river," according to Heckewelder. Me-cheek, "large"; Hobbe-nac, "potatoes;" hanna, "stream." The Swedes called the stream Opland, or Upland Kill, in an Indian deed, made to William Penn in 1685, it is called, "Macopanackhan, also Upland, now called Chester River or Creek" (Arch. Pa., I, 92, 1852). In another Indian deed of lands, made to Penn, in 1683, it is called, "Macopanackhan, als Chester River" (the same ref. 65). The first mention of a settlement at Upland was made by Huddie in the meeting with the Passayunk Indians in 1648. It is probable that Upland was settled in 1645. Court was first held at this place in 1672. "The Records of Upland" Court contain the records from 1676 to 1681. The jurisdiction of Upland Court was made as follows, "The court for the inhabitants of Upland shall have jurisdiction over the people on the east and the west side of Christina Kil and upwards to the head of the river" (Sept. 12, 1673). See Arch. Pa., Second Ser. VII, 758, 1878. The Justices of the Peace, appointed Sept. 23, 1676, were Peter Cock, Peter Rambo, Israel Helm, Lace Andrilsen, Oele Swen and Otto Ernest Cock. Their commissions were signed by Gov. Edmond Andros. According to the list of taxables at the various settlements on the Delaware in 1677, there were 17 persons (taxable) at Upland. William Penn made his first landing in America at Upland in 1682. It has been said that the exact date was October 27th., but Dr. Smith says that no man knows "the hour, the day, or the manner of his landing." Penn changed the name of Upland to Chester soon after his arrival. Consult; The Records of Upland Court, in Hist. Soc. Pa. Mem. VII, 1860; Colonies on the Delaware, Arch. Pa., Sec. Ser., V, 1890; Papers Rel. to the Dutch and Swedish Set. on the Delaware, Arch. Pa., Sec. Ser., VII, 459-820, 1878.

CHINKANNING. A former Indian village, near the mouth of Tunkhannock creek, Wyoming County, near the present Tunkhannock. See TUNKHANNOCK. Possibly a corruption of Chickhansink (noted by Heckewelder), which is a corruption of Tshickhansink, "where we were robbed, or, the place of robbery." The village was visited by Scarouady and Andrew Montour in Dec. 1755, as messengers form the Province to the Iroquois. At that time there were about 30 fighting men in the place. Tedyuskung was then at the village and informed them that he had been made a King.

Chickhansink. — Heckewelder, Indian Names. 242, 1872. **Chinkanning.**—Montour, Scarouady (1756), Col. Rec. Pa., VII, 66, 1851.

CHICORA.. A town in Butler County. The name given by the Spaniards, in 1521, to the coast of South Carolina, and to the Indian inhabitants of it. Gatschet says that the word is derived from the Catawba, Yuchikere, "Yuchi are there." See Handbook of American Indians, Part, 1 263.

CHICKASAW. A Muskhogean tribe, related to the Choctaw. Their chief landing place on the Mississippi River was at Chickasaw Bluffs, now Memphis, Tenn. They were a very warlike tribe. They claimed the region to the mouth of the Tennessee River—on the Ohio. They are frequently mentioned in the records of Penna., although they never played an important part in the Indian history of the State. Conrad Weiser in 1755 said that there were five or six Chickasaws living with the Shawnee at "Ostuacky" (at the mouth of Loyalsock Creek, Lycoming County). These had been living there for many years, and when Weiser was there they had been visited by two messengers from the Chickasaw nation. See Col. Rec. Pa., VI, 444, 1851. In 1756 there were a few Chickasaw living with the Shawnee, on the west side of the river near Wyoming (Col. Rec. Pa.. VII, 51, 1851). In 1757 two Indians were captured near Bedford by Capt. Paris and a company of Cherokee allies. One of these was a Chickasaw, who had been at Fort Duquesne with the French. He gave a great deal of valuable information concerning affairs on the Ohio (See Col. Rec. Pa., VII, 631, 1851.).

CHIEPIESSING. The name given to the lands in Bucks County, opposite the falls of the Delaware. The name is probably a corruption of Kschippehellen, "the water flows rapidly," with the locative "ing," signifying, "the place where the water

flows rapidly." The first mention of the place by this name is in the grant of land made to Capt. Hugh Hyde and Capt. Thomas Morley by Sir Robert Carr, in 1664.
Chiapiessnig.—Lovelace (1671), Arch. Sec. Ser., V, 642, 1890. **Chiepiessing.**—Lovelace (1671), Arch. Pa., Sec. Ser., XVI, 271, 1890. **Chiepiessinge.**—Moll (1680), Arch. Pa., Sec. Ser., VII, 803, 1878. **Chipassing.**—Minute Book "B" (1692), Arch. Pa., Sec. Ser., XIX, 87, 1893. **Chipussen.**—Carr (1664), Arch. Pa., Sec. Ser., V, 576, 1890.

CHILLISQUAQUE. A creek which enters the West Branch from the north in Northumberland County. Also the name of a township in the same county. Corrupted from Chililisuagi, "place of snow-birds," according to Heckewelder. There was a Shawnee village at the mouth of the creek, which had been settled soon after the Shawnee commenced to settle about Wyoming, evidently by members of this tribe who came over the old trail from the Ohio. Conrad Weiser passed through the place in 1737 on his way to Onondaga. The Count Zinzendorf and Martin Mack, the Moravian missionary passed through the region in 1742. See the Journals of both of these, in "Memorials of the Moravian Church," Vol. I, 1870. The first mention of the place in the archives of the State, is that in which it is called "Shallyschohking," in the petition from the Shawnee, signed by James Le Tort and Peter Chartier, in 1732. This letter was drawn up by Edmund Cartlidge. During the early years of white settlement the place was frequently visited by the hostile Indians, who carried away a number of captives from the "Chillisquaque settlement," as it was called. See Meginness. "Otzinachson," 237, 251, 260, 271, 306, 1856.
Chelisquaqua. — Crawford (1754), Archives, II, 133. **Chilisquaque.**—Scull map. 1770. **Chillesquaque.**—Board of Prop. (1783), Arch. Pa., Third Ser., I, 428, 1894. **Chillisquaque.**—Scull (1770), Arch. Pa., Third Ser., I, 289, 1894. **Chillisquaquy.**—Scull map, 1759. **Shallyschohking.** —Cartlidge (1732), Arch. Pa., I, 329, 1852. **Zilly-squachne.**—Weiser (1737), in Indian Names (Reichel's note), 242, 1872.

CHINKLACAMOOSE. A former Indian village, at the site of Clearfield, Clearfield County. There are nearly as many meanings given to the Indian name as there are various forms of the name itself. Heckewelder says that it is a corruption of Achtschingi-clamme, meaning "it al-

most joins"—having reference to the stream at this point. Ettwein gives the meaning, "no one tarries here willingly," evidently having reference to Punxsuatawney, as the legend he relates belongs to that place, according to Zeisberger (See PUNXSUATAWNEY). Hewitt gives the origin as, "Chinguaklakamoose, meaning large laughing moose." The later name, Clearfield, was given by the first white traders because of the clearings along the creek, due to the herds of buffalo which grazed over the region. C. F. Post passed over the trail through this village in 1758, when on his way to the council with the Indians at Kuskuski (Arch. Pa., III, 522, 1853). The main trail from Shamokin to the Ohio, as well as a branch of the Frankstown trail, passed through this place. This northern trail was used by the Indians during the French and Indian War. Many of the captives taken in the raids in the Cumberland Valley and along the Susquehanna, were taken to the Indian villages on the Allegheny and other western rivers, by this trail. See the "Narrative" of Marie le Roy, in Archives of Pa., Second Ser., VII, 405 etc., 1878. After the building of Fort Augusta at Shamokin in 1756, Col. Burd sent out scouting parties along this trail at various times. In 1757 it was reported that a body of French and Indians were on their way over this trail to make an attack upon Fort Augusta. Col. Burd sent out a detachment under the command of Capt. Patterson to scout as far as Chinklacamoose. This detachment returned within a few days, having met with no Indians. They found the town at C. burned and the place unoccupied (Arch. Pa., Sec. Ser., II, 777, 1876).

Chinglechamush. — Col. Burd (1757), Arch. Pa., Sec. Ser., II, 777, 1876 **Chingleclamoose.**—Heckewelder, in Hist. Sec. Mem., VII, 199, 1876. **Chinglecla-mouche.**—Scull, map, 1759. **Chingleo-lamlik.**—La Tour, map, 1784. **Chingleo-lamouk.**—Scull, map, 1770. **Chingleola-muk.**—Gussefeld, map, 1784. **Chinklaca-moose.**—Day, in Hist. Coll. of Pa., 231, 1843. **Chinklacamoose's Oldtown.**—Day, in Hist. Coll. of Pa., 231, 1843. **Jenkikla-muhs.**—Le Roy (1755), Arch. Pa., Sec. Ser., VII, 404, 1878. **Shingaclamoose.**—Armstrong (1778), Arch. Pa., VI, 612, 1853. **Shingelaclamoos.** — Bard (1758), Arch. Pa., III, 433, 1853. **Shinglacamuch.** —Col. Burd (1757), Arch. Pa., Sec. Ser., II, 780, 1876. **Shinglacamush.**—Col. Burd (1757), 777. **Shingleclamouse.**—Denny (1757), Arch. Pa., III, 116, 1853. **Shingle-Clamushe.**—Clapham (1756), Arch. Pa., 41. **Shinglimnce.**—Post (1758), Arch. Pa., 522.

CHIQUESALUNGA. A creek which enters the Susquehanna from the east in Lancaster County, above Columbia. A post office called, Salunga, and a station, called Chickies, in the same county, have abbreviated the name. The Indian name is a corruption of Chickiswalungo, "the place of the craw-fish." according to Heckewelder. The region along the Susqeuhanna, between Conestoga and Paxtang, was settled at a very early year in the 18th century, by the Scotch-Irish. Some of the early land grants along this creek were given to German people. Michael Shank and Jacob Graeff were each given 250 acres on this creek in 1724. Peter Allen and James Gilbraith were both living near the mouth of the creek in 1718, where they carried on a trade with the Indians. The author has often thought that these Scotch-Irish traders who first heard the name of the creek, not only corrupted it but also misplaced it. That the name applied to the hill near the mouth of the Conestoga, and not to the creek now known as Chiquesalunga. This hill was known as, "Turkey Hill," from earliest times. The Delaware word for turkey is T'schikenum, and the word for a round hill is, Wulumque. The compound word as it sounded to Scotch-Irish ears could easily be given the form Checkasolungas. On the Scull map of 1770, the creek enters the Susquehanna near a large rock, which is called, "Chickies Rock."

Checasolungas.—Minute Book (1724), Arch. Pa, Sec. Ser., XIX, 724, 1893. Checkaselunga.—Taylor ms. maps, No. 635, (1734), Hist. Soc. of Penna. Checkaselunga.—Taylor. No. 637, (1734), Hist. Soc. of Penna. Cheekaselunga.—Taylor, No 669, (1734), Hist. Soc. of Penna. Chickasalonge.—Blunston (1736), Arch. Pa., I, 532, 1852. Chickisalunga.—Howell, map, 1792. Chickisalungo.—Scull, map, 1759. Chickislungo.—Adlum, map, 1790. Chicques.—Morris, map, 1848. Chiquesatunga.—State map 1912, (an error). Chukusolungo.—Hempfield Manor map, in Hist. Soc. of Pa. Shecassalungas.—Minute Book "K" (1733), Arch. Pa., Third Ser., I, 31, 1894. Sheckasalungo.—Minute Book (1724), Arch. Pa, Sec. Ser, XIX, 749, 1893. Shickaselungo.—Taylor ms. No. 631, (1734), Hist. Soc. of Penna.

CHOCONUT. See *Chugnut.*

CHOWATIN. A creek mentioned by C F. Post in 1758. Was no doubt the present Mahoning, near Punxuatawney, in Jefferson County. The Indian trail crossed the Mahoning and the Little Mahoning near the forks of these streams. See Archives of Penna., III, 542, 1833.

CHOCTAW. A tribe belonging to the Muskhogean group. Their habitat was in southern Mississippi. Soon after the French and Indian War they began to move westward, across the Mississippi River. The greater part of those living in Miss. moved into Indian Ter. soon after the sale of their lands to the U. S. in 1832. They never had any relation to the affairs of Penna. History. A "Choctaw King, and his Queen" visited Philadelphia in 1787, with a delegation of Cherokee and Chickasaw on "business of the United States." They were given various presents, and their expenses paid while in the city, and for their return to Fort Pitt, on their way home. See Col. Rec. Pa., XV, 229, 232, 238, 240, 250, 277, 1853.

CHUGNUT. A creek which rises in Susquehanan County, called Choconut, enters the Susquehanna from the south, at Vestal, New York; also the name of a town in Susquehanna County. The name Choconut is a corruption of the Nanticoke word Tschochnot, according to Heckeweler. Cusick says that the name means, "place of tamaracks" (Aboriginal Place Names of N. Y., 27, 1907). Mooney, in Handbook of American Indians, gives the form Chugnut, as the correct one. He says that this was the name "of a small tribe living, about 1755, under Iroquois protection in a village of the same name." The name was not that of a tribe as Mooney says, but was a geographical group, composed of Iroquois, Delaware, Nanticoke, Conoy and Shawnee, to whom the name of the village in which they lived was applied. There were two villages to which this name applied. One was situated on the north side of the Susquehanna at the mouth of the present Nanticoke Creek, at the site of Union; the other village was on the opposite side of the river, at the mouth of the present Choconut Creek, at the site of Vestal, New York. A number of the Indians from this settlement were present at the Council at Easton in 1758. During the French and Indian War, as well as during the Revolution, it was a rendezvous for the Indians hostile to the settlers in Penna. In 1779, when the expedition of Gen. Sullivan went up the Susquehanna, the settlement here was destroyed. At that time there were 50 or 60 houses in the place, mostly on the south side of the river. The Brigade of Gen. Poor reached the village on Aug. 19, 1779, and destroyed it. The detachment under Gen. Clinton united with that of Gen. Poor at this place—hence the name of Union. The records of Penna. have the following forms of the name:

Choconotte.—Clapham (1756), Arch. Pa., III, 664, 1852. **Chooonut.**—Howell, map, 1792. **Chocquonote.**—Council at Phila. (1756), Col. Rec. Pa., VII, 171, 1851. **Chokenote.**—Pa. Council (1763), Col. Rec. Pa., IX, 46, 1852. **Choquonote.**—Pa. Coun. (1756), Col. Rec Pa., VII, 172, 1851. **Chughnut.**—Pa. Coun. (1756), the same, 68. **CHUGNOT.**—Pa. Coun. (1761), VIII, 644, 1852 **Chugnuts.**—Coun. at Easton (1758), Col. Rec. Pa., VIII, 176, 1852. The following forms are found in the "Journals of the Military Expedition of General Sullivan," 1887· **Chaconnut.**—Campfield, 55. **Choconant.**—Norris, 230. **Choconut.**—Flats. Fogg, 93. **Chokoanut.**—Hubley, 153 **Chuggnuts.**—Beatty, 24. **Chukkanut.**—Machin, 202. **Churamuk.**—Livermore, 185. **Cokanuck.**—Campfield. 55.

CLARION. The name of a county and of a creek. The creek enters the Allegheny River near Foxburg, Clarion County. Heckewelder gives the Indian name as having been "Gawunschhanne," meaning "brier stream." The name given upon the Scull map (1770) is Toby's Creek. C. F. Post calls it the "River Tobees" (Arch. Pa., III, 522, 1853). The Indian name was more likely to have been Topi-hanne, "alder stream," of which Toby's, or Tobees, is a corruption.

CLISTOWACKIN. A former Delaware village, situated on the path which led to the Minisinks on Martin's Creek, Lower Bethel Township, Northampton County. Zinzendorf visited the village in 1742, after having been at Tatemy's, near Stockertown. Five miles beyond Tatemy's he came to Clistonwackin, or Clistowackin. Brainerd, the missionary, preached here in 1744, when he lived in a cottage which he had built. (Consult: Mom. Mor. Church, 27-27; Loskiel, Hist. Miss., II, 24). The name is a corruption of Schigi, "fine," and Hacki, "land." The name is doubtless the same as that given on the map of Van Der Donck, 1656, as "t'Schichte Wacki," although on his map it is placed on the east side of the Delaware. The name, no doubt, applied to the region on both sides of the river, or was applied to the lands along Martin Creek after the Delawares moved there from New

Jersey. This region south of the Water Gap was occupied by the Delawares until they were driven away from it by the command of the Iroquois. (See *Delaware Water Gap, Lehigh,* etc.).

Clistowacka.—Loskiel (1794), in Hist. Miss., II, 24. **Clistowacki**—Brodhead, in Del. Water Gap, 46. **Clistowackin.**—Reichel, in Mem. Mor. Church, I. 27-28. **t'Schichte Wacki.**—Van Der Donck map, 1656.

CLEARFIELD CREEK. The stream enters the West Branch from the south at Clearfield. The name given upon the Scull map (1759) is Loyas Skutchanning," which is possibly a corruption of Lawi—"middle," kschiechi, "clear," and the locative ing, meaning "at the middle clear place." Or, it might be, 'at the place of the middle clear stream" — Kschiechi, "clear"; hanna, "stream," and the locative, ing.

COAQUANNOCK. The Indian name usually applied to the site of Philadelphia. Heckewelder gives its origin, from Cuwequenaku, "the grove of tall pines." The author of this article is, however, of the opinion that the name was that of the stream which was later known as Pegg's Run and which had its head springs in that part of the city of Philadelphia known as Spring Garden. The survey of the lands of Julian Hartsfielder was on the west side of the Delaware "at the lower side of Cohocksink Creek (later Mill Creek), beginning at the mouth of a small creek, or river, called Coach-que-naw-que." This survey was dated March 1, 1675. (See Arch. Pa., Third Ser., III, 315.) In "Minute Book "G" it is stated that Gov. Andros, by his Patent, dated March 25, 1676, granted to Jurian Hartsfielder, a tract of land, called Hartsfield. situated on the lower side of "Cohoesinck Creek." "The said Land beginning at the mouth of a Small Creek Or River Called Coo-ah-que-nunque" (Arch. Pa., Sec. Ser., XIX, 444). In 1679, Jurian Hartsfielder conveyed to Hannah (or Ann) Salter, a widow, all of the land mentioned in the above grant, save 100 acres. In April 23, 1681, Hannah Salter, of Tacony, deeded this land to Daniel Peage (meant for Pegg), "mey Land by Coakanake Creek" (Arch. Pa., XIX, 445). Daniel Pegg afterwards bought many other tracts of land in the same region. According to the return of the "Taxables" living within the jurisdiction of the "Court at Upland," in 1677, "Jurian hertsveder" is put down as living at Marr. Kill (Marcus Hook) In September 11, 1677, Jurian Hartswelder asked permission to resign his office as under-sheriff, on account of his "Remooveing his Living higher up the River" (See Records of Upland Court, 57, 80, 1860). It was no doubt at this time that Hartsfielder took possession of his lands in Philadelphia, "at the mouth of Coach-que-naw-que." According to the statement of John Reed, the "Northern Liberties" began on "Vine Street, then up the Delaware River to the mouth of Coach-que-naw-que; (which creek divides this from Jurian Hartfielder's land)." See Arch. Pa., Third Ser., III, 312.) In Proud's History of Pennsylvania, I, 211, 1798, it is said, "The Proprietary being now returned from Maryland to Coaquannock, the place so called by the Indians, where Philadelphia now stands, began to purchase lands of the natives, whom he treated with great justice and kindness." Proud, who is not always exact in his application of Indian place names, gave all of the future historians the name, which belonged to the creek, as the name of a village, or an Indian settlement. All of the later writers have followed the error which Proud evidently made. Clarkson, in his biography of Penn, says, "It appears that though the parties were to assemble at Coaquannock, the treaty was made a little higher up at Shackamaxon" (Vol. I, 264). The various reasons given as to why this change was made are "as a settlement had been long before made at Shackamaxon, by the Indians (natives) and by some Europeans" (Mem. Hist. Soc. I, 104, 1860). The real reason was that there was no Indian village at the mouth of this creek, and because Shackamaxon (more correctly, Shackamaxing) was a meeting place for the Indians. The author has been unable to find any reference whatever in which the name Coaquannock, in any of its forms, is applied to any place other than "Pegg's Run." According to various historical works, the name Coaquannock was the name of a village, and Cohoquinoque was the name of the creek. These names, and various others, are merely corruptions of the Indian name of the creek, known as Pegg's Run, after Daniel Pegg occupied the lands along its shore. The various forms of the Indian name are evidently corruptions of the compound

word which meant "tall pine tree stream." Some of the names recorded contain the Indian word hanna, or hannock, meaning "stream."

Coach-que-naw-que. — Survey of 1675, Arch. Pa., Third Ser., III, 312, 1894. **Coakanake.**—Deed of 1681, Arch. Pa., Sec Ser., XIX, 445, 1896. **Coaquannock.**—Heckewelder, Indian Names, 243, 1872 **Cooachquenauque.**—Deed of 1693, Arch. Pa., Sec. Ser., XIX, 182. **Coo-ah-que-nau-que.**—Deed of 1676, noted in Records of Upland, 57, 1860. **Coo-ah-que-nunque.** —Deed of 1676, Arch. Pa., Sec. Ser., XIX, 444. **Cohoquinoque.**—Wescott, in Eagle, Hist. of Pa., 1019, 1883. **Coquanoc.**—Wescott, in Eagle, Hist. of Pa., 1017. **Koo-ek-wen-aw-koo.**—Reichel, in Heck. Indian Nations, 142, 1876. **Kuequenaku.**—Heckewelder, Indian Nations, 142.

COCALICO. A creek and township in Lancaster County. Corrupted from Achgookwalico, meaning "where the snakes collect in dens to pass the winter," according to Heckewelder. The name means simply "snake dens." Achgook, "snake;" walak, "hole." There evidently had been an Indian village on this creek, before 1724. Eberherd Ream in that year made a request for 200 acres of land on a branch of the Conestoga Creek, "on which was a small Indian settlement called Cocallico" (Arch. Pa., Sec. Ser., XIX, 725, 1890). Many of the land surveys made by John Taylor, in 1733-34, were along this creek. The various survey maps are in the Taylor Papers, at the Historical Society of Pennsylvania.

COCK EYE'S CABIN. A prominent landmark on the Indian trail from Raystown (Bedford) to Shannopin's Town (Pittsburgh), mentioned by John Harris in his table of distances from Harris' Ferry (Harrisburg) to the Ohio,—"to Cock Eye's Cabbin— 8 Miles" (from Dunning's Sleeping Place). The next distance given, from Cock Eye's Cabin, is to the Four Mile Run—11 Miles" (Archives, 1I, 135). Christopher Gist mentions this place in his Journal of 1750 as "an old Indians camp" (Dar. Gist, 33). Darlington, in a note, says that this camp was that of Cock Eye, or Cockey, "a Delaware Indian, well known to the traders" (op. cit. 92). The situation of this place was probably on Bushy Run, near the scene of the Battle of Bushy Run, Aug. 5-6, 1763, near the present Harrison City, Westmoreland County. (See *Bushy Run*), according to Darlington (92). This is probably an error. Cock Eye's Cabin was probably on Brush Creek, near Trafford City. The distance from this "cabin" to Shannopin's Town, according to Harris, was 15 miles. According to Gist, the distance from the "old Indian's camp" to Shannopin's Town was twenty miles. Darlington may have been mistaken in identifying this "old Indian's Cabin" with "Cock Eye's Cabin," or the Indian had moved his cabin down Brush Creek in 1754. See *Dunning's Sleeping Place.*

Calico.—Howell, map, 1792. Also Cocalico. **Cocalico.**—German Clergy (1754), Arch. Pa., II, 186, 1853. **Cocallico.**—Pa. Land Rec. (1724), Arch. Pa., Sec. Ser., XIX, 725, 1890. **Cocolico.**—Scull, map, 1759. Also many of the Taylor surveys (1733). **Colico.**—Butcher (1736), Col. Rec. Pa., IV, 183, 1851.

COCOLAMUS. The name of a creek, and also of a Post Office in Juniata County. The creek enters the Juniata from the north at Millerstown, Perry County. The name given on the Scull map is Kakonlamus. There is a species of hawk, called by the Indians, "Kakon." The name may be derived from this word.

Cocalamus.—Morris, map, 1848. **Cockalamus.**—Scull, map, 1770. **Cockalanus.**—Howell, map, 1792. **Cocolamus.**—Recent state maps—R. R. map pub. by State, 1912. **Cokelamus.** — (date not given), Arch. Pa., Third Ser., III, 28⁰, 1896. **Kakonlamus.**—Scull, map, 1759.

COCOOSING. A branch of Tulpehocken Creek in Berks County. A village in the same county, called Cacosing. Corrupted from Gokhosing, "place of owls." Reichel says that Count Zinzendorf preached in a farm house on the Cocoosing, Dec. 28, 1742, during his visit to the Moravian Mission stations in Pennsylvania. (Heck., Indian Names, 244, 1872.) Some of the Taylor surveys, in 1733-34, were of lands along this stream.

Cacoosing.—Taylor, survey map, (1733), No. 626, in Hist. Soc. Pa., Coll. **Cacoosin.**—Taylor, survey map, (1734), No. 672, in Hist. Soc. Pa., Coll. **Cocasing.**—Scull, map, 1770. **Cocosing.**—Scull, map, 1770, (French map). **Coocosing.**—Scull, map, 1759.

CODORUS. A creek which enters the Susquehanna from the west at Star View, York County; also the name of a Post Office in the same county. The name is said to be derived from an Indian word meaning "rapid water." If such is the case, the original form of the word has been lost. The entire region along the Susquehanna, from the mouth of Codorus Creek, entered into the almost endless litigation between the Penns and the Calverts, in the boundary dispute between Pennsylvania and Maryland.

The first settlers in the Codorus Creek region were intruders from Maryland, who settled upon the lands which the Penns had not purchased from the Indians. In 1729, John and James Hendricks were given a license to settle on the lands west of the Susquehanna, by the authorities of the Province. In the same year, Charles Carroll was given a warrant for 10,000 acres, which included the Codorus Creek region, by the Governor of Maryland. In 1730, Thomas Cresap settled upon the lands near Wrightsville, and immediately there commenced the long fight between the rival settlers of the two colonies. (Consult: Col. Rec. Pa. (the letters of the Governors of Pennsylvania and Maryland), III, IV, 1851; Archives of Penna., 1853. Sec. Ser., XVI (the entire vol.), 1890. In 1736, the Province of Pennsylvania was purchased from the Iroquois, "All of the lands lying on the West side of the said River to the setting of the Sun" and, by so doing, alienated the great body of the Delaware and Shawnee, whose lands had been sold "under their feet." In trying to get ahead of the Colony of Maryland in the purchase of these lands, the Province of Pennsylvania brought upon itself the hatred and hostility of the Delaware and Shawnee, by ignoring them and by admitting that the Iroquois had the right to sell these lands. (See Treaty of 1736, in Col. Rec. Pa., IV, 79-94, 1851; Copy of the Deed, in Arch. Pa., I, 494-499, 1852). From this time forward the Delaware and Shawnee drifted away from the influence of the Province, to the Ohio River, where they sought to break away from the Iroquois yoke. The region west of the Susquehanna, in 1732, contained 400 persons who paid taxes to the Pennsylvania authorities. After the Treaty of 1736, the region about Codorus Creek filled up rapidly with both Scotch-Irish and German settlers. The County of York was created by an Act of Assembly, Aug. 19, 1749. In 1741, the town, called Yorktown, was laid out upon Codorus Creek. At the various elections held at this place, there was much disorder caused by the factional fights between the Scotch-Irish and the German elements. This contention kept up until the erection of Adams County, in 1800. In 1768, John Lukens made the return of the survey of the "Manor of Springetsbury," which included much of the land on

Codorus Creek, the present city of York being almost in the center of the plot. (See map No. 63, Arch. Pa., Third Ser., IV, 1895.) See *Conejohela*. **Codoras.**—Evans, map, 1749. **Codorus.**—Evans, map, 1755.

COHOCKSINK. A creek which entered the Delaware, below Kensington, in the present City of Philadelphia, later known as Mill Creek. The name is a corruption of Cuwenhasink, "where there are pine trees," according to Heckewelder. The name is compounded of the words, Cuwe, "pine," hacki, "land," and ink, the locative, which means "at the pine tree land." The name is first mentioned in the patent of the grant of land to Jurian Hartsfielder, by Gov. Andros, in 1676 (See COAQUANNOCK). The land north of this place was called Shackamaxon, and it may be possible that the Indian village of that name was situated on the northern bank of this stream (See Shackamaxon). Some of the early historical writers, Watson among them, thought that the Schuylkill River once entered the Delaware by way of the course of this creek, from near the Falls of the Schuylkill. William Penn purchased the lands included in this region in 1683 (See Arch. Pa., I 66-67, 1852). Consult; Watson, Annals of Philadelphia, I, 477 etc., 1850.

C o h o c k s i n c k s.—Records of Upland (note), 57, 1860. **Cohocksink.**—Reed, map, 1777. **Cohocksinks.**—Grant to Lasse Cock (1674-77), Arch. Pa., Sec. Ser., XVI, 321, 1890. **Cohocktincks.**—Hartsfielder, Deed (1676), Arch. Pa., 298. **Cohoesinck.**—Hartsfielder, Deed (1676), Arch. Pa., Sec. Ser., XIX, 444, 1890. **Cohoxin.**—Reed (1774), Arch. Pa., Third Ser., III, 344, 1896.

CONEJOHELA. A former Indian village, settled by Conoy and Shawnee, about 1707, on the west side of the Susquehanna River, near the place where Thomas Cresap settled in 1730. The situation of this village is so clearly determined from the various accounts of it, given in the Colonial Records and Archives, that is is not a matter of doubt. In the deposition of Cresap it is stated, "that he had lived on the West Side of Susquehanna River, in the said county, ever since the Sixteenth of March last—"that he heard the noises or report of three guns which were discharged at a rock, called Blew Rock, on the east side of the said river" (Arch. Pa., I, 311, 1852). This deposition was signed Jan. 29, 1731. The Blue Rock was situated at the site of Washington Borough, in Lancaster County, and is noted on Evans map of 1749, as well as on the Scull map of 1770. Blunston in a letter of 1731, says, "That William Penn had promised them (the Indians) they Should not be Disturbed by any Settlers on the west Side of Sasquehanah, but now contrary thereto, Several Marylanders, are Settled by the River on that side, at Conejohela; And that one Crissop, perticularly is Very abusive to them when they pass that way" (Arch. Pa., I, 295, 1852). In another letter of Wright and Blunston, it is stated, "At that time there were no English Inhabitants on the west Side of Sasquehanah River, in these parts, for About two Years before Edward Parnel & Several other families who Settled on the West Side of said river, near the same. Att a place Called (by the Indians) Conejohela" (Arch. P., I, 364). In 1736 Blunston, in speaking of the various disturbances caused by the Maryland settlers, said, that after one of these raids, they retired "to their ffortress at Conejohela" (the same 531). In 1737 Robert Anderson and John Montgomery, in a deposition, stated that "that they saw one Charles Hickenbottom, who told the Deponents that he was going up the next Day to a place called Conejohela, on the West Side of Susquehannah River." Hickenbottom (Higenbottum) wished Anderson and Montgomery to help him turning off some people who had taken possession of some land and who were "settled above Conejohela" (Arch. Pa., I, 536-537, 1852). Wright and Blunston, in a letter to the Governor of Maryland (1732), said that Edward Parnel, and the others settled at Conejohela, "were at the request of the Conestogoe Indians, removed by the Governor's Order from the said Place; the Indians insisting on the same to lye vacant for their Convenience, as their Right by Treaties with this Government formerly made. But about two years since, Thomas Cressop and some other People of loose Morals and turbulent Spirits, came and disturbed the Indians, our Friends and Allies, who were peaceably settled on those Lands from whence the said Parnel and others had been removed, burnt their Cabins and destroyed their Goods, and with much threating & ill usage drove them away" (Col. Rec. Pa., III, 470-472, 1852). At the Council at Conestoga, in 1722, Governor Keith, in answer to the complaints made by the Indians concerning the settlements on the west side of the Susquehanna, said, "I have fully considered this thing and if you approve my thoughts, I will immediately cause to take up a large Tract of Land on the other side of Susquehanna for the Grandson of William Penn, who is now a man as tall as I am; For when the Land is marked with his name upon the Trees, it will keep off the Mary Landers and every other Person whatsoever from coming to settle near you and disturb you." After his return to Philadelphia Governor Keith consulted with the members of the Executive Council, and then issued orders for the surveying of the Manor of Springetsbury on the west side of the Susquehanna. The reason given for making this region a Penn Manor was, "The Conestogoes, The Shawanoes & The Cawnoyes, are very much disturbed, and the Peace of this Colony is hourly in danger of being broken by persons, who pursuing their own private gain without regard to Justice, have attempted & others do still threaten to Survey and take up Lands on the South West Branch of the sd. River, right against the Towns & settlements of the said Indians— that a sufficient quantity of Land upon the South West side of the River Sasquehannah be surveyed and reserved the Proprietors hands, for accomodating the said Indian Nations when it may hereafter be thought proper & convenient for them to remove their Settlements further from the Christan Inhabitants." The Manor of Springetsbury was surveyed and the return made, June 21, 1722. (See Col. Rec. Pa., III 178-186, 1852). There is no doubt but that Conejohela was settled by various Conoy and Shanwee soon after this survey was made, and that the Indians remained at this village until the coming of Cresap in 1730. The purpose for which the Manor of Springetsbury was laid out was that the Indians east of the Susquehanna might have a place of refuge from the encroachments of the white settlers. Mr. Hanna, in "The Wilderness Trail," I, 151, 1911, places Conejohela at the site of Washington Borough, on the east side of the river, and makes this village and Dekanogah identical. Dekanogah occupied the site of Washington Borough, but Conejohela was directly opposite, on the west side of the river, in, not "directly across the river from that part of York County

which is still called Conejohela, or Conjocula Valley." The reason why this valley, and the creek was so called, was because the Indian village of Conejohela was at the mouth of the run, noted on Howell's map of 1792 as Conejohela Creek. Thomas Cresap's "plantation" and fort was a short distance above this village, near Wrightsville. Hewitt gives the meaning of the name, Conejoholo, "a kettle on a long upright object."

Conajacula.—Hendricks (1740), Arch Pa., Sec. Ser., XVI, 522, 1890. **Conajohola.**—Anderson (1737), Arch. Pa , I, 536, 1852. **Conedoughela.**—Stevenson (1758), Arch Pa., III, 395, 1853. **Conejohala.**—Blunston (1732), the same, 319. **Conejohela.**—Blunston (1731), the same, 295. **Conejohola.**—Anderson (1737), the same, 536-537. **Coneohela.**—Wright (1737), Col. Rec. Pa., III, 470, 1852. **Connejaghera.**—Prov. Coun. (1706), Col. Rec. Pa., II, 1852.

See *Dekanogah; Conoy Town; Codorus.*

CONEMAUGH. The name of a river, having its headwaters in Cambria County, and which unites with the Loyalhanna, at Saltsburg, Indiana County, to form the Kiskiminetas River. Also the name of a Post Office in Cambria County. The name is derived from Conunmoch, "otter." The form given by Brinton is Gunammochk. There was an Indian village called "Conemough Old Town," at the site of Johnstown, Cambria County, before 1731, composed chiefly of Shawnee and Delaware. According to the statement made by Le Tort, in 1731, there were in that year 20 families and 60 men in the village. All Delaware. (Arch. Pa., I, 301, 1852). This village was one branch of the trail which led from Frankstown to Kittanning. The Indian town called Kickenapawlings, through which C. F. Post passed in 1758, was not at this place, but on the trail leading to Ligonier. See KICKENAPAWLINGS. In 1787 a road was opened from Frankstown to the Conemaugh River, which followed, in the main, the old Indian trail. (Arch. Pa. XI, 186, 1853.)

Conemach Old T.—Scull, map, 1770. **Conemach Old Town.**—Scull, map, 1770, (French map). **Conemagh.**—Harris, (1787), Arch. Pa., XI, 186, 1855. **Conemaugh.**—Howell, map, 1792. **Conemough Old Town.**—Order No. 1683 (1770), Penn Papers, Hist. Soc. Pa. **Conimuch.**—Pownall, map, 1775. **Connumach.**—Le Tort (1731), Arch. Pa., I, 301, 1852. **Kunnumax.**—Traders, map, 1753.

CONESTOGA. A creek which enters the Susquehanna from the east at Safe Harbor, in Lancaster County. Also the name of one of the most historic Indian tribes in Pennsylvania, and the name of the village which they occupied in the early years of the XVIII Century. The name is derived from Kanastoge, "at the place of the immersed pole," according to Hewitt. Another meaning given is, Andastoegue, "people of the cabin pole." The tribe, which belonged to the Iroquoian group, was known by many names, chief of which are, Andastates, Conestogas, Gandastoques, Minquas, Susquehannocks, and various forms of all of these names. The French used the name Andastagues, or Andastaes; the Swedish and Dutch used the name Minquas, and the English the names Susquehannas, or Conestogas—although all of these names were used by the various writers. The tribe was first mentioned by Captain John Smith, in 1608, as Sasquesahannocks, and his map gives the name of their habitat as Sasquesahanough. The description of this tribe, as given by Smith, makes them to have been a people of gigantic size, who lived in palisaded towns "two days journey higher up than our barge could pass for rocks." If the rocks mentioned were at Port Deposit, Maryland, the two days higher would bring their situation at this time not far from the location of the Indian fort near Conestoga. But, it may be possible that the "rocks" mentioned were those near the mouth of the Conewago, which would put the Susquehanna at this time near the mouth of the Juniata. It is possible that the unidentified tribe, which lived on the Juniata River, was the Conestoga. The six towns which Smith mentions are, Sasquesahannough, Quadroque, Attaoc, Tesinigh, Utchowig and Cepowig. The situation of these towns cannot be determined with any degree of accuracy. But, if the "two days higher" puts the Susquehannas in the region of the Conestoga and Conewago Creeks, it is probable that the town of Sasquesahanough was within this region, and probably not far from the place to which the remnant of the tribe returned, after the Iroquios conquest, from the south. What is more likely than that the Conestoga town, known to history, was at or near the place where their ancestors had formerly lived? The site of the fort of 1670 is, beyond reasonable doubt, at the site of the historic Indian village of Conejohela, on the

west side of the Susquehanna, opposite Washington Borough, near the place where Cresap built his fort in 1730. Cresap, no doubt, well aware of the discussion between the Penns and the Calverts concerning the location of the fort, at issue, built his fort upon ground as close to, and yet south of the Indian fort, as possible. The discussion concerning the site of this fort takes up much of the entire volume, Arch. Pa., Sec. Ser., XVI, 1890. According to the map in this volume the fort, for which the Penns were contending, stood at the mouth of Octorara Creek. Cresaps place is just above the line, claimed as the boundary by the Calverts. This would put Cresap's fort two miles north of a line drawn due west from Philadelphia, which would give the location of "Cresap's Fort" almost exactly west of the present Washington Borough, at the site of the village of Conejohela, near which Cresap first settled. It is not possible in this article to go into the discussion of the matter more extensively. The Susquehanna, o r Conestoga, had as their mortal enemies the "Massawomecks." Mr. Hewitt identifies this name with M'cheuwaming, "at the great flats;" adding the animate plural, M'cheuomek. M'cheuoming is the word which has been corrupted by the English into Wyoming. According to nearly all the records of the various colonies on the Delaware the chief foes of the Conestoga, among the Iroquois, were the Seneca and Mohawk tribes. The geographic reason for this is evident. The Susquehanna River, by the north and the west branches, reached the country of these two most warlike tribes of the Iroquois. The Iroquois had for many years carried on a war with the Illinois. After this had ended they commenced their campaign for the destruction of the Conestoga. The Seneca had been the chief foes of the Illinois, reaching their country by way of the Ohio. Du Chesnau, in his memoir 1681, says, "The Iroquois having got quit of the Illinois, took no more trouble with them, and went to war against another nation called Andostagues, who were very numerous, and whom they utterly destroyed" (Arch. Pa. Sec. Ser. VI, 9, 1877). In 1673 the Seneca asked Count Frontenac to assist them in their war against the "Andastoguez, the sole enemies remaining." Gov. Andros, Oct. 21 1675, in writing to the Governor of Maryland, speaks of his desire to have the

"Macques" and the "Sinnecus" come to terms of peace with the "Susquehannahs." He said that he "found that the Susquehannahs being reputed by the Macques (Mohawks) of their Offspring, that they might be brought to some Peace, or concorporate again, and so take away the occasion of those Mischiefs or Inroads, though I find still the Sinneques (Senekas) wholly adverse to it; desiring their Extirpation (Arch. Pa., Sec. Ser., V, 706, 1890). The battle at the fort of 1670, near Conejohela Creek, and the final overthrow at the fort at the mouth of the Octorara, in 1675, completely subjugated the Conestoga to the Iroquois. The official ending of the war of the Iroquois and the Conestoga occurred in 1677. It is probable that the council of the Seneka and the Susquehanna at Shackamaxon in March 1677, mentioned in the Records of Upland Court, was the formal acceptance of the Iroquois demands by the Conestoga (Records of Upland, 49, 1860). The remnant of the Susquehannas, or Conestogas, became divided. Some were allowed to remain at Conestoga; others were taken into the Oneida country, where they became incorporated with that tribe, and a remnant fled southward to the Roanoke River, where they lived among the Occaneechi. The last mentioned quarrelled with the tribe among whom they had found a place of refuge, and returned to Conestoga. Here this remnant of the once powerful Susquehannas lived until 1763, when the 20 Conestoga Indians were blotted out by the Paxton gang of ruffians. (See any of the histories of this event.)

THE INDIAN TOWN. The historic Indian village of Conestoga, known as "Indian Town," was situated about 7 miles from Lancaster, near the present Millersville, Lancaster County. There is no doubt but that the entire region westward from this place to Washington Borough and along the Susquehanna, was once the site of a large settlement of Susquehannas. The entire region is filled with evidences of a lengthy and extensive Indian occupation. Indian relics of every kind have been found in great quantities over this entire region, on both sides of the river. The various Indian petroglyphs on the rocks below the mouth of the Conestoga Creek have been mentioned from early times. Soon after the settlement of the English

along the Delaware the Indian traders began going to Conestoga to trade with the Indians, whose ancestors had traded with the first Dutch and Swedish settlers at Upland (Chester). Various trails led from the lower Susquehanna to the Dutch and Swedish settlements on the Delaware, and one of the great trails led through Lancaster to the site of Philadelphia. Peter Bezalion, Martin Chartier, Peter Chartier, Edmund Cartlidge, John Cartlidge, Jonah Davenport, Nicole Godin, James Le Tort, Jacque Le Tort (perhaps one of the first), and many others had trading houses at this village soon after the English occupation of the Delaware, Jacques Le Tort trading at this place as early as 1696. In 1701, the Conestoga, or "Sasquehannah Minquays," with the Shawnee and Conoy, entered into a treaty with William Penn at Philadelphia. Among other things, the Conestogas promised that they would not allow "any Strange Nations of Indians to Settle or Plant on the further side of Sasquehannah, or about Potowmeck River"—"without the Special approbation and permission of the said Willm. Penn, his Heirs and Successors." (Col. Rec. Pa., II, 16, 1852.) The Shawnee frequently referred to this treaty in after years, when they were seeking to be brought back into the "league of amity" with the English. In 1705, the Conestoga appeared at Philadelphia, through Manangy, "the Indian Chief on Skuylkill," asking that permission be given to the Conoy, or "Ganawense," to settle at Tulpehocken, the Conestoga becoming their guardians (Col. Rec. Pa., II, 191, 1852). Gov. Evans visited Conestoga in July, 1707, at which time he met the Nanticoke, who were on their way to pay their tribute to the Iroquois (the same, 386-387). Gov. Charles Gookin visited the Indians at Conestoga in June, 1711. Civility (the War Captain), Queen Conguegoes, Opessah (the Shawnee King), and many others, appeared from time to time at Philadelphia, to bring their gifts, and to tell their complaints of the conditions existing at Conestoga. In 1714, the "old Queen," Conguegoes, died, and as the speaker (possibly Civility) said, the older generation had nearly all passed away. In 1719, Col. John French made a visit to Conestoga, followed in 1720 by one by John Logan. Both of these representatives of the Province held conferences with the Indians concerning the war expeditions of the Shawnee into the southern Colonies, which were the cause of much correspondence between the Governors of these Colonies and the Governor of Pennsylvania. Not only had the Shawnee been out on these war expeditions, but the Iroquois, in going southward against the Cherokee and Catawba, had been in the habit of stopping at Conestoga, both on their way out and upon their return with prisoners. This matter gave the Province much trouble, especially with the Colony of Virginia. The Indian could not realize that the various disputes between the various English colonies concerning boundary disputes was not similar to the disputes and wars carried on between the various Indian tribes, and that a war expedition of the Iroquois into Virginia, or South Carolina, was in no way a breach of their peace with the Province of Pennsylvania. This matter of warfare between the northern and the southern Indian tribes was never settled until the complete settlement of the State of Pennsylvania and Virginia, and the final migration of the Delaware and Shawnee beyond the Ohio. At the conference which Logan held at Conestoga, Civility spoke of the dissatisfaction felt by the Iroquois concerning the sale of the lands along the Susquehanna, and of the claim set up by the Cayuga as to their property right to all of these lands. Both of these matters became the subject of much argument, not only as to the Iroquois claims against Maryland and Virginia, but also as to the sale of the Susquehanna lands to the Governor of New York by the Iroquois, and of the subsequent purchase of these lands from New York by Pennsylvania. At a Council held at Albany, N. Y., in Sept., 1683, when the Governor of New York and the agents of the Penns were trying to come to an agreement with the Iroquois as to the purchase of the lands on the Susquehanna River, the chiefs of the Cayuga said, "The aforesaid Land belongs to us, Cayugas and Onondages, alone; the other three Nations vizt. the Sinnekes, Oneydes and Maquaas have nothing to do with it." (From Dutch Record C. No. 3— in Papers Relating to the Susquehanna, 396, 1796.) Father Lamberville, in a letter to M. De La Barre, in 1684, says, "It was this Oreouake (a Cayuga chief) that the English of Albany, formerly Orange, made use of to prevent Sieur Penn purchasing the

Country of the Andastogues who have been conquered by the Iroquois and the English of Merilande" (Paris Doc. II, in work cited). In 1684 the Cayuga and Onondaga, by an agreement with Lord Effingham, Governor of Virginia, and Col. Thomas Dongan, Governor of New York, made over these lands, in these words, "Thatt we do putt the Susquehanne River above the Washinta, or falls, and all the rest of our land under the Great Duke of York and to nobody else" (Lond. Doc. V, Robert Livingston, in work cited, 401). This subject came up again and again until the Treaty of Lancaster in 1744, at which time the whole matter was gone over by the Iroquois, by Canassatego, and the representatives of Pennsylvania, Maryland and Virginia. At that treaty Maryland claimed that that colony had bought the lands, for which the Iroquois demanded payment, from the Susquehannas, or Conestogas, in 1652, to the mouth of the Susquehanna River. The Iroquois replied, through Canassatego, that "the Conestoga or Susquehanna Indians had a right to sell those lands unto you, for they were then theirs, but since that time we have conquered them, and their country now belong to us, and the lands we demand satisfaction for are no part of the land comprised in those deeds—they are the Cohongorontas (Potomac) lands." The Maryland commissioners then paid for these lands. So far as the Iroquois claim against the lands on the Susquehanna River was concerned, it was shown that Gov. Dongan had bought these lands, which Penn bought from him in 1796, and which sale was confirmed by the Conestoga in 1699 and again in 1718, in the presence of the Onondaga deputies. Canassatego replied to this by saying that they had entrusted these lands to the Governor of New York, for safe keeping, and that he had gone to England, where he sold these lands to Penn for a large sum of money. When William Penn discovered how the Governor of New York had deceived the Iroquois, he paid them for their lands over again. Maryland paid the Iroquois £220, 15s., and made a present of $100 in gold. The release for these lands was signed by all of the leading Iroquois, save Shikellamy, the Oneida chief, who refused to sign it—and who never did sign it. Although Shikellamy did not give his views on the subject, his reason for refusing to sign this deed was no doubt based upon his feeling that this Indian title would give Maryland some claim to the lands which were claimed by the Penns in the boundary dispute, which was then at an acute stage. The Iroquois claims for the lands in Virginia were settled by the payment of 200 pounds in gold, and by granting the Iroquois an open path through Virginia to the Catawba country. This latter provision was the cause of frequent trouble with the Virginia settlers and authorities, and was never satisfactorily settled. The Iroquois understood it to mean that it gave them the right to "live upon" the country through which they passed. (Consult: Col. Rec. Pa., III, 78, 97, 99, 102, etc.; IV, 93, 235, 443, 561,— Treaty at Lancaster, 699,737, 1851; also later vols. of the Records and Archives.) In 1760, a conference was held at Lancaster by Richard Peters and the Conestoga Indians, (Col. Rec. Pa., VIII, 1852). On Nov. 30, 1763, the Conestogas sent a message of greeting to John Penn, grandson of William Penn, upon his arrival in the Province. On December 14, 1763, Edward Shippen wrote from Lancaster, informing the Governor of the murder of six of the Conestogas at their town, by frontiersmen. The survivors of this most cruel attack were removed for safe keeping to the jail in Lancaster. Here, on the morning of Dec. 27, 1763, the fourteen survivors of the historic Susquehannas were killed by a gang of "Paxton boys," numbering about fifty. (See Col. Rec. Pa., IX, 88, 89, 94, 96, 100, 102-103, 126, etc., 1852; Egle, Hist. of Penna., 112, etc., 1883; Life and Times of David Zeisberger, 290, 1870; Loskiel, History of Moravian Missions, Part 2 217, 1794, and the various histories of the United States.)

The murder of these Indians caused the widest excitement in Philadelphia and all over the country. The authorities of the Province feared that an attack would be made upon the Moravian Indians then kept, for their own safety, on Province Island. The reason used as an excuse for this blotting out of one of the most historic tribes in America was that the Indians at Conestoga had been giving refuge to the hostile Indians, who had been committing many crimes along the Susquehanna. There is as little evidence for the truth of this statement, as there is for that made as an excuse for the murder of the Delaware at Gnadenhutten, by the same class of frontiersmen in 1782. The Scotch-Irish settlers seemed to think that they had a direct commission from God to blot out the "heathen who inhabited the land." No historic proof has, however, been found for any such assertion to rest upon. The murder of the Conestoga, no matter how great the provication may have been, is one of the blackest pages in American history.

The leading synonyms of the name of the tribe have been noted previously. The following are those of the town and the creek.

Conestoga.—Hendricks (1690), Arch. Pa., Sec. Ser., XVI, 523, 1890. **Conestoga Creek.**—Scull, map, 1770; Taylor Papers. **Conestogo.**—Scull, map, 1759; Col. Rec. Pa., II, 22 (1707), 1852. **Conestogoe.**—Coun. Pa., (1701), Col. Rec. Pa., II, 70, 1852.

CONEWAGO. A creek which enters the Susquehanna from the east, at Falmouth, Lancaster County; also a creek which enters the same river from the west, in York County, a short distance south of the mouth of the former stream; also the name of a range of mountains along the streams in both counties. Heckewelder gives the origin from Guneunga, "they have been gone a long time," but the more probable origin is Ganowungo, "at the rapids." The name given to these falls, near the mouth of the Conewago, by the Iroquois was, Washinta, which is contracted from Tawasentha, the Mohawk word for water-fall. The Iroquois claimed the land along the Susquehanna to the "Washinta," or falls, and put this land into the keeping of the Governor of New York in 1684, who sold it to the Penns (See previous article). All of the troubles concerning the boundary dispute between the Penns and Calverts entered into the early history of the settlements in the Conewago valley. On Oct. 14, 1727, a grant of 10,000 acres of land was made to John Diggs, under a Maryland warrant, along the Conewago. This tract which was known as, "Diggs Choice in the Back Woods," was the cause of much trouble to the various claimants for land, under Penna. warrants (See Arch. Pa., I, 680, 713, etc., 1852; II, 28, 73, 93, 1852; Col. Rec. Pa., V, 582, 1851).

Conavaga.—Ross (1732), Arch. Pa., I, 333, 1852. **Conewaga.**—Cookson (1745), Arch. Pa., I, 680, 1852. Evans, map, 1749. **Conewago.**—Peters (1743), Arch. Pa., I, 637, 1852. Scull, map, 1759. **Conewoga.**—Evans, map, 1755. **Connevago.**—Seller (1749), Arch. Pa., II, 28, 1852. **Conewaga Falls.**—Graff (1789), Arch. Pa., XI, 602. 1855.

CONEWANGO. A river which enters the Allegheny River at Warren, from the north. Also the name of a Seneca village, at the site of Warren. The name is given the same origin as Conewago, and in addition to the meanings given, it is said to mean "a long strip," having reference to the long strip of bottom land along the river, which was used for the cultivation of corn. The French expedition under Celoron De Bienville (1749) made the portage from Lake Erie to Lake Chautauqua, and from there went down the Conewango to its junction with the Allegheny, where the first leaden plate, giving notice of the formal act of taking possession of the Ohio and its tributaries, was deposited. This plate was taken from Joncaire by the Seneca, and by them given to a Cayuga chief, who carried it to Sir William Johnson. At the Council at Mount Johnson, in 1750, one of the Cayuga chiefs said that the Iroquois had sent him to find out what this plate meant (Arch. Pa., Sed. Ser., VI, 85, 1877). This plate was sent to Governor Clinton, who then wrote to the Lords of Trade, giving an account of its finding, and later a copy of the inscription upon it (See Arch. Pa. Sec. Ser., VI, 83). Governor Clinton also sent a letter to Governor Hamilton of Penna., informing him of the matter. The expedition of Celoron was the commencement of the movement towards the Ohio, which ultimately resulted in the conflict between France and Great Britain for the possession of the Ohio Valley. The situation of the Indian village is noted on Father Bonnecamp's map of 1749 as, Kananaonagon. It is spoken of in his Relation as, Kananouangon (Jesuit Rel. LXIX, 165). The French expeditions which followed that of Celoron, to the Ohio region, went from Lake Erie by way of French Creek to the Allegheny. As a consequence Conewango was left out of the development of affairs on the Ohio. Darlington (Gist's Journals, 27, 1893) says that M. De Lery crossed from Lake Erie to Chautauqua Lake, and then by way of the Conewango, reached the Ohio in 1729, ten years before Celoron reached the Ohio by the same route. In 1756 the Seneca wrote to Governor Hardy of New York, concerning the murder of one of their warriors at Conewango by some Indian traders (Col. Rec. Pa., VII, 9, 35, 1851). In 1759 a number of the Indians from the upper Allegheny attended a Council with Governor Denny at Philadelphia. Among these were a number from Conewago and Buckaloons. One of these representatives was named, Canawaago, who is spoken of as "the Chief of the Indian Deputies near Bowclunce." It may be possible that the town and the river were both named for this chief, although he does not appear as a very prominent character in the events of this period. These Indians were given to understand positively that the English did not intend to settle on the Ohio, or beyond the Allegheny mountains, without the permission of the Indians (See Col. Rec. Pa., VIII, 264 etc., 1852). In 1778-1779 the raids from the Seneca country, on the upper Allegheny, became more and more frequent along the English frontiers in Westmoreland County. The hostile bands were led by Guyasutha, or Kiasutha (See Darlington's Gist, 210-213, 1893). Early in the summer of 1779, General Brodhead received permission of General Washington to make an expedition up the Allegheny River to destroy the Indian villages, and later join the expedition under General Sullivan, who had gone up the Susquehanna, for the same purpose. The hostile Indians and the British army was being supplied with corn from the villages in the Seneca country, at the headwaters of both of these streams. Brodhead left Pittsburgh in August, passing up the Allegheny River and destroying the corn fields and the deserted Indian villages on the way. He expected to find the Indians at Conewango. About 14 miles below this Indian village he met with a force of Seneca, with whom he had a fight, in which several Indians were killed. When the army reached Conewango the Indians had fled, evidently in a great hurry, as they left everything behind. In this village there were about 150 houses and in the fields along the river about 500 acres were planted in corn. Brodhead said that the plunder taken by the soldiers amounted to over $30,000 in value. "From the great quantity of corn in the ground and the number of new houses built and building, it appears that the whole Seneca and Munsee nations intended to collect in this settlement" (See Brodhead's letters, etc., Arch. Pa., XII, 155 etc.). There is little doubt but that Brodhead was correct in his supposition that the Seneca intended to make this place a sort of refuge should they be driven from the upper Susquehanna, as it was more distant from the American settlements and from danger of attack by the American army than almost any other place within reach from the Seneca country in New York. But, the expedition of General Sullivan which destroyed their villages from one side, and the expedition of General Brodhead from the other side, put an end to any hopes which the Seneca might have entertained, of ever holding their villages on the Allegheny. These expeditions put an end to the danger from the Seneca country. The importance of Brodhead's expedition, at this critical time during the Revolution, has never been given due credit. In 1789 Richard Butler and John Gibson were appointed to purchase the lands west of the Conewango from the Iroquois— the lands lying east of this river and west of the Allegheny being reserved for the use of the Seneca (See copy of Treaty, Arch. Pa., XI, 529, 1855). Among the chiefs who signed this Agreement, were Gyantwachia (Kiasutha), Gyashota (Big Cross), Xeandochgowa (Big Tree), Achiout (Half Town), and other prominent Iroquois chiefs. Two Munsee chiefs who signed these articles, did so, "as being residents on the land, but not owners." In 1786 General William Irvine had made a survey of these lands, west of the Conewango to the state line (Arch. Pa., XI, 51 1855).

Canawaago.—Prov. Coun. (1759), Col. Rec Pa., VIII, 264, 1852. Canawagy.— Scull, map, 1770. Evans, map, 1755. Canawaja.—Hardy (1756), Col. Rec. Pa., VII, 9, 1851. Canewago.—Irvine (1785), Arch. Pa., XI, 517, 1855, also Conewagoo. Conewango.—Adlum, map, 1790. Howell, map, 1792. Ganowongo.—Parker, in Bull. No. 530, p. 20, N. Y. State Museum, 1912. Kanaonagon.—Bonnecamp, map, 1749. Kananouangon.—Bonnecamp Rel. (1749), Jesuit Rel. LXIX, 165, 1902. Shenango. —Nuremberg, map, 1756, (the town).

CONEWANTA. A creek which enters the Susquehanna, from the south, in Susquehanna County. Corrupted from Guneunga, "they stay a long time," according to Heckewelder.

Conewaeta.—Howell, map, 1792. Conewanta.—Morris, map, 1848.

CONEWINGO. A creek which has its headwaters in Lancaster County and which enters the Susquehanna, from the east, in Maryland. Possibly the same origin as Conewago (q. v.).

Conewinga.—Certif. To Ewens (1728), Arch. Pa., Sec. Ser., XIX, 755, 1893. Conewingo.—Scull, map, 1759. Cononawingo.—Jones Petition (1726), Arch. Pa., Sec. Ser., XIX, 740, 1893. Conywingo.— Grant to Stuart (1735), Arch. Pa., Third Ser., I, 68, 1894.

CONNEAUT. A lake and a town

in Crawford County. A corruption of Gunniati, "it is a long time since they are gone," according to Heckewelder.

Conyeeyont.—Howell, map, 1792.

CONOCOCHEAGUE. A creek which flows southward from Franklin County to the Potomac, which it enters at Williamsport, Md. A corruption of Guneukitschik, "indeed a long way." Gu-ne-u, "long;" Hi-tschi-wi, "indeed." Having reference to the winding course of the stream. The Conococheague region is one of the most interesting parts of the historic Cumberland Valley. From the time of the Indian occupation, through the thrilling experiences of the French and Indian War, the Revolution and the Civil War, this most interesting region in Franklin County occupied a most prominent place. The Path Valley, which opens into the Cumberland Valley at Parnell's Knob, was traversed by various Indian trails. One of these ran northward, through Shirleysburg to Huntingdon, where it crossed the trail to the Ohio, and ran northward to the Bald Eagle Valley, and from there to Lock Haven, where it reached the West Branch, by which it went to Shamokin, or by way of Pine Creek, to the Iroquois region in New York. This trail was crossed by the various paths to the Ohio, which cut through the Kittatinny Mountains at Croghan's Gap, Roxbury Gap and other passes through the mountain ridge. The earliest trail westward, which this Tuscarora trail crossed was the Allegheny Path, which it joined at Fannettsburg. From here the latter trail led westward to Bloody Run (now Everett), where it was crossed by the other southern trail, called the Warriors Path, which crossed the Potomac near Old Town, Md. Down the Cumberland Valley ran the trail from the Susquehanna to the Potomac, which it crossed at the mouth of the Conococheague. All of these trails had various branches, which crossed from one main trail to another. The earliest Indian occupants of the region were the Shawnee, who came northward from the Potomac region in 1698. There can be little doubt but that the old Indian graveyard, at the site of the Presbyterian Church in Chambersburg, was a burial place of the Shawnee. James Le Tort and Martin Chartier (both of them associated with the Shawnee) had trading houses on the "branches of Patowmeck, within this Government," as early as 1708. There is every reason for thinking that one of the earliest trading points which Le Tort had in the Cumberland Valley, was at, or near, the site of Chambersburg. From this point the Potomac region could easily be reached, as could also the villages on the path to the Ohio. Le Tort afterwards had a trading post near Carlisle, of which the one on the waters of the Potomac was a branch. The Tuscarora did not come north until 1713, after which time they soon removed to the villages on the upper Susquehanna, near the Iroquois. The Shawnee and possibly a few of the Delaware remained in the Cumberland Valley until they were driven westward by the white settlements, just before the commencement of the French and Indian War. The majority of these went westward to the Ohio with Peter Chartier in 1720-27. After the Treaty of Lancaster of 1736, the Indians had nearly all left the region east of the mountains to the Ohio and its tributaries. It is said that the Indians, who had lived near Chambersburg, came back to the old burying ground for many years after they had left their old homes on the Conococheague (See Vol. I, Publications of Kittatinny Historical Society, 6, 1898). It is to be regretted that no one kept any account of what tribe these visiting Indians belonged. Nearly all of the first settlers of this entire region were Scotch-Irish, who went into all parts of the Cumberland Valley from about 1727. Joseph and Benjamin Chambers located at Falling Springs, in Chambersburg, in 1730. So rapidly had the population increased in this valley that in 1735 a petition was presented to the Court of Quarter Sessions, praying for the laying out of a road from John Harris' Ferry to the Potomac. The final viewers for the course of this road was signed by Randall Chambers, Robert Chambers, Benjamin Chambers, Robert Dunning and John McCormick (Docket No. 2, Quarter Sessions, page 31, Feb. 1744). This road was not completed for many years after it was commenced. As late as 1750 it was still in a very bad condition. (See, Old Roads of Cumberland County, J. D. Hemminger, 1909.) In 1755, when Gen. Braddock was organizing his expedition, against Fort Duquesne, at Fort Cumberland, a road was commenced at Shippensburg, which was completed as far as the Allegheny Mountains, beyond Bedford. This road was to connect with Braddock's Road near Turkey Foot, on the Youghiogheny River, but was never completed. The Indian hostility making work upon it impossible. Many of the supplies for this expedition were taken from various parts of Lancaster, York and Cumberland Counties to the mouth of the Conococheague, from which place they were taken to Fort Cumberland. After Braddock's defeat in 1755, the entire region along the frontier settlements was subject to disastrous Indian raids. The Conococheague settlement suffered severely (See Col. Rec. Pa., VI, 641, 673, 700, 767, 1851; VII, 118, 241, 399, 466, 479, 502, 1852; McCullough's, Narrative, Border Life, 88; Smith's, Narrative, Border Life, 13, (Pritt's) 1839). During 1756 various Frontier Forts were built in Franklin County, for the protection of the settlers. Among these were: Fort Chambers, on the west bank of the Conococheague, at the mouth of Falling Spring; Fort Davis, about nine miles south of Loudon, near the Maryland line; Fort Loudon, about a mile from the present Loudon, about two miles southwest of Parnell's Knob; Fort McCord, at the foot of the Kittatinny Mountains, north of Loudon; Fort McDowell, at McDowell's Mills, south of Fort Loudon; Fort Steel, perhaps the first of these defense works, about three miles east of Mercersburg, built by Rev. John Steel in 1755, around his church; Fort Lyttleton, about 20 miles southwest of Shirleysburg, at the site of the present Fort Lyttleton. All of these forts were scenes of thrilling events during the days which followed Braddock's defeat (See, Frontier Forts of Penna., I, 527-558, 1896). After the erection of Fort Pitt in 1758, and the ending of the Indian expeditions into the settlements after Col. Bouquet's expeditions in 1763-64, the "Conococheague Settlement" developed rapidly. The War of the Revolution, and the Civil War found this valley filled with rich farms, and a strong and loyal race of liberty loving people. (Consult Egle, History of Penna., 738,759, 1883, and any of the histories of the Civil War.)

The various attempts at spelling the name of this most historic creek are almost as interesting as the history of the creek itself. The maps give the following forms of the name:

Conococheague.—Scull, 1759, and 1770. Conegoge.—Pownall, 1776. Conegogee.—Evans, 1749.

The following are a few of the forms used in the various Records of the State, and by other early authorities: Canacoshick.—Bader (1756), Col. Rec. Pa., VII, 399, 1851. Conegachege.—Braddock (1755), Col. Rec. Pa., VI, 400, 1851. Conegocheague.—Pa. Coun. (1756), Col. Rec. Pa., VII, 118. Conegochege.—Trent (1755), the same, 641. Conegocheege.—Ind. Coun. (1742), Col. Rec. Pa., IV, 561, 1851. Conegochieque.—Forbes (1758), Col. Rec. Pa., VIII, 59, 1852. Conegogig.—Potter (1755), Col. Rec. Pa., VI, 673. Conehecheegoe.—Minute Book "K," (1734), Arch. Pa., Third Ser., I, 39, 1894. Conicochegue. — Croghan (1757), Col. Rec. Pa., VII, 479. Conigochegue.—Croghan (1756), the same, 466. Conogogee.—Morris (1755), Col. Rec. Pa., VI, 514, 1851. Connecocheege. — Dinwiddie (1755), the same, 465. Connecocheegue.—Shippen (1755), Col. Rec. Pa., VI, 459. Connegocheegue.—Burd (1755), Col. Rec. Pa., VI, 500. Connicocheeque.—Pa. Coun. (1757), Col. Rec. Pa., VII, 502. Kaneghuigik.—Vaudreuil (1756), Arch. Pa., Sec. Ser., VI, 362, 1877.

The early writers used almost every form possible, save that which is in use at present, Conococheague. Nearly all of the streams in this region, which once had the form *Cone*, have changed it to *Cono*. In other parts of the State the early form for such names has been kept. Heckewelder seems to have been the first writer to use of such forms as Conococheague, Conodogwinit etc., in place of the older form Conedogwinet etc. It would be well to return to the older, and more euphonious form.

CONODOGWINET. A creek, which enters the Susquehanna from the west at West Fairview, opposite Harrisburg. Also the name of an Indian village near the site of New Cumberland, Cumberland County, a few miles below the mouth of the creek. A corruption of Gunnipduckhannet, "for a long way nothing but bends," according to Heckewelder. A more correct significance of the name would be, taking the words used in its formation, "winding river"—one of the Indian names used for the Susquehanna. Gu-ne-u, "long"; P'tuk-hanne, "a crooked creek," or river. The correct form of the Indian name would be Guneptukhanne. The strip of land between the Conedogwinet and the Yellow Breeches, or Shawnee Creek, was occupied by the Shawnee after they commenced to move northward from Pequea Creek and the later villages in the neighborhood of Conestoga. Peter Chartier and James

Le Tort both had trading posts within this region at about 1720. The former Shawnee half-blood had his village near the mouth of the Conedogwinet, from which place he led his band westward to the Ohio in about 1727, although he did not leave this place permanently until later. James Le Tort built his cabin at Big Beaver Pond, at a deserted Shawnee village, at about the same time. Andrew Montour, who was also associated with the Shawnee, lived on the Conedogwinet in 1748. Thus these three most famous Indian traders and interpreters all lived along the two creeks of Cumberland County, and were associated with the Shawnee. When John Harris first settled at Paxtang, near Harrisburg, the Shawnee were living along the western shore of the Susquehanna, between the two creeks which entered it from the west. Before 1730, the majority of the Shawnee had left the lower Susquehanna, having gone westward to Chartier's Town, on the Allegheny River. The Provincial authorities realized the danger of these restless warriors being so far away from the English influence, and so made every effort to bring them back. In 1731, a letter was sent to Peter Chartier, informing him that the Commissioners of the Province had laid out a tract of land "between Conegogwainet & Shaawna Creeks five or six miles Back from the River, In order to Accommodate the Shaawna Indians or such others as may think fit to Settle there" (See Arch. Pa., I, 299, 1852). The Shawnee replied to this invitation, saying that they were very well satisfied where they were. But, the land which had been set aside by the Province as a Proprietary Manor, for the Shawnee, was the cause of much trouble later on. This tract of land, set aside for the Shawnee, included the Manor of Lowther, which was laid out in 1764. The Shawnee did not come back from the Ohio to occupy it, but later on they claimed the land, according to the Quaker element, which was at war with the Governor. When the hostilities of the Delaware and Shawnee became a vital subject, in 1755, the Assembly had to find some cause for this condition, which would show unjust dealings with the tribes. The Shawnee hostility was said to be due to the white settlers taking possession of these lands between the Conedogwinet and Yellow Breeches, which had been allotted to the Shawnee, and for which no settlement had been made. It was said by this Quaker element, which opposed every move which was made by Governor James Logan, that at the Treaty at Carlisle in 1753, the Shawnee had made complaint of the settlement of these lands which had been theirs, and for which the Province had not paid them. The entire matter was examined, and it was found that there had been no such complaint made at Carlisle, according to the reports of the treaty, but, as Isaac Norris said in his Message, "We are, however, convinced by original Minutes taken by the Commissioners at the Treaty at Carlisle, now lying before us, that the Shawonese Chiefs mentioned their Claim of theirs to the Lands in Question at that Time, and were promised that the matter should be laid before the Proprietaries" (See Col. Rec. Pa., VI, 710, 725, 746, 1851). The whole dispute was simply in line with all of the troubles between the Assembly and the Governor. There was not the shadow of a foundation for the Shawnee claim for these lands. They had never belonged to the Shawnee at any time, and were offered to them if they would return from the Ohio, which they never did do. The Indian village at the mouth of the Conedogwinet was known by the same name as the creek. In the report of Conrad Weiser's journey to Onondaga in 1743, concerning the disputes of the Iroquois with Maryland and Virginia, the village is mentioned as "Canadagueany." The Commissioners of Virginia wished to have the Iroquois go to Winchester to hold a Council, in the spring of 1744. This the Iroquois declined to do, on account of the place being so far away, but agreed to have such a Council at Conedogwinet. The Iroquois at Shamokin had agreed upon the same place, when Weiser visited them in the spring of 1743. When the time for the Council arrived it was discovered by the Provincial authorities that there would be such a large number of Indians, besides the various Commissioners of the three colonies, who would have to be provided with food and shelter, that the meeting place, with the consent of Canassatego, was changed to Lancaster, where the Treaty of 1744 was held. (See Col. Rec. Pa., IV, 648, 667, 705, 1851.) Conrad Weiser, after his return from the Ohio mission in 1748, informed Richard Peters that "Andrew Montour has pitched upon a place in the Pro-

prietors Manor, at Canataqueany" (Arch. Pa., II, 12, 1852). In 1752, Montour was given permission to "reside in such Place over the Kittochtinny Hills as you shall judge most central and convenient" (Col. Rec. Pa., V, 566-567, 1851). The place which Montour took as his place of residence was near the mouth of Montour's Run, on Shearman's Creek, between Landisburg and Loysville. "Montour's" was one of the points on the trail which led from Harris' Ferry to the Ohio, and is frequently mentioned in the various traders' tables of distances. George Croghan, who lived, from before 1747, near Silver's Spring, also crossed the mountains to Aughwick (Shirleysburg), in 1752 "Croghan's," at Silver's Spring, was also one of the points on the trail, which is frequently mentioned. In the table of distances given by John Harris, in 1754, "Croghan's" is given as 5 miles from Harris' Ferry (See Arch. Pa., II, 135, 1852). The trail which led through Croghan's Gap (now Sterrett's Gap), to the "Black Log," near Orbisonia, was called the "New Path" to the Ohio. The "Allegheny Path," which was the old path, ran along the Conedogwinet and went through the mountains at McAllister's Gap, now Roxbury Gap. The "New Path" and this older one united at the "Black Log," where the path divided, one branch going to Aughwick and on to Frankstown, the other ran westward to Ray's Town (Bedford), and on to the Allegheny. One branch of this new path possibly joined the old path at Concord, but it is hard to tell exactly where some of these cross trails met, as trails ran through nearly all of the mountain gaps, from the Cumberland to Horse and Tuscarora Valleys. In 1753, an important Council was held by the Commissioners of Pennsylvania with the Indians concerning the French occupation of the Ohio. Richard Peters, Isaac Norris and Benjamin Franklin represented the Province; James Wright and John Armstrong the Assembly, and Scarouady, Shingas, Pisquitomen, Delaware George, Nechecona and many other chiefs represented the Iroquois, Delaware, Shawnee, Twightwee and other Indian tribes. (See Col. Rec. Pa., V, 670, 686, 1851.) On Jan. 15, 1756, another Council was held at Carlisle, at which Governor Robert H. Morris, James Hamilton, William Logan, and Joseph Fox represented the Province. Conrad Weiser and George Croghan were the interpreters. The Belt, Silver Heels (Aroas), Jagrea, Newcastle, Seneca George and others represented the Indians (See Col. Rec. Pa., VII, 1-7, 1851). The Scotch-Irish were the first settlers along the Conedogwinet, following soon after the departure of Peter Chartier and his Shawnee to the Ohio. Many of them had crossed to the west side of the Susquehanna before 1730, and soon after this date built churches, a number of which organizations still exist. During the days when the danger from the raids of hostile Indians commenced, a number of forts, or stockades, were built. The date of the building of the first fort at Carlisle cannot be fixed with any degree of accuracy. It seems, from a letter of John O'Neill, that there was a garrison of 12 men guarding the stockade, which had been erected previous to 1753. The "stockade originally occupied two acres of ground square with a blockhouse on each corner, these buildings are now in ruin" (Arch. Pa., XII, 348, 1856). The date of the building of Fort Lowther at Carlisle is hard to determine from the records available. It would seem that it must have been built before 1754, as in an account published in 1755 there was a force of 50 men "at Fort Lowther in Carlisle;" in 1756, however, William Trent, in writing from Carlisle, says, "a Fort in this town would have saved this part of the Country, but I doubt this town in a few days will be deserted if this party that is out should kill any people nigh here" (Arch. Pa., XII, 348, 1856). In this letter of Trent's to Richard Peters, which is given in full in Arch. Pa., II, 575, Trent says that he was laughed at for thinking that "the Forts, as they were built, would be of no service." In 1757, Governor Denny, in writing to the Proprietaries, says, "Four Forts only were to remain over Sasquehannah, viz., Lyttleton, Loudoun, Shippensburg and Carlisle, which were to be garrisoned by the Eight Companies of Col. Armstrongs Battalion, two in each Fort" (Arch. Pa. III, 119, 1853). In May 30, 1757, Col. Stanwix encamped at Carlisle. Stanwix addressed his letters to Governor Denny from "Camp near Carlisle." He reported that he was at work upon his entrenchments, in July, 1757 (Arch. Pa., III, 239, 1853). During the preparations for Braddock's expedition, 1755; the expedition of Forbes, 1758; the Con-

spiracy of Pontiac, 1763; the Whisky Insurrection, 1794, and during both the great war of the Revolution and the Civil War, the Conedogwinet region was the arena in which many thrilling events took place. The place where General Stanwix built his entrenchments, and where the Hessian prisoners were kept, is now occupied by the United States Indian School, where the Red Men of today are taught the arts of peace, and the site of Fort Lowther is now occupied by business houses. The Public Square, where the Indians met in Council with the Commissioners of the Province of Pennsylvania, is today trodden by the feet of Indians from every tribe in the United States—a nation undreamed of when the first Indian Council was held in Carlisle, in 1753.

Consult: Carlisle, Old and New, 1907; Carlisle and The Red Men of Other Days, 1911; the various published papers of the Hamilton Library Association, Carlisle, Pa.; Frontier Forts of Pennsylvania, 1,508, 1896; the letters of Col. John Armstrong, William Trent, Gen. Stanwix, and others, in Vols. I, II and III, Archives of Penna.; Parkman, Conspiracy of Pontiac (any edition), under Carlisle, Fort Lowther or Bouquet; any history of the Civil War, read the Invasion of the Cumberland Valley; for information concerning the United States Indian School, send to the Superintendent, Carlisle, Pa.

Canadagueany.—Weiser (1743), Col. Rec. Pa., IV, 667, 1851. **Canataquamy.**—Weiser (1743), the same work, 648. **Canataqueany.**—Weiser (1748), Arch. Pa., II, 12, 1852. **Conedaguinet.**—Pa. Council (1771), Col. Rec. Pa., IX, 728, 1852. **Conedagwainet.**—Evans, map, 1749. **Conedagwinit.**—Deed of 1749, Arch. Pa., II, 34, 1852. **Conedegwenet.**—Evans, map, 1755. **Conedoguinet.**—Norris (1755), Col. Rec. Pa., VI, 710, 1851. **Conedogwainet.**—Penn Manor Survey, map, 1768, No. 38, Hist. Soc. Pa. **Conedogwenet.**—Pownall, map, 1776. **Conedogwinit.**—Scull, map, 1759. **Conidogwanet.**—Lowther Manor, map, (1764), No. 34, Arch. Pa, Third Ser., IV, 1895. **Connedoguinet.**—Pa. Council (1771), Col. Rec Pa , IX, 720, 1852. **Conodoguinet.** — Historical Map of Pa., 1875. Hist. Soc. of Pa.

CONOLLOWAY. A creek which flows southward in Fulton County, entering the Potomac at Hancock, Md. The branches of this stream were called the Little Conolloways, and the main creek Big Conolloways, in the early days of the white settlement. The origin of the name is not known. It may be a corruption of the name Conoy, or of the form Canhaways, The region along the creek was settled by people from Maryland as early as 1741 and 1742. On account of the boundary dispute between the Penns and the Calverts, the people settled along these creeks did not know whether they lived in Pennsylvania or Maryland. In 1750, when the settlers were removed from the unpurchased lands west of the Susquehanna, the Commissioners who had removed the "squatters" from Aughwick, Path Valley and other places, met at Shippensburg on May 28, 1750. The various Justices of Cumberland County declined to go to Little Cove and the Big and Little Conolloways. to remove the settlers, as those people had asked that they be permitted to remain until the line between the states should be determined, and the lands purchased from the Indians. Richard Peters explained that the sole purpose which the Province had in view was the prevention of an Indian war and offered these people lands east of the Susquehanna if they would remove. (Consult; Report of Richard Peters, Col. Rec. Pa., V, 444-445; Petitions from settlers, 453, 1851). In November 1755, after Braddock's defeat, the settlement on the Conolloway Creeks, with all of the others in the valley, were utterly blotted out by a band of about 100 Delaware and Shawnee, led by Shingas. The devastation caused by this raid, and others of a similar nature, awakened the Province to the great need of frontier forts. The survivors of the settlement in the Great Cove found refuge at "the Fort at Mr. Steel's Meeting House" (Col. Rec. Pa., VI, 675-676, 1851). There is no authority whatever for the form, Tonoloway, which is used on all recent maps of the state.

Canallowais.—Armstrong (1755), Col. Rec. Pa., VI, 676, 1851. **Conolaway.**—Scull, map, 1770; Howell, map, 1792. **Conolloways.**—Peters (1750), Col. Rec. Pa., V, 444, 1851. **Conolowaw.**—Scull, map, 1759. **Conoloway.**—Morris, map, 1848. **Tonoloway.**—State, map, 1912.

CONONODAW. A creek which enters the Allegheny from the west in McKean County, now called Potato Creek. Heckewelder gives the origin as Gunniada, "he tarries long." But the name is evidently not of Delaware origin, as this tribe did not occupy this region. It may be derived from, Gandadawayo, "running through the hemlocks"—which would be an appropriate name for the stream. Another suggested derivation is, Kendawyu, "a clearing." The valley, on one of the branches, has been known by the name Kushequa, from Gawshegwah, "a spear."

Cononotaw.—Adlum, map, 1790; Howell, map, 1792. **Potatoe Creek.**—Morris, map, 1848.

CONOQUENESSING. A creek which unites with Slippery Rock Creek and enters the Beaver River from the east, near the dividing line between Beaver and Lawrence Counties. Heckewelder, who makes the mistake of calling the stream a branch of the Allegheny, gives the origin from Gunachquenesink, "for a long way straight." The locative ink, or ing, would indicate that this was the name of a locality. In 1770 Sir William Johnson had a conversation with a chief named Conoquieson. The name may possibly be connected with the Indian town on this creek (Arch. Pa., IV, 373, 1853). G. F. Post passed through this village in 1758, on his way to Kuskuski from Fort Venango, at Franklin. He says, "We came to the River Conaquanosshan, an old Indian Town; we was then fifteen miles from Chshcushking" (Arch. Pa., III, 523, 1853). The Indian trail, which ran northward from Fort Duquesne to Fort Venango, crossed the branches of the Conoquenessing. This trail was crossed by the one leading from Kittanning to Kuskuski, by way of the Conoquenessing. Another trail ran northward from Logstown (Economy), crossed the Conoquenessing, near its junction with Slippery Rock Creek, and then ran on up along the valley of the former stream to Franklin, without touching the large Indian village at Kuskuski (New Castle). Christopher Gist and George Washington, in 1753, went northward from Logstown, crossing the Conoquenessing at the "Murthering Town," which was possibly at the site of the village mentioned by Post in 1758. This town must have been near the forks of the Conoquenessing and Slippery Rock Creeks, near Wurtemburg, according to Gist's map and Journal (See Darlington's Gist, 81, 1893). According to other maps Murdering Town was situated in Butler County, not far from Butler, where the trails between Kittanning and Kuskuski, crossed the trail from Fort Duquesne to Venango. General William B. Irvine made a survey of this entire region in 1785.

Canaghqunese.—Irvine (1785), Arch. Pa., XI, 517, 1856. **Conaquanosshan.**—Post (1758), Arch. Pa., III, 523, 1853. **Conaquenesing.**—Howell, map, 1792. **Cone-**

guenessing.—Morris, State map, 1848. Conequenessing.—Historical map of Pa., 1875. Hist. Soc. of Pa. Connekenness.—Denny (1794), Journal, Hist. Soc. Memorials, VII, 386, 1860. Connoquenessing.—Recent State maps. Map of 1912. Minacing Town.—Gist, map, 1753. Murderingtown.—Washington's Journal of 1753, Olden Time, I, 10, 1846. Muthering Town.—Gist (1753), Darlington's Gist, 81, 1893.

CONOY. A creek which enters the Susquehanna from the east in Lancaster County, at Bainbridge. Also the name of the Algonkian tribe which were given permission by the Treaty with William Penn, in 1701, to settle upon the headwaters of the Potomac, and in 1704 were permitted to settle near Conestoga, at the request of the Conestoga Indians. Very soon after this time they built a village at Conejohela. The first village of this name was on the east side of the Susquehanna, at the site of Washington Borough, but the majority removed to the west shore, near the mouth of Conejohela Creek, where they were when Cresap first moved to this place in 1731. (See Col. Rec. Pa., I, 448; II, 191, 516; III, 186, 218, 1852). This town became a stopping place for the Iroquois as they went southward on their war expeditions, and brought about much trouble between the authorities of Virginia and Pennsylvania on this account. As early as 1719 complaint was made because these war parties stopped at this place upon their return from their southern expeditions, with the prisoners which they had captured (Arch. Pa., I, 437, 1852; Col. Rec. Pa., III, 86, 1852). Because of the Conoy town being made a stopping place by the Iroquois, the Conoy Indians were constantly afraid that the Governor of Virginia would send an armed force against them. For this and other reasons the Conoy desired to remove higher up the river, which was consequently made as a request at the Council at Lancaster in 1744. This desire to remove from Conoy Town to the mouth of the Conedogwinet, Juniata or to Shamokin had been expressed in 1743 by "Old Sack," the chief at the town (Col. Rec. Pa., IV, 657, 1851). At the Council at Lancaster the Iroquois asked that satisfaction be given to the Conoy for the lands which they had left, in order to remove to Shamokin (See Col. Rec. Pa., IV, 657, 725-726, 745, 1851). At the Council at Philadelphia, in 1749 the Iroquois said that the Conoy at Juniata had requested them to present their claim for the lands which they

had left when they removed to the Juniata. Governor Hamilton replied that the Conoy had misrepresented the facts, and that they had no settlement due them (Col. Rec. Pa., V, 390-393, 1851). The Conoy gradually moved up the Susquehanna, to Catawissa, Wyoming, and then to Chenango, or Shenango, (near Binghampton, N. Y.). In 1760 the majority of the Conoy were living at this last mentioned place, on both sides of the Susquehanna River (Col. Rec. Pa., VII, 492, 1851). In 1766 John Penn said, to the Indians present in Phila., "We remember the Nanticokes and Conoys had a Council Fire formerly at the mouth of Juniata, and that they were afterwards admitted to the great Council at Onondaga, and that now they have a Council Fire burning at Chenango" (Col. Rec. Pa., IX, 332, 1852). In 1769, at a Council in Philadelphia, "Last Night, the Conoy King," said, in speaking of the friendship of the Conoy and Nanticoke, "Never yet since the beginning of the World have we pulled one scalp, nor even one Hair from your Head." He also said that they had "a Council Fire at Shenango, which is the Door of the Six Nations" (Col. Rec. Pa., IX, 332, 617, 1852). The small remnant of the Conoy were finally swallowed up in the Mohawk and Delaware. The Conoy Town, near Bainbridge, attracted the Indian traders to that place at a very early date. Peter Bezalion was perhaps one of the first. He had been trading at Conestoga as early as 1696. The old trail from the mouth of Conoy Creek ran directly east to Philadelphia, and a part of it was known as "Peter's Road." He was granted a tract of 700 acres along the river at this point in 1719.

Canayes.—Pa. Coun. (1728), Arch. Pa., I, 221, 1852. Cawnoys.—Wright (1728), the same, 213. Conay.—Gooch (1733), Col. Rec. Pa., III, 564, 1852. Connoi.—Gordon (1734), Arch. Pa., I, 437, 1852. Connois.—Pa. Coun. (1704), Col. Rec. Pa., II, 516, 1852. Conoy.—Treaty (1744), Col. Rec. Pa., IV, 734, 1851. Conoys.—Civility (1728), Arch. Pa., I, 233, 1852. Conoy-uch-such-roona.—Treaty (1744), Col. Rec. Pa., IV, 712, 1851. Ganaway.—Keith (1722), Col. Rec. Pa., III, 188, 1852. Ganawense.—Pa. Coun. (1704), Col. Rec. Pa., II, 191, 1852. Ganawese.—Pa. Coun. (1701), Col. Rec. Pa., II, 15, 1852. Piscataway.—Pa. Coun. (1704), Col. Rec. Pa., II, 191, 1852. Conay Town.—Pa. Coun. (1722), Col. Rec. Pa., III, 188, 1852. Conoi.—Pa. Coun. (1738), Col. Rec. Pa., IV, 313, 1851. Connoi Town.—Gordan (1734), Arch. Pa., I, 438, 1852. Conoy Town.—Spotswood (1719), Col. Rec. Pa., III, 86, 1852. Ganaway Town.—Pa. Coun. (1723), Col. Rec. Pa., III, 218, 1852.

CONSHOHOCKEN. The name of a hill, later known as Edge Hill, in Montgomery County, at the site of the present Conshohocken. The derivation, and meaning of the name has been variously given. It is said to mean, "Pleasant valley," but no such meaning can be found in any of the Indian words in the name. It may be a corruption of Guneu, "long"; schigi, "fine"; hacki, "Land", with the locative, ing, having the significance, "at the long fine land." In the deed to William Penn, 1683, of the lands between the Schuylkill and Chester Rivers, the line of the purchase commenced "on the West side of Manaiunk, called Conshohockhan." This deed was made out by Secane and Icquoquehan. The deed for the lands east of the Schuylkill, to Pemmapeckh Creek, run "So farr as ye hill called Conshohockin, on the said river Manaiunk." This deed is signed by Neneshickan, Malebore and Neshanocke. Catemus, "an Indian King," with Peter Rambo, Swanson, Philip Th. Lehnmann and Jos. Curteis, witnessed both of these deeds (See Arch. Pa., I, 65, 66, 1892). For the lands lying back of these lands a deed was made out in 1685, "Beginning at the hill called Conshohockin, on the River Manaiunck, or Skoolkill." This deed was signed by shakahoppoh, Secane, Malibor a n d Tangoras. It was delivered in the presence of Lassee Cock, Mouns Cock, Swan Swanson and others. (Arch. Pa., I, 92-93, 1852). The region about Conshohocken was settled soon after the landing of William Penn, chiefly by Swedes and Welsh. The "Swedes Ford," which is noted on Scull's map of 1759 was on the river near this place. It is noted on Scull's map (French) as "Swedes Fort"—an error. In 1723 a Petition was presented to the Provincial Council concerning a road from "the great Conestogae Road to the Swedes Ford over Schuylkill" (Col. Rec. Pa., III, 225, 230-21, 1852). During the War of the Revolution the American troops rendezvoued at the Swedes Ford, at which place the British army, under General Howe was later expected to cross in order to reach the American troops at Valley Forge. (Col. Rec. Pa., XI, 301, 1853; Arch. Pa., V, 615, 664, 1853). In 1777, when the American army left White Marsh, to go into winter quarters, it crossed the Schuylkill, on a bridge built of wagons, at the Swedes Ford and encamped at Gulph Mills, about a mile and half from the river and six miles from Valley Forge. Consult any of the histories of the Revolution, under title Valley Forge.

Conshockhan.—Deed, by Indians (1683), Arch. Pa., I, 65, 1852. **Conshockin.**—Deed, by Indians (1683), Arch. Pa., I, 66, 1852, also 92. **Conshohocken.**—Deed, by Indians (1685), Arch. Pa., I, 92. **Conshohockin.**—Deed, by Indians (1685), Arch. Pa., I, 92.

Another suggested meaning of the name is; Kitschii, "Great," hacki, "land," with locative, ing, meaning "at the place of the great land."

COPEECHAN. A creek which enters the Lehigh River near Catasauqua, in Lehigh County, now called Coplay Creek. The name is said to be derived from an Indian name, meaning "fine running streams," or "that which runs evenly." The only name found upon any of the maps is the name used at present.

Coplay Creek. Morris, map, 1848. Historical map, 1875.

CORNPLANTER. The name of a small creek, or run, which enters the Allegheny River from the west in Warren County, and the name of a run which enters the same river from the east, nearly opposite the former stream. Also the name of a Post Office in Warren County. Derived from the name of a famous Seneca chief, whose Indian name was Gyantwachia, but who was frequently called Captain John O'Bail and Cornplanter, by the English. His Indian name is said by Hewitt to be derived from Kaiiontwako, "by what one plants." He was born between 1732 and 1740 on the Genesee River near Conewaugus, N. Y. His father was a white trader, named John O'Bail. His mother was a full blood Seneca. Cornplanter occupied a prominent position in all of the negotiations concerning the purchase of the lands from the Indians in northwestern Penna. (See Arch. Pa., XI, 509, 1856; XII, 101, 1856; Sec. Ser. VI, 627, 1877). When he went to Philadelphia, in 1790, to present his claims to the Council and to meet Washington, he left his two wives and a number of children at Pittsburgh, in charge of the Commanding officer (Arch. Pa., XII, 300, 1856). While on his way to this meeting of the Council he stopped at Shippensburg. John Wilkins writes of him at this time, "I need not give you a character of the Cornplanter, his friendship for the people of Pennsylvania, his

pacific temper and integrity are sufficiently known" (the same ref. 321).
He appeared before the Council at
Philadelphia. October 23, 1790, at
which time he delivered an address,
which covered the various dealings he
had with the State of Penna., and
the United States, in the various sales
of lands, and other matters relating
to the various injuries done himself
and his tribe, the Seneca (Col. Rec.
Pa., XVI, 500-509). He took a prominent part in the Treaty of Fort Stanwix, 1784; the Treaty at Fort Harmer,
1789; and at the treaties with the
United States in 1797, and 1802. In
1789 Richard Butler advised the
granting of a tract of 1,500 acres of
land to "Captain Abeal, alias the
Cornplanter" (Arch. Pa., XI, 562).
This grant was made by a resolution
of the Legislature March 24, 1789.
In 1790 Cornplanter wrote a letter to
Gov. Mifflin concerning a settlement
for the lands which had been taken
in by the line of the purchase of
1789, but which had not been included in the land for which payment
had been made (Arch. Pa., XII, 322).
During 1794, when Major Ebenezer
Denny was stationed at Fort Franklin,
attending to the establishment at
Presque' Isle (now Erie), Cornplanter
frequently visited the fort, giving advice and warnings (Journal of Major
Denny, 397 etc., Hist. Soc. of Pa., Memoirs, VII, 1860). Cornplanter selected
for his own occupancy a tract of 640
acres, on the west bank of the Allegheny, about 14 miles above Warren.
He located on this in 1791, and lived
there until his death, February 18,
1836, at the age of over an hundred
years. For many years after the
settlement of the region along the
Allegheny the "Cornplanter Indians"
were engaged in cutting and rafting
timber. They were engaged in this
occupation until very recent years.
The Seneca still occupy the reservations along the upper Allegheny. One
of the towns, which was occupied by
Cornplanter was called Cayantha, or
Cayontona, and stood about a mile
north of the 195th mile post, from
the Delaware River, on the line between Pennsylvania and New York, on
the Conewago River. It is shown on
the map of Ellicott, 1787, as Cayontona.

Cyentookee or Cornplanter.—Pa. Coun.
(1790), Arch. Pa., XII. **Cyentwokee.**—
Jeffers (1790), the same ref., 86, 1856.
Captain Abeal, alias the Cornplanter.—
Butler (1789), Arch. Pa., XI, 562. **Cap-
tain O'Bale.**—Evans (1784), Arch. Pa.,
XI, 50, 1856. **Captain Obeal.**—Proctor

(1790), the same ref., 741. **Captain
O'Bail.**—Huffnagle (1786), the same ref.,
300. **Corn-planter.**—Nicholson (1790),
the same, 322. **Corn-Planter.**—Quit-Claim
(1791), Arch. Pa., Sec. Ser., VI, 627,
1877. **Corn Planter.**—Dickinson (1786),
Arch. Pa., X, 740, 1854. **Gaiant-waka.**—
Parker, in Code of Handsome Lake, 140.
Gyantwache.—Deed (1789), Arch. Pa.,
XII, 101. **Kiant-whau-ka, alias Corn-
planter.**—Treaty (1795), Arch. Pa., Sec.
Ser., VI, 803, 1877.

Consult: Papers Relating to the Es-
tablishment at Presqu' Isle, Arch. Pa.,
Sec. Ser., VI, 627-832, 1877; Albach,
Annals of the West, 432, 648, 1858.

**COSHECTON, COCHECTON, CUS-
HIETUNK.** The name of a small creek,
a range of mountains, and a former
Indian village in Wayne County. Also
the name of the falls in the Delaware
in the same region. The name, according to Heckewelder, is a corruption of Gischiechton, "finished, complete." Bauchamp gives the origin,
from Kussitchuan, "a rapid stream."
Boyd, "A finished small harbor." The
verb Gischicton, "to finish," with the
locative, unk, would give the form most
frequently found, Cushietunk, and
would signify "at the finished place"
—doubtless having reference to the
ending of canoe navigation at the falls.
The Indian village, or villages, were
situated on both sides of the Delaware,
before 1719, at the sites of Milanville,
Wayne County, Pa., and Cochecton,
Sullivan County, N. Y. When the line
was run between New York and New
Jersey in 1719, one of the stations for
the taking of observations was situated
on the New York side of the Delaware, at the place noted on Evans'
map of 1749 as "Station Point." James
Steel and Jacob Taylor made the survey of this line in accordance with the
agreement between New Jersey and
New York (Arch. Pa., Sec. Ser., XIX,
660, 1890). The falls near this point
now known as Coshocton Falls are
noted on Howell's map, 1792, as Cushietunk Falls. The Indian settlement
at this point was probably one of the
oldest on the Delaware. At the treaty
of 1749 the lands between the Delaware and the Susquehanna, south of
a line from the mouth of Lackawaxen
Creek to a point on the Susquehanna
below Shamokin (now Sunbury), were
deeded to the Penns (Arch. Pa., II,
33-37, 1852). The lands north of this
line were not purchased. This left
all of the lands about Wyoming out of
the purchase. At the Treaty at Albany in 1754 the Agents of the Con-

necticut Land Company bought the lands north of this line from the Mohawks, and started the endless controversy between Pennsylvania and Connecticut concerning the rights to these lands. This dispute, "involved the lives of hundreds, was the ruin of thousands and cost the State millions. It wore out one entire generation" (Gov. Hoyt, in Frontier Forts of Penna., I, 424, 1896). The first Connecticut settlers in this disputed territory built their log houses at the mouth of Calkins Creek in 1754 (Col. Rec. Pa., VI, 248, 1851). Tedyuskung, the Delaware chief, objected to this settlement, and brought the matter up at the Council at aston in 1758, and again at the Council at Philadelphia in 1760. Governor Hamilton issued Proclamations in 1761, 1763 and in 1769, warning the settlers to leave these lands, but they paid no attention whatever to these warnings (Col. Rec. Pa., VIII, 567, 594, 663, 1852; IX, 27, 588, 1852). In 1756 a number of the people at Cushietunk were attacked by the Indians, some were taken captive. The Indian trail from this point on the Delaware, ran through the Little Meadows across the Moosic Mountains to Capoose, where the trail led directly to Wyoming. The old trail was the first path between the Delaware and the Susquehanna that had been in use for generations by the Indians. The utter foolishness of the Connecticut settlers taking possession of this place, even had the Penns done nothing, is evident. The massacre of Wyoming and the fearful suffering which followed the settlement at this point, was simply a foregone conclusion. In 1762 John Williamson was sent to Cushetunk to see how many families were then living at the place. He reported that there were in all 16 families, which contained 40 men (Arch. Pa., IV, 83-84, 1853). The "Manor of Wallenpaupack," which was surveyed in 1751, for the use of the Proprietaries, was included in the lands claimed by the Connecticut land company, more properly the Delaware Company, and was included in the County of Westmoreland. The various disputes, the Indian troubles, and the hardships of the early settlers, on this historic ground takes up much space in the records of this period in Pennsylvania history. Consult: Archives of Penna., Sec. Ser., XVIII, the entire vol., 1890; Frontier Forts of Penna.,

I, 454, 1896; Egle, History of Penna., 1148-1149, 1883.

Cashetang.—Steel (1719), Arch. Pa., Sec. Ser., XIX, 660, 1890. **Cashiotan.**—Peters (1760), Arch. Pa., III, 754, 1852. **Cashiegtonok.**—Lotter, map, 1770. **Cashietank (Mts.).**—Lewis Evans, map, 1755. **Cashitunck.**—Gordon (1760), Arch. Pa., III, 756, 1853. **Cashishton.**—Stroude (1778), Arch. Pa., VI, 651, 1853. **Cosishton.**—Stroude (1778), Arch. Pa., VII, 63, 1853. **Cushichtun (Mts.)**—Scull, map, 1770. **Cushictunck.**—Gordan (1760), Arch. Pa., III, 760, 1853. **Cushietunk.**—Hamilton (1761), Col. Rec. Pa., VIII, 663, 1851. **Cushitunk.**—Chief Justice (1760), Arch. Pa., III, 754, 1853. **Cushyehtunk.**—Evans, map, 1749. **Cushyhunk.**—Coun. at Easton (1758), Col. Rec. Pa., VIII, 210, 1852. **Kuthichtun Falls.**—Adlum, map, 1790.

COVE SPRING. A point on the Indian trail from the Susquehanna to the Allegheny. Mentioned by John Harris, in his table of distances, in 1754. It was situated at what is now known as Trough Spring in Tell Township, Huntingdon County. See Arch. Pa., II, 135, 1852.

COWANESQUE. A branch of the Tioga River, which it enters from the west, at Lawrenceville, Tioga County. Heckewelder gives the derivation from Gawunshesque, "Overgrown with briers." This is questioned. A more probable origin is that which has been given by Hewitt, in a letter to the Hon. Charles Tubbs. "The word Cowanesque seems to be none other than Ka-hwe-nes-ke, the co for ka, marking grammatic gender, and meaning, it; wan, for hwe-n, the stem of the word o-whe-na an island; es, an adjective meaning long; que, for ke, the locative post position, meaning at or on; the whole signifying, "at or on the long island." Mr. Tubbs tells us that there was at one time an island in the river, which was about four miles long, between Osceola and Knoxville. "This long island in a small river, to the Indian mind, was its distinguishing characteristic" (Tubbs). This island is noted in the land Warrants, of the surveys made in the valley during 1785 and 1786 (See Warrants, 345, 416 and 529 in Land Office at Harrisburg). This same island appears on the surveys made by the Connecticut-Susquehanna Company, which sold lands in this region as late as 1790. The mill dams and other improvements made by the settlers cut out one branch of the stream around this island, hence it is not noted on any of the maps of the state after the white occupation of the region. Red Jacket was asked to define a list of Indian names given to him, Cowanesque among them. He said that it was a Seneca word, meaning "at the long island." The name Gawichnawane on Evans map of 1755, for the "Long Island," at the mouth of Pine Creek, on the Susquehanna, is probably a corruption of the same name (see BIG ISLAND; LONG ISLAND). Morgan gives Ga-weh-nasegeh, as "a long island." A name given to the Cowanesque, on a map of the survey of a State road in 1799, is, Ga-wa-nia-que,—on file at Harrisburg. In 1767 David Zeisberger, when on his way to the mouth of the Tionesta, passed to the headwaters of the Allegheny by way of the Cowanesque. On October 6th, he says, "We arrived before noon at Pasigachkunk, an old deserted Indian town. It was the last on the Tiaogee. Here Christian Frederick Post, during the late war, had to turn back while on his way to Allegheny, because the Indians would not allow him to proceed further. When we left this place we took the wrong path. Seeing that the route went too far South, we halted and John struck into the woods towards the North, in search of another path. He found one which we thought would be the correct one. We soon left the Tiaogee altogether and entered the great thicket, above which the Tiaogee has its source." (MS of Zeisberger's Journal of 1767). This town was evidently situated in the region of the "long island," near Knoxville, Tioga County. The author has gone over this region a number of times, from the Cowanesque to the Genesee and Allegheny, and is convinced that this was Zeisberger's route in 1767. This last town "the Tiaogee" (Cowanesque), was not far from the present town of Academy Corners, near Knoxville, where many Indian relics have been found. Just after leaving this place it was an easy matter to take the wrong path, as several valleys join the Cowanesque valley, at this point. They evidently took the valley running south, just beyond Knoxville, and then came back to the valley leading to the headwaters of the Cowanesque (See PASIGACHKUNK). Zeisberger crossed from the Cowanesque to the headwaters of the Genesee, near Ulysses, and then struck the waters of the Allegheny, near Gold, Potter County. He says, "After we had crossed a slight elevation we arrived at the source of the Allegheny, which is here no larger than Christan'

Spring." On the 9th., "We traveled along the Allegheny, keeping it to our left. This day we came out of the swamp (thicket) in which we had traveled four days." (These extracts are from the MS of the Journal of Zeisberger for 1767. Kindly copied by Charles Tubbs). The route followed by Zeisberger was down the Allegheny, through Coudersport, Potter County, beyond which they "came out of the swamp." Zeisberger was, in all probability, the first white man to pass over the divide between the Cowanesque and the Genesee and down the headwaters of the Allegheny. C. F. Post and John Hay's reached the site of the village of Pasigachkunk in 1760, but went no further, as they were warned to turn back by the Iroquois. Zeisberger returned by the same route, reaching the headwaters of the Allegheny on October 28th. and Pasigachkunk on the 31st. In 1768 he again made the trip over this same course. In 1787 Andrew Ellicott and Andrew Porter, who were running the boundary line between Pennsylvania and New York, reached Gawanishee Flats" on the 11th. of June, "where the 90th. mile-stone was set up last season." They crossed the divide to the Allegheny, and went on down the river until they "were ordered by the Indians to discontinue the Line 'till after a Treaty should be held." They had then reached the 167 mile-stone. This mile-stone was situated on the Tuneungwant Creek, near the present Tuna, McKean County, and was not far from the "most central of the Seneca towns," mentioned by Zeisberger as Tiozinossungachta, at the mouth of Cold Spring Creek, N. Y. The small Indian village at the mouth of Great Valley Creek, N. Y. was the nearest village to this point. The Cawwanishee Flats mentioned in Ellicott's letter, was situated on the Tioga River, at the site of Lawrenceville, Tioga County—where the 90th mile-stone was set up. (Arch. Pa., XI, 178, 1856).

Cawwanishee Flats.—Ellicott (1787), cited above. **Cawenesque.**—Adlum, map, 1790. **Cawenisque.**—Howell, map, 1792. **Cowanisque.**—Map of Connecticut-Susquehanna Land Co 1790. **Ga-wa-ni-a-que.** Survey of State Road (1799), Land Office, Harrisburg. **Tawanisco.**—Act of Legislature (1792), quoted by Tubb's.

Consult; Life and Times of David Zeisberger, 325, 1870; James Strawbridge, the Pioneer of Tioga County, by Charles Tubbs, 1906; The Centennial of Lycoming County, Charles Tubbs, 1895.

COWANSHANNOCK. A creek which enters the Allegheny from the east at Cowanshannock, Armstrong County. Possibly a corruption of Gawunschhanne. "brier-stream."
Cawanshannock.—Adlum, map, 1790. Cowanshanock.—Unappropriated Islands (1809), Arch. Pa., Third Ser., III, 477, 1896. Cowanshannock.—Warrant to B. Jacobs (1774), Arch. Pa., Third Ser., I, 400, 1894. Cowan Shannock.—Board of Prop. (1775), Arch. Pa., same vol. 396.

CROOKED CREEK. A stream which enters the Allegheny from the east, below Kittanning, Armstrong County. According to Heckewelder, the Indian name was Woak-hanne, "crooked-stream." Woaku, "crooked;" hanne, "stream."
Crooked Creek.—Scull, map, 1770; Howell, map, 1792.

CROSS CREEK. A stream which has its headwaters in Washington County, flows across the "Panhandle" of West Virginia, entering the Ohio from the east, opposite Mingo Junction, Ohio. According to Heckewelder the Indian name of the stream is, Wewuntschi-saquick, which means "two streams flowing into a river at the same point from opposite directions." The stream opposite this stream, in Ohio, is also called Cross Creek. Both enter the Ohio River on opposite sides. Cross Creek Village, in Washington County, was settled at about 1770. Many of the first settlers along Cross Creek took up land under Virginia warrants, and were under jurisdiction of the Virginia Court of West Augusta, at Washington, Pa. On account of the situation of this region, lying as it did between Fort Pitt and the Indian country beyond the Ohio River, the early settlements were frequently attacked by the Indians, whose old trails crossed from the Indian country in Ohio to the waters of the upper Ohio, at many points. Joseph Vance, who moved from Virginia to Washington County in 1774, built a stockade fort, about one mile north of the present Cross Creek village, which was known as "Vance's Fort." Mrs. Wallace whose death led to the massacre of Gnadenhutten, in 1782, was captured by the Indians near this fort. It is said that the scheme of this expedition was made out at this fort by a number of the residents of the Cross Creek settlement in the fall of 1781. Many of the men who took part in this most melancholy event were from the neighborhood of this settlement (For a list of names, consult Doddridge's Notes, 201, 1912 reprint). The majority of the settlers in this region were Scotch-Irish Presbyterians. Religious services were held under a tree, outside of the gate of Vance's Fort, on September 14, 1778, by Rev. James Power, D. D., the Pastor of the Presbyterian Church at Mount Pleasant, Westmoreland County, at which service a number of those who took part in the massacre were present. There were several other stockade forts in the neighborhood of the Cross Creek settlement. Among them were, Well's Fort, at the junction of the North and South branches, in Cross Creek Township; Marshall's Blockhouse, built by Col. James Marshall (or Marshel), in the same Township; Reynold's Blockhouse, about one and a half miles south of Cross Creek Village; Bayon's Blockhouse, in Cross Creek Township, and a few others in various parts of the same region.

Consult; History of Washington County, Boyd Crumrine, 1882; Frontier Forts of Penna., II, 416-417, 1896; Doddridge's Notes, 201, Reprint 1912; Old Redstone, Smith, 1854; History of the Presbytery of Washington, 260, 1889; History of Cross Creek Graveyard, Simpson, 1894; Arch. Pa., Third Ser., III (Virginia Certificates on Cross Creek), 505, 573, 1896.

CRUM CREEK. A creek which enters the Delaware from the west, in Delaware County. The Indian name given to this creek, Ockanickon, may possibly refer to the name of an Indian tribe. The record which contains this name reads, "The Ockanickon or Crum Creek Indians having removed from their old habitation before the Proprietors Departure, by his Order Seated, by Caleb Pusey etc., ...But the said Indians expressing great uneasiness at the uncertainty of their Settlements, pressed and several times Urged the Neighboring Friends that they might be Confirmed in Some particular place unter certain Metes and Bonds, that they Might live no more like Dogs, as they expressed themselves" (Arch. Pa., Sec. Ser., XIX, 341, 1893). This request was presented to the Commissioners of Property in 1702. The present name of the creek is a corruption of the Swedish name, Cromkill or Crumkill, meaning "Crooked Creek." On Lindstrom's MS. Map it is designated as, "Paperack La Riviere Courbie (crooked), ou La Riviere de Tenakons ou Peskohockon." John Printz, the Swedish Governor, established himself and built a fort, called New Gottenburg, on Tinicum island in 1643. A number of the colonists from Fort Christina came to Tinicum, settling along Crum Creek, near the fort. See CHESTER; MINQUAS KILL; DARBY; RIDLEY; TINICUM. Consult; History of New Sweden, Acrelius, N. Y. Hist. Soc. Coll., New Series, I, 409 etc., also edition of the Hist. Soc. of Penna.; Arch. Pa., Sec. Ser., V, 1890; Record of Upland, Hist. Soc. of Penna., Mem., VII, 1860; Annals of Phila., Watson, II, 227, 253, 1850, and the various Histories of the U. S.

Cromkill.—Upland Rec. (1677), work cited, 65. **Crumb Creek**—Minute Book "C," (1687), Arch. Pa., Sec. Ser., XIX, 15, 1893. **Crum Creek**—Minute Book "G," (1702), Arch. Pa. Sec. Ser., XIX, 341. **La Riviere Courbe.**—Lindstrom MS., map, Amer. Phil. Soc. **Ockanickon.** —Minute Book "G," (1702), Archives cited, XIX, 341. **Riviere de Tenakons.**— Lindstrom MS., map, cited.

CUSSEWAGO. A creek which enters French Creek at Meadville, Crawford County. Also the name of a former Munsee village, which stood on the south west shore of the creek of the same name. Custaloga, the head Chief of the Munsee tribe lived in this village. He was one of the Indians who had been at Venango, when the French drove away the English traders from that place in 1753. Among these traders was John Fraser, who afterwards lived at the mouth of Turtle Creek. This Chief was present at Venango when Washington and Gist were on their way to the French fort at Le Boeuf, at the present Waterford. Fraser wrongly locates this fort at Cussewago (Col. Rec. Pa., VI, 654, 1851). Later writers, who have followed his narration of events, have made the same error. Cussewago was on the trail from Lake Erie to the Allegheny, which was followed by the French army in their march to Venango in 1753. Washington went over this trail in 1753 to Fort Le Bouf (Western Annals, 115, 1858). Gist also mentions the place in his Journal, "We set out and travelled twenty-five miles to Cussewago, and old Indian town" (Darlington, Gist, 82, 1893). During the French and Indian War, and also during the Conspiracy of Pontiac, the town was occupied by hostile Munsee

and Seneca. It would seem that Custaloga continued to live at this place until after the British had driven the French from the region, as he, according to a letter of Col. Hugh Mercer, was living there in 1759 (Col. Rec. VIII, 313, 1852). His village, which is spoken of as being opposite the present Franklin, was evidently a temporary camp. Custaloga's Town, as noted in the various records is situated where Meadville now stands (Arch. Pa., III, 624-625, 1853). This chief was not a member of the Unalachtigo clan of the Delaware, as stated by many writers, but was the leading Chief of the Wolf Clan, or the Munsee, and was succeeded by the famous Captain Pipe. He had taken a leading part in the raids into the English settlements, and at various Treaties, at Fort Pitt and on the Muskingum, he returned some of the prisoners he had taken. He was the only one of the Munsee to sign the Treaty or agreement with Bouquet, in 1764, and for so doing he was called "an old woman," by the Seneca at Fort Pitt, in 1765 (Col. Rec. Pa., IX, 253, 1852). The two other tribes of the Delaware, the Turtle and Turkey, had not agreed to these terms, which Custaloga had signed. In 1788 a party of eleven men encamped near the site of the old Indian village of Cussewago. Among them was David Mead, who built a cabin above French Creek, surrounded by a stockade. In 1789 a number of other families joined this community, which became known as "Mead's Settlement." In 1791 these settlers were warned by "Flying Cloud," that a company of hostile Indians had been seen in the neighborhood. The women and children were gathered in Mead's blockhouse, and then were sent to Fort Franklin, at the site of the old French fort, Machault. Half-Town, a brother of Cornplanter, with 27 of his warriors protected the flight of these refuges by scouring the woods on each side of the creek. During this period there were many Indian raids into this then distant settlement. The defeat of the expedition of General Harmer, and later that of General St. Clair, gave the hostile Indians of Ohio greater courage in their raids upon the English settlements. During the years 1791-1792 many thrilling experiences were passed through by the settlers at this place (Consult: Frontier Forts of Penna., II, 623-627, 1896; Egle, History of Penna., 597-

611, 1883). In 1791, when Col. Proctor was at Fort Franklin on his mission to the Indians, the garrison at the fort was supplied with flour from the mills of David Mead (Col. Rec. Pa., Sec. Ser., IV, 571, 1876). Many of the supplies at this fort were received from Cussewago in 1794, when Major Denny was on his mission to Presque' Isle. He stopped at Cussewago on his way from Fort Franklin to Le Boeuf. He says, "Got to the settlement about three o'clock, where we found some people 'forted', as it is called. This the only place where a settlement has been attempted this side of Pittsburgh" (Denny's Journal, 388, 1860). While Major Denny was at Le Bouef he was visited by a delegation of Iroquois, who warned him that if he went on with the work at this point, that there would be trouble. They denied that they had sold the land, and said that the paper which they had signed at Fort Harmer was thought by them to be a treaty of peace, and not a deed to their lands (work cited, 390). After the treaty of Greenville, by General Wayne, the settlers commenced going into the region north of the Allegheny River in great numbers. Saw-mills were erected at Cussewago and other places along French Creek, and lumber was rafted down the creek to the Allegheny.

Caseoago.—Fraser (1753), Col. Rec. Pa., V, 659, 1851. **Casewago.**—Shippen (1753), same ref., 660. **Cassawaga.**—Proctor (1791), Arch. Pa., Sec. Ser., IV, 571, 1890. **Cusewago.**—Ellicott, map, 1788. **Cussawaga.**—Gist, map, 1753. **Cussawago.**—Gen. Neville (1793), Arch. Pa., Sec. Ser., IV, 751, 1890 **Cusseawago Town**—Ellicott (1794), Arch. Pa., Sec. Ser., VI, 775, 1877. **Cussewago.**—Gist (1753), Darlington's Gist, 82, 1893. **Cussewauga.**—Mead (1793), Arch, Pa., Sec. Ser., IV, 750, 1890.

The name of Custaloga has various forms, among which may be mentioned Castalogo, Custologo, Custaloga, Custelloga, Kastateelocaand Kustaloga. The last mentioned is the form used by Washington in 1753 (Washington's Journal, in Western Annals, 115, 1858).

Castologo's Town.—Mercer (1759), Arch. Pa., III, 624, 1853. **Cushtulogas Town.**—Mercer (1759), Col. Rec Pa., VII, 311, 1851. **Custalogoes Town.**—Mercer (1759), Arch. Pa., III, 625.

DAGUSCAHONDA. The name of a Post Office in Elk County. An early Land Company in the region had this name, the origin of which cannot be discovered.

DAHOGA. The name of a Post

Office in Elk County. May be a corruption of Diahago, or Deyohhogah, "where it forks." Same as Tioga (q. v.).

DEKANOAGAH. Hewitt gives the meaning, "between the rapids." Cusick gives as the name of the Mohawk Castle, Dekanoge, "where I live." Dekanoagah was the name given by Governor Evans for the Conoy village which was situated on the east side of the Susquehanna River, at the site of the present Washington Borough, Lancaster County. The name Conejohela was first given to this village, and then to the village on the western side of the river, nearly opposite. (See *Conejohela*.) It seems that the Conoy first settled at the site of Washington Borough, after entering the State, and soon after removed to the western side of the river, and then to Conoy Town (See *Conoy Town*.) The name Conejohela was given to both of the villages at this point, but more properly to the one on the western side of the river near which Cresap first settled after entering the Province. The name Dekanogah is used by Gov. Evans, who visited the place in 1707. At that time some of the Nanticoke were on their way to the Iroquois to pay their tribute.

Dekanoagah.—Evans (1707), Col. Rec. Pa., II, 386, 1852. **Dekawoagah.**—Egle, History of Pa., 843, 1883.

DELAWARE. The name of a state, river, county and various places in the United States. Also the name of the most historic of the Algonkian tribes, or confederation of tribes. The name is derived from that of the Governor of the English Colony at Jamestown, Lord De la Warre, who succeeded Sir Thomas Gates in 1610. The various documents relating to the Dutch, Swedish and English settlements on the Delaware are found in Archives of Pennsylvania, Second Series, V (the entire vol.); VII, 459-820, 1878; IX, 625-634, 1895; Records of the Court at Upland, Memoirs Hist. Soc. of Penna., VII, 9-203, 1860. According to Heckewelder, the Indian name of the river was Lenapewihittuck, "river of the Lenape," and Kit-hanne, "great stream." Zeisberger gives the form Kik-bit-tuk, "a large river." (See Heckewelder, Indian Nations, 51, 1876; Indian Names in Penna., 247, 1872). The name recorded in the first Indian Deed to William Penn, 1682, is "River Dellaware, alias Makeriskhickon" (Arch.

Pa., I, 47, 1852). This Indian name has been given various forms by later writers. Wats gives it as Makerish-Kitton (Watson, Annals, II, 180, 1850); Wescott, in Egle's Hist. of Penna., gives the form Makerisk-Kitton (Egle, 1019, 1883). Hecke-welder says that this name "denotes, I am inclined to believe, a spot either on the bank, or in the bed of the Delaware;—which conjecture I base on the termination kitton, evidently intended for kit-hanne or gicht-hanne, signifying the main stream," (Heck., Indian Names, 254, 1872.) Brinton and Anthony give the form Kittan, for "great river." The Delaware word Hikan signifies the ebb of the tide. The author thinks that this word enters into the compound word, which means, "the great tide-water river." The name may be a corruption of Maquaas-Kittan, "the great river of the Mohawks." The branch of the Delaware, now known as the West Branch, was formerly called the Mohawk Branch. This name was evidently applied to the main stream, as Allegheny or Ohio was the name of the river now known as the Ohio, as well as of the branch now known as the Allegheny. The most probable origin of the name Makeriskhickon is, therefore, Masquas-Kittan, "Great River of the Mohawks." The Mohawks were called Macquas, Maquas, Maquaas, Mackwaes, etc., by the early writers. Makerisk, or Makerish, may be a corruption of one of those early forms of the name Mohawk. From the time of Captain Cornelius Hendricksen (1616), the river was called South River by the Dutch and Swedish writers, who also called the bay "The Bay of the South River," even after it was called by the English "Bay de la Warre" (See Arch. Pa., Sec. Ser., V, 26-27, etc., 1890). The bay was discovered by Henry Hudson, an Englishman in the employ of the Dutch, on August 28, 1609. It is stated that Lord Delaware entered the bay the year following, when on his way to Jamestown, but this is doubtful. Cornelius Hendricksen explored the river in 1616 to about the site of Philadelphia (Arch. Pa., Sec. Ser., V, 11-12, 1890). The first attempt to settle on the Delaware was made by the Dutch at Gloucester, New Jersey, in 1623, when a trading post was established and a fort, called Nassau, was erected. In 1630, Samuel Godyn, and a few other merchants of Amsterdam, purchased from the Indians a tract of land on the western shore of the Delaware, which extended 32 miles north from Cape Henlopen and about 2 miles back from the river. In April, 2631, Captain DeVries and about 30 colonists landed at Whorekill, now Lewes, Delaware, at a place which they called Swaanendael, or Valley of Swans. During the absence of DeVries, this little colony was blotted out by the Indians (See Voyages of DeVries, Henry Murphy, translation, New York, 1853). The land and the jurisdiction of Swaanendael were transferred back to the Dutch West Indian Company in 1636. In April, 1638, a colony of 50 Swedes, under the direction of Peter Minuit, who had been a Director of the West India Company, but who had entered the newly organized Swedish West India Company, sailed up the Delaware River and landed at the mouth of Minquas Kill—later called Christina Creek by the Swedes. The spot chosen by Minuit for the erection of the trading-house and fort was about two miles from the mouth of the creek, at the site of the present Wilmington, Delaware. The Dutch at Fort Nassau informed Governor Kieft of the arrival of this Swedish colony on the western shore of the Delaware. Kieft at once issued orders to the Swedes not to intrude upon the possessions of the Dutch West India Company, but Minuit paid no attention to these orders. The Swedish colony prospered in its trade with the Indians. These severe winters of 1639-1640, however, nearly led the discouraged colonists to the abandonment of the place. The arrival of a new body of colonists in the spring of 1640, with plentiful supplies, put new life into the struggling settlement. In the spring of 1641, a colony of English colonists under Robert Cogswell sailed from Connecticut for the South River. They established a trading post at Salem Creek, New Jersey, near the mouth of the Schuylkill. The Dutch and the Swedes on the Delaware united to expel these "intruders." In 1643, Kieft instructed Jansen, the commissary at Fort Nassau, to expel these English colonists. Jansen was assisted by the Swedes from Fort Christina. The English were taken prisoners, sent to Manhattan and then to their homes in Connecticut. In the spring of 1643, John Printz arrived on the Delaware with the most thoroughly equipped colony which had ever reached the river. He was commissioned by Queen Christina as Governor of New Sweden.

The "Instructions" given to him were doubtless drawn up by Oxenstierna, the Chancellor of Sweden (See Arch. Pa., Sec. Ser., V, 797, etc., 1890). Printz established his government on the Island of Tinicum, where he built his house, which was called "Printz Hall," and a fort, which was named "New Gottenburg." He erected another fort about three miles below Salem Creek, called "Fort Elsinburg." In 2651, the Dutch Governor, Stuyvesant, built a fort, called "Casimir," near the present New Castle. Printz left the Delaware for Sweden in 1653, leaving his son-in-law, John Pappegoya, in charge of the colony. He was succeeded by Governor Risingh in 1654. One of the first acts of this new Governor of New Sweden was the taking of the Dutch fort, Casimir, which led to the invasion by Stuyvesant in September, 1655, and the complete downfall of the Swedish government on the Delaware. In March 1664, Charles II, granted to the Duke of York and Albany, a patent to all of the lands which included the New Netherlands. A squadron, under Col. Richard Nicolls, was sent to seize these lands. Stuyvesant surrendered Fort Amsterdam, on Sept. 8 1664, which then became known as New York. Robert Carr was sent with three ships to take possession of the lands on the Delaware (See Instructions to Carr, and other documents relating to the taking of the lands on the Delaware, Arch. Pa. Sec. Ser., V, 564 etc., 1890). In August 1673 the Dutch fleet of 23 ships under command of Cornelius Evertsen accomplished the recapture of New York, which again became a part of the New Netherlands. The colonies on the Delaware declared their submission. By the Treaty of Westminister, March 6 1674, the New Netherlands were ceded to the English. The Duke of York obtained a new royal patent on June 29, 1674, for the lands which had been granted in 1664. He appointed Major Edmund Andross Governor of this region, which the Dutch turned over to him on the 31st of October, 1674. Andross appointed Captain Edmund Cantwell and William Tom to take possession of New Castle and the forts and stores on the Delaware, November 6, 1674 (See Archives cited, 682, etc.). On June of the same year, the Duke of York had granted to Lord Berkley and George Cartaret the lands in the Province of New Jersey. Lord Berkley sold, in 1685, half of these lands to John Fenwick, in trust for Edward Byllinge and his assigns. Byllinge conveyed his interest in these lands to William Penn, Gawen Lawrie and Nicholas Lucas, in trust for his creditors. The Trustees sold rights to these lands to several people, who, with Sir George Cartaret, made a division of the Province, which was called West Jersey. Sir George Cartaret, the Proprietor of East Jersey, died in 1679. According to the direction of his will his rights to the lands in East Jersey was sold by his heirs to pay his debts. These rights were bought by William Penn and eleven others in 1681-2. In 1680 William Penn petitioned Charles II to grant him letters of Patent to lands in America, instead of the sum of 16,-000 Pounds which the government owed his father, Admiral Sir William Penn, for money advanced by him to the government and for pay in the sea service. The King signed the grant to the lands naming the Province Pennsylvania, in honor of Sir William Penn, the father of William Penn, March 4, 1681. Penn also received from the Duke of York, on August 24, 1882, a deed for the town of New Castle and the lands within a circle of twelve miles about it, as well as a release of the lands in the Province, granted by the King. William Penn landed at New Castle on October 24, 1682, and on the 29th. went to Upland, the name of which place was changed to Chester, at Penn's request. From Chester, Penn went to the mouth of the Schuylkill and to the site of Philadelphia, which was then settled by the Swedes, Dutch and the Quakers, who had come to America in the first colonies of settlers to New Jersey. The Treaty at Shackamaxon must have taken place at this time. (See Shackamaxon, Coaquannock, Darby, Tinicum, and other place names on the Delaware).

DELAWARE, FALLS OF. The falls of the Delaware, at Trenton, was regarded by the settlers on the Delaware as the limit of the jurisdiction of the Court at Upland. The Indian name for the place was Sankhikans (See note, Record of Upland Court, 31, 1860). This name, evidently is the same as that given by Heckewelder, Sankhicani, which he said was the Lenape name for the Mohawks. This name is the same as the Lenape word for gun-lock, according to both Heckewelder and Anthony. The former says that the name was given to the Mohawks by the Lenape, or Delaware, because the Mohawks used the muskets long before the former. The meaning "flint users" given by some authorities, would not have any special reference to the Mohawks, as all Indians were flint users, but the significance of "fire-striking people" is evident. The common Lenape word for flint was, "mahellis." Sankhikan was the word for "gun-lock." As has been stated in a previous note, the meaning of the Lenape word Hikan is "at the ending of the flow" of the tide. This may have some relation to the significance of the Indian name of the falls, although the meaning given seems to be more correct. The Mohawks, with the muskets purchased from the Europeans about New York, were likely first seen by the Delawares near the falls—to which place they could go in their canoes from the Mohawk Branch. At the meeting of the Court at Upland in Nov. 1677, Lawrence Cock, Israel Helm, John Dalbo and others made application for permission "to settle together in a Towne att the west syde of this river Just below the falls." This application was granted by the Court, but no such settlement was made at this time, as Gov. Andross was not willing that this land, which had not been purchased from the Indians, should be occupied until the Indian title should be extinguished (See Record of Upland, 75, 1860).

DELAWARE, FORKS OF. The name given to the triangular tract of land included between the Delaware and the Lehigh Rivers, at the mouth of the latter. The Blue Mountains form a natural boundary to this tract on the north. The Indian name for this place was, according to DeSchweinitz, Lechauwitonk. Heckewelder gives the form Lechauwake and Lechau-hanne—the former signifying, "where there are forks," and the latter, "forked-stream." Lechauwitank, "the place at at the forks" was the name given to the place where Easton is now situated. (See LEHIGH). The various Indian names for the "forks" were quite frequently shortened to Lecha, or Lechay, by the early settlers. In 1701 the Provincial Council was informed that John Hans Steelman, who was said to live in Maryland, was contrary to the law, trading with the Indians "at Lechay, or ye forks of Delaware" (Col. Rec. Pa., II, 21-22,

1852). In the same year the council ordered certain Indian chiefs to appear to be consulted with concerning the passing of a law prohibiting the sale of rum to the Indians. Among the chiefs mentioned was "Oppemenyhook at Lechay" (same ref. 26). There is good reason for thinking that "the forks of the Delaware" was the eastern end of one of the earliest, if not the earliest, trail leading to the Susquehanna and Ohio. The trail from the Old Indian town of Pechoquealin, just above the Water Gap, and the trail from "the forks" united just beyond the Blue Mountains, about 20 miles north of Easton (by way of the Wind Gap), and this main trail went on to Wyoming through the Pocono Mountain, Great Swamp and Shades of Death. (Consult the maps in the Journals of the Military Expedition of General Sullivan's Army, 1887.) This main trail was that which was followed by Sullivan's army in 1779—the branch trail from Easton being followed to the main trail (See Journal of Rev. William Rodgers, D. D., in work cited, 246-247). Various other trails entered the Lehigh valley; one of which crossed the river just below Bethlehem and then forked into various directions. Reichel thinks that the name Lechauweki, "the fork of a road," may have been given to the region in which these trails forked (Moravian Missions, 23, 1870). At the Council held at Philadelphia in 1728, Sassounan (or Allummapees) made complaint because the white settlers were going into the lands in this region, which had not been purchased from the Indians. The Provincial Council then presented a deed, made out in 1718, and signed by Sassounan, Opekasset and others, for lands between the Delaware and the Susquehanna, "from Duck Creek to the Mountains this side Lechay." This deed was acknowledged by the Indians, but they said that "their Lands on Tulpehocken were seated by the Christians" (Col. Rec. Pa., III, 321-323, 1852). These lands had been settled by the Germans from the Schoharie Valley, by permission of Governor Keith. They were not bought from the Indians until 1732, at which time a deed was made out for all of the lands in this region drained by the Schuylkill (Arch. Pa., I, 344-345, 1852). The "forks of the Delaware" had evidently been a meeting place for the Indians long before the coming of the white settlers into the region. In 1756, when the Provincial authorities were seeking to bring the Delawares back into friendship with the English, Tedyuskung insisted that the proposed Council must be held at Easton. This Council met July 27, 1756 (See Easton). The famous "Walking Purchase which had much to do with the alienation of the Delawares, and the necessity for this council, included the greater part of Northampton, a part of Carbon, Monroe and Pike Counties. This walk took place upon September 19, 1737 (See WALKING PURCHASE). The town of Easton was named by Thomas Penn, in honor of "my Lord Pomfret's house," September 8, 1751. At the time when the Delawares were ordered to leave "the forks" at the Council at Philadelphia, July 1742, among those present was Nutimus, who is frequently spoken of as "King Nutimus." He, with his followers, removed to the lands at Wyoming. On the Scull map of 1759 the village noted as, "Old King Neutimus" is placed on the west bank of the Susquehanna, a few miles north of the present Bloomsburg Columbia County. It was on the trail leading up the western shore of the river from Shamokin to Wyoming. (Col. Rec. Pa., IV, 578-579, 1851; Scull, map, 1759).

DELAWARE WATER GAP. The name given to the deep cut made by the Delaware River, as it passes through the Blue Mountains, about four miles below Stroudsburg, Monroe County. According to Heckewelder, the Indian name for this place was Buc-ka-buck-ka, "mountains butting opposite each other." The other form given by Heckewelder is Pochkapochka, "two mountains bearing down upon each other with a stream intervening." The creek, which enters the Lehigh River at Parryville, was known to the early settlers as Poco Poco, or Pohopoco,—a corruption of this Indian name. Reichel, in a note in Heckewelder's Indian names, says, that this name "was applied to the region of the Lehigh Water Gap, running back east of the river, and north of the mountain. Hence it was applied to the main stream in that region, now called Big Creek" (work cited, 262, 1872). Zeisberger gives the meaning of Poch-a-wach-ne, "a creek between two hills."

For the legends and traditions of the region consult, Brodhead, "Delaware Water Gap," Philadelphia, 1870.

DELAWARE INDIANS. When the first Dutch and Swedish explorers landed on the shores of the Delaware River they met the great tribe of the Algonkian group now known as the Delawares, and the great tribe of the Irquoian group, known as the Susquehannocks, or Andastes, as it was called by the French. The name given to the former by nearly all of the writers of the early records, was "River Indians," while the name given to the latter was "Minquaas." At that time the Minquaas, whose habitat was along the Susquehanna River, from the site of the present Sunbury down to the mouth of Octorara Creek traded and fished on the Delaware River. When the Swedes landed at the mouth of the creek, which they called Minquaas Creek, and which is now called Christiana Creek—instead of Christina, as it should be—they carried on a trade with these Susquehanna Indians, who came from the river of that name, by way of the trail down this creek. At this time the Delaware and the Susquehanna Indians were at peace with each other and the latter were the chief customers of the Swedes bringing great quantities of furs and peltries to the Swedish colony.

The Delawares called themselves "Lenape," or "Leni-Lenape," which signified "real men," or "Genuine men." The name by which they have been known in history was at first a geographic designation, the same as "Ohio Indians," which meant the Indians living on the Ohio River, without any reference to the tribal connection. Most unfortunately this English name has become the common designation of the most historic tribe of the Algonkian family. The man whose name has been given to this historic tribe of Red Men probably never even saw a "Delaware."

The name given to the Lenape by the French was "Loups," or "Wolves," possibly because the Munsee, or wolf clan, was the one most frequently met by the French explorers. The name was ultimately given by the French writers to the whole Lenape family. The Lenape who spread along the coast of New England were called Wapanachki, or "Easterners'—the name was shortened to "Abnaki." There is little doubt but that when the separation of the Lenape took place, after their first eastward migration, that the group of clans which went south were given the name of Suwano, or "Southerners," which has been corrupted to Shawnee. The Lenape, or Delaware proper, were divided into three main clans, called the Munsee, Unalachtigo and Unami, the Wolf, Turkey and Turtle clan. The legends and traditions of the Lenape are continued in a national history, called the Walam Olum.

When first met with by the Europeans the Lenape had their chief Council Fire at Shackamaxon, where William Penn held his first treaty with them in 1682. This site seems to have been a meeting place for the Minquaas, as well as for the Delawares. Shackamaxon was situated at the site of the present Kensington, a short distance above the business part of Philadelphia, on the Delaware River.

From the time of Penn's first treaty until 1729 all of the transactions of the English with the Indians for the purpose of buying lands within the Province, were carried on directly with the Delawares. The real commencement of the alienation of the Delawares began in 1736, when the Iroquois sold all of the lands of the Delawares south of the Blue Mountains. The Iroquois claim to the lands of the Delawares has never been satisfactorily settled. The tradition given by Heckewelder does not agree with the statements of the various Iroquois diplomats, given at various councils when these land purchases were under consideration. The Iroquois claimed these Delaware lands by right of conquest, but when this conquest was made has never been understood. After the Penn's had signed the papers, buying the lands south of the Blue Mountains, from the Iroquois, the wily diplomats of that Confederation realized that a precedent had been established, which would mean much to them, and the Delawares realized that the good old days of William Penn had gone by. From the time of Penn's landing in 1682 until that year the Delawares had dealt directly with the Proprietary government in all the affairs relating to the sale of land within the Province. Now they were put in the background and could not sell a foot of their own land without the permission of the Iroquois. We can possibly realize what this meant to the proud chiefs, who remembered the days when the Penns treated them with honor and respect, as the rightful owners of

the lands upon which their ancestors had lived for countless generations, to suddenly discover that they did not have a right to a foot of the ground upon which they lived, and that without any warning whatever, the Iroquois could sell the lands to which they had moved when they left their villages on the Delaware River.

In 1742, when the Province of Pennsylvania called a conference at Philadelphia for the purpose of paying the Iroquois for the land west of the Susquehanna River, which was purchased in 1736, the Delawares were informed that they were at liberty to come, provided they bear their own expenses. The decendants of Tammany, who had been treated by William Penn and his successors with dignity and honor, went back to their villages along the Upper Susquehanna and Ohio, to brood over their wrongs and to tell their young men of the change which had taken place. From the landing of William Penn until the treaty of 1736 there had never been a break in the peace between the Delawares and the English in the Province. The legend on the case which contains the Belt of Wampum, in the Historical Society of Pennsylvania, "Not Sworn to but Never Broken," is more than a mere sentiment. It is a historic fact. Until the Proprietors of the Province broke the terms of this treaty, the Delawares had kept it to the letter. The land sales of 1736 and 1742, and the land sale at the Treaty of Albany of 1754 drove the Delawares to the Ohio, and into the arms of the French. With the Delawares went the warlike Shawnee and the commencement of the hostility against the English settlers became a grim reality. Before the Delawares were won back to the League of Amity with the English the frontiers of the Province as, well as those of Maryland and Virginia, were drenched in blood.

There is now little doubt but that the power back of the Iroquois, and which led to the ascendency of that Confederation in Provincial affairs, was Conrad Weiser, the famous Indian interpreter and diplomat, who was himself an adopted Mohawk. Weiser came into power in Indian affairs just at the time when the policy of William Penn was on the decline. Walton, in his "Conrad Weiser," truthfully says, "Weiser helped Shickellamy sow the seed which drenched Pennsylvania in blood from 1755 to

1764." This able man whose sympathy was with the Iroquois, and who had little use for a Delaware or Shawnee, prevented the destruction of the English Colonies by winning the Iroquois, but he helped to bring on the war with the Delaware and Shawnee, which carried death into the white settlements along the entire frontier.

From the time of this Treaty of 1736 the Delawares began to feel more and more the wrong which had been done them, as they retreated beyond the Blue Mountains, seeking a refuge beyond the summits of the mountains in the Wyoming Valley, at Shamokin, along the West Branch, and even on the waters of the Ohio. No sooner had the lands been bought south of the Blue Mountains than a horde of white settlers commenced to invade the lands beyond the Susquehanna, which had not been purchased from the Indians. Again and again the Delawares and Shawnee complained to Shikellamy, the Iroquois deputy at Shamokin concerning the settlements which were spreading over these lands. Shikellamy complained to the authorities of the Province, and various efforts were made to remove these "white squatters." At the Treaty at Albany in 1754 the Commissioners decided to remove this cause of discord by purchasing the lands west of the mountains and south of the Ohio and Allegheny Rivers. At the same time the agents of the Connecticut Company, called the Susquehanna Company, had been bargaining on the quiet, with the Mohawks for the large tract of land in the Wyoming Valley. This fraudulent transaction was carried through by Woodbridge and Lydius, the Agents of this Company. When the Delaware and Shawnee realized that every foot of ground upon which they lived had been sold under their feet, they went home to their villages on the West Branch and on the Ohio, brooding over their wrongs and waiting for the day of reckoning. They did not have long to wait. The army of General Braddock was slowly cutting its way through the forests and over the mountains from Fort Cumberland to Fort Duquesne during the early summer of 1755. On the 9th of July it reached the fording of the Monongahela where its advance ended in utter defeat. Braddock's army paid with blood for the land sales of 1736 and 1754. From this time onward the frontiers of Pennsylvania were drenched in blood until the last of the Delawares had crossed the Ohio into the trackless forests along its northern shore.

The Delawares began to move to the region along the lower Ohio about 1750, and in 1751, at the invitation of the Huron, they moved in large numbers into the Tusearawas and Muskingum valleys. Within a few years the greater part of the tribe, along with the Munsee and Shawnee were settled within the present state of Ohio. The Delaware were the strongest foes to the advance of the white settlers into the region north of the Ohio River. In 1770, at the invitation of the Miami and Piankishaw, they removed into the region of the White River, in Indiana. In 1789 some of them removed to Missouri and Arkansas. After the Treaty of Greenville, in 1795, the greater part of the tribe had commenced to settle away from the rapidly approaching white settlements. By 1835 the greater part of the tribe had settled in Kansas, from which they removed in 1867 to Indian Territory where they became incorporated with the Cherokee. Remnants of the tribe became scattered over various parts of the west and Canada.

The history of the Moravian missions among the Delaware is one of the most interesting subjects relating to the wanderings of this people. The persecution and suffering of these "Moravian Delawares," as they were called, is one of the blackest chapters in American History. For reference, consult: Loskiel, "History of the Mission of the United Brethren Among the Indians of North America," London, 1794; DeSchweinitz, "Life and Times of David Zeisberger," Philadelphia, 1870; Zeisberger, "History of the North American Indians," Ohio Historical Society, 1910; Heckewelder, "History of the Manners and Customs of the Indian Nations," Philadelphia, 1876; Reichel, "Memorials of the Moravian Church," Philadelphia, 1870. Also various articles in "Handbook of American Indians," Bureau of American Ethnology, Washington, 1907-1910.

DEUNDAGA. See *Pittsburgh.*

DIAHOGA, DIAGO etc. See *Tioga.*

DUNEWANGUA. See *Tuneung-want.*

DUNNING'S SLEEPING PLACE. The name of a station on the Indian trail from Bedford to Pittsburgh. It was probably situated near the head of Brush Creek, Westmoreland County, not far from the present Harrison City. It was named for James Dunning, a prominent Indian Trader, who was robbed by Peter Chartier and a band of Shawnee, in 1745. He is frequently mentioned in the early records. Dunning's Creek and Dunning's Mountain, in Bedford County, were both named for this Trader. Robert Dunning, another Trader, lived near the present Carlisle. The Indian trail, from Harrisburg, ran to his home and then crossed to McAllister's Gap—then running up the Path Valley to near the present Concord, where it was joined by the "New Path," through Crogan's Gap, now Sterritt's Gap. Consult: Archives of Pa., II, 12, 43, 135, 1852. Dunning's Creek and Mountain are noted on Howell's map, 1792.

EAST MAUCH CHUNK. See *Mauch Chunk.*

EAST TEXAS. See *Texas.*

EDMUND'S SWAMP. A prominent landmark on the trail from Raystown (Bedford) to the Ohio. It is noted on Scull's map, 1770, and is mentioned in the table of distances to the Ohio, by John Harris, in 1754,—"to Edmund's Swamp—8 Miles, to Stoney Creek—6 Miles" (Archives, II, 135). In the table of distances of Patten and Montour it is mentioned,—"From Allegheny Mountain to Edmund's Swamp—8 Miles, From Edmund's Swamp to Cowamahony (Quemahoning) Creek —6 Miles" (Col. Rec., V, 750). This swamp was named in honor of Edmund Cartlidge, the Conestoga trader, who went to the Ohio to trade as early as 1727. He and the other early traders (Le Tort, Crawford, Fraser, etc.) followed this lower trail through Bedford to the Ohio. The swamp was situated near Buckstown, Shade Township, Somerset County. The run from it is wrongly named on the Morris map of 1848 as "Edward's Swamp Run." On the Howell's map of 1792 the swamp is situated near Burkets. The army of General Forbes crossed this swamp on its way to Fort Duquesne in 1758. The region where this swamp was situated is still swampy ground.

ELK CREEK. A branch of Penn's Creek, in Centre County. There are several creeks and runs in other counties of this name. See *Moshannon.*

ENDLESS MOUNTAINS. One of the names of the range of mountains which is more commonly known as the Kittatinny Mountains. See *Kittatinny.*

EQUINUNK. The name of a creek which enters the Delaware River on the west side in Wayne County. Also, Little Eqununk, a short distance below the above stream. The name is said by Heckewelder to be derived from an expression signifying "where articles of clothing were distributed." Also the name of a village in Wayne County.

Equinunk and Little Equinunk.— Howell's map, 1792.

ERIE. A county and city, on the lake of the same name. The name is probably a corruption of the Huron "yenresh," meaning "it is long-tailed," having reference to the panther. This word has been Gallicized into Eri and Ri, hence the locatives Erie, Rigue and Rique, signifying "the place of the panther." The name of the people occupying the region, Riqueronon and its various synonyms, meaning "people of the panther." The French word "chat" was a translation of the Iroquois word for puma, which also was the word for wild-cat. In all of the earlier French maps, and in the Jesuit Relations, the lake is called "Erie ou Du Chat," and the people "Erieehronons ou Nation du Chat" (See maps of d'Abbeville, 1656, and Hennepin, 1687). The Erie belonged to the Iroquoian family and occupied the region south of Lake Erie. Before their wars with the Iroquois they were spread over the region to the Ohio River and to the lands of the Susquehanna, at the divide between the waters of the Allegheny and the West Branch. The Wenrohronon, or Neutral Nation, occupied the lands on the eastern border of the Erie domain, probably near Cuba Lake, New York. This tribe is mentioned in the Jesuit Relation for 1640 and 1641. Little is known of the history of this early period concerning the Erie. It is possible that the unidentified "Black Minquas" were the Eries. The name given to the Allegheny, or Ohio River, on Herrman's map of Virginia and Maryland (1670) is "Black Minquaas River." The note on this map reads, "A very great river called the Black Minquaas River, out of which above the Susquehana fort meets a branch some leagues distant—where formerly those Black Minquaas came over as far as Delaware to trade, but the Sassquahana and Sinnicus Indians went over and

destroyed that very great Nation.'"
This note would make the Susquehanna
(Conestoga) Indians and the Seneca
the destroyers of the "Black Minquas."
These two tribes may have been united
in the expulsion of the Cherokee from
the upper Ohio. All were of the same
linguistic stock. As the Iroquois were
at war with the Susquehanna Indians
as early as 1608, it is more probable
that the "Black Minquaas," mentioned
by Herrman's note, were the Cherokees,
who were driven south. The unidentified tribe, which lived along the
Juniata, has also been supposed to be
the same as these "Black Minquaas,"
or "Black Mingoes."

The historic period of the Erie tribe
commences with its war with the Iroquois, before 1654. The cause of the
final war, according to the Jesuit Relation of 1655-56, was due to the acci-
dental killing of one of the Senecas
by one of the thirty Erie ambassadors.
These ambassadors had gone to the
Seneca capital, Sonontouan, to renew
the existing peace, when this happened.
The Seneca immediately put all of
the Erie deputies to death save five.
This final war commenced in 1653,
when the Erie made an attack upon
one of the Seneca towns, which they
captured and burned. Then they defeated a body of Senecas. These events
aroused the Iroquois, who raised an
army of 1,800 warriors, which made
an invasion of the Erie country. The
large village of Rique was finally captured, after a most strenuous defense
by the Eries. No quarter was asked
or given, and women and children
were slaughtered until "blood was knee
deep in certain places." This battle
at Rique, 1654, put an end to the power
of the Eries, but the war lasted until
1656, after which the Erie tribe was
entirely blotted out, either by the destruction of war or by the adoption
of the remaining members by the
Iroquois. The Erie were a brave and
war-like people. The estimated population of the tribe in 1654 was about
14,500. There were two Erie villages
whose names have been preserved,
Rique, at the site of the present city
of Erie, and Gentaienton, which was
probably in the southern part of Erie
County, New York.

Soon after the Marquis du Quesnes
became Governor-General of Canada,
he took steps towards the erection of
a chain of forts, which was to connect
the French possessions in Canada with
those on the Mississippi. Early in
Jan., 1753, Mons. Babier was sent with
300 men, for the purpose of building
a fort at the mouth of Chautauqua
Creek, where Celoron had disembarked
in 1749, when on his way to the Ohio.
The command of the expedition was
here assumed by Sieur Marin, who
arrived with an additional force of
500 whites and 20 Indians. Finding
that Chautauqua Creek was too shallow to float batteaux, he passed along
the shore of Lake Erie, where he at
last found a suitable place for the
erection of a fort. Here he built the
first of the French Forts, which was
named Presqu' Isle (Peninsula). This
fort stood at the site of the present
Erie. It was finished early in the
summer of 1753, as Duquesne writes,
Aug. 20, 1753, "Sieur Marin writes me
on the 3rd. instant, that the fort at
Presqu' Isle is entirely finished; that
the portage road, which is six leagues
in length, is also ready for carriages;
that the store which was necessary to
be built half way across this Portage
is in a condition to receive the supplies, and that the second fort, which
is located at the mouth (entree) of the
River au Boeuf, will be soon completed" (Archives of Pa., Second
Series, VI, 163, 1877).

Consult, Frontier Forts of Penna.,
II, 537-566, 1896; Archives of Pa.,
Second Series, VI, 161, 625-827, 1877;
Colonial Records of Pa., VI, 10, 1851.
Howell's map, 1792, gives the name for
the present Erie, Presqu' Isle. For
additional reading on Erie, consult
Jesuit Relations (Thwaites ed.), I—
LXXIII, 1896-1901; Handbook of
American Indians, Bureau of Ethnol-
ogy, I, 1907.

FISHING CREEK. Enters Susquehanna from the north in Columbia
county, at Rupert. Scull's map of
1759, "Namescesepong or Fishing
Creek." Is also the name of a branch
of Bald Eagle Creek. The name is
derived from Namees-hanna, according
to Heckewelder. The name given on
the Scull map is however more like
the Delaware "Na-mee-si-ponk," meaning , "it tastes fishy."

FRANKSTOWN. The name of a
prominent point on the trail from
Harris' Ferry, now Harrisburg, to
Kittanning and various other points
on the Allegheny River. It was named
for Frank Stevens, a prominent Indian trader, who went westward as
early as 1734. The tradition that the
place was named for Steven Frank,

a German trader, is due probably to the incorrect placing of an apostrophe in the table of distances given by John Harris. This is given (Archives of Pa., II. 136) as follows, "to Frank's (Stephen's) Town,—5 Miles." There should be no apostrophe in Stephen." Frank Stevens was a prominent trader, while there is no record of a trader named Stephen Frank. Frank's Town was situated at the site of the present Frankstown, Blair County, about two miles east of Hollidaysburg, on the Frankstown Branch of the Juniata. It had been the site of an old Indian village called Assunepachla (which see). A number of the Indian and traders trails intersected at this place. The main trail, known as the Frankstown Path, ran from Harris' Ferry (Harrisburg) to Kittanning, and then on to Shannopin's Town (Pittsburgh). One branch of this trail left it at Canoe Place (Cherry Tree) and ran northwest to Venango (Franklin), where it joined the Venango Path, which ran westward to the Shenango River, and then on to the Muskingum. Another trail ran north to the Bald Eagle Valley, and on to the Big Island (Lock Haven), crossing the Shamokin Path near the mouth of Marsh Creek. Another trail ran on down the Juniata to below the mouth of Lost Creek, where another branch ran northeast to Shamokin (Sunbury). The trail to the south ran through Three Springs, Huntingdon County, to Raystown (Bedford), where it joined the Allegheny Path, from which the Frankstown Path separated at Black Log (Orbisonia). These various trails had been used by the Indians long years before the coming of the white settlers and Indian traders. The trail down the Juniata may have been one of the paths of the "Black Mingoes," who once occupied the Ohio region and traded with the Dutch on the Delaware. The Juniata Valley was once occupied by a tribe of Indians which has never been identified (See JUNIATA).

The Frankstown Path was one of the most important, and much used, trails between the Susquehanna and the Ohio, for Indians, traders and settlers, until after the settlement of the lower Cumberland Valley and the opening of the military road to the Ohio by General Forbes in 1758. After that time the older Allegheny Road, and the "New Path" became more travelled, but the Frankstown Road continued to be used until after the building of the Pennsylvania Railroad. When Conrad Weiser went on his mission to the Indians at Logstown (Economy) in August, 1748, he went by the Frankstown route (Colonial Records of Pa., V. 348-358). At that time he saw no cabins or houses at the place, the Indians who had occupied the village had moved on westward to the Ohio. This was also the route of Col. Armstrong, and his company of frontiersmen, as they went to destroy the Indian settlement at Kittanning in 1756. John Harris gives a table of distances on this trail, and also of those on the Raystown branch, in Archives of Pa., II. 135-136. Consult; Hanna, Wilderness Trail, I. 147-273; also the various Colonial Records and Archives of Penna., under title.

Assunepachla.—Le Tort (1731), Arch. Pa., I, 302, 1852. **Frank's Town.**—Scull, map, 1759. **Franks Town.**—Montour (1752), Arch. Pa., II, 133, 1852. **Franks T.**—Lewis Evans, map, 1755. **Frankston.**—Daugherty (1782), Arch. Pa., IX 543, 1854. **Frankstown.**—Pa. Council (1790), Col. Rec. Pa., XVI, 434, 1853. **Franks, old Town.**—Adlum, map, 1789. **Frank's Town Road.**—Patten (1754), Col. Rec. Pa., V, 762, 1851.

FRENCH CREEK. The headwaters of this stream are in Chautauqua County, New York, west of Chautauqua Lake, in Erie County, Pa., at the town of Waterford. The creek runs south, through Cambridge Springs and Meadville and enters the Allegheny River at Franklin, Venango County. This historic stream has been known by several names. Dr. Eaton, in his history of Venango County (Egle's History of Penna., 1118) says that "The Indians seem to have known it as To-ra-da-koin. By the English as Venango River." I have been unable to find any authority for the name To-ra-da-koin. The Indian name was Onenge, "an otter," which has been corrupted into Venango. On the map of Lewis Evans, 1755, the name, which is blurred, is Toranadachkoa. Major Denny in his report to Secretary of War, Timothy Pickering, says, "It was formerly called Venango Creek, or rather Innan-ga-eh, and it is a beautiful, transparent, and rapid stream" (Frontier Forts, II. 584, 1896). Pownall's map of 1776, which is copied from Evans' map, gives the form Toranedachkoa. The French expedition, under Celoron de Bienville, passed the mouth of the creek on Aug. 3, 1749. He says in his journal, "I continued my route as far as the village at the River aux Boeufs, which is only nine or ten cabins." On the map of Father Bonnecamp, who was with Celoron, the creek is noted as, R. aux Boeufs. The creek is given this name in all of the French documents. George Washington, in his journal of 1753, calls the creek "French Creek" (See Washington's Journal of 1753, Olden Time, I. 10; also in Spark's Life of Washington). This name is given on Lewis Evans' map of 1755, and upon all of the later maps. Washington, no doubt, gave the name to the creek because the French Forts had been built upon it, and because he did not know the name of the stream. Christopher Gist, who was with him, does not mention the name of the creek, either in his journal nor upon his map, by any other name than that given to it by Washington. See Venango.

FRENCH MARGARET. The name of a former Indian village at the mouth of Lycoming Creek, Lycoming County, a few miles west of the Williamsport station. The site of this village is noted on all of the early maps, after those of Evans, 1749 and 1755, who notes "French T.", the village of Madame Montour, at the mouth of Loyalsock Creek. French Margaret was, according to Reichel, who probably takes the statement of Martin Mack as his authority, a neice of Madame Montour. Andrew Montour, the famous interpreter, is said by Mack, in his journal, to have been a brother of French Margaret, although Shikellamy said that Margaret Montour was a daughter of Madame Montour. Martin Mack called to see her in 1753. If she was a sister of Andrew Montour, then she was a daughter, instead of a neice, of Madame Montour, as the various Colonial Records clearly show that Andrew Montour was a son of Madame Montour. Martin Mack makes French Margaret to be a neice of Madame Montour and a sister of Andrew Montour, which is impossible. The husband of French Margaret was named Katarioniecha, or Peter Quebec, as he was called by the English. Their children were, Catherine, Esther, Mary, a son who was killed in the south in 1753, and Nicholas. The husband was a man of more than ordinary character. Margaret told Martin Mack, that he had not tasted

rum for over six years. French Margaret was the first person to put a "Local Option Law" into force in this early period, as she would not allow the use of rum in her town. The daughter known as "Queen Esther" was the most infamous of all who bore the name. She married a Munsee named Eghohowen, and in 1772 was living at Sheshequin, at the present Ulster, Bradford County. Soon after this date she removed to the place known as "Queen Esther's Town," opposite the present Athens. She took part in the fearful massacre of Wyoming on the 3rd. of July, 1778. (See QUEEN ESTHER'S TOWN). French Margaret attended a number of the Indian Councils, at Philadelphia, Easton and Albany. She was also a visitor to the Moravian institutions at Bethlehem, where she attended divine service. She is frequently mentioned in the various Journals of the Moravian missionaries, as well as in the records at Bethlehem. Consult; Archives of Pa., III. 741, 1853; IV. 52, 1853; Colonial Records of Pa. VIII. 499-500, 1852; Memorials of the Moravian Church, I. 330-331, 1870; Hanna, Wilderness Trail, 203-206, 1911. See MONTOUR.

French Margaret.—Scull, map, 1759.

(In Conrad Weiser's report of his journey to Shamokin, in Jan. 1742-43, he mentions, "Andrew Montour, the Son of Madame Montour." As Weiser knew Andrew intimately, this statement should settle any question as to his relation to Madame Montour. See Colonial Records, IV. 641)

GANAGARAHHARE. An Indian village, mentioned in the deposition of Stephen Coffen, in 1754, when he gave the account of the building of the French forts on the present French Creek. The village was situated at the mouth of this creek, at the site of Franklin. He says, "Mr. Morang (Marin) ordered Mosieur Bite with Fifty Men to a place called by the Indians Ganagarahhare, or the Banks of Belle Reviere, where the River aux Boeufs empties into it" (Col. Rec. Pa., IV, II, 1851). As this is the only mention of this village by this name, it is impossible to tell what the correct form was. The village at the site of Vernon, New York, bears a resemblance to the name—Ganowarehare, meaning "skull is fastenend to the top of it." See Venango.

GANOGA LAKE. A lake in Sullivan County. The name does not belong to this state. Ganogeh, derived from Ga-a-no-ge, which signifies "place of floating oil," was the name of the Cayuga village, at the site of the present Ganoga, New York.

GAWANGO. A town in Warren County. Cannot discover the origin. Is not a historic name in that locality. See JENNESEDAGO.

GENESEE. The name of a river, which rises in Potter County and flows northward into Lake Ontario; also the name of a village and township in the same county. The river possibly received its name from the Seneca village of Genesee, at the site of Genesee, New York, as this name was applied to the town when the river was known by other names. Genesee is derived from Tyo-nesi-yo, "there it has fine banks." Morgan gives the form Gen-nis-he-yo, signifying "beautiful valley." It is certain that there were two villages of the Seneca bearing this name. The older town was noted on the early maps as Chenussie, was situated at the mouth of Canaseraga Creek, on the eastern side of the Genesee River. This is where the village was located in the days of Mary Jemison. The Genesee Castle, of Sullivan's expedition, was situated on the west bank of the Genesee, near Cuylersville. The various Journals of Sullivan's expedition mention these two villages. The river was called Casconchiagon by Charlevoix in 1721 (See Bulletin No. 108, New York State Museum. 115, 1907). On the map of Lewis Evans, 1755, it is noted as, "Kaskuchse or L. Seneca R." Pownall's map of 1776, gives the name as, "L. Senekies or Kasconchiagon R." The "L" is an abbreviation for Little, and the two other names are possibly corruptions of the forms given by Harris, Gah-skesa-deh, signifying, "waterfalls." These waterfalls are the most wonderful and most striking natural features of the river. They begin at Portage, N. Y., where the falls, and the deep gorges, are strikingly beautiful. Mary Jemison is buried in Letchworth Park, which overlooks the Genesee River, near the falls below Portage. The scenery here is most beautiful. Howell's map 1792, gives the name as "Cheneesee River." Zeisberger, in the MS of his journey of 1767, in the Archives of the Moravian Church, at Bethlehem, gives the form "Zoneschie." He says, "still we pushed forwards and came across a large creek called Zoneschie, which flows into the land of the Senekas." Zeisberger crossed this stream near its headwaters in Potter County. Zeisberger and Cammerhoff visited the Seneca village in 1750. In his "History of the Mission of the United Brethren," Loskiel mentions this village by the name "Zoneshie" (Part II. page 122). Many other forms of the name Genesee are contained in the Journals of Sullivan's expedition, but these apply to the village in New York, and not to the river. Consult; Journals of the Military Expedition of Major General John Sullivan, Auburn, 1887; Handbook of American Indians, I. 489, 1907.

GENOSSA. Mentioned at the Council at Lancaster, 1757. Intended for Shamokin (Colonial Records, VII. 543-545). See *Shamokin*.

GLASSWANOGE. A former Indian village situated on the west side of Roaring Creek, at its mouth, in Montour County, near the present Roaring Creek. It is noted on the Scull map of 1770. On the Historical map of Penna. 1875, it is noted as "Glassawangoe." The origin of the name is not known.

GNADENHUETTEN. "Tents of Grace." There were five villages of this name, founded by the Moravian Church, and occupied by the Indian converts; First the village near the mouth of Mahoning Creek, Carbon County, at the site of Lehighton. This village was commenced in the spring of 1746, and was occupied by the Christian Indians from Shecomeco, who had found a temporary home at Bethlehem. The mission prospered under the influence of Martin Mack and his helpers. Various tracts of land had been purchased by the Moravian Church, until in 1754 there were 1382 acres in the mission tract, on both sides of the Lehigh. In 1747 a grist mill was built on the Mahoning. A saw mill and black-smith shop were added to the settlement. In 1749 Bishop Cammerhoff dedicated t h e chapel. Various additions were made to the population from Pachgatgoch, Wechquadnach and Meniolagomeka, from 1747 to 1754. In May 1754 the mission was transferred to the east side of the river, to the site of Weissport. This was the second Gnadenhuetten. In Dec. 1754 the mission numbered 137 Mohickon and Delawares, besides the converts living at Wyoming and Nescopeck. The entire village had been invited to remove to Wyoming, through the influence of Tedyuskung. In April 1754, 70 converts removed to Wyoming—fifteen of these afterwards removed to Nescopeck. The chapel at the second Gnadenhuetten was dedicated in 1754. At this time the defeat of Washington at the Great Meadows, and the conflict for the possession of the Ohio, was drawing many of the Delaware and Shawnee to the French influence. The defeat of Braddock in 1755 led to the open hostility of the Delaware and the Shawnee, who then commenced to make raids upon the settlements. The massacre at Penn's Creek (which see), and other acts of hostility aroused the white settlers throughout the entire frontier to a bitter hatred of the Indians. The mission at Gnadenhuetten was in charge of Mack, Grube, Schmick and Schebosh. These lived on the east side of the Lehigh, with the Indian converts. Many of the buildings were on the Mahoning. Anna Senseman, Gottlieb Anders, Martin Nitschmann and other Moravian helpers lived on the Mahoning. On the 24th. of November Zeisberger reached Gnadenhuetten, on the Lehigh, and was getting ready to go to the Mahoning, when Mack tried to persuade him to remain. But Zeisberger was determined to go on. He was fording the Lehigh when he heard the cry of horror from the mission house. He reached the other shore and then turned back. The Brethren at Gnadenhuetten had been attacked by the Delawares, when at supper. Ten were killed, and one captured. The buildings were destroyed Zeisberger carried the news to Bethlehem, where he arrived at 3 o'clock on the morning of Nov. 25th. The entire body of Indian converts fled from Gnadenhuetten, on the Lehigh, to Bethlehem. Susanna Nitschmann was the only captive taken. She died some months after at Tioga. The massacre created a great deal of feeling throughout the state. It was found out later that the party which made this attack was made up of Munsee, under Jacheabus (See KOBUS TOWN). The destruction of this village led to the attempt to build a fort at the site of Gnadenhuetten, on the Lehigh. On Jan. 1st. 1756, the savages made an attack upon the soldiers at this place, drove them

away, and burned the village. Benjamin Franklin arrived at the site of Gnadenheutten and at once commenced the erection of Fort Allen. Consult; DeSchweinitz, Life of Zeisberger, 220-240; Loskiel, Hist. Miss., II. 84-117, 133, 143, 151-171; Frontier Forts, I. 184 et seq.; Rec., V. 576; VI. 736, 747, 750, 759, 767, 772; VII. 15, 309; Archives, II, 460, 491, 515, etc.

The third Gnadenhuetten was a settlement of white persons at the site of Gnadenheutten the Second. The Fourth Gnadenhuetten was situated on the Tuscarawas River, Clay Township, Ohio, at the site of the present Gnadenhuetten, Ohio. This village was established in 1772, through the efforts of Zeisberger, who had been working on the Beaver River (See LANGUNTOUTENEUNK). This village thrived as had all of its predecessors. In 1781 Col. DePeyster of Detroit became convinced that the Indians on the Tuscarawas, who were midway between the British and the Amercian lines, were carrying information to Fort Pitt. The hostile Indians in Ohio threatened the Moravian villages because the Christian Indians would not join with them in their raids into the settlements of the Americans. The frontiersmen in south western Penna. threatened the Indians in these villages because they hated all Indians, regardless of tribe, or condition. Col. Brodhead had urged these Moravian Indians to remove to Fort Pitt, for their own safety. Both Zeisberger and Heckewelder were blind to the real situation in which these Christian Indian villages were placed at this time. In Aug. 1781 De Peyster removed these Indians to Sandusky. This removal was conducted by Capt. Elliott, Dunquat and Capt. Pipe. Before the Moravian Indians reached Sandusky nearly everything which they had, was stolen from them. The winter which followed was one of bitter privation and hardship. In the spring of 1782 a number of the Indians returned to Gnadenhuetten and Schoenbrunn to get some of the corn which they had left standing in their fields. Most unfortunately for these Indians the hostile Wyandot and Shawnee had been making raids into the settlements in the present Washington County, at this very time. The family of Robert Wallace, near Florence, was killed in Feb. 1782. The Indians who had committed this outrage returned to Ohio through Gnadenhuetten. John Carpenter, who was captured by this same party, said to the inhabitants of the village, "My captors will undoubtedly be pursued and tracked to this place" (Life of Zeis., 540). The Indians in the village were much alarmed, but the Moravian assistants quieted them. They remained, gathering their corn, and getting it ready to take away, when the company of frontiersmen, under Col. David Williamson, consisting of 75 to 100 mounted men, reached the village, and on March 8th. 1782 committed one of the vilest deeds in American History. A deed, which for blood-thirsty savagery has no equal in the Annals of Indian History. The whole number of the victims of these scoundrels was 90, men, women and helpless children. The crime is too black to even record. Consult; Loskiel, Hist. Miss., III. 174-184 DeSchweinitz, Life of Zeis., 513-557; Hassler, Old Westmoreland, 153-161; Crumrine, Hist. Wash. County, 102-103; Archives, IX. 496, 511, 540, 541, 552; Washington-Irvine Corres., 236-246; Heckewelder, Narrative 311-328). Doddridges Notes (1912 Ed.) 188-203; and any general history of the U. S. Gnadenhuetten, the Fifth, was founded after the return of the Christian Indians from Canada, upon the lands granted by Congress, June 1st. 1796. In the spring of 1797 Heckewelder returned to Gnadenhuetten and interred the bones of the converts who had been slaughtered in 1782. It was not until October 4, 1798 that the settlement was commenced by the Indians who returned from Canada (Consult; DeSchweinitz, Life of Zeisberger, 652 et seq.). See *Lawunakhannek, Languntouteneunk, Wyalusing*, etc.

GNAHAY. A former Indian village, mentioned in the statement of John Cox, who had been captured by the Delaware Indians near McDowell's Mill, near Fort Loudon, and carried to Kittanning. He was later taken to Tioga (Athens) from which place he went down the river to Gnahay to get some corn. Here he escaped and went to Shamokin, or Fort Augusta as it was then called. No other mention of this name can be found. Wyoming may be meant. Consult; Colonial Records, VII. 242-243.

GUYASUTHA. See *Cornplanter*.

GANAGAROHARRE. A former Indian village at the mouth of French Creek, in Venango County. Mentioned in the deposition of Stephen Coffen (Colonial Records, VI, 11). See *French Creek; Venango.*

GOSHGOSHING. A former Munsee and Delaware village at the mouth of Tionesta Creek, near the present Tionesta, Forest County. It was settled about 1765. The name is derived from Gosch-gosch, "hog," with the locative ing, signifying "place of hogs." It was the site of a Moravian mission which was established by David Zeisberger in 1767. There were three villages, one was two miles above, and the other four miles below this central one. Zeisberger left Wyalusing on September 30, 1767, with Anthony and John Papunhank, two Indians, as guides. They went up the present Chemung River, then down the Tioga, up the Cowanesque, across the divide, over the headwaters of the Genesee, and then down the Allegheny to the mouth of the Tionesta, which they reached on October 30th. Zeisberger was perhaps the first white man to pass over the region of the present Potter County. (Consult. DeSchweinitz, Life and Times of David Zeisberger, 321 et seq., 1870; Loskiel, History of Missions, Part III, 16, 23, etc., 1794; Egle's History of Pennsylvania, 734-738, 1884.) Zeisberger returned to Wyalusing to the Mission of Friedenshuetten, but returned to Goshgoshing in 1768, taking with him some mission helpers and several families of Christian Indians. They reached Goshgoshing in June. Things had not gone well during his absence. While the old blind chief of the village, Allemewi, was favorable, Wangomen, the heathen preacher of the town, opposed the mission. The Senecas also objected to the settlement of the region, saying that the English would build a mission, then a fort and then take possession. Zeisberger went to Zoneschio (Geneseo, N. Y.) to consult with the leading chief of the Seneca. This chief was away from home, but the leading chiefs ordered him to leave the village on the Tionesta. Accordingly, on the 7th of April, 1769, the station at the mouth of the Tionesta was left, the missionaries and the Christian Indians going to Lawunakhannek. This village was about six miles above the Tionesta, at the site of Hickory, near the mouth of Hickory Creek. None of the accounts of the distance to this village, from Goshgoshing, agree.

Loskiel says that it was fifteen miles further up the river, on the opposite bank. It is so placed on the map which accompanies his work. Heckewelder says (Narrative, 206, 1820) that it was fifteen miles to the southeast. It was situated about six miles up the Allegheny River, near the mouth of Hickory Creek. (See *Hickory Town, Lawunakhannek.*) Zeisberger had some very thrilling times during his stay at this village, and his life was in danger from the heathen Munsee, who opposed his mission, because of its interference with their drunken orgies. His preaching to the savages in the wilds of Forest County has been made the theme of the painting of Schuessele's painting, which was presented to the Moravian Society, by John W. Jordan, Jr. The Indian villages in the region were abandoned soon after Zeisberger moved to the Beaver River, April 17, 1770. (Loskiel gives April 7, 1769, as the date when the Mission was removed to Lawunakhannek, so that Zeisberger labored at that place for about one year.) Brodheads' expedition passed the place in 1779, when it was deserted (Archives, XII, 156, 1856). General Proctor passed through in 1791. He says, "We arrived this evening at an old Indian settlement called Hog's town" (Archives, Sec. Ser., IV, 572, 1876). General Irvine in a letter of 1785, says, "From Oil Creek to Cuskakushing, an old Indian Town, is about seventeen miles. From Cuskakushing to another old Indian Town, also on the Bank of the River, is about six miles; this place is called Caneacai, or Hickory Bottom" (Archives, XI, 516-517). The various names of this place are sometimes confused by writers with the names of Kuskuski, on the Beaver.

"Big Cush Cush Islands."—Archives (1806), Third Ser. III., 472, 1896. **Cuscushing.**—Brodhead (1779), Archives, XII., 156, 1856. **Cuskakushing.**—Irvine (1785), Archives, XI., 516-517 **Goschgosching.** — Heckewelder's Narrative, 106, 1820. **Goschgoschink town.**—Heckeweldor, Indian Nations of Pa., 294, 1876. **Goschgoschuenk.**—Loskiel's History of Missions, III., 16, 1794. **Goschgoschunk.**—DeSchweinitz, Life of Zeisberger, 336, 1870. **Gosgoskunk.**—Historical map of Penna., 1875. **Hog's Town.**—Proctor (1791), Archives, Sec. Ser., IV., 572, 1876.

See *Kushusdatening.*

HARRIS' FERRY. A prominent place on the Susquehanna River during the entire period of the early history of the region, at the site of the present Harrisburg. John Harris, Sr., was a native of Yorkshire, England. He came to America previous to 1698, and removed from Philadelphia to Conestoga Township before 1718, as his name is found on the tax list of that Township in that year. Harris was engaged in trade with the Indians, and soon after his arrival at Conestoga Township, he had discovered the advantage of having a trading house on the Susquehanna River. In 1733 he was given a Warrant for the purpose of "keeping of the ferry over the Susquehanna River at Pextan," and in 1734 he applied for permission to Build a small house on the west side of the said River for the conveniency of Travellers that may happen to come on that side in the Night Season or in Stormy Weather when the Boat or Flat cannot pass. He also requests the Grant of 200 Acres of Land on the same side of the River opposite to his Plantation where he dwells and whereon he would build the House. The Prop'r is pleased to grant him the Liberty of Building a small house on the west side of the said River for the use aforesaid during the term for which the ferry is granted provided the Indians be not made uneasy by it, but his further request for the 200 Acres of Land is referred" (Archives of Pa., Third Ser., I, 45, 1894). In 1731 Shikellamy complained to the Provincial authorities concerning a letter which he and Sassounan had sent to John Harris "to desire him to desist from making a Plantation at the Mouth of Choniata (Juniata), where Harris has built a House and is clearing fields." Shikellamy was informed that "Harris had only built that house for carrying on his trade; that his Plantation, on which he has houses, Barns &c. at Pextan, is his place of dwelling, and it is not supposed that he will remove from thence; that he has no Warrant or Order for making a Settlement at Choniata (Juniata)." Shikellamy then said that "tho' Harris may have built a House for the conveniency of his trade, yet he ought not to clear fields." (Colonial Records, III, 503, 504.) Harris' Ferry became a most important point on the trail from the Susquehanna to the Ohio, especially after the settlement of the Cumberland Valley. The various trails to the Ohio crossed the river at this point. The ferry was between the two present railroad bridges which cross the

Susquehanna at Harrisburg. John Harris, Sr., died December 17, 1748. He was buried beneath the tree to which he had been tied by the Indians in 1718 or 1719. This spot is now marked by a monument, with the inscription, "A CRUCE SALUS—John Harris—Of Yorkshire England—the friend of—William Penn—and Father of the—Founder of Harrisburg—Died Dec. 17, 1748—In the Communion of the—Church of England." His wife, Esther, was a woman of strong character, and the heroine of many thrilling events.

John Harris, Jr., the founder of Harrisburg, succeeded his father in the Indian trade and also in carrying on the ferry. His name occupies a most prominent place in the Colonial Records and the Archives of the State. During the various Indian Councils of the early days, he was a prominent figure. After the Massacre at Penn's Creek, Oct., 1755, he wrote to the Governor an account of the first massacre on the Susquehanna, and said that he had made a fort of his house. This was later surrounded by a stockade (Col. Rec., VI, 655; Archives, II, 635; III, 33). The log house which had been erected by John Harris, Sr., and in which John Harris, Jr., was born in 1726, stood on Front Street, below Mulberry, in the present city of Harrisburg. Here was the site of Fort Harris of 1755, which was one of the first, if not the first frontier forts of Pennsylvania. Nearly every prominent Indian chief, trader, explorer, traveler and settler of the early days had passed Harris' Ferry. See *Paxtang.*

The site of Harris' Ferry is noted on all of the early maps. Howell's map of 1792 is the first official map to give the name of Harrisburg. Consult; Archives of Pa., I. 657; II. 9-10 etc.; Colonial Records of Pa., V. 325, 614 etc.; Frontier Forts of Pa., I. 5-8; Egle's History of Pa., 640-643; Hanna's Wilderness Trail, (See Index); Walton's, Conrad Weiser, 73 etc.; Egle's, Notes and Queries.

HARTS LOG, HARTS SLEEPING PLACE, HARTS ROCK. There were two Indian traders by the name of John Hart. One of them was killed in a drunken fight at Allegheny in the fall of 1729. The letter giving this information is signed by James LeTort, Edmund Cartlidge and Shannopin, so that it is possible that he was killed in the region of Shannopin's

Town (Pittsburgh); (See Archives of Pa. I. 254). The other John Hart was licensed as an Indian trader in 1744. Edward Hart was also a trader as early as 1724 (Arch. Pa. Sec. Ser. XIX, 728). There were evidently two places known on the Frankstown Path as Hart's Log or Hart's Sleeping Place. The one was in Hart's Log Valley, in Huntingdon County, near Alexandria. The name was given because John Hart fed his horse out of a hollow log. John Gemmell offered proofs before the Board of Property, Jan. 26 1767, to show that James Starret had obtained a Warrant for 400 acres of land "at a place called Sleeping Place at Hart's Logg on Juniata" (Archives, Third Ser. I. 159). The valley and a small run still bears the name, "Hart's Log," or "Hartslog," as it is noted on the State Map of 1848. The other "Hart's Sleeping Place" was situated about 12 miles north of Ebensburg, Cambria County, on the Dry Gap road, near Carrolltown. It is noted on Scull's map of 1770. The former place, after the settlement of the region, was known as the "Hart's Log Settlement." In 1778 Col. John Piper asked that a guard of 30 men be placed in the region to protect it from the Indians (Archives of Pa. VI. 194). Hart's Rock, in the Ohio River near Steubinville, is noted on Lewis Evan's map, and later ones, as "A Rift (or fording place) called Hart's Rock." Mr. Hanna places this "Rock" at the site of the "Picture Rocks," at Smith's Ferry, which is too far north, as it is noted on all of the maps by an "X" placed just above "The 2 upper creeks" (Cross Creeks), and far below the mouth of Yellow Creek.

HARAORACKAN CREEK. The name of a creek, given in the Records of Upland, on which a tract of land, bearing the same name, was laid out for Eph. Herman and Lawrence Cock, in June 1680 (Records of Upland, 185, 1860). The author of the notes in this work identifies this name with Hackazockan, which is given on the Lindstrom MS. map for the region which was afterwards included in Pennsbury Manor. If such is the case this creek would be the present Scott's Creek, Bucks County (See note "E," page 203, in the work mentioned).

HIAWATHA. The name of a Post Office in Wayne County. The name of the hereditary chieftainship of the

Tortois clan of the Mohawk tribe. It was the name of the great statesman and lawgiver of the Mohawks, who was the founder of the League of the Iroquois, known as the Iroquois Confederacy or the Five Nations. He lived about 1570. He was the Moses of the Iroquois. The beautiful poem by Longfellow has made the name historic. But the poem makes no reference whatever to the real life and work of the real Hiawatha. Consult; A Lawgiver of the Stone Age, American Anthropologist, April 1892.

HICKORY TOWN. A former Delaware and Munsee village situated at the mouth of Hickory Creek, Forest County. There were evidently two villages of this name, one on the right bank and the other on the left bank of the Allegheny River, nearly opposite each other. The earlier, and larger, village was on the west, left, side of the river. The Moravian village of Lawunakhannek, according to Loskiel, was on the west side, at the site of Hickory Town. He says, in mentioning the removal of the Moravian village, "they quit Goschgoscheunk (near the mouth of the Tionesta) and retire fifteen miles further to a place called Lawunakhannek, situated on the opposite bank of the Ohio" (Allegheny). It is placed west of the Allegheny River on the map which is given in Loskiel (See Loskiel, History of the Mission of the United Brethren, Part III. 44, 1794). Gen. Irvine, in 1785, gives the distance above the village of Goshgoshunk as six miles, which is correct, and places it on the east side of the Allegheny, where Ellicott also places it in his very carefully prepared map of 1788 (Archives of Pa. XI. 517). The name given by Irvine is "Canenacai, or Hickory Bottom." The state map of 1848 places Hickory T. on the west side of the river. According to Col. Richard Proctor's Journal, the Delaware and Munsee had removed from this place to Catteragus in the month of April, 1791 (Archives, Second Ser. IV. 577, 1876). In 1794 the Indians had gone back to hunt between Oil Creek and Hickory Town (Archives, Second Ser. VI. 778, 1877). See *Lawunakhannek, Goshgoshunk.*

In July 1808 John Thompson applied for an island in the Allegheny River "about one mile above old Hickory Town" (Archives, Third Ser. III. 474), and in May 1809 Charles Holeman and John Thompson applied for an island in the same river "about one mile below Hickory Town" (the same, 477).

Canenacai, or **Hickory Bottom.**—Gen. Irvine (1785), Arch. Pa., XI., 517. **Hiccory T.**—Reading Howell's map, 1792. **Hickory Town.**—Ellicott, Boundary map, 1788. **Hickory T.**—Adlum map, 170R. **old Hickory Town.**—Archives (1808), Third Ser., III., 474.

HOCKENDAUQUA. The name of a creek in Northampton County, which enters the Lehigh River from the north. According to Heckewelder, a corruption of Hackiundochwe, signifying "searching for land." Zeisberger gives the words, Ha-cki, "land," Undoech-wen, "to come for some purpose." In a note in Heckewelder's Indian Names, Reichel says, "Surveyor-General Eastburn's Map of the Forks of Delaware, drawn in 1740, notes three surveys on Hockendauqua, one of 1800 acres, another of 1426 acres, marked William Allen, and a third of 1500 acres, marked John Page. These surveys were made prior to the walk of a day and a half in Sept. 1737. Lappawinzoe (whose portrait was presented to the Historical Society of Pennsylvania, by the late Granville Penn), at that time king of Hockendauqua, witnessed the walk in part, and expressed his dissatisfaction at the walkers in the memorable words—"No sit down to smoke, no shoot squirrel; but lun, lun, lun all day long." His village lay between Howells grist-mill and the mouth of the creek. Near it the tired walkers passed the night of the 19th and 20th of September, on the completion of a twelve hours' walk, bivouacking before a blazing fire, while the Indians in the village below prolonged a cantico till into the early hours of the morning (work cited, 248). Various corruptions of the name have been made.

Hockendocque. — Morris, map, 1848. **Hockyondocque.** — Scull, map, 1759. **Hockyondoque.**—Howell, map, 1792; also Scull, map, 1770. **Hockyondocquay.**—Historical Map of Penna, 1875. **Hokendauqua.**—State map, 1912—the Post Office, Lehigh County.

HOCKING JUNCTION. A station in Somerset County. The first part of the name is derived from the name of the Delaware village, at the site of Lancaster, Fairfield County, Ohio, which was a famous trading place in the early days. Its name, Hockhocking, signifies "place of gourds." This town was visited by Christopher Gist,

Andrew Montour and George Croghan in 1750, at which time the village consisted of but "for or five Delaware families" (Darlington, Gist, 42). While on this tour Croghan made an alliance with the western Indians, which the Penna. Council refused to ratify (Col. Rec. V. 552). William Trent mentions it (Archives Pa., II. 50)" a place called Hockhocken, about Three Hundred Miles from the Logs Town." The place was also called French Margaret's Town, possibly for an aunt of the French Margaret famous in Penna. history. Both the maps of Evans, 1755 and Pownall, 1776, give this name. The name does not belong to any historic place in Penna.

HOG'S TOWN. See *Goshgoshunk.*

HONEOYE. The name of a creek and village in Potter County; also the name of a lake, town and falls in New York. The name is a corruption of Hah-nyah, "his finger" and Ga-yah, "it lies." The Seneca village of this name was situated about half a mile from the northeast end of Honeoye Lake. Various traditions have been told concerning the origin of the name. Major Fogg, in his Journal of Sullivan's expedition, says, "This town took its name from a misfortune which befell an Indian here, viz;—the loss of a finger, which the word signifies" (Jour. Mil. Exped. Gen. Sullivan, 98, 1887). The map of Robert Erskine, of the survey made by Lodge, notes the lake as "Haunyauga Lake," and the English translation, "the open hand." There were a number of corn fields and apple trees about the village when it was destroyed by Sullivan's army in 1779. He left his supplies, worn out horses and sick men here, in charge of Capt. Cummings, with a guard of 50 men, when the army advanced towards Genesee. The army returned on Sept. 17 in high spirits because of the success of the expedition, and the prospect of a speedy return home. The village was destroyed and the return march, to Tioga, commenced on the 18th. The name has many variations in spelling—but a few of these are given, as they are all simply attempts to spell the name.

Angayea.—Campfield (1779), Sullivan's Exped., 59, 1887; Anyayea —Dearborn (1779), Sullivan's Exped., 74. **Annaquayen.**—Fogg (1779), Sullivan's Exped., 98. **Haunyauya.**—Grant (1779), Sullivan's Exped., 141. **Hannanyau.**—Blake (1779), Sullivan's Exped., 41. **Onnaya-**you. — McKendry (1779), Sullivan's Exped., 205.

HOOPANY CREEK. A name given to the creek, which enters the Susquehanna River from the south, in Wyoming County. The present name is Mehoopany, which is also the name of a village in the same county. According to Heckewelder, the name is a corruption of Hobbenisink, signifying "where there are wild potatoes." The only old map which gives this name to the creek is Howell's, 1792, which gives the form "Hoppeny." All other maps give the name Meshoppen, or Mehoopany, which Heckewelder gives as having a different meaning. The creek which enters from the north at present Meshoppen, and Mehoopany, on the south are given similar names on the early maps. Hoopany and other forms are possibly contractions, or corruptions, of Mechek, "large," and Hobbenac, "potatoes." See *Mehoopany, Meshoppen.*

INDIAN. The name which was given to the Aborigines of America by Christopher Columbus, in a letter of 1493, in which he speaks of the "Indios" he had with him. Columbus believed that he had reached India. Various attempts have been made to give a different name to the aborigines, but none of the names suggested has taken the place of this name which is now so associated with our literature, history and geography. Amerind, compounded of the two first syllables of American Indian, has been suggested, and has been somewhat widely used, but its usage has not become popular. "Indian" has been compounded with many place names, in all parts of the United States. In Pennsylvania, a county (Indiana), and various creeks, Post Offices and villages have been given the name Indian. Indian Creek (Fayette County), Indian Head (same county), Indian Orchard (Wayne County), Indian Run (Mercer County) and many other places are known by this historic name. The list of wild plants in Pennsylvania called "Indian" contains such familiar names as, Indian apple, Indian balm, Indian cherry, Indian cigar-tree, Indian corn, Indian cucumber, Indian elm, Indian mallow, Indian paint-brush, Indian potato, Indian turnip, Indian slipper, are but a few of the wild plants which have been given this name.

INGAREN, The name of a former Tuscarora village at the site of Great Bend, Susquehanna County. It was destroyed by Clinton's division of Sullivan's army, August 17, 1779. The origin of the name is not known. See *Tuscarora*.

Ingaren.—Beatty (1779), Mil. Exped. Sull., 24, 1887. **Tiscarora.**—Machlin, Mil. Exped. Sull., 202. **Tuscarora.**—Campfield, Mil. Exped. Sull., 55. **Tuskarora.** — VanHovenburgh, Mil. Exped. Sull., 278.

INOMOY. A name for a creek, and also an Indian "Nation" mentioned in the Colonial Records and Archives. The Indians are said to be "seated on Lake Erie & on the Inomoy Creek, that runs into that Lake" (Col. Rec., V, 97). The letter about these Indians was evidently written by a German trader, who was not well acquainted with either geography or orthography. The name may have reference to the Miami (Archives I, 737).

IROQUOIS. The name of the Confederation of Iroquoian tribes, known as the Five Nations, and later as the Six Nations, upon the admission of the Tuscarora in about 1713. Also known as the League of the Iroquois. The name Iroquois is a corruption of the Algonkin, Iriakhoiw, "real adder," with the French suffix, ois—"people." The Five Nations was made up of the Cayuga, Mohawk, Onondaga, Oneida and Seneca. The Delawares called them Mingwe, and the western Algonkins gave them the name of Nadowa, "adders." The date of the formation of the Confederation is not exactly known, but was possibly about 1570, through the efforts of Hiawatha. Soon after the formation of this union the Iroquois commenced to use firearms, which they received from the Dutch at New York. Their conquests spread their influence over a great extent of the region southward and westward. Champlain had joined the Algonkian tribes of Canada, in his early expeditions, against the Iroquois. This act made the Five Nations the enemies of the French, whom they opposed at every opportunity. And, while the Confederation was not always friendly to the English, the various Iroquois tribes were not friendly towards the French at any time during the conflict between France and Great Britain. The formation of the confederation of these Iroquoian tribes was one of the chief causes of the decline of the influence and power of the Algonkian tribes. These tribes, while far greater

in number, had no bond of unity, no organization, to withstand the firmly united and thoroughly organized Iroquois Confederation. As a consequence, the Iroquois swept everything before them. Had the Algonkian tribes been united, in the early days, under such a leader as Pontiac, it is not difficult to imagine what might have been the result during the hostility during the French and Indian War. But the Delaware and Shawnee and other Algonkian tribes seemed to have no realization of what they could do, if thoroughly organized. It is perhaps well for the English that they were not organized into a Confederation, such as that of the Iroquois. (For the general history of the Iroquois, Consult, Handbook of American Indians, 617-619, Part 1, 1907). While the historic habitat of the Iroquois was in the state of New York, yet the Iroquois had much to do with the early history of Pennsylvania. Because of their conquests of all of the tribes which inhabited the region covered by the state, they laid claim to all of the land from the Delaware to the Ohio, and southward to the Potomac. In fact, they laid claim to all of the land covered by Pennsylvania, Maryland, Virginia and West Virginia, which was inhabited by tribes belonging to their own linguistic family, as well as those belonging to the Algonkian group. They had conquered the Erie, the Susquehanna (or Andastes), and claimed to have conquered the Delaware. When, or how, this conquest of the Delaware was made is difficult to understand. But, however foolish the tradition of Heckewelder may seem, the fact is certain that the Delaware submitted to the condition and acknowledged that they were under Iroquois dominion. William Penn made his various treaties for land directly with the Delawares, in 1682. All of the various land purchases from this time until after the "Walking Purchase," 1737, had been made directly with the Delawares. After this famous "walk," the Delawares complained because settlers were taking up lands in Bucks County which had not been purchased. The Proprietors showed them the deed for the purchase of 1737, which was said to cover these lands, and also a note from the Iroquois saying that the Delawares owned no lands and had no right to sell lands. In 1742 a notice was sent to the Delawares that the deputies of the Iroquois would be in Philadelphia in May, 1742, and that they could come if they wished to do so, at their own expense. From this time onward the Iroquois were supreme in all of the Councils which were held with the Indians. At the Council of 1742, Canassatego, the Iroquois chief, in a severe speech to the Delawares, because of their refusal to leave the lands on the Delaware River, said, "But how came you to take it upon you to sell land at all? We conquered you, we made women of you, you know you are women, and can no more sell land than women" (Col. Rec., IV, 571, etc.). After this time the Delawares were obliged to submit to the dictation of the Iroquois in all matters pertaining to the sale of their own lands. They were driven to the Susquehanna, and then to the Ohio, where they hoped to escape from the power of the Iroquois, as well as get away from the white settlers. Shikellamy was appointed as the Iroquois deputy, with headquarters at Shamokin, and in 1745 he was made the Viceregent of the Iroquois, with full control of all of the Indian affairs in the Province. Scarouady had control of Iroquois affairs on the Ohio. This alliance of the Provincial authorities with the Iroquois alienated the Delaware and Shawnee, but it saved the English colonies by holding the powerful Iroquois Confederation in friendly relations during the period of the French and Indian War. During the frontier wars of the Province, from 1755 to 1763, the Iroquois as a body remained neutral. The Seneca, because of their intimate connection with the Delaware and Shawnee on the Ohio, by way of the Allegheny River and its tributaries, sided with the hostile Indians. At this period there were a number of Iroquois living in the various villages on the Ohio. These were, in the main, of the Seneca tribe. but were all classed as "Mingoes." These were hostile to the English. Consult. Walton, Conrad Weiser and the Indian Policy ·of Colonial Pennsylvania, 1900; Heckewelder, Indian Nations of Penna., 95, et seq., 1876; Hale, Iroquois Book of Rites, 1883; Loskiel, History of Missions, 1794, and many books and magazine articles on the Iroquois. See *Seneca, Susquehanna, Shamokin, Wyoming.*

JACK'S NARROWS, JACK'S MOUNTAIN, JACK'S CREEK. The very beautiful gorge cut by the Juniata through the mountains, just above Mount Union, Huntingdon County, as well as the mountain itself, is named for Jack Armstrong, an Indian trader who was killed by the Indians at the crossing of the Juniata, just above the present Mount Union. John Harris, in his table of distances on the Indian trail from the Susquehanna to the Ohio, mentions this place. He writes "to Jack Armstrong's Narrows, so called from his being there murdered—8 miles"—that is from the present Shirleysburg—(Archives Pa., II. 136). Armstrong had been killed ten years before Harris gave this table, that is in 1744. The Indian trail crossed to the north shore of the Juniata at Mount Union, where it joined the trail which came up the Juniata. John Armstrong and his two servants, Woodworth Arnold and James Smith, were murdered by some Delaware Indians. Armstrong was missed by his brother Alexander, who with a number of other traders, met at Joseph Chambers, in Paxtang, and held a conference. They decided to go to Shamokin and place the matter before the "Delaware King," Sassounan, and Shikellamy, the Iroquois deputy. This was done and these chiefs ordered eight Indians to go with the traders on the hunt of the missing persons. Three of the Indians left them the first night. The other five went with them to the last "supposed sleeping place" of Armstrong and his servants. They went to "the Narrows of Juniata, where they Suspected the said Murther to be Comited, and where the Allegheny Road Crosses the Creek." A shoulder bone of Armstrong's was found and also the bodies of the two servants (Archives of Pa. 643-644). John Mussemeelin, a Delaware, and John Neshalleeny, another Delaware, were arrested for having committed this crime. The former confessed to having killed John Armstrong and Woodward Arnold, and the latter to having killed James Smith. These two Indians were sent "to the settlements" by Shikellamy's sons, after having been found guilty by the Council at Shamokin. When they reached James Ferry's, about 40 miles above Harrisburg, Shikellamy's sons fearing the resentment of Neshalleeny's friends, released him, and took Mussemeelin to Lancaster. There he gave an account of the killing of Armstrong and his two servants to Thomas Cookson, who sent a report to the Governor (Archives

I. 646). The Governor brought the matter before the Provincial Council, which ordered Mussemeelin taken to the jail in Philadelphia for trial. It was also decided to request the chiefs who should attend the Treaty at Lancaster, to appoin. deputies to be present at the trial (Col. Rec. IV. 675-676). The Governor later reported to the Assembly that he had removed Mussemeelin to the jail in Philadelphia, and at the same time he requested Conrad Weiser to go to Shamokin to make inquiry concerning the entire case (the same, 678-679). Weiser went to Shamokin, held a conference with Sassounan, in the presence of Shikellamy, and made a report. According to this report Mussemeelin had committed all of the murders himself. Armstrong had taken a horse and a rifle from Mussemeelin, for a debt which the latter owed him. Later Mussemeelin paid Armstrong about 20 shillings, and offered a neck-belt in pawn for the remaining part of his debt, and then asked for the return of his horse. This Armstrong refused to do, but made the debt larger than it had been previously. This was the provocation for the crime (the entire story is given in Weiser's report, Colonial Records, IV. 680-685). At the Council at Lancaster, June 1744, the Governor made a report to the Indians on the case (the same, 714). In his reply Canassatego said that he had reproved the Delawares for this crime and had charged them to make satisfaction for the goods stolen and for the men who were killed (724). Many messages passed between the Governor and the Delaware "King," Sassounan, at Shamokin, concerning this case (Colonial Records, IV. 742-745). Walton says that Mussemeelin was finally released, but he evidently confuses Mussemeelin with the two other Delawares who were charged with the crime (Walton, Conrad Weiser, 119; Col. Records, IV. 724). Conrad Weiser, in a letter to Richard Peters, in 1747, says, "John Armstrong, the poor man had warning Sufficient to persuad him to do the Indians Justice but Covetnous prevented him, at last he payed to dear for his faults; our people are apt to forget such Exemples" (Archives Pa., I. 758-759). Several places bear the name of Jack Armstrong in the region in which he met his death. Jack's Mountain is the name of the beautiful ridge at Jack's Narrows,

and is also the name of a Post Office in Adams County; Jack's Creek, which enters the Juniata below Lewiston, Mifflin County. The creek is noted on Scull's maps of 1759 and 1770; Jack's Narrows on the map of 1759, and Jack's Mountain on the map of 1770. These are also noted on Howell's map, 1792. None of these natural features were named in honor of the mythical character "Captain Jack, the Wild Hunter of the Juniata," as some writers have stated.

JACOB'S CREEK, JACOB'S CABINS. The headwaters of the creek are in Westmoreland County. It enters the Youghiogheny River at Jacob's Creek. Jacob's Cabins is mentioned by Christopher Gist, in the Journal of his expedition to the French forts with Washington, in 1753. He says, "Set out (from his house at the present Mount Braddock), cross Big Youghiogany (at the present Connellsville), to Jacob's cabins, about twenty miles" (Darlington's Gist, 80). In Orme's Journal, of Braddock's expedition of 1755, he says, "We marched to Jacob's cabin. about 6 miles from the camp." With the march of 5 miles the day before, from the camp 2 miles from "Stewart's Crossing (Connellsville), this would make the distance from Gist's Plantation (at Mount Braddock) about 20 miles, which is the distance given by Gist. (Consult. Orme's Journal, in the History of Braddock's Expedition, 346, 1855.) Jacob's Cabin was possibly situated on "the Great Swamp," which extended from below the present Scottdale to Bridgeport, in the neighborhood of Iron Bridge.

"Captain Jacobs" was a famous Delaware chief, whose home was at Kittanning during the early years of Indian raids into the frontier settlements. He and Shingas, who also made the same Indian village his headquarters at this time, were the leading chiefs of the various bands of Indians which devastated the frontiers. (See *Shingas.*) It may be possible that the account given by Egle (History of Pa.. 940) has reference to this chief. He says that when Arthur Buchanan and his two sons encamped on the site of the old Indian town of Kishacoquillas, at the mouth of the creek of the same name, in Mifflin County, that the Indians were at first unwilling to sell the land. But the chief, whom he christened Jacobs, because of his resemblance to a "burly Dutchman," whom he had known in Cumberland County, finally made the sale. The chief and his followers, becoming dissatisfied because of the incoming of the settlers, destroyed their own village and left. The settlers soon after built a fort for their protection (See also Frontier Forts, I, 608). However true this story of Jacobs' relation to the early history of Lewistown may be, it is certain that "Captain Jacobs" was the destroyer of Fort Granville, at that place, in 1756. Edward Shippen, in a letter to Governor Morris, in April, 1756, says, in speaking of the men who had gone in pursuit of the Indians who had destroyed Fort McCord, west of Chambersburg, that they had killed fifteen of the Enemy, among whom they were confident Captain Jacobs was one" (Col. Records, VII. 77; Archives of Pa., 642). This evidently was not correct, as Col. Armstrong in his report of the capture of Kittanning, in Sept., 1756, says that Captain Jacobs was killed (Archives of Pa., II, 769). Col. Armstrong, in a letter to Gov. Denny, December, 1756. says, "A son of Captain Jacobs is killed, and a cousin of his, about seven feet high, called Young Jacob, at the Destroying of Kittanning" (Archives of Pa., III, 83). This is perhaps correct, as Captain Jacobs is mentioned in later documents. In the deposition of Peter Tittle, March, 1760, he said, in quoting Doctor John, an Indian, "they said they killed Captain Jacobs, but that he had another Captain Jacobs, a young, big man, bigger & stronger than him, that was killed" (Archives, III, 705). It is, of course, possible that the first Captain Jacobs was killed, and that the Captain Jacobs mentioned in Bouquet's documents was a son of the first. Captain Jacobs, who was the leader of the Indians at the capture of Fort Granville. 1756, said, "that he could take any Fort that would Catch Fire, and would make Peace with the English when they learned him to make Gunpowder" (Colonial Rec., VII, 232). See, also, Colonial Records, VI, 781; VII, 230. At the Indian Council at Fort Pitt, Sept. 17, 1764, Col. Bouquet delivered a speech to "Captain Jacobs and the Delaware chiefs with him" (Colonial Rec.. IX, 208). In October, 1764, a message was sent from Captain Jacobs. Captain Killbuck, Sunfish, and others, to Colonel Bouquet, at his camp on the Tuscarawas (IX, 212).

At the great Council of Indians, held at Fort Pitt, in April, 1768, at which 1103 Indians, besides women and children, were present. Captain Jacobs was among the Delaware chiefs present (Colonial Rec., IX, 515). Captain Jacobs is not mentioned in the later Archives of Pennsylvania.

JENUCHSHADEGA. A former Seneca village on the Allegheny River, at the site of the present Cornplanter Reservation, opposite Gawango, Warren County. This was one of the villages of Gaiantwaka (Cornplanter, or The Planter, as the name signifies), the famous Seneca chief. The name has various forms which bear little resemblance to each other. Some of them seem to be compounded of the names of Cornplanters' two villages. The correct form is Dionosadage, meaning "Burnt house," or "the place of the burnt houses." The name was probably given to the place after the burning of the Indian village at this site by Gen. Brodhead in 1779. It in all probability was the site of the village which Brodhead calls Yoghroonwago. or Yahrunwago, in his letters to General Washington and General Sullivan in 1779 (Archives of Pa., XII, 156, 165). The trail over which Brodhead's army passed crossed the Conewango and struck directly to this region. Cornplanter had another village on the Conewango just above the 195th mile post on the State Boundary survey, which was known as Cayontona (also Cayentona, or Obeals, as it is on Howell's map), near Fentonville, N. Y. This name is a corruption of one of the names of Cornplanter, which was written Cayentokee (See *Cornplanter*). Proctor gives the form Cayantha (Arch. Pa., Sec. Ser.. IV, 575). The village at the mouth of Cold Spring Creek, New York, was also one of Cornplanter's villages. It is noted Teushanushsonggoghta (Adlum map), Tushanushagota (Ellicott), Che-ua-shung-gau-tau (Narrative of Mary Jemison, 79), Tu-shanush-a-a-go-ta (B e a u c h a m p, Place Names in New York, 33), Tiozinossungachta (Zeisberger MS., 1767). The lower village of Dionosadega, or Dionesadage, was evidently the one which Proctor mentions in his Journal (1791) by the name of 'Tenachshegonchtongee. or the burnt house town" (Archives Pa., Sec. Ser., IV, 567, 1876). He also calls it "O'Beel's town." When he visited the place it contained 28 houses on the north side of the river. He was evidently at the lower Cornplanter town, as he later discovered that his Indian guide and canoeist had taken him up the river to this lower town, instead of taking him on up the river to the upper town, at the mouth of Cold Spring Creek. The name which he records is, however, that of the upper town. Zeisberger in his Journal of 1767 (MS) mentions the first town (going up the Allegheny) as Tiozinossungachta, and the second as Tiohuneaquaronta. These names probably were earlier names of these places, given before the destruction of the village in Pennsylvania by Brodhead in 1779. On Howells' map of 1792. Inshaunshágota is noted as the name of Cold Spring Creek, New York. In King's History of Ceres, page 13, mention is made of the missionaries sent by the Society of Friends to "Jennessie-Guhta," and on page 26, the name is given as "Genesinguhta." The Society of Friends sent missionaries to the Indian villages in this region as early as 1798. The missionaries were Joel Swayne, Halliday Jackson and Henry Simmons. Francis King, who was the first prominent settler in the upper Allegheny region, crossed the "divide" from the West Branch, over the portage to the present Port Allegany, in the spring of 1797. He settled at the present Ceres, on the Oswayo. He belonged to the Society of Friends, and was much interested in the mission among the Indians on the Allegheny. The reservation was about sixty miles from his home, which was six miles up the Oswayo (Consult: King. History of Ceres, 1896). The Society of Friends is still engaged in missionary work among the Seneca Indians in this region. The Morris map of Pennsylvania (1848) notes the village at the mouth of Cold Spring Creek as "Indian Village," and the site of Dionesadega as "Cornplanters." In the "Code of Handsome Lake, The Seneca Prophet," by A. C. Parker. the upper village is called, besides the names given, Cold Spring village (page 46), and the lower village as Cornplanter's town (page 12). Consult: De Schweinitz, Life and Times of David Zeisberger, 325, 1870; Loskiel, History of Missions of the United Brethren, Part III, 20, 1794; Parker, Code of Handsome Lake, The Seneca Prophet. See *Cornplanter; Yahrunwago.*

JUNIATA. A corruption of Tyunayate, signifying "projecting rock," which is said to have reference to a projecting rock, to which the Indians paid reverence (Hewitt). Also the name of an unidentified tribe of Indians which once occupied the Juniata Valley. The name has been perpetuated in the names of a river, a township in Perry County and a Post Office in Blair County. The sources of the river are in Bedford and in Blair Counties. The former stream is called the Raystown Branch, and the latter, the Frankstown Branch. These unite below Huntingdon, to form the main stream, which enters the Susquehanna at Logania, Perry County, a short distance above Harrisburg. The standing stone, which gave the name to the tribe, and to the river, was situated just below the mouth of Standing Stone Creek, on the Juniata River, at the site of the present Huntingdon, which was formerly called "Standing Stone" (See *Standing Stone*). This point was at the intersection of the Indian trails leading to the Bald Eagle Valley; to Frankstown; to Shamokin, and was on the "Warriors Path," which led from the Iroquois country to the Carolinas. Various attempts have been made to identify the tribe which once occupied the valley. Some writers have identified it with the "Black Mingoes. or Minquaas," mentioned by early writers. The author is inclined to believe that the people who once occupied the region of the "standing stone" was a branch of the Seneca. There are various reasons for this "opinion." The name Seneca is a Dutch corruption of the Iroquois name Oneniute, which in the Mohegan was A'sinne-ika," place of the stone." The Delaware name of the Senecas, according to Heckewelder, was Maechachtinni (Mechachtinni), which he translates "Mountaineers,' means "great mountains." This was a translation of the Iroquois Djiionondowanen-aka. "People of the Great Mountain." This was corrupted to Tsanondoaroons, or Tsandowanes, and the place which they occupied Tsanandowa (Wyoming). The "Great Mountain." according to all of 'the statements of the Iroquois and Delaware, at the various Councils in Pennsylvania, was the range now known as the Kittatinny, which is the Delaware for "great mountain." This range is cut by the Juniata River at the beautiful gap through which it enters the Susquehanna River. It is the longest and highest mountain ridge in the whole Susquehanna region. The great number of "projecting rocks" at the entrance to the Susquehanna. at the mouth of the Juniata, would strike any one, even now. The "Great Mountain People" would be a natural designation of the inhabitants living back of the great, blue ridge, through whose wonderful doorway of rock the Juniata enters the Susquehanna. The great gorge cut by the Juniata from Huntingdon (Standing Stone) to the mouth, through Jack's Narrows and Lewistown Narrows, is one of the most striking and beautiful natural features of the State (See *Standing Stone, Seneca, Kittatinny, Wyoming*). Within historic times there were but two Indian villages on the Juniata River. These are mentioned, in 1731, as Ohesson, which contained 20 families, with 60 men, chiefly Shawnee, of whom Miskakoquillas was chief—it was situated at the site of the present Lewistown (See *Kishacoquillas*). The other village was called Assunepachla, which contained 12 families, and 36 men, chiefly Delaware—it was situated at the site of the present Frankstown (See *Frankstown*). These villages were mentioned by Jonah Davenport and James LeTort, two Indian traders, in an examination before Governor Gordon, in October, 1731 (Archives of Penna., I, 299, 302, 1852). The trail which these traders followed to the Ohio was evidently up the Juniata River, through Huntingdon and Frankstown, from which they crossed to the Conemaugh, near Johnstown, and then on to Kittanning. The name Juniata is recorded in many forms. In 1748 Conrad Weiser mentioned the town of the Nanticokes at the mouth of the Juniata (Colonial Rec., V, 222). This town had been settled by the Nanticokes (or Conoy) soon after they left their villages on the lower Susquehanna, in 1743 (See *Conoy*). At the Council in Philadelphia, August, 1749, Canassatego, the Iroquois chief, complained because of the settlers invading the hunting grounds of 'our Cousins the Nanticokes" and other Indians living on the Juniata, where the former had been placed by order of the Iroquois (Colonial Records, V, 400-402). These "white squatters" on the Juniata had caused the Provincial authorities much trouble from 1721, in which year the Governor had ordered the removal of all of them. After the

purchase of all of the Indian lands south of the Kittatinny, or Blue, Mountains, in 1736, the white settlers had commenced to pour into this region along the Juniata in great numbers. About 1740, Frederick Starr and several German families had settled about 25 miles from the mouth of the Juniata. This was reported to the Iroquois Council, which demanded that these settlers be "thrown over the Big Mountain." This removal was made by order of Governor Thomas in 1743. In 1748, when Weiser went on his mission to the Ohio Indians, he had been ordered to order all of these squatters to leave. In writing from the "Tuscarora Path," in August, 1748, he said that he had read the Governor's Proclamation to the people, and that they had promised to remove the next spring. At the Council at Philadelphia, in the summer of 1749, Governor Hamilton was asked by the Iroquois chiefs, by what right the settlers were building cabins on the Juniata. The Governor said that these squatters had no right to invade these lands, and promised to see that they were removed. A Proclamation was issued ordering all of the white settlers to remove from the Juniata, and the region west of the mountains by the first of November, 1749. At a Council of a larger delegation of Indians, held a few months later, Canassatego offered to sell a strip of land east of the mountains, for these settlers to occupy. (Consult: Colonial Records, V, 399 et seq.). In the spring of 1750 a still larger number of settlers were on the Juniata. Governor Hamilton acted at once. Conrad Weiser and Richard Peters were commissioned to remove all of these settlers and burn their cabins. These Commissioners, with the Cumberland County Magistrates, reached the Juniata on May 22nd, west of the present Thompsontown, Juniata County. Four cabins were found at this place; those of William White, George Cohoon, George and William Galloway, and Andrew Lycon. The goods were removed from all of these cabins, which were then set on fire. Among those evicted from the Little Juniata (Sherman's Creek), was Simon Girty, who later became the relentless foe of the English (Consult; Colonial Records, V. 443). But, the settlers still kept pouring into the Juniata valley. Governor Hamilton could do nothing to keep them out. They laughed at every effort which the authorities put forth, and at every threat of the Indians, who were becoming hostile to the English. In 1753, when the French were commencing to win away the Indians on the Ohio, the Juniata was filled with white settlers. The Province could not remove these squatters, so it was decided that the only thing to do was to purchase the land from the Indians. This was done at the Treaty at Albany in 1754, and this last "land deal" robbed the Delaware of practically all of their lands west of the mountains. and south of the Ohio River. The Delaware and Shawnee then went over bodily to the French. Braddock's defeat followed in 1755, and then the whole frontier was drenched in the blood of the white settlers. The Juniata valley paid dearly for this last Indian purchase (Consult; Colonial Records, VI. 119, et seq.; Frontier Forts, I. 559-618, 1896). See *Burnt Cabins, Aughwick, Nanticoke, Ohesson, Kishakoquillas.*

The name Juniata is recorded under many forms, due chiefly to the attempts of various traders to write the name, as it sounded to their ears. Among these are the following; the maps of Lewis Evans (1749 and 1755), and Scull's map (1770), Howell's (1792), together with all later State maps give the form Juniata ;

Choniata.—Davenport (1731), Archives, I, 302, 1852. **Chiniotta.**—McKee (1742), Colonial Records, IV., 633, 1851. **Chiniotte.**—Weiser (1742), Colonial Records, IV., 640. **Johndachquanah.**—Minute Book K (1737), Archives, Third Ser., I., 87, 1894. **Joniady.**—Weiser (1749), Archives, II., 24, 1852. **Scokooniady.**—Weiser (1743), Colonial Records, IV. 648.

Beauchamps, says, "Tschochniade was the Iroquois name for Juniata River in 1752" (Aboriginal Place Names in New York, 262, 1907) but gives no authority.

KAKANKEN, KAKARIKONK, CARKOEN etc. See *Carkoen's Creek.*

KEEWAUDIN. The name of a station in Clearfield, and also in Sullivan Counties, *Keewahdin,* is the form given of the name on the state map (1911) for the former. The Post Office in Clearfield is given in Smull's Handbook (1912), as *Keewaydin.* The origin of the name is not known. It may be a corruption of the Canadian Keewatin.

KICKENAPAULING. A former Shawnee village, near the mouth of the Loyalhanna Creek, on the Kiskiminetia River, in Westmoreland County. Several writers have placed this village at the site of the present Johnstown, Cambria County (Egle, History of Pa., 470). This is an error. The site of the Indian village in that place was Conemaugh. The error is due to the misplacing of Kickenapauling's Cabin, which was on the Quemahoning, ten miles from "Edmund's Swamp" and was about eighteen miles from Ligonier. near the present Jennertown, Somerset County. This was, without doubt, the situation of the Cabin, mentioned by Gist, as well as the "Kekinny Paulins," mentioned by William West; the "Kackanapaulins," mentioned by Patten; the "Kickeny Paulin's House," mentioned by John Harris, and noted by other writers (Consult; Darlington's Gist, 33; Colonial Records, V. 761; V. 750; Archives, II. 135). The village on the Kiskiminetas is mentioned by Post, in his Journal of his second trip to the Ohio in 1758. He left the army of General Forbes at Ligonier and on the 11th. of November he reached this village. He says, "We started early, and came to the old Shawanese town called Keckkeknepolin, grown up thick with weeds, briars, and bushes, that we scarcely could get through" (Early Western Travels, Thwaites ed., 245).

Kickenapaulin, after whom this village and the cabin was named, was a Delaware, although Post speaks of the village as belonging to the Shawnee. It was possibly made up of both tribes, and was one of the villages which was settled soon after the migration of the Shawnee and Delaware from the Susquehanna, in about 1727. These came over the trail leading through Bedford and Shawnee Cabins. The village had evidently been deserted by 1748, as Weiser makes no mention of it when he crossed the river near that point in that year. The chief, after whom it was named, was one of the party which captured Mary Le Roy and Barbara Leininger, in 1755. The name given by these young women is "Kechkinnyperlin" (Archives, III. 633). In Croghan's Journal of 1758 (which is wrongly attributed to Post in the Archives), he is mentioned as "Kekkchnapalin" (Archives III. 565). He was present at the councils which

Post had with the western Indians, in 1758, when he is noted as, "Keykeynapalin" (537), and Kehkeknopatin" (Archives, III. 538). See *Black Leg's Village, Kiskiminetas, Quemahoning.* Consult; Hanna, Wilderness Trail, I. 267-269, 1911; Egle. History of Pennsylvania, 470, 1883.

KILLBUCK, KILL BUCK. The English nickname of *Gelelemend,* a famous Delaware chief. An island in the Allegheny River, directly opposite the site of Fort Pitt (which has since been removed), was called "Killbuck's, or Smoky Island." The name of the sub-station in the Pittsburgh Post Office is named Kilbuck. Gelelemend, or Killbuck, was a grandson of Netawatwes and was Chief Counsellor of the Turkey tribe, and after the death of White Eyes, he was the leading chief. He was born in about 1737 in the region of the Lehigh Water Gap, and died in 1811, in his 80th year. Shingas and Beaver were the leading chiefs of the Turkey tribe, Custaloga and Captain Pipe of the Wolf tribe and Netawatwes and Gelelemend of the Turtle tribe of the Delaware nation during the period of frontier wars, and during the wars with the Indians of Ohio. Gelelemend was a friend of the English during the former war and a friend of the Americans during the latter. It is said that when he escaped from his island near Fort Pitt, in 1872 during the raid made by Williamson's renegades, he lost the documents which belonged to the tribe, and that among these were the parchments given to the Delawares by William Penn, whose first treaties were with the Turtle clan of the Delawares. His friendship for the English and then the Americans made him the Tammany of the Ohio region. Netawatwes, Gelelemend (Killbuck), Welapachtschiechen (Captain Johnny), Machingwi Puschis (Big Cat), and Koquethagachton (White Eyes) were ardent advocates for peace among the Delawares during the period of the Revolution. When the British officers at Detroit were doing everything in their power, with the help of Simon Girty, Captain Pipe and the various Shawnee chiefs, to get the Delawares to "take up the hatchet" against the Americans, these chiefs did everything in their power to keep the great Delaware tribe at peace. The efforts of Netawatwes and White Eyes were particularly influential with the warriors of the tribe. During the ill-advised expedition of Lord Dunmore (called Dunmore's War), White Eyes was particularly influential in holding the Delawares back from an alliance with the Shawnee. The great majority of his own tribe looked at him as being false to his own people because of his attitude at this time. He was charged with trying to ingratiate himself with the Virginians, by whom this war was started. But, through it all he remained a faithful friend of the American cause, just before the outbreak which led to the Revolution. His most dramatic speech before the great Council at the Delaware capitol, Gekelemuckpecheunk, rivals that of Patrick Henry (Life and Times of David Zeisberger, 414 et seq. 1870). After Gelelemend became the leading chief of his tribe he adhered to this peaceful policy of the Delawares. None of these chiefs have been given the credit which they deserve. A war with the Delawares at this time would have been an evil, the result of which might have been the blotting out of every American settlement west of the mountains. Killbuck was present at many of the Indian Councils of the Province Colonial Records, VIII. 189, 308-383; IX. 212, 228, 280; X. 12, 62; Archives, III. 532; IV. 95, 498; V. 444; VI. 587, 601; VIII. 770; IX. 161; XII. 203). In 1778, owing to the hostility of his own tribe to him, on account of his friendship with the American cause, he removed to Fort Pitt, and was placed on the island which became known as "Killbuck's Island" —at the point, in the Allegheny River. He made an application for this island in a paper (Archives, XII. 305) which reads, "The Petition of Colo. Henry Killbuck, Late Chief, or King of the Delewer Tribes or Nation." In this he states the fact of his removal to the place of refuge at Fort Pitt, and asks the right to the island which he occupied, "in fee Simple as a Gratuity," or by "Right of Preemption at a Moderate Price." This application is recorded in 1806 (Archives, Third Ser. III, 472).

After the wanton destruction of the Moravian towns in Ohio and the vile murder of the Indians at Gnadenhuetten, in 1782, the gang of "Indian haters" made an attack upon these Indians on Smoky Island and killed two who had Captains' commissions in the American Army, besides several others. The balance of the Indians swam the river to Fort Pitt. Among these was Gelelemend. General Irvine, the Commandant of Fort Pitt, was away at the time of these crimes, which aroused the whole country. Upon his return from Carlisle, he wrote a letter to General Washington, stating the facts (Craig, History of Pittsburgh, 171, 1851). Gelelemend was baptized at the Moravian village of Salem in 1788, when he was given the name of William Henry, in honor of Judge William Henry, of Lancaster. He died at Goshen in 1811. DeSchweinitz says of him, "He was one of the last converts of distinction that had come down from the heroic times of the Mission, and bore an irreproachable character. The vices of the generation, which he had lived to see, caused him deep sorrow, and he protested, even with his dying breath, against its degeneracy" (Life of Zeisberger, 694). Consult: Heckewelder, Narrative, 145, 216, 1820; Heckewelder, Indian Nations, 233-238, 1876; DeSchweinitz, Life and Times of David Zeisberger, 436, 470, 479, etc., 1870; Loskiel, History of Missions, III, 85, etc. 1794. See *Gnadenhuetten; Tuscarawas.* (Gelelemend's father was also called Killbuck. Sometimes authors have confused the elder Killbuck, who was a son of Netawatwes, with Gelelemend.)

KING BEAVER'S TOWN. The name of a former Indian village, at the mouth of the Beaver River, also called Shinga's Town; the name of a village at the junction of the Big Sandy with the Tuscarawas River, in Ohio—this village was also called Tuscarawas. Both of these villages were named in honor of "King Beaver" (Tamaque, or Amochk), the leading chief of the Delewares, who belonged to the Unalachtigo, or Turkey, tribe. He was a brother of the no less famous Shingas (See *Shingas' Town*), whom he succeeded as leading chief. He was himself succeeded by "Captain Johnny," who was succeeded by "White Eyes." The term "King," which is often prefixed to his name, is misleading. It is doubtful whether the Delawares would look at the leading chief of the Turkey tribe as being "King." If any such an honor would be given to any chief, it would rather be given to Netawatwes, who was the leading chief of the Turtle tribe, which held the first rank. Killbuck (see article), who succeeded Netawatwes as leading chief of the Delawares, called

himself "King of the Deleware Nation." He was more apt to be so considered than any of the chiefs of the Turkey tribe. Tamaque, or The Beaver, was a relentless foe of the English settlers, as were nearly all of the leading chiefs of his tribe, or, rather, clan. The Turtle tribe, on the contrary, was almost without exception friendly to the English and also to the Americans. This may have been due to the first treaties of the Penns having been made with this tribe, which occupied the Delaware River region, between the Munsee, or Wolf tribe, and the Unalachtigo, or Turkey tribe. According to Deleware traditions, the Turtle tribe held the hereditary chieftanship. The chief place of residence of Tamaque was at Shingas Town, or Beaver Town, as it was later called. He also lived at Kuskuski and Kittanning. Until the time ·of Braddock's defeat, 1755, he was friendly towards the English. After that time he and his brother Shingas became the leaders of many of the expeditions against the white settlements. He was present at the Council with C. F. Post at Kuskuski in 1758, just previous to the advance of the army of General Forbes against Fort Duquesne. He was the chief speaker at all of the conferences which were held (Archives, III, 520; Thwaites, Early West. Travels, I, 267, 1904). He was present at many of the Councils which were held with the English. After the capture of Fort Duquesne he removed to the village on the Tuscarawas, which then became known as "King Beaver's Town." This town was on the trail which ran directly westward from the Beaver River to the Tuscarawas and Muskingum. During the Indian uprising of "Pontiac's Conspiracy," as it is called—tho' why "conspiracy" any more than the American Revolution was a "conspiracy," it is difficult to discover—he was a leader of the Indian raids into the frontiers of Penna. After Bouquet's expedition into the Tuscarawas region in 1764, he entered into peace with the English, through necessity. Shortly before his death, in 1770, he became a convert to Christianity at one of the Moravian Missions. He died, urging his people to become Christians. See *Shingas Town, Sawcunk, Tuscarawas.* Consult Colonial Records, V. 536; VI. 155, 781; VII. 381; VIII. 189, 305, 312, 382 etc.; IX. 215, 221, 226; Archives, III. 523, 573, 711 etc.

KINGSESSING. The name of a tract of land between Cobbs Creek and the Schuylkill River, mentioned in the records of the Dutch and Swedish settlements on the Delaware. It was evidently not a village, but rather a tract of land to which the name was first given by the Indians. In the report of Andreas Hudde, concerning the Swedish occupation of this region, he says, "At a little distance from this fort (the one at the mouth of the Schuylkill) was a creek to the fartherest distant wood, which place is named Kinsessing by the savages, which was before a certain and invariable resort for trade with the Minquas, but which is now opposed by the Swedes having there built a strong house. About half a mile further in the woods. Governor Printz constructed a mill on a kill which runs in the sea not far to the south of Matinnekenk, and on this kill a strong building just by the path which leads to the Minquas; and this place is called Kakarikonk. So that no access to the Minquas is left open" (Report of Hudde, 1745, Archives of Pa., Second Ser. V. III). This mill was erected by Governor Printz in 1643, and was the first water-mill ever erected in the entire region. It stood near the famous "Blue Bell Tavern," on the site which has recently been purchased for the Cobbs Creek Park and Parkway (1913). Evidently the name Kingsessing was applied to the region beyond this mill. Kakarikonk was the name of "Carkoens" Creek, or Amesland Creek, or Cobbs Creek. Governor John Printz, in his report of 1647, says, "Again a quarter of a mile higher up, by the said Minquas' Road, I have built another strong house, five freemen settling there. This place I have called Mondal, building there a water-mill, working it the whole year along" (Swedish MSS Archives, from note in the Records of Upland Court, 88, 1860). The "Minquas Road," noted by both Hudde and Printz, was the trail which ran from the Susquehanna River, by way of Conestoga Creek and Cobbs Creek, to the Swedish settlements at the mouth of the Schuylkill River. Hudde says, concerning this trade with the Susquehanna (Andastes, Conestoga), "and as these trading as before had been driven from Kingsessing, and we cannot otherwise approach the large woods to trade with the Minquas, by which consequently this trade being lost to us, the possession of this river, as I well observed before, would deserve very little consideration" (Archives, Sec. Ser., V. 120). Mattehoorn, one of the chiefs who sold the lands on the west side of the Delaware to Peter Stuyvesant, Director of New Netherlands, said, "that neither the Swedes nor any other nation had bought lands of them as right owners except the patch on which Fort Christina stood and that all the other houses of the Swedes, built at Tinneconhg, Hingessingh (Kingsessing) in the Schuylkill, and other places were set up there against the will and consent of the Indians" (same ref. 264). Alexander Boyer, Deputy-Commissary wrote to Director Stuyvesant. during the absence of Hudde, in Sept. 1648. "The Swede has at present few goods, so that were cargoes here now, we should, doubtless. have a good trade with the Minquas" (Archives, Sec. Ser., VII. 466). The trade with the Minquas, or Susquehanna, Indians was the chief cause of the rivalry between the Dutch and the Swedes on the Delaware. In June 1657 permission was given the Swedes to form villages at Upland, Passayonck, Finland, Kingsessing, on the 'Verdrietige hoeck,' or at such places as by them may be considered suitable" (same ref. 511). In the list of "responsible housekeepers and their families," living at the various Swedish settlements, Jonas Neilson, Peter Andrews, Barth. Sneeer, Elizabeth Dalbo, - - - Cock, - - - Otto, - - - Bone, are given as living at "Kincesse" (the same, 807). In the Records of Upland Court for June 8, 1680, the minute reads, "The Court therefore for ye most Ease of ye People haue thought fitt for ye future to sitt & meet att ye Towne of Kingsesse in ye Schuylkills" (171, 1860). Consequently the next court met, att Kingsesse for Upland County in Delowar River By his Mayties, authority october ye 13th, 1680 (the same ref. 175), The Court for the Swedish County of Upland was held at Kingsessing until the establishment of the English Colony of William Penn. This Swedish town of Kingsessing became an English Township before 1684. It is noted on Scull's map as Kinsess (1770), and on Howell's map, as Kingsess (1792). Owing to the many forms of the name, it is difficult to tell what the original form was. Hudde (see before) says that the place "is named Kinsessing by the savages." Some of the forms recorded are;

Kingsessingh.—VanRuyven (1656), Archives, Second Ser., V., 264, 1890. **Kincess.**—Upland Court (1680), Archives, Second Ser., VII., 807, 1878. **Kincesse.**—Upland Court (1680), Archives, Second Ser., VII., 805, 1878. **Kincessing.**—Hudde (1645), Archives, Second Ser., V., 111, 1890. **Kingcess.**—Board of Prop. (1736), Archives, Third Ser., VIII., 87, 1894. **Kingcessing.**—Minute Book (1722), Archives, Second Ser., XIX, 714, 1890. **Kinghsessing.**—Court of New Netherland (1657), Archives, Second Ser., VII., 511. **Kingsess.**—Minute Book K (1738), Archives, Third Ser., I, 100. (Also Scull map, 1759.). **Kingsessing.**—Minute Book G (Patent of 1670), Archives, Third Ser., XIX, 298. **Kingsesson Creek.**—Minute Book G (Patent of 1687), Archives, Third Ser., XIX, 298. **Kinses.**—Beekman (1660), Archives, Second Ser., VII., 628. **Kinsses.**—Beekman (1660), Archives, Second Ser., VII., 628. **Kingsessinge.**—Record of 1648, Archives, Third Ser., XVI., 237, 1890 (see p. 716). **Quinsessingh.**—Alricks (1658), Archives, Second Ser., V, 320.

The name has been perpetuated in the name of a sub-station of the Philadelphia Post Office, having the form Kingsessing.

KINZUA. The name of a creek and a village in Warren County. The creek has its source in McKean County, and enters the Allegheny River from the east in Warren County. According to Heckewelder the name is a corruption of Kentschuak, meaning "they gobble," having reference to the sound made by the wild-turkey. The creek may have been the resort of wild turkey's.

Kenjua.—Howell's map, 1792, also Morris' State map, 1848. **Kenzuaw.**—Adlum, map, 1790. **Kinzua.**—Maps after 1860.

KISHACOQUILLAS. The name of a creek which enters the Juniata River at Lewistown, Mifflin County; also the name of a valley in the same county; now the name of a Post Office, in the same county. Kishacoquilla was the name of a Shawnee chief, who lived at the village of Ohesson, which was situated at the mouth of the present Kishacoquillas Creek, before 1731. Heckewelder says that the name is a corruption of Gisch-achgook-walleu, Gischichgakwalis, which signifies, "the snakes are already in their dens." The village of "Ohesson upon Choniata" (Juniata) is mentioned in the examination of Jonah Davenport and James LeTort, before Governor Gordon, in October 1731. The village consisted of 20 families and 60 men of the Shawnee. "Kissikahquelas" was the chief of the village (Archives, I. 302, 1852). The

Shawnee at this time were leaving the Susquehanna region and were going westward to the Ohio, where they came under the French influence. Peter Chartiers had made a settlement on the Allegheny, to which many of the Shawnee from the lower Susquehanna had gone. The provincial authorities were anxious for these Shawnee to return to their villages on the Susquehanna. Kishacoquilla was friendly to the English, and remained so until his death. He was present at the Treaty at Philadelphia in 1739, when he signed the treaty of friendship (Colonial Records, IV. 347). At the treaty at Aughwick (Shirleysburg) in August, 1754 Conrad Weiser condoled with the Shawnee for the death of Kishacoquillas, who had died at Captain McKee's "last month" (August, 1754). In 1756 the sons of this chief notified the Governor of the death of their father, who before his death had sent a letter to Governor Hamilton "assuring him of his Love to this Province" (Colonial Records, VI. 421-422). Governor Morris, who had succeeded Governor Hamilton, sent a present to the sons of this faithful chief. His name occurs in the following forms;

Kaashawaghquillas.—L a w r i e (1739), Colonial Records, IV. 347. **Kishycoquillas.**—Morris (1756), Colonial Records, VI. 422. **Kissakochquilla.**—W e i s e r (1754), Colonial Records, VI. 154. **Kissikahquelas.**—LeTort (1731), Archives, I. 302.

The name of the creek and the valley has been recorded as follows;

Kishacoquilis.—A d l u m, map, 1790. **Kishequochkles.**—E v a n s, map, 1749. **Kishiquoquillis.**—Board of Prop. (1770), Archives, Third Ser., I. 313. Scull, 1770. Also Scull map, 1759, Kishicoquillis.

In 1755 George Croghan was ordered to erect three stockade forts, one of which was to be upon "Kishecoquillas" (Archives, II. 536). Governor Morris, in a letter to Governor Sharpe, January 29, 1756, says that he has erected another fort "near Juniata, where Kiskiquokilis falls into it" (same ref. 556), which he called Fort Granville. This fort was on the north bank of the Juniata, about one mile north of Lewistown. It was destroyed by the Indians, led by Captain Jacobs, in harvest time, July 30, 1756. The fort was burned by order of the French officer in command, and the prisoners, 22 men, 3 women and a number of children, were taken to

Kittanning. The destruction of Fort Granville, and the capture of these people, filled the entire frontiers with fear. Consult; Frontier Forts of Penna., I. 605-611; also Parkman's Conspiracy of Pontiac, under title Fort Granville.

KISKIMINETAS. The name of a river, formed by the union of the Conemaugh and Loyalhanna, which enters the Allegheny River opposite Freeport, Armstrong County. The Kiskiminetas and the Conemaugh Rivers mark the boundary line between Armstrong and Indiana Counties, on the north, and Westmoreland County, on the south side of the rivers. Various meanings have been given to the Indian name, of which the present name is a corruption. Heckewelder gives the form Gieschgumanito, signifying "make daylight" — from Gisch-gu, "day," and Ma-ni-toon, "to make." McCullough, all of whose other Indian names have a correct meaning given to them, gives the form Kee-ak-kshee-man-nit-toos, and the meaning, "Cut Spirit.' The Delaware for cut, with a knife, is Gischkschummen, and spirit, Manitto. Hewitt gives the meaning of "plenty of walnuts." Kiskiminetas was the name of a former Delaware village on the south side of the river, about seven miles from its junction with the Allegheny. It probably was situated near Deronda, Westmoreland County. The Indian trail crossed the river not far from the mouth of Carnahan's Run. Another trail crossed at the present Apollo (formerly Warren). It is possible that one of the Shawnee villages mentioned by Davenport and LeTort, as being on the Conemaugh River, was at the site of the later Delaware village (Archives I. 302). The Shawnee, however, soon moved to Chartier's Town, and then went on down the Ohio River. John Harris mentions the village in 1754, as Kiskemenette's Town," and gives the distance from the Allegheny River as six miles (Archives II. 136). Christopher Gist did not follow this trail down the valley from Loyalhanna (Ligonier), but crossed the present Westmoreland County by the direct trail to Shannopin's Town (Pittsburgh), when he went to the Ohio in 1750. Post mentions the place in his Journal of his second journey to Kuskuskl (New Castle) in 1758. He says, "At three o'clock we came to Kiskemeneco, an old Indian town, a rich bottom, well

timbered, good fine English grass, well watered, and lay waste since the war began" (Thwaites, Early Western Travels, I. 247). The Delawares probably left this village soon after Kittaninning became the central Delaware village for the Allegheny region, about 1755. (There was a village on the Ohio River, about eight miles above the mouth of the Kanawha River, having the name of "Kishkeminetas old Town" (Evans, map, 1755) also noted on LaTour's map).

The name of the village and the river in Pennsylvania has many forms, among which may be mentioned;

Gieschgumanito.—Heckewelder, in Transactions Amer. Philos. Sec., N. S. IV. 371, 1834. **Kee-ah-kshee-man-nit-toos.**—McCullough (1756), Border Life, 90, 1839. **Kiskemanetas.**—Pa. Council (1771), Colonial Records, IX, 1720. 1852. **Keskemenetas.**—Neville (1792), Archives, Second Ser., IV. 605, 1890. **Kiscominatis.**—Gist (1750), Darlington's Gist, 33, 1893. **Kiskamenitas.**—Board of Property (1770), Archives, Third Ser., I. 287, 1894. **Kishkemenetas Town.**—Scull, map, 1770. **Kishkemenetas (river).**—Scull, map, 1770. **Kishkeminetas.**—Evans, map, 1755. **Kishkimenetas.**—Pownall, map, 1776. **Kiskeminetoos.**—Weiser (1748), Thwaites, Early Western Travels, I. 23, 1904. **Kiskemontias.**—Denny (1758), Colonial Records, VIII. 238, 1852. **Kiskiminity.**—Findley (1791), Archives, Sec. Ser., IV. 1612. **Kiskomenetto.**—Ohio Co. Petition, Darlington's Gist, 230. **Kisscomenettes, old Town.**—Harris (1754), Archives, II. 135, 1852. **Kisskaminities.**—General Forbes (1758), Colonial Records, VIII. 234, 1852. **River d'Attique.**—Montcalm (1758), Archives, Sec. Ser., VI. 427. **R'Kikemenete.**—Pouchot, map, 1758. **Romanettoes.**—Ohio Co. Petition, Darlington's Gist, 230. **Tiscumenetis River.**—Campfield (1792), Archives, Sec. Ser., IV. 605.

KITTANNING. The name of the chief town of Armstrong County. The site of the important Indian village of the XVIII Century. According to Heckewelder the name is derived from Kit, "great." Hanne, "stream," with the locative ing, meaning "at the great stream." According to Brinton and Anthony, Kittan is the Delaware for "great river"—with the locative ing, would signify the same as the above. The Delaware name for the Ohio (which was the name for the Allegheny and the present Ohio) was, Kittan, or Kithanne, meaning "great river." The Indian village of Kittanning was the largest Indian settlement in Pennsylvania, west of Shamokin during the period from about 1730 until its destruction in 1756. The site was occupied by the

Delawares soon after they commenced their migration from the Susquehanna, in about 1723. From that time onward the Delaware and the Shawnee crossed the mountain ridges in increasing numbers, because of the land sales along the Susquehanna, and because of the debauchery of the rum traffic. In 1731 Davenport and Le-Tort two well known Indian traders, reported that there were at "Kythenning River" 50 families and 150 men, mostly Delawares (Archives, I. 301). The name Kittanning comprehended the Indian settlements on both sides of the Allegheny River. There were evidently several villages along the river front at this place, scattered along both sides the river. The term at "Allegheny on the Main Road," which is frequently used in the early records, no doubt had reference to this place, as well as others, on the "main road" of the Iroquois along the Allegheny River. This was the chief war path of the Iroquois to the Mississippi, and had been used by the Senecas in their war expeditions for many years before the coming of the Delaware and Shawnee to the region, within historic times. In the "Memoir" of 1718, it is stated, "The River Ohio (which was the name of the Allegheny and present Ohio), or the Beautiful River, is the route which the Iroquois take" (Archives, Sec. Ser., VI. 57, 1877). After 1731, when Kittanning was visited by LeTort, the villages must have been deserted for a time, as when Celoron passed in 1748, Father Bonnecamp says in his Journal, in speaking of Atique (the French name for Kittanning) "found no person here" (Jesuit Relation, Thwaites ed., LXIX. 170). At that time the Delawares had probably moved on down the river to Logstown and to the villages on the Beaver River. At the commencement of the war between France and Great Britian the villages of Kittanning, or "the Kittanning," as it was called, began to fill up with Delaware and Shawnee, who were hostile to the English. It was a strategic point, from which the settlements of the English could be reached over the "Kittanning Trail" and its various branches, and from which the other Indian villages on the Ohio, and its branches, could be easily reached by the river, as well as by the "Main Road," or great trail down the river, through Logstown, Sawcunk, Kuskuski and other prominent villages.

After Braddock's defeat, 1755, Kittanning became the chief rallying point for the Indian expeditions into the Cumberland Valley, the Juniata region, and to Virginia. A branch of the "Catawba Trail" ran directly southward across Westmoreland and Fayette Counties, to "Stewart's Crossings" (Connellsville), where Braddock crossed the Youghiogheny River, and then on southward into the Carolinas. The Braddock Road had opened the pathway to the Potomac, over which the raiding parties of French and Indians passed. At the Council at Carlisle, Jan. 1756, George Croghan reported that he had sent Delaware Jo, a friendly Indian, to "Kittannin, an Indian Delaware Town on the Ohio about forty Miles above Fort Duquesne, the Residence of Chingas (Shingas) and Captain Jacobs where he found one hundred and forty Men Chiefly Delawares and Shawonese, who had then with them above one hundred English Prisoners big and little taken from Virginia and Pennsylvania. That there the Beaver, Brother of Chingas, told him that the Governor of Fort Duquesne had often offered the French Hatchet to the Shawonese and Delawares, who had as often refused it." This offer had finally been accepted and the Delaware and the Shawnee had gone out against Virginia (Colonial Records, VI. 781, 1851). During 1756 many expeditions were sent out from this place to the various English settlements along the frontiers of Pennsylvania. The prisoners who were captured were taken to Kittanning, where they ran the gauntlet, were put to torture, or were adopted. Barbara Leininger and Marie LeRoy were taken to Kittanning, where they saw some of the cruel tortures which were inflicted upon the English prisoners after Col. Armstrong's expedition (Archives, Sec. Ser., VI. 403-412, 1878). The expedition of Col. Armstrong against Kittanning, for the purpose of destroying this starting point of Indian war parties, was undertaken in the summer of 1756. The force marched from Fort Shirley on August 30th, and reached Kittanning on the morning of September 8th, at which time he made the attack. The town was entirely destroyed and a number of prisoners were rescued (Consult; Colonial Records, VII. 257-263, 1851, which contains the account of the taking of Kittanning, by Armstrong).

Colonel James Smith, who was captured by the Indians in May 1755, was one of the first white prisoners to be taken to Kittanning (Border Life, 13-85, 1839). The destruction of Kittanning did not, as is sometimes stated, break up the gathering of Indians at this place. Although there were a few settlers in the southern part of Armstrong County after 1769, yet for many years after the white settlers began to take up land along the Forbes Road, Hannastown, a few miles north of the present Greensburg, Westmoreland County, marked the northern limit of the English settlements. Even as late as 1792 William Findley, in a letter to Secy. Dallas, said "Hannastown is now the frontier. You will perceive by the map that Westmoreland is now desolate to near the Center, and the rest of that is disturbed" (Archives, Sec. Ser., IV. 609). Owing to the trouble caused by the boundary dispute with Virginia, Arthur St. Clair, who was an adherent of the Penns, advised the building of a fort and town at Kittanning (Archives, IV. 545). Much correspondence passed between the various officers at Fort Pitt and General Washington during the Revolution, concerning the establishment of a fort at this point. Owing to the Indian hostility during 1778-79 Col. Brodhead erected a fort at Kittanning, for the security and protection of the frontiers of Westmoreland and Bedford Counties. This fort was called Fort Armstrong, in honor of General Armstrong, who had destroyed the Indian village in 1756. This fort was evacuated in November 1779, when the garrison was removed to Fort Pitt. This fort was never re-established, although there were various detachments sent to the place at a later time, as temporary guards for the frontiers (Consult; Frontier Forts, II. 449-485; Archives, III. 103, 116, 307; IV. 329, 431, 545, 557 etc.).

The famous "Kittanning Trail" crossed to Cherry Tree and then on to Kittanning Point (Horse-shoe curve) and then on down the Juniata to Frankstown, Standing Stone etc. (Consult; Archives, II. 133-34; Hanna, Wilderness Trail, I. 261 et seq.; Darlington's Gist, 139). The following are a few of the synonyms of Kittanning;

Adigia.—Guy Park. Conf. (1775), in N Y Col. Doc. Hist. 8, 557, 1857 Adigo.— Johnson Hall Conf. (1765), ibid VII 728, 1855. Atiga.—Bellin, map, 1744 Atique. —Bonnecamp (1794), Jesuit Relations,

Thwaites ed., LXIX, 170, 1904. Cantanyans.—Boudinot, Star of the West, 126, 1816 (the inhabitants) Cattanyan.— Smith (1799) in Drake, Trag. Wild, 263, 1841. Kattaning.—Harris, Tour, map, 1805. Killaning.—Pownall, map, 1776. Kitanning.—Pa. Gaz. (1756), quoted in Mass. Hist. Soc Coll 3rd. Ser. IV. 298, 1834. Kithannink.—Heckewelder, in Trans. Amer. Philos. Soc. N. S IV. 368, 1834. Kittanning.—Evans, map, 1755. Kittannin.—Croghan (1756), Colonial Records, Pa., VI. 781, 1851. Kittanny.— Leininger (1756), Archives, Pa., Sec. Ser., VII. 404. Kittany Town.—the same, 405. Kittanny Old Town.—Stewart (1791), Archives, Pa., Sec. Ser. IV. 556. Kittaones.—Lattre, map, 1784.

KITTATINNY. The name of the mountain range which crosses the State from the north-east to the south-west, and which forms the northern boundary of the Cumberland Valley; also called the North Mountain, Blue Ridge and other names in various localities. For many years after the settlements had been established along the seaboard, the region beyond this mountain range was an unknown wilderness, and for many years it marked the western and northern boundary of civilization in the State. It was not until after 1727 that the white settlers began to invade the Indian country beyond the Kittatinny mountains. The Susquehanna River cuts through this ridge in the beautiful gap just above Harrisburg, and from there southward it bounds the rich and fertile Cumberland Valley, which stretches on to the Potomac River. The various gaps in this ridge were the pathways of the Indians, and then of the traders and settlers. Going southward from the Susquehanna these gaps are, Croghans (Sterretts), Crains, Forty Shillings (or Long's), Hurley's (or Waggoner's), McClures, Doubling, Mac-Allister (or Roxbury), and Parnell's. The first of these, Croghans, and the last, Parnells, were perhaps the most important passes through the mountain, as the two most prominent trails to the Ohio entered the Tuscarora Valley through these. The word Kittanning is perhaps a corruption of the Delaware Kit, "great," and Atin, or Adin, "hill," or "mountain." As the name is nearly always mentioned by the Delawares as "Kittatinny Hills," it is possible that the name as first applied had reference to the "Kittuteney," "chief town," of the Delawares in the Minisinks. The signification would be "the chief town hills." However, the name is nearly always translated in the early deeds, as "Endless Mountains." According to the Deed of 1736 the ridge was "called in the language of the said Nations (the Iroquois) the Tyannutasacta, or endless hills, and by the Delaware Indians, the Kekkachtannin Hills" (Archives, I. 495, 498,). The form most frequently used by the early English writers was Kittochtinny Hills (same ref. 613). This mountain ridge was a prominent boundary line in all of the deeds of purchase from that of 1736 until the last one on the Susquehanna in 1754. In the release of the lands lying between the "mouth of the Sasquehanna and the Kekachtanium Hills" (1736), and the release of the lands on both sides of "the Sasquehannah as far South as this Province extends, and to the northward to those called the endless mountains or Kittochtenny Hills (1742), and in the purchase at Albany (1754), these mountains formed a prominent boundary line. This was the limit beyond which the Indians would not allow the white settlers to go until after the time of Braddock's expedition, when the land west of the mountain ridge was purchased from the Iroquois. Complaints had been made at nearly every Council with the Indians concerning the settlement of the region beyond the "Endless Mountains." This formed the boundary between the Indian country and the white settlements, according to the Indian's theory—just as afterwards the Ohio River was made the boundary line of the Indian country along its northern shore. But, by 1736 the white settlers had gone beyond this boundary, just as they later swept away the boundary of the Ohio. When the white settlers crossed the blue ridges of the Endless Mountains the Indian discovered that the term of his Deeds, "to the setting sun," meant, not to the top of the mountain ridge, below which the sun went down, but to the place where the sun went down over the waters of the Pacific. He sold his land to the "setting sun," as the white man understood the term, and not as he did. Consult; Colonial Records, IV. 88, 559; V. 152, 407, 567; VI. 118, 650, 651, 752; VII. 10; VIII. 211, 253, 653; IX. 554; Archives, I. 345, 495, 613, 629; II. 42, 43, 47, 452, 453, 545, 717; III. 707 etc. Some of the forms recorded are;

Katytena Hills.—Board of Prop. (1737), Archives, Third Ser. I. 87. **Keckach-**
tany Hills.—Deed of 1749, Archives, II. 34. **Keekachtanemin Hills.**—Deed of 1732, Archives I. 344. **Kekachtanium Hills.**—Colonial Records (1736), IV. 88. **Kekkachtannin Hills.**—Deed of 1736, Archives I. 495. **Killatining Mountains.**—Pownall, map, 1776. **Killatinny Mountains.**—Armstrong (1755), Archives, II. 452 **Kittatinney Hills.**—A r m s t r o n g (1756), Archives, II. 719. **Kittatinni Mountains.**—Instruc. to Evans (1750), Archives II. 47. **Kittatinny Hills.**—Morris (1756), Colonial Records, VII. 10. **Kittatinny Mts.**—Evans, map, 1749 (also Blue Mountains). **Kittatiny.**—W e s t (1760), Archives III. 707. **Kittektiny Hills.**—Orders to Reed (1756), Archives, II. 545. **Kittidany Hills.**—Weiser (1755), Archives, II. 453. **Kittochhinny.**—Pa. Council (1749), Colonial Records, V. 407. **Kittochtenny.**—Pa. Council (1742), Colonial Records IV. 559. **Kittochtinny Hills.**—Pa. Council (1742), Colonial Records, IV. 559. **Kitectiny Hills.**—Morris (1756), Archives, III. 557. **Kittochtisnny.**—Clarkson (1749), Archives, II. 43. **Tyannuntasacta, or Endless Hills.**—Deed of 1736, Archives, I. 495. **Tyoninhackta, or Endless Mountains.**—Deed of 1736 (release), Archives, I. 498.

There is a creek in Northampton County which has the name Kitatining.

KUSHEQUA. The name of a valley and Post Office in McKean County. Is probably the same as Kushaqua, in Franklin County New York. This is a corruption of Gaw-she-gweh, meaning "a spear."

KUSHUSDATENING. The name of a former Indian village, on the north side of the Allegheny River, a short distance below the present town of Irvineton, Warren County. The name may have been wrongly placed on Scull's map, for the village of Goshgoshunk, or Goschgosching—below the mouth of the Tionesta.

Kushusdatening—Scull, map, 1770. **Kuskusdutening.**—Pownall map, 1776.

KUSKUSKI. The name of a former Delaware village of much importance. There were Seneca villages having this name, the older one was situated at the junction of the Mahoning and Shenango Rivers, and the later one at the mouth of Neshannock Creek, on the Shenango, at the site of the present New Castle. Both Sherman Day and William Darlington wrongly fix the locality of these towns. According to Zeisberger's MS Journal these two villages had the situation as noted. The villages were evidently inhabited chiefly by Delawares of the Wolf and Turkey tribes, as nearly all of the chiefs mentioned in the various records as living there, belonged to these tribes, or clans. There were several Indian settlements in the region about the junction of the Mahoning and Shenango Rivers, to which the general name of "the Kuskuskies" applied, but the two historic villages had the sites noted previously. According to Heckeweder, the name is a corruption of Gosch-gosch, "a hog," with the locative ing, or unk, signifying "the place of hogs" (See *Goshgoshing*). On account of the situation of these villages on the trail to the Muskingum, to Venango, to Logstown and to the villages on the lower Ohio, the neighborhood became a center of trade among the Indians. The occupation of Fort Duquesne by the French, and later its occupation by the British, drove the Indians away from the upper Ohio to the Beaver and Muskingum Rivers, as well as down the Ohio. Sawcunk (Beaver) and Kuskuski became prominent villages during the period from 1755 until 1773. In the period just before the commencement of the French and Indian war it was the rival of Logstown (near Legionville). After the capture of Fort Duquesne by the British and until the final migration of the Indians from Pennsylvania, it was the most important Indian settlement in western Pa. At the time of Conrad Weiser's visit to Logstown, in 1748, the Indians at Kuskuski insisted upon the Council being held at their village. But George Croghan and Weiser both said that the Indians at Kuskuski had declined, the year previous, to hold the council in their village because of the scarcity of provisions, and so had made it necessary for the Council to meet at Logstown (Colonial Records, V. 349-350, 1851). In 1753 when Washington and Gist were on their way to the French forts, at Venango and Lé-Boeuf, they "encamped at the crossing of Beaver Creek, from the Kaskuskies to Venango about thirty miles" (Darlington's Gist, 81). The "Murthering town,' which is sometimes confused with Kuskuski, Washington and Gist encamped at the first night after they left Logstown. According to Gist's Journal, this town was about fifteen miles from Logstown, "on a branch of Great Beaver Creek." On their return journey this creek is mentioned as the "southeast fork of Beaver Creek"—evidently the Conoquenessing, which was about fifteen miles from Logstown (Consult; Washington's Journal, 1753, in Olden Time, I. 10). This was evidently the same town which Post mentions in his Journal of 1758, when he was on his way to Kuskuski—"We came to the river Conaquanosshan, where was an old Indian Town. We were then fifteen miles from Cushcushking (Archives, III. 523). According to Post, the village, or settlement, at this time consisted of four separate villages, the whole consisting of about 90 houses and 200 warriors. This mission of Frederick Post's was one of the most heroic enterprises of the entire period. The hostile Delaware and Shawnee in western Penna. had not been informed of the peace efforts of Tedyuskung. Post was sent in advance of the army of General Forbes, to urge these Indians to stay away from Fort Duquesne. He carried letters from Forbes to "Kings Beaver and Shingas." While holding this conference with the chiefs at Kuskuski, the French officers were doing everything in their power to gain the friendship of Beaver and Shingas. The Indian chiefs at first refused to pay any attention to the offers of peace, and said they had nothing to do with Tedyuskung. Post returned to Easton, and was immediately sent back to Kuskuski, passing the army of General Forbes at Ligonier. His mission was a success. The Indians stayed away from Fort Duquesne. The French, when they found that their Indian allies had deserted them, evacuated the fort, and the army of Forbes took possession. After the British occupation of the Ohio River, Colonel Hugh Mercer, the commandant at Fort Pitt, heard many reports concerning the gathering of Indians at Kuskuski, and of the attempt which was to be made by the French to retake the fort (Colonial Records, VII. 284, 292 etc.). Col. Mercer says in a letter, 1759, "The Delawares at the mouth of Beaver Creek intend to move to Kuskusky, they pretend at our request, but rather in my Opinion, tho' Diffidence of us, or to get out of the Way of Blows, if any are going, for depend upon it, they are desirous of fighting neither on the side of the English nor French, but would gladly see both dislodged from this Place" (Col. Rec. VIII. 305). Col. Mercer was correct in this opinion. The Indians at Kuskuski were given to understand that when General Forbes had taken Fort Duquesne, that the English would return east of the mountains. When this was not done they became suspicious. "The Beaver" at the Council at Fort Pitt with Col. Mercer, in 1759, said, "The Six Nations and you desired that I would sit down and smoak my Pipe at Kuskusky; what they desired me I intend to do, and shall move from Sacunk to Kuskusky." Col. Mercer said, "It is not the Desire of the English that you should move from Sacunk to Kuskusky. General Forbes in his letter, mentioned your sitting down and Smoaking your pipe at Kuskusky because he had heard of no other Great Delaware Town" (Col. Rec. VIII. 307-309). Col Mercer in a letter March 17, 1759, says, "the Beaver goes to the Forks of Siolas (Sciota) to Plant this Spring, and then return to Live at Kuskusky "(the same, 313). After this time "The Beaver" made his home at "Beaver Town" on the Tuscarawas, directly west from the mouth of the Beaver River, where his old town had been. (See *Beaver, Tuscarawas*). After the departure of Shingas and Beaver from Kuskuski, Packanke became the leading chief of the village, with Glikkikan as his war chief. These chiefs were instrumental in the removal of the Moravian Indians from the mouth of the Tionesta, to the village just below Kuskuski, which was called Languntouteneunk, or Friedensstadt, "City of Peace." Here these Christian Indians remained until the spring of 1773, when it was deserted for the Tuscarawas villages (See *Gnadehuetten, Languntouteneunk, Tuscarawas;* Consult, DeSchweinitz, Life and Times of David Zeisberger, 360 et seq.). Soon after the departure of the Moravian Indians and the commencement of the Revolution, the Indians from the Beaver River moved westward to the villages in Ohio. Gekelemukpechink, in Tuscarawas County, Ohio, became the capital of the Delaware tribes. The site of Kuskuski may have been occupied by wandering Delawares and Iroquois, but it was practically deserted after this westward migration of the Delawares. The forms of the name of the Indian settlement are many. A number of these follow;

Cachecacheki.—Vaudreuil (1759), in N. Y. Doc. Col. Hist., X. 949, 1858. **Cachekachheki.**—the same ref. **Cas-cagh-sagey.**—Clinton (1750), the same work, VI. 549, 1855. **Coscosky.**—Weiser (1748), Colonial Records, V. 349, 1851. **Cuschcushke.**—Heckewelder, in Trans. Amer. Phil. Soc., N. S. IV. 395, 1834. **Cuscuskie.**—Croghan (1750), in Rupp, West. Penna., Appx. 27, 1846. **Cuscuskey.**—

Bard (1756), Border Life, 117, 1839. **Cusausca Town.**—Map of 1753, in Darlington's Gist, 81. **Cuskcuskking.**—Post (1758), Archives, III 525, 1853. **Cuskuskus.**—Rupp, West. Penna., 138. **Kaschkaschking.**—Nar. Marie LeRoy (1756), Archives, Sec. Ser., VII. 406. **Kaskaskunk.**—Loskiel (1794), Mission of U. B., Part III. 55, 1794. **Kaskuskies.**—Gist (1753), in Dar. Gist, 81, 1893. **Kishkuske.**—Hutchins, map, 1764, in Smith's Boquet Exped., 1766. **Kshkushking.**—Post (1758), In Rupp, West. Penna., appx. 116, 1846. **Kushcushkec.**—Post (1758), in Drane, Book Inds., book, 5, 39, 1848. **Kushkushkee.**—Post (1758), in Rupp, West. Penna., appx. 80, 1846. **Kushkushkee Nations.**—Mercer (1759), Colonial Records, VIII. 393. **Kishkuskes.**—Lewis Evans, map, 1755. **Kushkuski.**—Pa. coun. (1759), Col. Rec. VIII. 265. **Kuskuskies.**—Lotter, map, 1770. **Kuskuskin.**—Alden (1834), in Mass. Hist. Soc. Coll., 3rd. Ser. VI. 144, 1837. **Kuskkusko Town.**—Washington (1753), in Rupp West Pa., appx., 1846 **Kuskusky.**—Peters (1760), in Mass. Hist. Coll., 4th. Ser. IX. 258, 1871. **Murdering Town.**—Washington (1753), in Rupp, West. Penna., appx. 48, 1846. **Murthering Town.**—Gist (1753), in Darlington, Gist, 81, 1893. These names are sometimes given in such a list. See the reference to this village under **Conoquenessing.**

LACOMICK CREEK. The former name of the present Sandy Creek, which enters the Allegheny from the west below Franklin, Venango County. A corruption of Lekauhannek, "sandy stream." Same as Lycoming (which see). Mentioned in Gist's Journal of 1753—"We set out from Venango (now Franklin) and travelled about five miles to Lacomick Creek" (Darlington, Gist, 84). The Indian trail crossed the river between this creek and French Creek, at a "Rift" noted on Evan's map of 1755.

Lacomic Creek.—Evans (1755), also Scull (1770). **Lacomick Creek.**—Gist (1753), Dar. Gist, 84. **Sandy Creek.**—Howell's, map, 1792.

LACKAWANNA. The name of a river which has its source in Susquehanna County, enters the Susquehanna River, above Pittston, Luzerne County. The name is a corruption of Lechau-hannek, "the forks of a stream." Zeisberger gives the form L'chau-hanne. The name is also applied to a mountain ridge and a valley in the same region. The Delawares must have occupied this "forks of the stream" from a very early time, as it was at the upper opening to the "great meadows" of Wyoming, and on the trail to the Minisinks, as well as on the trail to the Iroquois country in New York. There were two villages near the mouth of the stream within historic times (See *Adjouquay, Assarughney*). The attempt of the Connecticut settlers to take possession of this region was one of the chief causes of the trouble with the Indians, which finally resulted in the massacre of Wyoming (See *Wyoming*). The entire volume of the Archives, Second Series, XVIII, is taken up with this "Connecticut Dispute." In 1762 Tedyuskung, the leading chief of the Delawares, in a speech to Governor Hamilton, said, "Soon after I returned to Wyomink (Wyoming) from Lancaster, there came 150 of those people furnished with all sorts of Tools, as well for building as Husbandry, and declared that they had bought those Lands from the Six Nations, and would settle them, and were actually going to build themselves Houses and settle upon a Creek called Lechawanock, about seven or eight miles above Wyomink (Wyoming)" (Colonial Records, IX. 6). Christian Seidel and David Zeisberger preached at "Lechaweke, the Minnissing Town" in October, 1755 (Archives, II. 459). The army of General Sullivan encamped one mile beyond the mouth of the Lackawanna on July 31, 1779, and remained there until about one o'clock on Sunday, August 1st. A sketch of the site of the encampment is given in Colonel Hubley's Journal (Journal of Lieut. Col. Adam Hubley, Jr., 1779, edited by J. W. Jordan, 9, 1909). The site of this encampment was near the present Coxton. It is mentioned in all of the Journals of Sullivans expedition (The Military Expedition of Major General John Sullivan, 1887). There were several old Indian trails between the Delaware and the Susquehanna which crossed the path leading up to the Susquehanna River, near this point. A path ran from the Great Bend, near Lanesboro, across Wayne County to near the present Stockport on the Delaware. Another path ran from Minnisink Island, across Pike County to the head of the Lackawanna, and then down to the Susquehanna. A third path ran from Wyoming to the Delaware, by way of the Delaware Water Gap, Stroudsburg, where the trail was intersected by the trail from Easton to Wyoming, near the present Tannersville, Monroe County. From this point the trails passed over Pocono Mountain, through the "Great Swamp" and "Shades of Death" (Bar-

ren Hill, Luzerne County) and on to Wyoming (Wilkes-Barre). The map of Howell's, 1792, shows the course of this trail, a branch of which General Sullivan followed from Easton. Some authors have placed the Iroquois village of Hazirok at the mouth of the Lackawanna. See *Adjouquay, Assarughney*.

Lachawanuck.—Scull, map, 1770. **Lackawanick.**—Rogers (1779), Archives, Sec. Ser., XV. 271 **Lawahannock.**—Howell's map, 1792. **Lechaweke.**—Zeisberger (1755), Archives, II. 459.

In the Journals of Sullivan's expedition nearly every writer gives the name a different spelling. A few of these are;

Lacawaneck.—Blake (1779), Mill. Exped of Gen Sull. 39, 1887. **Lackawanna.**—Burrowes, the same ref. 50. **Laghawanny.**—Hardenburgh, the same ref. 123. **Leghewannunck.**—Nukerck, the same ref. 219 **Leighawaneuch.**—Gookin, the same ref. 104.

LACKAWANNOCK.
The name of a Township and a creek in Mercer County. The creek is a branch of Shenango River. The name has the same meaning as that given for Lackawanna. According to Heckewelder Hannock is the name for a rapidly flowing stream. Lechau-hannock, or hanna, would signify "the forks of a stream.

Lahawanick.—Howell, map, 1792 **Lackawannock.**—Morris, State Map, 1848

LACKAWAXEN.
A creek which enters the Delaware from the west. at Lackawaxen, Pike County; also the name of a Township in the same county. A corruption of Lechauwesink, "where the roads fork."

Lahawaxen.—Adlum, map, 1794. **Lahawaxin.**—Wetzel (1778), Archives, VI. 629 **Laxawacsein.**—Howell, map, 1792. **Lechawacsein.**—Evans, map, 1755. **Leighwackson.**—Hyndshaw (1761), Colonial Records, VIII. 614. **Lechawaxin.**—Scull, map, 1770.

LAMOCO.
The name of a tract of land granted to Albert Hendryx, at the head of Upland Creek (Chester). Mentioned in the Records of Upland Court, 1678.

Lamoco.—Records of Upland Court, 108, 1860. **Lemoky.**—same ref 126.

LAMOKA.
The name of a place in Bradford County. May be a corruption of the above. Name is not historic in the locality. Map of 1911.

LANGUNTOUTENEUNK.
Name of the Moravian Indian village,

on the east bank of the Beaver River, between the Shenango River and Slippery Rock Creek, in Lawrence County. The new town was on the west bank, near the same place. The German name, Friedensstadt, "City of Peace," is the name which is most commonly given to the place. The Indian name has the same meaning. On April 17, 1770, the Christian Indians left Lawunakhannek (which see) in fifteen canoes. They reached Fort Pitt on April 20th., and went on down the Ohio to the Mouth of the Beaver, and then went up that stream. When they reached the site of the level land below the mouth of the Mahoning River they commenced to build their village. Their first business was a visit to Packananke, the Munsee chief, at Kuskuski (New Castle). Abraham, an Indian convert, went with Zeisberger on this mission. Glikkikan, the war chief of Packananke, became a convert and joined the mission. This act made the chief at Kuskuski very angry, but he was finally brought back into friendly relations by Zeisberger's being officially adopted into the Munsee tribe on July 14th. This act of adoption brought many of the Munsees from the former village of Goshgoshunk to the mission on the Beaver. Towards the end of July Zeisberger laid out the new town on the west bank of the river. Here a church was built. General Irvine, in 1785, states in his report of his survey, "The distance from the above named line (McLain's survey of the Donation Lands) to an old Moravian Town is three or four miles, from thence to Shenango (the river), two and half or three miles: —from the mouth of Shenango to Cuskuskey, on the West Branch (the Mahoning River, is six or seven miles, but it was formerly all called Cuskuskey by the natives along this branch as high as the Salt spring, which is twenty-five miles from the mouth of the Shenango" (Archives, XI. 519). This would place the Moravian mission about at the site of the present Moravia, and at the site noted on Howell's map of 1792 as, "Moravian." It would also place Kuskuski, of 1792, near the present Edenburg. Zeisberger's Journals (MS) however place the Kuskuski of 1770 at the site of New Castle. The name Kuskuskies was applied to the entire region of level land along the Mahoning.River, and to the level along

the Shenango. On Christmas eve Glikkikan and Gendaskund were baptised. The mission then had 73 members. In March 1771 Zeisberger made his first visit to Gekelmukpecheunk, the Delaware capital in Ohio, where he was the guest of Netawatwes, the leading chief. He returned to the mission on the Beaver, where the church was dedicated on the 20th of June. Owing to the various difficulties which had to be encountered, chiefly the drunken Indians from Kuskuski, the mission was abandoned in the spring of 1773. The Moravian Indians were then removed to the new missions at Gnadenhuetten and Schoenbrunn in Ohio. See *Gnadenheutten*. Consult; DeSchweinitz. Life and Times of David Zeisberger, 360-386. 1870; Loskiel, History of Missions, Part III. 57-89, 1794; Heckewelder, Narrative, III. 1820; Darlington, Gist, 81, 101, 1893.

Moravian.—Howell's map, 1792. **Moravia.**—Morris, map, 1848.

LAWUNAKHANNEK. The name of the mission established by Zeisberger in 1769, three miles above Goshgoshing (which see). It was abandoned April 17, 1770. See article immediately preceeding. The name signifies "at the meeting of the streams," or more properly "the middle stream place." Consult; DeSchweinitz, Life and Times of David Zeisberger, 350 etc., 1870.

LEHIGH. A tributary of the Delaware River, which it enters from the west at Easton; also a creek which enters the Lehigh River from the south at Allentown; also the name of a range of mountains west of the Delaware River. The name is an English corruption of the German shortening of the Indian name, which was Lechauweeki, Lechauwiechink, Lechauweing, which the German settlers contracted to Lecha, and which the English corrupted to Lehi or Lehigh. Le-chau-woak, is a "fork." The name "Lechauwekink," and the other forms, signifies "at the forks," or "where there are forks." Heckewelder and others give the origin of the name to the place on the river, just below Bethlehem, where the Indian trails forked. The name however seems to be more commonly applied to the "Forks of the Delaware" at Easton. The Indians frequently gave this name to the junction of two streams. The Iroquois name for the junction of the two streams at the present Athens, was Tioga, or Diahoga. The Seneca name for the "Forks" of the Ohio was Diondega. Both of these words have the same significance as Lechauwekink, "at the forks." It seems more probable that the name was first used of the "Forks of the Delaware," than of the forking of the trails along the stream. It is nearly always so used in the Archives and Records. "The Forks of the Delaware" was a prominent place in the early history of the English occupation of the river, and had been a well known gathering place for the Indians long before the coming of the Europeans to the region. When the Delawares were finally driven from this place by the Iroquois, after the dispute concerning the "Walking Purchase," they objected because it had been the home of their fathers for countless generations. This sale, more than any one other thing, was the cause of the alienation of this great Algonkian tribe. It is first mentioned in the Colonial Records for 1701, when the report of a "Certain Young Swede arriving from Lechay" was given to the Provincial Council. The sale of rum was forbidden at this place, and John Hans Steelman, of Maryland, who was trading at the forks, had his goods confiscated by order of William Penn (Col. Rec. II. 20-22). In the Archives (1, 143) William Penn issued an order to "John Hans," the same person, in which he says, "I have ye-fore Stopt thy Goods intended for Lechay." The Swedes, no doubt, soon after forming the settlement at Chester, and at the mouth of the Schuylkill, carried on a trade with the Indians "at the Forks." DeSchweinitz gives the name Lechauwitonk, to the site of Easton. Heckewelder gives the form Laehauwake. Previous to the settlement of the valley, the river was known as the West Branch of the Delaware, and is so noted on the maps of Evans (1749), Scull (1759). Howell's map (1792) gives the present name, Lehigh. In all of the early documents the name is given as Lechay, Lecha, or Lehi. The Lehigh Hills are frequently mentioned in the Indian Deeds (1732), and came up in the disputes concerning the Walking Purchase. George Whitfield landed in Philadelphia in the spring of 1740 and went with his party to the "Forks of the Delaware" where he had purchased 5,000 acres of land. One of the members of this party was David Zeisberger, who was to be so closely associated with the Indian history of the Province. Owing to disagreements which arose, which led to the purchase of a tract of land ten miles south of Whitfield's improvements. In Sept. 1741 the corner-stone of the chapel was laid, and on Christmas day Count Zinzendorf, who was then on a visit to the mission, gave the settlement the name of Bethlehem. This little village became the center of the Moravian Church in America, and the head-quarters of this Church are still at the same place, which has grown into a busy city. See *Gnadenhuetten*. The city of Easton was laid out in the Forks of the Delaware in 1750, pursuant to an order of Thomas Penn, who said, "I desire that the new town be called Easton, from my Lord Pomfret's house, and whenever there is a new county that it shall be called Northampton." "The Forks" was then in Bucks County. A new county was organized in 1752, and given the name suggested. A number of Councils were held with the Indians at Easton during its early history. The most important of which was that which was held in October 1758. Tedyuskung, the leading chief of the Delawares, was present (Colonial Records, VII. 204-220). Conrad Weiser acted as interpreter and chief counsel for the Province. Another Council was held in November of the same year (the same ref. 311-338). A general Council was held in October 1758, at which all of the Indian tribes were represented (Col. Rec. VIII. 174-222). Another Council was held in the summer of 1761 (the same ref. 630-661). Consult; Archives and Records of Penna., under title Easton; Loskiel, History of Missions, 1794, under Gnadenhuetten; DeSchweinitz, Life of Zeisberger, 1870, under titles Bethlehem and Gnadenhuetten. See *Delaware, Forks of*.

Laihi.—Beatty (1779), Archives, Sec. Ser. XV. 253. **Leahy.**—Young (1756), Archives, II. 677. **Lecha.**—Spangenburg (1755), Moravian Missions, 248-Reichel ed. **Lechaig.**—Deed (1732), Archives, I. 344. **Lechay.**—Penn (1701), Archives, I. 143. **Lechey (creek).**—Evans, map, 1755. **Lecky.**—Archives (Burd Jour. 1758), III. 355. **Leheigh (creek).**—Scull, map, 1759. **Lehi.**—Hays (1760), Archives, III. 741. **Lehigh.**—Evans, map, 1749 (creek). **Lichy.**—Pa. Council (1757), Colonial Records, VII. 353.

LEHIGHTON. The name of a town in Carbon County; also the name of a creek, now Bushkill, which enters the Delaware at Easton. The name is a corruption of Lechauweting, or Lechauwetank, having the significance of "at the forks"—same as Lehigh.

Lehietan.—Scull, map, 1770 (small map).
Leheithan.—Scull, map, 1770 (large).
Lehieton.—Scull, map, 1759, also Howell's map, 1792.

The present name of Bushkill is probably a corruption of Bush-Hill, at which place Governor Hamilton held a conference with Tedyuskung in Oct. 1761 (Colonial Records, VIII. 667). Bushkill is not a historic name in the region.

Bush Kill.—Morris, map, 1848. **Bushkill.**—Later state maps (1912).

LENAPE. The name of a village and Post Office in Chester County. A part of the name of the Delaware Indians, who called themselves Lenni-Lenape, "real men," or "original men." See *Delaware Indians.*

LENNI MILLS. A part of the name of the Delaware, with Mills added. Lenni-Lenape, see *Delaware Indians.* The name of a village and Post Office in Delaware County.

LEPOS PETER'S TOWN, LAPACH PEETOS TOWN etc. The name of a former Delaware village, at the mouth Catawissa Creek, on the Susquehanna River (See *Catawissa*). Was situated at the crossing of the Warriors Path, to the West Branch and to Wyoming. Named in honor of a Delaware chief named Lapachpeton, corrupted to Labach Peters, Lepos Peters etc., who was a friend of the English during the period of Indian hostility after Braddock's defeat, in 1755. Conrad Weiser mentions him as having been present at a conference at Shamokin in 1742, by the name of Lapapeton (Col. Rec. IV. 641). In 1755 Weiser speaks of him as "Capachpiton, a noted Delaware, always true to the English" (Col. Rec. VI. 649). In 1757, after the Council at Easton, Conrad Weiser and Thomas McKee, in a Deposition state, "That the Delaware Indian, Lapachpeton, whom this Deponent knows to be of great Reputation among the Indians, interrupted Teedyuscung whilst he was speaking to the Governor, and in an Angry Way asked him, Why did you bring us down? We thought that we came down to make Peace with our Brethren

the English, but you continue to quarrel about this Land affair, which is Dirt, a Dispute we did not hear of until now. I desire you to enter upon the Business which we came down for. which is for Peace" (Archives, III, 257). The account of this dispute with Tedyuskung is given in the report of the Council at Easton, by Jacob Duche, who gives the name of the chief as, "Labboughpeton, a Delaware chief" (Col. Rec. VII. 701). Scull's map of 1759 notes "Lawpaughpeton's T." at the site of Catawissa (which see). In Col. Burd's Journal, 1756, as "Lapach Peetos Town, about ten miles from hence" (Archives, Sec. Ser., II. 795). Burd was then at Shamokin (Sunbury), which is more than ten miles from the mouth of Catawissa. The chief had evidently crossed the river and was living on the trail leading to Shamokin. In the examination of H. Fry and John Shmick, before Timothy Horsfield, in 1755, the former said, "we gave them the following instructions, vizt., "To go down the River on that side as far as Labach Peters, & there cross the River, & enquire at Lebach Peters (a small Indian Town) how it was at Shamokin" (Archives, II. 492). Fry and Schmick were at Wyoming. The trail from Wyoming ran along the western side of the river, opposite the mouth of the Catawissa, hence "that side" would be the western side.

LEQUEPEES. An Indian village, mentioned by LeTort and Davenport in 1731, consisting of "Mingoes mostly and some Delawares—4 settled families but a great Resort of those People" (Archives, I. 301). The name may be a corruption of Allaquippa's Town, which was situated at the mouth of Chartiers Creek,—the present McKees Rocks, below Pittsburgh. See *Allaquippa.*

LETORT'S SPRING. The name of a small creek, which enters the Conodogwinet near Carlisle, Cumberland County; also the name of a village in Lancaster County, where the name is given as Letart. Named for the famous Indian trader, James LeTort, who had a log cabin at the head of the spring, near the present Bonny Brook. He is frequently mentioned in the Archives and Records. His father, Jacques LeTort, was a French Huguenot who came to America in 1686, from London. In 1693 he and his wife, Anne, were engaged in the Indian trade on the Schuylkill. He began his Indian trade at Conestoga about 1695. The son, James, was put to many disadvantages on account of his French descent. He was put into the jail at Philadelphia, but was released on bond. He said that he was born in Philadelphia. He was granted a License as an Indian trader in 1713. After the death of his mother he removed to Bonny Brook, then called Big Beaver Pond, where he carried on a trade with the Shawnee. In 1719 he made application for 500 acres of land "between Paxtang and Conestoga, for convenience of trade with the Indians" (Archives, XIX (Sec. Ser.) 651). He was one of the first white men to enter the great wilderness beyond the mountains. He went as far west as the Miami, trading with the Indians at all of the villages along the way. His name has been perpetuated in the western region by names LeTort's Rapids, LeTort's Creek and LeTort's Island, in the Ohio River, just south of the Meigs County line. "LeTart's Falls" is noted on Evans map of 1755. Consult: Colonial Records, II. 100, 121, 138, 163, 170, 403, 471, 554, 539, 562; III. 330; IV. 237, 562, 574; Archives, I. 211, 214, 216, 255, 300, 328; Archives, II. 42, 43, 44; XII. 281. "LeTart's Spring," near Carlisle, is noted on Morris' map 1848.

LICK RUN. A creek which enters the West Branch of the Susquehanna, from the north at Farrandsville, Clinton County. It is noted on Scull's map of 1770 as, "Mianaquank." On Howell's map of 1792, and all later maps, it is noted as, "Lick Run." The name may be a corruption of Mawewiunk, "place of gathering"—however, its original form is doubtful. Mahoni was the Delaware word for "lick." Mahon-ing may have been its Indian name.

LITTLE BEAVER. A creek which enters the Ohio from the north at Smith's Ferry, Beaver County. Heckewelder gives the Indian name as, Tank-amochk-hanne, "little beaver stream." One of the trails to the mouth of Yellow Creek and to Wheeling evidently crossed the Ohio at this place. The Indian picture rocks on the bottom of the Ohio River at this point give evidence that this must have been a prominent gathering place for the Indians, as they passed down the Ohio. These were plainly visible during the low water a few years ago,

at which time many photographs of the strange petroglyphs were taken. Owing to the erection of the various locks on the Ohio these carvings are now submerged. The trail which crossed the river at this point cut across Hancock County, West Virginia, to the headwaters of Tomlinson's Run, and then on down to the crossing near Yellow Creek. Many Indian relics are still found along this trail. Arrow heads and other flint articles were evidently made at a point a few miles northeast of Pughtown (Fairview), as many flint clippings and various half finished articles are still found in that region. The famous Logan, or Tah-gah-jute, whose speech has been the cause of much controversy, had a number of his relatives murdered opposite the mouth of Yellow Creek, in 1774. It is also claimed that the fight between Adam Poe and "Big Foot" took place near the mouth of Tomlinson's Run (According to some writers Andrew, and not Adam, was the hero of this fight). The party of Indians were Wyandot, three of whom were sons of Dunquat, the "Half-King" (Consult: Doddridges Notes, ed. 1912, 232, etc.) This trail was frequently used by the Indians of Ohio in going into the white settlements of Washington County during the Revolution.

LITTLE CONEMAUGH. A branch of the Conemaugh River in Cambria County. Heckewelder gives the Indian name as, Gunamochki, "the little otter." The word for otter according to Zeisberger, is compounded of Gune-u, "long," and a-mochk, "a beaver." See *Conemaugh*.

LITTLE MOSHANNON. A branch of Moshannon Creek in Centre County. Heckewelder gives the name as, Tankimoos-hanne, "little elk stream." See *Moshannon*.
Little Mushanon.—Howell's map, 1792.

LITTLE SCHUYLKILL. A branch of the Schuylkill in Schuylkill County. Heckewelder gives the name as, Tamaque-hanne, "beaver stream." See *Schuylkill*.
Little Schuylkill or Tamaqua R.—Morris, map, 1848.

Tamaquay.—Scull, map 1759. **Tumauquay.**—Scull, map, 1770.

LOGANS VALLEY. A valley in Blair County, running from Tyrone to

Altoona. Said to be named for Captain Logan, a Delaware (not the famous "Mingo Logan"), one of whose cabins was near the site of the present Tyrone (Consult: Egle, History of Penna., 400, 1883).

LOGSTOWN. One of the most important Indian villages in the state during the period from the migration of the Delaware and Shawnee, about 1725-27, until the capture of Fort Duquesne by the British, in 1758. It was situated on the right (north) bank of the Ohio, about eighteen miles below the forks of the Ohio. The territory about the headwaters of the Ohio, where the Delaware and Shawnee settled, after their migration from the Susquehanna and Potomac, was claimed by the Iroquois. When the rivalry between France and Great Britain for the possession of the Ohio commenced Logstown was a prominent trading place. The village was inhabited by Delaware and Shawnee, with a number of Seneca, who became known along the Ohio as "Mingos." There were also a few Wyandot, Mohawk and Miami living in the settlement at various times. Tanachharison, the "Half King," was the leading chief in the settlement. Scarouady, who afterwards succeeded him, was also a resident of the place during the early days of the conflict with France. After the Treaty of Lancaster in 1744, the traders of Pennsylvania, Virginia and Maryland became more numerous along the Ohio and its tributaries. The great influx of these English traders soon aroused the jealousy of the French traders, chiefly because the former were charged with selling goods cheaper than the latter. The French traders influenced Peter Chartier, a Shawnee half-breed, to assist them in driving the English traders from the trade in Ohio. In 1747 a number of French traders were killed and scalped by some Indians, who had become enraged because of the low prices paid to them for their furs and peltries. The scalp of one of these traders was sent to the Governor of Pennsylvania, by three warriors at "Detroit," with a letter in which the senders promised to send more scalps. The letter and the scalp reached George Croghan, who sent the letter to the Governor, and urged that something be done to hold the offered friendship of these western Indians. Conrad Weiser also said that some-

thing should be done to hold these Indians in friendly relations, and suggested that a present should be sent to them if a suitable person could be found to take it. After much discussion the Provincial Council decided to send a present to the western Indians during the coming spring. The Assembly was opposed to the use of "bribes" to gain the friendship of the Indians, and was also opposed to doing anything to incite the Indians to hostility against the French. Governor Palmer wrote to the Governors of Maryland and Virginia, asking them to unite with him in collecting money to buy the proposed presents, and to appoint Commissioners to join those of this Province in the mission. Governor Gooch of Virginia heartily favored the plan, but his Assembly opposed it. The Governor then promised to assist Governor Palmer. Everything was made ready for the trip to the Ohio. The goods were purchased, George Croghan had gone on to his home to load his wagons, and Conrad Weiser was to start for the Ohio as soon as Spring would come. Then came a new difficulty. Shikellamy, the Iroquois deputy at Shamokin, became jealous of the attention which was being paid to these western Indians, who were subject to the Iroquois. He went to Weiser and told him that these western Indians could not make treaties or sell lands without the permission of the Iroquois, and that the trip to the Ohio was useless. He also told him that the Iroquois were going to send deputies to Philadelphia in the Spring, and that it would be necessary for him to be there to act as interpreter. Weiser did not know what to do. He finally sent a letter to the Provincial Council explaining the whole situation. Both he and Shikellamy were ordered to appear before the Council, which they did. After much discussion it was decided to postpone the sending of the presents until after the Iroquois had been to Philadelphia. But, in the meanwhile the members of the Council had become aroused over the matter. They saw the necessity of doing something at once to hold the friendship of the Indians on the Ohio, whom the French were gradually winning away from the Province. The Indian trade was worth trying to keep. So, it was decided to send Croghan at once with a present of about 200 Pounds value, and with the promise of a larger present later in the summer, when Weiser would meet with them in Council. George Croghan departed on this mission in April, 1748. When Croghan reached Logstown he found that a number of Miami Indians were on their way east to hold a conference with the English authorities. Weiser was informed of this mission and sent messengers to meet the delegates and conduct them to Lancaster. Here four Deputies of the Provincial Council met them and heard the cause of the visit. The result of this conference was the sending of Weiser as soon as possible to Logstown. Weiser started on the 11th of August, reaching Logstown on the 27th, 1748. This journey of Conrad Weiser was the first official mission of the English to the Indians beyond the mountains, and was the chief cause of the French expedition under Celoron DeBienville, the following year, and was the real commencement of the events which led to the struggle of France and Great Britain for the possession of the Ohio. This is why the causes leading to this visit have been presented in this article. While at Logstown Weiser asked for a list of the "fighting men" belonging to the tribes living on the Ohio. This list is of interest because it gives the earliest attempt at a Census of the Indians living in the region. "The Senecas 163, Shawonese 162, Owendats (Wyandot) 100, Tisagechroanu (Mississauga) 40, Mohawks 74, Mohicons 15, Onondagers 35, Cajukas (Cayuga) 20, Oneidos 15, Delawares 165, in all 789." As this list was made out by the representatives of the various tribes mentioned, it is more apt to be over-stated than otherwise. It comprehends "all the Nations of Indians settled on the Waters of Ohio." Most writers have a very exaggerated idea, not only as to the number of Indians living in the Ohio region before its first settlement by the English, but also of the number living on the Continent at the time of its discovery. Careful examination of all possible authorities lead to the conviction that the number of Indians now living on the American continent is about what it was when the continent was first discovered.

Weiser "Set up the Union Flagg on a long Pole" on September 1st, 1748, which was the first time which the banner of Great Britain was ever unfurled on upper Ohio, and just ten years before it was unfurled over the ruins of Fort Duquesne. Various conferences were held with the various tribes represented, the presents were distributed, the complaints of the Indians concerning the rum traffic were heard, and Tanachharison and Scarouady returned thanks to "Brother Onas" (Pennsylvania), and "Brother Assaraquoa" (Virginia) for the presents which had been given the Indians (Weiser's Journal, Colonial Records V. 348-358, 1851).

In the summer of 1749 Captain Celeron De Beinville with a detachment of French soldiers, descended the Conewango, Allegheny and Ohio, taking formal possession of the territory for France. He deposited leaden plates at the mouths of the various tributaries of the Ohio, on which was stated the fact of the act of possession. He reached Logstown, where he remained for two days, the 9th. and 10th. of August. Father Bonnecamp, who was with him, estimated the number of cabins in the settlement at 80. He said in his Journal, "we will call it Chiningue, from its vicinity to a river of that name" (Beaver). He also says, "The village of Chiningue is quite new; it is hardly more than five or six years since it was established" (Bonnecamp, Jesuit Relation, LXIX. 183). This French expedition, consisting of 250 Frenchmen, Canadians and Indians, went on down the Ohio, after having ordered the tearing down of the British Flag which had been put up by Weiser. The French visit to the Ohio aroused the Governors of Pennsylvania and Virginia to greater activity for holding the Indian trade on the Ohio. The latter Colony became especially active in its efforts. The organization of "The Ohio Company" in 1749 was the first organized effort for the taking possession of the lands along the Ohio River. Christopher Gist was employed by the Company, and given instructions concerning the exploration of the Ohio region. He reached Logstown on November 25, 1750. In his Journal he says "In the Loggs Town I found scarce any Body but a Parcel of reprobate Indian Traders, the Chief of the Indians being out a hunting" (Darlington Gist, 34). While Gist was at Logstown he was informed that George Croghan and Andrew Montour had passed through the place a week before, on a mission from Pennsylvania. Croghan's mission was caused by the report that the French Agent Joncaire was on the Ohio, seeking to win the Indians and to drive the English traders from the region. Croghan had been at Logstown on November 16th. and in his report to the Governor had given the first notice of the building of a fort on the Ohio. He said that the opinion of the Indians was "that their Brothers the English ought to have a Fort on this River to secure the Trade" (Colonial Records, V. 496-498). Croghan went on westward to the Muskingum, where he was overtaken by Gist (See Journals of Croghan and Gist, Colonial Records, V. 530 etc., Darlington, Gist). After Croghan had returned from this trip the assembly voted 700 Pounds for the purchase of presents, and employed Croghan and Montour to deliver them. They reached Logstown on May 18, 1751, where they were received "by a great number of the Six Nations, Delawares and Shawonese" (Col. Rec. V. 530). During this mission of Croghan's, the French Agent, Joncaire, arrived in Logstown with 40 warriors of the Six Nations, and sought by every possible means to win the Indians away from an alliance with the English. While Croghan was at Logstown a Dunkard from Virginia made a request for permission to settle on the Youghiogheny River," to which the Indians made answer that it was not in their power to dispose of Lands; that he must apply to the Council of Onondago." The Indians at Logstown again requested that the English build a fort on the Ohio. The Governor reported this to the Assembly of the Province, which declined to take any action. But, in the meanwhile the Ohio Company, and the ever active Governor Dinwiddie, of Virginia, were busily engaged in efforts for the actual taking possession of the Ohio region. This land was claimed, not only by virtue of the King's Charter, but also by the terms of the Treaty at Lancaster in 1744, by which the Iroquois sold to Virginia the lands "to the setting sun." Thus was commenced the struggle between France and Great Britain; the conflict over the Boundary between Pennsylvania and Virginia, and also the struggle between the Delaware and Iroquois, who claimed the lands "by right of conquest." All were fighting for the same territory about the Forks of the Ohio." During this early stage of affairs "the lack of organization was the weak spot in English trade. Local

contention and jealousy was beginning to destroy the fruit of what Conrad Weiser gained at Logstown in the summer of 1748" (Walton, Conrad Weiser, 195, 1900). In 1751 Governor Dinwiddie appointed James Patton, Joshua Fry and Lunsford Lomax as Commissioners to meet the Indians at Logstown. These Commissioners arrived at Logstown May 31, 1752, at which time various conferences were held with the Indians On June 13th the Commissioners had the Indian chiefs sign a ratification of the Treaty of Lancaster, 1744, allowing the English to form settlements on the south and east side of the Ohio, but at the same time the Indians denied the English claim to any lands west of the mountains (Consult: Loudermilk, History of Cumberland, 29, 1878; Dinwiddie Papers, I. 9; Darlington, Gist, 220 etc.; Virginia Historical Magazine, XIII. 143-174; Colonial Records of Pa., V. 730 etc.) The Governor General of Canada, Duquesne, was kept informed of all of these events which were taking place on the Ohio and early in 1753 he sent the expedition which commenced the erection of a series of forts, which was to connect the French possessions in Canada with those upon the Mississippi. The building of these forts led to mission of George Washington and Christopher Gist in 1753. The real intent of this mission was to hold the lands on the Ohio River for the "Ohio Company," and to enforce Virginia's claim to these lands, not only against the French but also against Pennsylvania. There was just as much rivalry between the traders of Pennsylvania and Virginia on the Ohio as there was between the traders of France and the English Colonies. This most unfortunate lack of harmony between the two great Colonies of Pennsylvania and Virginia was the chief cause of all of the lack of harmony in Braddock's expedition (1755), and the dispute concerning the route to be taken by General Forbes in 1758, and it was carried into almost every disaster which the English settlement of western Pennsylvania had to pass through. "The Virginia Dispute" was one of the most unfortunate incidents in the early history of western Pennsylvania.

Washington and Gist reached Logstown on November 24, 1753, where they remained until December 1st., when they departed for Venango (Franklin) accompanied by the "Half

King," Tanachharison, and two other Indian chiefs (Consult, Washington's Journal of 1753, in Olden Time, I. 10, Also in Spark's Life of Washington; Darlington, Gist, 81 etc.)

George Croghan reached Logstown on the 14th of January, 1754, after the departure of Washington and Gist. On the 16th of April, 1754, the French army under Contracoeur, descended the Allegheny River, from Venango, and captured the fort which was being erected by Edward Ward, at the forks of the Ohio. This fort was being erected by the Ohio Company, for the protection of its Indian trade on the Ohio (See *Pittsburgh*). After the French had taken possession of the Ohio, Logstown was deserted by the English traders. The two Iroquois deputies, Tanachharison and Scarouady left the village and later removed to Aughwick, after Washington's defeat at Fort Necessity. In 1756, at the Council at Carlisle, George Croghan reported that he had sent Delaware Jo, a friendly Indian, on a tour of investigation along the Ohio. He went "to the Log's Town, where he found about one hundred Indians and thirty English Prisoners taken by the Shawonese living at the Lower Shawonese Town from the western Frontiers of Virginia and sent up to Log's Town" (Colonial Records, VI. 781-782). Christian F. Post, who was sent on the mission of Peace to Kuskuski (which see), reached Logstown on August 23, 1758. When he returned from this mission he was immediately sent back. The army of General Forbes had then reached Ligonier. Post reached Logstown on December 2nd. He says in his Journal, "I with my companion, Kekiuscund's (Tedyuskung) son came to Log's-town, situated on a hill. On the east end is a great piece of low land, where the Old Logs-town used to stand. In the new Logs-town the French have built about thirty houses for the Indians. They have a large corn field on the south side, where the corn stands ungathered" (Thwaites, Early Western Travels, I. 281). After the fall of Fort Duquesne, and the British occupation of the Ohio, Logstown declined as a trading place, although Croghan and others had trading houses there. After the defeat of the Indians at the Battle of Bushy Run, in August, 1763, all of the trading houses in Logstown were destroyed by the Indians. In 1764

when Colonel Bouquet marched through the place on his way to the Muskingum, the place was entirely deserted. The Journal of this expedition reads, "October 5.—In this days march the army passed through Loggstown, situated 17 miles and a half, fifty-seven perches by path from Fort Pitt. This place was noted before the last war for the great trade carried on by the English and French, but its inhabitants abandoned it in the year 1758 (Historical Account of Bouquet's Expedition, (reprint, 45, 1869). In 1765 George Croghan passed through on May 16th. The village was then in ruins. After this time many travellers down the Ohio River make mention of passing through the site of the old Indian village. Rev. Charles Beatty and Rev. George Duffield passed through Logstown on September 11th, 1766, when on a missionary trip to the Ohio Indians. George Washington stopped here in 1770, when on his way to the Kanawha River (Craig's Olden Time, I. 418, 1848). Butler, in 1784, says, "I find the old fields quite grown up with shrubs, which have destroyed their beautiful appearance and verdure. There is still a great deal of fine blue grass among the plumb trees and other bushes" (Butler's Journal, Olden Time, II. 434). Arthur Lee, who passed through December 17, 1784, says, "The next place is Loggstown, which was formerly a settlement on both sides of the Ohio." (Olden Time, I. 338). Cummings speaks of it in 1807, as "a scattering hamlet of four or five log cabins" (Early Western Travels, IV. 97). Fordham's Personal Narrative, 1817, mentions it as "Indian Logstown 18 miles from Pittsburgh" (Fordham's Per. Nar., 81, 1906). A settlement on the south side of the river is called "Indian Logstown," in Western Navigation, 76, 1814.

General Wayne's army, known as the "Legion of the United States," encamped a short distance below Logstown from November 1792 until April 1793. The camp was called Legionville, which name still remains. A town called Montmorin was laid out at the site of Logstown in 1788, for which advertisements were published in the Pennsylvania Gazette for March 12, 1788. The proposed town never came into existence. In 1824 George Rapp, the head of the Harmony Society, established the settlement near the site of Logstown, which became one of the most prosperous communities in the United States. It was called Economy.

The origin of the name "Logstown" is difficult to figure out. There seems to have been no Indian name applied to the place, of which this was a translation, nor has any Indian name for the village been discovered. Shenango has been given as a probable name, but this has been due to the pronunciation of the French name Chiningue, which is similar. Thwaites states that the Indian name was Maughwawame (Wisconsin Hist. Coll., XVIII, 42), but no such name appears in any of the Records, Archives, letters, journals or maps, as applied to the site of Logstown. It was one of the names applied to Wyoming (Day, Penn. 431, 1843), and might have been applied to Logstown, so far as its signification is concerned—"g︢r e a t plains," or "great meadows"—but, it was never given by any early authority as a name for the place on the Ohio. Nearly all of the large Indian villages in Pennsylvania and Ohio were situated on "great plains" and might well have been called Maughwawame, or M'cheuwomink. The name "Mugguck" or "Maguck," on the Pickaway plains, south of Circleville, Ohio, evidently was a corruption of this word. The common name of the village, Logstown, was evidently a Traders name for the place, and may have been due to the great quantities of logs and driftwood spread over the level country after a flood in the river. The writer can remember how these great logs used to pile up along these levels during a flood on the Allegheny River. After the French occupation of the Ohio, as previously stated, a number of log houses were built here for the Indians. These may have been built from the logs which could be gathered from the highwater line. The present slackwater in the Ohio has changed the conditions along the river.

The name noted on Bonnecamp's map of 1749 is Chingue (not Chiningue, as often stated).

Chinengue.—Duquesne (1753), Archives, Sec. Ser., VI. 161, 1877. Chiningue.— Bonnecamp (1749), Jesuit Rel. LXIX. 183. De Chininque.—Joncarie (1751), Colonial Records, V. 540, 1851. Village de Chingue.—Bonnecamp, map, 1749. Leggs T.—Evans, map, 1775. Logg's Town.—Pa. Council, (1748), Col. Rec. V. 289. Log's Town.—Trent (1748), Archives, Pa, I. 17. Logs Town.—Trent (1750), the same ref. II. 50. Logstown.—

Weiser (1748), the same ref. II. 8. The Log's Town.—Gist, map, 1753.

Howell's map, 1792, notes Logs T. The Cary Atlas, 1801, notes Legionville; Morris' map, 1848, Economy. Logtown Run, on the opposite side of the river perpetuates the name in the region.

LONG ISLAND. An island in the West Branch of the Susquehanna, at the mouth of Pine Creek, Jersey Shore, Lycoming County. Scull's map of 1770 notes this island as "Cawichnowane, or Long Isle." The map of Lewis Evans, 1755, places this name at the site of the "Great Island" at Lock Haven. The legend at the mouth of Pine Creek (Evans map, 1755), is "A Conestoga Ind. F.," having reference to a fort of the Susquehanna, or Conestoga, Indians at this place. There was an old Indian burial ground on Pine Creek, in which the dead were said to have been buried in trenches. Meginness says there was a tradition that a great battle was fought between two hostile tribes (Otzinachson, 28). This may have been one of the battles between the Iroquois and the Susquehannas, who were finally driven down the Susquehanna River and finally overwhelmed by the Iroquois (See *Susquehanna*). The trail to the Seneca country passed up Pine Creek and across the divide to the Genesee. It is possible that the Wenro once had villages along the upper waters of the West Branch. In 1748 David Zeisberger and Martin Mack went up the West Branch from Shamokin (Sunbury). They found Ostonwakin and the other Indian villages entirely deserted. Zeisberger found a Delaware living on an island and asked him, "Where are all our brothers who used to hunt along this river?" For an answer the Indian drew aside the flaps of his tent and exposed to Zeisberger's eyes a number of Indians suffering with small-pox. The Indians at the Great Island were also afflicted with this disease. "Others were starving. A kettle of boiled grass constituted a luxury. Gaunt figures, huddled around fires, ate voraciously of such food" (DeSchweinitz, Life of Zeisberger, 145). The same condition existed on the North Branch also. It was one of the dreaded "starving times," when Famine, as well as Pestilence, stalked through the Indian villages. See *Big Island, Cowanesque.*

LOYALHANNA. The name of a tributary of the Kiskiminetas, which rises in Westmoreland County; *Loyalhanning*, the name of a former Indian village on this stream, at the site of the present Ligonier. The name is a corruption of Lawel-hanna, "middle stream," and with the locative ing, "at the middle stream." The Loyalhanna is midway between the waters of the Juniata and the Ohio Rivers, on the trail from Raystown (Bedford) to Shannopins Town (Pittsburgh). The Loyalhanna unites with the Conemaugh at Saltsburg to form the Kiskiminetas, which enters the Allegheny River opposite Freeport. The Indian village at the site of Ligonier, was probably settled by Delawares soon after the commencement of their migration from the Susquehanna, 1727. It is mentioned by Christopher Gist in 1750, as "Loylhannan, an old Indian Town on a creek of Ohio called Kiscominitis" (Darlington, Gist, 33). In the table of distances to the Ohio, over the Raystown Path, given by John Patten, it is mentioned (1754) as, "Loyal Hannin Old Town," and the distance to Shannopin's Town is given as 50 miles (Colonial Records, V. 751). In the expedition of General Forbes, 1758, this point was the western outpost of the army. Col. Henry Bouquet, who was in command of the outpost at Bedford, sent forward Col. Burd to open the road to Loyal Hanna. After the occupation by the army the site was called the "Camp at Loyalhannon." Col. Henry Bouquet reached the place on the 7th of September. General Forbes, who was so ill that he had to be carried in a litter, did not reach Loyalhanna until about Nov. 1st. While the army was here awaiting the arrival of General Forbes, Major James Grant went on his ill-fated expedition on Sept. 9th, with a force of 37 officers and 805 privates. He reached the place in the present city of Pittsburgh known as "Grant's Hill," where he was attacked by the French and Indians, whom he had drawn out of Fort Duquesne, and defeated with a loss of 273 killed, wounded and captured. The French then made an attack upon the camp at Loyalhanna on October 12th, with about 1200 French and Indians, and after a severe fight were driven away. The British loss was 12 killed, 18 wounded, 31 missing. Col. James Burd was in command at Ligonier at the time of this engagement. (Consult: Archives, Sec. Ser.,

VI. 427-430; Colonial Records, VIII. 224-225, 229, 232; Frontier Forts, II. 194-290). The stockade fort which was built at Loyalhanna was called Fort Ligonier, in honor of Sir John Ligonier, Lord Viscount of Enniskillen. After the arrival of General Forbes at Fort Ligonier it was decided at a council of war to advance no further, but to wait until spring. The weather had become quite cold, and the mountains were covered with snow. But the reports which came from Fort Duquesne, by scouts and Indians, changed this plan, and it was decided to advance at once. The advance left Ligonier on Nov. 12th, followed by General Forbes, with the main army of 4,300 men, on Nov. 17th. On the 24th, the entire army was encamped at Turtle Creek, about 12 miles from the French fort. On the 25th the entire army advanced and took possession of the fort which the French had set on fire, and then deserted.

During the Conspiracy of Pontiac Fort Ligonier was the only military post west of the mountains, save Fort Pitt, which had not fallen into the hands of the hostile Indians. Venango, Presqu' Isle and LeBoeuf had all fallen. Lieut. Archibald Blane was shut up in Fort Ligonier from early in May. Communication with Fort Pitt was cut off. Col. Bouquet, who was then in Philadelphia, was ordered to the relief of Fort Pitt. When Bouquet reached Carlisle he sent 30 Highlanders in advance to the relief of Fort Ligonier, which post was absolutely necessary for his advance to the Ohio. When this detachment reached the fort at Ligonier it was surrounded by Indians, who fired upon them as they entered the fort. Bouquet reached Fort Ligonier on August 2nd, 1763, and then went on to Bushy Run, where he defeated the Indians in the battle of August 5th and 6th (Consult: Parkman, Conspiracy of Pontiac, under title Fort Ligonier). By 1775 the Ligonier Valley was filled with settlements. A number of block-houses were built for the protection of these settlements (Consult: Boucher, History of Westmoreland County; Hassler, Old Westmoreland, etc.).

La-el-han-neck, or Middle Creek.—McCullough (1756), Border Life, 90, 1839. **Lewlhannon.**—Fry & Jefferson, map, 1755. **Loyal Haning.**—Harris (1754), Archives, II. 135. **Loyal Hannin.**—Patten (1754), Colonial Records, V. 750. **Loyal Hanning.**—Shippen (1758), Archives, III. 510. **Loyalhannin.**—West (1752),

Colonial Records, V. 761. **Loyalhanning.**—Evans, map, 1775. **Loyal Hannon.**—Forbes (1758), Colonial Records, VIII. 224. **Royal Amnon.**—Vaudreuil (1759), Archives, VI. Sec Ser., 553. **Royal Hannon.**—Malartic (1759), Archives, VI. Sec. Ser., 564. **Royal Hannon.**—M o n t c a l m (1758), Archives, VI. Sec. Ser. 428. **Fort Legioner.**—Stanwix (1759), Archives, III. 696. **Fort Ligonier.**—Armstrong (1759), Archives, III. 688. **Legonier.**—Mercer (1759), Archives, III. 625. **Ligonier.**—Mercer (1759), Archives, III. 674.

LOYALSOCK. A creek which enters the West Branch of the Susquehanna from the north at Montourville, Lycoming County. A corruption of Lawisaquick, "middle creek." Is about midway between Lycoming and Muncy Creeks, on the north side of the river. The name is also that of a Post Office and station in Lycoming County. The entire region along the West Branch was evidently occupied by the Susquehannock, or Conestoga, and then by the Seneca, before the historic period of its occupation by the Delaware and Shawnee (See *Susquehanna, Long Island, Pine Creek, etc.*). Within historic times there was an Indian village at the mouth of the creek (See *Otstonwakin*). After the building of Fort Augusta at Shamokin (which see) the settlers spread along the West Branch Valley, beyond the line of the lands purchased from the Indians. These "squatters" caused much trouble to the Province, and also brought severe punishment to the settlers (See *West Branch*). During 1777 and 1778 many families were killed, or taken captive in the region of Loyalsock Creek (Consult: Archives VI. 516, 565, 589, 590, 599, 603; Meginness, Otzinachson, 195, 203, 222, 224). Among the most famous men killed near the creek was James Brady, a son of Capt. John Brady, who was a younger brother of the famous Capt. Sam Brady (see last work cited, 222).

Layal Sock.—Potter (1778), Archives, VI. 603. **Loyal Sack.**—Potter (1778), Archives, VI 516. **Loyal Sock.**—Scull, map, 1759. **Loyalsock.**—Howell, map, 1792. **Lywasock.**—Map of 1755, in Gist (Darlington ed.)

LYCAMAHONING. A creek which enters the Allegheny River from the east at Redbank, now called Redbank Creek, one of the sources of which is now called Sandy Lick Creek. The name is a corruption of Legauwi-mahoni, "sandy-lick." The bend which the Allegheny River makes just above the mouth of this creek, is called Brady's Bend. This was the scene of the conflict between the Indians and a detachment of 20 soldiers and the Delaware chief, Nonoland, under command of Captain Sam Brady, in June, 1779. This incident did not take place during Brodhead's expedition in August, 1779, as is frequently stated. Captain Brady went on this scouting expedition in June for the purpose of trying to find the party of Seneca Indians which had been raiding the white settlements along Sewickley Creek, in Westmoreland County Brady fell in with a party of seven Indians near the mouth of Redbank Creek, or "about fifteen miles above Kittanning" The Indians were attacked, and in the fight Brady killed the chief "Bald Eagle" (See *Bald Eagle*), recaptured six horses, released two prisoners and took all of the plunder which the Indians had taken from the settlements (Consult: Archives, XII. 131-132, Brodhead's letter to Washington: Meginness. Otzinachson, 236. 240. 253. 337. 489-518; Border Life, 254, etc.) Many of the incidents related of Capt. Sam Brady are very much overdrawn, as the official reports in the Archives show. Some of these incidents have given rise to some of the traditions concerning "The Indian Hunter of the Susquehanna," "The Wild Hunter of the Juniata," "Captain Jack, the Avenger," and similar mythical characters. The incidents ascribed to all of these characters are practically identical. There is, of course, a small part of every such tradition which is true—the balance is the work of the imagination. Captain Sam Brady really did enough of the heroic, without the addition of purely imaginary episodes.

Lecamick.—Map of western Pa., in Gist, 1755. **Lycamahoning.**—Scull, map, 1770. **Red Bank Creek.**—Morris, state map, 1848. **Redbank Creek.**—State maps, 1911 etc. **Sandy Lick Creek.**—Howell, map, 1792.

LYCOMING. A creek which rises in Tioga County, and which enters the West Branch of the Susquehanna on the north, at Newberry, Lycoming County; also the name of a county. A corruption of Legaui-hanne, "sandy stream." The name which the Delawares always gave to the stream, according to Heckewelder. In 1745 Bishop Spangenberg, accompanied by Conrad Weiser, who was on his way to Onondaga (in May, 1745), wrote in his Journal, "at dark came to the 'Limping

Messenger,' or Didachton Creek, and encamped for the night." Weiser mentions this creek, in his Journal of 1745, as Diadagdon (Colonial Records, IV. 778). In the Indian Deed of 1768 it is mentioned as Tiadaghton (Col. Rec. IX. 554). In the discussion concerning what creek the Indians called by this name, the Commissioners of the purchase of 1784 appealed to the Iroquois for a statement of the exact meaning of the terms of the Deed of 1768. The Iroquois answered, "With regard to the Creek called Teadaghton mentioned in your Deed of 1768, we have already answered you and again repeat it, it is the same you call Pine Creek, being the largest emptying into the West branch of the Susquehanna" (Archives X. 357-358). By many of the authorities of the period this name was supposed to apply to Lycoming Creek, as Weiser falsely called it by the name which belonged to Pine Creek (See *Pine Creek*). There was an Indian village at the mouth of Lycoming Creek called French Margaret's, or French Town (See *French Margaret's*). A prominent Indian trail ran to the headwaters of this creek, one branch of which crossed the divide to the Tioga River and went on into the Seneca country; another branch crossed to the headwaters of Towanda Creek, and thence to Sheshequin (which see). Before the Purchase of 1784, when Lycoming Creek was understood to be the legal boundary of the Purchase of 1768, there was much trouble caused by the settlers occupying lands beyond the mouth of Lycoming Creek. These settlers were ordered to leave in 1773. There were then about 40 "improvements" between Lycoming Creek and the Big Island (Lock Haven), where William Dunn, who said that he was paying rent to the Indians for his land, lived (Archives, VI. 570). During 1777 and 1778 a number of settlers were killed and scalped by the Indians along the creek (Consult: Archives, VI. 596, 599, 603; XII. 286; Meginness, Otzinachson, 239, 245, 247, 266). See *Lacomick, Lycamahoning*. There had evidently been an Iroquois, or Susquehanna village at the mouth of this creek before its occupation by Margaret Montour. The early maps give the name Ostonage, or Ostwagu, as the name of Lycoming Creek. This name may be derived from Ostenra, " a rock."

Lecamick.—Map of West. Penna., 1755, in Darlington's Gist. **Licoman.**—Potter (1778), Archives, VI. 599. **Licoming.**—Cook (1773), Archives, XII. 286. **Lycawmick.**—Scull, map, 1759. **Lycoming.**—Scull, map, 1770. **Ostonage.**—Evans, map, 1755. **Ostwagu.**—Evans, map, 1749.

MACHALOOSIN. See *Wyalusing*.

MACOPANACKAN. See *Chester Creek*.

MACUNGIE, MACUNGY. The name of a town in Lehigh County; also of two Townships, Upper and Lower Macungie in the same county. The village was formerly called Miller's Town (Howell's Map, 1792). The site of the present Emaus was formerly called Maguntsche, a corruption of the Indian name, as also is Macungie, Machkunschi, "feeding place of bears." The most frequently used form of the name is Macungy. The region drained by the Little Lehigh, now Lehigh Creek, was settled by the Germans before 1735. In that year an application was made for a road from "Macousie" to "New Cosshehoppa," and thence to Philadelphia. The name was evidently applied to the region in which these German settlements were made, about Emaus and the present Macungie. The Moravian missionaires labored in this settlement as early as 1742, when the field was occupied by Gottlieb Pezold. In 1761 the Moravian village within this region was established and named Emmaus, not Emaus as the name is now written. The Township of Macungie, or Macungy, was divided, in 1832, into Upper and Lower Macungie, or Macungy. The present town of Macungie was formerly called Miller's Town, or Millerstown, in honor of Peter Miller, who laid it out in 1776.

Maccongy.—Scull, map, 1759. **Maccoungo.**—Wetzel (1778), Archives, VI. 551. **Macousie.**—Pa. Council (1735), Colonial Records, III. 590 **Macungy.**—Howell, map, 1792, also Morris, map, 1848. **Maguntsche.**—DeSchweinitz, Life of Zeisberger, 65, 1870. **Maquenusie.**—Return of Road (1736), Colonial Records, III. 617.

MAGHINQUECHAHOCKING. The name of a former Indian village, destroyed by General Brodhead in 1779, which was situated "about 20 Miles above Venango (Franklin, Venango County) on French Creek, consisting of 35 large houses were likewise burnt." The Historical Map of Pennsylvania (1875) places this village on the upper Allegheny River.

The name seems to be a corruption of Mequachake, one of the clans of the Shawnee, and hackí, meaning "land of the Mequachake." The name is similar to several of the place names of the Shawnee in Ohio. It may be a c o r r u p t i o n of Meech-schinghacki "great level land," and have reference to the long stretch of level land along the Allegheny River, or along the upper waters of French Creek. The name is found in no other writer save Broadhead.

Maghinquechachooking.—Quoted in Albach, Western Annals, 305, 1858. **Mahusquechikoken.**—Brodhead (1779), Report of Exped., Archives, XII. 157. **Mehusquehicken.**—Historical Map of Penna., 1875.

MAGUCK. A name which does not belong in Pennsylvania, but which is frequently mentioned in the early Journals and records. The name of the level stretch of land known as Pickaway Plain, in Pickaway County, Ohio, about 3 miles south of Circleville. This region was occupied by the Shawnee, previous to their removal to the Cumberland River, Kentucky, and to the Potomac. This was evidently the home of the Shawnee, before their southern migration. The Iroquois said to the Shawnee chiefs, in 1732, "You Shawanese look back toward Ohio, the place from which you came, and return thitherward" (Archives, I. 329). The Shawnee returned to the Ohio, from the Potomac and Susquehanna, in 1727-1754, and from there went to the Sciota by permission of the Wyandot (N. Y. Doc. Col. Hist. IX. 1035), occupying the land which had previously belonged to their fathers. The name Maguck is probably a corruption of Mequachake, "red earth," which was the name of one of the Shawnee clans, and which, like the name of one of the other clans, or divisions, the Piqua, was given to places occupied by the people of the clan, or division. The same holds good concerning the two other divisions of the Shawnee, the Chillicothe and Assiwikale, who left the names Chillicothe and Sewickley. The name may be a shortening of the Delaware Maughwawame, meaning "great plains," as applied to other localities, such as Wyoming. The former origin, however, seems more in accordance with the facts of history. Christopher Gist visited the locality in 1751, when he mentions it in his Journal—"to the Maguck, a little

Delaware Town of about ten Families, by the N side of a plain or Clear Field, about 5 M in Length—2 M broad, with a Small Rising in the Middle" (Darlington, Gist, 42). Governor Sharpe mentions it in 1754—"not far from the Maguak" (Archives, II. 213). In 1758 George Croghan (wrongly stated in the Archives as Post), said that the Delawares had informed him that "the lower Shanoes (Shawnee) had remoov'd off the River up Sihotta (Sciota), to a great Plain Call'd Moguck, and had sent for those that live here (on the upper Ohio) to come there and live with them & quit the French" (Archives, III. 560). In 1759 Col. Mercer and George Croghan send a report concerning conditions at Fort Pitt to General Stanwix, who was then at Fort Bedford, that "Two Shawanese came here from Maguck (Colonial Records, VIII. 379, also repeated 395).

Maguck.—Croghan (1759), Col. Rec. VIII. 379. **Maguck Town.**—Gist (1751), Darlington, Gist, 42. **Meguck.**—Croghan (1759), Col. Rec., VIII. 395. **Moguck.**—Croghan (1758), Archives, III. 560. the **Maguak.**—Sharpe (1754), Archives, II. 213. the **Maguck.**—Gist (1751), Dar., Gist, 42.

MAHAKENSINK, MACKHACKA-MACK. A former Indian village, at the mouth of the present Neversink River, at the site of Port Jervis, N. J. The point of land between the Neversink and the Delaware was formerly called Mohockamack Fork. The present Neversink River was called Mackhackamack, or Mohocamac. The name of the village is probably a corruption of Mahack, or Mohawk, with the locative ing, meaning "place of the Mohawk." Mahack was a corrupt form of the name Mohawk. At the Council at Philadelphia in 1758, the village is mentioned, "The Senecas, whose chief is Tagee-iskatt-a, and lives at Mahakensink" (Colonial Records, VIII, 159). It is also mentioned in 1761, in the Deposition of Capt. James Hyndshaw, in the Connecticut settlement dispute,—"to a Tavern kept by Peter Kuykendale, on or near, the River Delaware, at Mackhackamack, in Sussex County, West New Jersey" (same ref. 612). The "old mine road" which was constructed by the early Dutch settlers of Esopus, now Kingston, on the Hudson River, to reach the copper mine in Walpack Township, Warren County, N. J., followed the Mamakating Valley, and continued in the Mahackamack branch of the Delaware. The mine was situated about three miles north-west of Nicholas DePui's house. Nicholas DePui, or Puy, or Depew settled in the region in 1725. (Consult; Delaware Water Gap, 235, 1870). The map of Lewis Evans, 1749, gives Mohocamac, as the name of the river. Howell, map, 1792, gives the form Mohocam Cr. Consult; Gen. Sull. Mil. Exped., 117, 214, 1887. See *Minisink*.

MAHANIAHY. See *Wyoming*.

MAHANOY, MAHONING, MAHONY. A name which is much used over the entire state, chiefly as a name of various creeks and runs, but also as a village and town name, with various compounds. Is a corruption of Mahoni, "a lick," and with the locative, ink, or ing, "at the lick," having reference to the "licks" which were frequented by deer, elk and other animals. The principal streams having the name are; the stream, now called Mahoning, which enters the Lehigh River from the south, opposite Weissport, Carbon County; the creek which enters the Susquehanna, from the east in Northumberland County, now called Mahanoy; the creek which enters the Allegheny River, from the east in Armstrong County, formerly called Mohulbucteetam (which see); the stream which enters the Beaver from the west, at Lawrence Junction, Lawrence County, called Mahoning River; the stream, now called Penns Creek which enters the Susquehanna, from the west, at Selinsgrove, was formerly called Big Mahonoy, or Mahony. There are several other s m a l l e r streams in various parts of the state, which have the same name, with various modifications. The name of the above streams are recorded as follows;
(1). Mahoning, on the Lehigh;

Mahoney.—Morris (1755), Archives, II. 526. **Mahoning.**—Scull, map, 1759; Evans, map, 1749; State map, 1912. **Mahonoy.**—Morris (1755), Archives, II. 520. **Mahony.**—Spangenberg (1758), Archives, III. 501.

(2). Mahoning, on the Susquehanna, from the east;

Cantaguy (Iroquois name).—Deed of 1749, Archives, II. 42. **Machanoy.**—Scull, map, 1770. **Maghonioy.**—Deed of 1749, Archives, II. 42. **Mahanoy.**—State map, 1912; Morris, map, 1848. **Mahonoy.**—Scull, map, 1759. **Mahony.**—Howell, map, 1792. **Mochany.**—Map of Deed of 1749.

(3). Mahoning, on the Susquehanna, west side;

Big Mahonoy.—Scull, map, 1759. **Mahanoy (or Penns Creek).**—Harris (1755), Colonial Records, VI. 645. **Mahonia.**—Terrence (1755), Colonial Records, VI. 648. **Mahoning.**—Hunter (1778), Archives, VI. 570. **Penns Creek.**—Scull, map, 1770. Morris, map, 1848 etc.

(4). Mahoning, on the Allegheny. See *Mohulbucteetam*.
(5). Mahoning, on the Beaver;

Mahoning.—Howell, map, 1792, and all later maps. **Mohoning.**—McCullough's Nar., Border Life, 100, 1839. **West Branch (of Beaver).**—Evans, map, 1755.

MAHONTANGO, MAHANTANGO. The name given to two creeks, one of which enters the Susquehanna from the east in Northumberland County, and the other which enters from the west, nearly opposite, on the line between Snyder and Juniata Counties. The latter stream is now called West Mahontango, and the former Mahontango. According to Heckewelder, the name is a corruption of Mohantango, "where we had plenty of meat to eat." The name given on the map of the Deed of 1749 (Archives II. 42), is Kind Creek. Scull's map of 1759 gives the name as, Mahatango, or Kind Creek. The Delaware word for "kind" is Gettemagelentin. On the traders map of Isaac Taylor, 1727, the name given for this creek is Quatoochatoon (or Quatooesiatoon). This is probably a corruption of the Iroquois name. On account of Shamokin being the chief Indian village on the Susquehanna, and because of the various trails leading along the river, the region along the eastern shore of the Susquehanna was travelled by many of the early Indian traders and the various missionaries who visited Shamokin. Count Zinzendorf passed along the river, on his way to Shamokin with Conrad Weiser, in 1742. He named the creek Benigna's Creek, in honor of his daughter (Memorials of the Moravian Church, 81, 1870). John Scull had a trading post above the mouth of the creek as early as 1725, which is noted on Taylor's map of 1727. Captain Thomas McKee, the well known trader, had a house about three miles above the mouth of the creek. The rapids in the river near this place are noted on several of the early maps, and mentioned in the Archives, as McKees Riffles (Archives, Third Ser. III. 412). "McKees" is noted on Scull's map, 1759, and "Mackees" on Evans map, 1755. This trading house stood near the present Georgetown. A trader named Welsh had a store just at the mouth of the creek. In 1748 Bishop Cammerhoff, when on his way to Shamokin, was obliged to turn back, in an attempt to reach McKees before night, and spend the night of Jan. 12th. at a house at the mouth of the creek, which he calls "Benigna's Creek." The next morning they reached "Thomas McKee's, the last white settlement on the river below Shamokin" (Cammerhoff's Journal, Penn. Mag. of Hist. XXIX, 168-169, 1905). Cammerhoff says that McKee's wife "who was brought up among the Indians, speaks but little English." McKee, who was then ill, requested that the Bishop baptize his child upon his return. After the commencement of Indian hostilities in 1755, Capt Thomas McKee was authorized to get such supplies as were needed for the defense of the settlers, at Fort Hunter, six miles above Harrisburg (Archives, II. 553 etc.). There has been much discussion as to the location of McKee's Fort. Some writers placing it on the western side of the river, but this is hardly possible. The direct line of communication between Fort Augusta and Fort Hunter would be on the eastern shore, where McKee had his trading house. There would be no reason for placing a fort on the western shore, out of touch with the two other forts (Consult: Frontier Forts, I. 621, etc.). There was a branch of the Indian trail which crossed the Susquehanna near McKee's and then connected with the trail leading to the Juniata from Shamokin. It joined the Juniata Trail near Mifflintown. In 1756 Governor Morris wrote, "On the west side of Sasquehana the forts are already ordered, one at a River Call'd Machitongo, about twelve miles from the Sasquehana, which I have call'd Pomfret Castle" (Archives, II. 556). This fort was situated at Richfield, although there has been much discussion as to its situation (Frontier Forts, I. 593 et seq.). Many writers have stated that Patterson's F o r t, a t Mexico, Juniata County, and Pomfret's Castle, were identical although Governor Morris stated that the fort on Mahantango was called by the latter name. Patterson's Fort was not on this stream. Apart from the few notices of this fort by Governor Morris, is that of Elisha Salter, who states, " on the 29th. of March (1756) Pomfret Castle was fir'd on by a party of Indians, who took one Hugh

Mitchettree prisoner" (Archives, II. 611). Governor Morris writes, April 8th., 1756, "Metcheltree, taken last week within sight of Patterson's fort, call'd to the Garrison, told them the Indians were but six in number, and desired to be rescued, but none went, he was carry'd off" (Archives, II. 617). The names of the two creeks are differently given on the various maps. The creek which enters the Susquehanna from the east;

Benigna's Creek.—Zinzendorf (1742), Mem. Mor. Church, 81. **Kind Creek.**—Map of Deed of 1749, in Archives, II. 42; also, Evans, map 1755. **Mahantango.**—Howell, map, 1792. **Mahatango, or Kind Cr.**—Scull, map, 1759. **Mohontongo.**—Board of Prop. (1795), Archives, Third Ser., III. 412. **Quatoochatoon.**—Taylor, Map, 1727.

The creek, on the west side of the river;

Mahantango.—Evans, map, 1755; Scull, map, 1770. **Mahatango.**—Scull, map, 1759. **Matchitongo.**—Morris (1756), Archives, II. 556.

Both creeks are now called Mahontango.

MAKERISK-KITTON. See *Delaware River.*

MAKOOMIHAY. See *Wyoming.*

MALSON. A former Shawnee village, mentioned by Sadowsky, an Indian trader, in 1728. Its location is difficult to make out. He mentions it, when writing of the Indians having hanged Timothy Higgins to a cabin pole, "at Sauanos, that is Malson" (Archives, I. 227). This is also mentioned as "the Shawanese town called Malson (Colonial Records, III. 330). It may have been situated on the West Branch, near Shamokin, it could have referred to Shamokin, as the same writer mentions that place as "Siamocon." Or, the town may have been one of the Shawnee villages in the region of Wyoming. No other mention of the place can be found.

MANADA. See *Monody.*

MANAHAN. According to Heckewelder this was the name of a branch of Yellow Breeches Creek, in York County, and is a corruption of Menehund, "where liquor had been drunk."

MANALTIN. Said to be corrupted from Menaltink, "where we drank liquor to excess." See the account of the killing of some Indians by Walter and John Winter, in 1728, in Archives, I. 215, 220, 224. Malanton.

MANATAWNY. A creek which rises in Berks County, enters the Schuylkill at Pottstown, Montgomery County. Heckewelder gives this as a corruption of Menhaltanink, "where we drank liquor." The road from Harris' Ferry ran through Reading, across Manatawny to Philadelphia. Governor John Evans, upon his return from the Council with the Indians at Pecquea and Conestoga, in 1707, returned by this route, remaining in Manatawny over night—possibly with Edward Farmer (Colonial Records, II. 390). In 1712 Governor Gookin received a letter from Mounce Jones, of Manatawny, saying that "four Indian Kings" were there and desired to meet him. On the 19th. of May, 1712, the Governor met these Indians at "White Marsh, at ye House of Edwd. ffarmer." Among the Indians present was "Sasunnan" (Sassounan), and eleven others. These Indians said that they were on their way to pay tribute to the Iroquois. They explained the meaning of the various belts, which they had with them (Colonial Records, II. 545-546). In 1728 there was much trouble caused between the settlers in the region and some Shawnee from Pechoquealin (Colonial Records, III. 305, 312, 324). The region about Manatawny Creek was settled before 1704 by Germans.

Mahanatawny.—Gordon (1728), Colonial Records, III. 305. **Manatawny.**—Pa. Council (1707), Col. Rec., II. 390; also all early maps. **Manahatay.**—Pa. Council (1728), Archives, I. 221. **Manatanny.** —Pa. Coun. (1712), Colonial Records, II. 545.

A station and a Post Office, besides the creek, perpetuate the name.

MANAYUNK, MANAIUNK. The name of the Schuylkill River, mentioned in the early Indian Deeds for lands along this river. Said by Heckewelder to be a corruption of Meneiunk, "where we go to drink." Mentioned in the Deeds for lands, to William Penn, 1683, as "Manaiunk, als Schuylkill" (Archives, I. 65). Also in the Deed of 1685, as "River Manaiunck or Skoolkill" (same ref. 92). See *Schuylkill.*

MANCKATAWANGUM. A former Indian village at the site of Barton, Tioga County, New York. Mentioned in a number of the Journals of Sullivan's expedition, 1779. The village may have been situated on the south side of the Susquehanna, opposite Barton. The name is a corruption of Machkachtawunge, meaning "red bank of a river." It is translated Red Bank in several of the Journals. Beatty's Journal mentions it as opposite "Fitzgeralds Farm" (Mil. Exped. Gen. Sull., 25, 1887). All of the Journals, which mention the place, speak of it as an old Indina village in ruins.

Mackatawando.—Campfield (1779), Jour. Mil. Exped. Gen. Sull., 55, 1887. **Macktowanuck.**—Norris, the same ref., 230. **Macktowanunk.**—Dearborn, ditto. 70. **Mauckatawangum, or Red Bank.**—Jenkins, ditto. 171. **Mawkuatowough (alias Red Brook).**—Fogg, ditto, 92. **Mawkuhtowonguh.**—Fogg, ditto, 93.

MANHATTAN. The name of a Post Office in Tioga County. The Indian name does not belong in this state. The name is derived from that of a tribe of the Wappinger, that occupied Manhattan Island, and the eastern shore of the Hudson River, called Manhattes etc. The name is said by Tooker to be derived from Manah, "an island," and Atin, "hill," meaning "the hill island." Heckewelder derives it from Manachachtanienk, meaning "the island where we all became intoxicated" (Heckewelder, Indian Nations, 77, 262, 1876). Some Delaware Indians said, "We called that island Manahatouh, "the place where timber is procured for bows and arrows." The word is compounded of N'manhumin, "I gather," and tanning, "at the place" (See Aboriginal Place Names in New York, 129, 1907). Consult; Tooker, Place Names on Long Island, 95. 1911.

MARCUS HOOK. The name of a prominent place in the early history of the settlement of the Delaware, at the site of Marcus Hook, Delaware County. The origin of the name has been variously given. Armstrong, in the note (page 135) in the Record of Upland Court, says, "As the designation Marcus Hook was earlier applied to the region than Marreties Hook, which latter is supposed to have its origin from 'Maarte', the name Marrettie and Marcus were doubtless distinct titles, and neither a corruption of the other." The author of this note thinks otherwise, for the following reasons; Hudde says, in 1648, "That I too should build there on which two of the principal sach-

ems, as Maarte-Hoock and Wisseme-
nets, planted with their own hands
the colors of the Prince of Orange,
and ordered that I should fire a gun
three times, as a mark that I had
taken possession" (Archives, Sec. Ser.,
V. 120). In 1650 Van Tienhoven said,
"Martin Gerritson's bay, or Martinne-
houck—the smallest stream runs up in
front of the Indian village called Mar-
tinnehouck, where they have their
plantations. This tribe is not strong
and consists of about thirty families"
(Archives, Sec. Ser., V. 320). The
small stream was the creek mentioned
in the Records of Upland, as marretties kil," now Chichester Creek, and
evidently was the home of Maarte-
Hoock. The present Marcus Hook is
mentioned a number of times in the
Record of Upland Court, as "marreties hook," or "marretties hoek"
(135 etc.). In 1662, Beekman says,
"They do not know that this land has
ever been the property of one Hans
Ammonsen, or his heirs, or that he
has carried on any farming on it,
but they have heard one Elias Hullen-
green say (after the arrival of Governor Rysingh) that his wife's father
had received by a rescript of Queen
Christina, a donation of a certain
piece of land situate between Mary-
ties Hoek and Upland kil" (Archives,
Sec. Ser., VII. 689). This land was
granted to Captain John Admunsen
Besk in 1683. This tract of land was
situated between Chichester and Chester Creeks. On the Lindstrom MS
map the "hook" is designated as,
"Furu udden, Le Cap des Pines," and
a l s o "Kackimensi, Memachitonna,"
and the creek as "Memanchitonna
and Marikes Kyl, Le Riviere de Marikes." In 1677 a census was made of
all of the taxable persons in the
Swedish settlements. There were then
living on "MARR:KILL" nineteen persons, among them was Jan Jansen,
who had made application for 100
acres on "oplonds kill" (Chester
Creek), after having sold his land on
"marretties kill" to Richard Noble
(Records of Upland Court, 73, 80).
In 1680 a census of the housekeepers at "Marquess Hook," and at
"Marquesse Kill," was taken. Among
those living at the former was Charles
Janses, and at the latter, John Hendrickson (Archives, Sec. Ser., VII.
808). In 1682 Governor Markham
allowed the inhabitants to change
the name of the place, Marcus Hook,
to Chichester, but its old name remained.

Consult; Archives, Sec. Ser., V.
(entire vol. concerning the Colonies on
the Delaware); VII. 459-820 (Dutch
and Swedish Settlements on the Delaware); XVI. (the entire vol. on the
Boundary Dispute with Maryland);
Records of the Court at Upland, from
1676-1681, 1860; Tooker, Place Names
on Long Island, 115-116, 1911.

MASGEEK-HANNE. According to
Heckewelder, the name given to the
stream which runs through the swamp
in Monroe County, "swamp stream."
The word for such a stream, according to Brinton, is "Maskehanne."
Zeisberger gives Mas-keek, as the
Delaware for swamp. This may have
reference to the present Red Run,
which was noted on the early maps
as Mud Run (Scull, 1770).

**MATINICUM, M A T I N I C U N K,
MATINICONK** etc. The name has
been applied to the islands below
Philadelphia, now known as Tinicum,
and also to the island, now known as
Burlington Island. This name was
applied by both the Dutch and the
Swedish writers to both of these
islands, as was also the name which
was the more commonly used of the
island below Philadelphia, Tinicum.
The name is probably a corruption of
Menatey, "island," with the locative
suffix, onk, ink, unk, meaning "at the
island." Tooker gives, "M'attinne-
auke-ut, "at the place of observation"
—but, this seems incorrect. The common name for island among the Delaware was Menatey, and some of the
earlier forms of the name (Matinicum,
Matineconk) are simply corrupted
from the original form. The island
near Burlington is mentioned in the
first deed to William Penn in 1682, as
Mattinicunk Island, and in the dispute with the government of West Jersey, in 1683 it is mentioned as "Matinicum" (Archives, I. 48, 58). The
Deed noted was executed at the house
of Lasse Cock, in Kensington, at the
site of the famous Treaty of Shackamaxon, when this Deed was probably
made. In the Records of Upland
Court, 1679, an action in trespass
was brought by Peter Jegou against
Thomas Wright and Godfrey Hancock,
in which he "declares that in ye
yeare 1668 hee obtayned a permit &
grant of Governor Philip Cartret, to
take up ye Land Called Leasy Point
Lying and being ouer agst. mattinag-

com Eyland & Burlington to settle himself there & to build and keep a house of Entertaynment for ye accomodation of Trauelors; He then goes on to state that he had held these lands and improvements, "until ye Yeare 1670; att wch. tyme yor Plt. was plundered by the Indians, & by them utterly Ruined as is wel knowne to a ye world" (141, Upland Records). On the Lindstrom MS map this island is noted as "Tinnekoncks Eyland, Ile de Tinnedonck." In 1711 it was surveyed "to Lewis Morris as agent of ye West Jersey Society," and by him called "Matoneconk Isles" (note, 141, Upland Court). On page 149 of the Court Records it is called "Tinnagcong Island." As all of the various names applied to this island are corruptions of the names applied to Tinicum, a complete list of synonyms will be found under *Tinicum*.

MATTAWANA. A corruption of the name of the creek in Duchess County, New York, Matteawan, meaning "good furs." Other meanings are "enchanted furs" and "enchanted skin." The name of a Post Office in Mifflin County. The name does not belong to the state.

MAUCH CHUNK. The name of the county-seat of Carbon County, also the name of a Township. The name is derived from Machk, "a bear," and Wach-tschu, " a hill, or mountain," Machk-tschunk, "at the bear mountain." The region about Maunch Chunk was not settled until about 1815. Previous to that time it was a wilderness. Mauch Chunk.—Morris, map, 1848.

M A U N Q U A Y, MIANAQUAUNK. The former name was applied to an Indian village at the mouth of the present Young Woman's Creek, in Clinton County. The Indian name of the creek was Mianaquaunk. The present North Bend occupies the site of the Indian village. Young Woman's Town, noted on Morris' map of 1848, was on the opposite side of the creek, which enters the West Branch of the Susquehanna from the north. The name may mean "place of meeting." One of the paths which led up to the West Branch to the Sinnemahoning evidently forked at the mouth of the creek, running north along the present Young Woman's Creek and connected with the trail up Pine Creek, and then over the divide to the waters of the Genesee, in Potter County.

Maunquay.—Scull, map, 1759. (May be a corruption of Minqua, the Susquehannas). **Young Woman's Town.**—Morris, map, 1848. **North Bend.**—State map 1911. **Mianaquaunk.**—Scull, map, 1770. **Young Woman's Creek.**—Howell, map, 1792.

MAXATAWNY. The name of a Post Office and Township in Berks County, with the spelling Maxatawny; also the name of a creek, a branch of Saucon Creek. The name is a corruption of, Machksit-hanne, "bear path stream." Zinzendorf preached at the house of Jacob DeLevan, in this Township, in 1742.

Maxatany.—Howell, map, 1792. **Maxetawny.**—Scull, map, 1759. **Maxitawny.**—Weiser, (1757), Archives, III. 218. **Maxatawny.**—Heckewelder. Place Names, 255.

MECHEEK-MENATEY. The Delaware name for the "Great Island," at Lock Haven. See *Big Island*. It was a resort for the Indians during historic times, and was no doubt a site of one of the villages of the Andastes (Conestoga), before they were driven southward by the Iroquois.

MEECH-HANNE. "The main stream," a name used by the Delaware, according to Heckewelder, for the main branch of the Lehigh River, as it was larger than either the Tobyhanna or the Tunk-hanna, the other sources of the Lehigh.

MEGGECKESJOUW. A former Indian village, mentioned by Beekman, in 1663. It was probably situated near the present Trenton, New Jersey (Archives, Sec. Ser. VII. 713). Meggeckessou. — Beekman (1659), Archives, Sec. Ser., VII. 581. Meggeckosjou.—same ref., 615. Machihachansio.—same ref., V. 149 (1649). Mageckqueshou.—Van Der Donck map, 1656.

MEHEAHOMING. See *Wyoming*.

MEHOOPANY, LITTLE MEHOOPANY. The first stream enters the Susquehanna from the south in Wyoming County, at North Mehoopany; the smaller stream enters just above it. The name was originally Hoppeny, from Hobbenisink, "place of wild potatoes." Howell's map, 1792, gives the form Hoppeny. Morris' map, 1848 gives Mehoopany. There was a settlement made near this point in 1775 by Amos York, who afterwards removed to Wyalusing. Elijah Phelps, finding the house vacant, moved in, without York's permission. Henry

Love settled near the mouth of Little Mehoopany in 1796. Zephaniah Lott settled near the mouth of Mehoopany (or Big Mehoopany) in 1791. The present name is probably a corruption of Meech-Hoopeny, with the meaning "Big Hoopany"— the common name of the stream. The Historical Map (1875) gives the name as, Mahcopany.

MENIOLOGAMEKA. A former Indian village in Eldred Township, Monroe County, eight miles south of Wind Gap, on the north bank of the Aquanshicola, at the intersection of the old Wilkes-Barre Road, which crosses the mountain at Smith's Gap. Heckewelder gives the meaning as, "a rich spot of land surrounded by barren lands." Heckewelder (Narrative, 37), states that the Moravian Missionaries visited this place by invitation of the Delawares, in 1747. Count Zinzendorf visited the village in 1742 (DeSchweinitz, Life of Zeisberger, 107). According to Loskiel the mission was established here by the Moravians, Cammerhoff and Seidel, in 1749. The chief of the place was "George Rex," who was soon after baptized at Bethlehem. The missionaries stationed at Gnadenheutten frequently visited the place. In 1751 the condition of the Moravian Indians in this village became filled with danger, as the white settlers were trying to drive them from the place. At the end of April 1754 the Christian Indians removed to Gnadenheutten (which see). Reichel gives the date of this removal as June, 1754. The removal was caused by Richard Peters, who owned the lands upon the Aquanshicola, upon which the village was situated. He had requested the removal of the Indians in 1750. See *Aquanshicola.* Consult; Loskiel, History of Missions, Part II. 25, 116, 130, 151; Reichel, Memorials of the Moravian Church, I. 30, 35, DeSchweinitz, Life of Zeisberger, 107.

MESHOPPEN, LITTLE MESHOPPEN. The name of two streams which enter the Susquehanna from the north, at Meshoppen, Wyoming County. The name is a corruption of Maschapi, "corals, or beads" with the locative, ing. Scull gives the name of this creek as Massape. Amaziah Cleveland was probably the first settler at the mouth of this creek, where he built a saw mill. Mason Alden, and others came soon after 1775, it is

said. All of the settlers left this region before 1779, when the army of General Sullivan passed through. The army crossed the creek at its mouth on Aug. 4th, and encamped a few miles beyond at Vanderlip's Plantation (near Black Walnut), and at Williamson's Plantation, about one mile beyond. Frederick Vanderlip, or Van der Lippe, and Williamson had both deserted their farms and had joined with the Tory and Indian troops, before Sullivan's advance. Norris says in his Journal, "we passed several places that were once the habitations of retirement and domestic peace, but now the solitary haunts of savages" (Sull. Exp. 228). Rodgers says in his Journal, "a creek, viz; Machapendaarre ran between the two encampments" (57). This creek is noted on Scull's map, 1770, as Machapendaawe. It is the small creek just below Black Walnut station. All of the Journals of Sullivan's expedition make mention of the encampment at Vanderlip's. The large walnut trees are mentioned by a number of the writers. Hubley says that some of the trees "were not less than 6 feet over, and excessive high" (Hubley's Journal, Dr. Jordan ed., II, 1909).

Mashaw.—Barton (1779), Journals MIL. EXPED. Gen. Sull., 5, 1887. **Massape.**—Scull, map, 1770. **Massappe.**—Hubley (1779), Hubley's Jour., Jordan, ed. 11, 1909. **Masshappen.**—Rogers (1779), Jour. Mil. Exped. Gen. Sull., 257. **Meshapon.**—Grant, same ref., 138. **Meshawmin.**—Roberts, same ref. 242. **Meshoking.**—Machin, same ref., 194. **Meshoping.**—Dearborn, same ref, 67. **Meshoppen.** — (Howell's map, 1792). **Meshopping.**—Norris, map. 228. **Moshoping.**—Lodge, map, 1779.

The present form is Meshoppen. Map of 1911.

MIANTONOMAH. The name of a mountain in Susquehanna County. A corruption of the name of the famous chief of the Narraganset, Miantonomo. Consult; Handbook of American Indians, Part 1, 855, 1907.

MILWAUKEE.. A station in Lackawana County. The name is a corruption of Milo, "good," and Aki, "land." The name of a former Indian village near the site of Milwaukee, Wis. Another meaning is given, "there is a good point," from Mine-wagi. Is not a historic name in this state.

MINGO BOTTOM. The name of the level on the Ohio River three miles below Steubenville, Ohio. So named because of the occupation of this beautiful spot by the Mingo Town, at the site of the present Mingo. This village in 1766 consisted of about 60 families. In 1770 General Washington stopped at the place, on his tour of the Ohio. It then consisted of 20 cabins and about 70 inhabitants. When Washington was there 60 Iroquois passed through on their way to the Catawba Country. The name Mingo was applied to all of the Iroquois, who lived on the Ohio, regardless of their tribe. It is a corruption of Mengwe, meaning "s t e a l t h y," or "treacherous," and was the name applied to the Iroquois by the Algonkian tribes. The Mingo Town was at the Ohio end of the trail to Will's Town. near Duncan Falls, Ohio. Pownall stated (1776) that it was 71 miles from Fort Pitt. Mingo is 70 miles, by the river from Pittsburgh. The village was also called Crow's Town. Col. David Williamson's gang of renegades crossed the Ohio River at this point, March 4, 1782, when on the way to murder the Indians at Gnadenhuetten (which see). They here divided their spoil after their return from their expedition of death. Strangly enough it was at this same place that the expedition of Col. William Crawford gathered on May 20, 1782, and elected Crawford as the commander, by a majority of five votes over Williamson, who had conducted the previous expedition. If ever a body of men were doomed for destruction it was the devoted band of 480 men whom Crawford led to the Muskingum. The massacre of Gnadenheutten had aroused the Indians of the Ohio region to a frenzy or rage, and justly so. The majority of the men in Crawford's Regiment were Scotch-Irish, from the Monongahela, Youghiogheny region who had first stolen the Indian land, driven them to the Ohio, and were now on the way to "blot out the heathen." Sad as was Crawford's death, it came when he was on an expedition to do to the Indian, just what the Indian did to him. Nothing but blood could satisfy the Virginia element in southwestern Pennsylvania, in all of their relations with the Indians. (Consult: Old Westmoreland, 162-169; Archives, Sec. Ser., XIV. 753-54; 690-727).

MINGO CREEK. The name of a creek which enters the Monongahela in Washington County; also a creek which enters the Schuylkill, in Philadelphia.

MINISINK. The name of the chief village of the Minsi, a branch of the Munsee clan of the Delawares, situated on the eastern side of the Delaware River a few miles south-east of Milford, nearly opposite Minisink Island, Pike County; also the name given to the lands on both sides of the Delaware River, north of the Water Gap, in Pennsylvania, New Jersey and New York. This region is frequently noted in the early writings as "the Minisinks." The name signifies, "the place of the Minsi." Min-ach-sin-ink signifies, "where the stones are gathered together,"—the name of the Munsee. It is possible that the name Minisink is a corruption of Menichink, which signifies "gathering," or "assembly," and may have reference to the village having been the meeting place of the Minsi, or of the entire clan of the Munsee. The Minsi are frequently confounded with the Munsee. The Munsee was the Wolf clan of the Delawares, and the Minsi was the Wolf clan of the Munsee. The Minsi living along the Hudson River became incorporated with the Wolf clan of the Mohawk, while the Minsi along the Delaware, in Pennsylvania and New Jersey, gradually moved westward to the Susquehanna and Ohio, after the Walking Purchase, of 1727, when their lands along the Delaware were sold. Because of the various land sales the Munsee became the most hostile of the clans of the Delawares towards the white settlers. They were the most warlike of any of the Delaware clans, and because of their relationship, as well as by natural characteristics, they were associated with the Shawnee, throughout the entire period of the history of the settlement of the Province. The Shawnee settled in the Minisink country about 1694, coming with Arnold Viele, the Dutch trader who had taken a band of Shawnee home to the Ohio in 1692. These "Far Indians" as they are called in the early records of the conference with Governor Fletcher, came to trade with the Europeans along the upper Delaware, and were taken home to the Ohio by Viele, who returned with a number of them in 1694. The Shawnee built a village, called Pechoquealin, on the east side of the Delaware, a few miles south of the mouth of Flat Brook Creek, Sussex County. Another village was situated on the west shore, near Shawnee, Monroe County. There evidently was another Shawnee village near the mouth of Pequea Creek, Warren County, New Jersey. (See *Pequea, Pequehan, Pechoquealin, S h a w n e e*). Vanderdonck's map, 1656, gives the names of four Minsi villages; Schichtewacki, Schepinaikonck, Meoechkonck, and Macharienkonck. Shapnack Island, twenty miles south of Port Jervis, no doubt was the site of Schepinaikonck, which name is preserved in that of the island. The first mention of the Minisink Indians in the Archives of Pennsylvania occurs in the letter of William Beekman, written at Altena (Chester, Pa.), April 28, 1660, in which he says, "Michael Karman came here a few days ago from above, where he had been trading with the savages and said, that eleven Minissingh savages had been killed by those of the Esopus, on which account these behave very hostilely and are inclined to go against the Dutch" (Archives, Sec. Ser. VII. 633). On June 17, 1660. Beekman again writes to Director Stuyvesant, "On the first inst. 7 canoes full of savages with women and children came down the river and proceeded to the Minquaes country (on the lower Susquehanna). It was said that they had lived near the Menissing Indians and had fled for fear of a certain Manitto" (same ref. 642). The trade with these Minisink Indians was carried on by the Dutch on the lower Delaware, as well as by the Dutch traders from Albany to Esopus. The route followed by the latter was over the "old mine road," which ran from Esopus (Kingston, N. Y.) following the valley north of the Shawangunk mountains, and its continuation in the Mackhackamack, or Neversink, valley to the copper mines in the Minisinks, east of the Delaware. This mine was worked by the Dutch at a very early day. It was situated about three miles northwest of the house of Nicholas Dupui (about 5 miles east of Stroudsburg), in Warren County, New Jersey. This old road was used by Nicholas Dupui and the other Dutch families in the region for carrying their farm products to Esopus and Albany. Nicholas Dupui (or DePui, or DePew) settled in the Minisink in about 1725. He bought the two large islands in the Delaware (Shawnee and Manwalamink), as well as the level land including the present Shawnee, in 1727, from the Indians. Various travellers passed through the Minisink region in the

early days, leaving the records in various ous Journals. Among these Journals may be mentioned that of Capt. Arent Schuyler, who visited the Minisink in 1694 (See Hanna, Wilderness Trail, I. 140-141) ; the Journal of Count Zinzendorf who passed through the Minisink in 1742 (See Memorials of the Moravian Church, I. 47-61). Soon after the coming of the white settlers to the region the Minsi commenced their migration westward to the Susquehanna, taking the trail which led to the headwaters of the Lackawanna, and then down that stream to the Susquehanna. At the Council at Conestoga in 1728 Governor Gordon was informed that the trouble at John Burt's house was committed by "one of the Menysincks who are of another Nation" (Col. Rec. III. 314), and at the Council at Philadelphia, later in the same year, he was informed "that the Menysineks live at the Forks of Sasquehannah above Meehayomy (Wyoming), & that their Kings name is Kindassowa" (same ref. 326). The "Forks of Sasquehannah" evidently refers to the junction of the Lackawanna and the Susquehanna, to which place the Minisinks mentioned had removed from the Delaware. The Shawnee from the villages on the Delaware and from the lower Susquehanna also removed to the region of Wyoming at about the same time. The Walking Purchase, of 1737, was the chief cause of this migration of the Minsi and other Delaware tribes from the Minisinks, which was included in the purchase. Many of the Delawares asked that permission be given them of living in this region, which their fathers had occupied for generations, but this was refused by the Provincial authorities, and at the Council at Philadelphia in 1742, Canassatego, the Iroquois, ordered the Delawares to remove at once to Wyoming or Shamokin (Col. Rec. IV. 579-580). The sale of these Minisink lands, by the Walking Purchase, and the driving of the Delawares to the Susquehanna marked the commencement of the hostility of this great group of tribes, which had always been friendly towards the Province (See Deed of Walking Purchase, Archives, I. 541-543). After 1742 nearly all of the Delawares had left the shores of the river where they had lived for many generations, and where they were first met by the Dutch, Swedish and English settlers.

Consult; Reichel, Memorials of the

Moravian Church, I. 46, 51, 58, 69; Heckewelder, Indian Nations, 52; Egle, History of Penna. 947, 1051; Broadhead, Delaware Water Gap, 215-272; Hanna, Wilderness Trail, I. 92 etc.; Colonial Records, III. 15, 326; IV. 513, 420, 446; V. 1, 470, 576 etc.; Archives, II. 97, 459, 532, 538, 746; III. 32, 34, 57, 67, 346, 420 etc.; Frontier Forts of Penna., I. 192, 277, 284-285, 300 etc.; Minisink Valley Historical Society, Bicentennial celebration of the settlement of the Minisink Valley, 1890.

Manessings.—Kregier (1663) in N. Y. Doc. Col. Hist. XIII. 339, 1881. **Menesincks.**—Pa. Coun. (1740), Col. Rec. IV. 413. **Menessink Indians.**—Weiser (1756) Archives III. 67. **Menissens.**—Beekman (1663) Archives, Sec. Ser. VII. 705. **Menissing.**—Beekman (1660) Archives, Sec. Ser. VII. 642. **Menysincks.**—Pa. Coun. (1728) Col. Rec. III. 314. **Menysineks.**—Pa. Coun. (1728) Col. Rec. III. 326. **Minesinks.**—Hawley (1756) Col. Rec. VII. 13. **Minisikk.**—Hamilton (1755) Archives, II. 538. **Minisincks.**—Pa. Coun. (1740) Col. Rec. IV. 447; also Swartwout (1662) in N. Y. Doc. Col. Hist. XIII. 229. **Minisink.**—Thomas (1745) Col. Rec. V. 2. **Minisink Tribe.**—Weiser (1756) Archives, III. 32. **Minisingh.**—Beekman (1660) Archives, Sec. Ser., VII. 633. **Minissinks.**—Weiser (1750) Col. Rec. V. 470. **Minnisinks.**—Parsons (1756) Archives II. 746. **Minnissing Town.**—Horsfield (1755) Archives II 459. **Minusing.**—Proud, Pa., II. 320, 1798. **Monnesick.**—A d d a m (1653), in Drake Bk. Inds., bk. 2, 79, 1848.

MINNEQUA. A town in Bradford County. A recently applied name, which is made up of Indian sounds, rather than words. It is said to mean "to drink." The Delaware word for "to drink" is Menen, and "to drink with each other," Menachtin. It may be a corruption of one of these words, but such is doubtful.

MINOOKA. A town in Lackawanna County. The name does not belong in the region. There is a town of the same name in Grundy County, Illinois. The name seems to be a corruption of Mino, "good" and Aki, "land."

MINQUAS CREEK. The early name of the present White Clay and Christiana Creek, the former of which rises in Chester County. The main stream enters the Delaware below Wilmington, Del. It was called Minquas Kil by the Dutch; Christina Creek, in honor of the child Queen Christina of Sweden; th English corrupted the name to Christiana. The Indian name of the stream was Suppeckongh or Supeskongh; also Sittoensaene, by various

early Dutch writers. The Swedes, under Peter Minuit, landed on the Delaware in April 1638 and purchased the lands on the western side of the river, from the mouth of Minquas Creek to the Falls, at Trenton, from the Indian occupants. Near the mouth of the creek they erected a fort, called Fort Christina (not Christiana, as frequently written), in honor of the Queen of Sweden, who was a daughter of Gustavus Adolphus (Consult; Bancroft, History of U. S., I. 503, 1880). The Swedes called the creek, upon their arrival, Minquas Kil, because it was one of the main trails from the land of the Minquas, or Susquehannas (Conestogas), on the lower Susquehanna River. The villages of this famous Iroquoian tribe were spread along the Susquehanna River to the mouth of Octorara Creek. The trails by which they reached the lower Delaware ran up Octorara and Pequea and Conestoga Creeks, and then across to the creeks running into the Delaware. At the time of the Swedish occupation of the Delaware these Minquas reached the settlement at Christina by way of Octorara and Pequea Creeks from where they then had villages on the Susquehanna. Andreas Hudde says, in 1645, "Further up the river about three miles, on the west shore, on a creek called the Minquas Creek, so named as it runs near the Minquas land, in another fort named Christina" (Archives, Sec. Ser., V. 110). In 1651, Stuyvesant, the Dutch Governor, built a fort near the present New Castle, which was named Fort Casimir. At various times in July, 1651, Stuyvesant purchased various tracts of land along the Delaware, including the lands previously claimed by Minuit. On July 9, 1651, he purchased a tract on the west side of the river "from the west point of the Minquaas Kill, where Fort Christina stands, called in their language Supeskongh, unto Boompgens hook (Bombay Hook), in their language called Neuwsings" (Archives, Sec. Ser., V. 265). On July 30, 1651, he also purchased from the Indians, who said that they had never sold the lands to the Swedes, the land "on the west shore beginning at a certain little Kill, named Neckatoesingh, extending westward from the river unto Sittoensaene otherwise called Minquaas Kill, where fort Christina stands" (Archives, Sec. Ser. V. 261). The Indian chief who claimed the right to sell these lands was named Wappingzewan, a Delaware. The various conflicts between the Dutch and the Swedes for the possession of the river, and the rich trade with the Minquas, ended in the final overthrow of the Swedish fort, Christina, by Stuyvesant, September 11, 1655 (See *Tinicum*. Consult ; Egle, Hist. Pa., 30 et seq., 1883 ; Bancroft, Hist. U. S., I. 500 et seq., 1888 ; Scribner, Hist. U. S., II. 150 et seq., 1897 ; Acrelius, New Sweden, or Swedish Set. on Del., N. Y. Hist. Soc. Col. (N. S.) II. ; Hist. Soc. Pa., Memoirs, III, 1834 ; Records of the Court at Upland, Introduction (pages 11-33), 1860 ; Archives of Pa., Sec. Ser., V. (entire vol.) ; VII. 458-820).

Christeen Creek.—Evans, map, 1749. **Christiana Creek.**—Scull, map, 1759. **Christina Creek.**—Stuyvesany (1657), Archives Sec. Ser., VII. 501. Lindstrom maps. **Mingas Creek.**—Dutch. Rec. (1648), Archives, Sec. Ser., XVI. 237. **Minquaas Kill.**—VanRuyven (1651), Archives, Sec. Ser., V. 261. **Minquas Creek.** —Hudde (1648), Archives, Sec. Ser., V. 110. **Minquas Kill.**—Schelluyne (1649), Archives, Sec. Ser., V. 148. **Settoen soene.**—Dutch Rec. (1656), Archives, Sec. Ser., V. 253. **Sittoensaene.**—VanRuyven (1651), Archives, Sec. Ser., V. 261. **Supeskongh.**—Deed of 1651, Archives, Sec. Ser., V. 265. **Suppeckongh.** —Deed of 1651, Archives, Sec. Ser. V. 266.

MITCHELL'S SLEEPING PLACE. One of the points on the trail from Harris' Ferry (Harrisburg) to the Ohio. Mentioned by John Harris (Archives, II. 135), "t o T h o s. Mitchell's Sleepg. place 3 miles" (from Tuscarora Hill). Thomas Mitchell was an Indian trader, who gave his name to the place where he used some sort of a shelter for staying over night. The trail ran from Andrew Montours, near Landisburg, Perry County, to Tuscarora Hill, near Fort Robinson, and then on to Liberty Valley, where this sleeping place was situated, on what is known as the old "Meninger farm," three miles beyond the present Centre Post Office, Perry County. During the period of Indian hostility after 1755 the settlers in the valley along Shearman's Creek were frequently attacked by the bands of Indians, which came over the trails from the Ohio. In July 1756 a party of these Indians made an attack upon Robinson's Fort, killing several and taking captive Hugh Gibson and Betsey Henry. Robert Robinson was also taken captive during the same summer. His narrative is given in Frontier Forts, I. 613-616.

MOHOCAMAC, also MACKHACK-

AMACK. The former name of the present Neversink River, which enters the Delaware from the east at Port Jervis, near which place formerly stood a village called Mahackensink, or Mackhackamack (See *Mahackensink*). The name is a corruption of Mohawk, with the locative ing. The region along the river was the route of the "old mine road" (See *Minisink*), which was the course followed by one of the divisions of Sullivan's army to the camp at Easton, in 1779 (See Hardenbergh, Journal, Sull. exped. 117).

This route was followed by Arnold Viele, from Albany, in 1692 and 1694, and by Capt. Arent Schuyler in 1694 (See Schuyler's Journal, Hanna, Wilderness Trail, I. 140). The name Mackhackamack was evidently first applied to the Indian village at the mouth of the Neversink River (See *Neversink*). This village was the point to which the Commissioners of Pennsylvania, New York and New Jersey ran the boundary line in 1719, supposing that this point was near the Latitude of 41 degrees 40 minutes. It was discovered that Mackhackamack was 17 miles south of this point, which was found at Cashietunk (Cochecton), 37 miles above Mackhackamack on the Delaware River. The line was drawn from Mackhackamack to the Hudson River. Port Jervis is near the point where this line between New York and New Jersey strikes the Delaware River (Archives, Sec. Ser., XIX. 660-661). In the report of the Commissioners Mackhackamack is mentioned as "a Dutch Town on the East Side of Delaware River." The name may signify, "fishing place of the Mohawks."

Haurnanack.—H a r d e n b e r g h (1779), Jour. Sull. Exped., 117. **Mackhackamack.** —Taylor (1719), Archives, Sec. Ser., XIX. 660. **Mackhackemack.**—Reichel, in Mem. Mor. Church, 45. **Maggaghkamieck.**—Schuyler (1694), in Hanna, I. 140. **Mahackamack.**—Note in Jour. Sull. Exped., 117. **Mahakemack.**—VanCampen (1779), Archives, VII. 603. **Mohocamac.** —Evans, maps, 1749, 1755. **Mohocam.**— Howell, map, 1792. **Mohochomack.**—Adlum, map, 1790.

MOHOCKS BRANCH OF DELAWARE. The former name of the present West Branch of the Delaware, the Popacton Branch being the East Branch. Called M o h a w k's Branch because it was the chief stream by which the Mohawk reached the Delaware River. The name Mohawk is derived from Mahowauuck, "they eat (animate) things," hence "man eaters." Their name for themselves was Kaniengehaga, "people of the place of flint." According to Heckewelder the Delawares called them Sankhicani, from Sankhican, a gun lock. The name was given because the Mohawks were the first to use muskets, among the Indians. The name has the significance, "fire striking people."

Among the Iroquois, the Mohawk belong to the "Three Elder Brothers," the Seneca and Onondaga being the other two. The Mohawk carried on a warfare with the Abnaki, the Algonkin and the Susquehanna. They had many ups and downs in these conflicts until about 1614 when they were furnished with firearms by the Dutch, when they at once began to gain a position of power over all of their enemies. The early use of firearms gave the Mohawk and the other Iroquois tribes an advantage over the Delaware and other tribes to the southward—even as far westward as the Mississippi. The Dutch along the Delaware were brought into trade relations with the Mohawk soon after their settlement at Fort Christina. The Mohawk on the east and the Seneca on the west of the Iroquois country were the most warlike, and most active in the various efforts against the white settlers in the Province. Consult; Handbook of American Indians, I. 921-924; Bancroft, Hist. U. S., I. 583; Archives, Sec. Ser., V. 101 etc. There were evidently several Mohawk villages along the Delaware just above the Minisink region. Mackhackamack, at the site of Port Jervis, was probably one of the early villages of the Mohawk in the region south of the historic Mohawk habitat.

Mohawks Branch.—Pownall, map, 1776. **Mohock branch of Delaware.**—Scull, map, 1770. **Mohocks Branch.**—Evans, map, 1755. **Mohocks Br.**—Carey, map, 1801.

MOHULBUCTEETAM. The former name of the present Mahoning Creek, which enters the Allegheny River from the east in Armstrong County. The name is a corruption of Mochoolpakiton, "where canoes are abandoned." A-mo-chool, "a canoe," Paki-ton, "to throw away." The creek is noted on all of the early maps by this Indian name. A few miles below the mouth of the creek, at the

site of the present Templeton, on the flat, level land, Howell notes Mahoning Town, map of 1792. This was the site of a Delaware village for a few years before the white settlement of the region. Brodhead mentions "a place called Mahoning, about 15 Miles above Fort Armstrong" (Kittanning), in his letter to Washington in 1779 (Archives, XII. 155). The creek was given this name in later documents and maps, although Howell's map of 1792 gives the Indian name for the creek.

Mochulbuch Riturn.—Pownall, map, 1776. **Mochulbuckiklum.**—Evans, map, 1775. **Moghulbuchtitum.**—Scull, map, 1770. **Mochulbuchtetum, or Stump Creek.**—Board of Prop. (1783), Archives, Third Ser. I. 434. **Mogwolbughtitum.**—Irvine (1786), Archives, XI. 520. **Mohulbucktitem.**—Adlum, map, 1790. **Mohulbucktitum.**—Howell, map, 1792. **Mohulbucteetam.**—Heckewelder, in Ind. Names, 256, 1872.

The name "Stump Creek," noted above, may suggest a different origin than that given by Heckewelder. Tschachgachtin, is the Delaware for "stump." With the word Mechek, "big," as a prefix, the compound would signify "big stump." The former origin however seems the correct one.

MOKOMA. The name of a Lake and village in Sullivan County. The origin of the name cannot be discovered. It is of recent origin in the locality.

MONCANAQUA. The name of a village in Luzerne County. Cannot discover origin. The name is not historic in the region.

MONOCASY. The name of a creek which enters the Lehigh from the north at Bethlehem, Northampton County. A corruption of Menagassi, or Menakessi, meaning "a stream with several large bends," according to Heckewelder. Reichel says in a note (Ind. Names, 256) that Menagachsink was the name given to the site of Bethlehem by the Delawares.

Manakisy.—Scull, map, 1759 and 1770. **Manookisy.**—Morris, map, 1848. **Monacasy.**—Evans, map, 1749. **Monocasy.**—Recent maps, State map 1911.

MONOCKONOCK. The name of an island in the Susquehanna River, near the present Wilkes-Barre. It was the scene of a part of the massacre of Wyoming, July 1778. The name is probably a corruption of Menachhenonk, meaning "at the island," or "island place." Consult; Egle, Hist. Pa., 904. See *Wyoming*.

Manaughanung Island. Map of Abrahams Plains, Archives, Third Ser. IV. Map No. 77.

MONODY. The present Manada Creek, a branch of the Swatara Creek, in Dauphin County. Heckewelder says that the name is a corruption of Menatey, "an island." The cut in the Kittatinny Mountains, through which the creek flows, is called Manada Gap. The region along Swatara Creek and its branches was settled by the Scotch-Irish, who came in great numbers to the region of Paxtang in 1720-1735. The "Old Hanover Church," or "Monnoday Church" as it was called, was established about 1735, on Manada Creek, about eleven miles from the present Harrisburg. Owing to the Indian hostility after Braddock's defeat in 1755 the settlements along Swatara and Manada Creeks were frequently invaded by parties of Indians. In order to protect the settlements a number of stockade forts were erected along the Kittatinny Mountains. Manada Fort was erected on Manada Creek, near Manada Gap. Besides this one Brown's Fort, Fort Swatara, Fort at Harper's and Robinson's Fort were also erected in the region drained by Swatara Creek. Many persons were killed, or captured by the Indians during 1756-1757 (Consult; Frontier Forts of Pa., I. 26 et seq.). The The Manada Gap and Tolihaio, or the "Hole," the Gap now known as Swatara Gap were the doorways through the Kittatinny Mountains, by which the Indians could reach the settlements from the Susquehanna River and its West Branch. The trail through latter Gap was probably the course which was taken by Count Zinzendorf and Conrad Weiser to Shamokin in 1742. (See *Swatara, Quitopahilla, Tolheo*).

MANADA. Recent maps. Present form. Also perpetuated in Manada Hill, Manadaville, Dauphin County.

Manady.—Morris, map, 1848. **Manity.**—Weiser (1756), Archives. **Mannadys.**—Patterson (1757), Archives, III. 331. **Monaday.**—Bussee (1756), Archives, II. 552. **Monady.**—Galbreath (1756), Archives, II. 740. **Monaidy.**—Pa. Coun. (1757), Col, Rec. VII. 706. **Monday.**—Scull, map, 1770, 1759. **Monody.**—Howell, map, 1792.

MONONGAHELA. The name of the river which unites with the Allegheny

River at Pittsburgh, to form the Ohio. Corrupted from Menaungehilla, "high banks, breaking off and falling down at places." Various writers have stated that this name is not correctly translated, as the river does not have "falling in banks." The very opposite statement is correct. The large deposits of clay, under the shale and sandstone, at the river surface, was washed by the water until the clay was carried away and the bank then fell. The writer can remember how the waters of the Monongahela, during flood stage, could be clearly traced for a number of miles below the union with the Allegheny, because of the heavy deposits of red and yellow clay which the waters of the former stream contained. This falling in of the banks of the Monongahela has ceased to a great extent since the river banks have been covered with the slag from the steel mills, and the improvement of the river front, but in the early days this "falling in" of the banks was a marked feature of the river. L. E. Flint, in his article on the Monongahela River (Historical Magazine, Monongahela Old Home Association, 1908), says, "The widening of the stream is without doubt due to the wave action of steamers undermining the clay banks, causing them to cave in. In the lower reaches of the river the caving of the banks has practically ceased, many miles of the shore being now prevented from further erosion by the almost vertical walls of slag or other protection" (208). Mr. Flint was not giving the reason for the river having such a name, but was simply explaining, from an engineer's point of view, the various changes in the river, and in its channel. Darlington says (Gist's Journal, 141), "The correctness of these definitions is doubtful, the banks of this river do not 'fall in' or 'break off' more than those of the Ohio, Allegheny, and many other streams, nor is it known that they ever did, and the Indians invariably gave accurate descriptive names." Mr. Darlington made a mistake in this statement. The river banks did "fall in," for the reasons stated, until the banks were protected within recent times. A more accurate, descriptive name could not have been given. Its "falling in banks" was the one thing which made the Monongahela entirely different from the Allegheny and the

Youghiogheny. The waters of these latter streams was clear, because of the geological formation of the region through which they passed, while the Monongahela River was nearly always muddy because of the clay banks being washed into its water almost continually. The clay deposits along the upper waters of this stream at Greensboro and other places, constitutes one of the distinctive geological features of the formation along this stream. The river was one of the paths followed by the Tallegewi (Allagewi, after whom the Allegheny was named. See *Allegheny*), as they were driven southward by the Iroquois (See Problem of the Ohio Mounds, by Cyrus Thomas, 38 et seq., 1889). The various earthen mounds, called forts, which were scattered along the northern shore of the Monongahela, at Redstone "Old Fort" (Brownsville), and at the mouth of Little Redstone Creek, and other places, were probably made by the Tallegewi, who were the ancestors of the Cherokee. The warfare which was carried on by the Iroquois against these southern Indians, according to the statement of various Iroquois chiefs, had existed "since the world began" (See *Cherokee*). The various mounds along the Youghiogheny were also probably the work of the same tribe. The Cherokee and the Shawnee were both builders of these earthen mounds, even within historic times. If these Monongahela and Youghiogheny "Indian forts" were not made by the Tallegewi (as well as the mounds at McKees Rocks), then they must have been built by the Shawnee as they migrated from the lower Ohio and Cumberland Rivers to the south. The trail from the present Brownsville, which was known as Nemacolin's Trail, may have been one of the earliest routes of the Shawnee, as they passed from the Ohio to the Potomac, before the commencement of the period when the Shawnee moved northward from the Potomac to the Susquehanna, and then back to their original habitat in Ohio, upon the Pickaway Plains. The region in which these mounds are found was not occupied by any Indian villages within historic times, but was traversed by trails running southward into the Carolinas, from the Iroquois Country in New York, and by various trails running between the Potomac and Ohio. Various of these

"Indian Forts" are noted on Scull's Map of 1770 (Consult; Thomas. Problem of the Ohio Mounds. 1889; Ellis, History of Fayette County, 19-22; Veech, Monongahela of Old, and notes in Atlas of Fayette County, 1872).

It is not possible to give more than a mere outline of the various events which have made the Monongahela one of the most historic rivers on the continent. The river did not come into historic prominence until the commencement of the struggle for the possession of the Ohio by France and Great Britain, as nearly all of the early trading trails between the Susquehanna and the Ohio ran north of this river, by way of the various tributaries of the Allegheny. The chief southern trail being the one which ran from Bedford to Kittanning and Shannopin's Town. The region south of this line of travel, in the present state of Pennsylvania, was an unexplored wilderness until Christopher Gist passed through it in 1750-51 for the Ohio Company. After that time it became the scene of the most important events in the history of western Pennsylvania. Before Gist's trip of exploration the history of the entire region is purely mythical. Nothing whatever is known concerning what the Red travellers through it did. Various legends are told of great battles between the Indians, along the mountain ridges of Fayette and Westmoreland, and the great quantities of flint arrow heads, Indian graves, and earthen mounds give evidence upon which to base such traditions. But, no priest or explorer left any record of any events which took place in this region south of the Allegheny River. Conrad Weiser was the first official visitor of the white race to the Indians on the Ohio. His mission in 1748 was the first throwing open of the doors of actual history on the Ohio, in Pennsylvania. The Ohio Company was organized in 1748 by John Hanbury, of London, Thomas Lee, President of the Council of Virginia, and a number of others. The King granted them 200,000 acres of land on the south side of the Ohio River, upon condition that they should settle 100 families and build a fort upon this land, within seven years. When the Company should fulfill these conditions, it would receive 300,000 acres more land, joining the first grant. The Company then erected a store house opposite the mouth of Will's Creek, at the site of the present Cumberland, Md., and sent to England for a cargo of goods. In 1750 Christopher Gist was sent by the Company to explore the region west of the mountains. He set out on this journey, from Thomas Cresap's, at Old Town, Md., October 31, 1850, going northward over the Warriors Path to Bloody Run (Everett), east of the present Bedford, where he struck the trail called the Allegheny Path, which led westward to Shannopin's Town, by way of Ligonier. He explored the entire region along the Ohio to the Kanhawha River, returning to his home on the Yadkin River, by an overland route from the Ohio. In 1751 he was again sent by the Ohio Company to discover and mark the most direct route from the Company store on Will's Creek to the Monongahela. He set out from the Company Store at Will's Creek on November 4, 1751, going over the trail which was surveyed the next year by Gist, Cresap and Nemacolin. He reached the mouth of Dunlap's Creek on December 9th., where he met Nemacolin (Nemicotton), who was then living about 7 miles from the present Brownsville on Nemacolin's Creek (Dunlap's Creek). Here he crossed the Monongahela River and went on southward (See Darlington's Gist, 1893). Gist returned to Will's Creek on March 29, 1752. While the general course of the route followed by Gist at this time was somewhat to the north of that which he, Cresap and Nemacolin opened in 1752-53, yet its general direction was about the same. The Trial, known as "Nemacolin's Trail, ran from Will's Creek to the mouth of Dunlap's Creek. This was the course followed by Washington and Gist in 1753, as far as Gist's Plantation (Mount Braddock), where they struck the Catawba Trail running to Stewart's Crossing (Connellsville), and then by way of Mount Pleasant, Hunkers etc. to the mouth of Turtle Creek. This course was that which was taken by Braddock in 1755, and also by Washington as far as the Great Meadows and Gist's Plantation in 1754. In 1753 Gist went with Washington to Venango and LeBoeuf, to warn the French troops from the region. The course followed was the same as noted, via Gist's Plantation, where a new settlement had been made upon the tract of land which Gist had received from the Ohio Company. This settlement, at the present Mount Braddock, Fayette County, was without doubt the first white settlement in western Pennsylvania, beyond the mountains. Washington and Gist left Will's Creek on November 14, 1753, and returned on Jan. 6th. 1754. In February 1754 Captain William Trent built a Store House, or Hangard, near the mouth of Redstone Creek, and then went on to the Forks of the Ohio where work was commenced on the fort which the Ohio Company intended to build to protect its trade on the Ohio. The Store House at Redstone was to be a branch of the Store House at Will's Creek. From Redstone the goods were to be taken by water to the Ohio, where other store houses would have no doubt been built—had plans carried out. It must be borne in mind that this whole enterprise of taking possession of the Ohio was a business proposition, and not a purely patriotic one. The Ohio Company was a business enterprise, and the Store House at Redstone and the fort at the present Pittsburgh were simply means for carrying out the plan of a lot of business men, who were associated in a money making scheme. While Trent was back at Will's Creek, the French army under Contracoeur descended the Allegheny River and demanded that Ensign Edward Ward surrender the fort which was only beginning to exist. Resistance was impossible, and on April 17, Ward surrendered the fort and returned to Will's Creek, by way of Redstone. Thus the French occupation of the Ohio took the merely business proposition of the Virginians, associated in the Ohio Company, out of the domain of merely personal affairs and made of it an issue which was to ultimately drench the world in blood. The King, in Council, decided that the valley of the Ohio was within the domain of the Colony of Virginia, and that the encroachments of the French should be resisted by force of arms. The very active Governor of Virginia, Dinwiddie, at once took steps to drive the French from the Ohio. George Washington, who had been over the region in 1753, was commissioned a Major, and then a Lieutenant-Colonel. Colonel Joshua Fry, who was to command the expedition did not assume command, on account of ill health, so the command fell upon Washington. The engagement with Jumonville, on May 28, 1754, which "set the world on fire"; the surrender to the French commander, Coulon deVillers on July 4; the retreat to Will's Creek are matters of general knowledge (Consult; Frontier Forts, II. 3 et. seq.; Loudermilk, History of Cumberland, Maryland, 1878; Bancroft, Parkman, Scribner. Sparks under title, Washington, Fort Necessity, French on the Ohio).

Washington's defeat at Fort Necessity left the French in absolute control of the entire Ohio and Mississippi valleys. No other flag floated over the entire region west of the mountains. DeVillers destroyed all of the English settlements at Gist's, Stewart's Crossing, and at Redstone destroyed the Store House of the Ohio Company (Consult; Archives, Sec. Ser. VI. 168 et seq.) The Expedition of General Edward Braddock against Fort Duquesne, which had been erected at the "Forks of the Ohio" was the next historic event which made this region memorable. The army passed over the trail from Fort Cumberland, on Will's Creek, near where the Ohio Company Store House had stood, to Gist's Plantation, which was reached on June 27, 1755. From this point Braddock followed the Catawba Trail, which crossed the Youghiogheny River at Connellsville. The Monongahela was crossed below the mouth of Crooked Run, on July 9th, and then recrossed just below the mouth of Turtle Creek. Here, near where John Fraser's trading house stood, was fought the memorable "Battle of Monongahela," at the site of the present Braddock, in which Braddock's army was almost blotted out. Braddock, who was wounded, was carried back to Gist's Plantation, which was reached on July 10, at 10 o'clock at night. The next day the remnant of the army retreated to Dunbar's Camp, and then to camp near the Great Meadows, where Braddock died on July 13th, and was buried near the spot where the present Braddock Park is situated. Washington read the burial service (Consult; Sargent History of Braddock's Expedition, 1855; Loudermilk, History of Cumberland, 1878; Archives of Pa., II. 203, 288, 290 etc.; Col. Rec. Pa., VI. 200, 280, 294 etc.) Many of the scenes of the Whisky Insurrection of 1794 occurred along the Monongahela River (Consult; Brackenridge, History of the western insurrection in western Penna., 1859; Crumrine, History of Washington County, 262-306, 1882; Findley History of the insurrection etc., 1796; Archives of Pa., Sec. Ser., IV. 1876). For general reference, consult; Bancroft, Life of Washington, I. 12-39, 1826; Chapman, French in the

Allegheny Valley, 30-59, 1887; Craig, History of Pittsburgh, 21 et seq., 1851; Parkman, Conspiracy of Pontiac, I. 102-105, 1897; Parkman, Montcalm and Wolfe, I. 133-167, II. 339-346, III. 268-270, 1894-98; Sparks, Life of Washington, 30-63, 83-94, etc., (abridged ed.); Hulbert, Braddocks Road, 1903. There has been much discussion as to the first settlement of the white race in the region west of the mountains. It has been stated that some of the French traders, who came into the region along the Monongahela before the coming of the English, married Indian women and lived at various places—the mouth of Georges Creek is mentioned as one such place. But, while this may be true, there is no record of any such settlement, either in the Archives of Pennsylvania or in any of the French documents. Wherever French or Canadian settlers went, the French priest went with them. None of the Jesuit Relations make mention of any settlement in this region. The first actual written record which is found in the French documents is that of Celeron DeBienville, and his Chaplain and cartographer, Father Bonnecamp, and neither of these make mention of any French settlement on the Monongahela in 1749. Bonnecamp does not even note the name of the river on his map. The first actual settlement was that of Christopher Gist, at the site of the present Mount Braddock, Fayette County. Gist selected the land, the most level and best adapted for farming in the region, when on his trip of exploration in 1751-52, but possibly did not make any settlement until the spring of 1753. Washington makes mention of this "new settlement" in his Journal of 1753. Upon his return from this trip Washington reached Gist's on Jan. 1, 1754, where he bought a horse and saddle, and on his return to Will's Creek, a few days later, he met "some families going out to settle" (Consult; Washington's Journal of 1753, Olden Time, I. 12-26, 1846). That Gist had made this settlement before the fall of 1753 is evident. Veech, in Monongahela of Old, makes Wendell Brown and his two sons, who settled first on Proviance's Bottom, in 1751-52, the first settlers in the region. And says that the Brown's supplied corn and beef to Washington's army when it was encamped at the Great Meadows. But, this is mere tradition. There is no evidence whatever that the Brown's were living in this region, which was an uninhabited wilderness in 1751-52, and it surely is not possible that a frontiersman, living at such a far distant point could have had corn and beef enough to help supply an army. Gist's exploration of the region in 1751-52 was the first notice of the wilderness beyond the mountains in southwestern Pennsylvania. The Brown's probably settled soon after Gist's settlers went out, but most certainly they did not go before that time. The only other settlement which was made at the time of Washington's defeat at Fort Necessity was that of William Stewart, at Stewart's Crossings (Connellsville), which, according to his sworn statement, was made in 1753 (Ellis, History of Fayette County, 57). All of the settlers at Gist's and Stewart's Crossing and any other places in the region, went back to Will's Creek after Washington's defeat at Fort Necessity, July 4, 1754. The French army on its return to Fort Duquesne, destroyed all of these settlements (Archives, Sec. Ser., VI. 168). After the British occupation of Fort Duquesne, 1758, a number of the settlers returned to the region, and others came in. As these lands had not then been purchased from the Indians, this invasion of white settlers caused much trouble. They were warned again and again to leave the region, but persisted in staying until the Indian hostility of Pontiac's Conspiracy, when they became terrified and left their settlements. After 1765 they again returned in large numbers, settling at the mouth of Dunlap's Creek, Turkey Foot, Stewart's Crossing, Gist's Plantation, along the Cheat River, and in other places. Most of these settlers were from Virginia and Maryland, and some were from the Cumberland Valley. The majority were Scotch-Irish Presbyterians. The Indians continued to complain of the occupation of these unpurchased lands, and of the killing of their warriors as they passed to the south against their "natural enemies," the Cherokee and Catawba. Governor Penn and Governor Fauquier issued proclamations ordering the settlers to leave the lands at Redstone, along the Monongahela Valley and on the Youghioghenny. Troops were sent from Fort Pitt in 1766-67 to Fort Burd (Redstone) to expel these squatters, but they returned after the troops had left. Finally in 1768 Governor Penn issued a Proclamation warning the settlers to leave, and stated that those convicted occupying these lands "shall suffer death, without the benefit of clergy." Soon after this Proclamation was issued the Governor appointed Captain John Steel (Captain, Pastor of the Presbyterian Church at Carlisle) and several others, to visit these settlements and urge the people to comply with the law. In Steel's report of this mission the names of the settlers residing at Redstone, Gist's Turkey Foot are given, but this list is not complete as many names of persons of prominence who were then living in the region are not given (Consult; Colonial Records, IX. 323, 353, 507, 531, 540; Ellis, History of Fayette County, 60-61). The Indians showed the greatest patience and sympathy with the Provincial authorities in their efforts to remove these settlers, who would not comply with the orders of the Governor. They even did not wish that any severe measures should be adopted which might incur the ill will of these settlers. The speech of Kiasutha is worthy of reading. He said, "And we shall be very unhappy, if, by our Conduct towards them at this time, we shall give them Reason to dislike us, and treat us in an unkind Manner, when they again become our Neighbors. We therefore hope, Brethren, you will not be displeased at us for not performing our Agreement with you, for You may be assured that we have good Hearts towards all of our Brethren, the English" (Col. Rec. IX. 542). The thing which the Indians would not do was to go to Redstone to warn the settlers to leave. The conduct of the Indians during this time, when law and justice was on their side, is in marked contrast to the conduct of the very people who lived in this region ten years later, when they rushed into the Indian country beyond the Ohio on expeditions, the justice of which has rightly been questioned. The very people whom the Indians permitted to stay at this time, with a desire to win their friendship, were the very people who, without any just cause whatever, were anxious in 1779 and 1792 to kill all Indians on sight. After the Treaty of Fort Stanwix, 1768, and the purchase of all of these lands in southwestern Pennsylvania from the Iroquois, who claimed the land by right of conquest, the region rapidly filled up with settlers from Virginia, Maryland and eastern Pennsylvania. The great majority, however, were from Virginia. The Boundary Dispute with Virginia caused almost endless trouble between the settlers south of the line of the Forbes Road and those living along the course of this road. The Braddock Road, and all of its near settlements was peopled chiefly by Virginians, while the Forbes Road, and all of the settlements, was thoroughly under the influence of Pennsylvania. The rivalry of the two Colonies for the possession of the Indian trade on the Ohio, which had commenced before 1748, was carried on in the bitter struggle between the two Colonies for the possession of the domain. The Penns claimed the region by right of Royal Charter, and Virginia claimed it by right of Purchase from the Iroquois, at the Treaty of Lancaster in 1744, as well as by right of Charter, and the Grant to the Ohio Company in 1749. Virginia also claimed the region by right of actual occupation (Consult; Archives, Third Ser., III. 483-573; Ellis, History of Fayette County, 114-125; Crumrine, The Old Virginia Court House at Augusta Town, 1905; Crumrine, Annals of Carnegie Museum, I. 525 et seq., III. 6 et seq. (containing the Minute Books of the Virginia Courts); Archives of Pa., IV. 435, 479, 481-84, 522, etc.; VII. 133, 467; VIII. 713; IX. 4, 193, etc.; X. 8, 56, 72, 81, 95, 279 etc.) The various Presbyterian and Baptist Churches were established throughout this region at an early day (Consult; Smith, Old Redstone, 1854; History of Washington Presbytery, 1889; Doddridge, Notes on the Settlement and Indian Wars, 1824, revised edition 1912). During the War of the Revolution, even with the Boundary Dispute at its height, the great majority of the settlers in the Monongahela region enlisted in the various Regiments of Pennsylvania and Virginia. Chiefly through the efforts of Col. William Crawford, who lived at Stewart's Crossing, the Seventh Virginia was recruited from the region along the Youghiogheny and Monongahela. Crawford was made Lieut. Col. of the Fifth Virginia, and then Colonel of the Seventh Virginia. The Thirteenth Virginia, known as the West Augusta Regiment, was recruited in the same region. Crawford was

later Colonel of this Regiment. Besides these Virginia regiments, the Monongahela region furnished eight companies for the Pennsylvania Line. These companies belonged to the Eighth Pennsylvania Line (Consult; Ellis, History of Fayette County, 73-86; Hassler, Old Westmoreland, 60 et seq.; Archives, Sec. Ser., XIX, 673 et seq.) Besides these Regiments many others were recruited in part by the inhabitants of the region included in the present Westmoreland, Fayette and Washington Counties. The greater part of the army making up Crawford's Sandusky Expedition of 1782 was from the Monongahela and Youghiogheny region, and nearly all were Scotch-Irish (Consult; Hassler, Old Westmoreland, 162-169; Archives, Sec. Ser., XIV. 690-727; Butterfield, Historical Account of the Expedition against Sandusky, 1873). See *Allegheny, Ohio, Redstone, Stewart's Crossings, Youghiogheny; Catawba* (Trail), *Nemacolin* (Trail).

The various forms of the name are simply attempts to spell the Indian name, Menaungehilla (or Mehmonauangehelak, as Darlington gives it). A few of these forms are:

Malangaillee.—Vaudreuil (1757), Archives, Sec. Ser., VI. 402. **Maneuquile.**—Pouchot, map, 1758. **Minongehelo.**—Weiser (1755), Colonial Records, VI. 551. **Minongelo.**—Weiser (1755), Col. Rec., VI. 589. **Mohongahela.**—Morris (1755), Col. Rec., VI. 233. **Mohngaly.**—Gist (1751), in Dar. Gist., 68. **Mohongealo.**—Morris (1755), Col. rec., VI. 452. **Mohongeyela.**—Ohio Co. (1751), in Dar. Gist Jour., 67. **Mohongialo.**—Hamilton (1753), Col. Rec. V. 698. **Mohungahalo.**—Traders map, 1752-53. **Monaungehela.**—Evans, map, 1755. **Monongahala.**—Hendrick (1769), Archives, IV. 346. **Monongahela.**—Gist (1751), in Dar. Gist Jour., 81. **Monongahalia.**—Archives, IV. 425. **Monongahila.**—Morris (1755), Col. Rec., VI. 318. **Monongehala.**—Johnson (1756), Col. Rec., VII. 342. **Monongohela.**—Pa. Coun. (1756), Col. Rec., VII. 49.

MONSEYTOWN. See *Muncy, Munsee.*

MONTOUR. The name of a county, creek, mountain, village and several Townships in the state, named in honor of Andrew Henry Montour, or Sattelihu, or of his mother Madame Montour. Perhaps the only place named in honor of the mother is Montoursville, Lycoming County—the others are named for Andrew her eldest child. The Montours occupied a prominent place in the early history of Pennsylvania. Many of the stories told about the various members of the family are without any foundation, but enough of these are true to make the name famous, or infamous in some cases. Even Conrad Weiser in his Journal of 1737 falls into the error of calling Madame Montour "a French woman by birth." Madame Montour was a daughter of a French nobleman, named Montour, and an Indian woman. This Frenchman settled in Canada about 1665. By his Indian wife he had a son and two daughters. The son was killed by order of Vaudreuil, Governor of Canada, in 1709, for alienating the Indians beyond Montreal from the French trade. The daughter known as Madame Montour was captured by the Iroquois in about 1694, when about ten years of age, and at maturity she was married by a Seneca, named Roland Montour. By this husband she had four (or five) children; Andrew, (Henry), Robert, Lewis and Margaret. After the death of her first husband Madame Montour married the Oneida chief, called Carondowanen, or "Big Tree," who also had the name Robert Hunter, the name of the Governor of New York. Carondowanen was captured by the Catawaba, when on a war expedition to the south in 1729, and was put to death (Archives, I. 240-241, 328, 671). On account of the killing of her brother by Vaudreuil, she was always bitterly opposed to the French. Various efforts were made by the French Governor to have her remove to Canada. Her sister who had probably married a Miami Indian, was sent to offer her many inducements to leave the English and join the French. The Governor of New York realizing the value of the influence of Madame Montour, sent for her in 1719 to come to Albany. She was then given a man's pay, as interpreter, and from this time forward acted as interpreter for the English. In 1727 she was interpreter at a Council in Philadelphia. Various early authorities, who met Madame Montour, claimed that she was a French-Canadian, without Indian blood (Marsh, Zinzendorf etc.). But the culture, polish, refinement and other qualities noted by these writers was no doubt very much intensified by the writers. Count Zinzendorf visited her at Ostonwakin, at the Mouth of the Loyalsock Creek, in 1742. Here he met her son Andrew, whom he describes in his

Journal (Memorials of Moravian Church, I. 95). This description is of interest. He says, "Andrew's cast of countenance is decidedly European, and had not his face been encircled with a broad band of paint, applied with bear's fat, I would certainly taken him for one. He wore a brown broadcloth coat, a scarlet damasken lappel-waiscoat, breeches, over which his shirt hung, a black Cordovan neckerchief, decked with silver bugles, shoes, and stockings, and a hat. His ears were hung with pendants of brass and other wires plaited together like the handle of a basket. He was very cordial, but on addressing him in French, he, to my surprise, replied in English" Andrew Montour served the Province as interpreter and messenger for many years. In May 1745, he went with Conrad Weiser to Onondago. From this time onward he acted as interpreter at nearly all of the Councils with the Indians. In 1752 he was granted permission to select a place of residence for himself beyond the Kittatinny Mountains. He selected a tract of 143 acres of land, near the junction of the present Montour's Run and Shearman's Creek. His house stood near the present Landisburg, Perry County. In 1761 he was granted 1500 acres on Kishacoquillas Creek. In a number of the land grants and official documents he is called both Andrew and Henry. He was with Braddock on the ill-fated expedition of 1755. He served Virginia and Maryland, as interpreter, at various councils, and during his life he travelled over nearly all of the region east of the Mississippi on official missions for the various Colonies. In 1769 he was granted a tract of land, including Montour's Island (below Pittsburgh), containing 300 acres. This tract was called Oughsaragoh. Montour's Iroquois name was Oughsara, or Eghisara. The name of his grant was, therefore, "Eghisara Place,—a name which should be given to some of the beautiful "places" in this region now. The oldest son of Andrew—John Montour—lived on Montour's Island, until 1789. Craig says that Andrew Montour died on Montour's Island, prior to 1775. It is stated that Mary Montour, a niece of Andrew's, was married to the "White Mingo," who lived at the mouth of Pine Creek, on the Allegheny River. John Montour, Andrew's son, and the "White Mingo" were associated in many missions during the time that General Brodhead was at Fort Pitt, taking part in Brodhead's Expedition up the Allegheny in 1779. It is possible that Craig made a mistake in stating that Andrew died on Montour's Island, and that he died at the home of the "White Mingo," at the mouth of Pine Creek, near Sharpsburg.

This "White Mingo Town" was settled soon after the erection of Fort Pitt by the Mingo (tramp Iroquois) from the Mingo Town near Steubenville, Ohio.

Consult; Handbook of American Indians, Part I. 936-937; Darlington, Gist's Journals, 152-158, 163 et seq.; Hanna, Wilderness Trail, I. 223-246; Reichel, Memorials of the Moravian Church, I. 68, 95, 102, 132, 281; Walton, Conrad Weiser, 84 etc., 1900; Loskiel, History of Missions, II. 32, 1794; DeSchweinitz, Life of Zeisberger, 112, 132-137, 1870; Also Colonial Records III. 271, 295; IV. 778 etc.; Archives, I. 211; II. 9, 12, 31, 45 etc. (See Index Vol. under title).

The other Montours mentioned in the early writings are; Esther, the "fiend of Wyoming," a daughter of French Margaret, and a grand-daughter of Madame Montour; Catherine Montour, another daughter of French Margaret. She was the wife of Telelemet, known also as Thomas Hudson; Mary Montour, a sister of the two previously mentioned. She was the wife of the "White Mingo," or Kanaghragait, a Seneca chief. She was baptized in Phila. by a Catholic priest, and yet she was among the converts of the Moravian Mission, which removed from Salem, Ohio, in 1791, to Canada. DeSchweinitz says, "One of the latest converts who accompanied him (Zeisberger) was a sister of Andrew Montour. She was a living polyglot of the tongues of the West, speaking the English, French, Mohawk, Wyandot, Ottawa, Chippewa, Shawanese, and Delaware languages" (op. cit. 621); Lewis Montour, brother of Andrew's was also employed as an interpreter; John Montour a son of Andrew's, was employed by General Brodhead on a number of missions, and was with him when he destroyed the Seneca villages on the Allegheny River in 1779. The name has been perpetuated in the various places mentioned previously. See *French Margaret's, Otstonwakin, Queen Esther's Town, Sheshequin, Wyoming.*

MOOSIC. The name of a mountain range in Wayne and Lackawanna Counties; also a Lake and a village in Lackawanna County. Probably a corruption of Moos, "elk," with the locative, ink, signifying "elk place." Moosic Lake.—State map 1911. Moosick Mount.—Adlum, map, 1790; also Morris, map, 1848.

MORAVIA. The name of a town in Lawrence County. Derived from the Delaware Indian. Moravian Mission, called Friedensstadt, or Languntouteneunk, which was near the place in 1771-73. See *Languntouteneunk.*

MOSELEM. A branch of Maiden Creek, in Berks County. A corruption of Meschilameek - hanne, "trout stream."

Moselem.—Scull, map, 1770; 1759; Howell, map, 1792. **Moselin.**—Evans, map, 1749.

MOSHANNON. A creek which enters the West Branch of the Susquehanna between Clearfield and Centre Counties; also a branch, in Centre County, called Black Moshannon; also a town in Centre County; also a town, Moshannon Mills, in the same county. The name is a corruption of Mooshanne, "elk stream." One of the earliest Indian trails from the Susquehanna to the Ohio was that which led from Shamokin (Sunbury), up the West Branch to the Big Island (Lock Haven), and then up Bald Eagle Creek, Marsh Creek, to near Snow Shoe, across the Moshannon, through Clearfield to Chinklaclamoose (Clearfield), to Punxsutawney, and then to Kittanning, on the Allegheny. This was one of the routes followed by the Delawares as they migrated to the Ohio in about 1724-27. It was also the route taken by C. F. Post, as he went westward to Kuskuski (New Castle) in 1758, on his Peace Mission (Archives, III. 520 et seq.). This was also the route taken by Ettwein, who was leading the Christian Indians from Wyalusing in 1772 (Ettwein's Journal, in Hanna, I. 214-216; DeSchweinitz, Life of Zeisberger, 376-377). This trail was also used by the various scouting parties from Fort Duquesne between 1755 and 1758, as they investigated the British situation at Fort Augusta (Sunbury). While Col. Burd was at this fort in 1756-57 he sent out scouting parties along this trail to the present Clearfield (Archives, Sec. Ser., II. 780). As the Military roads were opened westward from the Cumberland Valley, and because of the more rapid increase of settlements along the southern trails, this northern trail was little used. Even in the Indian days it yas not as prominent a trail, because of the very steep hills and also the scarcity of game along its course. See *Shamokin, Chinklaclamoose.*

Mushannon.—Scull, map, 1759. **Mushanon.**—Scull, map, 1770; Howell, map, 1792. **West Moshannock.**—Ettwein (1772), in Hanna, I. 214.

The present Black Moshanon;

Little Moshanon.—Morris, map, 1848. **Little Mushanon.**—Howell, map, 1792.

MUCKINIPATTUS. A branch of Darby Creek, near its mouth, in Delaware County. The first recorded form of this name is in the grant of land, by Stuyvesant, to "Israel Helm, Hendrick Jacobson, Olle Koeck (Cock) and Jan Minsterman," June 18, 1668 (Archives, I. 28), where it is called "Mokornipalas Kill." In 1677 the Court of Upland granted to Hans Boen (Boon) 200 acres of land "on the East syde of a Little Creeke wch. comes out of amesland Creeke (Darby Creek) called mohurmipati" (Records of Upland Court, 71). The place on this creek was called "moherhuting"" (op. cit. 65, 71). The author of the "Records of Upland Court" (Edward Armstrong) says that a friend of his met Andrew Boon, a descendant of Hans Boon, at this place in 1857. The Grant to Andres Boon was called "Boon's Forest"—April 13, 1680. The name has been corrupted by various writers to Mackinipa, Mackinipattus, and finally to Muckinipattus, the name given on the U. S. Geological Survey map of 1909. It is difficult to tell what the original form of the name was. The corruption of the name is complete—from Mokornipalas to Muckinipattus.

MOWHEWAMICK. Mentioned in Archives (1761) IV. 60-61. See *Wyoming.*

MOYAMENSING. The name of a creek which entered the Delaware a short distance above Gloucester Point, probably the stream known later as Hay Creek; also the name of the Township in Philadelphia County in 1741. This Township was incorporated as a district on March 24, 1812. It was consolidated with the City of Philadelphia in 1854. The first mention of the name is found in the Grant of land to Swen Gonderson, Swen Swenson, Oele Swenson and Andrew Swenson, by Gov. Nicholls and confirmed by Francis Lovelace, in 1664. In this grant it is noted "as Moyamensink kill." (Watson, Annals of Phila., I. 147, 1850). In 1677 Lasse Andries, Oele Stille, Andreas Benckson and John Mattson, "Inhabitants of Moyamensinck," were granted permission to take up 25 acres each "of marrsh or meddow between the hollanders Kill (Hollander's Creek) and Rosemonds kill (not marked on the MS. Map of the Department of Surveys, of Philadelphia, of 1787 (Records of Upland Court, 100). In the Census of the "responsible housekeepers," taken by John Brigs, for Gov. Edmond Andros, in 1680, the name is given as, "Moy Mansy" (Archives, Sec. Ser., VII. 806). According to the tax list of the Court of Upland, 1677, "oele stille, andries Benckes and Jan mattson" are given as residents of "Taokanink" (Tacony). (Consult; Records of Upland Court, 77-78). The origin of the name is doubtful. It may be a corruption of Menantachk "swamp," with the locative ing. The original form of the name, however, cannot be found.

MUNCY. A name used in many places in the state, and in various combinations. Is a corruption of Munsee (from Min-asin-ink, "where stones are gathered together"), the name of the Wolf clan of the Delawares. Their council village was at Minisink, in Sussex County, N. J. (See *Minisink*). After the Walking Purchase of 1737 nearly all of the Munsee left the Delaware and settled upon the lands at Wyoming, and at various places along the Susquehanna and the West Branch. They gradually moved on westward to the upper Allegheny, where some of them had settled as early as 1724. The various Moravian Missions in Pennsylvania and Ohio were made up chiefly of this clan of the Delawares (See *Lawunakhannek, Languntouteneunk, Sheshequin, Wyalusing, Gnadenhcutten etc.*). They were the most warlike of the Delaware clans, and were associated with the Shawnee and Seneca in nearly all of the Indian wars of Colonial days in Pennsylvania, and also in Ohio. One of the chief reasons of hostility of the white settlers towards the "Moravian Indians" was perhaps due to the fact that they were nearly all members of the Munsee clan. Many of the Munsee settled above Tioga (Athens) on the branches of the Susquehanna. This region is frequently mentioned after 1755, as the "Munsey Country." Sheshequin, just below this point, was at one end of the trail to the West Branch, known as the "Sheshequin Path. The trail which ran up Muncey Creek, and then across to Wyoming (Wilkes-Barre) was perhaps one of the most prominent in that region. The Munsee living along the North Branch became associated with the Mohawks in the various raids into the white settlements, in the region from which the Munsee had been driven. There seems to be many reasons for thinking that the Delaware names which are found in the Iroquois Country in New York are due to the settlement of the Munsee among the Seneca, with which tribe, no doubt, many of them became incorporated. The entire region along the headwaters of the Susquehanna, the West Branch and the upper Allegheny became a real "Munsee Country," after 1749, and continued to be so until the final migration of the Indians of Pennsylvania to the region of the present Ohio, about 1794. The region along the West Branch, and along the present Chemung River, which had been occupied by the Susquehannas (Conestoga), was then occupied by the Seneca 1675), and then by the Seneca and Munsee, with the latter in the majority. After the removal to Ohio the Munsee became incorporated with the Delawares. Some of them joined the Chippewa and Shawnee. Some of the clan became incorporated with the Cherokee, in Indian Territory, about 1868. Others moved to Canada, where they joined with the Chippewa in Canada. On account of the hostility of the Munsee to the white settlers in Pennsylvania they are frequently mentioned in the Archives and Colonial Records. Egohowen was the leading chief of the tribe in 1758. He was married to a daughter of "French Margaret" named Esther Montour, known as "Queen Esther," who was known as the "fiend of Wyoming" (See Queen Esther's Town, Sheshequin, Wyoming). After the death of her husband "Queen Esther" became the woman chief of the village where she lived, Sheshequin, at the site of Ulster, Bradford County. About 1772 she removed to

Queen Esther's Town, about 6 miles north of her old village, opposite Tioga Point (Col. Rec. VIII. 159). There were a number of Munsee villages along the West Branch, chief of which were those at Muncy, Big Island (Lock Haven) and at Bald Eagle's Nest (Milesburg), on the Bald Eagle Creek (See these, under title). The Indian settlement at the "Big Island" (Lock Haven), was called Monsey Town by the white settlers and travellers. It is mentioned as such in Loudon, Indian Narratives, and in Meginness, Otzinachson (Hanna, I. 242; Meginness, 22). The beautiful flats which stretch along the West Branch, from Lock Haven to the present Muncy, were called "Monsey Flats," or "Monseytown Flats," in many early writers. The Manor of Muncy was surveyed by Joseph J. Wallis and John Henderson, May 1776. It ran along the West Branch, from above the mouth of Muncy Creek, down the river 636 perches, and included the improvements of Mordecai McKinney, Peter Smith, Paul Sheep, John Brady, Caleb Knapp and John Scutter. This Manor included Muncy Creek for some distance from its mouth-about 554 perches. It contained about 1615 acres, and allowances (Manor of Muncy, map, in Archives, Third Ser., IV. Map No. 42; Meginness, Otzinachson, 37, 155, 216 etc.). The land along the West Branch was purchased from the Indians at the Treaty of Fort Stanwix, 1768, to the mouth of Pine Creek (See Tyadaghton). The rush of the white settlers into this region before the land had been purchased from the Indians was the causes of much trouble to the Provincial authorities, who issued repeated orders for these settlers to remove. The exact line of the boundary was not settled until the second Treaty at Fort Stanwix, 1784. The Proprietors issued proclamations forbidding settlers to take up lands beyond Lycoming Creek, but the settlers pressed on into the forbidden region (See Lycoming, Big Island). During the days when the bands of hostile Indians made raids upon the white settlements along the West Branch, various frontier forts were erected. Among these was Fort Muncy, which stood about 4 miles above the present Muncy, about half a mile above Hall's Station (Consult; Frontier Forts, I. 390-392; Meginness, Otzinachson, 236, 240, 253,

270 etc.). Captain John Brady was killed near this fort in 1779. The present Muncy Creek is noted on the old maps, and in the early records by the following names;

Canascoraga.—Evans, map, 1749. **Canaserage.**—Evans, map, 1755. **Canasoragy.** —Weiser (1755), Col. Rec., VI. 443-444. **Canasserago.**—Scull, map, 1770. **Loneserango.**—Meginness, Otzinachson, 155 (an error. Never so written). **Muncy Creek.**—Howell, map, 1792. **Occohpocheny.**—Meginness, Otzinachson, 155, 1856. **Ocockpochong.**—Scull, map, 1759. **Oughcapochany.**—Board of Prop. (1770), Archives, Third Ser., I. 291.

Count Zinzendorf and his companions passed along this trail over Muncy Creek in 1742. In Aug. 26, 1753 Mack and Grube, the Moravian missionaires, passed "Muncy Creek" (Consult; Reichel, note, Heckewelder's Indian Names, 257). Bishop Spangenberg, who accompanied Weiser to Onondaga in 1745, mentions the creek as "Canachriage." In Weiser's Journal of his trip to Onondaga in 1750, he mentions "Canasoragy," but this village visited by Weiser was the Tuscarora village, on Canaseraga Creek, Sullivan, New York, which was visited by Gansevort's men, Sept. 23, 1779. The name of this village was Ganasarage. The former name of Muncy Creek is a corruption of this name, which means "among the mandrakes," or at the place of mandrakes." Other meanings have been given, "among the milkweeds," "Slippery-elm" etc. The former is that given by J. N B. Hewitt, of the Bureau of Ethnology.

MUNSEE, See *Muncy.*

MURDERING TOWN. An Indian village mentioned in Gist's Journal, of 1753, as Murthering town (Dar. Gist's Journal, 81). He places it about 15 miles from Logstown, "on a branch of Great Beaver Creek." He again refers to the place on the return trip. Here they met an Indian, whom Gist says they had seen at Venango. This Indian, who was mistrusted by Gist, fired at them. (op. cit. 84-85). Washington mentions the town as "Murdering Town," in his Journal of the same trip, and also mentions the incident noted (Albach, Western Annals, 119; also any of the copies of Washington's Journal of 1753). On Gist's map of 1753, the town on this branch of Beaver Creek is noted as "Minacing Town." The village was probably that which was noted by C. F. Post, in 1758, as Conoquenessing. The Creek of that

name is the branch of "Great Beaver Creek," mentioned by Gist. See *Conoquenessing.* The name Murdering Town was probably given to the place by Washington and Gist, because of the incident noted.

MUSCANETUNK. The name of a creek which enters the Delaware from the east in new Jersey, opposite Northampton County. Now called Musconetcong. Probably a corruption of Maskhanneunk, "a rapid stream."

Maskenycunk.—Howell, map, 1792. **Muscanetcunk.**—Evans, map, 1749. **Muscanetkunk.**—Scull, map, 1770. **Muscanetunk.**—Scull, map, 1759. **Musconecunk.**—Adlum, map, 1790. **Muskonetoung.**—Morris, map, 1848.

NAAMAN'S CREEK. A creek which enters the Delaware from the west, just below the Pennsylvania line. Named in honor of a Delaware (Ferris says that he was a Minqua, or Susquehanna), who lived upon this creek at the time of its first settlement. Naaman is mentioned by Lindstrom as one of the chiefs who attended a conference with Gov. John Rysingh at Tinicum Island, June 17, 1654. Acrelius states that the name is of Swedish origin, and gives the form "Nyman's Kihl" (Acrelius, 64). Lindstrom gives the name as "La Riviere de Naaman" (MS map). It is mentioned in the Records of Upland Court (48) as, "namans creeke." The two grants of land, from Gov. Lovelace in 1673, to Capt. Edmund Cantwell and Johannes de Haes, "between Dog Creek and Namon's Creek," are mentioned in the Boundary Dispute between the Penns and Calverts (Archives, Sec. Ser., XVI. 279). Also the grant of 1000 acres by Gov. Edmund Andros to Charles Jansen, and others, in 1674-77, in which it is mentioned as "Naaman's Creek" (op. cit. 317). The temporary line between Pennsylvania and Maryland, run by Talbot in 1683, was from the mouth of Naaman's Creek to the mouth of Octorara Creek, on the Susquehanna. The present circular line runs from the Delaware, just above the mouth of this creek. Besides the forms noted, the early maps give the following:

Naamans Creek.—Scull, maps, 1759, 1770. **Namans Creek.**—Howell, map, 1792.

NANTICOKE. The name of a town in Luzerne County. Derived from Nentego, a variation of Unechtgo, Unalachtgo, "tide water people." The

Turkey Clan of the Delawares. They were living on the Nanticoke River in Maryland in 1608, where Smith located their chief village of Nanticoke. In the Walam Olum (10th. verse of the Fifth Song) it is stated, "The Nentegos and the Shawanis went to the south lands." The region in which they were living at the time of this separation is called "Talega land," which was evidently the land of the Tallegewi, or Tallegwi (See *Allegheny*), mentioned in Heckewelder's tradition of the eastward migration of the Delaware and Iroquois. This legend of the Nanticoke and that of the Shawnee is the same (Brinton, Lenape Legends, 139, 1885). This "Talega" land was no doubt on the Ohio River, and perhaps on the present Allegheny, and the migration southward was from this place. The traditions of the Shawnee, as those of the Delaware (Walam Olum) fix this region along the Ohio, in the present state of Ohio, as the place from which both of these tribes made their migration southward. The Pickaway Plains in Ohio, where the Shawnee finally were re-united, after being driven from the east, is mentioned by the Iroquois as the place from which they came (See *Maguck, Shawnee*). By the time of the landing of the English at Jamestown the Nanticoke had become very different in manners and customs, and had developed a dialect which differed greatly, from those of the Delaware tribes living along the Delaware River. They were at war with the English settlers in Maryland until 1678, when they made peace at a treaty. From this time forward the Maryland authorities placed the Nanticokes on reservations, or as the chiefs said later, after they came to Pennsylvania, "put a fence around them." This was the first adoption of the "reservation" system, in dealing with the Indians. The Conoy and Nanticoke were associated in a league, with a King, or Emperor, of Nanticoke lineage at its head, according to a statement made to the Governor of Maryland in 1660. But this was not true in the later history of the two tribes in Penna., when "Last Night," a Conoy, was the accepted King of the two tribes. In 1706, the Conestoga Indians, who had gone to Philadelphia to see Gov. Thomas, showed him a large Belt of Wampum, which had been given to the Nanticokes by the Onondagas, when the former became tributaries of

the Five Nations, as a pledge of peace. They said that the Nanticokes, who were then at Conestoga, on their way to pay tribute to the Iroquois, had another similar Belt. (Colonial Rec. II. 246-247). In 1707, when Gov. Evans went to Dekanoagah (which see), he held a conference with the Shawnee, Conestoga, Conoy and Nanticoke. The latter said that they had been at peace with the Iroquois since 1680. The names of the seven Nanticoke villages in Maryland are given. No interpreter was used as the Nanticoke present all understand English. This was true of all of the Nanticoke with whom Councils were held later in Penna. history. They were on their way to pay tribute to the Iroquois (Col. Rec. II. 386-387). In 1722 the Nanticoke again were on their way to pay tribute, stopping at the Conoy Town on the Susquehanna, where James Le Tort and James Mitchell held a conference with them. Sir William Keith, Governor of the Province, sent a letter to the Conoy King, Winjack, concerning this visit of the Nanticokes, and also sent a present (Col. Rec. III. 187-189). At the Council at Phila. in 1742 in the list of Indians present are the names of several. "Indians of the Nanticokes, by Us called the Cannoyios." Weiser acted as interpreter and probably gave this list, with the comments (Col. Rec. IV. 585-588). In 1743, when Weiser was on his mission to Onondaga, he met the 6 Nanticoke chiefs who were present, and acted as their interpreter, speaking English (op. cit. 662). Some of the Nanticoke had probably settled at the Conoy villages on the lower Susquehanna soon after the Conoy were permitted to enter the Province, in 1704. They came in small numbers at various times, living in the villages of the Conestoga and Conoy along the lower Susquehanna until about 1742, when they removed to the mouth of the Juniata with the Conoy. This move was made in order that both the Conoy and Nnaticoke might get away from the war parties of the Iroquois, who went southward and returned with their prisoners, stopping at their villages. This action of the Iroquois made the Nanticoke and Conoy liable to charges of harboring these war parties. Hence the move (See *Conoy*). This move was made by the authority of the Iroquois, by whose permission the Conoy and Nanticoke "kindled a Council Fire at the mouth of the Juniata." By 1748 the village at this place was made up chiefly of Nanticoke. They were represented at the Council at Lancaster in 1748, and at the Council at Philadelphia in 1749. At the latter Council, Canassatego, the Iroquois, made complaint concerning the white settlements on the Juniata, "as this is the hunting Ground of our Cousins the Nanticokes and other Indians, Living on the waters of Juniata" (Col. Rec. V. 222, 307, 388, 400-402). Canassatego then speaks of the Nanticoke having removed from Maryland because of the "differences between the People of Maryland and them we sent for them and placed them at the mouth of Juniata, where they now live" (op. cit. 402). The Nanticokes had told Canassaatego that there were still three settlements of their tribe left in Maryland. These wished to join their relatives on the Juniata, but "the Marylanders kept them in fence & would not let them." Canassatego asked that the Governor, Hamilton, write to the Governor of Maryland, asking him to "have the fence in which they are confin'd removed, and that they be permitted to settle with their relatives on the Juniata. He also complained because the Inhabitants of Maryland made slaves of these Nanticokes, and sold their children. In 1751 several Nanticokes went to Phila., from Wyoming. One of these said that, "We passed about nine Years ago by your door, we came from Maryland and asked your leave to go and settle among our Brethren the Delawares, and you gave us leave" (Col. Rec. V. 544). This would make the time of the arrival of the Nanticoke in the Province, about 1742. The Governor was informed that the Nanticokes from Juniata had removed to Wyoming, and asked his permission to make this change of residence. Governor Hamilton gave them permission to make this change, provided the Indians at Wyoming made no objection. The place which was occupied at this time by the Nanticokes was below Wyoming, near the present Nanticoke, Nanticoke Creek and Nanticoke Falls, in Luzerne County. It is noted on the Manor of Stoke, map, of 1768, as "Old Nanticoke T." (Archives Third, Ser., IV. Map No. 66). Previous to settling at this site the Nanticoke had lived at the various small villages along the Susquehanna (Glass-

wanoge, Nescopeck etc.). In 1755 Scarouady, the Oneida deputy, went up the Susquehanna to where the Nanticokes then lived, and informed them of Braddock's defeat, and again in 1756 he went up to their chief village of Chenango (See Shenango), at the site of Binghamton, New York. There were 30 cabins and 60 men in the village, in which Skayanas (The Fisher) was chief. The village was made up of Conoy, Nanticoke and Onondaga. At the Council at Easton, 1757, the Nanticoke congratulated the English upon the conclusion of the Peace with the Delawares, and asked permission to go to Lancaster to remove the bones of the Indians killed at Lancaster. They were also at the Council in Phila. in 1760 and 1761 (Col. Rec. VI. 685-687; VII. 65, 707; VIII. 484, 492, 614). At the Council in Phila. in 1761 the Nanticokes said that they had gone to Maryland 7 years before with a Belt, asking permission to get their relatives there, but had been informed that it would be necessary for them to bring a letter, as a Belt could not be understood (VIII. 651). Seneca George, the friend and messenger of the Province, who was living at Chenango in 1761, told of his poverty and of his need of several articles, which the Governor promised to give him. Governor Hamilton wrote a letter to Governor Sharpe, of Maryland, recommending Robert White, a Nanticoke, and the business upon which he went to Maryland—to get his relatives. Robert White, whose Indian name was Ullauckquam, was a faithful friend of the English during the period of hostility, 1755-1764. He is frequently mentioned in the records (VIII. 656, 661,729). At the Council at Phila. in 1763 the Nanticoke and Conoy from Chenango were present. The former stated that they formerly had a Council Fire at Juniata, but that after they had been admitted to the Council at Onondaga, they were given a Council Fire at Chenango (Col. Rec. IX. 44, 328, 385). At a Council at Shamokin, in Fort Augusta, in 1769, for the purpose of condoling with Seneca George for the death of his only son, who had been killed by some unknown white settlers near the mouth of Middle Creek, about 55 Indians, chiefly Conoy and Nanticoke were present. Col. Francis, Rev. Dr. Smith and other representatives of the Province were present. On account of the high esteem in which Seneca George was held, not only by the Indians, but also by the English, the death of his son caused wide-spread sorrow. Genquant, the Onondaga chief, and Last Night, the Conoy King, were present as the speakers for the Indians. Seneca George made one of the most pathetic speeches which has ever been recorded, and his final speech of friendly forgivness is one of the most dramatic events recorded in the Colonial Records. On Sabbath, August 20, 1769, Rev. Dr. Smith preached at Fort Augusta, the service being attended by all of the Indians, at their request. Last Night, the Conoy King, said in his address, "The Nations to which I belong, the Nanticokes and Conoys, never yet since the beginning of the World, pulled one Scalp, nor even one Hair from your Heads, and this I say gives us the Right to call ourselves your Brothers." And this statement is true. No record can be found of a Conoy or Nanticoke having engaged in any of the hostile expeditions against the English. He also said, "There is a Council Fire at Shanango (Chenango), which is the Door of the Six Nations." Chenango was so regarded by the Iroquois. This and not Tioga, as is sometimes stated, was the Door of the Iroquois Country, on the south. The Conoy, Nanticoke and Mahican residents of the village were placed there to "guard" this Doorway. All news from the south reached the Council at Onondaga by way of Chenango. In 1775 a number of Nanticoke and Conoy went to Phila., and were given assistance by order of Governor John Penn (Col. Rec. IX. 44, 77, 328, 385, 611, 617; X. 238 etc.). By 1784 the majority of the Nanticoke had moved westward with remnants of the Mahican and Wappinger, where they became incorporated with the Delawares of Ohio. Besides the villages mentioned, the Nanticoke also lived, in small groups, at Sheshequin, Chemung and other places along the upper waters of the Susquehanna. Among the strange customs which this historic tribe had was that of carrying the bones of their dead to their new homes. Heckewelder and other writers mention this custom. They went to their old habitat in Maryland from the upper Susquehanna, to get the bones of their dead (Heckewelder, Indian Nations, 53, 92; Reichel, Memorials of Mor. Church, I. 74, 311, 341, 346; DeSchweinitz, Life of Zeisber-

ger, 36 70, 186, 204, 206, 222-23). DeSchweinitz says that by 1794 the Nanticokes had "dwindled to four or five families." The name has been perpetuated in various places in the region about Wyoming (Wilkes-Barre), where they lived for a time.

NAYAUG. Said to be the Indian name of Roaring Creek, which enters the Susquehanna from the south in Luzerne County. Consult; Egle, Hist. Pa., 883.

NEBRASKA. A town in Forest County. Not a historic name in the state. The name of the State, from which it is no doubt taken, is said to mean "shallow water."

NEKODA. A village in Perry County. Seems to be made up of Indian sounds.

NEMACOLIN'S TRAIL. Nemacolin was a Delaware, who was living at the mouth of Nemacolin's Creek, afterward Dunlap's Creek, in 1751 when Gist was on his second trip to the Ohio. Gist then stopped at the camp of this Indian, where he met Charles Poke, a Donegal trader, who had formerly lived on the Potomac, near the site of Hancock, Md. The father of Nemacolin had lived on the Brandywine, from which he had been driven by the white settlers, who took up his lands. Nemacolin was the chief's oldest son. The letter of this chief to Gov. Gordon, in 1729, is found in Archives, I. 239-240. In 1730 Cachuscunt and Memcollen, complained because of the abuses which they had received from Isaac Miranda (op. cit., 266-267). This chief had removed to the Susquehanna before 1718. Nemacolin had probably gone down over the Warriors Trail to the Potomac to the region of Col. Thomas Cresap's before his removal to the mouth of Dunlap's Creek, as his acquaintance and friendship with the Cresap family would indicate, as would also his knowledge of the trail from the Potomac to the Monongahela. Charles Poke, Michael Cresap, Christopher Gist and others who were associated with Nemacolin, had probably first met this Indian when he was at Cresap's, at Old Town selling his furs and peltries. He was employed in 1752 by Col. Thomas Cresap and Gist to blaze the trail from Will's Creek to the mouth of Dunlap's Creek (or Redstone, as it is called, although Dunlap's Creek is the one meant).

This blazed trail was afterwards used by Washington, 1754, and Braddock, 1755, as far as Gist's Plantation, at Mount Braddock. Previous to that time the trail was little known, save by a few traders from the Potomac, who went to the mouth of Dunlap's Creek. It was called by later writers Nemacolin's Trail, but is never so mentioned on any of the early maps, or in any of the early Journals. This trail was little used by the Pennsylvania or Virginia traders, before 1752. Even Gist went by the Warriors Trail to Bloody Run, and then over the Raystown Path on his first journey in 1750. See *Redstone, Will's Creek, Stewart's Crossing, Raystown, Frankstown, Catawba Trail*, and other related articles. Consult; Col. Rec. III., 45, 47.

NESCOPEC. The name of a town, creek, mountain and valley in Luzerne County, and the name of a former Delaware and Shawnee village at the site of the present Nescopec. The Wyoming Path ran along the opposite side of the Susquehanna, from Shamokin. This trail was intersected by the Warriors Path, at the mouth of Catawissa Creek. A short distance below Nescopec, on the Wyoming Path was the village of King Nutimus, the Delaware chief who had been driven to the place by the sale of his lands by the Walking Purchase. His sons lived at Lepos Peters Town in 1757 (Col. Rec. IV. 312; Archives, Sec. Ser., II. 800). After Braddock's defeat, 1755, Nescopec became a rallying point for the Indians who were hostile to the English. The building of Fort Augusta, at Shamokin, drove all of the hostile Indians away from the region of Nescopec. In 1756, Aroas, or "Silver Heels," an Iroquois, was sent to investigate the condition of affairs on the Susquehanna. He found no Indians at Shamokin, but did find about 140 warriors at Nescopec, who were all very bitter against the English, and who were getting ready to make a raid on the frontier settlements (Col. Rec. VI. 783). In the same year Conrad Weiser reported to the Provincial Council that he had interviewed John Shikellamy (Tachneckdorus), who had moved from Nescopec to Wyoming, because of the hostility of the Indians of the former place to the English. At that time the Indians who were hostile had warned all hostile Indians to move from other villages to Nescopec. Be-

cause of this Shikellamy had moved away from Nescopec, and had gone to Wyoming, where Paxinosa, the Shawnee chief, who was friendly to the English lived. When the Delawares at Nescopec became afraid of being attacked by the English, after the erection of Fort Augusta in 1756, they moved on up the river to Assarughney (which see), where about 100 warriors were living (Archives, II. 606; Col. Rec. VII. 51-52). After the Conspiracy of Pontiac various settlements were made in this region by the English, but in 1778 Col. Hartley reported that all of the settlements on the north-east branch of the Susquehanna, as far as Nescopec, had been abandoned (Archives, VII. 81). In 1758, when Charles Thompson and C. F. Post were on their way to Wyoming on their Peace Mission, they were stopped about 15 miles from Wyoming, at the Nescopec Hills, by some Indians who were on their way to Bethlehem. They were told that the woods were full of hostile Indians, and that it would be dangerous for them to go further. They went to Wyoming for Tedyuskung, who came and held a council with them (Col. Rec. VII. 132-135).

Consult; Archives, II. 550, 558, 561, 565, 606; III. 507; Col. Rec., VI. 35, 771, 783, VII. 54, 56; VIII. 132; XVI. 83, 213, 259.

Naskepack Falls.—Barton (1779), Jour. Gen. Sull. Mil. Exped., 4. **Nescopack.**—Hartley (1778), Archives, VII. 87. **Nescopeak.**—Burd (1757), Arch. Sec. Ser., II. 695, 1890. **Nescopecka.**—Evans, map, 1755. **Nescopeck.**—Scull, map, 1770. **Nescopecken.**—Weiser (1756), Col. Rec., VII. 52. **Nescopeckon.**—Morris (1756), Archives, II. 561. **Nescopekum.**—Thompson (1758), Col. Rec., VIII. 132. **Nescopekun.**—Tattamy (1758), Archives, III. 507. **Neshkopeckon.**—Weiser (1756), Col. Rec., VII. 52. **Neskapeke.**—De-Schweinitz, in Life of Zeis., 214. **Neskopeken.**—Morris (1756), Col. Rec. VI. 771. **Neskopekin.**—Morris (1756), Archives, II, 606. **Nishkibeckon.**—Morris (1756), Col. Rec., VI. 35.

The name is probably a corruption of Neskchoppeek, "black," or "deep and still water." Nees-i-ku, "black." Tup-peek, "a spring." Niskeu, "dirty."

NESHAMINY. The name of a creek which enters the Delaware in Bucks County; also the name of a village in the same county. A corruption of Nischam-hanne "two-streams," or "double stream," signifying a stream formed by the joining of two branches. Is mentioned in the Records of Upland Court, 1677, as nishammenies Creeke," and Nisham-

menies Creeke" (63, 64), when 300 acres were granted to Jan Claassen and Paerde Cooper, and 100 acres were granted to Thomas Jacobse, next to the previous claim. Is also mentioned as "Nieshambenies Creeke" in a petition for 100 acres of land, by "Dunk Williams" in 1678 (Records of Upland Court, 106). In 1680 Mr. Erik Cock was appointed as a Constable "to officiate between the Schull Kill & nieshambenies Kill (op. cit. 184). The creek is mentioned in the first Deed of land from the Indians to William Penn, in 1682, and is also mentioned in six other Deeds from 1683 to 1697 (Archives, I. 47, 62, 63, 64, 124). At the Council held with the Indians at Crosswicks (N. J.) in 1758, Tedyuskung, the leading Delaware chief, claimed at tract of land on this creek, called "Neshannock" (Archives, III. 345).
See *Neshannock*.

Kesheminck.—Deed of 1683, Archives, 1. 63. **Neshameneh.**—Holme, map, 1689. **Neshameny.**—Evans, map, 1749-1755 **Neshamineh.**—Deed of 1683, Archives, I. 63. **Neshaming.**—Howell, map, 1792. **Neshaminy.**—Deed of 1697, Archives, I. 124. Scull, map, 1759. **Neshamene.**—Pownall, map, 1776. **Neshammonys.**—Archives, I. 47, Deed of 1682. **Nesheminck.**—Deed of 1683, Archives, I. 63. **Neshemineh.**—Deed of 1683, Archives, I. 64. **Neshamineh.**—Board of Prop. (1701), Archives, Sec. Ser., XIX, 250. **Neshamoning.**—Temporary Line, map, 1739, Archives, I. 594. **Nesheminah.**—Board of Prop. (1690), Archives, Sec. Ser., XIX. 61. **Neshannock.**—Council at Crosswicks (1758), Archives, III. 345. **Nieshambenies Creek.**—Records of Upland (1678), 106. **Nieshambenies Kill.**—Records of Upland (1680), 184. **Nishammenies Creek.**—Records of Upland (1677), 63. **Nishambanack.**—Grant from Gov. Andros (1674), Archives, Sec. Ser., XVI. 321.

(One of the chiefs who signed the Deed to William Penn, in 1683, was named Neshanocke; Archives, I. 66).

NESHANNOCK. The name of a creek which enters the Beaver River in Lawrence County; also the name of a town and Township in Mercer County; also a town called Neshannock Falls, in Lawrence County. The name is a corruption of the same name as above. Heckewelder gives the form, Nishannok, "both streams," or "two adjoining streams." Some of the Delawares from the region about the Neshaminy settled along the Beaver River, near Kuskuski. It seems a coincidence that this stream should be given the name of the historic stream on the Delaware. And, in addition among the first settlers of the white race in this region were some of the Scotch-Irish Presbyterians, who also carried the name of the historic Neshaminy Church, and the memories of William Tennen and his famous "Log College" into the western country. Neshannock Church was organized in 1799. It, and Westminister College are both situated at New Wilmington, on one of the branches of Neshannock Creek. The Indians remained in this region until after Wayne's Treaty, 1795, after which all had removed to the present states of Ohio and Indiana. Washington and Gist who crossed this creek in 1753, when on their mission to Venango, do not mention the stream by its name, but mention it simply as one of the "head branches of Great Beaver Creek." See *Kuskuski, Murdering Town, Venango.*

Neshanock. Howell, map, 1792; Morris, map, 1848.
Neshannock. Recent maps.

NESQUEHONING. The name of a creek, and town in Carbon County; also with the word Junction, a town in same county. The creek enters the Lehigh from the south above Mauch Chunk. A corruption of Neska-honi. "black-lick," or Niskeu-honi, "dirty lick." This creek was just beyond the Mahanoy, or Mahoning, beyond Fort Allen, and is probably referred to in the report made by Conrad Weiser of the information received from an Indian. Zaccheus, that 40 Indians were coming from Tioga to "Nishamekachton," three miles beyond Fort Allen (Col. Rec., VII. 317). It may also be referreed to as "Nixhisaqua (or Mahony)," in Col. Rec. VIII. 748, beyond which the Indians desired the Penns to make no settlements. Although this may refer to the creek on the Susquehanna, below Shamokin (Sunbury), which was also called the Mahony, now Mahoning.

Nesquehoning.—Howell, map, 1792. **Nesquehoning.**—Scull, map, 1770. **Nesquehoning.**—Morris, map, 1848 (a place at site of present town of Nesquehoning). **Nesquhoning.**—Morris, map, 1848.

NEVERSINK. The present name of the branch of the Delaware, which was formerly called the Mackhackamack, or Mohocamac (which see). Howell's map of 1792 gives the older name, as does also Pownall's map of 1776, which gives the name Niversink to a river above it. The name Neversink is a corruption of Navasink, which means, "at the promintory."

It was the name of a tribe of the Delawares which lived in the Navesink highlands of N. J. It belonged to the Unami clan. They are referred to by Beekman, in 1660, as "Nevesin," and by Andros in 1675, as "Nevisans" (Archives, Sec. Ser., VII. 636, 767). There were a number of Minsi villages along this river, and on the Delaware near its mouth. The chief village of Minisink, according to some maps, was on the eastern shore of the Delaware a few miles below the mouth of the Neversink. The four Minsi villages on the map of Vanderdonck, 1656, places the village of "Meoechkonck" on the north side of the Neversink, quite a distance above its junction with the Delaware. There are many variations and corruptions of the name Navesink, or Neversink. Consult; Handbook of American Indians, Part 2. 46. See *Mohocamac*.

NEWTOWN. The name of an Indian village situated on the left bank of the Chemung River, five miles below Elmira, New York. There were several Indian villages along the river from near the present Chemung to Elmira. All of these went by the name of Chemung. Old Chemung was near the present Chemung; New Chemung was a few miles above it; Newtown was a few miles above the former, above the present Lowman; Middle Town was opposite the Big Island; and Kanawohalla was at the site of Elmira. All of these village sites were passed through by the army of General Sullivan, August 1779. The Battle of Newtown was fought on August 29th. between the British Tories, led by Col. John Butler; the Indians led by the famous Mohawk, Joseph Brandt (Thayendanegea), and the army commanded by General John Sullivan (Consult; Journals of the Military Expedition of Major General John Sullivan, 1887; Journal of Lieut. Col. Adam Hubley, Jr. 1779, John W. Jordan, Editor. 1909; Beatty's Journal, Rodger's Journal, Letter of William Gray, in Archives of Penna. Sec. Ser., XV. 220-293, 1893).

NEWTYCHANNING. A former Iroquois village at the site of the present North Towanda, Bradford County, on the west bank of the Susquehanna, at the mouth of Sugar Creek. The origin of the name is not known. It was on the site of one of the villages of the Susquehanna (Conestoga) before they were driven from

the region. This town was called Oscalui (which see). When the place was reached by Col. Proctor, of Gen. Sullivan's army, on August 8, 1779, the village which consisted of 28 log houses, from which the inhabitants had fled. The houses were burned (Jour. of Campfield, Mil. Exped. Gen. Sull., 54).

Newtychaning.—Campfield (1779), op. cit. 54. **Newtycharming.**—Craft, in op. cit., 350.

NIANTIC. A village in Montgomery County. The names of a river, village and bay in Connecticut. Name said to mean, "at the point of land on a tidal river." The name does not have any historic significance in this state.

NIPPENOSE. The name of a creek, valley and town in Lycoming County. The creek enters the West Branch of the Susquehanna, opposite Jersey Shore, draining Nippenose Bottom. A corruption of Nipeno-wi, "like the summer"—signifying a pleasant situation. Ni-pen, "summer," Nipenaschen, "summer hunt." Meginness, in his "Otzinachson" (437), gives the following unique origin of the name, "The name is a corruption of that of an old Indian called Nippenucy, who had his wigwam there, and the Bottom of the same name, where he lived and hunted alternately. This is the true origin of the present title." On the very fine map of Morris (1848), the Nippenose Valley is noted as "Oval Limstone Valley." During the Indian hostility Lieut. Col. Henry Antes erected a fort on the east side of Nippenose Creek, on the high ground above, almost opposite Jersey Shore, at the present Fort Antes station on the P. R. R. Col. Antes was one of the most prominent men along the West Branch during the period of its settlement. It is stated that he went to the mouth of Nippenose Creek as early as 1772. Here he built a house and a mill. The region is most beautiful. The creek cuts through a gap in the Bald Eagle Mountain. The stockade fort was built during the summer of 1777. During this year and the year following the Indians made many raids into the white settlements along the river. Pine Creek, which enters the Susquehanna on the oppo site of the river, was one of the trails which led directly from the Seneca country in western New York, and the West Branch led to the divide between the Allegheny and the Susquehanna, while the Bald Eagle Valley was the course of several trails to the Ohio. The Indian trail to Chinklaclamoose (which see) crossed the West Branch at the present Lock Haven. All of these trails leading directly from the Indian wilderness to the west and north made the situation of these settlements particularly dangerous at the period when the various stockades were built. Fort Augusta, at the present Sunbury, was the only source of supply for arms and ammunition. Because of the various British efforts to harass the army of General Washington, by the various Indian attacks from the Seneca country, arms and ammunition, as well as men, were hard to get at these little stockade forts. Various thrilling events took place about this frontier fort. Job Chilloway, a friendly Delaware who is frequently mentioned in the Archives, was one of the frequent visitors to this fort. In the early part of the summer of 1778 Col. Hunter sent word from Fort Augusta to Fort Muncy (see Muncy) that it would be necessary for all of the inhabitants above the Muncy Hills to abandon their settlements and seek refuge at Fort Augusta. Robert Covenhoven was sent on this dangerous mission of carrying this message to Fort Antes. All of the settlements above Fort Muncy were abandoned. Then came the abandonment of Fort Muncy and all of the other points on the West Branch. The entire region was deserted. This flight of the settlers to Fort Augusta was known as the "Big Runaway." The letters of Col. Hunter at Fort Augusta, and the other letters of this period are filled with the thrilling events which were taking place along the West Branch. Consult; Meginness, Otzinachson, 216, 222, 236, 240, 245, 248, 270 etc.; Frontier Forts, I. 394-405; Archives, VI. 636-637, 664, 666 (and the various letters of Col. Hunter in this vol.); VII. (See Hunter's letters).

Nepanose (valley).—Howell, map, 1792. Antess, noted at mouth of creek. **Nipenoses.**—Scull, map, 1770. **Nippenose.**— Morris, map, 1848.

NITTABAKONCK. According to Acrelius this was the name of one of the Indian villages in the region of Philadelphia (Watson, Annals, I. 230). It is also mentioned in Egle, Hist. of Penna., as Nittabaconk (1017). According to the MS. map of Lindström, "Mittabakonck" was the name of the Schuylkill, or Menejackse (Manayunk) River. Nittabakonck is evidently simply an error (or visa versa), and should have "M," instead of the "N." While Heckewelder gives the derivation of Manayunk (Mene-iunk), "where we go to drink," the more probable derivation is, Menach-hen, "an island," with the locative onk, signifying "at the island." The name Mittabakonck may simply be a corruption of the same name. The other name, Menejeck, or Menejackse, may be a corruption of Menantachk, "a swamp." It is difficult, however, to give any accurate history of the name, with but the two forms—both of which are in fact the same, with the change of a single letter. See *Schuylkill, Manayunk.*

NITTANY. The name of a mountain and valley in Centre County. The name may be a corruption of Nekti, "single," and attin, "mountain," or "hill," or it may be a shortening of some other combination of the word attin, or adin, with some other Indian word. Is noted by the name Nittany on the maps of Scull (1770), Howell (1792), Morris (1848), and on later maps.

NOCKAMIXON. The name of a Township in Bucks County. Heckewelder gives the derevation from Nochanichsink, "where there are three houses."

Nockamixon.—Scull, map, 1759.

NOLAMATTINK. According to Heckewelder this was the name which the Delawares gave to that part of the Nazareth Tract, upon which Gnadenthal and Christian's Spring lay, and which abounded in mulberry trees. The name means, "where the silkworm spins." Reichel says in a note (Indian Names, 258) that in June 1752, Philip C. Bader, who was conducting the culture of silk-worms at Bethlehem, removed his cocoonery to Christian's Spring, and suggests that the name was given because of this circumstance.

NORTH MEHOOPANY. See *Mehoopany.* (A village in Wyoming County).

NORTH SEWICKLEY. See *Sewickley.* (A village in Beaver County).

NORTH TOWANDA. See *Towanda.* (A town in Bradford County).

OCTORARO. The name of a creek which enters the Susquehanna from the east at Rolandville, Maryland. Its headwaters are in Chester County, and its course is on the line between Chester and Lancaster Counties. When the Dutch and Swedes made their settlements on the Delaware they carried on a trade with the Minquas, or Susquehannas, from the region of Octoraro Creek. These Indians reached the Delaware by way of Octoraro Creek, Christina and Minquas Creek. John Smith in his map and Description of Virginia, locates a village of the Susquehannas above the mouth of this creek. This was the site of the "Susquehannock Fort," the exact situation of which had much to do with the dispute between the Penns and Calverts, as the southern boundary of Pennsylvania was marked by it. This fort is mentioned by Vice-Director Alrichs, in a letter to Director Stuyvesant, in 1657. He says, "Afterwards a Minquaas savage with some other savages came here into the Colony (at Chester), who commands in the fort nearest here in the Minquaas' country, and brought some wampum and other things, which they had taken from the savage there, who had perpetrated the crime," which was the killing of Lourens Hansen, a trader from Christina, or Altena, as it was called by the Dutch (Archives, Sec. Ser., VII. 512). In the Documents relating to the Boundary Dispute, a number of statements were taken from various persons concerning the exact situation of this fort. James Hendricks, in his statement says, "That the Affirmant was then told, by some of the Indians there residing (at the mouth of the creek), that they called the same Place Meanock, which they said, in English, signified a Fortification or Fortified Town. Has also seen the Ruins of another such Fortified Town on the East side of Susquehannah River aforesaid, opposite to a Place where one Thomas Cresap lately dwelt. That the land there on both sides of the said River was formerly called Conajocula" (See *Conejohela*). This latter fort was the one which stood on the western side of the Susquehanna, a few miles below the present Wrightsville, York County, opposite Washington Borough, Lancaster County. This was the site of Cresap's Fort, and also of the Susquehanna Fort of 1670. The name which Hendricks gives to the village at the mouth of Octoraro Creek, "Meanock," is used of other fortified places. Menachk, is an enclosed place, hence a fortification. Menachkhasu, is the word which Zeisberger gives for "fortified place." The papers relating to the situation of this fort are found in Archives of Penna., Second Series, XVI. 522-525 (the entire vol. is taken up with the Boundary dispute). The line due west, from the most southern part of Philadelphia (old city) crosses the Susquehanna a few miles south of Cresap's Fort; the line agreed upon by His Majesty's order in 1739 crosses the Susquehanna above the mouth of Octoraro Creek, about 15 and a quarter miles due south of the other line (Map of the Survey of 1739, in Archives, I. 564). The Temporary line run by Talbot, in 1683, ran from the mouth of Namaan's Creek, on the Delaware, to the mouth of Octorara Creek. The dispute concerning this line caused much bitter strife between the settlers along the lower Susquehanna, and was the cause of much feeling between the two Colonies. In 1684 it was reported to William Penn that "Jonas Askins heard Coll. Talbot say, that if Govr. Penn should come into Maryland, he would Seize him & his retairee (retinue) in their Journey to Susquehannah fort" (Col. Rec. I. 114). The Minquas, or Susquehannas (Conestoga), who lived along the Susquehanna River, at the time of John Smith and the Dutch and Swedish settlement of the Delaware, were conquered and almost blotted out by the Iroquois in 1675 (See *Susquehanna*). Consult; Hanna, Wilderness Trail, I. 29 et seq. Archives, I. 348 et seq.; Archives, Sec. Ser. XVI. (entire vol.). In 1707 Governor Evans, when on his way to hold a Council with the Indians at Conestoga and other villages, went from New Castle, Del. to the mouth of Octorara Creek, where he was given various presents by the Indians then living there (Col. Rec. II. 386).

Auchteraroe.—Keith (1722), Colonial Records, III. 179. **Octarara.**—Hamilton (1734), Colonial Records, III. 561. **Octararoe.**—Board of Prop. (1713), Archives, Sec. Ser., XIX. 571; **Octoraro.**—Wright (1732), Archives, I. 364; Boundary Map (1739), 564. **Otararoe.**—Board of Prop. (1717), Archives, Sec. Ser., XIX. 626. **Otteraroe.**—Evans (1707), Col. Rec., II. 386. **Ouchteraroe.**—Keith (1722), Col. Rec., III. 179.

OGHQUAGY. See *Oquaga*.

OGONTZ. A village in Montgomery

County; also the name of a young woman's school called Ogontz, in same county. Said to be the name of an Indian chief. Can find no authority for the statement.

OHESSON. See *Kishacoquillas*.

OHIOPILE, or OHIO PYLE. The name of the falls in the Youghiogheny River, in Fayette County. A corruption of Ohiopehelle, signifying, "water whitened by froth"—by falling over rocks. When Washington was at the Great Crossings, May 20, 1754, on his way to Redstone, his army encamped near the present Somerfield, he went down the Youghiogheny with Lieut. West, three soldiers and an Indian to explore the river. He may have had an idea of making his base of supplies on this river, instead of on the Monongahela, and wished to discover the possibility of sending his supplies, and army, down this river, instead of crossing the mountains. He explored as far as Turkey Foot that night. The next morning he went on down the river about ten miles, in a canoe, and was obliged to go ashore. The river was more rapid and full of rocks. It is possible that Washington may have gone down to the falls. See *Turkey Foot*.

Great Falls.—Scull, map, 1770. **Ohiopile Falls.**—Howell, map, 1792. **Ohiopyle Falls.**—Evans, map, 1755.

OHIO. There has been much discussion as to the exact origin and meaning of this name of the river, which from its source in Potter County to its mouth on the Mississippi, was known as the Ohio, or Allegheny River. The present river, Ohio, was looked at as being a continuation of the stream which is now known as the Allegheny. The Monongahela was simply a tributary of this stream. It will not be possible in this note to enter into the entire discussion concerning this name, by which the river was known to all of the early explorers and travellers. Heckewelder says, "There are persons who would have had me believe that the Ohio signified "the beautiful river," and others "the river red with blood," or the "bloody river." He said that the Delawares always called the river Kit-hanne, "great river," or "main stream." Hence, Kittanning, "on the great river." Heckewelder then goes on to give the various meanings of Indian (Delaware) words,

similar in sound to Ohio—such as Ohiopeek, "white with froth," Ohiopeekhanne, "a stream whitened by froth," and other forms, in which the Delaware word, or sound, Ohio, is found. He mentions the fact (which the author has frequently noticed), that the river, during an up-stream wind, is covered with white caps, and says that the Indians would exclaim, "Ohiopeek, it is very white"; or, "Ohiophanne, the stream is very white." And such is the meaning which he gives the name. But, the river had the name Ohio, or Oyo, before the Delawares had migrated to the banks of the stream, and when they were living on the banks of the Delaware. The earliest French maps give the name Ohio, and invariably translate it, "La Belle Riviere," or "The Beautiful River." When the French explorers, LaSalle, DeLery Celoron and others first reached the river they came in contact with the Seneca, or other Iroquois tribes, who gave them the name, which they translated. Ohio is not a Delaware word, but a Seneca word, or compound, which does signify "Beautiful River." Ohio was the Seneca name for the river. Alligewi-sipu, or more properly, Tallagewi-sipu, was the Delaware name (hence Allegheny, which see). Ohi-io is the form used in the "Code of Handsome Lake," the Seneca prophet (Code of Handsome Lake, 20, 1913). This is the form given by A. C. Parker (op. cit.), with the significance "River Beautiful." The various derivations, and meanings, given by Spafford, "endless river," as the meaning of Allegheny; Trumbell (Welhik-hanne—Allegheny), "fairest river," and the meaning of Ohio, as given by Mary Jemison, "bloody river," are simply interesting, but have no foundation whatever. They are similar to the confusion in names made by Trumbell, who says, "The Indian name of the Alleghenies has been said—I do not remember on whose authority to mean "endless mountains" (Aboriginal Place Names in New York, 25, 1907). The name used is not Allegheny but Kittatinny, which was so translated—"endless mountains"—and the authority is the Indian Deed of 1749, and other Indian Deeds for the Susquehanna lands (See *Kittatinny*).

Herrman's map of Virginia and Maryland (1670), in the legend at the top of the map, calls the river "the Black Minquaas River." Who these

Black Minquaas were has never been discovered. They belonged to the Iroquoian stock, and were destroyed by the Iroquois and the Susquehannas (Conestoga) before 1670. Previous to that time they carried on a trade with the Dutch and Swedes on the Delaware. According to Van der Donck they were called Black, "because they wear a black badge on their breast, and not because they are really black" (Handbook of Amer. Ind., II. 659). They are mentioned by Hudde, in 1656, as "Southern Indians (called Minquas) and the Black Indians"—the former name having reference to the Susquehanna. These Indians were then carrying Beaver skins to the Delaware (Archives, Sec. Ser., V. 250). In 1662 William Beekman informed Director Stuyvesant, "The Chiefs informed us among others, that they were (the Susquehannas) expecting shortly for their assistance 800 black Minquas, and that 200 of this nation had already come in, so that they were fully resolved to go to war with the Sinnecus next spring and visit their fort. They asked therefore, that we Christians should not neglect to provide them with ammunition of war against payment" (Archives, Sec. Ser., VII. 695). There seems some grounds for thinking that these "Black Minquas" were either the Erie or the Wenro. While the term Sinnecus was applied to the Iroquois in general, it was the name of the present Seneca. In 1681 Jacob Young stated before the Council at St. Mary's (Maryland), after a visit to the Indians to the northward, and accompanied by an Onondaga and an Oneida, from whom he got his information, "They likewise say that another nation called the Black Mingoes, are joined with the Sinnondowanes, who are the right Sinniquos; that they were so informed by some New York Indians whom they met as they were coming down. That they told then that the Black Mingoes in their way coming to the Sinniquos, were pursued by some Southern Indians, set upon and routed, several of them taken and bound, till the Sinniquos come unto their relief" (Hanna, I. 68-69). On Louis Franquelin's map (1684), the river is marked as, "Ohio ats Mosopeleacipi ats Olighin." The Mosopelea was a tribe which has not been identified. It is noted on Marquette's map (1681), as having a village on the Mississippi,

just below the mouth of the Ohio. In 1682 LaSalle met a Mosopelea chief who was living among the Taensea, to which place he had gone after the destruction of his villages by some unknown enemy. On Franquelin's map, about midway up the Ohio there is marked "Mosapelea. 8 Vil. detruit" (Mosopelea. 8 villages, destroyed). These villages were situated about midway on the river Ohio, or between the Sciota and the site of Pittsburgh. On De l'Isle's map of Louisana, on the southern bank of the Ohio there is marked, "les Tongoria" (the Iroquois name for the Ontwaganha, which means "foreigners," and included the Miami, Shawnee and other alien tribes). This name is placed about south of Franquelin's "Mosapelea"— on the opposite side of the Ohio. These were probably the Shawnee. The region from which the Mosopelea were driven, and their villages destroyed, was about the region in which the various earthen mounds are found. In Cyrus Thomas' Problem of the Ohio Mounds (Washington, 1889) he gives many reasons for thinking that these mounds were built by the Tallegwi (Heckewelder's Allegewi), who were the ancestors of the present Cherokee. These Tallegwi, as well as the Cherokee, were mound builders. The most important point in his very fine argument is however the fact that "when this tradition (of Heckewelder, See *Allegheny*) was first made known, and the mounds mentioned were attributed to this people, these ancient works were almost unknown to the investigating minds of the country. This forbids the supposition that the tradition was warped or shaped to fit a theory in regard to the origin of these antiquities" (op. cit. 45). There can be little doubt but that the Tallegwi (Cherokee) were the builders of these mounds in the Sciota valley, and probably those along the Ohio River above this region. Is it then not possible that the Mosopelea and the Tallegwi were one and the same people, and that the name "Mosopeleacipi" (River of the Mosopelea), and "Olighin" (or Heckewelder's Allagewi-sipu) are simply names for the same people who lived along the shores of the Ohio, the Tallegwi? And may it not also be possible that the "Black Minquas," the Mosopelea and the Tallegwi were simply different names for the same Iroquoian tribe? The mound builders were

evidently the most prominent tribe
which lived on the Ohio in this period
before the historic days, and in the
period before 1670 the "Black Minquas" were the most prominent and
warlike tribe living on the Ohio. The
Eries, who were destroyed by the
Iroquois in 1654-56, may have been a
tribe which separated from the main
body of the Tallegwi, as the former
occupied the region which joined that
of the latter along the Allegheny and
Ohio. Both were of Iroquoian stock.
VanKeulen's map of New France
(1720) marks the river, "Riv. d'Ohis
autrement apelec Acansea Sipi," or
River of the Akansea." Gravier
stated, 1701, that the Ohio was known
to the Miami and Illinois as the
"river of the Akansea" because that
people had formerly lived upon it.
The Akansea, or Arkansa, is a Siouan
tribe which was living in that year on
the Arkansas River. The traditions
of the Osage, Kwapa and Omaha all
have traditions which carry them back
to the headwaters of the Ohio, as the
land from which they migrated westward. Catlin, Sibley, Dorsey and
others heard this same tradition from
the various tribes related to the
Akansea (Consult; Mooney, Siouan
Tribes of the East, 10 et seq., 1894).
It is of passing interest to notice that
Catlin seems inclined to think that the
earthen mounds in Ohio were built
by the "Welsh colony, the followers
of Madoc," who sailed up the Mississippi and then up the Ohio to the
region of the Muskingum, where they
flourished until the savages about them
became jealous and assaulted their
settlements. They then built the
earthen fortifications, as a protection
against the savages. They then left
the region, going to the Missouri, and
then on up that river to the country
where Catlin met the Mandans, whom
he regarded as the descendants of
these Welsh colonists. This theory
was advanced by Catlin because of
the various peculiar facts he mentions, in the appearence of these Indians—hair of all colors, of civilized
society, blue eyes, hazel eyes etc.
(The George Catlin Gallery, 459, 1886;
Catlin's Eight Years, I. 206-207). In
all of the French documents and
letters of the historic period, after
1748, the river is always mentioned
as, "Ohio ou La Belle Riviere," and
so it became known to the British,
who first entered the region (officially)

in 1748. See *Allegheny, Logstown,
Conewango, Venango etc.*
Consult; Colonial Records, IV. 736;
V. 122, 137, 139, 146 etc.; VI. 180, 205,
219, 257 etc. Archives, II. 144, 171,
173, 209 etc.; III. 369, 459 etc.; Second
Ser. VI. 110 etc.

OHIO INDIANS. A geographic
group, mentioned in the Archives and
Records (Archives, I. 144 etc.). Included all of the various tribes living on the Ohio. The same as Allegheny Indians.

OHIO, TRAIL TO. A name given
to the various trails leading to the
Ohio from the Susquehanna, and also
the Great Trail from the Iroquois
country down the river. The Allegheny Path, Frankstown Path, Nemacolin Trail, Shamokin Trail, and the
trail down the Ohio, were all referred
to in various records as Trail, or
Path, to the Ohio. See *Allegheny, Kittanning, Frankstown etc.*

For the Forts on the Ohio, See *Logstown, Pittsburgh, Venango, etc.*

The following legends from the various maps, arranged according to date
of map, may be of interest. Other
names will be found under note on
Allegheny.

Black Minquaas River.—Herrman's map,
1670. **Ohio ats Mosopeleacipi ats Olighin.**—Franquelin's map, 1684. **Ohio on
la Belle Riviere.**—De l'Isle's map, 1718.
**Riv.d'Ohis autrement apelec Acansea
Sipi.**—VanKeulen's map, 1720. **I'oyo ou
la Belle Riviere.**—Bellin's map, 1744.
**Ohio or Allegeny R.or La Belle R.and
Palawa Thepiki by the Shawanese.**—
Evans, map, 1755. **Ohio River (as at
present).**—Scull's map, 1770. **Fleuve de
l'Ohyo.**—Crevcoeur's map, 1787. **Ohio
River.**—Howell's map, 1792.

The first Indian traders to cross
the mountains were those whose
names are noted in various notes relating to the history of the Indian
villages on the Ohio (See *Logstown,
Kuskuski, Venango, Kittanning etc.*).
The first of these of whom any records can be found, were Arnold Viele,
James LeTort, Edmund Cartlidge,
Hugh Crawford, George Croghan,
Christopher Gist, John Fraser etc.
These traders crossed the mountains
and went to the Ohio, and on to
the Muskingum before 1727. Some of
them possibly before 1717. The first
white traveller down the Allegheny
and Ohio was probably the Dutch
trader, form Albany, Arnold Viele,
who went from the Delaware, *via*
the Wyoming and Shamokin Paths, to
the Ohio, in the fall of 1692. He
returned from the Shawnee villages

along the Ohio in 1694, bringing with him a number of Shawnees who settled above the Delaware Water Gap. James LeTort was perhaps the first Pennsylvania trader to go to the Ohio region. He was carrying on a trade with the Ohio Indians before 1727 (See *Le Tort's Spring*).

The first official mission to the Ohio was that of Conrad Weiser, who held a Council with the Indians at Logstown in 1748 (See *Logstown*). The expedition of Celoron de Bienville in 1749, and other Ohio expeditions are noted under *Logstown, Pittsburgh, Venango, Kuskuski, Redstone etc.*

OKEHOCKING. The name of the Indian town or reservation which was established by William Penn in 1701. Pokahis, Sepopawny and Muttagooppa and their people were given this tract by Penn after their lands had been purchased. The site, four miles west of Newtown Square and 17 miles west of Philadelphia, was marked by the Pennsylvania Historical Commission and the Chester County Historical Society, June 21, 1924.

OKOME. The name of a village in Lycoming County. May be an Indian name, or a corruption of one. There is a river in Georgia called Okomi, which is said to mean "great water." The name is not historic.

OLD TOWN. A term frequently to former Indian villages by the early settlers, and also noted on some of the early maps, in various localities. Chartier's Town, Shawnee Town, and other places were referred to as Old Town, or with the name prefixed, as Chartier's Old Town etc. Old Town, Maryland, below the present Cumberland at site of Oldtown, was the most prominent place so c a l l e d. C o l. Thomas Cresap lived at this place, after his removal from the Susquehanna. His house was on the trail which led through Cumberland to the Ohio, via Nemacolin's Trail, and was also near the place where the Warrior's Path crossed the Potomac. Christopher Gist made this the starting place for his journey to the Ohio in 1750 (Gist's Jour., 32, 90, 219). The site is noted on Evan's map (1755) as, Crassops, and on Scull's map (1770) as, Col. Cressops. The name "Old Town" was given because the flat had previously been occupied by the Shawnee. The wide flats along the Potomac at this point are similar

to those along the Susquehanna, Ohio and other rivers where the Indians had extensive corn f i e l d s. The "Shawno Indian Fields d e s e r t e d," along the Potomac River, between the Little Cacapon and the Savage Rivers, are noted in two places on the survey maps of the land belonging to the Rt. Hon. Lord Fairfax Baron Cameron, as surveyed in 1736-1737. This map, dated 1745, is in the Library of Congress. In 1779, when Col. Daniel Brodhead was in command of Fort Pitt, he wrote to General Washington, "The quantity of flour on hand at these Magazines is very small, and I am informed that there is none at Cumberland, or Old Town." And he also wrote to Col. George Morgan, "I am informed that there is no flour at Old Town' (Archives, XII. 147, 153). In 1781 he wrote to President Reed (of Penna.), "And now I have the mortification to be informed by his (Mr. Wilson's) Brother, who is just arrived form Old Town, that a Prohibitory Law of the State of Virginia will prevent his getting the Cattle he may have purchased for consumption here" (Archives, VIII. 707). The cause of the lack of provisions at Fort Pitt at this time, which made it necessary to send to Old Town for flour and supplies, was due in a great measure to the severe winter of 1779-80, which was called "the Winter of the deep snow." The snow was four feet deep in the woods and on the mountains. The farmers in Westmoreland County were unable to feed their stock. Because of the deep snow in the woods game of all sorts perished. This winter was followed by a summer which was noted for its large harvests. The settlers however were not anxious to sell their flour or cattle because Col. Brodhead paid them in due bills. This "money" was of little value. The troops at Fort Pitt were in a starving condition. At last Brodhead had to resort to sever measures. He sent Capt. Sam Brady to take cattle, by force, if necessary. Even this did not bring the needed supplies, as the farmers drove their cattle into the woods to hide them. A great many Delawares were driven to Fort Pitt for food. Brodhead was obliged to tell them his condition. The settlers in Westmoreland County, who hated all Indians went to Fort Pitt, intending to kill these friendly Delawares. Brodhead threw a guard about the

Indian camp, and western Pennsylvania was spared placing another blot on its history. After Brady had failed to get the needed cattle, Brodhead made arrangements with the Indians to go on a hunting expedition to the Kanawha region. He hoped to keep his garrison from starvation by the buffalo and other game which these Indians would bring (Consult; Archives, VIII. 487, 514-515, 536, 558, 559, 583, 589, 596; Craig, Olden Time, II. 377-378).

OLEY. The name of a Township in Berks County; also a mountain ridge in the same county. A corruption of Olink (also Wahlink, Woalac) "a hole," also a "cove," a tract of land surrounded by hills. This was one of the earliest settlements in Berks County. Many of the first settlers were German emigrants from the Palatinate, French Huguenots a n d Friends. Among the latter were Arthur Lee and George Boone (ancestor of Daniel Boone). Isaac Turk was one of the first of the French Huguenots to settle at Oley. He took up land at Oley in 1712. John Le-Dee and some others took up land at "a place called Oley, about 50 Miles Distant from Philadelphia, and settled thereon, but without any agreement or survey," in 1709. "The said John, which (should be "with") Isaac de Turck and John FFrederick-fields (all Germans), by further leave Granted them, procured the Surveyor (p. J. L. ord'r) to lay out to John Le-Dee 300 acres, to Isaac de Turck 300 acres, to John FFrederickfields 500 acres, for which they agree to pay ten pounds p. hundred" (Archives, Sec. Ser., XIX. 517). This Isaac de Turck was the father of John de Turck in whose house at Esopus the Synod of the United Brethren met in 1742, during the visit of Count Zinzendorf (Memorials of the Mor. Church, I. 180). According to the Archives Isaac de Turck was at Oley in 1709, and not at the later date given for his removal from Esopus—1712. Oley was one of the first fields occupied by the Moravian Church in Pennsylvania. Consult; Loskiel, Hist. of Mor. Miss., II. 19-20; Reichel Mem. Mor. Church, I. 75.

Oley.—Board of Prop. (1712), Archives, Sec. Ser., XIX. 517. **Oley Hills.**—Evans map, 1749. **Olly Hills.**—Scull, map, 1770. **Oly.**—Loskiel, in Hist. Miss. of U. B., 1794.

ONEIDA. The name of a town in Butler County; also a village in Schuylkill County. Named after the tribe of the Iroquois confederation. A corruption of the name or term, Tiionen-iote, "a standing stone"—set up by some one. The tribe occupied the region south of Oneida Lake, and the Upper Susquehanna. The tribe has three clans; Turtle, Wolf and Bear. The tribes on the Susquehanna, chiefly the Conestoga, were conquered chiefly by the Oneida, Cayuga and Seneca. The sale of the lands at Wyoming by the Mohawk, who had not helped in the conquest of the Susquehanna Indians, led the Council at Onondaga, in 1728, to appoint Shikellamy, an Oneida, as vice-gerent of the Iroquois on the Susquehanna, with headquarters at Shamokin (w h i c h see). The great body of the Tuscarora and Oneida were neutral during the Revolution. The hostile Iroquois burned one of the Oneida villages, because of this friendliness towards the Americans. Some of the Oneida were with Sullivan's army, as guides, in 1779. In 1683 the Cayuga and Onondaga claimed that the Oneida, Seneca and Mohawk had nothing whatever to do with the Susquehanna lands. They said that they had conveyed these lands four years before to the Governor of New York (Dutch Record C. No. 3, Albany. Also in Papers Relating to the Susquehanna River, 396). See *Susquehanna.* The number of the Oneida at various times are merely estimates. In 1660 they were estimated at 500; 1677, 1000; 1795, 660. and in 1906 about 3,220. The Oneida are frequently mentioned in the Archives and Records, in their relation to the affairs in the Province of Pennsylvania. Consult; Records, IV. 707, 776,; VI. 112, 117, 289, 342, 651; VII. 67, 68; VIII. 586, 746; Archives, I. 657, 756; II. 428; X. 63 etc.

ONEOQUAGY. See *Oquaga.*

ONOKO, GLEN. A beautiful glen and water falls on the Lehigh, in Carbon County. The site is not noted by its present name on the early maps. The name is of recent origin. It may be a corruption of the Delaware Woakeu, "it bends." There are variations of this name in other places. as Onunk, Onuc, etc.

ONONDAGA. The name of a village in Jefferson County. Named after the tribe of the Iroquois confederation, the name of which is derived from Ononta-ge, "on the hill, or mountain top." Among the Iroquois they were known as Hodisnnageta, "they, the name bearers." They lived in the region of the present Onondaga County, New York. Their chief village of Onondaga was situated before 1654 in the present town of Pompey (N. Y.). The village was removed in 1681 to Butternut Creek, where the fort was burned in 1696. In 1720 it was moved back to Butternut Creek. Onondaga was the capital of the Iroquois confederation. In 1535 Cartier was informed that the Iroquoian tribes on the St. Lawrence were being warred against by the enemies to the south, probably the Seneca. In 1686 they were at war with a tribe called Cherermons, probably Shawnee. All of these various conflicts between the Iroquoian tribes led to the formation of the League of the Iroquois, in about 1570. The Onondaga was the last of the five tribes to enter this league (Consult; Parkman, Bancroft, Handbook of American Indians, under title). During the Colonial period, Pennsylvania, Virginia and Maryland sent a number of messengers to Onondaga, to hold conferences with the Council of the Iroquois at that place. These conferences had to deal with the various land disputes of the Iroquois with Virginia, Maryland and Pennsylvania. Conrad Weiser went on a mission to Onondaga in 1743 (Col. Rec. IV. 660-669). He was sent again in 1745 (Col Rec. IV. 778-782). Another mission was made in 1750 (Col. Rec. V. 470-480). An Onondaga chief (Connodaghtoh) was present at a Council in Philadelphia in 1701, when the "Articles of Agreement" between the Provincial authorities and the Conestoga, Shawnee and Conoy were made (Col. Rec. II. 15). From this time onward the Onondaga are frequently mentioned in the Records and Archives (Col. Rec. II. 159, 204; III. 123, 570; IV. 80; V. 388, 474, 637, 642, VI. 77, 128, 188, 193, 340; VII. 13, 20, 22, 26, 68, 116, 128, 244, 503, 762; VIII. 121, 615, 644, 647, 762; Archives, I. 230, 649; II, 24, 32; IV. 107 etc.). The Onondaga were given various names, a few of which are; Anandagas, Honnontages, Montagnes, Mountaineers, Onandages etc.

ONTELAUNEE. The name of a R. R. station in Berks County, wrongly printed on the state map (1911) as Ontelauntee; also the Indian name of the present Maiden Creek (a l s o wrongly, Maidens Creek, on the state map). All of the early maps (Evans 1749; Scull, 1759 etc.) give the name as Maiden Creek. Count Zinzendorf passed over this creek in the summer of 1742 on his way to the home of Conrad Weiser at Heidelberg (Mem-Mor. Church, I. 31). Bishop Cammerhoff mentions "the Ontelaunee" in his Journal of 1748 (Pennsylvania Magazine of Hist., XXIX. 162). He spent the night at the home of Moses Starr, a Quaker. Watson (Annals of Phil., II. 475), says "It is told as a tradition that the Indians called the river (Schuylkill) the mother, and that what is called 'Maiden Creek', a branch of the Schuylkill above Reading was called Onteelaunee, meaning "little daughter of a great mother."

OPASISKUNK. The name of an Indian village, mentioned in a Deed to William Penn in 1683, from Kekelappan (or Kekerappan), for lands between the Delaware and Susquehanna. The village was probably on the Susquehanna River, in the region of Conestoga Creek. Opasiskunk is not mentioned elsewhere (Archives, I. 67).

OPESSA'S TOWN. There were two Shawnee villages bearing this name; one was situated on the Susquehanna River, possibly near Shamokin, or Wyoming, and the other was at the site of Oldtown, Maryland. Opessa, or Opetha (also Wopaththa was the Shawnee "King" who entered into the Treaty of Peace with William Penn in 1701, after the arrival of the Shawnee in the Province in 1698. This tribe first settled at the mouth of Pequea Creek, where they were visited by Governor Evans, at their village of Pequehan in 1707. In 1711 Opessa deserted his tribe and gave up his "Kingship," in order to go with the Delawares of Sassouan's tribe. Various traditions are told concerning this "King" having fallen in love with a Delaware maiden, who would not leave her tribe, so he gave up his position as leading chief of the Shawnee, in order to be with his beloved maiden. In 1714 the Shawnee elected Cakundawanna as King, to take the place of Opessa (Col. Rec. II. 574). In 1730 Joshua Lowe, in a letter to Governor Gordon, speaks of Patrick Boyd coming down from "Opessa Toune," when he was at "Pechston (Paxtang)—so that the town must have been above Paxtang (Archives, II. 269). As Opessa had gone with the tribe of Sassounan, who lived at

Shamokin, it is probable that this Opessa Town was in that region. It is probable that the Opessa Town, at the site of Oldtown, Maryland, was so called because it had been occupied by the Shawnee, under Opessa, before —and not after—he had given up the chieftainship of the tribe. This town was called Opessa's Town in 1725 (Maryland Archives, VIII. 443). The Shawnee villages along the Potomac were deserted before 1737, as they are so noted on the various survey maps made in 1737-39.

Consult; Colonial Records, II. 510-11, 574, 599, 608; IV. 234, 346; Archives, II. 269.

The name Wopaththa may be a corruption of Wapalaneathy, "an eagle."

ONONTEJO, ONONTIO. The Iroquois name for the Governors of Canada. Was frequently used at the various Indian Councils in referring to the Governor of Canada, or to Canada. The term, which means, "great mountain," is also used of the King of France. During the French and Indian War the French King, Governor of Canada, and the French power was nearly always mentioned by the Indians by this name. The form is sometimes Onontiquoah (Col. Rec., V. 475); Onontejo (Col. Rec. III. 444); Onnontio (Archives, Sec. Ser., VI. 110).

OQUAGA. A former Iroquois village, on both sides of the Susquehanna River, and also an island, at the site of the present Colesville, New York. The name is of Mohawk origin, and means "place of wild grapes." In 1754 the Rev. Gideon Hawley, a Presbyterian Minister, established a mission in this village among the Oneida and Tuscarora residents. The settlement consisted of three villages about two miles from each other in 1756. The Indians from this settlement are frequently mentioned in the records as "Oneocquagos," "Oghquagis" etc., at the various Councils. A number of these were present at the Council at Albany in 1754 (Col. Rec. VI. III. 128, 468; VII. 11-12, 43, 68, 72). The "Tuscarora village," which is mentioned in the Journal of Beatty (1779) as being about three miles below the village at which General Clinton's Brigade encamped, is called "Lower Tuscarora Onohoquage," in a letter from Angus, a Tuscarora chief, in 1762. This letter was written by Rev. Eli Forbes, a missionary in the set-

tlements (Col. Rec. VIII. 722-23; Beatty's Journal, Archives, Sec. Ser., XV. 232). In 1763 the settlement was made up of Delaware, Tuscarora, Oneida and Munsee (Col. Rec. IX. 46). The settlement was partially destroyed by Gen. Butler, with the Fourth Penna. Regt., on October 8 and 9, 1778 (Archives, Sec. Ser., X 495). General Clinton's Brigade, on its way to join the army of General Sullivan, encamped here on August 14-17, 1779. In the Journal of Lieut. E. Beatty (afterwards Major), who was with Clinton's Brigade, he mentions this as one of the neatest Indian towns on the river. The settlement was on both sides of the river, containing about 60 houses and a Church. According to the map of Capt. William Gray, this church was on the east side of the river (Archives, Sec. Ser., XV. 232, 289). Beatty mentions the ruins of an old fort being at this place.

A c q u a g u a.—VanHovenburgh (1779), Jour. Sull. Exped., 277. **Anaquago.**—Butler (1778), Archives Sec. Ser., X. 495. **Ocquaghho.**—Peters (1754), Col. Rec., VI. 128. **Ocquago.**—McKendry (1779), Jour. Sull. Exped., 201. **Oghquagis.**—Penna. Coun. (1756), Col. Rec., VII. 72. **Oghquagy.**—Adams (1756), Col. Rec., VII. 43. **Onaghquage.**—Johnson (1769), Archives, IV. 349. **Onehaghguagy.**—Claus (1755), Col. Rec., VI. 468. **Oneocquago.**—Penn (1754), Col. Rec., VI. 111. **Oneocquagos.**—Penn. Coun. (1756), Col. Rec., VII. 90. **Oneoquage.**—Penna. Coun. (1756), Col. Rec. VII. 68. **Oneoquago.**—Penna. Coun. (1756), Col. Rec. VII. 12. **Onnaquaugo.**—McKendry (1779), Jour. Sull. Exped., 202. **Onoghquagy.**—Johnson (1768), Archives, IV. 290. **Onohaghguago.**—Letter from (1757), Col. Rec. VII. 763. **Onohoquaga.**—Penna. Coun. (1763), Col. Rec. IX. 68. **Onohoquage.**—Forbes (1762), Col. Rec. VIII. 723. **Onohoquagey.**—P e n n a. C o u n. (1763), Col. Rec. IX. 46. **Onohquage.**—Hawley (1756), Col. Rec. VII. 12. **Ononaughquagy.**—Gray, map, 1778. Archives, Sec. Ser., XV. 289. **Onoquaga.**—Beatty (1779), Jour. Sull. Exped., 23.

ORECHTON ISLAND. An island in the Delaware, opposite Trenton, on the western side of the river. Probably the island now known as Biles Island. In 1679 the Indians informed Edmund Cantwell that they would make no objection to the laying out of lands "from the beginning of the Falls downe to the lower end of Orechton Island and no further" (Archives, Sec. Ser., VII. 801). Ockenichan is mentioned as one of the chief owners of the land in this region. In the Deed to William Penn (the first Deed of Indian lands to him), July 15, 1682, Okonikon is one of the owners of the land deeded, and Orecton acts for Nannacussey. This Deed covers the islands in the Delaware, "knowne by the severall names of Mattinicunk Island, Sepassincks Island, and Orecktons Island, lying or being in the sayd River Dellaware (Archives, I. 47-48). On the Historical Map of Pennsylvania (1875), the island now known as Moon Island, is marked "Orictous Is."

OSCALUI. A former Susquehanna (Conestoga) village, at the mouth of Sugar Creek, Bradford County. The word is said to mean "fierce." In various writings it is said that there was a village at this place called Ogehage (note by Gen. John S. Clark, Jour. Sull. Exped., 124). Ogehage was the Mohawk form of the name of the Conestoga, and is the name of of the people, rather than of the village. It is given on Hendricksen's map of 1616. Carantonannais is also a name of the Conestoga, or Susquehanna. Carantouan, which was one of the chief palisaded towns of the Conestoga in 1615, was situated above Oscalui at the site of Waverly, New York, and on what is now known as "Spanish Hill" in Bradford County, nearly opposite. In 1615 when Champlain, with the Huron allies, made his attack upon the Onondaga fort, in Fenner Township, Madison County, New York, he had sent his interpreter, Estienne Brule, to Carantouan to get the 500 warriors which they had promised to send to assist the Huron. Brule did not return with the promised warriors. Champlain returned to France, having given up the attack upon the Onondaga fort. He returned to Canada in 1618, when he met Brule and received an account of his failure to reach Champlain. Brule had gone to Carantouan, which was then a strongly fortified place, defended by 800 warriors. After various experiences the 500 Conestoga warriors were gotten ready, but did not reach the Onondaga fort until after Champlain had departed. They then returned to Carantouan, where Brule was obliged to remain all winter because he could not get an escort to take him home. Brule then spent the time in exploring the region along the river to the southward, until he reached the sea. He then returned to Carantouan until some of the Indians offered to take him home. The three towns of the Carantouannais were Carantouan (at Waverly, and then at Spanish Hill) ; Oscalui, at

the mouth of Sugar Creek (Towanda, at the mouth of Towanda Creek, was probably a part of this settlement), and Gahontoto, at the site of Wyalusing. The early writers and travellers make mention of the existence of long deserted villages of unknown tribes being found at three places (See *Towanda, Wyalusing*). The Carantouannais, Andastes, Ogehage, or Susquehannocks before 1615 occupied the entire region along the Susquehanna to the mouth of Octorara Creek. They were finally overcome, and almost destroyed by the Iroquois in 1675 (See *Conestoga, Susquehanna*). Conrad Weiser, in his Journal of his mission to Onondaga in 1737, gives the name Oscahu to the present Sugar Creek.

Ogehage.—Hendricksen, map. 1616 (in N. Y. Doc. Col. Hist., I. 1856). **Oscahu.**—Weiser (1737), Pub. Hist. Soc. Pa, Coll. I. 1853. **Oscalui.**—Clark, in Jour. Mil. Exped. Sull., 124. (note). **Osculi.**—Egle, Hist. Pa., 409. See NEWTYCHANNING.

The form given by Bishop Spangenberg, in his Journal of 1745, is Osgochgo, and by Bertram, in his Journal of 1743, Uskoho (Hanna, I. 32).

OSCEOLA. A town in Tioga County ; also as Osceola Mills, a town in Clearfield County. Named in honor of the Seminole chief, who was falsely betrayed by Gen. Jesup, while holding a conference under a flag of truce. He died at Fort Moultrie, Florida, in January 1838. The name is a corruption of Asi-yaholo, "Black-drink halloer." Osceola was in no way connected with the history of Pennsylvania.

OSEWINGO. See (*Chenango*) *Shenango*.

OSKOHARY. A former Indian village at the mouth of Catawissa Creek, Columbia County, which was also called, at a later date, Lapachpitton's Town (See *Lepos Peters Town*). In 1754 Conrad Weiser sent his son, and James Logan (the lame son of Shikellamy), from Shamokin to "Oskohary (Catawissa), Nishkibeckon (Nescopec), and Woyamock (Wyoming)." The Delaware chief Lapapitton, after whom the village was named, was then at "Skohary" (Colonial Records, VI. 35.

OSTONWAKIN. A former Indian village at the mouth of Loyalsock Creek, made up of a mixed population, at the site of the present Montoursville, Lycoming County. The old Indian village is marked on the early maps as on the west side of the creek, at its mouth. It was probably on both sides of the creek, with the home of Madame Montour on the west side. It was also called French Town, because of the residence of the Montours (See *Montour*). The name is probably derived from Ostenra, "a rock." Weiser in his Journal of 1737 says that it was so called "from a high rock which lies opposite" (Pub. Hist. Soc. Pa., Colls. I, 1853). The village was visited by Count Zinzendorf, his daughter Anna, Conrad Weiser, Martin Mack and his wife, in 1742. Andrew Montour, the famous interpreter, was then in the village. Zinzendorf had a conversation with Madame Montour, who wished him to baptize two children (Zinzendorf's Jour. in Mem. Mor. Church, 95-98). The visit is also mentioned in the Journal of Martin Mack (op. cit. 100). Zinzendorf and his party, guided by Andrew Montour, went from this place to Wyoming, reaching the Shawnee village near the present Plymouth, in five days. In his proposed plan of operations for the Moravian Missions Zinzendorf made Ostouwakin, "the center of operations among the French halfbreeds, who are to be reached through Andrew Montour, alias Sattelihu, and the rendezvous of missionaries appointed to labor" (op. cit. 137). Bishop Spangenberg and Conrad Weiser passed through the village in 1745, on their way to Onondaga. In 1755 Conrad Weiser was sent to the village to build a fence about the corn-fields of the Indians (Col. Rec. VI. 443), by order of Governor Morris. At that time nearly all of the Indians had left the village because a heavy frost on the night of the 29th. of May had killed all of their corn. The village was deserted soon after the commencement of the Indian hostility, after Braddock's defeat, and then was occupied by various mixed bands of Indians, hostile to the English, until the building of Fort Augusta, 1756.

Ostanwackin.—Meginness, Otzinachson, 25. **Ostonwaxin.**—Zinzendorf (1743), Mem. Mor. Church, 132. **Otstonwakin.**—Zinzendorf (1742), Mem. Mor. Church, 95. **Otstnacky.**—Weiser (1755) Colonial Records, VI. 443.

On the map of Lewis Evans, 1749, the present Loyalsock Creek is marked, Ostwagu. His map of 1755, gives the form Ostonage. Pownall's map of 1775, gives the form Ostonwage. These maps note the village as "French T." See *Loyalsock*.

OSWAYO. The name of a river, town and Township in Potter County. The river, now known as Oswayo Creek, rises in that county and enters the Allegheny River from the east near Portville, New York. Heckewelder, wrongly, gives this name as a corruption of Utscheja, "place of flies," from Ut-sche-wak, a Delaware word. The name is not of Delaware but of Seneca origin. The derivation given by Morgan, O-so-a-yeh, "pine forest," is correct. The largest pine forests in the state were found along this stream by the early settlers, and the "Oswayo white pine" was considered the finest pine timber to be obtained, by the early lumbermen. The Seneca village of Ishua (Eighso etc.), and several others stretched along the Allegheny River bend, from the present Olean to Warren Penna., in the days before the white settlement. Canadea, the most southern Seneca village on the Genesee River, was over the divide between the Genesee and Allegheny Rivers. Francis King formed the first white settlement on the Oswayo, in 1797, reaching the creek by crossing the divide from the West Branch of the Susquehanna, by way of the portage to the Allegheny, and then down that stream to the Oswayo. The present village of Ceres was the site of this settlement. The Seneca were then living in their villages along the Allegheny, near the present Salamanca, where the Seneca still live (History of Ceres, 1896).

Oswaya.—Howell, map, 1792; Ellicott, map, 1787. **Oswaye.**—Adlum, map, 1790. **Oswayo.**—Morris, map, 1848, and all present maps.

OTSININGY. See *Shenango*.

OTTAWA. The name of a town in Montour County. Named for the Algonkian tribe, which was called Adawe, "to trade." So called because they were great traders, even before the coming of the Europeans. The name was applied not only to the tribe which has been given the name of Ottawa, but also to the Cree, Chippewa, Nipissing and Montagnais, all of whom were great traders. The Ottawa lived on Manitoulin Island and along the northern shore of Georgian Bay, when first met with by the French. After 1680 they had joined the Hurons at Mackinaw. After the removal of the Hurons to the neighborhood of Detroit, the Ottawa removed to the western shore of Lake Huron—about 1700. From this point they spread out along the entire Lake region, even as far east as the Beaver River, Pennsylvania. The greater part of the tribe remained in southwestern Michigan. The celebrated Pontiac was a member of this tribe. (Consult; Parkman, History of Pontiac's Conspiracy; Schoolcraft, in Hist. Sketches of Mich., 53-89, 1834). During the various Indian wars in Pennsylvania, as well as elsewhere, the Ottawa were allied with the French interests. Soon after the building of the French forts on the Ohio, Allegheny and on French Creek, the Ottawa on the Ohio began hostile action against the English traders, killing them and stealing their goods (Colonial Records, V. 629). In 1754 George Croghan stated that the French at Fort Duquesne had been joined by 300 "Coniwagos and Outaways" (Col. Rec. VI. 181). There were doubtless a number of Ottawa with the French army, under Coulin de Villers, which defeated Colonel George Washington at Fort Necessity, July 3, 1754, and among the 600 Indian allies with the French force which defeated General Braddock, July 9, 1755, were many Ottawa. The tribe is frequently mentioned in the Colonial Records and Archives. Consult; Col. Rec., V. 462, 629; VI. 181, 654; VIII. 137, 294, 307, 392, 735; IX. 63, 219; Archives, II. 213, 404; Second Ser., VI. 44, 52, 109 etc.

OTZINACHSON. The name of the West Branch of the Susquehanna. Zinzendorf says in his Journal of 1742, after leaving Shamokin (Sunbury), "To the left of the path, after crossing the river, a large cave in a rocky hill in the wilderness was shown us. From it the surrounding country and the West Branch of the Susquehanna are called Otzinachson, i. e. the 'Demon's Den'; for here the evil spirits, say the Indians, hold their revels" (Mem. Mor. Church, I. 94). Zinzendorf crossed the North Branch, to the present Northumberland, and then went along the trail leading up the West Branch. The author was informed, upon inquiry about it, that there had formerly existed a cave in the hill to the left of the trail, which was still visible before the improvements were made along the river at Northumberland. It is possible that the story told to Zinzendorf was the correct origin

of the name, which was first applied to the region at the mouth of the West Branch, and then to the river itself. Mr. Hanna thinks that the name "Otzinachson", was the Iroquois name for Shamokin. The quotation from Weiser, which he gives, in which Weiser makes mention of "2 Machson" has been misread by him. Weiser does not give this as the name of Shikellamy's town, but of the West Branch. It reads, "I arrived at Shamokin the 20th of April. Found that two of the Shickcalamys being about thirty miles off on the northwest branch Susquehanna, commonly called 2 Machson" (Col. Rec. VI. 35; Hanna, I. 196). According to this statement Weiser applied the name to the river, and not to the village of Shikellamy, either at Shamokin or at the mouth of Shikellamy's Run. And this is in accordance with all of Weiser's statements, in which both the name Otzinachson and Shamokin are mentioned, as referring to different places. Otzinachson was the name which was applied to the entire region at the mouth of the West Branch, to the present Northumberland and to the West Branch of the Susquehanna. Even the name "Otzenachse" which Shikellamy applied to Shamokin, had reference to the larger region all about Shamokin, at the mouth of the West Branch. It was very much like the expression "at Allegheny," which included Venango as well as Shannopin's Town. At the Council at Philadelphia in 1740, the Indians at Otzenaxa, and also at Shamokin are both mentioned (Col. Rec. IV. 443). In the memorandum of the message delivered to the Indians of Shamokin, at the house of Joseph Chambers, in Paxton, by Conrad Weiser, in 1747, the record reads, "Brethren: You that Live at Zinachson (Shamokin)," Weiser uses the name of the region, which would be unfamiliar to the members of the Provincial Council, and adds the common name of the village, in that region. (Col. Rec. V. 84). In 1754, when Weiser was on a visit to Shamokin he was informed that about 100 Delawares were going to remove from the Ohio, for the security of their wives and children, to "Big Island upon Zinacksy River (Col. Rec. VI. 37). At the Council of Albany in 1754, Secy. Richard Peters, mentions the "Western Branch of Sasquehanna, called in their Language Senaxe (the Iroquois) (Col. Rec. VI. 112). In 1755 Weiser mentions the rumor concerning a body of French and hostile Indians, being on their way to the Susquehanna, at the place "Zinaghton River comes out of Allegheny Hills" (Col. Rec. VI. 649), and in the same letter he again mentions "the River Zinachton (the North West Branch of Sasquehannah" (650). He again mentions this report concerning the French and Indians, who "crossed Allegheny Hills at the Head of Rinacson River (evidently a misprint, should be Z, instead of R (op. cit. 659). In 1755 Weiser informed Governor Morris that a company of Iroquois, led by Jonathan Cayienquilyquoah, and a company of Shawnee, intended to make a town the next spring "on Westrn. Branch of Susquehana, Comonly Called Otsinackson, at a place Called Otstuagy, or French town, about 40 miles above Shamockin" ((Archives, II. 259). These Indians asked the Governor to build a fence about the corn-fields at this place. This request the Governor granted, and later commissioned Weiser to build the fence.

See *Ostonwakin.* The West Branch Valley begins at Northumberland and ends at Lock Haven, where it is joined by the Bald Eagle Valley. Beyond this point to the headwaters, and the divide between it and the Allegheny, the valley is but a narrow gorge. This valley had been occupied by the Conestoga, and probably by the Wenro, long before the commencement of the period of its occupation by the mixed Indian population of historic times. Hewitt mentions the Conestoga village at Utchowig, mentioned by John Smith in 1608, as being situated at the Big Island, at Lock Haven. It is more probable that this village was at the mouth of Pine Creek, upon the broad levels at Jersey Shore. There was evidently a very ancient burial ground along Pine Creek, in which the bodies were buried in trenches. These burial grounds were found by the early settlers at various places from the Big Island to Sunbury. The valley was crossed by a number of Indian trails. The Shamokin Path crossed the North Branch at Northumberland, then up the river to the mouth of Warriors Run, through the gap in Muncy Hills to Muncy, and then along the northern shore of the river to Lock Haven, where it crossed the West Branch, ran along the Bald Eagle Creek to Marsh Creek, and from the headquarters of that creek it cut across to the present Clearfield and on to Kittanning. This path branched at Muncy, running up this creek to its headwaters, crossed to Fishing Creek, and then through Nescopec Gap, to Wyoming. The Wyalusing Path ran up Muncy Creek to its head, crossed to Loyalsock Creek, and then struck Wyalusing Creek, in the northest part of Sullivan County, and down it to Wyalusing. The Shamokin Path ran on up to Big Island, where it crossed. A branch ran on up the river to the headwaters of the West Branch, then over the divide from Emporium Junction, to the headwaters of the Allegheny, and on to the Seneca country, in western New York. Another branch of this trail ran up Pine Creek to its headwaters, and then over the divide in Potter County, to the Genesee River. The Northern Central R. R., and the State Road to Elmira, which runs up the Lycoming Creek from Williamsport, follows the course of the trail to Onondaga, over which Weiser and Bishop Spangenberg passed in 1737. This trail strikes the Tioga River by a branch, but the main trail went on almost due north to South Creek, and then on to Elmira etc. An ancient fortification and burial ground existed on this trail from Shamokin, near the mouth of Wolf Run. It was on a high cliff, surrounded by a deep ditch. It was palisaded, and is said to have had wooden doors. It was probably built by the Andastes (Conestoga), whose chief villages of Carantouan and Oscalui were not far distant on the Chemung Branch of the Susquehanna. These ancient burial grounds and forts in this region south of the Chemung would indicate that the Andaste village of Utchowig was probably on the West Branch, in the region of Williamsport or Jersey Shore. When Weiser passed the above fort in 1737 it was a crumbling ruin. The Sheshequin Path, which went down Towanda Creek, and then crossed to the Lycoming Creek, would be an easy means of going from the Andastes villages in the region of Towanda, Wyalusing and Waverly, or Spanish Hill, to the West Branch. This trail was probably the means of communication between the Andaste villages on the Susquehanna, and Utchowig on the West Branch. The site of the burial ground, which was near this fort, was visited as late as 1839, when skulls, pipes etc. were taken from the graves. This fort stood near the present Halls, at the mouth of Wolfe Run. Some of these relics are now in the possession of a collector a t Muncy. The Sheshequin Path ran through the present city of Williamsport, along West Fourth Street. There are various other old trails along the West Branch valley, which was one of the leading highways of the Seneca into the settlements in the Susquehanna and Cumberland valleys during the days of Indian hostility. There were a number of Indian villages along the valley from the Sinnemahoning to Shamokin (See *Big Island*, *Ticquamingy Town*, *Ostonwakin*, *Muncy*, *Patterson's Town*, etc.). The land along the West Branch, bounded on the north and west by Towanda and Pine Creeks, and along the south side of the West Branch to Cherry Tree, then to Kittanning, and then down the southern shore of the Allegheny and Ohio, was purchased from the Indians at the Treaty of Fort Stanwix, in 1768 (Col. Rec. IX. 554-555). There was much dispute as to what stream was intended by "Tiadachton," mentioned in this Deed. At first the present Lycoming Creek was thought to be the boundary, but later it was explained that the real Tiadachton was the present Pine Creek (See *Tiadachton*). The lands west of Pine Creek were purchased at Fort Stanwix in 1784. During the period between 1768 and 1784, when the white settlers were pushing into this valley, the Indians objected to the occupation of the region. Warnings were issued to the settlers to remove, but they continued taking up land, even beyond Pine Creek. As a consequence there were many Indian raids into the valley during 1778-79 especially. To protect themselves against the Indians the settlers erected various stockade forts, among these were Fort Horn, Fort Antes, Fort Brady, Fort Muncy, Fort Meninger, Fort Freeland, Fort Reid and others (Consult; Frontier Forts, I. 374 et seq.). The various synonyms and references are given in the body of this article. For many interesting narratives of the West Branch Valley, consult; Meginness, Otzinachson, 1856; Shoemaker, Susquehanna Legends, 1913.

OUAQUAGO MOUNTAIN. A mountain at the Great Bend of the Susquehanna River, in Susquehanna County. The name is a corruption of Oquaga (which see).
Oquago Mt.—Morris, map, 1848. Ouaquago Mountain.—Egle, Hist. Pa., 1088.

OWEGO. A former Indian village, of mixed population, among which were a number of Shawnee, at the site of the present Owego, about two miles from the Susquehanna, on Owego Creek, Tioga County, New York. The name is probably a corruption of Ahwa-ga, or A-o-we-gwa, "where the valley widens." In 1756, during the Indian hostilities, Scarouady and Andrew Montour, who had been on a trip to Onondaga the previous fall, reported that they had visited Wyoming, where they had learned of the hostile intent of the Delaware and Shawnee in that settlement. Paxinosa, the Shawnee chief, and about thirty of his followers had separated themselves from these hostile Indians, and were living by themselves. Because of the known friendship of Paxinosa towards the English, he and his followers were advised to remove from Wyoming to Owego for their own safety. This they did not wish to do in the severe weather of winter, but promised to do so in the following spring (Col. Rec. VII. 65-66). Scarouady and Montour then went on up the Susquehanna to Tioga, and then up the North Branch to Owego, which is mentioned as an "Old Indian Town, deserted" (op. cit. 68). Paxinosa did not remove to Owego, but later removed to Tioga, where he was living in 1758. He then said that he was going to remove to his lands on the Ohio, "where he was born" (Col. Rec. VIII. 126). The Shawnee at this time were very uneasy because of the bringing of the Cherokees, to help General Forbes in his expedition. As a consequence of the stories told about the intention of the English, in regard to these Cherokees (op. cit. 129). Some of the Shawnee had removed before this time to Chenango and Owego. In 1763 there were still some Shawnee at Owego (Col. Rec. IX. 46). Owego was the point at which the line for the purchase of 1768 commenced. (Deed, Col. Rec. IX. 554). The Indians had removed from the village in 1758, when it was visited by Charles Thompson and C. F. Post (Archives, III. 421). It was occupied after this time, probably after the conclusion of the Indian hostility, known as the Conspiracy of Pontiac, in 1763. At the commencement of the War of the American Revolution, it was occupied by Indians hostile to the Americans. When General Poor's Brigade encamped there on August 17, 1779, it had been deserted by the Indians just after corn planting the spring previous.

It consisted at that time of 20 houses, which were destroyed on Aug. 19th. **Awaigah.**—Pa. Coun. (1763), Col. Rec. IX. 46. **Awegen.**—Esnaults and Rapilly Map, 1777. **Owages.**—Norris (1779), Jour. Sull. Exped., 230. **Owago.**—McKendry (1779), Jour. Sull. Exped., 202. **Owaygo.**—VanHovenberg (1779). Sull. Exped., 278 **Owego town.**—Beatty (1779), Sull. Exped., 24. **Owegy.**—Evans, map, 1749. **Oweigey.**—Mt. Johnson Conf. (1755), N. Y. Doc. Coll, Hist., VI. 984. **Oquegan.**—VanHovenberg (1779), Jour. Sull. Exped., 284.

PAGHAGHACKING. A creek, evidently in the region of Delaware County. A tract of land is mentioned in 1648 as lying on this creek. In the Indian Deed, to William Penn, 1685, among the owners of the land deeded, between Duck Creek and Chester Creek, was Packenah. The name may be a corruption of his name, with the Delaware Haki, "land," and the locative ing. Paghaghacking. Hudde (1648), Archives, Sec. Ser., V. 121.

PAINT CREEK. A branch of the Conemaugh River in Cambria County. Said by Heckewelder to be a translation of the Indian name, Wallamink, "where there is paint."

PAHKEHOMA. A creek mentioned in a Deed to William Penn, by Maughoughsin, in 1684, Archives, I. 88.

PANAWAKEE. An Indian village mentioned by Zeisberger, in his Journal (MS.) of 1767. A corruption of the Seneca Ganawaca, or Ganowongo, "at the rapids" (See *Conewango*).

PASSIGACHKUNK. A f o r m e r Indian village, of Delaware and Seneca, on the Cowanesque River, Tioga County. It was probably situated near the present Academy Corners and Knoxville. John Hays and C. F. Post visited the village in 1760, when on their way to the Ohio, but were not allowed to advance, but were ordered to go back, as the Iroquois did not allow white men to go over this trail. Hays, Post and Tedyuskung (the Delaware chief) reached the village on June 7, 1760. Hays says, in his Journal, "arrived at Paseckachkunk about four o'clock, after Crossing the River five times; this town Stand on the South side of the River, and is in two parts, at the space of a mile Distance, where there is two Sorts of people; the Nearest part is peopled with Wonamies (Unami, one of the Delaware tribes), Quitigon is their Chief, and the Upper part is Mingoes

(Seneca), which Commands all that Country. We halted at the Lower town and in the Evening there Came nine or ten from the Mings Town, and Looked very Sower and Divilish but went of after some time" (Archives, III. 738-739). The lower town at which Hays and Post stopped was possibly Academy Corners, which is on the south side of the river. Knoxville, about a mile away was probably the site of the "Mings Town." The Cowanesque valley is very broad and level at this place. Well adapted for corn-fields. The ground is fertile. Tobacco of a fine quality is still raised along the valley. Many Indian relics, such as arrow points, pipes, etc., have been found at the northern side of the valley at Academy Corners. After remaining here for several days, Post and Hays were obliged to turn back, as the Senecas would not allow them to advance any further. In 1756 Samuel Clifford, Leonard Weeser and Henry Hess, who were captured by the Indians, were examined upon their return. The first was taken to Tioga, and "afterwards from thence up the Cayuga Branch, about forty miles to an Indian camp"; the second, Weeser, was taken to Tioga "till the Planting Time, & from thence they went to Little Passeeca, an Indian Town, up the Cayuga Branch"; the third, Hess, was also taken to Tioga until planting time, when the Indians removed "to a place up the Cayuga Branch near its head, called Little Shingle". Tedyuskung, the Delaware "King", was the leader in the party of Indians making these raids (Archives, III. 44, 46, 56-57). In 1757 when the Governor, Denny, was trying to find Tedyuskung, in order to get him to the Council at Easton, he wrote to the Proprietaries, concerning the news given to him by some of the chiefs of the Six Nations, who were seeking Tedyuskung at Tioga, "When they heard nothing from him, nor that he was returned from the Seneca Country, where they were told he was gone, as they passed thro' the Diahogo (Tioga) Town, where he lived, in their Way from Sir William Johnson's to this Province" (III. 193). In June, 1757, Governor Denny sent two Indians, Nathaniel and Zacharias, with a message to Tedyuskung. Upon their return they made a report of their journey. "After We set out, we were Eleven Days before we arrived at Diahoga (Tioga, now Athens), And then were obliged to go to Passekawkung; there we came to Teedyuscung's Habitation, and were Twenty-six Days in performing Our Journey" (Col. Rec. VII. 588). During the period of hostility, before the Treaty at Easton, Tedyuskung and his sons left Tioga and went to this village, which was far enough away from the white settlements to be beyond danger of attack. Here he planted corn, and to this place he carried the prisoners which he captured. After the Council at Easton, 1757, Tedyuskung became a prominent advocate for peace. In 1767 when David Zeisberger was on his way to the mouth of the Tionesta, he reached "Pasigachkunk" on October 6th. He says in his Journal for this date, "Before noon we arrived at Pasigachkunk, an old deserted Indian town. It was the last on Tiaogee. Here Christian Frederick Post, during the late war, had to turn back while on his way to the Allegany, because the Indians would not allow him to proceed further. It is possible to travel thus far on the waters of Tiaogee" (from MS in Archives of the Moravian Church at Bethlehem). Zeisberger calls the Cowanesque "Tiaogee," giving the name of the stream of which it was a branch. It is not possible to make the descriptions given in his Journal, fit any other course than that up the Cowanesque and then over the divide to the Allegheny. The author has gone over this region with Zeisberger's Journal as a guide. He went on to Tionesta and returned to this village on October 31st. In 1768 he again made this journey, reaching this village on May 19th. Zeisberger was the first white man to cross the divide between the Susquehanna and the Allegheny, in the present Potter County. The name of the village is probably a corruption of Passikachk, "a board," with the locative, unk— with the meaning, "board place." The name Little Shingle, and Little Passeeca, no doubt were attempts to translate this word. "Little" was given as the name of the smaller village in which the Delawares lived. The large village was occupied by Senecas.

Pacihsahounk.—Hays (1760), Archives, III. 737. **Paseckachkunk.**—Hays (1760), Archives, III. 738. **Pasigachkunk.**—Zeisberger (1767), MS. at Bethlehem (Oct. 6). **Passekawkung.**—Nathaniel (1757), Col. Rec., VII. 588. **Passigachgungh.**—Zeisberger (1757), MS. at Beth., (Oct. 31). **Passigachkunk.**—Zeisberger (1768), MS. at Beth., (May, 19). **Little Passeeca.**—Weeser (1756), Archives, III. 46. **Little Shingle.**—Hess (1756), Ar-

chives, III. 56. **Secaughceeny.**—Pa. Coun. (1762), Col. Rec., VIII. 508. (?).

The name given as the home of Cornelius, one of the Indians killed by Frederick Stump and John Ironcutter, in 1768,—"Paghsekacunk, on the Susquehanna. Six Miles below Diahoga" is evidently intended for this village, which is incorrectly located (Col. Rec. IX. 470).

PASSYUNK. The name of one of the Townships in Philadelphia County in 1741. Now a part of the city. The name is derived from the Indian name for the tract of land between the Delaware and the Schuylkill. at the mouth of the latter. There probably was an Indian village on the eastern shore of the Schuylkill. The name is a corruption of Pachsegink, or Pachsegonk, "in the valley." The name is first mentioned in the Archives by A. Hudde, at Fort Nassau, in 1748. He says, "It happened now that on the fourth of the same month, some of the sachems came to me from the savages of Passayonk, who asked me why I did not build on the Schuylkill, that the Swedes has already then some buildings constructed" (Archives, Sec. Ser., V. 120). In 1657 permission was given to the Swedes to build a village there, and at other places (Arch. Sec. Ser., VII. 511). In 1667 Richard Nicolls granted to Robert Ashman and others, a tract of land which was bounded on the north by the tract of Peter Rambo (Arch. Sec. Ser. XIX. 137-8. A grant was made to Peter Rambo by Governor Andres, dated Mar. 25, 1676 (Arch. Third Ser., I. 43. In 1680 a Census was taken of all those living in the Swedish villages on the Delaware. There were then 12 living at Passyunk (Arch. Sec. Ser., VII. 806). In 1684 a grant was made to "Lassey Cock and Mathias Holston" (Arch. Third Ser., I. 44). In 1693 Mathias Houlsted (same as Holston) conveyed a tract of land to William Carter (Arch. Sec. Ser., XIX. 161. A grant of land was made to Andrew Bankson in the "Township of Passiunk" same ref. 91). In 1714 the Commissioners granted to Andrew Haney the land which had been formerly granted to "Lacey Cock" (same ref. 19). Various other land grants in Passyunk are noted in the Archives, and in the Records of Upland Court. The situation of these, and other grants are shown on Holmes map of Pennsylvania (1681-1684). The Indians living in this region at the time of its settlement by the Swedes, belonged to the Unami, or Turtle, clan of the Delawares. Passayunk (as the name should be) was probably a village of this clan.

Bahsayunck.—Holmes map, 1681-84. **Pasiunk.**—Nicolls (1667), Arch. 2 Ser., XIX. 137-8. **Passajonck.**—Alricks (1658), Arch. 2 Ser., V. 320. **Passajongh.**—Beekman (1661), Arch. 2 Ser., VII. 651. **Passayonck**—Permit to Swedes (1657), Arch. 2 Ser., VII. 511. **Passayongh.**—Beekman (1660), Arch. 2 Ser., VII. 629. **Passayonk.**—Hudde (1648), Arch. 2 Ser., V. 120. **Passayunck**—Com. of Prop. (1702), Arch. 2 Ser., XIX. 353. **Passayvncke.**—Tom (1673), Arch. 2 Ser., VII. 756. **Passiunk.**—Com. of Prop. (1692), Arch. 2 Ser., XIX. 91. **Passiyunk**—Com. of Prop. (1693), Arch. 2 Ser., XIX. 161. **Passyunk**—Com. of Prop. (1705), Arch. 2 Ser., XIX. 457. **Passyunck.**—Com. of Prop. (1734), 3 Ser., I. 41.

Consult; Records of the Court at Upland, 138, 1860.

PAUPACK. The name of a Township in Wayne County; also a creek in Pike County. The name is probably one of the corruptions of Wallenpaupack, the stream of which the creek is a branch. The Township name is probably a corruption of the name of the branch of the Delaware, now called Popacton Branch. Papeek, is "a pond." See *Popacton, Wallenpaupack.*

PAXINOUS. The name of a village in Northumberland County. Probably named in honor of Paxinosa, the leading chief of the Shawnee, who was always a friend of the English, even when the great majority of his tribe became hostile. According to his own statement, he was born on the Ohio. One of the chief reasons for his friendly attitude towards the Province was the fact that his wife, Elizabeth was baptized at Bethlehem, by the Moravians, in 1755 (Mem. Mor. Church, 109). He lived at Wyoming until the commencement of the Indian hostilities, when he removed to the village at the mouth of the Lackawanna (Archives, III, 413). He attended the Council at Philadelphia in 1755 (Col. Rec. VI. 360), and soon after removed from the neighborhood of the hostile Delaware and Shawnee. His youngest son, Kolapeeka (or Sammy), lived at Tioga (Col. Rec. VII. 187-8). He was present at the Council at Easton in 1757. In 1758 Paxinosa, his sons, sons-in-law, and whole family, were at Tioga. His sister was living at Chenango, and the "Old King" was getting ready to move to the Ohio, where he was born (Col. Rec. VIII. 126). He removed to the Ohio in May, 1758, and was present at the Council at Fort Pitt in 1760. His name is variously spelled, Paxinous, Paxinosa, Backsinous, Buckshinutha, being a few of the forms. Cyrus Thomas says in the article in the Handbook of American Indians (II. 217) that Paxinos was a Minisink. This is an error, if Mr. Thomas means that Paxinosa was a Minisink by birth. According to his own statement, he was born on the Ohio. He was probably among the Shawnee who came from the Ohio, at an early date, to trade on the upper Delaware, and finally settled in the Minisink country. This accounts for his being mentioned with the Delawares, or Minisink, and also for his acting as interpreter for the Delawares, as well as for the Shawnee. His long residence with the Delawares made him a Delaware at heart, but he was a Shawnee by birth. Although the Shawnee from the south came into the Province in 1698, some of them from the Ohio had settled on the upper Delaware, where they came to trade, before the arrival of those from the south, at the mouth of Pequea creek (See *Pequea, Shawnee, Pechoquealin*).

PAXTON, formerly **PAXTANG, PESHTANG** etc. The name of a creek, town and also two Townships, Middle and Upper Paxton, in Dauphin County; also the name of a former Indian village, near the mouth of the creek, which enters the Susquehanna at Harrisburg. The name is a corruption of Peekstank, "where the waters stand," or possibly, Peeksting, "the place of springs"—from Tup-peek, "a spring, or pond," with the locative, ing. The name was probably given because of the beautiful springs, and ponds which were along this creek. Some of these still exist in the region of Paxtang Park, near Harrisburg. The suggestion of Mr. Hanna that the name has the same origin as Pequea, or Pict's Town, because of its settlement by the Shawnee tribe, the Piqua, does not seem to be well founded. Heckewelder is not always reliable in his tracing of the origin of Indian names, but in many cases his derevation is correct. Peekstank is a name which well describes the region of the present Paxtang creek (Consult; Hanna, Wild. Trail, I, 145). The Delawares commenced moving to the Susquehanna soon after the settlement of the Delaware River, and the various land purchases by William Penn. Some of them had probably settled at Paxtang before 1700. The overthrow of the Conestoga, and the submission of the Delawares, made the Iroquois the masters of the Susquehanna. This ending of the war between the Iroquois and the Conestoga probably was ratified at a treaty at Shackamaxon in 1677. It seems probable that the subjugation of the Delawares took place at the same time, and was due to their having been associated with, and giving harbor to, the Conestoga, during their conflicts with the Iroquois. The Delaware, Conestoga, Conoy, Nanticoke and Shawnee were associated in nearly all of the villages along the Susquehanna. All were subject to the Iroquois. Sassounan, the Delaware "King," was living at Paxtang previous to 1709. After signing the release of 1718 he removed to Shamokin. Many of the Delawares removed from the Delaware River to the Susquehanna before this date, and after 1718 nearly all of them from the lower Delaware, had removed to the various villages on the Susquehanna. They soon after this date commenced their migration to the Ohio. When the first white settlers commenced to cross the Susquehanna, about 1725, all of the Indians commenced to leave that region. The great Delaware migration westward was from 1724-1727. After that period few remained on the lower Susquehanna. All had removed to the upper Susquehanna (Shamokin, Wyoming, Big Island, etc.). Paxtang became a prominent trading place soon after its occupation by the Delaware and Shawnee. There were various Indian villages in the region, among which were the Shawnee village, at the site of New Cumberland; the village on Duncan's Island, at the mouth of the Juniata; Paxtang, at Harrisburg, and all of the villages on the Juniata, Susquehanna, and even on the Ohio, could be reached from this point. Various trails ran up the river, down the Cumberland Valley and over the mountains to the Ohio, or to the Potomac. All of these trails became trading paths for the various Indian traders who soon came to Paxtang. Among these were, Peter Bezalion, James LeTort, Edmund Cartlidge, Peter Chartier, Nicole Godin, Joseph Jessop, Hugh Crawford and many others. The one trader who was to make the place memorable was John Harris, the father of the founder of Harrisburg, who came to Paxtang before 1733. There is no question but

that the John Hans, whom Egle and others, identify as John Harris, was John Hans Steelman, the Maryland trader, who is frequently mentioned in the records of the period. John Harris was granted permission to keep a ferry at Paxtang in October, 1733, and not in 1753, as stated by Mr. Hanna. He was also given permission to "Build a small house on the west side of the said River for the conveniency of Travellers that may happen to come on that side in the Night Season or in Stormy Weather when the Boat or Flat cannot pass." He also asked for 200 acres on the west side of the river opposite his plantation (Archives, Third Ser., I. 45). Shikellamy complained concerning the erection of this house, and the clearing of the fields, at the mouth of the Juniata. According to the previous record noted, the land which Harris asked for was opposite his plantation. It would seem that the place called Paxtang was opposite the mouth of the Juniata, above Harrisburg (Col. Rec. III. 503-504). Or, the name Paxtang was applied to all of the region between Paxtang Creek and the Susquehanna River (See *Harris' Ferry*). John Harris, Sr. died in 1748. His son John Harris, who was born at Paxtang in 1726, inherited 700 acres of land. Upon a part of this Harrisburg was laid out in 1785. The region was settled by the Scotch-Irish, from 1720-1730. The name Paxtang very naturally became Paxton. The Presbyterian Church, at Paxton, was organized in 1733. The congregation had been served previous to this time by Rev. James Anderson. In 1738 Rev. John Elder became pastor. This minister became a Colonel in the Provincial service. The various companies which were organized for the protection of the settlements from the Indians during the period of hostility, 1755-1764, were known as "Paxton Boys." A part of these "Boys" exterminated the last remnant of the Conestogas in December, 1763 (See *Conestoga*). They also held Philadelphia in terror by their march on that city, which was for the purpose of demanding that the Quaker Assembly give them an equal representation with the other counties in the Assembly. Governor Penn realized that the demands for representation which had been made again and again, and that this so called "riot" was simply a demand of the same sort that men in all ages have made for the right of representation.

It was the same sort of a "riot" which later developed into a "revolution." There should be no excuse made for the crime at Conestoga. But, the march on Philadelphia was to demand their rights, and not to kill Indians. The whole affair was most unjustly interpreted by the entire Quaker influence, which was hostile to everything Presbyterian, and especially the attitude of these frontiersmen, whose wives and children had been killed, and whose homes had been burned by the very Indians, whom the Quakers regarded more than they did their own countrymen (Consult; Archives, IV. 147-148, 153, 162, 165; Colonial Records, IX. 132, 138, 142 etc.; Egle Hist. Penna., 114-122; the various U. S. histories, under title, Paxton). The memorial which was presented to the Provincial authorities by Col. Matthew Smith and James Gibson, reveals the real purpose of the so called "riot" (Col. Rec. 138-142). The various pamphlets which were issued in Philadelphia at this time have been used as the foundation for so called historical writings, which have no basis whatever in fact. The very same conditions which led the "Paxton Boys" to protest against the injustice of being governed without right representation, led to the Declaration of American Independence at a later day. And the first step towards that end was taken by the very people who at this time were called "rioters." The spirit of the "Paxton Boys" was the one thing which made the American nation possible. The "Paxton Boys" and their descendants fought upon every battlefield of the Revolution for the very same principles for which they were fighting in 1763-4. History has not only been unjust, but also untrue in dealing with the "Paxton riot" in Philadelphia. Not a single historical document of the period, including the letters of Governor John Penn, give the slightest basis of real fact for the various tirades which have been written about the "Paxton Boys." The pamphlet of Benjamin Franklin, which was written for political effect, is a sample of "profane history," which is conducive to real historical profanity. John Harris used the form, Paxton, in all of his letters, which the author has seen recorded.

Paxtang.—Com. of Prop. (1719), Arch. 2 Ser., XIX, 651. **Paxton.**—Harris (1755), Col. Rec. VI. 457. Archives (1734), I. 425; Evans map, 1749. **Pochston.**—Lowe (1730), Archives, I. 268. **Peixtan.**—Pa. Coun. (1707), Col. Rec., II. 389. **Poshtang.**—Pa. Coun. (1709), Col. Rec., II. 471. **Peshtank.**—Blunston (1728), Archives, I. 216. **Pextan.**—Pa. Coun. (1718), Col. Rec., III. 47. **Pextang.**—Pa. Coun. (1736), Col. Rec. IV. 152; Scull map, 1759. **Poxton.**—Pa. Coun. (1721), Col. Rec., III. 153.

PECHOQUEALING. The name of a former Shawnee village, on the east side of the Delaware: the name of a region on the west side of the Delaware, above the Water Gap and to the region of Dingman's Ferry (Pike county); also an Indian village, near the latter place, and probably an Indian village near Durham Iron Works (now Durham, Bucks County). The mountain, a part of the Kittatinny or Blue Ridge, in this region was also called by this name, the origin of which is doubtful. The Shawnee, under Kakowwatchky, came to this region in 1694, under the guidance of Arnold Viele, the Dutch trader. They settled on the Minisink lands, a short distance below the Neversink River. These Shawnee belonged to the Pequa clan of that tribe. Pequea Creek, in New Jersey, south of this region, and other names were left by these Shawnee. Pechoquealing, Pacoqualin etc. may be a corruption of Pequea-ling, "the place of the Pequa." Mr. Hanna gives its origin as Pohaqualing, "a mountain with a hole or gap in it." In 1724 "Nich. Schoonover, of Sopus, requests the Grant of some low Ground on Delaware, between Pehaqualon and Machacamac (Neversink)" (Arch. Sec. Ser., XIX, 721). In 1728 "John Smith and Nicholas Skolehoven" (doubtless the same as "Nich. Schoonover"), Messengers from the Chief of the Shawanese, at Pechoquealin," were given instructions to carry to a message to Kakowwatchy (Archives, I. 223). They were asked to request this chief to meet the Governor at Durham some time this year. In the same year (September) Henry Smith and John Petty, who were going to the Susquehanna, were asked to see Shikellamy, and others at Shamokin, and if possible to see Kakowwatchky, and ask him why he had left "Pechoquealin, after they had promised to meet me at Durham Ironworks" (op. cit. 228). In 1732 the Shawnee on the Ohio sent word to Governor Gordon, through Edmund Cartlidge as to why they had left Pechoquealing, and then why they had left Wyoming. The Five Nations had said to them, "Therefore, you Shawanese Look back towards Ohioh, The place from whence you Came, and

Return thitherward, for now wee Shall Take pitty on the English and Lett them have all this Land. And further Said now Since you are Become women, Ile Take Peahohquelloman, and putt itt on Meheahoaming (Wyoming) and Ile Take Meheahoaming and putt itt on Ohioh, and Ohioh Ile putt on Woabach (Wabash), and thatt shall be the warriours Road for the future" (Archives, I. 329). At the Coucil at Easton, in 1758, the Provincial authorities bought from the "Minisinks and Wapings," all of the lands between the Provinces of New York and New Jersey. The lines about this purchase are given. In part this line was from "Laametang Falls on the North Branch of Rariton River; and thence on a Straight Line to Pacoqualin Mountain, where it joins on Delaware River; and thence up the Delaware to Cushyhink (Cochecton). A few days later this land and line were referred to, as follows, "then to the Mouth of Rariton, then up that River to Laometung Falls, then on a Straight Line to Pasqualin, where it joins on Delaware River" (Colonial Records, VIII. 110, 220-221). This New Jersey line, of 1745, is shown on Evans map of 1749. It strikes the Delaware about the mouth of the present Dingmans Creek, in Pike County. This region between the Water Gap, where the Kittatinny crosses the Delaware River, was probably the region known as Pechoquealing. The town in New Jersey gave the name to this tract on the western side of the river. It was just south of the village of Minisink, as noted on Evans map of 1755. The Indian town of "Cashetang" (See *Cashietunk*), where James Steel and Jacob Taylor, took their observations, when surveying the line between New York and New Jersey in 1719 (hence Station Point) was on both sides of the river, as was also the case with all of the Indian villages along the Delaware. The village in Pennsylvania, named Pechoquealing, was probably nearly opposite the one in New Jersey of the same name. The Shawnee, as has been noted, left this region in 1728, when some of them went to Shawnee Flats (Plymouth) Wyoming, and then went to the Ohio. They belonged to the same clan which had settled at the mouth of Pequea Creek, Lancaster County, in 1698 (See *Pequea, Shawnee*). Consult; Colonial Records, III, 309, 317, 329, 330, the Durham Iron Works

is probably mentioned as it was the nearest settled or convenient place for the meeting with Kakowwatchky, and does not signify that Pechoquealing was at that locality. **Pacoqualin.**—Pa. Coun. (1758), Col. Rec. VIII. 110. **Pahaquelan.**—Steel (1719), Archives, Sec. Ser., XIX. 662. **Pasqualin.** —Pa. Coun. (1758), Col. Rec., VIII. 221. **Peahohquelloman.**—C a r t l i d g e (1732), Archives, I. 329. **Pechoquealin.**—Gordon (1728), Archives, I. 223. **Pehaqualon.**— Board of Prop. (1724), Archives, Sec. Ser., XIX. 721. **Pehoquealin.**—Pa. Coun. (1728), Colonial Records, III. 329.

PENN'S CREEK. A creek which enters the Susquehanna from the west at the present Selinsgrove, Snyder County. The Iroquois name of the stream was Kayarondinhagh. The land north of the Kittatinny mountains, north of the Purchase of 1749, to the mouth of Penn's Creek, was purchased from the Iroquois at the Treaty at Albany in 1754, at the same time that the Mohawks sold the lands on the Susquehanna River to the Connecticut Company (Col. Rec. VI. 117-123). For this tract the Penns paid 400 Pounds in coin. The sale of these lands was very displeasing to the Delaware and Shawnee, and had much to do with the hostility which followed. Braddock's defeat, July 9, 1755, led many of these Indians to the French influence. The storm clouds which had been gathering for many years suddenly broke in the fall of 1755, when the hostile Delaware and Shawnee commenced their raids upon the white settlements. The first of these raids were made upon the settlers on Patterson's Creek, on the Potomac, and upon Penn's Creek. The latter was the first Indian massacre, or act of hostility, in the Province, after Braddock's defeat. The Indians, numbering about 14, were led by Kickenapauling (which see), who had gathered his band at Kittanning. They fell upon the settlement on Penn's Creek, at George Gabriel's (See Scull's map, 1759), and killed, or carried away, 25 persons. The account of this raid is given in the Narrative of Marie LeRoy, whose father Jacob LeRoy (or King) was killed at the time of the raid, October 16, 1755 (Archives, Sec. Ser., VII. 401 et seq.). This massacre caused the wildest excitement along the entire frontier, and was the direct cause of the building of the chain of frontier forts along the entire boundary of the settlements. It also was the cause of the bitter strife between the Governor, Morris, and the Quaker Assembly. Conrad Weiser, who was most active in the activity which followed this massacre, had evidently written to Thomas Penn, telling him the entire situation, and evidently advising the exclusion of the Quakers from the Assembly. Penn wrote in reply, telling Weiser, "It was not thought wright here to exclude the Quakers by law from the Assembly, yet as they have been told they will be excluded in case they do not withdraw at the next session" (MS. Hist. Soc. Pa., quoted by Walton, Conrad Weiser, 312). The whole miserable discussion between the Governor and the Assembly which followed was one of the prime causes of the utter lack of anything like unity of purpose in the plans which were made against the French and Indians. Immediately after this massacre on Penn's Creek, John Harris gathered a company of 45 men and went to the scene of the disaster to bury the dead. Finding that this had been done, he went on to Shamokin, to prevail upon the Indians there to remain neutral. He found many Indians in the place, painted black. The next morning as Harris and his party were about to leave, they were advised by Andrew Montour not to go down along the trail on the western side of the river, but to take the old trail along the eastern shore. But, distrustful of Montour's friendship, they went down the western trail. When at the fording place on Penn's Creek, where the stream divides near the river, they were fired upon, killing four. Harris and his men took to the trees, firing upon the Indians and retreating to the river. Four or five men were drowned in trying to cross the Susquehanna (Consult; Col. Rec., VI. 644-660). Harris reached his home at Harris' Ferry and wrote an account of this affair to the Governor. The Indians were killing and scalping and burning the white settlers and their homes in the Great and Little Coves. Conrad Weiser was busy gathering the Germans south of the Blue Mountains for the defense of their homes. Weiser divided these sturdy men into companies of 30, and at once commenced the defense of the settlements south of the mountains. Governor Morris was pleased with this action and made Weiser a Colonel (Col. Rec., VI. 657, 660 etc.; See *Swatara, Tulkeo* etc.). Weiser, with all of his failings, was the most thorough-ly efficient man in the whole Province at this time (Consult; Walton, Conrad Weiser, entire book; Meginness. Otzinachson, 60 et seq.). The killing of a number of Indians by Frederick Stump on this creek and Middle Creek, on Jan. 10, 1768, led to a very serious state of affairs. The Iroquois were complaining of the "white squatters" on the lands along the Monongahela and Youghiogheny Rivers, and were also very unfriendly because of the various acts of hostility against the Indians, committed by the white settlers. The relations between the Iroquois and the Province were sorely strained. Frederick Stump and John Ironcutter had killed the "White Mingo," a friendly Seneca, three other Indian men, two Indian women, at his house near the mouth of Middle Creek, on Jan. 10th., and had gone the next day to an Indian cabin, about 14 miles up the creek, and murdered an Indian woman, two girls and a child. These Indians had formerly lived at the Big Island (Lock Haven), and had moved to Middle Creek in the spring of 1767. They were all friendly with the settlers, who treated them kindly. Stump said that he had killed all of these with his own hands. Two hundred Pounds were offered for the capture of Stump. Capt. William Patterson, whose exploits afforded ground for many of the tales about "Captain Jack, the Wild Hunter of the Juniata," went with 20 men to the house of George Gabriel, on Penn's Creek, where he arrested Stump and took him to the Jail at Carlisle, where he and his servant, John Ironcutter, were confined. On Jan 29th. a company of 70 or 80 men made a raid on the Jail at Carlisle and released Stump and Ironcutter. The Quaker Assembly was more aroused because these two men had escaped than they had before been aroused because of the murder of all of the white settlers in the Province (Col. Rec. IX. 414-468, 500-501, 510, 512, 517). The Assembly put the entire affair upon the shoulders of Gov. John Penn (op. cit., 473-480). The entire situation was one of grave danger. The Indians threatened another general war. Matters were finally settled at the Treaty of Fort Stanwix in 1768, when the lands south of the West Branch and the Allegheny and Ohio were purchased, and the Indians "condoled" for their losses. Consult; Meginness, Otzinachson, 111-119; Walton, C o n r a d

Weiser). Stump and Ironcutter were hidden for a time by their friends, and then escaped to Virginia. Neither were ever captured, or punished for this crime.

Andrew Montour was granted a tract of 820 acres at the head of Penn's Creek in May 19, 1767, above the Great Spring, which he called Succoth. The probable reason of Stump's hatred of the Indians, previous to this time, was due to the fact that the Indians had complained of his settlement at the place where he lived, in 1766. This had led to the issuance of a Proclamation of Gov. John Penn, Sept. 23, 1766, ordering Stump and the other settlers to remove (Col. Rec., IX. 327-328). Stump paid no attention to this Proclamation, but continued on his place until the time of his arrest. There were various trails leading to this point on the Susquehanna. The trail down the west shore ran on to the mouth of the Juniata, where it connected with the trail up that valley. The trail down the eastern shore, from Shamokin, crossed near the head of the island to the mouth of Middle Creek, and then ran overland, along the foot of Narrows Mountain to the Juniata, where it connected with the trail to Standing Stone. The trail down the western shore, from Shamokin, crossed where the branches of Penn's Creek separated, near the river. It was at this point that Harris and his party were surprised by the Indians. The topography has been much changed at this place in recent years. The spot was nearly opposite the upper end of the "Isle of Que," where the creek formerly entered the river (See *Que, Isle of*). The name Penn's Creek was given in honor of Governor John Penn. It had also been known as Mahoning, or Big Mahanoy (See *Mahoning*).

Mahanoy (or Penn's Creek).—Harris (1755), Col. Rec., VI. 645. **Mahoney.**— Penn (1768), Col. Rec., IX. 436. **Mahonia.**—Terrence (1755), Col. Rec., VI. 648. **Mr. Penn's Creek.**—Harris (1755), Col. Rec., VI. 646. **John Penn's Creek.**— Weiser (1755), same ref., 647. **Kayarondinhagh or John Penn's Creek.**—Coun. at E. (1758), Col. Rec., VIII. 203. **Kayarondinhagh.**—Deed of 1754, in Col. Rec., VI. 120. **Kayarondinagh.**—Coun. at Albany (1754), same ref., 118.

Scull's map, 1759, gives the name as Big Mahanoy Cr.; Scull, 1770, as Penn's Creek.

PENNYPACK. A creek which enters

the Delaware in Philadelphia County. It was also called Dublin Creek, in the early records. This name in its present form shows how corrupt an Indian name can become. It is first mentioned in the order of Gov. Francis Lovelace to Capt. Edmund Cantwell, to see that the land was seated and cleared, in August 1672. This land was received, by Patent, by Richard Gorsuch, who assigned it to Lovelace (Archives, Sec. Ser., V. 65). The name used in this order was "Pemecacka." In 1677 Ephraim Herman and "Pelle Rambo." (Peter Rambo) were each granted 300 acres of land between this creek and Poquessing Creek by order of the Court of Upland (Records of Upland Court, 61), and in 1678 Ephraim Herman was allowed to take the remainder of the land between these creeks (op. cit. 115). In 1678 Peter Rambo was granted, by the same court, a survey of his land, called "Rams Doep," on the north-east side of the creek (op. cit. 124). In 1679 Peter Herman gave up his right to his land, in order that it might be otherwise disposed of (op. cit. 143). In 1680 Hans Kien sold his land on the west side of the creek, opposite the plantation of Peter Rambo, about half a mile from the mouth of the creek (op. cit. 179). These lands, and their occupants, or owners, are noted on Holmes map (1691-94), on which creek is marked "Dublin Creek." In 1683 Tammany deeded to William Penn, his lands between this creek and Neshaminy Creek, and in various other deeds which follow, this chief and others mentioned, deed the land on this creek to William Penn. In the Deed of 1697, Tammany, or Tamanend, and Weheeiand, his brother, and Weheequeckhon alias Andrew, "who is to be king after my death," Yaqueehon alias Nicholas, and Quenameckquid alias Charles, "my sons," are the signers (Archives, I. 62-64). The son, who was to be king, "Weheequeckhon," has been identified by A. L. Guss, as Sassounan, the leading chief of the Delawares at Shamokin, but there is no authority for this statement. Tammany, as the head chief of the Turtle tribe, occupied the position of leading chief of the Delawares, and as such was given the title of "King." In all of the Councils of the Delaware Nation, the head chief of the Turtle tribe held a superior place. The head chief of the Wolf and Turkey tribes were both of less dignity. The leading chief of the Delawares could not be a Wolf or a Turkey chief. The title "King," as bestowed by the English upon Beaver and Shingas, and others, was not properly bestowed, as these chiefs were heads of the Turkey tribe. In the later history of the Delawares in Ohio, Netawatwes was the "King" of the Nation, as was also his grandson, Gelelemend. Both of these chiefs were Turtle head-chiefs, and as such were recognized by the Delawares themselves. The head-chief of the Turtle tribe kept all of the official records, wampum, treaties etc. It is said that when Gelelemend (See *Killbuck*) had to swim the Allegheny River, from his island near Fort Pitt, in order to escape from the renegades who made the attack upon the village, that he lost all of the records of the Delawares, among which were the treaties made with William Penn. There is little doubt but that Shackamaxon (which see) was the capital of the Delaware Nation, as was Gekelmukpecheunk (which see) at a later date, in Ohio, during the time of Netawatwes (or Newcomer). The entire region about Philadelphia was occupied by the Turtle tribe. They were bounded on the north by the Wolf tribe, and on the south and east by the Turkey tribe. Because of the friendship, and the "League of Amity," made with William Penn, the Turtle tribe, and its chiefs, were always friendly with the English, as a tribe. Even in the period of the Revolution, when other tribes were hostile, the chiefs of the Turtle tribe were strongly in friendly relations with the Americans. The massacre of Gnadenheutten, Crawford's Expedition, and similar uncalled for events sorely tried the friendly Delawares, but Netawatwes, Gelelemend, White Eyes and others were firm in their friendship for the Americans. The wise and friendly chiefs of the Turtle tribe, from Tammany to Netawatwes and Gelelemend, have never been given the credit due them.

Th land lying between Pennypack Creek and Chester Creek was purchased by William Penn, in 1685, from Shakhoppoh, Secane, Malibor and Tangoras. In the Deed for these lands the creek is called "Pemapecka, now called Dublin Creek" (Archives, I. 92). Secane, one of the signers of this Deed, had also signed the Deed, 1683, for the lands between the Schuylkill and Chester Creek. Essepenaike one of the signers of the Deed of 1683, also signed the Deed for the lands south of Chester Creek to Duck Creek, in 1685 (Archives, I. 63, 95). It would seem that the Turtle tribe claimed all of the lands along the west side of the Delaware (from about the Water Gap to Chesapeak Bay (the autographs of these various chiefs are found in Archives, I. 100). In 1692 Tammany, Tangorus, Swampes (Swanpees, in Deed of 1683), and Hickoqueon (Icquoquehan, in Deed of 1683), deeded the land between Neshaminy and Poquessing, to, William Penn (Arch. I. 116).

Pemapeck.—Deed of 1683, Archives, I. 63. **Pemapecka.**—Deed of 1685, Archives, I. 92. **Pemecacka.**—Lovelace (1672), Archives, Sec. Ser., V. 651. **Pemepeka.**—Board of Prop. (1735), Archives, Third Ser., I. 60. **Pemibaccan.**—Records of Upland (1678), Rec. Up, 115. **Pemibackes.**—Records of Upland (1680), Rec. Up, 179. **Pemippackes.**—Records of Upland (1678), Rec. Up, 124. **Pemopeck.**—Deed of 1697, Archives, I. 124. **Pemmapeck.**—Pa. Coun. (1701), Col. Rec., II. 34 **Pemmapecka.**—Deed of 1683, Archives, I. 62. **Pemneapecker.**—Deed of 1683, Archives, I. 64. **Penepack.**—Evans Map, 1749. **Pennypack.**—Scull Map, 1759. **Pennypack.**—Howell Map, 1792. **Pemmapecka.**—Deed of 1683, Archives I. 63 (evidently an error).

There are various other corruptions of this name. The maps commenced the work of fixing the present corrupt form of Pennypack, which should be changed back to its early form of Pemapeck, which is not far from the original Indian name of Pemapeek or Pemapaki, "lake land."

PENOBSCOT. A village in Luzerne County; also, Penobscot Knob, in same county. The name of the tribe of the Abnaki confederation. The meaning of the word is variously given. Penaubsket, "it flows on rocks" (Vetromile); Penobskat, "plenty stones" (Gerard) etc. The tribe lived along the Penobscot River in Maine. The name does not have any historic significance in this state.

PEQUEA. The name of a creek, which enters the Susquehanna from the east in Lancaster County, at Pequea; also the name of a former Shawnee village at the site of Pequea. Named after the Piqua tribe of the Shawnee. The name means, "dust" or "ashes." The time of the establishment of this Shawnee village is somewhat doubtful. According to Drake 70 families came to the place in 1677, from South Carolina. This date seems too early. According to the statement made to Governor Morris, in 1755, the Shawnee, about 60 families came to the region of Conestoga, in 1698, and upon application of the Conestoga they were allowed to remain. That soon after this time (1701) William Penn gave them permission to stay, and from that time onward they came in great numbers (Col. Rec. VI. 726). The "Shallnarooners" mentioned as having visited Ann LeTort, near Conestoga in 1692 were probably Shawnee who had come up from the Potomac to trade, and were not then settled on the Susquehanna (Col. Rec. I. 396-397, 435-436). The Treaty of 1701, made by William Penn and the Conestoga, Conoy, Nanticoke and Shawnee was the first official relation of the latter with the Province. The permission given to the Shawnee to settle, under the control of the Conestoga in 1698, was agreed to and an agreement made with these tribes (Col. Rec. II. 15-16). Some of these Shawnee, who settled at Pequea, may have been of the tribe which Martin Chartier followed from the region of Fort St. Louis, on the Mississippi, and settled in Cecil County, Maryland, but the majority were from South Carolina, which they commenced to leave in 1677. They probably settled on the Potomac, in the region of Old Town, and then went to the Susquehanna. Opessa, the Shawnee "King," came to the village at the mouth of Pequea Creek, from Old Town (See *Opessa's Town*). The "Shawnee Fields, deserted" on the Potomac must have been occupied for some time after this migration from South Carolina, as the broad fields at Oldtown were evidently used for some years. The Shawnee at the mouth of Octorara Creek and at Pequea were visited by Governor Evans in 1707 (Col. Rec. II. 386-390). The Indian traders settled in the Conestoga and Pequea region at an early date. Martin Chartier, who had married a Shawnee, and his son, Peter, who also married a Shawnee, possibly came with the Shawnee to Pequea (See *Chartier's Town*). Peter Bezalion, James LeTort and other noted Indian traders carried on a large business with these Shawnee, who gradually moved up the Susquehanna to Wyoming, and across the mountains to the Ohio.

(See *LeTort's Spring, Shawnee Cabins, Shawnee, Wyoming*).

Peckquea.—Pa. Coun. (1707), Col. Rec.,

II. 390. **Pequehan.**—Evans (1707), Col. Rec., II. 386. **Paquea.**—(Cr.) Board of Prop. (1713), Archives, Sec. Ser., XIX. 580. **Pecquea.**—(Cr.) Board of Prop. (1733), Archives, Third Ser., I. 29. **Pecque.**—(Cr.) Board of Prop. (1734), Archives, Third Ser., I. 47. **Pequa.**—(Cr.) Board of Prop. (1715), Archives, Sec. Ser., XIX. 600. **Peque.**—(Cr.) Evans, Map, 1749, 1755.

Howell's map (1792), and Scull's map (1759), both have the form Pequea, for Cr. The creek, which enters the Delaware from the east in New Jersey, now called Peques Creek, is so noted on Evans (1749), and Scull (1759). Adlum (1790), and Howell's (1792) both give the form Pequest.

PERKIOMEN. A creek which enters the Schuylkill from the north in Montgomery County; also a village called Perkiomenville, in same county. The name is a corruption of Pakihmomink, "where there are cranberries." Pakihm, "cranberry," with locative, ing, or ink. The region along this creek was settled by the Welsh and Germans soon after the arrival of William Penn. The land on the creek was purchased from Maughhoughsin in 1684 (Archives, I. 88). Robert Edwards seated himself upon a tract near this creek, soon after this time. Richard Lewis, who married a daughter of Edwards, purchased the 300 acres from the Penns in 1715 (Archives, Sec. Ser., XIX. 600). The Manor of Gilberts was laid out on the northern side of the creek, along the Schuylkill, and the Manor of Lowther was laid out along the headwaters of the creek (Holmes Map of Penna. 1691; Map 49, in Archives, Third Ser. IV). The Manor of Richland (Map 53, in Archives cited). The name Richland was given to Lowther, and that name given to the Manor in Cumberland County.

Pahkehoma.—Deed of 1684, Archives, I. 88. **Parkcominck.**—Board of Prop. (1714), Archives, Sec. Ser. XIX. 600. **Parkeocoming.**—Board of Prop. (1714), Archives, Sec. Ser. XIX. 647. **Parkeomink.**—Board of Prop. (1714), Archives, Sec. Ser. XIX. 610. **Parqueaming.**—Board of Prop. (1717), Archives, Sec. Ser. XIX. 677. **Perkiomen.**—Morris, map, 1848. **Perkiomy.**—Evans, map, 1749; Map of Richland Manor, No. 53. Archives, Third Ser. IV. **Perkiony.**—Scull, map, 1759. **Perquecominck.**—Board of P. (1704), Archives, Sec. Ser., XIX. 439. **Perqueominck.**—Board of Prop. (1704), Archives, Sec. Ser., XIX. 439. **Perquicominck.**—Board of Prop. (1712), Archives, Sec. Ser., XIX. 517. **Perquiominck.**—Board of Prop. (1701), Archives, Sec. Ser., XIX. 225. **Perquiomin.**—

Richland Manor, survey (1788) MS. Penn and Taylor Papers. **Perquioming.** —Adlum, map, 1790.

PETERS CREEK. A creek which has its headwaters in Washington County, and which enters the Monongahela River from the south, below West Elizabeth, Allegheny County. Said to have been named for an Indian, who is mentioned in the report of the Commissioners who went to Redstone, to warn the settlers to leave (Colonial Records, IX. 507). This Indian, who is also mentioned in the Minutes of West Augusta Court, evidently lived opposite "Redstone Old Fort," as Michael Cresap was granted a license for a ferry from that place to "Indian Peters," February 23, 1775 (Annals of Carneige Museum, I., Minute for Feb. 23, 1775). Many of the Virginia land grants were given along this creek (Archives, Third Ser., III. 508 etc.). A map of the grant, called "Coxburg," which was on this creek (was made to Gabriel Cox in 1780) is in the maps in Appendix I-X, to Third Series of Archives. This tract was situated in Washington County, Nottingham Township, in which Cox had settled in 1769. The Deed for this tract was made at "Coxes Fort," which was situated on the Monongahela River, about a mile from Shire Oaks (Consult; Frontier Forts, II. 432-433).

Peters Creek.—Scull, map, 1770; Howell, map, 1792.

PINE CREEK. A creek, which heads in Potter and Tioga Counties, and which enters the West Branch of the Susquehanna, near Jersey Shore, on the line between Clinton and Lycoming Counties. According to Heckewelder the Delaware name for the stream was, C u w e n h a n n e, "pine stream," a stream flowing through pine lands. The Iroquois name for the creek, and the name used in the various Deeds, was Tiadachton, or Tyadachton. The latter name was first mentioned in the Treaty of Fort Stanwix, 1768, when the purchase of all of the lands south of a line, which commenced at Owegy, running down the Susquehanna to the mouth of Towanda Creek, then up that creek to its headwaters, then down Tiadachton Creek, up the West Branch and across to the present Cherry Tree, and then in a straight line to Kittanning, down the Allegheny and Ohio. The present Lycoming Creek was

understood to be the creek called Tiadachton, but the Iroquois explained at the Treaty of Fort Stanwix, in 1784, that this name applied to the creek, known as Pine Creek. The map of the purchase of 1768 in the Archives, shows the line down Lycoming Creek, with "Tiadaghton" Creek marked west of it. On both of Lewis Evans Maps (1749-1755) the name is wrongly placed as that of Lycoming Creek. These maps were probably responsible for the error which was made. Beauchamp places "Ti-a-dagh-ta Creek" on the "west fork of the east branch of the Susquehanna." This may refer to some other creek, but as no reference is given, it is difficult to know where this creek was, unless the author has made an error in placing the creek in the wrong place (Place Names in New York, 175). There is no doubt what ever as to where Tiadachton Creek was. They said that they meant the creek now known as Pine Creek (Archives, X. 357). It is probable that the Susquehanna (Conestoga) had a village, and a fort at the mouth of this creek. A "Conestoga Indian F." is noted on both of Evans' maps, at the mouth of "Tiadachton," but if he was mistaken in the name of the stream, this Conestoga fort belongs at the mouth of Lycoming Creek, above Williamsport, at the site of Newbery. There were probably Conestoga villages at both places, as the old grave-yards at both places prove that these Indians had settlements there. These mounds and burial places were there when the region was first occupied by the Delaware, Shawnee and Seneca. One of the main trails to the Seneca country in western New York, ran up Pine Creek, over the divide to the Genesee and then down to Canadea and the other Seneca villages. The region was soon occupied by the settlers, after the Treaty of 1768. Some of these were beyond the line of the purchase and caused much trouble to the Provincial authorities, who warned them to leave. In 1778 and 1779 there were many Indians raids into the settlements along the West Branch (Consult; Meginness, Otzinachson; Shoemaker, Legends of the Susquehanna). Conrad Weiser first mentions this stream when on his mission to Onondaga in 1737. He says, "the stream we are now on the Indians call Dia-dachlu (the lost or bewildered) which in fact deserves such a name."

Weiser's Journal to Onondaga, in Pennsylvania Historical Society Collections, I. 9. See *Big Island, Muncy, Otzinachson*, etc.

Diadachlu.—Weiser (1737), Pa. Hist. Soc. Coll., I. 9. **Teadaghton.**—Kirkland (1748), Archives, X. 357. **Tiadaghton.** —Penn (1769), Col. Rec. IX. 554. **Tiadaughton.**—Atlee (1784), Archives, X. 357. **TiadaXton.**—Evans, map, 1749 (the "X" is the same as "ch"). **Tyadaghton.**—Evans (1784), Archives, XI. 509.

PITTSBURGH. Heckewelder says that the Delawares called the site, after its occupation by the French, Menachk-sink, "where there is a fence." Menachk, "a fence," is also "a fort." Zeisberger gives the word, Menachkhasu, "a fortified place." In the boundary dispute with Maryland, concerning the situation of the Conestoga fort at the mouth of Octorara Creek, James Hendricks said that some Indians told him that the Indians called the site, "Meanock, which, they said, in English signified a Fortification or Fortified Town" (Archives, Sec. Ser., XVI. 522). This word is the same as both Heckewelder and Zeisberger give, Menachk. Darlington gives the Iroquois form, Cheonderoga, as being the name of the place at the junction of the two rivers (Gist's Jour. 273). The Seneca name, which has been variously corrupted, was Diondega. This is the name used in "The Code of Handsome Lake, the Seneca Prophet" (20, 140). The "Gaiwiio" reads, "They land at Diondega. It is a little village of white people. Here they barter their skins, dried meat, and fresh game for strong drink. They put a barrel of it in their canoes. Now all the canoes are lashed together like a raft. Now all the men become filled with strong drink. They yell and sing like demented people" (p. 20). The "Gaiwhiio" then goes on to tell of the drunken fights, debauchery and crime caused by "goniga-nongi" (strong drink). The various Seneca names given by various writers are all, no doubt, corruptions of this name, which probably gave Washington and other early visitors to the place, the common English name of "The Forks." Pownall's note, which Darlington uses, in explaining the situation of "Trois Rivieres," which he places at Pittsburgh, is the cause of Darlington's error. "Trois Rivieres," as used in all of the French documents, had reference, not to the site of Pittsburgh, but to the "Three Rivers," on the north side of the St. Lawrence River, in Canada. While the name "Trois Rivieres" might have been applied to the site of Pittsburgh, by the French writers, it never was so used, but was, without a single exception, used of the place in Canada, long before the site of Pittsburgh had been visited by a white man. All of the children of Pierre Couc were born at "Three Rivers." Andrew, the first to bear the name of Montour, was born there in 1659 (Egle's Notes and Queries, Fourth Ser., II. 327, 1895). Father Lambing, in "The Centenary of the Borough of Pittsburgh," (p. 10) says, "Da-un-da-ga, which stood directly in the forks—the name is of Seneca origin, and is said to mean simply "the forks." He also says that he can find no authority for this name (Consult, Frontier Forts, II. 163-164). The name used by Father Lambing and others is a corruption of the name Diondega as used in the Code of Handsome Lake, before mentioned. This Seneca name is a form of the other Iroquois names used for the junction of the two branches of the Susquehanna at Tioga Point. This name, variously written, Diahoga, Tionioga, etc., has been corrupted to Tioga (which see). The "Written Rock" village mentioned by Celoron in 1749, was not, as is stated in Frontier Forts (II. 164) at the site of Pittsburgh, but at the present McKees Rocks, where "Queen Allaquippa" was then living (See *Allaquippa*). The only Indian village at the site of Pittsburgh, at the time when the region was first visited by the French and English, was Shannopin's Town (which see). The Iroquois, chiefly Seneca, used the Allegheny and Ohio Rivers as a war trail to the villages in the Illinois region, long before the occupation of these rivers by the Delaware and Shawnee, of historic times (Archives, Sec. Ser., VI. 57). The earliest name, therefore, for the site of Pittsburgh, was probably the Seneca name Diondega. The first white man to travel down the river past the site of the present city was probably Arnold Viele, the Dutch trader from Albany, who went from the Minisink country on the Delaware, to Wyoming and then over the Shamokin trail to the Ohio in 1692. He returned from the Shawnee region along the lower Ohio in 1694, with a band of Shawnee, some of whom probably settled on the upper Delaware (See *Allegheny, Minisink, Ohio, Shawnee*). James LeTort was probably the first Pennsylvania trader to cross the mountains to the site of Pittsburgh (See *Le Torts Springs*). At about the same time, before 1727, Hugh Crawford, Edmund Cartlidge, Peter Chartier, and other traders from the Susquehanna were trading at the Indian villages along the Ohio and Allegheny, and going westward to the Muskingum and Sciota Rivers. Thomas Cresap, George Croghan, Barney Curran, Jonas Davenport, James Dunning, and a host of Pennsylvania, Virginia and Maryland traders were on the Ohio before the commencement of the French and Indian War (Mr. Hanna gives a very complete list. Wilderness Trail, II. 326-343). A list of traders licensed by the Province from 1743 to 1748, is found in Archives, Sec. Ser., II. 619-621, and from 1762 to 1775, in same vol. from 621 to 627. The Ohio region, about the "forks," came into the field of real history about 1731, when Jonah Davenport, James LeTort and Edmund Cartlidge, Indian traders, were examined by the Provincial authorities concerning this then almost unknown wilderness (Archives, I. 299-306). The examination of these traders revealed the fact that a Frenchman, named Cavalier (the family name of LaSalle) had been trading on the Allegheny in the Kittanning town, every year, save 1729, since 1726. The rivalry of these French and English traders on the Allegheny was destined to bring the region into world history. This was the actual commencement of the events which led France and Great Britain into the struggle for the possession of the Ohio. The migration of the Delaware and Shawnee from the Susquehanna commenced in about 1724. This migration drew the Pennsylvania, Maryland and Virginia traders to the Ohio, where they came into conflict with the French traders from Canada. As early as 1732 William Jamieson and Edward Warren, two traders who were employed by Peter Allen, reported that the "french People, from Canada, were busy building a Fort with Loggs, at or near the said River Ohio" (Archives I. 309). It is possible that this "Logg" building was erected at the site which became known as "Loggstown," the historic Logstown (which see). From this time onward

the "forks of the Ohio" occupied an important place in the history of the development of the "woods," as the region west of the mountains was called. Pennsylvania and Virginia were pitted against the French power in Canada. The Shawnee, because they had left the Susquehanna against the wishes of the Iroquois, were seeking the protection of the French in Canada, and were also seeking to draw the Delawares from the Susquehanna, and into an alliance with them. The struggle which was soon to commence on the Ohio was not only between France and Great Britain, but also between the Shawnee and Delaware and their conquerors, the Iroquois. The various expeditions, Weiser, in 1748; Celoron, 1749; Gist, 1750-51; Washington and Gist, 1753; Washington, 1754; Braddock, 1755; Forbes, 1758, led to the final occupation of "the Forks" by the British, November 25, 1758 (Consult: Frontier Forts, II. 1-194; Darlington, Gist Journals; Weiser Jour., Col. Rec., V., 348-358; Post Jour., Archives, III. 520 et seq.; Thwaites, Early Western Travels; Parkman, Conspiracy of Pontiac; Sargent, Braddock's Expedition; Smith, Bouquet's Expedition of 1764; Albach, Western Annals; Craig, History of Pittsburgh; Boucher, History of Westmoreland County; Crumrine, History of Washington County; S. H. Church, History of Pittsburgh; Ellis, History of Fayette County; Chapman, French in the Allegheny Valley; Loudermilk, History of Cumberland, Md.; Sparks, Life of Washington; Craig, Olden Time; Rupp, History of Western Penna.; Walton, Conrad Weiser, and the various vols. of the Colonial Records and Archives). See *Chartier's Town, Kittanning, Logstown, Shannopin's Town, Allaquippa, Allegheny, Ohio, Venango, Conewango*, etc.

There were a number of historic Indian Trails which led to "the Forks.' The oldest of these was probably the Iroquois Trail, which came down the Allegheny River, from the Seneca country. This was used by the Iroquois on their war expeditions to the Mississippi and to the Carolinas. The Kittanning Trail ran eastward to the Susquehanna, by way of the Juniata. The Shamokin Trail, which was perhaps the oldest trail eastward, ran by way of Clearfield, Lock Haven, Williamsport, Sunbury, Wyoming, etc., to the upper Delaware. The Allegheny Path, which ran by way of

Ligonier, Bedford, Fort Loudon, Chambersburg, Carlisle to Harrisburg (this was perhaps the path which the Shawnee and Delaware followed westward from the Susquehanna. Some of them going by way of the Juniata and Frankstown Trail to Kittanning). A later Trail followed along this course to the Kittatinny Mountains, and then cut through "Croghan's Gap (now Sterritt's) to the Cumberland Valley, and then up to Harrisburg. The Monongahela River was used by the Seneca as a trail to the Catawba and Cherokee country. This water trail was joined by a branch which crossed Westmoreland and Fayette Counties, which is frequently mentioned as the "Catawba Trail." Even after the British occupation of the Ohio, the Seneca went down the Allegheny and then up the Monongahela, and across Virginia to the Carolinas (Col. Rec. IX. 252). It is probable that the Monongahela and Youghiogheny Rivers were both used by the Shawnee, as they went southward, when expelled by the Iroquois, before the commencement of the historic period. Nemacolin's Trail ran from the mouth of Dunlap's Creek (Brownsville) to Gist's Plantation, and then across the mountains to the Potomac, at Cumberland, Md. This trail crossed the Catawba Trail, which ran across from Kittanning to the mouth of Dunkard's Creek. Nemacolin's Trail was followed by Washington (1753 and 1754), and also by Braddock (1755) to the present Mount Braddock, where it then joined the Catawba Trail, running northward through Connellsville, Mount Pleasand and Hannastown to Kittanning. Near Turtle Creek the trail to Pittsburgh left a branch of this Catawba Trail. This trail down the valley to McKeesport was that followed by Washington and Braddock. General Forbes in 1758 followed the trail from Bedford, through Ligonier, Hannastown, Harrison City, to Pittsburgh, via Penn Avenue (For distances along these trails from Harrisburg to Pittsburgh, consult; Archives, II. 12, 24, 47-48, 133-136; Col. Rec. V. 750-760; VI. 84). Consult; Hanna, Wilderness Trail; Hulbert, Historic Highways. See *Frankstown, Kittanning, Raystown*, and the notes on any of the places along any of these trails. For other data relating to the region of Pittsburgh, see *Allegheny, Ohio, Shannopin's Town*.

In 1731, according to the estimate of Jonah Davenport, there were 300 Delaware, 260 Shawnee, 100 Asswekalaes (Shawnee, see *Sewickley*), and some "Mingoes" (Seneca), living on the Ohio in this region (Archives, I. 299). As the Indian trade increased on the Ohio many other villages were settled by Delaware, Shawnee, Iroquois, with a mixture of Miami, Wyandot and other tribes living in Ohio. See *Venango, Kittanning, Chartier's Town, Shannopin's Town, Logstown, Shinga's Town, Kuskuski, Shenango*, etc. After the British occupation of Fort Pitt the Indians commenced leaving the villages in the entire region, going westward into Ohio, Indiana and Illinois, and northward along the upper waters of the Allegheny. A number of important Indian Councils were held at Fort Pitt (Col. Rec. VIII. 264, 382, 429, etc.; Archives, III. 744; IV. 471, 531, etc.).

PLAYWICKY. A former Delaware village, the home of "King" Tammany, who sold the lands to William Penn between Neshaminy and Pennypack Creeks, June 23, 1683. The site was marked by the Pennsylvania Historical Commission and the Colonial Dames, October 17, 1925, by the placing of a marker upon a hill about half a mile west of Neshaminy Creek, two and a half miles west of Langhorne, Bucks County.

PLUM CREEK. A branch of Crooked Creek in Armstrong County. Said by Heckewelder to have been called Sipuas-hanne, "plum stream," by the Delawares. Sipuassink, "where there are plums," or "plum place." Howell's map, 1792, gives the name as Plumb Creek.

POAKOPOHKUNK. See *Pochapochkunk.*

POCAHONTAS. A town in Somerset County, named for the famous daughter of the "King Powhatan," immortalized by John Smith. The name according to Heckewelder is a corruption of Pockohantes, "a run between two hills," from Pochko, "a rock," or "rocky hill," and "Hanne," "a stream," with the diminutive suffix, tes. Strachey, however said, "So the great King Powhatan called a young daughter of his, whome he loved well, Pochahuntas, which may signify little wanton. Tooker agrees with this statement, saying that the name is derived from Poachau, "he or she plays," ontas, the diminutive,

Poachau-untas, "the little frolic," or "little wanton" (American Anthropologist (N. S.) VIII. 24, 1906). Strachey says of this young woman, "Pochahuntas, a well featured, but wanton young girle, Powhatan's d a u g h t e r sometymes resorted to our fort, of the age then of eleven or twelve yeares, get the boyes forth with her into the markett place, and make them wheele, falling on their hands, turning their heeles upwards, whome she would followe and wheele so herself, naked as she was all the fort over." (Historie, 65). In her riper years this young "girle" was called Amonaute-from amonateu, "she gives warning," probably having reference to the warning which she gave Smith in 1609 (Tooker). Pocahontas was married to John Rolfe, in April, 1613. In 1616 she went with him to England. She was received with great honor. When about to start for America, March 1617, she was taken ill with smallpox and died in her 22nd year. She left an only son (John Rolfe's child called Thomas Rolfe, who afterwards went to Virginia. He became a man of wealth and prominence. He left an only daughter, from whom descended, on the mother's side, John Randolph, of Roanoke. The father of Pochahontas, Powhatan, was the head of the confederacy which bears that name. Mr. Tooker derives this name from Powah, which is equivalent to the Massachusetts Pauwau, he "uses divination," or "powwaw" a "priest, or wise man"—hence our adopted word "powwow." The village of this chief was "Pawwau-atan," which means the "hill of divination," where Powhatan held his "powwows" (American Anthropologist (N. S.) VI. 467, 1904). Heckewelder gives, "Pawat-hanne," "stream of wealth or fruitfulness"; Trumbull, Powhat-hanne, "falls in a stream." The village was situated on the north bank of the James River, at the falls, near Richmond, Virginia. The name has no relation to the history of Pennsylvania.

POCHAPUCHKUG. A former Indian village near the Lehigh Water Gap, visited by Count Zinzendorf in 1742, when on his way to Meniologameka. It was probably on the present Big Creek, or Pohopoco Creek, which enters the Lehigh above the gap. The name is probably a corruption of Pochkapochka, "two mountains opposite each other, with a creek between," with the locative ung. The Brethren

of the Moravian mission give the form Buck-ka-buch-ka, "rock aside of rock." Pock-a-wach-ne, signifies "a creek between two hills." Captain Harris, a Delaware, the father of Tedyuskung, lived at this village when the surveyors of the Walking Purchase stopped in the village in 1737, to rest after the walk. Nicholas Scull mentions him as "Captain Harrison" (Col. Rec. VII. 400). This chief was also there when Zinzendorf visited the place in 1742 (Loskiel, Hist. Miss., II. 25). Reichel seems to place this village near the later Moravian mission at Wechquetank, or Wequetank, which was on the north side of Wire Creek, near Brodheadsville, Monroe County Mem. Mor. Church, I. 38).

Poskopohkunk.—Scull (1757), Col. Rec. VII. 400. **Pochapuchkung.**—L o s k i e l (1794), Hist. Miss., II. 25.

POCONO. The name of a mountain, Township and Lake and creek, in Monroe County; also with compound Manor and Pines, in same county. Said by Heckewelder to be a corruption of Poco-hanne, "a stream between mountains."

One of the earliest Indian trails between the Susquehanna and the upper Delaware, ran from Wyoming across Monroe County to Stroudsburg. This was probably the course followed by Arnold Viele in 1694, when he returned with a party of Shawnee, from the Ohio. It was also, from the point about 22 miles north of Easton, the course followed by the army of General Sullivan to Wyoming in 1779. A fine map of the exact route of Sullivan is found in the "History of the Military Expedition of General Sullivan in 1779." The old trail from the Delaware to Wyoming is also noted on Scull's map of 1770. Sullivan's army left Easton on June 17, 1779, and went by way of Wind Gap, Great Swamp, Shades of Death, to Wyoming, which was reached on the 23rd of June. The Pocono Mountain is the divide between the waters of the Delaware and Susquehanna, in this region. In Carbon County, Morris (1848) notes this range as Pohopoko. It is probable that Pocono, or Pokono, and Pohopoco, or Pohpoko, are corruptions of Pochkapochka, "two mountains bearing down, or near each other, with a stream between."

Second Mountain Pocono.—Howell, map, 1792. **Pokono Point.**—Scull, map, 1770.

The various Journals and maps in Sullivan's Expedition have the following forms of the name:

Pocono point.—Blake (1779), Jour. Exped. Gen. Sull. 38. **Poconoco.**—Gookin (1779), Jour. Mil. Exped. Gen. Sull. 103. **Poconogo.**—Livermore, (1779), Jour. Mil. Exped. Gen. Sull. 181. **Pogono point.** —Norris, (1779), Jour. Mil. Exped Gen. Sull. 224. **Pokanose point.**—G r a n t, (1779), Jour. Mil. Exped. Gen. Sull. 107. **Pokono.**—Rogers, (1779), Jour. Mil. Exped. Gen. Sull. 247. **Pokonno.**—Map 103 A. (1779), Jour Mil. Exped. Gen. Sull. (in cover).

POCOPSON. A creek and town in Chester County. The creek is a branch of the Brandywine. Said to be from an Indian word meaning "roaring creek."

POHOPOCO. A creek which enters the Lehigh from the north, now known as Big Creek, was also formerly called Heads Creek. Said to be a corruption of Pochkpochka, or Buchkabuchka, 'two mountains bearing down on each other," or "rock beside rock" (See *Pocono*). Scull's map of 1770 is marked "Poopoko or Heads Cr." His map of 1759, and Howell's map of 1759 give the latter name alone. Morris' map (1848) gives the name Pohopoko to the mountain in Carbon County, which is noted as Pokono in Monroe County. Both names are probably corruptions of the same Indian word. The name is written Pocopo by Reichel, who also gives the name Hoeth's Creek, as the name of Head's Creek. The Moravians bought lands at the head of this creek in 1760, to a village which was called Wechquetank (which see). Consult; Reichel, Mem. Mor. Church, 29, 33, 38. Frederick Hoeth lived on this creek in 1755, when his house was attacked by the Indians. He and his wife and several children were killed (Col. Rec. VI. 758-759).

Pocho Pochto.—Parsons (1755), Col. Rec. VI. 759. **Poopoko or Heads Cr.**—Scull, map, 1770.

POKETO, now PUCKETTA. A creek which enters the Allegheny River from the south between Westmoreland and Allegheny Counties. Said to be a corruption of Pa-ki-ton, or Pachgita, "throw it away," or "abandon it" (Heckewelder). The name seems rather to be a corruption of Pock-ates, with the significance "little creek." An Indian trail, which branched from about Apollo, crossed the Allegheny River just about the mouth of this

creek, and then crossed to the Beaver and Mahoning Rivers, joining the path which led from Venango to Kuskuski. Many of the Indian raids in the region south of the Allegheny were made by parties coming over this trail from the Ohio Indian country in 1777-1780. In order to protect the settlements a fort was erected just above the mouth of this creek, in May, 1778, and was named Fort Crawford, in honor of Col. William Crawford, who built the fort, and who commanded it at intervals from 1778 to 1780. The fort was evacuated by order of Col. Brodhead in Nov., 1779, but was again occupied in the spring of 1780. During the Indian troubles in 1791-93 the fort was occupied by various frontier troops. It stood in the present Parnassus, above the mouth of the creek. Consult; Frontier Forts, II. 337-44; Archives, XII. 129, 160, 171, etc.

Pochketos.—Scull, map, 1770 (evidently an error). **Pocketoes.**—Howell, map, 1792. **Pocketos.**—Brodhead (1779), Archives, VIII. 38. **Pucatees.**—Lochry (1780), Archives, VIII. 77. **Pucketos.**— Frontier Forts, II. 340. **Puckety.**— Frontier Forts, II. 340. **Punkety.**— Frontier Forts, II. 337 (an error). **Pucketta.**—Present maps (1911).

POPACTON. The name of one of the branches of the Delaware River, which it enters from the east. Said to be a corruption of Popocus, "partridge," with the locative, ing (Beauchamp). This derivation does not seem satisfactory. It is more probably from Papagonk, "at the pond." The name of a tribe, or band of Munsee, which lived along this river.

Paupacton.—Morris, map, 1848. **Popachtunk.**—Evans (1755), Scull (1770), Howell (1792). **Popochtunk.**—Pownall, map, 1776. **Popachton.**—Adlum, map, 1790. **Popacton.**—Map, 1911.

POPOMETANG. A creek which enters the Susquehanna from the south, in Northumberland County, source in Columbia County. Now called Roaring Creek. There was an Indian village at its mouth called Glasswanoge (which see).

Popemetang.—Board of Prop. (1773), Arch., Third Ser., I. 297. **Popometang.**— Scull, map, 1770. **Roaring Creek.**—Howell, map, 1792.

POPONOMING. The name of a pond or small lake in Monroe County. Heckewelder derives the name from Papennamink, "where we were gazing." It may be from Papeek, "a pond," with the locative suffix. It is now called Long Lake. On Morris' map (1848) it is called Long Pond; the present name of a Post Office, near the lake.

POQUESSING. The name of a creek which enters the Delaware from the west at the north-east boundary of Philadelphia. There may have been an Indian village at, or near, the mouth of this creek. Heckewelder gives the origin from Poquesink, or Poquesing, "the place of mice." Achpo-quees, "a mouse," with the locative, ink, or ing. The name is frequently mentioned, under various forms, in the Records of Upland Court, and also in the Archives of the Province. In 1677 Ephraim Herman and Pelle (Peter) Rambo were granted 300 acres of land on the south side of the creek (Records of the Court at Upland, 61), and in the same year Capt. Hans Moens (Moensen) was also given a grant of land on the creek (op. cit. 64). In 1678 Ephraim Herman was granted the remaining land between this creek and the creek now known as Pennypack Creek (op. cit. 115), and in the same year James Sanderlands and Lawrence Cock were given a tract, called "Poat-Quessink," on the northeast side of the creek (op. cit. 123). In the same year Henry Hastings was given a tract, called "Hastings Hope," one mile above the mouth of the creek, and bounded by the grant made to James Sanderlands and Lawrence Cock (op. cit. 125). In 1681 William Biles was appointed overseer of the highways between the Falls and Poquessing (op. cit. 194). These various tracts, and others, are noted on Holme's map of Pennsylvania. In 1692 a Deed was made to William Penn, of the lands between this creek and Neshaminy, signed by Taminent (Tammany), Tangorus, Swampes, and Hickoqueon, who stated that these lands were "claimed by Us from the beginning of the World to the day of the date hereof" (Archives, I. 117). The tract granted to Joseph Growdon, for a Manor, by William Penn, is mentioned in Archives, Sec. Ser., XIX. 250-251). This lease and release, was dated 1681, consisted of 10,000 acres. In 1702 Joseph Growden granted to David Lloyd, who had married his daughter, 1000 acres of this land (op. cit. 302). There were various disputes about this land, which Penn had

granted to Joseph Growden (also Growdon). (Consult; op. cit. 309, 330, 352, 374 etc.).

Pequossin.—Evans, map, 1749. Paequossin.—Rec. Upland (1677), Records of Upland, 61. Paequessink.—Rec. Upland (1677), Records of Upland, 64. Poat-Quessink.—Rec. Upland (1678), Records of Upland, 123. Poattquessink.—Rec. Upland (1678), Records of Upland, 125. Poat quessink.—Rec. Upland (1678), Records of Upland, 125. Poetquessink.—Rec. Upland (1678), Records of Upland, 115. Poquassin.—Howell, map, 1792. Poquessing.—Deed (1692), Archives, I. 116. Potquessin.—Holme, map, 1691-4. Poyquessing.— Board of P. (1683-1717), Archives, Sec. Ser., XIX. 614.

PORTAGE CREEK. A creek which enters the Allegheny, from the south, at Port Allegany, McKean County. Called Portage Creek because its source was in the divide between the waters of the West Branch and the Allegheny Rivers. Between these streams a "portage" of about 23 miles was made. This is the only "portage" necessary between the Atlantic Ocean and the Gulf of Mexico, via the Susquehanna, West Branch, Allegheny, Ohio and Mississippi. This is perhaps the longest canoe trip possible on the American continent. There was a portage road, over the Indian trail, from Emporium Junction, on the waters of the West Branch, to Port Allegany, on the Allegheny River. This road was used by the first settlers to the Allegheny and Oswayo region. Driftwood may have been the end of canoe navigation for these settlers, who then crossed to Canoe Place, now Port Allegany. Francis King made this trip to the Oswayo in 1797, when he established the settlement at Ceres. The name of this creek, as noted on Howell's map (1792). The line of the The creek which enters the Driftwood branch of the Sinnemahoning, at Emporium Junction, is also noted as Portages Creeks, and the Allegheny River, It is called Koshekotoes Creek on Howell's may (1792). The line of the P. R. R., between Lock Haven and Olean, practically follows the Indian trail up the West Branch, the Sinnemahoning, the Driftwood Branch, Portages Creeks, and the Allegheny river, to the former Seneca villages along the "Big Bend" of the Allegheny. The former "portage" from Emporium Junction to Keating Summit, is perhaps the longest steep R. R. grade in the state. These points are 16 miles apart, with a difference of 857 feet in elevation—Emporium Junction being 1019 feet above sea level, and Keating

Summit, 1876 feet. Adlum's map (1790) gives the form Kocheketow for the latter creek, from Driftwood to the divide, and the distance from Driftwood to Port Allegany as 23 miles. The distance is 42.4 miles, so that the 23 mile portage commenced at Emporium Junction, which is 24.4 miles from Port Allegany.

PORT ALLEGANY. A town on the Allegheny River, in McKean County. Formerly Kingsville (Morris, map, 1848), and previous to the settlement of the region in about 1798, it was known as Canoe Place. Here the Indians, in crossing from the Allegheny to the West Branch of the Susquehanna, were obliged to make a portage to the other Canoe Place, over the divide, at Driftwood, or Emporium Junction. This was one of the trails from the Seneca villages in western New York, to the Susquehanna. It was also probably the trail followed by the Wenro, from their villages near Cuba Lake, N. Y., to the Susquehanna. When the Andastes, or Conestoga, were all powerful on the Susquehanna, it was probably one of the trails by which they reached the villages of the Seneca. See *Conestoga, Susquehanna, West Branch, Canoe Place,* etc.

Canoe Place.—Howell map, 1792. **Kingsville.**—Morris, map, 1848. **Port Allegany.** —Recent maps. **Port Alleghany.**—Hopkins, map, 1872.

POTOMAC. The name of an important river, which heads in the Allegheny mountains, formed by two main branches which unite about 20 miles south-east of Cumberland, Md. For the greater part of its course it is the boundary line between Virginia and Maryland. It cuts through a most beautiful gap in the Blue Ridge at Harper's Ferry. It flows into Chesapeake Bay, above which the river is from 6 to 8 miles wide. Many historic events have taken place along the course of this stream. The attempted settlement of the Spanish colony, under Don Louis, a converted Mexican Indian, in 1570; the desertion of this little colony by Don Louis; its destruction; the arrival of Menendez in the Potomac, and the failure of Spain to make a settlement on this river which they called Espiritu Santo; the expedition of John Smith up Chesapeake Bay in 1608, and the other events connected with the early exploration and settlement of the river are narrated in the various histories of the United States, and the settlement of Virginia.

Potomac was also the name of an important tribe in the Powhatan confederation, which occupied the south bank of the river in Stafford and King George Counties, Virginia; also the name of the chief village of this tribe, situated on the peninsula formed by the Potomac River and Potomac Creek, about 55 miles due west of Chesapeake Bay, in Stafford County, Virginia. The river takes its name from this village, which was supposed to be the name of the river when first heard by Henry Spelman, in about 1613. Spelman in his Relation of Virginia, calls the ruler of the village "King Patomecke," and the tribe the "Patomeck." Heckewelder gives the origin of this name from Pethamook, "they are coming by water." This is evidently a mistake. Gerard gives its derivation from Patomek, meaning "something brought," and as applying to a place, "where something is brought," and suggests that it was given because the tribute was brought to this village by the tribes subject to the chief. The chief of this tribe was said to be as powerful as Powhatan himself. Within historic times the river was occupied by various groups of the Conoy, Nanticoke and later by the Shawnee, and because this river was connected by trails with the Delaware, Susquehanna and Ohio, it is frequently mentioned in the Archives of Pennsylvania, chiefly in the various disputes between the Iroquois and the colonies of Virginia and Maryland, concerning the various purchases of lands along its course. After the Iroquois had been paid for the lands in Pennsylvania, south of the Kittatinny mountains, along the Susquehanna River, they then demanded that Virginia and Maryland also pay for the lands which lay along the western boundaries of these colonies. The various Iroquois raids into the country of the Cherokee and Catawba had been made across Maryland and Virginia, where various depredations had been done by the bands of warriors passing through the region. The two colonies demanded satisfaction for these damages. An Iroquois war with these two colonies was imminent, after the Council of 1736, when Pennsylvania undertook to settle the dispute with the Iroquois. These disputes had come before the Council at Philadelphia in 1736, and again in 1742. After much correspondence between Governor Thomas, of Pennsylvania, and Governor Ogle of Maryland, it was decided to send Conrad Weiser to Onondaga to invite the Iroquois to a Council at Harris Ferry the following spring to talk over the entire matter. Maryland was anxious to settle the matter, but Virginia denied the Iroquois claim and was unwilling to do anything. In 1743 things had reached a critical point. The Iroquois were on the very verge of a war with Virginia, which would make Pennsylvania a passage way for the hostile Iroquois on their way southward. After the Treaty of 1742 a number of Iroquois went southward, against their enemies, the Catawba, and in Crossing Virginia they killed a number of hogs and cattle belonging to the settlers. This led to a conflict in which a number of settlers were killed. The Iroquois were complaining of the white settlers pressing over the mountains of Pennsylvania along the Juniata; the Shawnee were being alienated by the French on the Ohio, and the Delawares were becoming more and more unfriendly because of the various land sales, and the war of the Austrian Succession was about to bring on a struggle. In this impending conflict the American colonies simply could not afford to enter into a war with the Iroquois. It was one of the most critical periods which the British interests in North America ever had to meet. Conrad Weiser went to Shamokin, where he held a conference with Shikellamy, and returned to Philadelphia with his report. Governor Gooch, of Virginia, had in the meanwhile written to the Governor of Pennsylvania, in which he opened the way for a conference with the Iroquois. Weiser was sent back to Shamokin, and upon his return was sent to Onondaga with a present from Virginia, which he represented at the Council (Consult; Col. Rec. IV. X 632 et seq.; Weiser's Jour. IV. 640-650; 660-669). In 1644 the Treaty of Lancaster was held. All of these matters of dispute came up for consideration. Maryland claimed that the Colony had bought all of the lands on both sides of Chesapeake Bay, to the mouth of the Susquehanna, from the Minquas (Conestoga) in 1652; that in 1663 eight hundred Seneca and Cayuga were defeated by the Minquas assisted by the Marylanders. The Minquas, reduced by famine, were finally defeated by the Iroquois, after the Marylanders had withdrawn from the alliance. The Iroquois then claimed these lands, by right of conquest, to the head of Ches-

apeake Bay. Pennsylvania had purchased these lands as far north as the Blue Mountains in 1736 (after having previously bought them before from Gov. Dongan in 1696). The Commissioners of Maryland brought up these points, to which Canassatego, the Iroquois diplomat, replied. He reviewed the various purchases made by Pennsylvania, and acknowledged the validity of all of the purchases made from the Minquas (Conestoga) before they were conquered by the Iroquois, but denied that Maryland had been in possession of the Cohongorontas (Potomac) lands before that time. Canassatego was amply able to defend the position taken by the Iroquois. He said, "We have had your Deeds Interpreted to Us, and we acknowledge them to be good and valid and that the Conestogoe or Sasquehannah Indians had a Right to sell those Lands unto you, for they were then their's; but since that time We have Conquered them, and their Country now belongs to Us, and the Lands we demanded satisfaction for are no part of the Lands comprized in those Deeds—they are the Cohongoroutas Lands" (Col. Rec. IV. 708-709). In answer to the Virginia Commissioners Canassatego said, "All the World Knows we conquered the Several Nations living on Sasquehanna, Cohongoronta, and on the Back of the Great Mountains in Virginia. The Coney-uch-such-roona, Coch-nan-wasroonan, Tokoa-irough-roonan, and Connutskirr-ough-roonaw, feel the effects of Our Conquests, being now a Part of Our Nations, and their Lands at our Disposal. We know very well it hath often been say'd by the Virginians that the Great King of England and the People of that Colony conquered the Indians that lived there, but it is not true. We will allow that they have conquered the Sachdagughroonan (Nanticoke) and Drove back the Tuscarroraws, and that they have on that Account a Right to some Part of Virginia, but as to what lies beyond the Mountains, we conquered the Nations residing there, and that Land, if ever the Virginians get a good Right to it, it must be by Us" (op. cit. 712). The disputes concerning these lands were finally settled by Virginia and Maryland making payment for the lands claimed by the Iroquois. The Deed to Maryland was made to include "all those Lands lying two Miles above the uppermost Fork of Patowmack or Cohongoruton River, near which Thomas

Cressap has a Hunting or Trading Cabbin by a North Line to the Bounds of Pennsylvania (op. cit. 719). Shikellamy did not sign this Deed at this time, and never would sign it. Probably because he was made to realize that it would have some bearing in the Boundary Dispute, which was then a vital question, between Pennsylvania and Maryland. Shikellamy was wise enough to see that he could not do anything which might be used against the Province, in which he lived and which had always been so willing to listen to his advice. Conrad Weiser may have had much to do with the attitude taken by this chief (Consult; Treaty at Lancaster, in Col. Rec. IV. 698-736). This treaty ended with feelings of good will among the Indians for the three Colonies represented. Col. Thomas Cresap had established a trading house at Old Town, Md., in 1742-43. The situation of this house is noted on Evan's map of 1749. He was an Agent of the Ohio Company. Old Town was near the point where the Warriors Trail crossed the Potomac River. Cresap. Gist and Nemacolin blazed the trail, later known as Nemacolin's Trail, from the mouth of Will's Creek, 15 miles above Cresap's house, to the mouth of Redstone Creek. Gist started on his trip of exploration of the Ohio, from Cresap's in 1750 (See *Old Town, Gist's, Redstone*, etc.; Consult; Darlington's, Gist). Fort Cumberland at the site of Cumberland, Md., was the starting point of Washington's expedition of 1754, and also of Braddock's expedition of 1755, and was also the point of departure for Washington and Gist in 1753 to the French forts (Consult; Washington's and Gist's Journals of 1753; Sargants, Braddock's Expedition of 1755). The Ohio Company erected a store house at the mouth of Will's Creek on the Potomac, which was to be the chief distributing point for the trade on the Ohio (Consult; Lowdermilk, History of Cumberland, Maryland). After the time of Braddock's defeat, 1755, the trade with the Ohio, from the Colonies, ended until after 1758, when the French were driven from the Ohio. The road which led from the Potomac to the Ohio then became a well used pathway for the settlers going to the Ohio country. Braddock's Road, as Nemacolin's rail was then called, became one of the chief highways to the "Great West," between the Potomac and the Ohio. Its general course was

later followed by the National Pike, which connected the east with the west (Consult, Searight, The Old Pike, A History of the National Road, 1894). It is probable that the Shawnee who lived along the Potomac, near Old Town, migrated to the Ohio at about the same time that he Shawnee from South Carolina entered the lower Susquehanna region—between 1698 and 1724. The course which they followed westward may have been the same as that previously followed by their ancestors when they were driven from the Ohio by the Iroquois. Evidently some of the Shawnee returned to the Ohio by way of the trail, later used as Braddock's Road. Some of the Shawnee went northward along the Warriors Path to Bloody Run (near Everett), and then went westward over the trail leading through Bedford, Shawnee Cabins, Ligonier, etc. to the Allegheny, at Chartiers Town (which see). The following forms of the name Potomac are simply those taken from the Archives and Records of Pennsylvania—they cover nearly all of the forms used in the various records of Virginia and Maryland.

Patowmack.—Weiser (1744), Col. Rec. IV. 717. **Patowmeck.**— H e r m a n n (1670), Map of Maryland and Virginia. **Pawtowmeck.**—Spotswood (1722), Col. Rec. III. 205. **Potomack.**—Harris (1755), Col. Rec. VI. 646. **Potomock.**—Logan (1701), Archives, I. 145. **Potowmach River called Cohongoronta.**—Mayo, map, 1737. **Potowmeck.**—Scull, map, 1759. **Potowmeck.**—Pa. Coun. (1721), Col. Rec. III. 114. **Cachwangarodon (Patowmeck).** —Weiser(1750), Col. Rec. V. 477. **Cohongoronta.**—Canassatego (1742), Col. Rec. IV. 561. **Cohongoronto.**—Scull, map, 1770; also Fry and Jefferson map, 1755. **Cohongoroonton.**—Weiser (1744), Col. Rec. IV. 716. **Cohongoroutas.**—Canassatego (1744), Col. Rec. IV. 708. **Cohongoruton.**—Canassatego (1744), Col. Rec. IV. 719.

In "Aboriginal Place Names in New York" (p. 27) Mr. Beauchamp says, "Co-hon-go-run-to, a name of the Susquehanna, according to Colden, which may mean either a river in the woods, or one which serves as a door." Mr. Colden is mistaken. This name was that used by the Iroquois for the Potomac River.

PUNXSUTAWNEY. The name of a town in Jefferson County; the name of a former Delaware village at the same place. A corruption of Ponks-uteney, "gnat town." Heckewelder says in his Narrative (121) that the place was infested with these gnats, or sand-flies. "That not a moment's rest was to be expected at this place otherwise than by kindling fires throughout the camp, and sitting in the smoke." He relates the tradition, told in 1772, that about 30 years before a hermit lived there on a rock. This Indian was a magician, who would appear in various form to frighten travellers, some of whom he killed. Finally a chief killed him. Thus far the story is said to have been true. The chief burned the hermit's bones to ashes. These were thrown into the air to be thrown away, but turned into Ponksak, "sand-flies"— hence the trouble to the travellers and horses in later years. Ettwein, who passed over the trail from the West Branch, with the Moravian converts, says in his Journal (1772), "In the evening the ponkis were excessively annoying, so that the cattle pressed towards and into our camp, to escape their persecutors in the smoke of the fires. This vermin is a plague to man and beast, both by day and night. But, in the swamp, through which we were now passing, their name is legion, and hence the Indians call it Ponks-utenink, i.e., "the town of the Ponkis" (Quoted in Hanna, I. 215). C. F. Post returned from his mission to the Ohio in 1758, by this route, on his way to Shamokin. He says, "In the afternoon we twice crossed Chowatin (now Mahoning Creek) and came to Ponche-stanning (an Old town that lies on the same Creek)" (Archives, III. 542). The old trail from Shamokin (now Sunbury) to Kittanning passed through this point. Not far from the swamp which was west of the present town, the trail crossed the branch of the Frankstown Path, leading to the mouth of the Tionesta, and also to Venango. Post had travelled over both of these paths. Marie LeRoy and Barbara Leininger, who were captured below Shamokin in 1755, were taken over this trail to Kittanning. In the Narrative of the captivity of these young women it is stated, "There we stayed ten days and then proceeded to Puncksetonay or Eschentown" (Eschen is the German for Ponkis, or sand-flies) (Archives, Sec. Ser., VII. 404). The trail from Shamokin to Kittanning, via the West Branch, Bald Eagle, Marsh Creek, Clearfield and Punxsutawny was one of the oldest between the Susquehanna and Ohio. After the southern trail via Bedford, Ligonier and Kittanning, or the Frankstown Path, via the Juniata, Kittanning Point, Cherry Tree, etc., were used (after 1758) this northern

route was abandoned to a great extent, because of its various disadvantages, such as lack of game, difficult grades and sand-flies, which were exceedingly annoying to the traders horses.

Puncksotonay.—LeRoy (1755), Arch., Sec. Ser., VII. 404; also, Eschentown, 404. **Punystawny.**—Morris, map, 1848. **Ponchestanning.**—Post (1758), Archives, III. 542. **Ponks-utenink.**—E t t w e i n (1772), Hanna, I. 215. **Ponks Utenay.**—Heckewelder, in Narrative, 121, 1820. **Punxsutawney.**—Recent maps, and official form.

While it is stated by most writers, Post included, that there was a village at this point, it is doubtful. The Indians would hardly locate a village at a point where there were no advantages, and where they would be afflicted with the sand-flies, when so many good village sites were so easily found. The Indians evidently knew the place, because of the great number of sand-flies, as Ponks-utenink, "the town of the sand-flies," and no doubt these were the only occupants of the place.

PYMATUNING. The name of a creek which rises in Ohio, flowing south-east into the Shenango River, near Sharpsville, Mercer County, Pa.; also the name of a former Indian village near the mouth of the creek, near Clarksville. According to Hutchin's map of 1764 the village was situated on the left, west, side of the Shenango river, below the present Clarksville, Mercer County. On Scull's map of 1770 the village is on the east side of the Shenango River. Howell's map of 1792, has the village just below the mouth of Lackawanna Creek, on the west side of what is noted as Pymatuning Creek, but which is the present Shenango River, just below Big Bend, Mercer County. The trail up the Shenango River ran past this village to the head of the Big Bend, where Hutchin's says were a number of Indian graves, which must have been near New Hamburg, at the place noted on Morris' map of 1848 as Delaware Grove. Here the trail turned east, running to the head of Sandy Lake, then about two and a half miles along the ridge to the crossing of Sandy Creek, then down the creek for about two miles, and then over the hills to Venango (now Franklin). Heckewelder gives the origin of the name from Pihmtomink, "where the man with the crooked mouth resides," and says in a note, "I was acquainted with the person to whose deformity there is allusion in the name of the creek" (Indian Names, 263). Pim-e-u, "slanting," W'doon, "mouth."

Pematuning.—Hutchins, map, 1764; Pematuning Town. Howell, map, 1792. **P e m e y t u n i n g.**—Hutchins (1764), in Hanna, II. 201. **Pymatooning (Tp.)**— M o r r i s, map, 1848. **Pymatuning.**— Howell, map, 1792 (both town and creek).

QUAKAKE. The name of a creek which enters the Lehigh from the west in Carbon County; also the name of a Township and Hill in the same county, and of a village in Schuylkill County. A corruption of Cuwenkeek, "pine lands." Cuwen-hanna would signify, "pine stream." Is mentioned in the observations of Stephen Balliets, in 1787, concerning the possibility of a road to Wyoming through this region. He says, "I suppose the distance from the Delaware to the mouth of Quakake, along the course of the Lehigh, to be about Sixty miles" (Archives, XI. 131, 133, 135). He also mentions the gap in Quakake Hill, as a suitable course for the road to Wyoming. Quakake Hill and Valley are noted on Morris' map, 1848, and Quacake Valley and creek on Howell's map, 1792. **Queekeek.**—Hays (1758), Archives, III. 413.

QUEEN ESTHER'S TOWN. A former Indian village opposite Tioga point, below the junction of the Chemung with the Susquehanna, near the site of the present Green's Landing, Bradford County. Named in honor of Esther Montour, the daughter of French Margaret, and a grand-daughter of Madame Montour (See *Montour*). Esther was the most notorious of all of the family, and is known as "the fiend of Wyoming" (Consult; Frontier Forts, I. 458; (See *Wyoming*). She was the wife of a Munsee chief called Eghehowen (also Egebund, Echegohund), and after his death she became the leader of his village tribe (Col. Rec. VIII. 152, 159, 196, 209, 435; Archives, III. 506, 740; IV. 90). Her village in 1772 was Sheshequin (which see). Soon after this time she removed about six miles north to the Susquehanna, opposite Tioga Point, where her village was destroyed by Col. Hartley in the fall of 1778. He says, "We burnt Tioga, Queen Hester's Palace or Town, & all the settlements this side" (Archives, VII. 6). Some of the writers have confused Esther with her sister Catharine, called "Queen Cath-

erine," whose village, called Catharine's Town, or She-o-qua-ga, was situated south of Havana, N. Y. (See *Sheoquaga*). The army of General Sullivan crossed the Chemung to Tioga, at this point on August 10, 1779. The place is noted in nearly all of the Journals of Sullivan's expedition. It is probable that Esther Montour removed up the river to Chemung, previous to the destruction of her village by Col. Hartley in 1778.

Estherton.—Hand (1779), Archives, VII. 344. **Queen Esther's Castle.**—Grant (1779), Jour. Mil. Exped. Gen. Sull., 139. **Queen Easter.**—Roberts (1779), Jour. Mil. Exped. Gen. Sull., 244. **Queen Esther's Palace.**—Hubley (1779), Jour. Mil. Exped. Gen. Sull., 151. **Queen Esther's Flats.**—Barton (1779), Jour. Mil. Exped. Gen. Sull., 5. **Queen Esther's Plantation.**—Norris (1779), Jour. Mil Exped. Gen. Sull., 229. **Queen Esther's Plains.**—Shute (1779), Jour. Mil. Exped. Gen. Sull., 270. **Queenchester.**—Livermore (1779), Jour. Mil. Exped. Gen. Sull., 184. **Queen Hester's Palace or Town.**—Hartley (1778), Archives, VII. 6. **Queen Hester's Plains.**—Grant (1779), Jour. Sull. Exped. ,109.

QUE, ISLE OF. An island in the Susquehanna River opposite Selinsgrove, Snyder County. Was evidently a gathering place for the Indians before the time of the Delaware and Shawnee. It was probably a stopping place for the Iroquois, as they went down the river, and was possibly the site of one of the early villages of the Conestoga, or Susquehannas. Meginness in his "Otzinachson" (99) says that the name is a "misspelling, being in fact Isle a Queue, (Tail Island) a title which was undoubtedly given by the French traders.—It was probably a translation of the Indian name long since forgotten." It is hardly probable that this name is of French origin. There were very few French traders on the Susquehanna River at any period. It is more probably a corruption of Cuwei-menatey, "pine island," or "isle of pines." Penn's Creek, which enters the river opposite the head of the island, was called Kayarondinagh by the Iroquois. (See *Penn's Creek*). This was the point mentioned in the Purchase of 1754 (Col. Rec. VI. 118-121). There was a burial ground at the lower end of this island, from which many relics were taken when the region was first settled. Consult; Meginness, Otzinachson, 99 et seq.

QUEMAHONING. A branch of Stony Creek, in Somerset County; also the name of a village in the same county. The name is a corruption of Cuwei-mahoni, "pine tree lick," with the locative, ing. There may have been an Indian village on this creek, near its mouth. It was on the trail from Bedford to Pittsburgh, known as the Raystown Path. This trail was one of the most used in the state, between the Susquehanna and Ohio. Gist travelled over it in 1750, from Old Town, Md., going by way of the Warriors Path to where it crossed this trail at Bloody Run (Everett, east of Bedford, and then followed it from that point to the Ohio. (Consult; Gist's Journal). It was also the course taken by C. F. Post in 1758, when he made his second trip to the Ohio, in advance of the army of General Forbes, who was then building the road from Raystown (Bedford) to Fort Duquesne (Consult; Post's Journals, Early Western Travels, I.). The trail later became known as the Forbes Road, because of it having been opened in 1758 for the expedition against Fort Duquesne. In the table of distances given by John Harris, in 1754, is given, "to Stoney Creek (from Edmund's Swamp)—6 miles. To Kickeney Paulin's House (Indian)—6 miles" (Archives, II, 135). In the table given by Patten in 1754, is noted, "From Edmund's Swamp to Cowamahony—6 miles. From Cowamahony to Kackanapaulins—5 Miles" (Col. Rec. V. 750). Kickenapaulings (which see) was evidently situated at the mouth of Pickering's Run, on the Quemahoning, near the present Jenner Cross Roads. The old trail crossed Stony Fork of the Quemahoning east of Stoystown. The distances agree with those given by Harris and Patten. After the British occupation of Fort Duquesne this trail became the chief means of communication between the Susquehanna and the Ohio, and was used for many years for carrying supplies to Fort Pitt, and was later used by Col. Bouquet in his expedition for the relief of that place during the Conspiracy of Pontiac (See *Frankstown, Raystown, Shawnee-Cabins*, etc. In 1785, according to a census taken there were living in Quemahoning Township, between the ages of 18 and 63, 93 white males (Archives, X. 512). The region about the Forbes and the Old Glade roads, was settled by GeGrmans, who made the country a garden spot.

Cowamahony.—Patten (1754), Col. Rec. V. 750. **Quemahone.**—Scull, map, 1770.

Quemahoning.—Howell, may, 1792. **Quomahonning.**—Traders map, 1753.

QUENISCHASCHACKI. According to Heckewelder this name was given to the long reach in the West Branch of the Susquehanna, in Lycoming County. "Hence they called the West Branch Quenischachachgek-hanne, which word has been corrupted to Susquehanna" (Indian Names, 264). According to Gerard the name is an attempt to write from memory the word Kwinishukuneihaki, "panther land." The meaning given by Heckewelder is more nearly the correct one. Schachachgachne is the Delaware for "the straight course of a river." The West Branch along the region where the Indian village of this name was situated has a "long reach," or straight course. It is probable that the name is a corruption of Cuwi-achachagachne, meaning "the long reach, with pine trees," or Quin-achas-chack-ki, "long, straight," —reach in the river. It is hardly possible that the name was corrupted to Susquehanna. The Delaware village of this name stood at the site of the present Linden, Lycoming County. It was deserted in 1758 when C. F. Post passed through on his way to Ohio. Ettwein and the Moravian converts passed the site of the village in 1772, when on their way to Ohio. The creek was also known by the same name as the village.

Quenashawakee.—Post (1758), Archives, III. 521. **Queenshohoque.**—Morris, map, 1848. **Queneshahaque.**—Scull, map, 1770. **Queneshohaque.**—Howell, map, 1792. **Quenishachshachki.**—Meginness, in Otzinachson, 431. **Quenishchachaki.**—Ettwein (1772), in Hanna, I. 214. **Quenshehague.**—Hopkins, atlas, 1872; Pa. Geo. Sur., Lycoming County, 35, 1880. **Quinishahaquy.**—Scull, map, 1759.

QUEONEMYSING. A former village of the Unami Clan of the Delaware, situated in the great bend of Brandywine Creek, in the present Birmingham Township, D e l a w a r e County, about three miles south of Chadds Ford and about seven miles north of Wilmington. It was the village of Secetareus and his followers. This land was purchased by William Penn December 19, 1683.

The site was marked by the Pennsylvania Historical Commission and the Delaware County Historical Society, October 4, 1924.

QUESSINAWOMINK. The Indian name of the present Tacony Creek, in Philadelphia. This name was applied to the stream now known as Tacony, for its entire length above and below its junction with the Wingohocking. Peter Cock was granted a tract on this creek (Nov. 24, 1675, a return of survey was made), which he called "Quessmacemink." It is mentioned in Archives, Sec. Sec., XVI. 321. See *Tacony*.

Quessmacemink.—Records of Upland (note), 63. **Quessinawomink.**—Records of Upland (note), 63. **Quessinawominck.**—Grant of land (1675), Archives, XVI (2nd. Ser.) 321. **Quissinomink.**—Holme (1675), Arch. Third Ser., III. 312, 316.

QUILUTAMEND. The name of an Indian village about 7 miles above the Lackawanna River, near Ransom, Lackawanna County. Heckewelder says that the Delawares told him that they had surprised and captured a body of Iroquois at this place in their early wars. He gives the meaning as, "we came unawares upon them." Quilutamen is the Delaware for "to fall upon." The village was deserted in 1760 when John Hays and C. F. Post passed through. Hays speaks of it as an "Old Indian Town called Quelootamaa." The army of General Sullivan encamped here on the night of August 1, 1779. and remained all of the next day, leaving on the morning of the 3rd.

Quailuternunk.— Machin (1779), Jour. Sull. Exped., 194. **Quialutimunck.**—Rogers (1779), Jour. Sull. Exped., 256. **Quialutemac.**—Craft, in Jour. Sull. Exped., 348. **Quilitumack.**—Nukerck (1779), Jour. Sull. Exped., 215. **Quilutimac.**—Shute (1779), Jour. Sull. Exped., 269. **Quilutimack.**—Norris (1779), Jour. Sull. Exped., 221. **Quilutimunk.**—Hubley (1779), Jour. Sull. Exped., 147. **Quialutimunk.**—Hubley (1779), (Jordan ed. 9, 1909). **Willimanck.**—Roberts (1779), Jordan ed. 9, 1909), 241.

QUING QUINGUS. A creek which enters the Delaware from the east in Delaware, now Duck Creek. A corruption of Qui-quin-gus, "large duck," the Delaware name for the large, wild duck, known as mallard. The creek is mentioned in the Deed of 1685, for the lands from "Quing Quingus Called Duck Creek unto upland Called Chester Creek all along the West Side of Delaware River" and as far backwards as a man can ride in two days (Archives, I. 95; Sec. Ser., XVI. 389-90).

QUITAPAHILLA. A branch of Swatara Creek, in Lebanon County. A corruption of Cuwe-pehelle, "pine spring." ·Heckewelder gives the form Cuitpehelle or Cuwitpehelle, "a spring

that flows from the ground among pines." One of the leading Indian trails from the Delaware crossed this stream. It ran through the present Reading to Tulpehocken, and then northward to Shamokin (now Sunbury). This trail was frequently used by Conrad Weiser, Bishop Cammerhoff and others. Shikellamy, Tedyuskung and other chiefs from Shamokin used it in going to the Councils at Philadelphia. It was a much shorter route than that which was the leading trail to the Ohio, through Reading to Harrisburg, where a trail ran northward to Shamokin. Cammerhoff's Journal of 1748 gives a very good description of this trail from the Quitapahilla region to S h a m o k i n (Penna. Mag. of Hist., XXIX, 160-179, 1905). The Quitapahilla was settled by Germans from the Palatinate about 1723-29.

Quattapahilla.—T r i m b l e (1790), Archives, XI. 681. **Quetapahilla.**—Lloyd (1790), Archives, XI. 677. **Quitapahill.**—Morris, map, 1848. **Quitopahella.**—Reynolds (1759), Archives, III. 678. **Quitipihilla.**—Scull, map, 1770; Howell, map, 1792. **Quitopahilla.**—M a t l a c k (1790), Archives, XI. 693. **Quitopehill.**—Loskiel (1794), Miss. Mor. Church, II. 108, 1794. **Quittapahilla.**—Mifflin (1794), Colonial Records, XVI. 275. **Quittopohille.**—Cammerhoff (1748), Mag. Hist. (Penna.), XXIX, 163, 1905. **Quittopohela Spring.**—Parsons (1756), Archives, II. 748.

RACCOON CREEK. A c r e e k which rises in Washington County, entering the Ohio from the south in Beaver County. According to Heckewelder the Delaware name of the stream was Nachenum-hanne, "raccoon-stream." The M e m o r i a l of Charles Sims concerning the land along this creek, and at Montour's Island is found in Archives, XI. 160-162; Col. Rec. XV 242 (See also Archives, Third Ser. III. 402-504). In 1779 Col. Brodhead, in a letter to Washington, mentions the capture of two boys by the Indians on this creek (Archives, XII. 148).

RAY'S TOWN. A prominent place on the Indian trails between the Ohio and the Susquehanna, which was probably named for John Wray, an Indian trader, who lived at this place before 1750. He may have had a cabin, or trading house, at this point in 1732, when he accompanied a party of Shawnee to Philadelphia, where he acted as interpreter, together with Edmund Cartlidge and Peter Chartier, all of whom were trading on the Ohio as early as 1727 (Col. Rec. III. 459). Previous to Wray living at this site he had traded on the Potomac in the region of Old Town, where some of the Shawnee had formerly lived. A trail ran along the foot of Will's Mountain from the mouth of Will's Creek to Raystown (now Bedford). At the foot of Warriors Ridge, east of Bedford, the Warriors Path crossed Bloody Run (at Everett), running southward to Cresap's at Old Town, Md., and northward to Shamokin (now Sunbury), and then up the Susquehanna to Wyoming. The main trail from Harris' Ferry (Harrisburg) to the Ohio, ran down the Cumberland Valley to Shippensburg, then around Parnall's Knob, at Fort Loudon, then up the Valley to Fort Lyttleton, and then almost due west to the present Bedford, and on through Shawnee Cabins, Edmund's Swamp, Ligonier to Shannopin's Town (Pittsburgh). A trail ran northward from Bedford to Frankstown, where it connected with the Venango and Kittanning trails, and also with the trail leading up the Bald Eagle Valley to the Big Island (Lock Haven), Shamokin and Wyoming. A branch of this trail ran down the Frankstown Branch of the Juniata to Standing Stone (Huntingdon), down the Juniata to Shirleysburg, formerly Aughwick, and connected with the trail leading through Croghan's Gap (now Sterritt's Gap) to Harris' Ferry. This trail, via Croghan's Gap, was called the "New Path" (Evans, map, 1749). The "Allegheny Path" went down the Cumberland Valley, from Harris' Ferry, and cut through Roxbury Gap, west of Shippensburg (Now McAllister's Gap, or Roxbury Gap), and another trail went on down the valley and cut through the mountains at Fort Loudon (at Parnall's Knob). These westward trails from the Cumberland Valley were branches of the great road which run from Harris' Ferry to the Potomac, which crossed the various trails east and west, at Carlisle, Shippensburg and Chambersburg. At Chambersburg this trail crossed the trail leading east to Lancaster, and west to the Ohio, via Fort Loudon, Fort Lyttleton, Bedford, Ligonier to Pittsburgh. It is now the course of the State Road from Pittsburgh, which forks at the Public Square in Chambersburg, for Harrisburg, Gettysburg, Baltimore etc. The "New Path" and the "Allegheny Path," before men-

tioned, united at the "Black Log," east of Orbisonia, where it again forked, one branch running to Frankstown, and the other to Raystown. Conrad Weiser went to the Ohio in 1748 by way of the trail leading to the Black Log, via Croghan's (near Carlisle), and then to Frankstown (Col. Rec. IV. 348-358), and from there to the Ohio. John Harris went from his ferry, at Harrisburg, to Logstown in 1753. He gave an account of the course of this trail to the Provincial Council in 1754. His course was from Paxtang (Harris' Ferry), to Croghan's (near Silver's Springs), 5 miles; to the Kittatinny Mountains (through Sterrett's Gap), 9 miles; to George Cowan's House (about 6 miles northwest of the Gap) 6 miles; to Andrew Montour's (between Landisburg and Loysville) 5 miles; to Tuscarora Hill (near Centre P. O.) 9 miles; to Thomas Mitchell's Sleeping Place (in Perry County) 3 miles; to Tuscarora Hill (near Concord P. O.) 14 miles; to Cove Spring (near McNeal P. O.) 10 miles; to the Shadow of Death (Shade Gap) 8 miles; to the Black Log (east of Orbisonia) 3 miles. This is the point where the trail forked for Frankstown and Raystown. The trail to Frankstown ran to Aughwick (Shirleysburg) 6 miles; to Jack Armstrong's Narrows (now Jack's Narrows, above Mount Union) 8 miles; to the Standing Stone (Huntingdon) 10 miles; to the Last Crossing of Juniata (near Alexandria) 8 miles; to Water Street (east of Water Street P. O.) 10 miles; to the Big Lick (near Canoe Creek P. O.) 10 miles; to Frank's (Stephen's) Town (now Frankstown) 5 miles; to Beaver Dams (Beaver Dam branch of Juniata) 10 miles; to Allegheny Hill (at Horseshoe Bend) 4 miles; to Clearfields (near Chest Spring P. O.) 6 miles; to John Hart's Sleeping Place (about 3 miles north of Carrolltown) 12 miles; to the Head of Susquehanna (at Cherry Tree, Indiana County) 12 miles; to the Shawnee Cabins (about a mile from Cookport) 12 miles; to P. Sheaver's Sleeping Place (about half mile from mouth of Ramsey's Run) 12 miles; to the Eighteen Mile Run (near Shelocta) 12 miles; to the Ten Mile lick (near Spring Church P. O., Armstrong County) 6 miles; to Kiskemenettes Town (about a mile below Apollo) 10 miles; to Chartier's Landing (near Tarentum) 8 miles; to Kittanning, up the river, (Kittanning) 18 miles; to

Venango (Franklin) 70 miles; down the river form Chartier's Landing, to Pine Creek (at Etna) 14 miles; to the Logs Town (near Economy) 17 miles. From the Black Log (Orbisonia) the Ray's Town path went to Three Springs (Three Springs, P. O.) 10 miles; to Sideling Hill Gap (near Dublin Mills P. O.) 8 miles; to Juniata Hill (near Well's Tannery P. O.) 8 miles; to Juniata Creek (near Breezewood P. O.) 8 miles to Snake Spring (near Everett) 8 miles; to Ray's Town (Bedford) 4 miles; to S h a w a n a (Shawnee) Cabbins (near Schellsburg) 8 miles; to Allegheny Hill (directly west of Schellsburg) 6 miles; to Edmund's Swamp (near Buckstown) 6 miles; to Stony Creek (Quemahoning, near Stoystown) 6 miles,; to Kickeney Paulin's House (near Jenner X Roads) 6 miles; to the Clear Fields (about 2 miles west of Jennerstown) 7 miles; to Other Side of Laurel Hill (almost due north-west to a point above Ligonier) 5 miles; to Loyol Haning (Ligonier) 6 miles; to the Big Bottom (near Kingston) 8 miles; to the Chestnut Ridge (near Latrobe) 8 miles; to the Parting of the Roads (probably near the Unity Presbyterian Church, or St. Vincent's School) 4 miles (just below St. Vincent's may be the place where these trails forked); to the Big Lick (on one of the branches of the Loyalhanna) 3 miles; to the Beaver Dams (on headwaters of Jack's Run) 6 miles; to James Dunning's Sleeping Place (near Harrison City) 8 miles; to Cock-Eye's Cabin (must have been on Bushy Run near Trafford City. There is a great difference in the various accounts of these distances) 8 miles; to Four Mile Run (Negley's Run) 11 miles; to Shanoppin's Town (at mouth of Two Mile Run, opposite Herr's Island) 4 miles; to Logs Town (above Economy) 16 miles. This trail from Carlisle, by way of Shippensburg, Chambersburg, Fort Loudon, Fort Lyttleton, Bedford, Ligonier and Hannastown (north of Greensburg) was on the course, in the main, of the Forbes Road of 1758, and the route of Col. Henry Bouquet in 1763 (Nearly all of the points mentioned on these trails are noted under the articles in this book). Consult; Col. Rec. V. 750, 759-60; Archives, II. 12, 133-136; Hemminger, Old Roads of Cumberland County, 1909; Hanna, Wilderness Trail, I. 247-289; also any of the papers relating to the Forbes Road, or

Forbes Expedition of 1758. The expedition under General Forbes, 1758, went by way of this route to Fort Dusquene, after much discussion concerning the advantages of the route followed by General Braddock in 1755, from Will's Creek to the Monongahela. The Virginia and Maryland officials favored the Braddock route. Col. George Washington also favored the route with which he was familiar, but the Pennsylvania influence finally overcame all opposition to the more direct route which was chosen. Each route had its advantages. In many respects the Braddock route was better suited for such an expedition as its general topography is better suited for road building, as the U. S. Government decided in the building of the National Pike. The Forbes Road, after the British occupation of the Ohio, became the main highway between the east and the west, and over it went the cattle and the farm products of the Ohio Valley for nearly a century. Various valuable papers dealing with the history of this road are found in the published volumes of the "Kittochtinny Historical Society," of Chambersburg, and also in the published papers of the Hamilton Library Association, of Carlisle (Consult; Kitt. Hist. Soc., I. 12; V. 9, 223; VI. 93, 140; VII. 152; Ham. Lib. Asso., Old Roads of Cumb. County, 1909; Hist. Walnut Bottom Road, J. R. Miller, and other papers of these societies). Fort Bedford was erected on the Raystown Branch of the Juniata, at the site of the present Bedford in 1758. Previous to that time various companies had been sent out from Carlisle to scout the region about Raystown. In April 1757 Governor Denny ordered John Armstrong, to encamp with 300 men near Raystown (For the history of Fort Bedford, Consult; Frontier Forts, I. 476-489; Col. Rec. VII. 504; VIII. 352, 376-77, 754 757; IX. 34, 211, 304, 386; Archives, III. 510, XII. 339-341; Albert, Hist. Westmoreland County, 27-31, 1882; Boucher, Hist. Westm'd. County, I. 13-24, 1906; Loudermilk, Hist. Cumb., Md., 231-252, 1878; Parkman, Montcalm and Wolfe II. 131-163. 1894-98; Post's Jour., Early West Trav., I. 175-291, 1904; Olden Time, 1. 99-125, 1846; and any general accounts of the expedition of 1758). For the accounts of Bouquet's Expedition of 1763, Consult; Parkman, Conspiracy of Pontiac, II. 132-206; III. 72-118, 227-232, 262-

269, 1897-98; Frontier Forts, II. 509-536; Smith, Hist. of Bouquet's Exped., 1868; Olden Time, I. 203-221, 241-261, 1846—some of these references contain the account of the expedition of 1764 also). During the Whiskey Insurrection of 1794 Bedford was the most western point reached by General (President) Washington, with the Federal army. Washington reached Bedford October 19, and remained for a few days and then returned to the Capital (Consult; Archives, Sec. Ser., IV., and the various works dealing with the Whiskey Insurrection, cited under *Redstone*). For general references to Raystown, Consult; Col. Rec. VI. 368, 396, 404, 431-33, 436, 461, 466, 589; VII. 445, 531, 598, 629, 633; VIII. 168, 224, 769; Archives, II. 115, 299, 611; III. 117, 202, 212, 269, 271, 448, 480, 487, 489, 510, 551; IV. 459. Among the early Deeds recorded at Bedford are those made by the Indians to George Croghan, dated Fort Pitt, Nov. 29, 1770, for the lands which the Indians had sold to Croghan in 1749, and a Deed to Garrett Pendergrass, from the Indians for the land where Bedford was situated, made out in 1770. Both of these Deeds are mentioned in various Pennsylvania and Virginia archives. Croghan's grant of land was the cause of considerable litigation. The same Deed was recorded in the Virginia Court of Augusta County, Sept. 23, 1775 (Annals of Carnegie Museum, I. 554). Croghan was anxious to have this Deed recorded in both of the Courts, which might ultimately have jurisdiction (See also, Darlington, Gist's Jour., 190-192). The entire grant came up at the Treaty of Fort Stanwix.

REDSTONE CREEK. A creek which enters the Monongahela from the east below Brownsville, Fayette County. Heckewelder says that the Delaware name for this stream was Machkachsen-hanne, "redstone stream." Machk-e-u, "red"; Ach-sin, "stone;" hanne, "stream." The creek first came to the attention of the civilized world through the organization of the Ohio Company, in 1749, when Col. Thomas Cresap, a member of the Company, was guided from Old Town, Md., where he had a trading house, to the mouth of Dunlap's Creek (formerly Nemacolin's Creek) by Nemacolin, a Delaware, whose father, Checochinican, had formerly lived on the Brandywine (Col. Rec. II. 643; III.

36; Archives, I. 239, 266). Nemacolin had probably removed to the mouth of Dunlap's Creek from the Susquehanna, to which his father had removed about 1718. From this place he had probably gone to the trading house of Col. Cresap at Old Town (which see), over an old trail which had been used by the Shawnee as they retreated from the Ohio region, before the commencement of historic times, when the Shawnee were expelled from the Ohio by the Iroquois. In 1749 Nemacolin guided Cresap to the Monongahela, as the best course for the Ohio Company to follow, in order to reach that river and the Ohio. In 1752 Nemacolin, with Cresap and Gist, blazed the trail from Will's Creek to the mouth of Dunlap's Creek. Redstone Creek enters the Monongahela about a mile below the mouth of Dunlap's Creek, and yet the old earthwork, known as Redstone Old Fort, was at the mouth of Dunlap's Creek. This "fort" was a large earthen mound overlooking the Monongahela River. It was in existence when the first white settlers came into the region. There were several other "forts" of a similar sort along the Monongahela below this one. These are noted on Scull's map of 1770. Many relics have been found at this point. The mounds were probably built by the Shawnee, who were no doubt the builders of many of the Ohio mounds, as they retreated up the Monongahela and Youghiogheny Rivers to their southern habitat of historic times. There is no record of any other tribe having occupied this region. Nemacolin was living at this place in 1750-52, when Christopher Gist passed through the region on his tour of exploration for the Ohio Company (Gist's Jour. 1752, 70). The creek was first known as Nemacolin's Creek, and afterwards as Dunlap's Creek—named for an Indian trader, named William Dunlap. Charles Poke, mentioned by Gist, was one of the traders who went to the Ohio before 1734. He is mentioned in the list of traders (Archives, I. 425). In 1737 he had a trading house on the Potomac, near Hancock, Md., from which place he went by way of Will's Creek (Cumberland) over the trail to Dunlap's Creek. He later removed to Cross Creek, W. Va., and then to Shelby County, Ky., where he was living in 1799 (Jefferson, Notes on Virginia, 368, 1801). Nemacolin, after whom the trail to the Potomac was named, later removed to the Ohio River and then went to Blennerhassett's Island, below Parkersburg. In 1785 General Richard Butler, in his Journal, mentions passing "Nemacolin's Island," which was probably at the island mentioned. In 1754, in order to protect the interests of the Ohio Company, Gov. Dinwiddie, of Virginia, sent Capt. William Trent, with John Fraser as Lieut., and Edward Ward, as Ensign, with about 33 men to the Ohio to build a fort at "the Forks." Trent went over the trail which had been followed by Washington and Gist in 1753, as far as Gist's Plantation, and then followed Nemacolin's Trail to the mouth of Dunlap's Creek, where they built a store-house for the Ohio Company, called the Hangard, and then went on to the "Forks," which they reached on Feb. 17, 1754, and at once commenced the erection of a fort. Soon after the commencement of the work, Trent returned to Virginia, by way of the Hangard; Fraser had gone to his trading house, at Turtle Creek, and Edward Ward, George Croghan, Christopher Gist and others were engaged in getting the fort completed, when the French army, under Captain Contracoeur, descended the Allegheny, on April 17, and demanded the surrender of the "fort." Ward and his party were allowed to return to Will's Creek, which they did by way of Redstone. In Washington's expedition, 1754, he intended to advance to the Hangard, fortify the place, and await for reinforcements. He had advanced beyond Gist's Plantation, when he retreated to the Great Meadows, where he erected Fort Necessity. Here he was obliged to surrender to M. Coulon de Villers, the French commander, on July 4, 1754. The French army had advanced up the Monongahela to the Hangard, which he reached on June 30th. He says in his Journal, "Came to the Hangard, which was a sort of fort built with logs, one upon another, well notched in, about thirty feet in length and twenty in breadth; and as it was late and would not do any thing without consulting the Indians, I encamped about two musket-shots from that place." DeVillers left the Hangard, in charge of a detachment of 20 men, and advanced to Gist's Plantation on July 1st. He sent out scouts, who made their report, and the French commenced to retreat to the Hangard, on July 2nd, when some Indians came from the Hangard with a prisoner, whom they had captured. The account given by this deserter from Washington's army caused the French commander to advance. In the letter of Capt. Robert Stobo (one of the hostages given by Washington to the French commander, after the surrender at Fort Necessity), written at Fort Duquesne, July 29th, he gives a list of the prisoners and deserters at the French fort. Among these he mentions Barnabas Devan, of Vanbram's Company, and says in a note, "This man is the Cause of all our Misfortunes; he deserted the Day before the Battle; the French got to Guest's (Gist's) at Dawn of Day, surrounded the Place imagining that we were still there; gave a general Fire; but when they found We were gone, they were determined to return with all Expedition, thinking We had returned to the Inhabitants, when Up comes Mr. Driscall (does he mean Devan); told them he deserted the Day before and that the Regiment was still at the Meadows in a Starving Condition, which caused his deserting, and hearing they were coming deserted to them; they confined him, told him if true he should be rewarded, if false hanged; this I had from the English Interperter" (Col. Rec. VI. 142). This statement agrees, in the main facts, with that given in DeVillers Journal (De Villers Jour., Olden Time, II. 210-212; also, in part, Archives, Sec. Ser., VI. 168-172). The French army returned to the Hangard on July 6th. DeVillers captured a number of English soldiers who had been with Washington's army (Col. Rec. VI. 142-143). The Hangard was burned and DeVillers returned to Fort Duquesne. After the capture of Fort Duquesne in 1758, General Stanwix commenced the erection of Fort Pitt. In the latter part of 1759 Col. James Burd commenced the erection of a fort at Redstone, by order of Col. Henry Bouquet, then at Carlisle. This fort, called Fort Burd (wrongly Fort Bird), was built during September, 1759, was erected on the site of the "Redstone Old Fort," before mentioned, and was nearly always mentioned by the earlier name of "Redstone Old Fort," in the early writings. Col. Burd, in his Journal, speaks of it as "being on a hill in the fork of the River Monongahela and Nemocollin's Creek," or "Nemoralling's Creek," as it is given in some of his papers (Archives, XII. 346-347; Frontier Forts, II. 382-388). At some time before 1774 Capt. Michael Cresap took up a "Tomahawk Claim" to the land about this fort, and was later given a Virginia title to the land, including the site of the fort. On February 23, 1775, he was granted a license to run a ferry across the river from Redstone fort to the land of Indian Peter, opposite (Minute Book of the Virginia Court for the District of West Augusta, in Annals of Carnegie Museum, I. 525, etc.). The Iroquois made many complaints concerning the settlement of this region before the land had been purchased from them. The Provincial authorities had made many attempts to drive the "squatters" away from Redstone, and other places in the region. In 1769 the Rev. John Steel, of Carlisle, and a number of others were commissioned to go to all of these points and warn the settlers to leave. The Indians had been complaining of these settlers since 1766. The Commission, appointed by Governor John Penn, visited Redstone, Gist's, Turkey Foot and other places and warned the inhabitants to leave (See lists of inhabitants at these places, Col. Rec. IX. 508-509). Very few of these people paid any attention to the warnings, and remained. The moderation shown by Kiasutha, and the other Iroquois chiefs, at this time, stands in striking contrast to that of these same people a few years later. Kiasutha said, in speaking of the attitude of the Indians, "They say they would not choose to incur the ill Will of those People; for if they should now be removed, they will hereafter return to their Settlements when the English have purchased the Country from us, And we shall be very unhappy, if, by our Conduct towards them at this Time, we shall give them Reason to dislike us, and treat us in an unkind Manner, when they again become our Neighbors" (Col. Rec. IX. 542). A few years later these very people, whom the Indians were anxious to conciliate at this time, were over anxious to go on expeditions into the Indian country beyond the Ohio. A great majority of the various expeditions into the Muskingum region were made up in this very region about the Monongahela and Youghiogheny. After the purchase of these lands at the Treaty of Fort Stanwix, in 1768, the region

filled up, chiefly with people who were under the jurisdiction of the Virginia courts. Michael Cresap sold his land to Thomas and Basil Brown, who in 1779 received a Virginia Deed to these lands. This Deed was made out at Redstone Old Fort on Dec. 16, 1779. John McCulloch received a Deed for the lands, including "Fort Bird," Aug. 15, 1784, in pursuance of an order of survey, dated July 3, 1769 (Both of these documents are reproduced in the Appendix I-X, Third Ser., Archives. The latter showing "Fort Bird"). During the troublesome times of the Virginia Boundary Dispute Redstone Old Fort, and the Region about, was under the jurisdiction of the Virginia Courts (Consult; Minutes of the Virginia Courts, Carnegie Annals, I. 525 et seq., III. 6 et seq.; Archives, Third Ser., III. 483-573). During "Dunmore's War," the Revolution, and the Whisky Insurrection, Redstone Old Fort occupied a prominent position in the thrilling events of these periods. During the Whisky Insurrection many of the most important meetings were held at this place. (Consult; Archives, Sec. Ser. IV; Ellis, History of Fayette County, 52-129; Hassler, Old Westmoreland; Brackenridge, Hist. West. Insur., commonly Called the Whis. Insr. of 1794, 1859; Carnahan, Penna. Insur. of 1794, in N. J. Hist. Soc. Pro., 113-152, 1853; Findley, Hist. of the Insur. of 1794, 1796, etc.). Consult; Col. Rec. VI. 29, 137; IX. 321-23, 344, 350, 403, 479, 494, 483, 506, 508-9, 539, 540; Archives, III. 685, 251, 296, 298, 306, 346, 412, 424, 477, 481; VIII. 280; IX. 352; XII. 276-78; Darlington, Gist's Jour., 70, 140.

The land which the Brown's had about Redstone Old Fort was laid out as a town, which was incorporated in 1815 as Brownsville. The National Pike, or Cumberland Road, which was completed in 1820, passed through Brownsville to Washington, Pa. (Consult; Searight, The Old Pike, 1894). Many writers have been misled in their study of the route of Braddock's Road and the Cumberland Pike. While the general direction of these roads was the same, the course which they followed was different. Braddock's Road crosses and runs along the course of the Pike in various places, but the two are by no means identical. The course followed by the army of General Braddock, in 1755, was the same as that followed by

Washington in 1754, as far as Gist's Plantation—beyond which point Washington did not go in 1754. Braddock's Road crosses the National Pike at Braddock's Memorial Park, and then strikes northward along the mountains to the present Mount Braddock, where Gist's Plantation was situated. Uniontown is left to the south, and Brownsville is about 15 miles to the northwest. Washington's Road ran from the mouth of Will's Creek to Gist's Plantation. Braddock's Road ran from this point to Braddock, on the Monongahela. Burd's Road ran from Gist's Plantation to Redstone Old Fort. Dunlap's Old Road ran from the Great Rock (Rock Fort, or Half-King's Rock), in the mountains, where it left the course of Washington's Road, to the mouth of Dunlap's Creek. This was probably the original Nemacolin's Trail. It descended the Laurel Mountain to Lick Hollow, and then almost directly to the mouth of Dunlap's Creek. The Catawba Trail crossed the Burd Road at Gist's Plantation. From this point, northward, Braddock's Road followed the course of the Catawba Trail, through Connellsville and Mount Pleasant, to the point near Turtle Creek, where Braddock left the Indian trail, in order to avoid the narrow defile in the Turtle Creek Valley. It is, however, certain that the Catawba Trail was left after Braddock had reached the crossing of Sewickley Creek, near Hunker's Station. The Catawba trail went northward to the Allegheny River, which it probably reached at Kittanning. This trail was not, as has been stated, the Warriors Path southward. The Warriors Path ran along the eastern slope of Warriors Mountain, crossing the Potomac at Old Town, where Col. Thomas Cresap had a trading house. The trail across Westmoreland and Fayette Counties was a branch trail, used by the Seneca in going southward to the Catawba and Cherokee country, on war expeditions. This was a distinctively war trail, and was never used as a trader's path (See *Catawba, Cherokee, Old Town, Warriors Path*, etc.). The course of the Braddock Road, as shown on the Historical Map of Penna. (1875) is incorrect. It did not touch Uniontown, as it is marked. It ran along the ridge of the Laurel Mountain to the place marked Gist's, from which it went north to "Stewart's Crossings" (now Connellsville).

Braddock's Road, from near Dunbar's Camp (Jumonville School), to Gist's ran along the boundary of the present Wharton and Dunbar, and North Union Townships. From this place (Gist's) Burd's Road ran along the boundary lines of Dunbar and Franklin, and North Union, to the crossing of Redstone Creek, at Vance's Mill. Dunlap's Road was the boundary line between the Virginia counties of Yohogania and Monongalia (Consult; Archives, Third Ser. III., map op. p. 482; also various returns of Road Viewers, in Court Records at Uniontown; also various Road surveys in Minutes of the Virginia Courts for the District of West Augusta, Annals of Carnegie Museum, I. 525 et seq., III. 6 et seq.). The first map to note Redstone Creek was that of Lewis Evans, 1755. On Scull's map (1770) it is marked Red Stone Creek. Dunlap's Creek is also noted on the Scull map. Namacolin's Creek is called "Nemoralling's Creek" by Burd in 1759 (Archives, XII. 347—where the name is also "Nemocalling's Creek"). Gist gives the name as Nemicotton, in 1751 (Darlington, Gist, 70).

SAGAMORE. A village in Armstrong County. Derived from the Abnaki Sang-man, "a ruler;" the same as the Delaware Sakima, "a chief, or ruler."

SAGINAW. A village in York County, named for the town of Saginaw, Michigan, where a former Indian village, of the same name, was situated. A corruption of Saginawa," "mouth of a river." The same as the Delaware Sakuwit, or Sakwihillak, which has been corrupted to Sacunk, Sohkon, etc. See *Sawcunk.*

SAKHAUWOTUNG. A former Indian village on the west bank of the Delaware, near Allen's Ferry, Northampton County, about 7 miles below the Gap. Visited by Count Zinzendorf in 1742. Brainerd, the Presbyterian missionary, built a cabin here in 1744, and preached to the Delawares about the region from 1744 to 1746. He visited Shamokin each year during his stay at this place. Consult; Reichel, Memorials of the Moravian Church, 27, 67.

SALT LICK. Heckeweider speaks of Salt Lick Creek," a branch of the Youghiogheny in Fayette County." This is the creek now known as Jacob's Creek, which is noted on

Scull's map of 1770 as "Salt Lick Cr. or Jacob's Cr." (See *Jacobs Creek*.) The Indian name was Sikhewi-mahoni, "salt lick." Sikei-hanne, "a stream from a salt-lick." One of the camping places of Braddock's army in 1755 was called "Salt Lick Camp," which was reached on July 3, after the swamp had been repaired. It was six miles from Jacob's Cabin, which was about 12 miles from the "Stewart's Crossings," which would put Jacob's Cabin in the region of Bridgeport. The note in Orme's Journal, therefore, must be made to refer to the previous camp at the crossing of the Youghiogheny, near Connellsville. Jacob's Cabin would be 6 miles from this camp, or about 7 miles from the river, which would place it near Iron Bridge, or Prittstown. The march on July 3 was about 6 miles to Salt Lick Creek, which was reached just below Mount Pleasant. Here Braddock held a Council of War. Braddock was in doubt as to the advisability of waiting here for Col. Dunbar's detachment, or to advance. It was decided by the Council to advance (Sargant's, Braddock's Expedition, Orme's Jour., 346-349). Scull's map, 1770, Salt Lick Cr. or Jacob's Cr.

SALT LICK TOWN. This town is mentioned in a number of places in the various early records and narratives. There were other places known as Salt Lick, or Salt Lick Town. The village on the West Branch of the Beaver, or the present Mahoning (which received its name from these licks) was situated about one mile northwest of Niles, Ohio. It is noted on Evans' map of 1755, and is mentioned in McCullough's Narrative (Border Life, 96, 1839) as "Kseek-heoong, or Salt Lick." The Indian name was Sikheunk, "at the salt spring." The place is also mentioned in Hutchin's MS. in the Historical Society of Penna. as "Salt Lick Town," and is noted on Hutchin's map of 1764 as "Salt Lick T." At the Council at Philadelphia, 1760, Tedyuskung said that he had gone as far as the Salt Lick Town "towards the head of Beaver Creek" (Col. Rec. VIII. 497). On Crevcoeur's map of 1878 it is noted as "V. de la Saline." When McCullough was taken, as a captive, to this place, in about 1758, he says that it was a new town, which is hardly possible. The place had evidently been known to the Indians for

many years previous to this time as a place to which they went to make salt. There were a number of salt springs in this region. The "Salt Spring" is noted on Morris' map of 1848. Mahoning, another town on the river, was situated near Youngstown, or Struthers, Ohio. The river takes its name from these Mahoni, "licks." A salt lick, as before mentioned, was called Sikhewi-mahoni. A town at a salt lick would be Sikei-mahoning. Gen. Wm. Irvine says that "from the mouth of Shenango to Cuskuskey (Kuskuski), on the West Branch, is six or seven miles, but it was formerly all called Cuskuskey by the natives along this branch as high as the Salt Spring, which is twenty-five miles from the mouth of Shenango" (Archives, XI. 519). The trail to Shenango, Indian village, crossed the Mahoning River at Salt Lick Town, and struck the Shenango River near the present Sharon, near which the Indian village of Shenango must have been situated—according to Hutchin's description Shenango was 9 miles below Pymatuning, which must have been near Big Bend. If Pymatuning Indian town was at the mouth of Pymatuning Creek, Shenango would be in the region of South Sharon. The early maps, and tables of distances do not agree concerning the situation of the Indian villages on the Shenango River, probably because it was not much traveled by white traders. See *Kuskuski, Mahoning, Shenango.*

SANDY LICK CREEK. A creek which enters the Allegheny River south of Franklin, Venango County. Now Sandy Creek. Was formerly called Lycomick Creek. In 1785 Gen. Irvine mentions it as "Sandy Creek, by Hutchins and Scull called Lycomie" (Archives, XI. 515). Lycomick is a corruption of Legauwi-mahoni, "sandy lick." See *Lycomick, Lycoming.*

SANKINACK. The name of a small creek, or run, which enters the Lehigh below Weissport, Carbon County. Mentioned in a letter to Count Zinzendorf in 1747 as "two miles below Gnadenhuetten" (Heck. Ind. Names, 264). A corruption of Sankhanne, "flint stream." Reichel identifies it with Tar Run.

SALUNGA. A village in Lancaster County. The name is a contraction of Chiquesalunga, which see.

SAUCON. The name of a creek

which enters the Lehigh from the south in Northampton County; also the name of two Townships (Upper and Lower Saucon), and a village in the same county; also, as Saucony, a town in Berks County; also a village in Lehigh, as Saucona. The name is a corruption of Sakunk, "the mouth of a stream." There were several Sakunks in the State, the most famous of which was perhaps that at the mouth of Beaver River (See *Sawkunk*). The creek by this name was early occupied by Germans, who bought the land from a group of Philadelphia speculators. The Saucon Valley was rich and fertile. It soon became filled with thrifty German farmers. As early as 1743 the Moravians settled in the valley. The present, South Bethlehem occupies the Moravian farm, the Union Station standing on the site of the old Crown Tavern. In 1724 a grant of 1200 acres of land was made to Peter Wents and Lawrence Sweitzer at "Sawcany" (Archives, Sec. Ser., XIX. 725). In 1752 a petition was made for a road to connect the Saucon settlements with the region along the Delaware, near Durham (Col. Rec. V. 576-577). See *Bethlehem*, *Gnadenhuetten*, etc.

Saucon.—Evans map, 1749; Scull map, 1759, etc.,
Sawcany.—Board of Prop. (1724), Archives, Sec. Ser., XIX. 725. **Sawcunk, Sacunk,** etc.. See **Shingas' Town. Scahantowano.**—See **Wyoming.**

SCHUYLKILL. The origin of this name has been variously given. In 1684 Gerrit VanSweeringen's Account of the Settling of the Delaware by the Dutch and Swedes, he says, "The Sweeds ship sailed up as high as Tenacum hideing themselves in a creeke, therefore is called to this day the Schuylkill, in English Hideing Creeke" (Archives, Sec. Ser., V. 779). Watson gives the meaning as "Hidden River," because its mouth was not seen, as it was passed on the Delaware (Watson, Annals, II. 475). Capt. Cornelius Hendricksen, the Dutch Skipper probably was the first European to sail up the Delaware to the mouth of the Schuylkill. Hendricksen appeared before the Dutch Assembly on August 18, 1616, and gave an account of his discoveries between New France and Virginia, or between 40 and 45 degrees Latitude. He made this trip of exploration in a vessel called the "Onrust" (or Restless). Between 38 and 40 degrees of Latitude

he had discovered a bay and three r:vers (Archives, Sec. Ser., V. 10-12). In 1623 the Dutch, under Capt. Cornelius Mey, landed on the South River (the Delaware) and landed near the present Gloucester, where Fort Nassau was erected. In 1638 the Swedes purchased the lands along the western shore from the Indians to the falls, near Trenton. Peter Minuit, who had been with the Dutch West India Company for 9 years, and who had changed his service to Sweden, landed on the Delaware in April 1638, and at once commenced the erection of a fort at the mouth of Minquas Creek, which he name Christina River, in honor of the young Queen of Sweden. The fort was also named in her honor. This little colony of 50 persons would have perished, had not the arrival of a new colony, with abundant supplies, in the spring of 1640 reached the settlement. In 1642 a still larger colony arrived, under Lieut. John Printz. Printz was commissioned as Governor of New Sweden, and at once established his seat of Government at Tinicum, where he built a house and a fort, called Gottenburg. He also built a fort about 4 miles below Salem Creek, which was called Elsinburg. The various conflicts between the Dutch and Swedish powers for the possession of the rich trade of the Minquas (Conestogas) makes up much of the history of the various conflicts on the Delaware at this period. Everything in the way of the trade with the Susquehanna Indians was in the hands of the Swedes, who occupied the western shore of the river, and all of the creeks leading to the Minquas country. The Report of Andreas Hudde, the Dutch Commissary on the Delaware, shows how successful the Swedes had been in getting possession of this rich trade, which was the one thing for which both Dutch and Swede were struggling (See *Chester Creek*, *Minquas Creek*, *Tinicum*, *Delaware*, etc.); Consult, Archives, Sec. Ser., V; VII. 459-820; Records of Upland Court, and also the various histories of the Dutch and Swedish Settlements on the Delaware. The name Schuylkill has been recorded under many forms. These are of little value, as they are simply attempts to spell the Dutch, or Swedish name. Some of these forms are;

Schole Kill.—Lovelace (1669), Archives, I. 29. **Schulkil.**—Holme, map, 1681-4. **Scoolkill.**—Pa. Coun. (1685), Col. Rec.

I. 126. **Schuyl Kill.**—Van der Donck, map, 1656. **Sculkill.**—Pa. Coun. (1693), Col. Rec. I. 373. **Skolkill.**—Deed of 1683, Archives, I. 65. **Skoolkill.**—Pa. Coun. (1690), Col. Rec. I. 334.

The present form of the name was used by Hudde and others of the early officials on the Delaware (Archives, Sec. Ser., VII. 462 etc.). The Indian name of the river, which is mentioned in the Deed to William Penn in 1683, was Manaiunk, which has been corrupted to Manayunk (Archives, I. 65). See *Manayunk*.

SCIOTA. A village in Monroe County. Taken from the name of the river in Ohio, the name of which is probably a corruption of Ough-scan-oto, "deer." Ouasiota (the name for the Cumberland Mountains), Sonnioto (the Shawnee village at the mouth of the Sciota), Sinhioto (Bonnecamp, 1749), Souyoto (Vaudreuil, 1760), and other corruptions, or variations of the name occur in the early records. The name has no historic significance in this state.

SECANE. A village in Delaware County. Derived from the name of the Delaware chief who deeded the lands between the Schuylkill and Chester Rivers to William Penn, in 1683 (Archives, I. 65).

SEEKAUGHKUNT. An Indian village, mentioned by Charles Thompson and C. F. Post, in the report of their mission to Wyoming in 1758, upon which they were stopped at the Nescopeck Hills. They were told "That Backsinosa (Paxinosa) was at Seekaughkunt, but that he was preparing to go somewhere" (Archives, III. 413). The place is mentioned again in the same report, "that Backsinosa, with about 100 men, lives yet at Leekaughhunt (422)." At this time Paxinosa was living at the mouth of the Lackawanna, according to many authorities. In the same year (1758) Lawrence Burck wrote to Secy. Peters, concerning the removal of Thomas Hays and his wife, to "Seconghcan," also written "Seconchan" (478). At the Council at Easton, in 1758, Tedyuskung said that he had sent the Belts to Diahogo (Tioga), Assintzin (Painted Post), and thence to Secaughkung. He also said that "Lapackpeton" (See *Lepos Peter's Town*) was then living at this place, and said that the Delawares, Unamies, Mohickons and Wappings, were settled "as far as Secaughkung" (Col. Rec. VIII. 200-201). Before Post went to this Treaty Tedyuskung had been at a place called Passigachkunk (which see), to which place he had evidently been accustomed to go. At the Council at Philadelphia in 1762, one of the Cayuga chiefs said that after the Council at Onondaga was over, that the Senecas sent 5 of their Indians to the Cayuga Town, where they were informed that some of them would "come down the Cayuga Branch by Secaughcunk, and that they would bring the prisoners from Allegheny, as well as from other parts" (Col. Rec. VIII. 699). Several of the prisoners which were returned at this time were from Passigachkunk. On April 26, 1758, Tedyuskung went to Philadelphia with a Messenger, named Daniel, "of the Wanami Nation" (Unami), who had been sent "from the Council of the Indians at Seekaughkoonta" (Col. Rec. VIII. 86-87). Tedyuskung's son, John Jacob, was with him at this time. In that year John Jacob was living at Passigachkunk. In Hay's Journal of 1760 he speaks of being at Passigachkunk, one part of which was settled by "Wonamies" (VIII. 469). Leonard Wesser, who was captured by a party of Indians led by Tedyuskung, was taken to "Passeca, an Indian Town, up the Cayuga Branch," in 1755. At that time Amos and Jacob, the sons of Tedyuskung, were there, as was also Daniel, the Messenger before mentioned (Archives, III. 46). Henry Hess, who was captured by Tedyuskung on New Year's Day, 1756, was taken to Tioga, and then "up the Cayuga Branch, near its head" to a place called "Little Shingle." There were then other prisoners at the village (Archives, III. 56). At a conference in Philadelphia in 1762, with three Delawares from "Secaughcung," the murder of Doctor John, an Indian who had been killed near Carlisle in 1760, the Indians speak of passing "Wighhalousing" (Wyalusing) on their way down (Col. Rec. VIII. 709-712). All of these facts prove that this village of Seekaughkung and Passigachkunk were one and the same place. It was situated on the Cowanesque, near Academy Corners, Tioga County, on the trail which Zeisberger followed to the Allegheny in 1767. This may have been the route taken by Paxinosa as he, and his tribe of Shawnee removed to the Ohio, after leaving Wyoming. He wished to get back to the region in which he had been born (See *Paxinous*). On account of the distance of this village from the English settlements, and because of the difficulty in reaching it, it no doubt was a point to which many of the white captives were taken. Many Indian relics have been found along the Cowanesque at this point (See *Cowanesque*, *Passigachkunk*).

Leekaughhunt.—Thompson (1758), Archives, III. 421. **Secaughoung.**—Pa. Coun. (1762), Col. Rec., VIII. 709. **Secaughcunk.**—Pa. Coun. (1762), Col. Rec., VIII. 699. **Secanghkung.**—Pa. Coun. (1758), Col. Rec., VIII. 200. **Seconchan.**—Burck (1758), Archives, III. 478. **Seconghcan.** Burck (1758), Archives, III. 478. **Seekauphkoonts.**—Pa. Coun. (1758), Col. Rec., VIII. 86. **Seekauphkunt.**—Thompson (1758), Archives, III. 413.

SENANGELSTOWN. A village mentioned by James LeTort in 1731, as containing 16 families, 50 men, Delawares. The chief is called Senangel (Archives, I. 301). This was probably the village known as Shannopin's Town, although the distance given from Kittanning is but 16 miles. The figures, in the list, may have been wrongly placed. The "50" probably belongs to the distance to Senangelstown. See *Shannopin's Town*.

SENECA. The name of a village in Venango County, also used in various combinations with hill, place, etc. Named after the Iroquoian tribe, which occupied a very prominent place in the various Indian wars in this State. The Iroquoian ethnic name of Oneida, or Oneniute-a-ka, "people of the standing stone," was corrupted by the translation of the sounds from the Dutch, and then the English, until the name Seneca was finally produced. The name Sinnecus, or Sinnekus, as used by the early Dutch and Swedish settlers on the Delaware, was applied to the Iroquois, rather than to the particular tribe now known by the name Seneca, although it is probable that the first Iroquois to reach the settlements on the lower Delaware were members of the Seneca tribe, who went down the Susquehanna, and then by way of Minquas Creek, reached the settlements along the Delaware River. The derivation of the name Seneca from the Mohegan was from a'sinni, "a stone," ika, "place of," with the Dutch genitive plural ending, ens. The Delaware name of W'tassone, in which assone is simply another form of a'sinni. The French called the Seneca, Sonontouans, which

is a corruption of the Iroquois name for the Seneca, Djiionondowanen-aka, "People of the Great Mountain," of which the Delaware form was Mechachtin-ni, "great mountain." The French form is often used in the early records of Pennsylvania as Tsanondowaroonas. The land about Wyoming is often referred to as Tsanandowa (Col. Rec. III. 150, 273). According to all of the early records the name "Great Mountain," or "Endless Mountain" (Mechach-tin-ni," or Kitta-tin-ni) referred to the range of mountains which cross the Susquehanna, near the mouth of the Juniata. May it not be possible that the Seneca once occupied the region of the Juniata, Standing Stone, and later the Wyoming region, previous to their being driven out of this region by the Andastes (Conestoga)? The name Juniata, Standing Stone, and others in the region are similar in origin to that of the Seneca (to the Oneida also, but the direct connection by trails, and rivers, of the Juniata region, and the region of the "Great Mountain" was with the Seneca country of Sonontouan, in New York, by way of the West Branch, as well as by the present Chemung). The oldest trail of the Iroquois, southward, led from the Seneca country, down the West Branch to Shamokin, or down the Chemung to Wyoming and Shamokin, and then along the Warriors Path from Shamokin, to Standing Stone (now Huntingdon), and then southward along Warriors Ridge, crossing the Potomac at Old Town, Maryland. This trail had been used by the Seneca long before the westward migration of the Delaware and Shawnee. It was an Iroquois trail, but it was also a distinctively Seneca trail. The indications seem to point to the Seneca having entered their historic habitat in New York from the south, by way of the Susquehanna, both branches. At the time of the separation of the Delawares and the Iroquois, when they first migrated eastward, according to tradition (See *Allegheny*), the separation probably took place on the upper Ohio. The Delawares crossed the mountains, settling along the Delaware River, and the Iroquois went northward by way of the various rivers to their historic habitat in New York. The Seneca, who occupied the extreme western end of the Iroquois country, probably reached it by way of the Conemaugh, Juniata, Susquehanna, West Branch and Chemung. An earlier northward movement may have gone by way of the Allegheny and Genesee. The Seneca who occupied the Juniata and the West Branch Valley followed later, going over the divide to the Genesee, or going up the Susquehanna, by way of Shamokin and Wyoming to the Chemung, and then up that river to the historic Sonontouan, between the Genesee River and Seneca Lake. All of the wars, the trails and the movements of the Iroquois, in historic times, seem to point to a northward movement of the Iroquois to their historic habitat. This northward migration took place before the formation of the Iroquois Confederation, and before the wars of that Confederation with the kindred tribes, the Andastes, Erie, Wenro, Neuter and other tribes which the Confederation overthrew. These tribes remained behind, as the Seneca and other tribes of the Five Nations moved north. The Tuscarora went south, the Andastes remained on the lower Susquehanna, the Erie occupied the region from the Ohio to Lake Erie, the Wenro and Neuter to the east of the Erie, and the Seneca occupying the Conemaugh and Juniata, and then the West Branch and the Wyoming Valley, and finally joining their fellow tribesmen in western New York. The Seneca probably were driven from the Juniata, and then from Wyoming and the West Branch, by the Andastes, who had become their rivals for the possession of the hunting grounds along the Juniata. At the commencement of the historic period the Andastes had driven the Seneca beyond the Pennsylvania limits to their historic habitat in the Sonontouan, of the early French writers. The northern limit of the Andastes country was then at Carantouan, just at the boundary between New York and Pennsylvania, on the Susquehanna. When written history commenced the Seneca were occupying the Sonontouan, of the early maps, between the Genesee and Seneca Lake, having reached this region from the south. All of the prominent rivers to the south of this region had Iroquois names, at the very commencement of the relations of the English with them, and long before the Iroquois had any historic villages to the south of their New York habitat. Otzinachson, Juniata, Ohio, Cohongarunta and many other Iroquois names were common names of the streams south of the Seneca country, long before the Iroquois had occupied these streams, within historic times. The great range of the Kittatinny Mountains was called by the Iroquois name of Tyannuntasacta, or Endless Hills (See *Kittatinny*). These trails of Iroquois names to the south of the historic Seneca habitat mean much. The later Delaware names were simply translations of the earlier Seneca names. Kittatinny, or Mechachtinni, were translations of the Iroquois name for the mountains, which was also used as one of the names of the Seneca themselves by the Delawares. The French name for the Seneca country, Sonontouan, or as it was also written, Tsantouan, was, as has been noted, the corruption of Djiionon-do-wanen," people of the great mountain." This name was corrupted by the English, and also by the French, to Tsandowanes. Tsandowana was one of the earliest names of the place known as Wyoming (which see), and Tsandowannes was a name used of the inhabitants of Wyoming (Col. Rec. III. 273, 425, 435). The name Tsanandowans was frequently used of the Seneca, and Tsanandowa of Wyoming (Col. Rec. III. 449, 512, 513, 578). The Tsandowana was corrupted to Schahandowana, and this was translated into the Delaware M'cheuwomink, "upon the great plains," which has been corrupted to Wyoming. May it not be possible that Sonontouan, Tsantouan, Tsanandowan, and the other variants of the Seneca name of the region in New York, and Tsandowan, Tsandowana, Schahandowana, Shenandoah—all of which have the same significance as the Delaware M'cheuwomink—are simply synonyms and corruptions of the Iroquois name for the Senecas, Djiionon-do-wanen? The Sonontouan of the historic period included the present counties of Ontario, Monroe and Livingstone, New York. The Seneca villages of this period, 1657-1687, were Gandougarae (south of Victor), Totiakto (near Honeoye Falls, at Rochester Junction), Gandagora (near Victor), and a number of smaller villages in the region about each of these larger villages. Each of these village sites has been examined by the Buffalo Academy of Natural Sciences (Consult; The Seneca Nation from 1657 to 1687. Vol. X. No. 2, 1912, Bull. B. S. of Nat. Sci.). The Jesuits commenced work among the Senecas in these villages in 1657. The mission of La Conception was at Totiakto; St. Jacques, at Gandagora, and St. Michael at Gandougarae (Jesuit Rel. LVII. 191; LIX. 77; LX. 175). These missions had as their ultimate purpose the winning of the Senecas to the French influence. In this they were not successful. The Seneca tribe was the great barrier in the way of the French dominion of Canada and the Ohio Valley. The destruction of the Huron tribes in 1649; the overthrow of the Tionotati at about the same time; the destruction of the Neuter Nation in 1651; the complete overthrow of the Erie in 1656; the almost complete destruction of the Andastes in 1675, and the conquests of the Illinois and Miami in 1686 made the Senecas absolute masters of the region southward to the Potomac and westward to the Mississippi. They controlled the Ohio and Susquehanna Rivers from their head springs to their mouths. In 1684 the Senecas were bringing furs and peltries from the Illinois country, by way of the Ohio River, to trade at Albany for the merchandise of the Dutch and English. The entire length of the Ohio River was at this time absolutely under the dominion of the Seneca. On Herrmans map of Virginia (1670) the Ohio River is called the "Black Minquaas River." Much has been written concerning these Black Minquas, who have not been identified. By 1679 the Senecas were in complete control of the Ohio from its source to its mouth. The Erie and Neuter had been overthrown, and the conquests of the Seneca reached to the Mississippi. If any other Iroquoian tribe, worthy of having the great Ohion named for it, was then living on the upper river that tribe has not left a trace behind it. The river ran into the Seneca country, from which every foe had been driven. May it not be possible that the name Black Minqua was simply a name for the Seneca, who in 1670 used the Ohio as a war-path from the Genesee region, reaching it by the portage from Canadea to about the present Olean, or by the trail from Lake Erie down the Conewango? No other Iroquoian tribe dominated the Ohio River in 1670, and this is the only Iroquoian tribe mentioned in the French documents of the period as being a barrier in the way of the French plans for the possession of the Ohio and Mississippi

trade. All of the efforts of the French to occupy the region south of Lake Erie and westward to the Mississippi were thwarted by the possession of this region by the Seneca. (Consult; Archives, Sec. Ser., VI. 3-45).

From the very commencement of their relation with the French, the Seneca were hostile. They objected to the attempts of La Salle to build the fort at Niagra, in 1679, and were hostile to the work of building the Griffon above the falls. The Seneca stood in the way of all of the French plans for the conquest of the Ohio. All of the French documents of this period dealing with the question of the extension of the French trade westward and southward, mention the necessity of getting rid of the Senecas. Denonville, in his Memoir on the state of Canada, 1685, says, "The Senecas being the strongest are the most indolent. Their subjugation need never be expected except we be in a position to surprise them. This cannot be effected without approaching nearer to them; occupying some post into which supplies may be thrown for troops that will go in quest of those savages" (Arch. Sec. Ser., VI. 27). The French did not wish to make a war upon the Iroquois, because Gov. Dougan of New York, claimed that the Iroquois were subjects of the King of Great Britain, and a war upon the Five Nations, chiefly the Seneca, would bring on a war with Great Britain, which it ultimately did. De la Barre, the Governor of Canada, made an attempt to subjugate the Senecas in 1683, because of the invasion of the country of the Illinois, Ottawas and Hurons by these warlike Iroquois, but his plans utterly failed, and the Senecas became more hostile and carried on still greater wars against the Indian allies of France. In 1686 the Senecas returned from the Miami country with 500 captives (N. Y. Doc. Col. Hist., III. 489). In 1687, Denonville who had succeeded De la Barre, as Governor of Canada, had the King of France approve his plan for the humiliation of the Senecas. His force of 140 Mohawks and 2000 French soldiers, was joined at Irondequoit by about 1000 western Indians, under Tonty and others. He left 440 men at this place under D'Orvillers, and marched towards Gandagora. On Aug. 13, the army reached the pass where the Senecas were in ambush. These were driven back, and the army marched on to Gandagora, which was burned on the 14th. Denonville remained in the Seneca country for ten days, destroying the villages and the great stores of corn—estimated at 1,-200,000 bushels and took possession of the region in the name of the King of France, by planting his Majesty's Arms, and proclaiming "in a loud voice, Vive le Roi" (Doc. Coll. Hist. N. Y. IX. 334). After the destruction of their villages, the Senecas, who had fled before the French army, never rebuilt on the same sites, but returned to the region along the Genesee and near the sites, of Totiackto, Gandagora and their former villages, where they built the villages which were destroyed by the army of General Sullivan in 1779. After this period the Seneca power began to decline, but they still remained the most warlike and aggressive of the Iroquoian tribes. In 1694 the Seneca and Onondaga sent belts to the Delawares, "who say that you Delaware Indians do nothing but stay at home and boil your pots, you are like women, while we Onondagas and Senecas go abroad and fight against the enemies." The Delawares present at this conference with Gov. Markham, were Hithquoquean, Tammany, and others. The former said, "The Senecas would have us Delaware Indians to be partners with them to fight against the French, but we have always been a peaceable people, and resolving to live so, and being weak and very few in number, cannot assist them, and having resolved among ourselves not to go, do intend to send back this, their belt of wampum" (Col. Rec. III. 447). It was probably because of this refusal of the Delawares to help them in their wars, that the Iroquois called them "women," and which had led to the subjugation of the Delawares, with the Andastes, in 1677, at Shackamaxon, when the official subjugation of the Delaware and Andaste took place (Records of Upland, 49). In M. Du Chesnau's Memoir on the Western Indians, 1681, he speaks of the war which the Iroquois waged against the Illinois "for these three years past," and then says, "The Iroquois having got quit of the Illinois, took no more trouble with them, and went to war against another nation called Andostagues, who were very numerous, and whom they entirely destroyed" (Arch. Sec. Ser., VI. 8-9).

This war with the Andastes (Conestoga) was brought to a close in 1675, when the Andastes were completely overcome at their fort on the lower Susquehanna (See *Conestoga, Octoraro, Susquehanna*). After the termination of this war, which was done at a Treaty at Shackamaxon in 1677, the Iroquois laid claim to all of the lands which had been previously occupied by both the Delaware and the Susquehanna Indians, including all of the lands along the Susquehanna River. In the sale of these Susquehanna lands to Governor Dongan the Cayuga and Onondaga stated that these lands belonged to them exclusively, and that "the other three Nations vizt. the Sinnekes, Oneydes and Maquaas have nothing to do with it" (Dutch Record C. No. 3, in Papers Relating to the Susquehanna River). The sale of these lands, or rather the conveying of the trust of them, to Governor Dongan, in 1679, was reaffirmed in 1683, at a Council with the Cayuga, Onondaga, Oneida and Mohawk, at Albany, Sept. 26, 1683. In 1720 the Cayuga made the claim that the Susquehanna lands belonged to them alone (Col. Rec. III. 101). At the Council at Albany, 1754, the statement was made by Conrad Weiser, who had held a number of conferences with the Indians, that "the Lands now under Consideration did really belong to the Cayugas and Oneidas in Right of the Conquest of the Sasquehannah Indians" (Col. Rec. VI. 117). After the Deed was made out for these lands, it was stated that the Province had paid for these lands three times; first to Gov. Dongan, then to the Conestoga, and finally to the Six Nations, in 1754 (Col. Rec. VI. 124). All of the Six Nations entered into the Deed for this last purchase. At several later Treaties in Pennsylvania the Iroquois confessed that the land sales of the Conestoga, before their defeat by the Iroquois, had a right to sell the Susquehanna and Potomac lands, but after that time the Iroquois alone had a right to dispose of these lands.

It is evident from all statements made at the early Councils concerning the Susquehanna lands that the Cayuga and Onondaga, or the Cayuga and Oneida, were the tribes which had defeated the Conestoga (Andaste, or Susquehanna) Indians, and in none of the references are the Seneca mentioned as having had anything to do with the conquest of the Conestoga.

This seems to be a strange fact, as the Seneca country was the most directly on the path to both the West Branch and the Chemung. Neither the Seneca or the Mohawk, the guardians of the "Doorway" of the Iroquois "Long House" were instrumental in defeating the Susquehanna Indians, whose river ran directly to the Seneca country. After the various land sales had driven the Delaware and Shawnee to the upper Susquehanna, and later to the Ohio, the Munsee, Shawnee and Seneca became associated in the various villages which were established. The Munsee and the Seneca, while of different linguistic families, seemed to have a natural affinity for each other. During the period of hostility, between 1755 and 1790, these two tribes were the most persistent enemies of the white settlers. After the French occupation of the Ohio many of the Seneca came under French influence and joined the western Indians in their raids upon the settlements in Pennsylvania. While the majority of the Delaware tribe which had made the treaties with William Penn (the Unami) remained friendly during the early period of hostility, and sought to win the Shawnee and Munsee back to friendship, the majority of these tribes, together with the majority of the Seneca, were hostile to the English. The villages on the West Branch, on the upper Allegheny, on the Ohio and Beaver Rivers were filled with hostile Munsee, Shawnee and Mingo, among whom were many Seneca of mixed blood. The Seneca, as a tribe, was seeking to restrain the hostile Delaware (chiefly Munsee) and Shawnee, by order of the Council at Onondaga, but the great majority of the Indians who committed the various raids into the settlements during 1756-1790 were of these tribes. While the Delaware were under Iroquois control they were directly under the control of the Seneca (Col. Rec. VII. 623). For some reason the Seneca themselves were under the influence of the Minisink branch of the Delawares during this period, and the only way to reach the Seneca was to gain this tribe (Col. Rec. VIII. 747). The Minisink was the Wolf clan of the Munsee, which was the Wolf tribe of the Delawares. During the hostility of the greater part of the Indians in western Pennsylvania in the period of the Conspiracy of Pontiac, 1761-64, the Seneca were nearly all engaged in the conflict against the

English settlements and forts. Kiasutha was a leader in many of these Indian raiding parties. Even after the conclusion of the Indian war at this period the Seneca were hostile to the English. During the War of the Revolution the Seneca, as a tribe, were on the side of the British. Many of the worst Indian raids in western Pennsylvania during 1778-79 were made up of Seneca warriors. The stand of the tribe at this time was due to a very great extent to the influence of Sir William Johnson. This hostility of the Seneca led to the expedition of Gen. Sullivan up the Susquehanna, into the Seneca country in western New York, and to Col. Brodhead's expedition up the Allegheny to the Seneca villages, in the summer of 1779. The greater part of the Seneca country was devastated by these two expeditions. All of the villages were destroyed, and the tribe never recovered from its ruin at this time (Consult; Journals of the Military Expedition of Gen. John Sullivan, in 1779; Brodhead's Expedition, in Archives, XII. 149-159). The last Indian raid into the settlements of Western Pennsylvania, during the Revolution, was that on July 13, 1782, when Hannastown, in Westmoreland County, was destroyed, and a number of settlers killed and captured. Kiasutha, or Guyasuta, was the leader of about 300 Indians, chiefly Seneca, in this raid (Consult; Frontier Forts, II. 290 et seq.; Old Redstone, 225 et seq.; Olden Time, II. 351 et seq.). Mr. Hewitt is of the opinion that the Seneca on the upper Allegheny during this period were chiefly made up of outlying colonies of the Seneca, and were adopted and conquered tribes, among which were the remnants of the Erie and Conestoga. This is no doubt true to a certain extent, but there were many Seneca among those who were engaged in the conflicts with the Americans at this time. Kiasutha and Cornplanter, and many of the other chiefs along the upper Allegheny were Senecas. The Purchase of the lands west of the Purchase of 1768, from Pine Creek, made in 1784, was followed by the Purchase of 1792, when the lands in north-western Pennsylvania were deeded by the Iroquois. This Deed was signed by Gyantwachia (Cornplanter), Gyashot (Big Cross), Kanassee (New Arrow), Achiout (Half Town), Anachkout (the Wasp), Chishekoa (Wood Bug), Sessewa (Big Bale of a Kettle), Sciawhowa (Council

Keeper), Tewanias (Broken Twig), Souachshowa (Full Moon), Cachunevasse (Twenty Canoes), Cageahgea (Dogs about the Fire), Sawedowa (the Blast), Kiondashowa (Swimming Fish), Onesechter (Leaded Man), Kiandochgowa (Big Tree), and Owenewah (Thrown-in-the-Water). These were all Seneca chiefs. This Deed was also signed by one Tuscorarar, one Onondaga, one Oneida, two Cayuga, and two Munsee "as being residenters on the land but not owners" (Archives, Sec. Ser., VI. 730-735). According to the terms of this sale the Seneca reserved the tract upon which their villages were situated, between the Allegheny River and the Conewango River. In 1791 Cornplanter, Half-Town and Big Tree had signed a release of their lands to the state of Pennsylvania (op. cit. 627). Cornplanter's Reservation, above Warren, was occupied by the Seneca for many years. The majority of the Seneca, now living, are located along the upper Allegheny River near Salamanca, New York. Consult; Handbook of American Indians, Part 2, 502-508: See *Allegheny, Conewango. Cornplanter, Otzinachson, Shamokin, Susquehanna, Venango, Wyoming,* etc. A complete list of synonyms follow the article in the Handbook of American Indians. In the Colonial Records and Archives, besides the common forms of the name, such as Sennekaes, Sinakers, etc., the following corruptions of the Iroquois name of Djiionondowanenronnon, are mentioned:

Isanandonas.—Pa. Coun. (1721), Col. Rec., III. 133. **Jenontowanos.**—Treaty at Lan. (1744). Archives, I. 656. **Tsanandowans.**—Weiser (1732), Col. Rec., III. 449. **Tsanondowaroonas.**—Pa. Coun. (1721), Col. Rec. III. 150. **Tsanundowans.**—Pa. Coun. (1754), Col. Rec. VI. 124.

The various synonyms for Wyoming, such as Chanandowa (Col. Rec. IV. 92), Tssnandowa (Col. Rec. III. 273), Scahantowano (Archives, I. 657), Scha, han, do, a, na (Arch. Sec. Ser., VI. 69), and the other corruptions of this name, may be corruptions of the Iroquois name of the Seneca, and not the Iroquois name, which Heckewelder translated M'cheuomi "great flats, or meadows." The Seneca is the one tribe of the Iroquois, whose name and associations, as well as direct trails, was associated with Wyoming, and it was the one Iroquois tribe which seemed to have nothing to do with the conquering of the Susquehannocks (Andastes), in

1675. In 1696 the Deed of Gov. Dongan to William Penn, of the Susquehanna lands, mention is made of Dongan having purchased, or received by gift, these lands from the "Sennica Susquehanna Indians." Dongan knew enough concerning the use of the term "Sennica" as to not use it as a synonym for the Iroquois, as was done before this time (Archives, I. 123). The probability is that the unidentified tribe on the Juniata, before the commencement of the historic period, was the Seneca tribe, which was gradually driven north to Wyoming by the Andastes, with whom they had previously been closely connected after the separation of the Iroquois and Delawares. The Seneca were gradually driven from Wyoming by the Andastes, who were successful in the early years of the conflict with the Iroquois. The Wyoming Valley was therefore, probably the habitat of the Seneca, after their expulsion from the Juniata, and previous to their occupation of their historic habitat in New York. Sonontouan, Tsontouan, Shenandowana, Tsanandowana, bear a striking resemblance to Djiionondowanen, and the above mentioned facts all seem to connect the Seneca of history with the Susquehanna valley, as well as with the Ohio valley, previous to their final residence in New York. In several of the early records of Pennsylvania the Seneca are mentioned as the "real Sennica," as if the "Susquehanna Sennica" were offshoots from the parent stock. "The Great Mountain," as always understood by the Iroquois, was the Kittatinny ridge, which crosses the Susquehanna near the mouth of the Juniata. The people living beyond the great ridge, as seen from the Susquehanna, could have no more fitting name than "Djiionondowanen-aki," "People of the Great Mountain" (See *Juniata, Kittatinny*).

The Iroquois name for the Kittatinny mountains, as stated in various Deeds, was Tyannuntasacta, which was variously translated as "Great Mountain," or "Endless Hills" (Archives, I. 495). This name as recorded was no doubt a corruption of Djiionondowanen-aka. This mountain range was one of the most frequently mentioned natural features in the entire state, in all of the early records of the land purchases. This mountain was the one above all others which an Iroquois of the early period would identify as "The Great Mountain." It is mentioned in nearly every Indian Deed as

Kittatinny, Mechachtinni, or by the Iroquois Tyannuntasacta.

SEPASSINCKS ISLAND. An island in the Delaware River below Trenton, mentioned in the Deed to William Penn, in 1682. It is also mentioned in the Deed of August 1, 1682, in which "ye Land called Soepassincks, & of ye island of ye same name," is mentioned. Also mentioned in the instructions of the Commissioners, who were appointed in 1683, to the Treaty with West Jersey, as Sepassing (Archives, I. 48, 49, 59). This name is probably a corruption of Chiapiessing, or Chipussen, which is first mentioned in 1664 (Archives, Sec. Ser., V. 576). It was the name given to the lands in Buck's County, opposite the Falls of the Delaware. It is probably a corruption of Kschipehellen, with the locative ing, meaning "the place where the waters flow rapidly" (See *Chiepiessing*).

Sepassincks.—Deed of 1682, Archives, I. 48. **Sepassing.**—Instructions to Comm. (1683), Archives, I. 59. **Soepassincks.**—Deed of 1682, Archives, I. 49.

SERECHEN. A name given by Heckewelder, as a corruption from Selehend, or Sinuehund, "place of milking." No location given.

SEWICKLEY. The name of a creek in Westmoreland County; a town in Allegheny County, and of a former Shawnee village on the north side of the Allegheny River, below Tarentum, and of another Shawnee village on the Big Sewickley Creek near West Newton; also a creek, known as Little Sewickley, which enters the Ohio River, near the present Sewickley. The name is a corruption of the name Asswekales, the common name given to the Hatha-wekela division of the Shawnee by the English traders. The name is first mentioned in the Archives of Pennsylvania in 1731, when Le Tort and Davenport gave an account of the Indian villages on the Ohio. Among these are mentioned, "On Connumach Creek there are 3 Shawanese towns, 45 families, 200 men. Okowela. Asswikales 50 families lately come from S. Carolina to Ptowmack, & from thence thither, making 100 Men; Aqueloma, their Chief" (Archives, I. 302). Edmund Cartlidge said, 1731, that there were about 500 Indians on the Allegheny, "Delaware, Shawanah, Asseekales & Mingo" (op. cit. 305). The members of this tribe of Shawnee probably came from the region of Old

Town, on the Potomac, by way of the Warriors Path to Bloody Run, and then westward over the trail through Bedford and Ligonier. The Shawnee Cabins, near Shellsburg, was probably a stopping place of these Shawnee, who settled near Chartier's Town, on the Allegheny River. The Sewickley Old Town, noted on Evan's map of 1755, was a few miles below Chartiers Town, at the mouth of Dick's Run, below Tarentum. There was another Sewickley Town, which was mentioned in the grant of 60,000 acres which George Croghan received at the Treaty of Fort Stanwix in 1768, for lands lying on the Youghiogheny River. This village was probably at the mouth of the Big Sewickley Creek, below West Newton, or near Markle's old mill, about two miles east of West Newton, on the flat where Col. Lochry's detachment encamped, on their way to the Ohio Indian country, in Aug. 1781. The region south of where the Braddock Road crossed the Big Sewickley creek was filled up with Scotch-Irish settlers soon after the capture of Fort Duquesne. It was known as the Sewickley Settlement. One of the branches of the trail from Bedford, left the main path a few miles west of Bedford, and crossed through the present Somerset, and Mount Pleasant to Robb's Town (now West Newton) on the Youghiogheny River. This trail later became the Old Glade Road. By this course many of the settlers reached the Big Sewickley, which was well adapted for water mills. The Shawnee who settled at these two villages, belonging to the same clan of the Shawnee, no doubt soon removed to Logstown, hence the name there, before going on down the Ohio to the Lower Shawnee Town. In Ecuyer's Journal (Darlington, Fort Pitt, 85) of 1763, mention is made of Col. William Clapham, who had removed to the Sewickley Old Town, soon after 1761, to occupy the grant which had been made to himself and Croghan. There were a number of Indian raids into the Sewickley Settlement during the period of Indian hostility, before 1778. Col. Clapham was killed in one of these Indian raids, while living at his home on Sewickley Creek during the Indian uprising in the Conspiracy of Pontiac. One of the articles in the demand which Col. Bouquet made of the Indians in Ohio in 1764 was the surrender of the murderers of Col. Clapham. This matter was spoken of by Bouquet at the Council with the Indians at Tuscarawas in October, 1764 (Col. Rec. IX. 218). The Sewickley settlement, being made up of Scotch-Irish, soon organized a Presbyterian Church, which was known as the Sewickley Church. It was situated between Long Run and West Newton. It was organized in 1776 by Rev. James Power, Pastor of the Mount Pleasant Church. In Minutes of Redstone Presbytery for April 9, 1781, the meeting of the Presbytery at "Seweekly," was not held "A sufficient number of members not attending, by reason of the incursions of the savages" (Minutes of Redstone, 4, 1878; also, Old Redstone, 314, 1854). At this time the entire settlement in Westmoreland County from Ligonier and Hannastown to the Youghiogheny River was terrorized by the many Indian raids, which commenced early in the spring. Many of the men who enlisted in the expeditions of General George R. Clark and Col. Lochry, in the summer of 1781, were from these Presbyterian settlements. Col. William Crawford, famous in the Virginia Boundary Dispute, and also because of his ill-fated expedition to Sandusky, lived just above the mouth of the Big Sewickley at Stewart's Crossings (now Connellsville). All of the Virginia adherents were anxious to support Clark, while the Pennsylvania adherents were anxious to see the expedition fail. Among the former were, Crawford, Pentecost, Canon, Cox, Leet and other strong Virginia supporters. The Virginia controversy not only divided the military and political movements of the time, but also the Presbyterian congregations. Nearly all of these men, as well as all of the men making up the expeditions of Clark and Lochry, were members of the Presbyterian Church, with few exceptions. (Consult ; Archives, IX. 23, 137, 141, 239, 247, 559, etc.; Frontier Forts, II. 194; Archives, Sec. Ser., XIV. 730 et seq.; Frontier Forts, II. 334; Archives, IX. 574, 733). The Shawnee who occupied both of the Sewickley Old Towns removed to Logstown soon after 1731, and then removed on down the Ohio to the mouth of the Sciota, and to the Lower Shawnee Town.

Sewickly's old T.—Evens, map, 1755 —on Allegheny River. **Sewicklys Old Town.**—Scull, map, 1770—on Allegheny River. **Ancient Village des Chaouanons.** —Bonnecamp, map, 1749, on Allegheny River. **Asseekalos.**—Cartlidge (1731), Archives, I. 305—the tribe. **Assekelaes.** —Gordon (1731), Archives, I. 302—the tribe. **Asswekalaes.**—Davenport (1731), Archives, I. 299—the tribe. **Asswikales.**

—LeTort (1731, Archives, I. 302—the tribe. **Sewickly C.**—Evans, map, 1755 —the creek. **Sewickly Creek.**—Scull, map, 1770—the creek (the French map has Sewichly Cr.). **Big Sewickley Creek.** —Howell's, map, 1792. On Howell's map the two creeks above Logstown are marked Big Sewickley Creek, and Little Sewickley Cr. The former is now known as Sewickley Creek, and the latter as Little Sewickley Creek. **Saweckly.**—Brodhead (1779). Archives VII. 505—the settlement on the creek. **Seeweekley.** — McFarland (1774), Archives, IV. 555—the settlement on the creek. **Seweekly.**—Minutes of Redstone (1782), Min. Red. Presby., 4, 1878—the settlement on the creek. **Sewickley.**— Perry (1781), Archives, IX. 52—the settlement on the creek. **Sweakley.**— Mason (1781), Archives, IX. 238—the settlement on the creek.

SHADES OF DEATH. The name applied to the great Swamp, or rather to the western end of this swamp, which is noted on Scull's map of 1770, and also on Evans, map of 1755. One of the oldest trails from the Delaware to the Susquehanna ran from Wyoming through this swamp to Pechoquealin, on the Delaware. Another trail joined this one about 22 miles north of Easton, leading through the Wind Gap to Easton. This trail was followed by Sullivan's army in 1779 to Wyoming, from Easton, and is frequently mentioned in the Journals of this expedition. In the Journal of Rev. William Rogers, D.D., Chaplain to Hand's Brigade, he says, for June 21, "This day we marched through the Great Swamp and Bear Swamp. The Great Swamp, which is eleven or twelves miles through, contains what is called on our maps, the 'shades of death,' by reason of its darkness ; both swamps contain trees of amazing height, viz., hemlock, birch, pine, sugar-maple, ash, locust, etc." (Jour. Mil. Exped. Gen. Sull. 247). This swamp was situated in the north-western part of Monroe County, on the headwaters of the Lehigh. It was known as "The Shades of Death" long before the fugitives from Wyoming sought refuge in it, as stated by several writers. It is so noted on Scull's map of 1770.

SHADOW OF DEATH. A prominent point on the Indian Trail from Harris' Ferry to the Ohio. It is mentioned by Conrad Weiser in his Journal to Aughwick, now Shirleysburg, in 1754 (Col. Rec. VI. 151), and is also mentioned in the Table of Distances, given by John Harris, in 1754 (Archives, II. 133-34). This point was situated at the present Shade Gap, Huntingdon County. For the course of this trail, see *Frankstown, Raystown.*

SHACKAMAXON. The name of the former chief village of the Turtle clan of the Delawares, situated on the Delaware River in the present Philadelphia, at Kensington. Heckeweller, and others, give the derivation of this name from Schachamesink, "place of eels," from Scha-cha-meek, "an eel," with the locative ing. It is more probably from Sakima, "a chief," with the locative ing, meaning, "place of chiefs," or Sakimaucheen, "the place where chiefs are made." Shackamaxon was no doubt the chief town of the Unami tribe of the Delawares, as Minisink was the chief town of the Minsi tribe, and as such was therefore the Capital of the Delaware. The leading Unami chief was regarded as the head chief of the Delaware Nation, and his village as the Capital of the Delawares, as was the case when Gekelemukpecheunk became the Delaware Capital in Ohio. Tammany as the leading Unami chief would be considered as the head of the Delaware Nation. As such he was given the title of "King" by the English. The head chief of the Unami kept all of the official belts of wampum of the tribe, and presided at all of the Councils of the Delawares. Shackamaxon was the official village of Tammany, and here all of the Councils of the tribe were held. There is no reason to doubt the tradition of Penn's Treaty being held at this place. The Delaware, and all other tribes, were extremely conservative about holding their important Councils at the place where their "Council Fire" had always burned. Entirely apart from the tradition which fixes Shackamaxon as the place where this Council and Treaty was held, is the fact that the official ending of the war between the Iroquois and the Andastes (Conestoga), and the submission of the Delawares to the Iroquois, took place at Shackamaxon in March, 1677. Clarkson, the author of the biography of William Penn, says, "It appears, that though the parties were to assemble at Coaquannock, the treaty was made a little higher up, at Shackamaxon." In the Memoir on the Locality of the Penn Treaty, Roberts Vaux says, in commenting on this statement, "The probable reason for this change of the place of meeting with the Indians was their own convenience, as well as that of the proprietor and those who attended him, as a settlement had long before been made at Shackamaxon" (Memoirs, Hist. Soc. Penna., I. 103-104). This may be true, but the real reason why the Indians wished the meeting to take place was because this was the Council village of their tribe. No other such place is mentioned in any of the records of this period. As no other meeting place of the Indians is mentioned, on this part of the Delaware, the presumption is in favor of Shackamaxon (Consult; Memoir, in Memoirs of Hist. Soc. Penna., I. 90-106). The Belt of Wampum, which is now in the Historical Society of Pennsylvania, was probably given at this Treaty (Consult; Memoirs, Hist. Soc. Penna., VI. 205-281). The minute of the meeting of Upland Court, March 13, 1677, reads, "Att a meeting held by ye Commander (Capt. John Colier) & Justicea att uppland, uppon the news of the Simeco Indians comming downe to fetch the Susquehanno that were amonghts these River Indians, etc March 13th. annoq Dom. 1676-77 (1677) * * * * Itt was concluded uppon the motions of Rinoweha the Indian Sachomore for the most quiet of the River viz. That Captain Colier & Justice Israell helm goe upp to Sachamexin (where att p'sent a great number of Simico & other Indians are) and that they Endeauor to prswaede the Simecus the Sasquehannes & these River Indians to send Each a Sachomore or Deputy to his honor, the Governor, att New Yorke, and that Justice Israell helm goe wth. them ; for to heare & Receive his sd. honors. Resolucons & answer to their demands" (Records of Upland Court, 49). At the meeting of the Court on June 14, 1677, "Lace Cock" presented a bill of 250 "Gilders" for the expenses of the Commander and Justices, for the expenses of this meeting at Shackamaxon, from March 14 to 18, 1677. (Records of Upland, 53). In 1656 the Delawares conveyed to Director Peter Stuyvesant, the land on the western shore of the Delaware, known as "Tinnecongh," to the "bounds and limits of the Minquaes country." This Deed was witnessed by four of the Minquas (Andastes) chiefs (Archives, Sec. Ser., V. 266-267). The close association of the River Indians (Delaware) and the Minquas (Andastes, or Conestoga) during this period, and the fact that later on when the latter were overcome by the Iroquois, they sought refuge with the Delawares, show that these two tribes, of different linguistic families, were in close affiliation. The Delaware, because of this association with the Minquas, were probably included in the terms of submission to the Five Nations, at this official ending of the Iroquois war with the Andastes (Minquas) at Shackamaxon in 1677. The Iroquois, at the later Councils at Lancaster and Philadelphia, refused to grant the validity of any of the land sales of either the Delaware or Minquas, after the latter had been conquered by them in 1675. Because the Delawares refused to help the Iroquois in their wars with the French, 1678-86, they were called "women." There is no record of any war of the Iroquois with the Delaware, save the war in which the Delaware granted aid and protection to the Minquas, when the latter were at war with the Five Nations, or rather with the Cayuga and Oneida (See *Seneca*). The land called Shackamaxon, or Shakha Mexunk (Reed's map), was situated on the north side of Cohocksink Creek, in the present Kensington. Peter Cock received 600 acres in this tract in 1664 (Archives, Third Ser., III. 315-316). Lawrence Cock, and Martha Cock, his wife, deeded to Elizabeth Kinsey (who became wife of Thomas Fairman) 300 acres of land "att the toune or neighborhood Called and Knowne by the name of Sachamexing" (Records of Upland Court, 116-118). This Deed is also mentioned in 1791, after Elizabeth Kinsey had become the wife of Thomas Fairman (Archives, Sec. Ser., XIX. 72-73). Various other transactions at Shackamaxon are noted in the references which follow. At the time of Penn's Treaty, 1683, there was quite a settlement at this place, made up chiefly of Swedes, who had previously been under the jurisdiction of the Court at Upland.

Soon after the English occupation of the Delaware the Indians began to move westward to the Susquehanna. By 1718 only a small remnant was living on the Brandywine, and in other places in the region. After the various land purchases about the Delaware Water Gap, and south of the Kittatinny mountains, all of the Delawares moved to Wyoming, Shamokin or to the West Branch and the Ohio. The Unami tribe, which had occupied the region about Philadelphia, was the most friendly towards the English, even during the period of Indian hostility. They boasted of their friendship for the English, when the Munsee were bitter foes. Even in the period

of the Revolution the Unami, or Turtle clan, as a tribe, remained true to the American cause. Gelelemend, and many others of the Turtle clan, who were the direct descendants of Tammany, and the chiefs who met William Penn, remained true to the League of Amity which their fathers had made a century before.

Sachamaxeing.—Upland Court (1678), Records of Upland, 117. **Sachamexin.**—Upland Court (1677), Records of Upland Court, 49. **Sachamexing.**—Upland Court (1678), Records of Upland Court, 117. **Shacamaxin.**—Board of P. (1774), Archives, Third Ser., III. 344. **Shackamaksen.**—Board of P. (1691), Archives, Sec. Ser., XIX, 70. **Shackamaxon.**—Board of P. (1691), Archives, Sec. Ser., XIX. 69. **Shackamaxson.**—Board of P. (1691), Archives, Sec. Ser., XIX. 72. **Shackamexunk.**—Board of Pa. (1664), Archives, Third Ser. III. 315. **Shakamakson.**—Board of P. (1691), Archives, Sec. Ser., XIX. 65. **Shakha Mexunk.**—Reeds map, 1774. **Shakamxunk.**—Board of Prop. (1691), Archives, Sec. Ser., XIX. 68. **Sharamaxen.**—Board of Prop. (1691), Archives, Sec. Ser., XIX. 58. **Shaxamaxin.**—Board of Prop. (1691), Archives, Sec. Ser., XIX, 76. **Shaxamaxing.**—Board of Prop (1691), Archives, Sec. Ser., XIX. 73. **Shaxamaxsen.**—Board of Prop. (1690) Archives, Sec. Ser., XIX. 51. **Shaxamaxsin.**—Board of Prop. (1690), Archives, Sec. Ser., XIX. 57.

SHALLYSCHOHKING. See *Chillisquaque.*

SHAMOKIN. The name of a town, creek and mountain in Northumberland County; also the name of a village, called Shamokin Dam, in Snyder County; also the name of one of the most historic Indian villages in the state, formerly situated at the site of the present Sunbury, Northumberland County. The name is said by Heckewelder to be a corruption of Schahamoki, or Schahamokink, "the place of eels." He says that it was later called Schachhenamendi, "the place where gun barrels are straightened," because it had become the residence of a Delaware, named Nutamees, who repaired the bent fire-arms of the Indians. Heckewelder is mistaken both in the statement concerning the origin of the name, and also the black-smith shop in this place. The Moravians built a smithy at Shamokin in 1747, under the direction of Joseph Powell and John Hagen. The latter died at Shamokin, Sept. 16, 1747, and was buried there. Bishop Cammerhoff, in his Journal of 1748, says, "During the day I visited Hagen's grave, which is in the corner of a field near the Susquehanna" (Penna. Mag. Hist., XXIX. 172). The various smiths employed at this shop were, Schmidt, Wesa and Kieffer. The smithy was in operation until 1755. Cammerhoff says in his Journal, before noted, "Our smith is kept constantly employed, many Indians coming from a great distance" (op. cit. 173). During the past summer (1913) the stone anvil which must have been used in this smithy was dug up near the site of Fort Augusta. It is now in the "Relic Room" at the home of Mrs. Amelia Gross, on the site of the old fort. If Shamokin ever had the name suggested by Heckewelder, it was due to the presence of this Moravian smithy. Gerard gives the origin of the name from Shumokenk, "where antlers are plenty." The more probable origin is that suggested by Reichel, from Sakima, "a chief, or ruler," with the locative, ing, signifying "the place of chiefs, or rulers." Shamokin was not only the residence of the Iroquois deputy, Shikellamy, but also of the Delaware "King," Sassounan, or Allummapees, who was the successor of Tammany. Shamokin was the Capital of the Delaware tribe, after the removal of the Delawares to the Susquehanna. Shackamaxin had been the former Capital on the Delaware. In later years Logstown became a sort of Capital, but the real Delaware Capital on the Ohio was Gekelemukpecheunk, the home of Netawatwes, head chief of the Delawares. Shamokin was the largest and most important Indian village in Pennsylvania from 1727 until 1756, after which time the majority of the residents had removed up the West Branch to the Big Island, up the North Branch to Wyoming, or to the Ohio. The old Indian village was situated just opposite the island in the Susquehanna, facing the West Branch. It was one of the most central points in the entire state. The trail to Wyoming and the upper Delaware, the trail up the West Branch to the Big Island, the Bald Eagle Valley and the Ohio; the trail down the Susquehanna to the various villages on the lower river; the Warriors Path to the Juniata, and on to the Potomac, at Old Town, and many other branch trails to the east, west, north and south, all centered here. There is no doubt but that it had been a site of one of the important villages of the Susquehannocks (Minqua. Andaste, Conestoga). The villages of this great tribe of Iroquoian Stock were scattered along the West Branch to Lock Haven, and up the North Branch to the site of Carantouan, near Waverly. N. Y. This was a favorite meeting place for the Iroquois as they went on their raids into the country of the Cherokee and Catawba, and here they held their celebrations before returning to their homes in New York. The historic Indian village of Shamokin was probably settled about 1718, after the removal of the Delaware and Shawnee from about Paxtang, the mouth of the Juniata and in part from the Delaware. The village was situated in the upper part of the present Sunbury, opposite the island in the Susquehanna. It spread to the island and to the present Northumberland. Chenastry, or Chenasshy, was the name applied to the village occupying the land at the forks of the West Branch, at the site of Northumberland. where James Le Tort (See *Le Tort's Spring*) had a trading house before 1725. The name was probably a corruption of Otzinachson (which see), the name applied to the West Branch, or at first to the entire region about the mouth of the West Branch. Because of its situation on the trail to Wyoming, Shamokin was on the main path leading from the upper Delaware to the Ohio, and was no doubt one of the first paths taken by the Delawares from "the Forks of the Delaware to the Susquehanna. West Branch and Allegheny. As early as 1721 the Delawares were in the habit of going westward to the Ohio to fish, going in the fall and returning in the spring (Col. Rec., III. 116). Allummapees, the head chief of the Delawares, succeeded Skalitchy in 1715. He lived at Paxtang in 1718, and soon after removed to Shamokin. He remained here until his death in 1747, at which time Weiser suggested that "Lapaghuitton" (See *Lepos Peters*) was the most suitable successor for him, as the "King" of the Delawares, but that he declined to serve (Col. Rec. V. 138-139). "King Beaver" was afterwards appointed by the Iroquois as "King" of the Delawares, but the Delawares themselves never acknowledged him as such, as they had not elected him, and as neither he, or his brother, Shingas, were members of the Unami, or Turtle tribe, but belonged to the Unalachtigo, or Turkey tribe, from which the head chief was never chosen. Allummapees, or Sassounan, was the leading chief of the Unami tribe, and as such was the head chief of the Delaware Nation. The statement of Mr. Hanna that Shingas, Beaver and Pisquitomen were children of a sister of Allummapees is hardly probable, as these were members of the Turkey tribe, while both Allummapees and his sister belonged to the Turtle clan, or tribe. The head chief of the Unami tribe kept all of the official wampum of the Delawares. This was in the possession of Allummapees, and what he had left, after "drinking up" the most of it, passed to Netawatwees, and then to Gelelemend (See *Killbuck*). The Delawares commenced moving to the Ohio, from Shamokin, by way of the Big Island, soon after 1724. From that time until 1727 there was a continual migration of Delaware and Shawnee to the Ohio. The village of Kittanning (which see) was established at this time, as was also Logstown (which see). In 1728 Governor Gordon was informed that all of the Indians, save Allummapees and Opekasset, had removed from Shamokin (Col. Rec. III. 330; Archives, I. 211, 227). In 1728 Shikellamy, an Oneida chief, was appointed by the Iroquois as their deputy at Shamokin, having special oversight of the Shawnee (Archives, I. 228). After the Council of 1742 at Philadelphia, Canassatego ordered the Delawares to leave their lands on the Delaware, about the "Forks" and remove at once to Wyoming or Shamokin (Col. Rec. IV. 579-580). From this time onward until 1755 Shamokin was the Indian Capital of the Province. All matters relating to the Delaware and Shawnee, as well as all matters relating to the various land sales, were referred to the Iroquois deputy at this place. Shikellamy died in 1748, and was succeeded by his son, Taghneghdoarus (John). The visit of Weiser on his official mission to the Ohio, in 1748, and the expedition of Celoron de Bienville, in 1794, began to arouse the three colonies of Pennsylvania, Virginia and Maryland to the need of doing something to hold the Indian trade, which had passed from the Susquehanna to the Ohio, and which was becoming imperilled by the French activity in the Ohio Valley, to which the Delaware and Shawnee had removed in great numbers. Every effort was made by the authorities of the Province, to draw these Indians back to the Susquehanna, and away from the French influence. Even the Iroquois threatened a war with the Delawares, if they would not come back from the

Ohio. But, all of these efforts were in vain. The Delaware and Shawnee refused to return. The Indians of the Susquehanna were being massed on the waters of the Ohio. Shamokin, as a center of Indian affairs, had seen its day, and Kittanning, Logstown, Sawcunk, and Kuskuski had become the important Indian villages when the struggle for the possession of the Ohio between France and Great Britain was impending. The Moravian Church was active in missionary efforts in Shamokin, almost from the time of its historic settlement. Count Zinzendorf visited Shamokin in 1742, under the guidance of Conrad Weiser. He met Shikellamy, who ever after was a firm friend of the Moravians (Zinzendorf's Journal, Memorials of the Mor. Church, I. 84 et seq). Among the missionaries who labored at Shamokin, were Mack, Post, Pyrlaeus, and Zeisberger. David Brainerd, the Presbyterian missionary, also visited Shamokin each year during his residence at the "Forks of the Delaware." In 1745 he said that the Indian village was on both sides of the river, and on the island. It then contained about 50 houses and upwards of 300 inhabitants, one half of whom were Delawares, and the other half, Seneca and Tutelo. The village was the scene of great drunken revels, during these visits of Brainerd (Mem. Mor. Church, 67). In 1749 all of the Indians were obliged to remove from Shamokin because of a famine which was then raging through the entire region (Archives, II. 23). After Braddock's defeat, in 1755, the entire region was overrun by hostile Delaware, Shawnee and Seneca. Governor Morris spoke of his intention of building a fort at this place in 1755, because of the demand of Scarouady that such a fort be built for the protection of the friendly Indians (Col. Rec. IV. 665, 686, 701). This request was made at the treaty at Carlisle, and again at the Council at Philadelphia, in 1756 (Col. Rec. VII. 6, 54). During the spring and summer of 1756 this fort was erected (Archives, Sec. Ser., II. 745-820, 1890). The fort was called Fort Augusta. It stood just below the junction of the two branches of the Susquehanna, facing the West Branch, and opposite the Blue Hill, through which ran one of the trails to the Bald Eagle Valley, and the big Island. The site of this fort is now most suitably marked by Mrs. I. M. Gross, who occupies and owns the fort site. A marker erected by the D. A. R. Chapter at Sunbury, stands on the bank of the river at one corner of the fort. Just above this fort was the old Indian burial ground, in which Shikellamy, and also, probably Allummapees were buried. On the river bank, opposite the end of the island, stood the Store House. Many Indian relics, and many relics from Fort Augusta, have been found along the river near the site of the fort. Col. Hunter, who commanded the fort in its later history, is buried in a small grave yard, not far from the fort. Fort Augusta, which was the most important of the frontier forts during the period of Indian hostility, was the scene of many of the thrilling events in the history of the West Branch valley (For a history of Fort Augusta, Consult; Frontier Forts, I. 354-363; Burd's Journals, in Archives Sec. Ser., II. 743-820, 1876; VII. 413 et seq.). A number of important Indian Councils were held at Fort Augusta by Col. Francis in 1769 (Col. Rec. IX. 610-620). In Jan. 1748 Bishop Cammerhoff, accompanied by Joseph Powell, visited Shamokin. Shikellamy was then living, and visited the Bishop, with whom he had a lengthy conversation concerning the Moravian smithy. The Journal of Cammerhoff gives a very good description of the trail from Bethlehem to Shamokin, and also of the various persons then living along its course (Consult; Penna. Magazine of Hist. and Biog., XXIX. 160-179, 1905). The various trails which entered Shamokin, were as follows; the Wyoming Path, which ran up the Susquehanna to Wyoming, and then on to Tioga where it branched for the Iroquois country up the Chemung and for the various villages along the North Branch. One branch of this trail left Wyoming, going east through the Shades of Death, Great Swamp, to the Delaware; from Shamokin this trail continued westward up the West Branch, on the North side, to the mouth of the Muncy Creek, and on to the Big Island, at Lock Haven, where one branch continued on up the West Branch to the Sinnemahoning, and over the divide to the Allegheny—another branch went up Pine Creek, from Jersey Shore, to the headwaters and then over the divide to the Genesee. Still another branch went up Lycoming Creek, and another branch up Muncy Creek, to Sheshequin (which

see.) The main Shamokin Path went on up the Bald Eagle Creek, to Marsh Creek, and then along it to the divide, and then over to the Allegheny River, near Kittanning. Southward from Shamokin ran the path to Harris' Ferry, and to the region of Bethlehem. Another path, the Warriors Path ran from the mouth of Penn's Creek, having crossed the river at Shamokin, to the Juniata, and then to Standing Stone, and southward along the eastern side of Warrior's Ridge, to the Potomac, at Old Town, Maryland. This was the Iroquois War Trail to the Carolinas. It crossed the various trails leading from the Susquehanna to the Ohio. One of the trails to the upper West Branch crossed the river near Shamokin, and cut directly through the gap in the Blue Hill. A short trail to Wyoming left the site of Fort Augusta, going directly up along the valley of Shamokin Creek, or rather on the divide between the creek and the Susquehanna River, which was reached at the mouth of Roaring Creek. Many other minor trails entered Shamokin from various points along the West Branch and the Bald Eagle Valley. Conrad Weiser frequently visited Shamokin. (Consult; Weiser's Journals, Col. Rec. IV. 640-680; Post, Jour., to Ohio, Archives, III. 320 et seq.). For general reference consult; Hanna, Wilderness Trail, I. and II., under title; Colonial Records, and Archives, of Penna., under title. Many of these follow in the list of synonyms.

Fort Augusta. — Scull, map, 1759, **Fort Schamookin.**—LeRoy (1755), Arch. Sec. Ser. VII. 403. **Samokin.**—Lattre, map, 1784. **Schachhenamendi.**—Heckewelder, in Indian Names, 266. **Schomako.**—Zinzendorf (1742), Mem. Mor. Church, 133. **Shahomaking.**—Allummapees (1727), Archives, I. 214. **Shamaken.**—Blunston (1728), Archives, I. 216. **Shamockin.**—Burd (1757), Arch. Sec. Ser., II. 665, 1890. **Shamokin.**—Weiser (1743), Col. Rec. IV. 640; Weiser, map, 1749. **Shaumoking.** — Brainerd (1745), Day, Penn., 525, 1843. **Shawmokin.**—Harris (1754), Archives, II. 178. **Shoahmokin.**—Cartlidge (1730), Archives, I. 254. **Shomhomokin.**—Weiser (1744), Archives, I. 661. **Shomoken.**—Bard (1755), Border Wars, 121, 1839. **Shomokin.**—Weiser (1745), Archives, I. 673. **Siamocon.**—Sadowsky (1728), Archives, I. 227. **Skamoken.**—Vaudreuil (1757), Archives, Sec. Ser., VI. 404.

The following forms of Otzinachson (which see) are included under Shamokin, because they refer to the region in which Shamokin was situated. Before the occupation of the

Indian village at Shamokin, by the Delawares, the region about the junction of the West Branch with the Susquehanna was known by the Iroquois name of Otzinachson. This name was used by the Indians and the traders just as "at Ohio," or "at Allegheny" was used, before the settlements at Kittanning, Venango, Logstown, etc., had been formed. "At Zinachson" was as indefinite as "at Ohio." On Pouchot's map, 1758, Fort Augusta is placed at "Schinanchen," and in Vaudreuil's letter, 1757, it is stated, "This fort is on the upper part of the river Zinantchain" (Archives. Sec. Ser., VI. 404). I have been unable to find any proof that this name was ever used, save as stated. It was the name of a river, and of a region along that river.

Chenastry.—Weiser (1728), Col. Rec., III. 295. **Chenasshy.**—Logan (1728), Archives, I. 210. **Chinasky or Shamokin.**—Taylor, map, 1727. **Schinanchen.**—Pouchot map, 1758. **Zinachson.**—Weiser (1747), Col. Rec., V. 84.

The "(Shamokin)" which follows this name in the Col. Rec. was evidently added by the editor of the MS. notes. The record reads, "Brethren: You that Live at Zinachson (Shamokin)." See *Big Island, Ostonwakin, Otzinachson, Wyoming.* The Manor of Pomfret, situated between Shamokin Creek and the upper end of the island, containing 4,766 acres and allowances, was surveyed on Dec. 19, 1768 (See map No. 52, Archives, Third Ser., IV. 1895).

SHANNOPIN'S TOWN. A former Delaware village, upon the south bank of the Allegheny River, below the mouth of Two Mile Run, opposite to Herr's Island. It was about two miles from the "Forks" of the Allegheny and Monongahela, between the present Penn Avenue and the river, north of Thirtieth Street. It was named for the chief of the village, Shannopin, who signed a letter, evidently written by one of the Indian traders who were present when it was composed. These traders were, Edmund Cartlidge, James LeTort and Joseph Davenport. The first mentioned probably wrote the letter, which was concerning the killing of John Hart, a Shamokin trader, and the shooting of David Robeson by a Shawnee woman, and various matters relating to the drunken brawls, due to the unrestricted sale of rum to the Indians, The letter was written to Governor Gordon, requesting that he put a stop to the carrying of such large quantities of rum "into the woods." The letter, which is dated "att Alleegaeening on the Main Road," April 30, 1730, was signed by "Shawannoppan" (Shannopin), and other chiefs (Archives, I. 254-255). Edmund Cartlidge, Jonah Davenport and Henry Baly (Baily) wrote a letter to Gov. Gordon in 1730, in which they state that for three years past they have ventured "further than any person formarly Did," and that because of this they had bought great quantities of furs and peltries. In order to hold the trade of the Indians at "Alleegeneeing" they had extended credit to them each fall. The Indians had regularly paid these debts each spring, until a lot of new traders came into the region, with a small quantity of goods and a large quantity of rum. As a consequence the Indians were debauched, and unable to pay their debts. These debts had increased until they then amounted to about 2000 pounds worth of peltries" (Archives, I. 261). Such were the conditions on the Allegheny in 1730. If the "Senangel's Town," mentioned by James LeTort, in 1731, is the same as Shannopin's Town, which is probable, it then contained 16 families and 50 men, of the Delaware tribe (Arch. I. 301). The village was a prominent gathering place for the Indian traders to the Ohio. George Croghan, William Trent, Robert Callender and Michael Taafe and a number of other traders had trading houses at the mouth of Pine Creek (at Etna), on the trail from Kittanning and Chartier's Town, to Logstown. The "Main Road" from Harris' Ferry crossed the Allegheny at Shannopin's Town, where, according to Lewis Evan's Analysis of the Map of the Middle Colonies (25, 1775) "At Shannopin's there is a fording place in very dry times and the lowest down the river." Shannopin's Town was on the "Main Road" between the Susquehanna over which many of the traders carried their goods to the Ohio, and returned with their furs and peltries. In the table of distances, given by John Harris in 1754, between Harris' Ferry and the Ohio, Shannopin's Town is given on the Ray's Town branch of the trail (the course of this trail is noted under the article on *Raystown*). This trail ran through Bedford, Ligonier, Hannastown etc. to Shannopin's, and then on to Logstown. The Frankstown trail crossed the Allegheny at

Chartier's Landing, and ran down the river through Etna, joining the "Main Road" opposite Shannopin's Town (Col. Rec. V. 750-751; Archives, II. 135-136). The distance given by Harris, from Harris' Ferry (Harrisburg), to Shannopin's Town, was 230 miles, and 16 miles more to Logstown. According to the computed distance of William West, 1752, the distance to Shannopin's Town, from Three Springs, was 145 miles—with the added distance from Harris' Ferry to Three Springs. 82 miles, this would make 227 miles to Shannopin's from Harrisburg (Col. Rec. V. 760-762). Each of the points along both the Frankstown and the Raystown trails are noticed under title. Conrad Weiser passed through Shannopin's Town in 1748, when on his mission to Logstown (which see). Weiser travelled over the Frankstown Path to Chartier's Town, where he hired a canoe, in which he reached Shannopin's Town, where he was kindly treated by the Indians. He remained in the village on the night of August 26, and left in the morning for Logstown, going by water (Col. Rec. V. 348-349). Shannopin was present at the Council at Logstown. In 1749 Celeron de Bienville passed down the Allegheny River, taking possession of it and its tributaries in the name of the King of France. He stopped at the village, which is noted on Bonnecamp's map as "Village du Loups" (Village of Delawares). In 1750, when Christopher Gist was on his tour of investigation for the Ohio Company, he stopped at Shannopin's Town. He says, "The River Ohio is 76 Poles wide at Shannopin Town. There are about twenty families in this town" (Darlington, Gist's Jour., 34). Gist crossed the Allegheny at this place, going along East and West Ohio Streets to Beaver Avenue, and then down it and along the river bank to Logstown, near Economy. Washington and Gist were at Shannopin's in 1753, when on their way to Logstown, and the French Fort at Venango. They went through Shannopin's Town to the mouth of the Allegheny, where they "swimmed our horses over Allegheny, and there encamped that night" (Dar-Gist Jour., 81). The place where Washington and Gist spent this night was probably near the foot of Monument Hill, on the North Side. It was on this trip that Washington spent some time examining the land at "the Forks." He says in his Jour-

nal of 1753, "I spent some time in vewing the rivers, and the land in the fork, which I think is extremely well situated for a fort, as it has absolute command of both rivers." (Olden Time, I. 10 et seq.). Washington and Gist returned from Venango on Dec. 29, 1753, when they built a raft and reached the island above Shannopin's Town. As Gist's fingers were frozen, and as Washington had fallen from the raft into the icy water, and as it was dark, they encamped on the island that night, and the next morning were able to walk over the river on the ice, going directly to John Fraser's at the mouth of Turtle Creek (Gist Jour. 86; Washington's Jour. Olden Time, I. 10 et seq.). The island upon which Washington and Gist spent this night was Herr's Island. In Nov. 1753 Lewis Montour said that the Half King (Tanachharison) and Scarouady (his successor), had been at the Lower Shawnee Town, at the mouth of the Sciota, and had returned "thence home, that is to Shannopin, about three miles above the Forks of Monhongialo, forthwith called together the Indians of their own Nations, about twenty in number, to a Meeting, and likewise the Indian Traders who were then in the Town." The speeches which were made at this meeting were taken down by Reed Mitchel a trader who was present (Col. Rec. V. 702). Ensign Ward, in his deposition, states that the French army, under Contracoeur, was first seen descending the Allegheny River "at Shannopin's Town about two Miles distant from the Fort the 17th of April last" (Ward's deposition was taken in 1754, Consult; Darlington, Gist's Jour., 275). This fort which Ward was building was surrendered to the French Commander, and Ward returned to Will's Creek (See *Pittsburgh, Redstone, Venango*). George Croghan, when on his way to Logstown in Jan. 1754, was overtaken by Andrew Montour and John Patten, who were on their way to the western Indians with two Shawnee, who had been held in captivity in South Carolina (Col. Rec. V. 731). In 1754 Croghan in a letter to Richard Peters, said, "I am Surprised to think that the Gentelmen of Philadelphia are So Litle acquainted with ye back parts of this Province, for I ashure you that from ye three Springs (which is about Eight Miles west from My house, and Cartanly Some Miles Est from Philip Daveys,) butt 70 Miles to ye Lowrel Hill, ye Road we Now Travel, which I Supose may be About 50 od Miles on a Streat Course, and from Lowrel Hill to Shanopens is butt 46 Mile, as ye Road Now goes." Croghan also voices the wish of many later investigators, when he says, "I Wish with all My hart Some gentelmen who is an Artist in Philadelphia, and whos Acount wold be Depended on, whould have ye Curiosety to take a Journay in those parts, whos Return, I Dear Say, wold give A Ginrel Satisfaction to ye whole Province" (Archives, II. 132-133). The army of General Forbes passed through Shannopin's Town, in 1758, having gone over the Old Indian trail from Fort Loudon, to Bedford, Ligonier, Hannastown, and then over the Frankstown Road to Shannopin's Town. Forbes' course through Pittsburgh was not down Forbes Street, as often stated, but down Penn Avenue, along the old Indian trail to Shannopin's Town. When the army of General Forbes passed this site, many of the bodies of the Scotch Highlanders who had been captured in Col. Grant's ill-fated expedition, were still found along the river front, where they had met death at the stake. Grant had evidently reached the place, since known as Grant's Hill, by way of the trail down the Turtle Creek Valley, taking the direct path from Hannastown, over which Bouquet marched in 1763, instead of taking the course which was later followed by General Forbes. He probably followed the general course of Forbes Street, which should be called Bouquet Street, while Penn Avenue should be called Forbes Avenue—if historic naming is to mean anything. The Delaware chief, after whom the village was named, was present at the Council at Philadelphia in 1740 (Col. Rec. IV. 447). He wrote a letter to Governor Gordon in 1732, thanking him for the present of a cask of rum (Archives, I. 341). He died between 1749 and 1751, as Governor Hamilton, in a letter to the Indians at Logstown in 1751 says. "Shawanapon and Others are since dead" (Col. Rec. V. 519). The name has been perpetuated on the Ohio in the name of a town called Shannopin, Beaver County.

Alleegaeening.—Cartlidge (1730), Archives, I, 255. **Allegaeniny.**—Doc. of 1730, cited by Darlington, Gist Jour.,

93. **Schahanapan.**—Coun. at Phil. (1740), Col. Rec. IV. 447. **Senangelstown.**—LeTort (1731), Archives, I. 301. **Shanapins.**—Washington (1753), Jour. 13, 1865. **Shanapin's Town.**—Washington (1753), quoted by Rupp, West. Penn., app. 46. **Shanappins T.**—Pownall, map, 1775. **Shannapins.**—Washington (1753), Jour., 37, 1865. **Shannopen T.**—Evans, map, 1755. **Shannopin Town.**—Gist (1750), Dar. Gist Jour., 33. **Shannopin's Town.**—Dar. Gist. Jour., 34. **Shannopin's town.**—Gist (1753), Dar. Gist Jour., 80. **Shannopin Town.**—Gist (1750), Dar. Gist Jour., 34. **Shanopens.**—Croghan (1754), Archives, II. 132. **Shanopins.**—Washington (1753), Jour., 39. **Shanoppin.**—Patten (1754), Col. Rec., V. 750. **Shanoppin's T.**—Evans, map, 1755. **Shannopon T.**—Trader's map, 1753. **Shanoppin's Town.**—Croghan (1754), in Thwaites, E. W. T., I. 74. **Shawanapon.**—Pa. Hist. Soc. Coll., I. 29. **Shawanasson.**—Weiser (1748), Col. Rec. V. 355. **Shawannoppan.**—Cartlidge (1730), Archives, I. 255. **Village du Loups.**—Bonnecamp, map, 1749.

SHAWMUT. The name of a village in Elk County. Is probably a shortening of Mushauwomuk, the Indian name of Boston, Mass., which was corrupted to Shawmut. The name is said to mean, "he goes by boat." The name, in Elk County, may be a corruption of Shummonk, "the place of antlers." The name in Elk County is not historic.

SHAWNEE. The name of a number of places in the State, in Cambria, Montour, Lancaster, and Luzerne Counties; also of Shawnee-on-Delaware, in Monroe County; also of several small runs, named in honor of the Algonkian tribe, known as the Shawnee. The name is derived from Shawun, "south"; Shawunogi, "southerners;" Schawaneu is "southward;" Schwanewunk, "southward, or south place;" Schawanachen, "south wind." It is not possible in this historical note to discuss the various problems presented by the Shawnee, nor to give a history of the many migrations of this most mysterious tribe. In many respects the history of the Shawnee is the most interesting of any of the tribes connected with the early history of the region east of the Mississippi. Their wandering habits connect their history with that of the entire region east of the Mississippi and south of the Ohio basins. In all probability they were the builders of many of the earthen mounds found throughout the Ohio, Monongahela and Youghiogheny Valleys. According to the traditions of the Walum Olum, the Shawnee, Delaware and Nanticoke were at one time united, before the expulsion of the Talligewi from the Allegheny and Ohio Rivers. It would seem from the study of the various early maps and records, as well as from the various places in which the Shawnee are known to have lived, and also from various statements made by the chiefs who migrated from the Susquehanna, just before the reunion of the Shawnee in Ohio, that the habitat from which the Shawnee first commenced their migrations, after their separation from the Delawares, was in the basin of the Ohio River, from about the site of Pittsburgh to the mouth of the Mississippi, and possibly along the western shore of the Mississippi, in the region of New Madrid, Mo. This region of earthen mounds was in all probability occupied by the Shawnee previous to their occupation of the two separated habitats in Tennessee and South Carolina, in which they were on friendly terms with the Cherokee. It is possible that this friendship between these tribes commenced when they both occupied the region along the Ohio, below the Allegheny basin, to which the Cherokee had been driven by the wars of the Iroquois. The map of Franquelin, 1679, places the Chaouanons, the French name for the Shawnee, on the eastern side of the Mississippi, below the mouth of the Ohio. In 1673 Marquette says, in speaking of the Ohio, "This river comes from the country on the east, inhabited by the people called Chaouanons, in such numbers that they reckon twenty-three villages in one district, and fifteen in another, lying quite near each other." The Iroquois were at this time carrying on a war with these Chaouanons. It is probable that the Shawnee were at this period, before their southern migration, living along the northern shore of the Ohio, in the region in which the tribe was reunited after its migration from South Carolina to Pennsylvania, and then back to the various Shawnee towns in Ohio and along the river to its mouth. While the settlement of Shawneetown, Gallatin County, Illinois, belongs to this later period, there is every reason to believe that this place had been occupied long before that time, and for a long period, by the Shawnee. The author visited this place a few years ago and examined a number of the very large pots, which had been used for boiling salt, which had been

dug up within the present Shawneetown. Along Saline River the broken fragments of similar pots are found in great piles, covered with trees and rubbish. On the opposite side of the Ohio River at this point, there evidently were extensive burial grounds. Even now the Ohio River, after high water, opens many of these burial places. The entire region along Saline River, and, in fact, the entire peninsula between the Ohio and Mississippi, was evidently occupied by a large Indian population for many years. The Indians came from great distances to the saline springs to make salt. This may have been the site of a number of these prehistoric Indian villages, which were occupied by the Shawnee. The author examined a number of the perfect examples of pottery found here, and compared them with some found at the mound near New Madrid, Mo. They were evidently of the same period and made by the same people. This entire region was no doubt their habitat before the migration of the tribe to the Cumberland River, and to South Carolina (Consult; Problem of the Ohio Mounds, by Cyrus Thomas, 1889; Hanna, II. 86 et seq.; Handbook of American Indians, II. 530 et seq.). The various names given by Mr. Hanna (I. 119) as synonyms of Shawnee cannot so be understood. Sawwanew, Sawanoos, Sauwanoos, as used by De Laet, Van der Donck and other Dutch writers, before 1676, evidently simply means "southerners," in the sense of being south of New York, and cannot refer to the tribe known as Shawnee. The Shawnee were living in the Cumberland basin, in Tennessee, and along the Savannah (another form of Shawnee) in South Carolina. Here they were living in 1669-70 when first noticed by the English. It is possible that the Chillicothe tribe remained on the Ohio, or in the Ohio region, as the Shawnee chiefs who came northward into Pennsylvania belonged to the Piqua and Hathawekela (Assiwikale) tribes. The Shawnee which were on the Mississippi, about Fort St. Louis, were some which had been drawn there by La Salle. Joutel says, "They (the Shawnee) have been there only since they were drawn thither by M. de La Salle; formerly they lived on the borders of Virginia and the English Colonies" (Margry, III. 502). These were possibly the Shawnee who occupied the village noted on Franquelin's map. The company of Shawnee which Martin Chartier took to the mouth of the Susquehanna River in 1692 were taken from this Shawnee village near Fort St. Louis (Maryland Coun. Pro., III. 341-345, 350). This Martin Chartier was the father of Peter Chartier, who later was associated with the Shawnee on the Susquehanna and Ohio (See *Chartier's Town*). He was married to a Shawnee, as his son Peter also was (Maryland Coun. Pro., III., 458, 486, 517). The first migration of the Shawnee to Pennsylvania was in 1698, and not in 1678, as stated by Drake. They were driven from South Carolina by the English, who favored the Catawba at the expense of the Shawnee. The migration from the south commenced in the year which Drake gives as their entrance to Pennsylvania. But, the Shawnee did not go to the mouth of Pequa Creek until 1698, spending the years between on the Potomac near Old Town, Maryland, where Opessah's Town was situated. They remained on the Potomac until their migration to Pequea Creek in 1698. At the time that Opessah and 60 families removed to the Susquehanna, some of the Shawnee, of the Hathawekela tribe, removed from the Potomac to the Allegheny, where they founded several villages, known as Sewickley's Old Town (which see), under the chief of their clan, named Aqueloma. These "Asswikale" Shawnee did not go to the Susquehanna, but to the Potomac, from South Carolina, and then over the Warriors Trail to Bloody Run, and then westward through Bedford, beyond which place, near Schellsburg, they left their name in "Shawnee Cabins" (which see). Some of them lived for a time on the branches of the Conemaugh River, and then moved to Sewickley Creek, in Westmoreland County, and then to the Allegheny River, where they had a village known as Sewickley's Old Town (which see). They gradually moved on down the Ohio River to Logstown, and then later to Shawnee Town, and Lower Shawnee Town, at the mouths of the Kanhawha and Sciota. The Pequea tribe, under Wopaththa, or Opessah, removed from the Potomac to the mouth of Pequea Creek, where they settled the village known as Pequea (which see). Soon after their arrival on the Susquehanna they went to Conestoga, and requested that the Conestoga take them under

their protection. This the Conestoga did, by the permission of the Province. In 1701 the Conestoga and Shawnee appeared before William Penn, who gave them permission to settle on the Susquehanna, under the care of the Conestoga, and under the dominion of the Five Nations. This fact was distinctly stated. The Shawnee in joining with the Conestoga, who were subject to the Five Nations, made themselves subject to the Five Nations also. This fact was insisted upon at the later Indian Councils, when the Iroquois were requested to bring the Shawnee back to the Susquehanna from the Ohio. Shikellamy, the Iroquois deputy at Shamokin, and Scarouady, on the Ohio, were chiefly delegated by the Iroquois to look after all affairs relating to the Shawnee. At the Treaty of 1701, with William Penn, "Articles of Agreement," between the Conestoga and Shawnee and the Province, were drawn up. These articles were signed in the presence of James Le Fort (error, should be Le Tort), and John Hans Steelman, two traders who had been associated with the Shawnee in Maryland, and who, no doubt, had much to do with their removal to the Susquehanna (Consult; Col. Rec. II. 15-18; VI. 726 et seq.). Soon after this treaty of 1701, many Shawnee removed from South Carolina to the Susquehanna and the upper Delaware, where they established the various villages of Pechoquealin (which see). There were some Shawnee at the latter place, who had removed thither with their chief Kakowatcheky from the Ohio, under the leadership of Arnold Viele, the Dutch trader from Albany, who had visited the Shawnee on the Ohio in 1692-93. In 1727, because of various conflicts with the traders in the Province, and because of a number of crimes with which they were charged, the Shawnee commenced moving westward to the Ohio, to escape from the Iroquois, rather than because of any fear of the Province (Col. Rec. III. 302, 309, 310-330, etc.). In 1728 Kakowatchey and the Shawnee left the upper Delaware, and removed to Wyoming. Shikellamy was appealed to as the deputy of the Iroquois having charge of the Shawnee, to find out why this move had been made (Col. Rec. III. 330-31). The various troubles of the Shawnee with the English in the Province at this time were due to the unlicensed traffic in rum, concerning which they complained again and again. In 1731 Shikellamy gave the Provincial authorities to understand that friendship with the Six Nations could no longer be expected to last, unless this traffic in rum with the Delawares and Shawnee was better regulated (Col. Rec. III. 407). Many of the Shawnee from the upper Delaware and from the lower Susquehanna villages had gradually moved to Wyoming, from which place they removed to the Big Island, and then to the Ohio. Peter Chartier had taken a number westward from the village at the mouth of Yellow Breeches, and from the Conodogwinet, to the Allegheny River, where Chartier's Town was established. Others followed from Wyoming and the Big Island. In 1732, at the Council in Philadelphia, the Iroquois were urged to recall the Shawnee from the Ohio, where they were coming under French influence more and more (Col. Rec. III. 445-446). The Iroquois deputies said that it would not be kind to cause the Shawnee to remove while their corn was growing, and winter coming on, but that they would order them to remove in the following spring. The Proprietary, Thomas Penn, had a tract of land surveyed on the western side of the Susquehanna, called the Manor of Conedogwinet. Here the Shawnee, who owned no land in the Province, were invited to settle. In 1735, at the Council in Philadelphia, the Iroquois reported that they had sent a number of their chiefs to the Ohio to request the Shawnee to return to the Susquehanna. The Shawnee had listened to all of the speeches, but refused to leave the Ohio, "which they said was more commodious for them." Shortly after this conference with the Shawnee a "Tsanandowas" chief, named Sagohandechty, who lived at Allegheny, went with the other Iroquois chiefs to prevail upon the Shawnee to heed the recall to the Susquehanna. This Seneca chief pressed the Shawnee so closely that, after the other Iroquois chiefs had left, the Shawnee killed this Seneca. As a consequence the Iroquois were determined to avenge this crime. When asked what tribe had committed this crime, they replied, "the Tribe of Shawanese complained of is called Shaweygira (Hathawekela, or Assiwikale) & consist of about thirty young Men, ten old Men & several Women and Children; that it is now supposed that they have returned

from the place from whence they first came, which is below Carolina" (Col. Rec. III. 609). The French were not slow in making the most of the alienation of the Shawnee, who were not only getting away from the English influence, but also from the control of the Iroquois (Archives, I. 325, 327). In 1732 the Shawnee on the Ohio sent a message to Governor Gordon, written by James Le Tort and Peter Chartier, in which they explain the reasons which influenced them to move to the Ohio. The Iroquois had said, "you Shawanese Look back toward Ohioh, The place from whence you Came, and Return thitherward, for now wee Shall Take pitty on the English and Lett them have all this Land." Other reasons were given, among which was the fact that several slaves had run away from the south, seeking refuge among them, and they were afraid that the English would blame them for giving protection to these slaves (Archives, I. 329-330). They promised to send some chiefs to Philadelphia during the summer. Later in the spring these chiefs sent a letter to Governor Gordon, in which they complained of the sale of rum on the Ohio, and asked that permission be given them and Peter Chartier to "break in pieces all the Cags" brought into their villages (op. cit. 394-5). Again in 1738 a resolution signed by a number of the "Sheynars" (Shawnee) on the Allegheny, was sent to the Governor, in which they state that all rum brought into their towns will be spilt. This "resolution" was signed by Laypareawah, Opessah's son, and a large number of the Shawnee chiefs (op. cit. 549-553). In 1739 Kakowatcheky and twenty other Shawnee from the Ohio held a council with Governor Thomas Penn in Philadelphia. At this Council the history of the various dealings of the Province with the Shawnee, from the time of their first entering it, "about Forty years ago," when they came from "the great River that bears your Name." Articles of agreement were signed by the chiefs present, and by Thomas Penn, George Thomas and Thomas Fraeme, Jr. (Col. Rec. IV. 336-347; See also 91, 234). At the Treaty at Lancaster in 1744 there was but one Shawnee chief present. Upon an investigation being made it was discovered that the reason the Shawnee were absent, was due to the fact that they were not on good terms with the

Iroquois, who feared that in case of a war with the French that the Shawnee and the Delaware both would be on the side of the French. There is no doubt but that the growing feeling of hostility of the Shawnee towards the Iroquois, and the influence of the former over the Delawares, had as much to do with the alienation of the Delaware and Shawnee from the English interest as either the land sales, or the traffic in rum. The Shawnee had gone to the Ohio to escape the Iroquois dominion over them, and had been flattered by the French, with whom thew had always been better treated than with the English. The French realized that there was no hope in winning the friendship of the Iroquois, so they were making use of the feeling of revolt on the part of the Shawnee against the Iroquois and English. The Shawnee were seeking to draw the Delawares from Shamokin and other places on the Susquehanna to the Ohio. Conrad Weiser was at this critical period in complete power, so far as the Indian policy of the Province was concerned. Weiser had no use for either a Delaware or a Shawnee (Col. Rec. IV. 739). The land sales, the rum traffic, the Shawnee hatred of the Iroquois, the Delaware friendship for the Shawnee, Weiser favoritism for the Iroquois —all of these things were driving the Shawnee to the French alliance. In 1745 Peter Chartier left the village on the Allegheny for the Lower Shawnee Town, where he was brought directly under the influence of the French on the Mississippi. Chartier took a number of the Shawnee with him (Col. Rec. IV. 757-759). The amount of damage done by the band of Shawnee under Chartier was greatly overestimated, as was also the number of Shawnee who went with him. Shikellamy was given full power to deal with the Shawnee on the Susquehanna, and Scarouady was given the same power on the Ohio. In a short time Scarouady had won back the greater part of the Shawnee who had gone with Chartier (Col. Rec. V. 21, 300). At the Council at Lancaster in 1748, Kakowatcheky and a number of Shawnee from the Ohio (Logstown) came before the Commissioners, and in the most abject manner confessed their folly in being misled by Chartier, and asked to be forgiven. They presented the Agreement of 1739 and asked that it be signed afresh, "and all former crimes

buried and forgot." Now was the time for the Province to win these independent warriors. But, the influence of Weiser was supreme. The Commissioners refused to sign the Agreement. It was handed back to them with the statement, and telling them that it would be time enough to sign it when they had "performed that Condition" (Col. Rec., V. 311, 315-816). The English revealed in this utterly foolish refusal to sign this Agreement the lack of the very wisdom which was revealed in all of the dealings of the French with the Shawnee. Through the eyes of Conrad Weiser the Province was able to understand the Iroquois, but after the time of William Penn the Province was blind in all of its dealings with the Shawnee and Delaware. It was well, in the long run, that this folly won the Iroquois, even at the expense of the Delaware and Shawnee friendship, but it drenched Pennsylvania in blood, none the less. The Indians at the Treaty of Lancaster all received presents, save the Shawnee, who had their guns mended. They went from Lancaster, after having been humiliated before the Iroquois, back to the Ohio, to be welcomed into the arms of the French. In 1745 Conrad Weiser, when at a Council at Onondaga, learned that the Iroquois were in favor of a war against the Shawnee. In 1753 Neucheconneh, the Shawnee "King," and a number of other chiefs, were present at the Treaty at Carlisle. All of the facts bearing on the French movements on the Ohio were related at this Council, together with the various warnings which had been given the French army by the Half King and Scarouady. Three warnings had been sent them, in accordance with the Indian custom, urging them to advance no further. These warnings had all been disregarded. Now nothing remained for the Indians to do but declare war against the French. The Delaware, Shawnee and other Indians at Carlisle all renewed the League of Amity with the English (Col. Rec. V. 665-686). The army of Col. George Washington was defeated by the French force at Fort Necessity in July, 1754. At a Council held at Aughwick (which see) in August and September, 1754, at which a few Shawnee chiefs were present, Weiser discovered that the Delaware and Shawnee "are very strictly united together, and that the French made them large Presents, desiring them to stand their Friends or Neuter." The "Twightwees" (Miami) had sent a message to the Shawnee, in which they charged them with sitting still while the French invaded their country, and urging them to "take up the hatchet" against the French. To this the Shawnee replied that they had been asked by the Six Nations to sit still, and not pay any attention to the French." Because this answer had been sent by the Shawnee, without consulting the Half King (Tanachharison, who had charge of the Shawnee on the Ohio, and Scarouady, the Oneida deputy, were not very well pleased" (Col. Rec. VI. 159-160. There is no doubt but that the Delaware and Shawnee were simply waiting to see how things would turn out before they took any side in the conflict between the French and the English. After the defeat of Gen. Braddock's army, July 9, 1755, the Delaware and Shawnee went over bodily to the French side, throwing away the "skirts of women" and declaring their independence from the Iroquois. Many of the Delaware on the Susquehanna remained faithful to the English, but the great majority of the tribe together with the Shawnee took up the hatchet against the Province and the English. Pennsylvania had to pay dearly for the short-sighted policy which had alienated the friendly Delawares and the warlike Shawnee. During 1755, 1756 and 1757 the entire frontier was drenched with the blood of the white settlers. The great majority of the hostile Indians were Delaware, Shawnee and Seneca, who had moved to the villages on the Ohio. The Half King, Tanachharison, and Scarouady remained faithful to the English. The former had died in 1754, soon after Washington's defeat. He was succeeded by Scarouady, who always remained true to the English. He even favored the Declaration of War which was made against the Delawares in April, 1756 (Col. Rec. VI. 771-772). During the entire period of Indian hostility from the time of the French and Indian War, until after the Revolution, the Shawnee, as a body, were hostile to the English and then to the American cause. The many expeditions into the "Indian country" beyond the Ohio, during the period of the Revolution, were chiefly against the Shawnee and Delaware. In Dun-

more's War various expeditions were sent into the region along the Ohio. These expeditions terminated with that of Gen. Anthony Wayne's expedition of 1795, which was followed by the Treaty of Greenville, which put an end to the long war in the Northwest Territory. The history of the Shawnee, after their reunion in Ohio, about 1750, belongs to the history of Ohio, rather than to Pennsylvania. (For a history of these various expeditions, consult; Hassler, Old Westmoreland; DeSchweinitz, Life and Times of David Zeisberger; Heckewelder, Narrative; Border Life; Doddridges, Notes; and all of the general histories dealing with the expeditions of Clark, Lewis, Brodhead, Bouquet, Wayne, etc.; Parkman, Conspiracy of Pontiac; Hanna, Wilderness Trail; the various publications of the Ohio Valley Historical Society, etc.). In 1869 the Shawnee became incorporated with the Cherokee, with whose history they have always been associated, in Oklahoma, where the great majority of them are now living. The Shawnee have produced some of the strongest characters in Indian history. Among these may be mentioned Cornstalk and Tecumseh. The history of the various Shawnee villages in Pennsylvania will be found under the title of the various villages. See *Conedogwinet, Chartier's Town, Logstown, Paxtang, Pequea, Old Town, Sewickley,* etc. For a complete list of synonyms, see Handbook of American Indians, II. 537-538.

SHAWNEE CABINS. A prominent land mark of the Ray's Town Half, between Bedford and Pittsburgh, situated about 8 miles west of Bedford and about half a mile east of Schellsburg, Bedford County. It was probably a temporary stopping place of the Shawnee as they migrated from the Potomac, by way of the Warriors Path and the Ray's Town Path, to the Ohio in the early part of the XVIII Century. These Shawnee came directly from the Potomac, about Old Town, Md., to which place they had gone from South Carolina. The letter of the two traders. Callendar and Taffe, dated, "September 28th. 1753, Shawonese Cabbins," was probably written at this place (Col. Rec. V. 684). The place is mentioned in John Harris' Table of Distances, in 1754, "to the Shawana Cabbins—8 miles" (from Ray's Town, or Bedford)

(Archives, II. 135). Patten and Montour, in the same year, give the distance, "From Ray's Town to the Shawonese Cabbin—8 Miles" (Col. Rec. V. 750). It is also noted on Scull's map of 1759. There was another Shawnee Cabin on the south branch of Two Lick Creek, in Indiana County, about one mile south of Cookport. This place is mentioned by Conrad Weiser, in 1748, when he was on his way to Logstown, — "Came to Shawonese Cabbins, 34 Miles" (Col. Rec. V. 348). It is also mentioned by John Harris, in 1754, as one of the points on the Frankstown Path,——"to the Shawana Cabbins,—12 Miles" (Archives, II. 136). The former place is also noted on Scull's map of 1770, and on Hutchins map of 1764. This place was evidently occupied for some time, as there was a point on the Shawnee Run, near Schellsburg, where flint arrow heads were made. Great quantities of these are found along the run at this place. The author has quite a number of them. They are very roughly made. The site is similar to that of many of the Shawnee village sites. Beautiful, rolling, but level land.

SHAWNEE FLATS. The name given to the broad valley along the Susquehanna River below Wyoming (now Wilkes-Barre), on both sides of the river. The name as first used was applied to the region on the western side of the river, at the present Plymouth, Luzerne County, but was later applied to the entire flats of the Wyoming Valley (See *Wyoming*). In 1728 Kakowatcheky, the Shawnee chief at Pechoquealin, in the Minisinks, removed with his followers to the site of Plymouth, leaving their corn standing in their deserted village (Col. Rec. III. 309, 330, 506). This chief had probably gone to the Delaware with Arnold Viele, from the Ohio, in 1694. He remained at Wyoming, as the entire valley was called, until 1743, when he and a number of his followers went to Logstown on the Ohio. He was succeeded by the Shawnee chief Paxinosa, who removed from Paxtang to Wyoming soon after the departure of Kakowatcheky. In 1756 the friendly Delaware removed from Wyoming to Tioga, and were soon followed by Paxinosa and the Shawnee. These lived at various places along the river until about 1759, when Paxinosa removed to the Ohio, to which many

of the Shawnee had been going since 1728. Conrad Weiser stopped at Wyoming on his return from Onondaga in 1737. At that time the settlement consisted of Shawnee and Mahickon. Count Zinzendorf visited the Shawnee at the site of Plymouth in 1742, in the hope of establishing a mission among them (Mem. Mor. Church, I. 69, 103, 105, 113, 137, 355; Loskiel, Hist. Miss., II. 32, 80, 181). The Manor at Sunbury, surveyed in 1768, included all of the lands on the western side of the river along the Wyoming Valley. The site of the "Old Shawanese T," and the path to Shamokin are noted on this survey map, as is also the site of Wyoming, on the eastern side of the river. The Manor of Stoke, along the eastern side of the river notes the site of Wyoming and also the Old Nanticoke Town (Archives, Third Ser., IV., maps Nos. 60 and 67). The Tract, called Abraham's Plains, which joined the Manor of Sunbury, notes the island in the Susquehanna, called "Manaughanung" (op. cit., map No. 77). The various Indians occupying the beautiful Wyoming Valley had always demanded that Wyoming be kept as a perpetual reserve, which the Indians would never sell, and which the whites should never buy (See *Wyoming*). They had been driven to this place of refuge from the lower Susquehanna and from the Delaware, by the various land sales. The occupation of the Valley by the settlers from Connecticut, led to the final stroke for the possession of the "vales of Wyoming," in what has been called the "Massacre of Wyoming." (For the various forts erected in this region for the protection of these settlers, Consult ; Frontier Forts, I. 423 et seq.). Shawnee Flats are frequently mentioned in the Journals of Sullivan's expedition of 1779. In the Journal of Lieut. S. M. Shute, he says, in a foot-note, "Shawney flatts is situate on Susquehanna about four miles from Wyoming contains about 500 acres of. exceeding good land, and the best bottom in the world & only wants a little cultivation to make it the best land in this part—It was but lately inhabited by New England people, they were all killed about a year ago. There is now a family of Yankeys whose names are as follows—mens— Almarin & Lloyd—Females Artemisia, Dustimona, Alethica, Sereptica all belonging to the tribe of Gad & the household of Mary" (Jour. Sull. Exped., 268). Whatever family the writer means, it is most certain that they belonged to the same tribe of Classical New Englanders, who have left a trail of Classic names, in place of the Indian names, from Athens to Ithaca. The various forms of the name as used in these Journals are of little value. They are simply attempts to spell Shawnee (Shawney, 182; Shawny, 122; Schawne, 83). Evans map of 1749 places "Wioming" on the west side of the river, at the site of Plymouth, as does also his map of 1755. Scull's map of 1759 places "Wioming," on the eastern side of the river, near the present Wilkes-Barre. Scull's map of 1770 places Wyoming at the same site, and "Old Shawanese Town," near "Shawanese Lake"—Harvey's Lake. The Morris map of 1848, notes Shawney Town, at the site of Plymouth, and Old Wyoming, just below Wilkes-Barre.

SHAVER'S SLEEPING PLACE. A point on the Frankstown Path, mentioned by Harris in 1754; situated about half a mile above the mouth of Ramsey's Run, in Indiana County, about 12 miles from Indiana. Archives, II. 136.

SHEHAWKEN. The name of a village in Wayne County; also the name of a creek, in the same county; also the name of a pond, or small lake. The name of the village has the form given. The present state map gives the form Chehocton, as that of the creek, and the lake is called Chehocton Pond. Heckewelder gives the form Shohokin, as a corruption of Schohacan, "glue," and Schohacanink, "where glue is made." This derivation does not seem satisfactory. The name seems to be a compound of some word with hacki, "land," but it is difficult to tell just what word was prefixed.
Chehocton.—State map, 1911. Chehocton Pond.—State map, 1912. Shehawken.— (present P. O.) Map, 1912. Shehocking. —(creek) Howell, map, 1792. Shohokin. —(creek) Morris, map, 1848.

SHELOCTA. The name of a town in Indiana County. The name has the form Shalocta upon the Morris map, 1848. It is possible that the name is a short corruption of Schachgeu, "straight," with some compound, which has disappeared. The name of the present Plum Creek, as recorded on the early maps, was Plumb Creek. This creek enters Crooked Creek, and there is little doubt but that the name Plumb, was a translation of the early Indian name, meaning straight. Heckewelder

gives the name Sipuas-hanne, "plum stream," for this creek. The Scull map (1770), and Howell's map (1792), and the Morris map (1848) all give the name as Plumb Creek, which was no doubt the true name, and not Plum Creek, as given on later maps. Near the mouth of this creek, near Shelocta, James LeTort had a trading house, which was near the forks of the Frankstown Path to Kittanning and Chartier's Town. This is mentioned in some of the early records of Indiana County as James Le Tort's (or Litart's) Town. This was also the site which is noted on Scull's map (1770) as "Tohogases Cabbins" (not Town, as stated by Mr. Hanna). Tohogases, or Tohoguses, is a corruption of Ontwaganha, the Iroquois term, which has the derived significance of "alien." It was used by the Iroquois in speaking of the Algonkian tribes, and was frequently applied to the Shawnee. The name therefore, is simply the Iroquois name for "Shawnee Cabins." This may have been the point mentioned in some of the early journals. There were, however, several places in the region about Shelocta, where the Shawnee had cabins, or temporary dwelling places. Because of its situation near the forking of the two trails, the trading house at the mouth of Plum, or Plumb, Creek, was probably well patronized.

SHENANDOAH. A town in Schuylkill County, given to the place by some lover of Indian names. It does not belong to this state, but is derived from the name of the river in Virginia. Heckewelder gives this name as a corruption from Schindhandowi, "the sprucy stream." It is more probably a corruption of Scahhentowanen, "it is a very great plain." This name was applied to the Wyoming Valley, by the Iroquois. It was corrupted to Skehandowana, Tsanandowana etc., by various writers. The name was, no doubt, first applied to the valley, now known as the Shenandoah Valley. See *Wyoming*.

SHENANGO. The name of a Township and town in Mercer County; also the name of a branch of the Beaver River; also the name of a former Indian village on the Shenango River. Also, with the form Chenango, the name of a river which enters the Susquehanna from the north at Binghampton, New York; also, with the same form of the name, a former Indian village about 4 miles from the mouth of this stream. The name was also used in various other places, under various forms. The name is a corruption of Ochenango, "large bull thistles." This name as applied to Logstown, was simply a corruption of the French name Chiningue or Chininque, which was given the place by Bonnecamp and Celoron de Bienville, in 1749, because it was near the Beaver River. It will be necessary to notice the two chief locations wnown by the name, separately. First: the CHENANGO on the north Branch of the Susquehanna. This village was situated on Chenango River, near Binghampton, New York. A later village, of the same name was up the Chenango River, about 4 miles. The village of Ossewingo, noted on Evans map of 1749, was also at the mouth of this creek, south, or west, of Chenango. The statement made in the Journal of Thompson and Post, 1758, that Chenango was "about half way between Owegey anl Ossewingo," is evidently an error. No map so shows the site of Ossewingo, save at the mouth of Chenango River. The only possible way to place Chenango midway between these places would be to place Chenango at the mouth of Nanticoke Creek, near the present Union. This was the site of a later Indian village, and it may possibly have been the site of Chenango, but it is more probable that Chenango was at the mouth of Chenango River, and then later about 4 miles up this creek, or river. Osewingo (Evans, 1749) is shown as being at the mouth of Chenango, on the west bank. His map of 1755 also notes it at this place. Scull's map of 1770 places "Chenango T." a few miles up the Chenango, on the east bank, while Chugnutt, or Choconut, is directly opposite the mouth of the Chenango, nearly opposite Binghampton, instead of at the site of Vestal, where it is commonly placed. It is possible that Ossewingo was the name of a much older village, than Chenango. The Conoy and Nanticoke were formerly at the mouth of the Juniata, where they had a Council Fire. They removed to Wyoming about 1750, where they lived in the Nanticoke Town. From here they removed to Chenango in about 1753-55, where they established the village of Chenango, which figures in the history of the Indian affairs until its final destruction in 1779. According to various statements made by the Conoy and Nanticoke chiefs, at various Councils

(See *Nanticoke*), Chenango was the "Door of the Six Nations." All of the official belts of wampum, messages and messengers from the south, had to pass through Chenango, in order to reach Onondaga. This was the chief Nanticoke village of 1758. There were then about 50 fighting men in the tribe, most of whom lived at Chenango (Archives, III. 421). During the period of hostility from 1755 to 1758 various Councils were held at Chenango between the Six Nations and the various subject tribes, and various Conoy and Nanticoke chiefs from this settlement visited Philadelphia and Shamokin. Among these were Robert White and Last Night. Seneca George, the prominent messenger anl interpreter, lived in this village during a part of this period (See *Conoy, Nanticoke;* Col. Rec., VII. 66, 107, 139, 223, 382, 435, 486). In 1757 Chenango was perhaps the most important Inlian settlement on the Susquehanna, not excepting Wyoming. Here all of the important matters relating to the attempts to win back the Delaware and Shawnee were discussed, and here these hostile warriors promised to "lay down the hatchet" (Col. Rec. VII. 538, 628). At the Council at Philadelphia, John Curtis, a Nanticoke, brought messages from the Conoy, Nanticoke, Onondaga and Mahickon at Chenango (Col. Rec. IX. 46). During the Revolution the village was a center of hostile Indians, who gradually moved northward into the Iroquois country in New York. In 1779, when Major Parr's detachment went up the river to destroy the village they found it deserted and burned. It was then situated 4 miles up the Chenango River, and had consisted of 20 houses, which had been deserted the year before. This was evidently a later village than the one first settled by the Nanticokes, hence —the confusion in various accounts concerning the situation of Chenango. Rev. David Craft, and others, make the statement, "Many have incorrectly located this town at Binghampton" Jour. Sull. Exped., 354). The village destroyed, and visited by Sullivan's army, was not at Binghampton, but at the site 4 miles above, but the early Nanticoke and Conoy settlement, known as Chenango was at the mouth of the Chenango River. The village of Ossewingo is included with Chenango, simply because its situation is given at the mouth of the Chenango River.

Osewingo.—Evans, maps, 1749, 1755. Ossewingo. — Thompson (1758), Archives, III. 413.

The following are the forms recorded of the name of the village on Chenango River: **Chenango.**—Coun. at Phil. (1760), Col. Rec., VIII. 484. **Cheningo.**—Letter (1757), in Col. Rec., VII. 763. **Chewango.** —Adlum, map, 1790. **Chinango.**— Beatty (1779), Jour. Sull. Exped., 24. **Oksiningo.**—Wraxall (1758), Col. Rec., VIII. 154. **Otsanango.**— Denny (1756), Col. Rec., VII. 223. **Otsaningo.**—Pa. Coun. (1756), Col. Rec., VII, 107. **Otseningo.**—Hartley (1756), Col. Rec., VII. 100. **Otsineange.**—Coun. at Phil. (1756), Col. Rec., VII. 66. **Otsiningo.** —Pa. Coun. (1756), Col. Rec., VII. 107. **Otsininky.**—Weiser (1756), Col. Rec., VII. 139. **Schemanga.**—Post (1760), Archives, III. 708. **Shanango.**—Coun. at Ft. Aug (1769), Col. Rec. IX. 611. **Shenengo.**—Van Hovenburgh (1779). Jour. Sull. Exped., 278. **Ziningo.**— Loskiel, in Hist. Missions, 1794, III. 16.

SHENANGO. The river in western Pennsylvania, unites with the Mahoning, just below New Castle, Lawrence County, to form the Beaver River. Various trails ran along and across the Shenango Valley, from the Salt Springs on the Mahoning, near Niles, Ohio, to the Indian village of Shenango, and then on up the valley to Pymatuning. A branch of this trail ran eastward to Venango, where it joined the trails to the Allegheny and Ohio villages. A trail ran down the Shenango Valley to Kuskuski, where it was joined by the trail up the Mahoning Valley, and then went down the Beaver River to Shingas' Town, where it joined the trails to Logstown, up the Ohio, and the Great Trail westward to the Muskingum. The Indian village of Shenango was situated about 20 miles above the mouth of the Mahoning, which distance would place it just below Sharon, possibly on the broad valley at the present South Sharon, Mercer County. The trail from the Mahoning, near Niles, reached the Shenango River at this point. The Venango Path left this trail 6 miles above this village, while the main trail ran on up the river to Pymatuning, and then across by the upper end of Sandy Lake to Venango. This region, south of Lake Erie, was probably once occupied by the Erie, who were destroyed by the Iroquois in 1656. From that time until the occupation of the Ohio valley by the Delaware and Shawnee, which commenced about 1727, the entire region south of Lake Erie, was an uninhabited wilderness, filled with great droves of wolves, which had increased in great numbers. The various villages along the Beaver and Shenango, were peopled chiefly by Delawares. (See *Kuskuski, Pymatuning, Shingas' Town, Venango*, etc.).

John McCullough, who was captured by the Indians in the Cumberland Valley in 1756, was taken to Presqu Isle, then to LeBoeuf, and then to Shenango. Here he remained for two years and a half, and then removed to the Salt Springs on the Mahoning, near Niles. While he was at Shenango a number of Iroquois warriors came to the village, on their return from a raid into the settlements. They had a number of scalps, and a prisoner, a young man of about twenty-five years of age. These warriors were on their way to Presqu' Isle (Erie), beyond which place they lived (McCullough's Narrative, Border Life, 97, 1839). Marie Le Roy states in her Narrative that when the French and Indians were defeated at Ligonier (1758) that all of the Indions took their wives and children from all of these villages in the Beaver and Shenango region, to the Muskingum (Archives, Sec. Ser., VII. 406).

Schomingo.—LeRoy (1759), Archives, Sec. Ser., VII. 406. **Shaningo.**—Hutchins, map, 1764. **Shaningo's T.**—Evans, map, 1755. **Shenango.**—Exam. of Indians (1757), Col. Rec., VII. 531. (May refer to Logstown.) **Shenanggo.**—McCullough's Nar., in Border Life, 94, 1839. **Shenang-go.**—McCullough's Nar., in Border Life, 95, 1839.

SHEOQUAGA. Commonly called Catharine's Town, or French Catharine's Town. It was situated a short distance south of Havana, New York, about three miles from the head of Seneca Lake. It was the residence of Catharine Montour, a daughter of French Margaret (which see), and a grand-daughter of Madame Montour. Her husband's name was Telenemut, or Thomas Hudson, a Seneca chief. The village was destroyed by Sullivan's army, Sept. 1, 1779. The village then consisted of 30 or 40 houses, well built. The name She-o-qua-ga, is said to mean "falling water," or "tumbling water." The village is mentioned in nearly all of the Journals of Sullivan's Expedition. Only the forms of the Indian name of the village are given, in this note. For the other forms, which are simply various spellings of French Catharine, see the work cited.

Cheoquoc.—Jenkins (1779), Jour. Sull. Exped., 173. **Queauchguaga.**—McNeill (1779), Archives, Sec. Ser., XV. 756.

Shequaga.—Jenkins (1779), Jour. Sull. Exped. 176. **She-o-qua-ga.**—Clark, in Jour. Sull. Exped. 129. **Shughquago.**—Shute, in Jour. Sull. Exped. 271.

SHESHEQUIN. A former Indian village, on the west shore of the Susquehanna, at the site of Ulster, Bradford County, about 6 miles below Tioga Point. The name is a corruption of Sheshekwan, "a gourd rattle," and with the locative ink, or ing, "at the place of the gourd rattle." This rattle was used in the ceremonies of the pagan Indians. Loskiel says in his History of the mission at this place, "About half a mile from Tschechschequannink the savages used at stated times to keep their feasts of sacrifice." He then goes on to tell of the noise which was made at these feasts. These feasts, and the use of the ceremonial gourd rattle, probably gave the place its name (Loskiel, Hist. Miss. III. 37). The settlement was divided by Cash's Creek. The northern part was occupied by the pagan, and the southern part by the Christian Indians. Queen Esther lived at this place until about 1772, when she removed to Queen Esther's Town, just below Tioga Point. Her village there was destroyed by Col. Hartley in the fall of 1778. The Moravian mission at this village was established by John Roth February 4, 1769 (Loskiel, III. 36). In 1771 all of the inhabitants of the settlement were obliged to abandon it for several days, owing to a great flood in the Susquehanna (op. cit. III. 67). In 1772 the Moravians were invited to remove to the Beaver River. They left Sheshequin June 11, 1772, going in two parties, one of which led by John Ettwein, going by land, and the other, led by John Roth, going by water to the Big Island (Lock Haven), where they then took the trail overland to the Allegheny River (See Shamokin Path). This party consisted of 204 persons, 151 of whom were from Wyalusing and 53 from Sheshequin. Among the latter were two sons and a nephew of Tedyuskung, the Delaware "King" (DeSchweinitz, Life of Zeis., 377). In 1778 Col. Hartley, whose army gathered at Fort Muncy, went by way of the Sheshequin Path to this settlement, which he destroyed, together with Queen Esther's Town and Tioga (Archives VI. 773; VII. 5-6). The next year, 1779, the army of Gen. Sullivan encamped on the 9 and 10 of August, at Sheshequin Flats, opposite Ulster. Part of the army forded the Susque-

hanna the next day to the west shore, near Ulster, but the main body of the army forded the river at Milan, and again crossed the river to Tioga Point, after passing through Esther's Town. The flats along the river on both sides were called Sheshequin Flats. The name is perpetuated in Sheshequin, Bradford county.

Schechschiquanunk. — DeSchweinitz, in Life of Zeis., 712. **Shackanack.**—Gookin (1779), Jour. Sull. Exped., 104. **Shekenunk.**—Grant (1779), Jour. Sull. Exped., 138. **Shesheck.**—Blake (1779), Jour. Sull. Exped., 39. **Sheshecunuuk.**—Elmer (1779), Jour. Sull. Exped., 84. **Sheshehung.**—Hardenburgh (1779), Jour. Sull. Exped., 124. **Sheshekonunk.**—Dearborn (1779), Jour. Sull. Exped., 69. **Sheshequannunk.** — Campfield (1779), Jour. Sull. Exped., 54. **Sheshekonuck.** Norris (1779), Jour. Sull. Exped., 229.

The above are a few of the forms in the Journals of Sullivan's expedition. **Sheshecununk.**—Hartley (1778), Archives, VII. 6. **Shesheken Flats.**—Howells, map, 1792. **Sheshequon.**—Heckewelder, in Narrative, 106 **Shesiken.**—Hunter (1778), Archives, VI. 773. **Tschechschequannunk.**—Loskiel, in Hist. Miss., III. 36.

The Sheshequin Path ran up Muncy Creek, and then across to the Towanda, and down it to the flats. Another path ran up Lycoming Creek to its head and then across to the headwaters of Towanda, and down it to the Susquehanna. There were other branches of these trails connecting the Susquehanna and the West Branch Valley.

SHICKSHINNY. The name of a creek which enters the Susquehanna from the north at Shickshinny, Luzerne County; also the name of the mountain range along the Susquehanna at this place. The mountain is noted on Howells map, 1792, as "Fishing Creek Knob." On the Morris map, 1848, both the creek and the mountain are called "Shickshinny." The name is said to mean "five mountains" but there is no authority whatever for this meaning. The name may be a corruption of Schigi-hanna, "fine stream." **Shecsheny.**—Adlum, map, 1790. **Shickshinny.**—Morris, map, 1848. **Shicsheny.**—Howells, map, 1792.

SHIKELLAMY'S TOWN. This place of residence of Shikellamy, the Oneida chief, was situated about a mile below Milton, Northumberland County, on the West Branch, opposite the mouth of Sinking Run, or Shikellamy's Run, as it was formerly called. This chief lived here before his appointment as the representative of the Six Nations, in 1728. After that time his headquarters were at Shamokin. He may have lived at this place until 1745, when he was appointed vicegerent of the Six Nations. He then lived at Shamokin until his death, Dec. 17, 1748. Shikellamy could not have spent much of his time at this village, as from 1728 until his death he was constantly at Shamokin. See *Shamokin*.

SHINGAS' OLD TOWN. A former Delaware, Shawnee and Mingo (Iroquois of various tribes) village at the site of the present Beaver. The village was situated about one mile below the mouth of the Beaver River, on the high bluff above the Ohio River. This settlement was known by various names, Sawcunk, Shingas' Town and Beaver's Town. The first mentioned may have been first situated at the site of West Bridgewater, but it evidently was later the name used of the village known as Shingas' Town, as both names are used of the same place. Weiser says in his Journal of 1748, "I went to Beaver Creek, an Indian Town about 8 Miles off (from Logstown) chiefly Delawares, the rest Mohocks, to have some Belts of Wampum made. * * * * We both (himself and Montour) lodged at this Town at George Croghan's Trading House" (Col. Sec. V. 349). On account of its situation, on the trails down the Ohio to the Muskingum, and up the Beaver to Kuskuski and the Mahoning Valley, this village soon became one of the most important trading points in western Pennsylvania, and continued to be so until the capture of Fort Duquesne by the British in 1758. At that time it was for a time deserted. Christopher Gist, in 1750, travelled from Logstown to the mouth of Beaver River, where he met Barney Curran, the trader who was with Washington on his mission to the French forts in 1753. Gist and Curran went on to Ohio. They evidently did not pass through the village situated on the bluff, but kept along the bottom, after crossing the Beaver River, taking a northwest course to New Lisbon, Ohio (Dar. Gist, Jour., 35). Shingas was not living at this place in 1753, when Washington passed down the Ohio to Logstown, but at the mouth of Chartier's Creek, or on the northern shore of the Ohio opposite the present McKees Rocks (Dar. Gist., 81). "King" Beaver (Tamaque) and Shingas (Shingask, "a bog, or swamp") were brothers, and leading chiefs of the

Turkey (Unalachtigo) tribe of Delawares. Neither of them could have been leading chiefs of the Delaware Nation, as only a Turtle (Unami) chief could ever be "King." This was a custom which the Delawares never broke. Tammany, Tedyuskung, Netawatwes, Gelelemend, all of the "Kings" of the Delawares belonged to the Turtle tribe. Beaver, and then Shingas were head chiefs of the Turkey tribe, only as such does the title "King" apply. These two chiefs were of a wandering nature, as they had residences at Kittanning, Kuskuski, and later on the Tuscarawas. In 1756 Governer Morris mentions "Shingas' Town, called Kittanning" (Col. Rec. VII. 98). In 1758, when C. F. Post was at Kuskuski, he was entertained by "King Beaver" at his house in that place (Archives, III. 525). Shingas was present at the Treaty at Carlisle in 1753 (Col. Rec. V. 685), but Beaver was not there. Pisquitomen, another brother, who later was with Post, was present. In 1754 when Croghan was at Logstown, Shingas said, "It is true that I live here on the River Side, which is the French Road" (op. cit. 735). The Beaver was present at Aughwick in 1754, when Weiser held a conference with the Indians, after Washington's defeat at Fort Necessity. Beaver made a speech to the Six Nations, in which he said that, "I still remember the Time when You first conquered Us and made Women of Us" (Col. Rec. VI. 156). After Braddock's defeat, July 9, 1755, both Shingas and Beaver sided with the French. The former became the leader of many of the raids into the frontier settlements. His name became dreaded in every log cabin along the mountains west of the Cumberland Valley. Shingas and Captain Jacobs were two of the most bitter foes of the English during this entire period of hostility. Many of the Indian captives, later returned to Col. Bouquet, were taken at this time by Shingas and Jacobs in the Big and Little Coves, along Shearman's Creek, and various other places (Col. Rec. VI. 643, 675). During this period of bitter hostility both Beaver and Shingas lived at Kittanning, which was the chief gathering place for the hostile Indians. After the destruction of this village by Col. Armstrong in 1756, Beaver, Shingas and other hostile Delawares moved to the Muskingum. This was probably the time of the settlement of Beaver's Town, at Tuscarawas Beaver was not as active in his hostility as was his brother, and he was not in favor of taking up the hatchet against the English (Col. Rec. VI. 781; VII. 230, 242, 381). In 1758 both Shingas and Beaver were living at Kuskuski, where C. F. Post was entertained in the house of the former. During this visit of Post at Kuskuski, he went to "Saconk," where he was very unwelcome. The two hostile Delaware chiefs talked with Post concerning the reasons why the Indians had taken up the hatchet against the English. These Red Men were not as unreasonable in their attitude, as has often been pictured. They said to Post, "Why dont you and the French fight in the old country, and on the sea? Why do you come to fight on our land? This makes everybody believe that you only want to take and settle the Land." Post gave these chiefs to understand that the English were not after the land, and urged them to return to the friendship with the English. Shingas was afraid that after he had killed so many English, that he would be hanged, as a price had been set on his head. Post won these hostile warriors to the English interest, and in so doing made the desertion of Fort Duquesne by the French a foregone conclusion. The Indians were made to believe that when the British had driven the French from the Ohio, that the former would go back over the mountains, leaving the Indians in possession of the Ohio. When they discovered that the British intended to stay, the hostility of the so-called Conspiracy of Pontiac followed. This "conspiracy" was simply an attempt to force the British from the region which the Indians believed had been taken from them by a fraud (Archives, III. 520-544). The Ohio Indians were informed at a Council at Philadelphia, in reply to the question which they had asked, "What is the Reason that you did not return to your Own Country from Pittsburgh, as the Commanding officer there had, at your request, related what had passed between the English and the Delawares, and between the Six Nations Deputies and the Indians at Kushkuski, and the other Town on Beaver Creek?" "The General (Forbes) knows the French have told the Indians that the English intend to cheat them of the Land on the Ohio, and settle it for themselves, but this he assures you is false. The English have no intention to make Settlements in your Hunting Country be-

yond the Allegheny Hills, unless they shall be desired for your Conveniency to Erect Store Houses, in order to establish and carry on a trade which they are ready to do on fair and just terms" (Col. Rec. VIII. 265-269). When the Indians discovered that the English had no intention whatever of leaving the Ohio, as Forbes promised them, they arose in a "conspiracy" to drive the English out. The chief cause of the Indian hostility in western Pennsylvania during the "Conspiracy of Pontiac" was due to this fact. The Indians had left their alliance with the French, on the understanding that the British would drive them out and leave the Ohio to the Indians. They discovered that this promise, like every other promise ever made to an Indian, down to the present moment, concerning their lands, was of no value whatever. Had the Delaware and Shawnee remained at Fort Duquesne, General Forbes would likely have met the same fate as did General Braddock. At the time of the expedition of General Forbes there may have been no intention of the British to occupy the Ohio, permanently. That was what the Indians were given to understand, both by Post and by General Forbes himself. If that was not what the Indians were given to understand, then language has no meaning whatever. The letters which General Forbes sent by C. F. Post, as well as the letter which was written by Lieut. James Grant, by the order of General Forbes, can have no other construction than that placed upon them by the Indians. While it is frequently stated that the Indians moved from the mouth of the Beaver just after the British occupation of Fort Duquesne, this is not true. Col. Mercer stated in a letter to Richard Peters, March 1, 1759, "The Delawares at the Mouth of Beaver Creek intend to move to Kuskusky, they pretend, at our request; but rather in my Opinion, thro' Diffidence of us, or to get out of the Way of Blows, if any are going, for depend upon it they are desirous of fighting neither on the side of the English nor French, but would gladly see both dislodged from this Place" (Col. Rec. VIII. 305). Col. Mercer was correct. Why should the Indians desire either the French or the English to remain on the Ohio? They realized fully that the fight was between France and Great Britain for the possession of the Ohio, and that all of the protestations of the benevolent schemes of the British were mere "hot air." The great trouble was that the Indians were not so foolish as the British authorities seemed to imagine. Their voice was the voice of Jacob, but their hand was the hand of Esau. They said that they did not want the lands on the Ohio, but in the meanwhile they went on building a fort, in order to hold it. The great trouble in the English, and American, method of dealing with the Indian was due to this constant misjudgement of the Indian's ability to see through flimsy excuses. The Indian was a diplomat by nature. All of his methods of hunting and fighting were based on his ability to deceive. Deception was an art, and yet the British officers and the Colonial authorities imagined that they could beat the Indian at a game, in which he was an expert, and they mere bunglers. The Indian was never deceived, in the sense in which an ignorant child is deceived. They saw through every scheme, but had to pretend they did not, in order that they might get what little they could get out of the wreck.

The Indians on the Ohio had supreme faith in Christian Post, and Post, no doubt believed the messages which he delivered from the Province and General Forbes. Consequently they remained away from Fort Duquesne, and the French army, forsaken by their only hope, deserted the post, and left the Ohio forever. But, the Indian owed a debt to the English, which he paid, with interest, in 1763 and again in 1778-79. In 1759 the Delawares at Shingas' Town, or Sawcunk, stated that they were anxious to remove from the place to Kuskuski, in order that they might keep the promise made to General Forbes. Col. Mercer explained that Forbes mentioned "your sitting down & Smoking your Pipe at Kuskusky, because he had heard of no other Great Delaware Town. Your Brothers, the English, desire to see you live in Peace and Happiness, either at Sacunk, Kuskusky, or wherever you think proper, and by no means intend to Limit you to one Place or another" (Col. Rec. VIII. 309). In the summer of 1759 a Council was held at Fort Pitt, at which both Beaver and Shingas were present, when they delivered a number of the captives which they had taken (op. cit. 383 et seq.). In 1762 both of these chiefs wrote a letter to Governor Hamilton, in which they stated that they were anxious for peace (op. cit. 676). All the while the forces of the Indian in the wilds of Pennsylvania, and along the great lakes, and in the depths of the Ohio forests, were gathering, as silently as spirits, for the great struggle against the white invaders of the Red Man's country. This storm broke in the year of 1763, in what is called "Pontiac's Conspiracy." After the defeat of the Indians at Bushy Run, in Aug. 1763, the Indians deserted the villages along the upper Ohio, and retreated to the Muskingum. It was at this time that Shingas' Town, or Sawcunk, was finally deserted by the Delaware, Shawnee and Mingo, who had lived there. Beaver and Shingas both retreated to the Tuscarawas. They were with C. F. Post, in 1762, when he was leading the Indian captives to Carlisle, from the Tuscarawas (Archives IV. 92 et seq.). After Bouquet's expedition to the Muskingum in 1764, the Beaver entered into a half-hearted peace with the English. He died about 1770, a zealous Moravian convert. When Bouquet's expedition passed through Sawcunk in 1764, the chimneys of the log houses which the French had built for the Indians, were still standing. Hutchins the engineer of the expedition, says that this village was deserted by the Indians in 1758, which is not correct, as has been noted. It was not deserted until after the battle of Bushy Run, in 1763. During the Indian hostility of 1778-79, Fort McIntosh was built on the site of this former Indian settlement. This fort was built in Sep. 1778, by General Lachlin McIntosh, Commander of the Western Department (Consult; Frontier Forts, II. 485 et seq.; Old Westmoreland, 60-79). The various names of the Indian village at this place were, Sawcunk, Beaver's Town and Shingas' Town. Sawcunk is a corruption of Sakunk, "at the mouth." of a stream; Beaver, a translation of Amochk, or T'amochk, which was corrupted to Tamaque, "beaver," or "the Beaver"; Shingas, or Shingiss, a corruption of Shingask, "a bog," or "swamp." Heckewelder says that the Beaver River was called Amochk-hanne, or Amochk-sipu, "b e a v e r-stream," or "beaver river," but that the Indians called it Kaskaskie-sipu, from the prominent town of Kuskuski, or Kaskaskie, at its head (See *Beaver*, *Kuskuski*). A few of the synonyms of these various names follow;

Beaver Creek.—Weiser (1748), Col. Rec.,
V. 349. **Ksack-hoong.**—McCullough,
Nar. (1759) in Border Life, 101, 1839.
Saccung.—Post (1758), quoted by Proud,
Penn. II., app. 124, 1798. **Sackum.**—
LeRoy (1759), Archives, Sec. Ser., VII.
406. **Sackung.**—Post (1758), Archives,
III. 533. **Saconk.**—Post (1758), Ar-
chives,, III. 527. **Sacunk.**—Post (1758),
Archives, III. 533. **Sakonk.**—Post
(1758), Archives, III. 533. **Sawcung.**—
Post (1758), Early West. Trav. I. 251.
Sawkunc.—Post (1759), Archives, III.
581. **Soh-kon.**—Darlington, in Gist's
Jour., 106. **Shingas Old Town.**—Pur-
chase of 1784, Archives, XI. 508.
Shingoes T.—Evans, map, 1755. **Fort
McIntosh.**—Howell's, map, 1792.

SHOHOLA. A creek which enters
the Delaware from the west, at Shohola, Pike County; also the name of
a village, township and falls, in the
same county. Heckewelder gives this
as a corruption of Schauwihilla,
"weak." An old Indian trail, from
the Minisinks, near Milford, to Wyoming, crossed this creek, a few miles
beyond Lord's Valley P. O., where it
was joined by a trail from the Delaware Water Gap, going westward to
the Lackawanna, and down it to its
mouth, and then to Wyoming (Wilkes-
Barre). The intersection of these
trails in Pike County was near the
place marked Shoholy House, o n
Scull's map.

Shohola.—Howell's, map, 1792; also
Shohola House. **Shoholy.**—Scull, map,
1770; also, Shoholy House.

SHOHOKIN. See *Shehawken.*

SINNEMAHONING. The name of
the main tributary of the West
Branch of the Susquehanna, which
it enters at Keating, Clinton County.
The Sinnemahoning has as its chief
tributaries; First Fork, or East Fork,
which flows from the north, entering
the main stream at Sinnemahoning,
Cameron County; above this point
the main stream is called Driftwood
Branch, which has as its tributaries,
Bennetts Branch, which enters from
the west at Driftwood, and Portage
Creek, which enters the Driftwood
Branch, from the north, at Emporium.
The Sinnemahoning rises in the divide
between the Allegheny and the Susquehanna, in Potter County, having
three main branches, East Fork, South
Fork and Freeman's Run. These
tributaries have their heads in the
hills south of Coudersport, Potter
County. The name is a corruption of
Achsinni-mahoni, "stony lick." An Indian trail ran up the West Branch,
from Shamokin (Sunbury), to the

Big Island (Lock Haven), and then
on up the West Branch, along the
northern shore to the Sinnemahoning,
and then up the Driftwood Branch
to Emporium, and then over the divide to the Allegheny, which it
reached at the present Port Allegany, McKean County. This trail
later became the pathway of the early
settlers, who crossed the "divide" from
Emporium to Port Allegany. The
present line of the P. R. R. to Buffalo
follows the course of this trail nearly
all of the way from Lock Haven to
Olean, New York, or, in fact, from
Sunbury to Olean. There were several branches of this trail, at various
points, leading northward into the
Genesee Valley. These were chiefly
Seneca paths to the main trail down
the West Branch. In 1781 a party of
Seneca Indians made an attack upon
the settlement at Buffalo Valley killing a few people. To avenge this
act of hostility Peter Grove and three
others followed the Indians up the
West Branch. They found them encamped near the mouth of the Sinnemahoning. Grove and his companions made an attack upon the
Indians, killing a few of them, and
then making their escape. This fight
took place at the mouth of Grove's
Run, in the town of Sinnemahoning
(Consult; Otzinachson, 294-295). Peter
Grove the hero of this affair, was
a famous Indian fighter, whose various exploits rival those of the famous
"Captain Jack," of the Juniata, and
various other places. Almost every
valley in the state had such a character, around whose exploits, real
and imaginary, various romances have
been woven. Meginness gives a number of the adventures of Grove at the
end of his work, Otzinachson, 488 et
seq. There were a number of small
Indian villages, or rather hunting and
fishing camps, at various points along
the West Branch, in the region of the
Sinnemahoning. One of these was at
the mouth of Sterling Run. The
Susquehanna, or Conestoga, probably
had hunting camps in this same region,
which is still the wildest and most
sparcely settled in the entire state.
John Adlum, Samuel Maclay and
Timothy Matlack were commissioned
in 1789 to explore the West Branch
Valley and then go over the
divide to the Allegheny (Archives,
XI. 681, 683, 692). The first settlers
in Potter, McKean and Clinton (also
later Cameron) Counties went up this

West Branch trail to Canoe Place, and then over the divide to Canoe Place on the Allegheny. See *Canoe Place, Port Allegheny etc.*

Cinnamahoning.—Instr. to Com. (1790), Archives, XI. 683. **Seninghoning.**—Potter (1778), Archives, VI. 603. **Sennemahoning.**—Matlack (1790), Archives, XI. 692. **Sinnamahoning.**—Lloyd (1790), Archives, XI. 678. **Sinemahoning.**—Adlum, map, 1790. **Sinnemahoning.**—Howells, map, 1792. **Shenemahoning.**—Scull map, 1759.

The eastern township in Cameron County is named Grove, in honor of Peter Grove.

SKEHANDOWANA. See *Wyoming.*

SKIPPACK. One of the townships in Philadelphia County in 1741, and in 1762, and in 1784, upon the organization of Montgomery County, it became a township in that county; also the name of a creek, which enters Perkiomen Creek from the east, in the same county; also the name of a town and P. O. in the same county. Heckewelder gives the origin of the name from Schki-peek, "a pool of stagnant, offensive water." It is more probably from Skappeu-hacki, contracted to Skappack. meaning "wet land." All of the early maps, Scull (1759) Scull (1770) and Howell's (1792), give the form Skippack. Evans map (1749) gives Skepack.

SLIPPERY ROCK. The name of a creek and township and town in Lawrence County. The creek is a branch of the Conoquenessing, which flows into the Beaver River, from the east. Heckewelder gives the Indian name as Weschachachapochka, "slippery rock." Zeisberger gives W'schacheu, "slippery." Washington and Gist crossed the headwaters of this creek in 1753, when on their way to Venango (Gist's Jour., 81). Gist simply calls it "one of the head branches of Great Beaver Creek." The place where they encamped on the night of December 3, 1753, was at the headwaters of this creek, in Mercer County, about 15 miles from the present Franklin. near the boundary of Butler and Venango Counties. They made the first crossing of this creek near the present Wurtemberg, Lawrence County. Such was the course as noted on Gist's map of this trip. Gen. William B. Irvine, in exploring this region in 1785, traveled from Venango (Franklin) over this trail. He says, "From Venango, I returned along the path leading to Pittsburgh to within about seven miles of Flat Rock Creek (Slippery Rock Creek)—here I took a West course along a large dividing Ridge, already noticed, about ten miles, where I struck a branch of Canaghquenese, or Beaver, about thirty yards wide, and which joins Flat Rock before it empties into the main branch of Canaghquenese" (Archives, XI. 519). The trail from Venango to Fort Pitt ran directly south from the former place. Irvine left this path and went westward by the trail which C. F. Post had gone to Kuskuski, from Venango, in 1758. See *Conoquenessing.* One of the numerous fights of Capt. Sam Brady with the Indians is said to have taken place on this creek, some time after Brodhead's expedition up the Allegheny River. This fight is not mentioned in the Archives. It may be founded upon the fight with the Indians near Kuskuski (Archives, VIII. 378). As the trail from Fort Pitt to Venango crossed this creek, it is possible that many Indian "fights" took place along its course, by scouting parties from both of the forts. The Venango Path, which left the Ohio opposite the mouth of Saw Mill Run, is mentioned by Gen. Iryine (Archives, XI. 514, 515).

Branch of Beaver Creek.—Scull, map, 1770. **Chippery Rock Creek.**—Adlum, map, 1790. **Flat Rock Creek.**—Irvine (1785), Archives, XI. 519. **Slippery Rock Creek.**—Morris, map, 1848.

SNAKE TOWN. On September 27, 1727, James Logan informed the Provincial Council that he had received a letter from John Wright, one of the Justices of Chester County, in which he informed him of the killing of Thomas Wright, who was killed by some Indians at the house of John Burt, "at Snaketown, forty miles above Conestogoe," during a drunken carousal (Col. Rec. III. 285). "The Members of the Board observed that this was the first Accident of the kind that they had ever heard of in the Province since its first Settlement" (op. cit. 286). This murder, as was also the first one on the Ohio, was caused by the traffic in rum, at the very time that the Delaware and Shawnee were complaining about the great quantities of rum which the traders carried into the "woods." At a Council in Philadelphia in August, 1728, Governor Gordon was informed that this crime had been committed by the Minisink Indians, who were living above Wyoming (op. cit. 326). Nearly all of the troubles between the Indians and the traders and settlers were caused by this traffic, which the Provincial authorities tried in every way to regulate. Snaketown must have been a popular name for one of the trading points along the Susquehanna River, in the neighborhood of Paxtang, or at the mouth of the Juniata. It may possibly have been the name of the village at the mouth of Yellow Breeches Creek, at the site of New Cumberland. John Burt, the trader at whose house this crime was committed, had been granted a License, as a trader, in 1726. The statement is made, "for that tho' this Burt had been recommended for a License, it was scarce possible to find a man in the whole Government more unfitt for it" (op. cit. 286-7).

Snaketown.—Pa. Coun. (1727), Col. Rec., III, 285. **Snake town.**—Pa. Coun. (1728), Col. Rec., III. 326.

STANDING STONE. There were two places in the State known by this name. The most prominent was at the site of the present Huntingdon, where, at the mouth of Standing Stone Creek, once stood a famous "standing stone," which was a prominent landmark on the trail to the Ohio. John Harris, in 1754, says that this stone was 14 feet high and 6 inches square (Archives, II. 136). This stone is supposed to have been erected by one of the tribes of the Iroquois, probably the Seneca, who may have at one time occupied the valley, previous to their migration into New York (See *Seneca*). Heckewelder gives the name of this place as Achsinnink, "where there is a large stone," or "the place of the large stone." The Seneca name was Tyu-na-yate, "projecting rock." A name which Mr. Hewitt says "is said to refer to a standing stone to which the Indians paid reverence." There is little doubt but that the "standing stone" at this place was a meeting place for the Iroquois tribes, returning from their war expeditions to the south, and that they here celebrated their victories. This stone was at the intersection of a number of the Indian trails, from the Susquehanna to the Ohio, and from the West Branch and North Branch, leading southward across the State by way of the War-

riors Path, which ran along the foot of Warriors Mountain to Old Town, Maryland, where it crossed the Potomac, and ran on southward into the Carolinas. The trail to Bald Eagle Valley, to Shamokin, down the Juniata, across the Cumberland Valley, to the Potomac, to Kittanning, to Raystown, to Bedford, all centered here. It was a central point for all of the great trails of the Indians. From this point every part of the entire system of trails could be reached. This stone, no doubt, gave the name to the river Juniata, which is a corruption of Tyu-na-yate, the Seneca name for the place. The original stone, which stood at the mouth of Standing Stone Creek, was removed by the Indians after the Purchase of 1754. A memorial stone has been erected in Huntingdon bearing the inscription:

> "Onojutta,
> Juniata,
> Achsinnink.
> Erected September 8,
> 1896,
> As a Memorial of
> the Ancient Standing Stone,
> Removed by the Indians,
> in 1754."

The author spent some time at this place studying the course of the various trails, which centered here. The spot was an ideal site for an Indian village and yet there is no record of a village having been here, within historic times, at least. The reason why no Indian village stood at this beautiful spot was probably because of its situation on the pathway of the various war parties of so many different tribes. It was a sort of Neutral Ground, or a Hague tribunal of War, instead of Peace. One can only realize the real situation of the place, as a "Trail Center," by studying Scull's map on the spot, with the various mountains and valleys in view. To the southeast the Juniata passes through the narrow gorge, called Jack's Narrows, near the present Mount Union, where the trail forked to Aughwick (Shirleysburg); to the northwest runs the valley through which the trail ran to the Bald Eagle Valley; to the west ran the trail to Frankstown, and to the south ran the Warriors trail to the Potomac. The Raystown Branch of the Juniata enters the river just below Huntingdon. Conrad Weiser passed through this place in 1748, on his way to the Ohio, from Harris' Ferry (Col. Rec. V. 348). He mentions it as "the Standing Stone." John Harris gives the place in his table of distances to the Ohio, in 1754, "to Jack Armstrong's Narrows, so called from his being there murdered,—8 miles (from Aughwick), to the Standing Stone,—10 Miles, At each of these last places we cross Juniata" (Archives, II. 136). The trail crossed the Juniata, from the south, just above Mount Union, ran along the northern bank of the Juniata to Standing Stone, crossing the river again near the present bridge, and then ran westward to Frankstown, or southward to Everett, and Old Town, Md. The site is noted on all of the early maps, Evans (1755), Scull (1770), and is mentioned in many of the early Journals. Hugh Crawford, the Indian trader, was one of the first settlers in this region. In 1768 the Board of Property recorded the following minute, "In 1755 Barnaby Barnes took out a Warrant for Mr. Teas Use for the place in dispute. In 1763 Mr. Teas Received from George Croghan 10 Pounds 13 Shillings to take out a Warrant for Charles Coxe in the name of William Paxton for 200 A's on the North Side of Juniata between Hugh Crawfords place at the Mouth of Standing Stone & Sheavers Run in the County of Cumberland. In 1766 Doctor Smith took out an Application for the same place as Mr. Teas Warrant" * * * By Mr. McClay's Information there is but one place between Hugh Crawfords place and the Mouth of Shavers Creek on the North Side of Juniata which could be the Object of a Warrant." After an examination of the case Doctor Smith, Provost of the University of Pennsylvania, was granted the land (Archives, Third Ser., I. 216-217). Doctor Smith laid out a town on this tract which he gave the name of Huntingdon, in honor of Salina, Countess of Huntingdon (England), who had made a gift to the University. The place still continued to be called by its old name for many years after its settlement. The few white settlers living in this region before. 1762 erected a stockade fort, which was abandoned during the Conspiracy of Pontiac, 1763. After the return of the settlers to the Juniata, after the Treaty of 1768, the fort was strengthened, or rebuilt. During the Revolution it was a meeting place for the Tories of Sinking Valley, who made an attack upon the settlers, who had taken the oath of allegiance, and drove them away. Gen. Daniel Roberdeau says in a letter, April 23, 1778, "The insurgents from this Neighborhood (Standing Stone), I am informed are about thirty." On April 24, 1778, Lieut. Carothers, in writing from Carlisle, says, "a body of Tories, near 320, in and above Standing Stone, had collected themselves together & Drove a number of the inhabitants from Standing Stone Town" (Archives, VI. 436-439, 603, 610, 650). Consult; Frontier Forts, I. 579-586; Walton, Conrad Weiser, 186. See *Jack's Narrows, Aughwick, Kishacoquillas, Frankstown, Raystown*, etc. It is possible that the Delaware village, mentioned by Le Tort, in 1731, as Assunnepachla "upon Choniata," which contained 12 families and 36 men, was at this place, instead of at Frankstown. The distance given, however, would be too great for this place. The name Assunnepachla, however, may be a corruption of Assun, or Achsin, "stone," and Pachgen, "to turn out of the road," having the significance, "the stone, where one turns out of the road," or "the stone, where the road turns." See *Frankstown*.

STANDING STONE. A large rock on the west bank of the Susquehanna River, opposite the present Standingstone, Bradford County. This large rock was not set up by the Indians, but evidently fell from the top of the mountain into the river. It is mentioned in the Journals of Sullivan's expedition as being about 10 miles above Wyalusing. The army encamped near this place on the evening of August 8, 1779. Rogers says in his Journal, "Just upon entering these flats, I saw the stone from which they take their name. It is upon the opposite shore, on the cap of the water with which it is usually surrounded. Its height is twenty feet. Its breadth is fourteen feet. Its thickness two and a half feet. At the back of it is a large rock forming more than a semicircle upon which it is supposed a considerable tenement might be erected" (Jour. Sull. Exped., 259). A few families had been settled at this place before 1779, but deserted their farms and joined the Tories.

Standing Stone.—Elmer (1779), Jour. Sull. Exped., 84. **Standing Stone Bottom.**

—Barton, Jour. Sull. Exped., 5. **Standing Stone Flats.**—Rogers, Jour. Sull. Exped., 259. **Standing stone flatts.**—Grant, Jour. Sull. Exped., 138. **Standingstone.**—Blake, Jour. Sull. Exped., 39. **Long Standing Stone.**—Shute, Jour. Sull. Exped., 269.

ACHSINNING, ASSINNISSINK, ATSINSIN, ATSINSINK, etc. The name of a prominent Munsee village in 1756-62, situated at the site of Corning, on the opposite side of the river, near the junction of the Canestio with the Tioga River, New York. It is strange that this village which has been so accurately located, should be put in so many different places. Zeisberger says in his Journal of 1757, MS. at Bethlehem, for October 3, 1767 "About noon we arrived at Assinissink, where the noted chief of the Monsy tribe, Jachaebus who burnt the settlement on the Mahoni lived. His town was burnt and laid waste by the Mohocks later on, but he gave up his life as a prisoner in the late war. Curosities in the shape of pyramids of stone, which look as if they were made by man are here to be seen. From them this place derived its name. * * * "Here the Tiogee (Tioga) divides itself into two branches; the one goes toward the north into the land of the Senikas while the other along which we pursued our way extends towards the west." The place called Painted Post was a short distance north of this point, on the north side of the river, at the mouth of the Conhocton River. The late Charles Tubbs, who made a careful study of the region, said in a letter to the author a short time before his death. "My father often saw the so-called pyramids of stone; chimneys they were called by the early settlers. The road that ran by them was called "The Chimney Narrows." About 20 years ago he pointed out to me the site they (the part of them, at least) occupied below Corning on the opposite side of the river. They were demolished in 1881 in the building of the D. L. & W. R. R. I often go to Elmira on the Erie, also on the D. L. & W. and the N. Y. C. R. R. I think I never pass the mouth of the Conhocton River, and the Canestio, that I do not think of these diaries of Zeisberger." Zeisberger reached this place on his return journey, on Nov. 2nd. 1767. He was again at the place in May 15, 1768, when on his way to the mouth of the Tionesta. The trail up the Chemung, from Tioga Point, to this place, and then to the headwaters of the Allegheny, was one of the oldest in the region between the the Susquehanna and the Allegheny. It was a distinctively Indian trail, over which white men were not allowed to go. C. F. Post was turned back by the Indians, when on his his way to the Allegheny, "because the Indians would not allow him to proceede any further" (See *Passigachkunk, Cowanesque*). The origin of the name Assinsink, was due, as stated by Zeisberger, to these stone pyramids. Its meaning is "place of stones," or "place where stones are gathered together." The town was the home of the Munsee chief, Jachaebus, and also of Kobus, another Munsee chief, in whose honor the village was sometimes called Kobus Town. The latter name was not bestowed because of the place being the residence of the former, as stated by Beauchamp, who gives the town a wrong situation, but was given for the latter. Both of these chiefs were at the Council at Lancaster in 1762 (Archives, IV. 90). During the period of Indian hostility this was a gathering place for the Munsee tribe, and also a meeting place of the Iroquois. Various Councils were held here during 1759 (Archives, III. 737; Col. Rec. VIII. 416, 419, 423, 425, 464, etc.). It was the headquarters of the Minisink Indians during this period. Many of them went to the various Councils at Philadelphia and Lancaster, during 1760-1762 (Col. Rec. VIII 723-774). Egohohowen (also written, Echhoan, Echobund etc.) the famous Munsee chief, who was married to a daughter of French Margaret (Montour), named "Queen Esther," after his death, when she became the ruler of his village below Tioga Point. This woman was the most infamous of all the Montour family, being known as the "Fiend of Wyoming" (See *Queen Esther's Town, Sheshequin, Wyoming.* In 1758 Moses Tatamy and Isaac Hill visited this place. In their Journal they say, "We reached the side of the mountain Aghsinsin, and lodged at the house of one Kobus, a Delaware Indian. In this Town called Kobus Town are three large Houses and about 10 small ones, about 100 People, men, women and children. Here we saw a white woman at a distance in a corn Field." (Archives, III. 505). In 1760 John Hays was at this village. He says in his Journal, for May 23, 1760, "Set out early and arrived at Asinsan in the Evening, there stayed all night. Satturday, 24th. Sent a string to the Mingoes at Pachishahcunk to call them to Council, and staid for the Return; this Day the Indians Began to Sacrifice to their God, and Spent the Day in a very Odd manner, Howling, and Danceing, Raveling Like Wolves and Painted frightful as Divels. Sunday, 25th. * * * Indians went on in the Same Manner as Yesterday. Monday, 26th. The Indians Haveing Got Rum Got Drunk, all in General, Except some old men, and Teedyuscung Behaved well on this Ocasion, for when his Sone brought in the Kegg with Rum He would not taste it" (Archives, III. 737). Egohohowin was at this place during Hays' visit. Many of the captives which were returned after peace had been proclaimed, 1758-59, were delivered by the Munsee and Seneca from these villages on the Chemung, Tioga and Cowanesque. There is no doubt but that the existence of so many Delaware names in this region in New York State, is due to the occupation of these towns by the Minisink clan of the Munsee. Many of them moved into the Seneca country and became a part of that tribe, during this period, 1756-1762. The Munsee and the Seneca formed a sort of union at this time. Both were hostile to the English, and later to the American cause. Some of the Munsee from this region drifted westward to the Allegheny, then to the Ohio, and to the Muskingum. After Sullivan's expedition, 1779, the destruction of the Seneca villages drove the Munsee and other Indians from this region.

Achsinning.—Heckewelder, in Ind. Nations, 184. Aghsinsin.—Tatamy (1758), Archives, III. 503. Asinsan.—Hays (1760), Archives, III. 740. Assinnissink.—Coun. at Lan. (1762), Archives, IV. 90. Assinitzin.—Coun. at Easton (1758), Col. Rec. VIII. 200. Assunsing.—Tedy. (1759), Col. Rec. VIII. 416. Atsentsing.—Coun. at Phil. (1763), Col. Rec. IX. 47. Atsintsing.—Hamilton (1759), Col. Rec., VIII 423. Atsintzing.—Coun. at Phil. (1760), Col. Rec., VIII. 485. Atsunsing.—Coun. at Phil. (1759), Col. Rec., VIII. 419. Atsuntsing.—Pa. Coun. (1760), Col. Rec. VIII. 435. Citsintsing.—Pa. Coun. (1760), Col. Rec. VIII. 507.

STARRUCCA. A creek which enters the Susquehanna from the southeast in Susquehanna County; also the name of a village in the same county, and also one in Wayne County. The name is evidently of Indian origin, but has been so corrupted that its original form cannot be figured out. There were no settlers in this region before 1787. The Great Bend, in the river, commences near the mouth of this creek, where the river makes a sharp turn to the west.

Starucca.—Howells, map, 1792. Starrucca.—Present maps, 1912.

STILLWATER CREEK. A creek which heads in Warren County, and flows northeast into the Conewango near Frewsburg, New York. Cornplanter's village, Cayantona, was a short distance south of this creek, on the Conewango. The various names recorded on the early maps, as the name of the present Stillwater Creek, may be corruptions of this name—Cay-an-tha (or Cayontona), which is translated, "cornfields." Ellicott records the name in 1787. The other maps have taken Ellicott's map as the base for their maps of this region, but have mistaken Ellicott's "n" for a "w", or "u."

Cannenniendah.—Ellicott, map, 1787. Caweeneindah.—Howells, map, 1792. Couwnyanda.—Morris, map, 1848. Stillwater Creek.—Recent maps, 1911.

STONY CREEK. A branch of the Quemahoning Creek, in Somerset County; also the name of the creek formed by the union of Stony Creek and Quemahoning, which enters the Conemaugh River at Johnstown, Cambria County. Heckewelder gives the Delaware name of the stream as Sinne-hanna, or Achsinne-hanne, "stony stream.' The creek is frequently mentioned in the early records, as it was one of the landmarks on the trail from Bedford to Pittsburgh. John Harris, in 1754, gives the distance from Edmund's Swamp, "to Stoney Creek—6 Miles," and from this point to "Kickeney Paulin's House (Indian) —6 Miles" (Archives, III. 133). John Patten, in 1754, gives the distances, "From Edmund's Swamp to Cowamahony (Quemahoning) Creek—6 Miles. From Cowamahony to Kackanapaulins —5 Miles" (Col. Rec. V. 750). The trail crossed Stony Creek, east of Stoystown. Kickenapaulin's was at the present Jenner Cross Roads, or Jenners, Somerset County. Christopher Gist passed over this trail in 1750, on his way to Shannopin's Town. He does not mention either point by name (Dar. Gist's Jour., 33). He says, "I went into an old Indian Cabbin where

I stay'd all Night" (this was Kickena-paulin's Cabin). The creek is noted on Scull's map (1770), and also on Howell's map (1792). See *Kickena-pauling's, Edmunds Swamp*, etc. C. F. Post went through to the Ohio on his second mission in 1758, by this route. He passed the artillery on Laurel Hill, just before reaching Loyalhanna (Ligonier). The expedition of General Forbes went over this trail from Bedford to Fort Duquesne, in 1758. C. F. Post again passed over the trail in 1762, when leading the Indians from the Tuscarawas to Lancaster. Beaver, Shingas and other famous chiefs were then in the company. The party encamped on Stony Creek on the night of July 14th. (Archives, IV. 95). General Stanwix wrote from Pittsburgh, Dec. 24, 1759, to Governor Hamilton, "I have likewise ordered all the Pensilvanians on this side of the Mountains, viz., Pittsburg, Wetherhold, Fort Ligonier, and Stony Creek, to march immediately to Lancaster, to be paid and broak" (Archives, III. 696). This would show that the detachment which had been stationed at the breastworks at Stoystown, which had been erected as one of the stations on the line of the Forbes Road, was abandoned at this time, instead of in 1763, as often stated. A number of the surveys in the Penn Papers, at the Historical Society of Penna. for 1770, are for lands along Stony Creek, and the Conemaugh River. Several of these show the course of the Forbes Road, and old trail, from Edmund's Swamp to Stony Creek. The region was occupied by the white settlers soon after the Treaty at Fort Stanwix in 1768. Many of those who settled in this region were of the thrifty Germans of Lancaster County.

SUGAR CABINS. The name of a prominent landmark on the trail through Fulton County, via Cowan's Gap to Raystown. The Sugar Cabins were situated at the site of the present Fort Lyttleton, Fulton County. One of the old Indian trails from the Cumberland Valley, and from the Potomac, passed through Cowans Gap, in the Tuscarora Mountains, by way of the Gap in the Kittatinny Mountains at Parnell's Knob, near Fort Loudon, then up the Path Valley to Cowan's Gap, and then westward through Burnt Cabins, etc., to Bedford. This trail was joined by several other branches from the Cumberland Valley, through Roxbury, Doubling, McClures and other Gaps in the Kittatinny Mountains. A trail ran southward to the Potomac, near the mouth of Conococheague Creek. One of the early Iroquois War Trails ran down the Cumberland Valley to the Potomac River, and then on through Winchester to the Catawba and Cherokee country. As the Cumberland Valley was settled very early after the migration of the Delaware and Shawnee to the Ohio, and in 1754 there was a large Scotch-Irish population in the region along the Conococheague. This settlement commenced as early as 1732, in the "slate lands," which were not covered with a heavy growth of trees. There is every reason to believe that this part of the Cumberland Valley was covered with meadow grass, much as were the prairies in the west. The Indians soon left this region, going westward to the Ohio, and the Iroquois moved their trail to the south, to the eastern slope of Warriors Mountain, crossing the Potomac at Old Town, Md. All of these trails into the Cumberland Valley, and to the Potomac became veritable trails of blood during the hostility which commenced in the early summer of 1755. When General Braddock's expedition was getting ready to march to Fort Duquesne, Sir John St. Clair, who had been given charge of the selection of a route from Will's Creek to the Ohio, selected the course which Washington had taken in 1754. He however realized the importance of having the supplies sent from the settlements of Pennsylvania by a shorter route. There was a wagon road from Philadelphia, through Lancaster and York, to the mouth of the Conococheague, but no road from that point to Will's Creek along the northern shore of the Potomac. As a consequence he decided that a road must be made to connect with the Great Virginia Road, from Harrisburg down the Cumberland Valley to the Potomac, leading westward to join Braddock's Road near the Great Crossings, or at Turkey Foot, at the confluence of the three branches of the Youghiogheny River in southwestern part of Somerset County—near the line of Fayette County. Sir John St. Clair wrote to Governor R. H. Morris, Feb. 14, 1755, "For this Reason I must press upon your Excellency in the most earnest manner, to open a Communication by cutting or Repairing, the Roads towards the Head of Yougheagany, or any other way that is nearer to the French Forts" (Col. Rec. VI. 300). In the Minutes of the Provincial Council, Feb. 18," the Council judged that it would be absolutely necessary to open a Road from Shippensburg to intersect the Road of the Army from Will's Creek to Fort Duquesne thro' Ray's Town" (op. cit. 317). The Council decided that a Commission should be appointed by the Governor to explore the region west of the mountains. The Governor issued such a Commission to George Croghan, John Armstrong, James Bird (Burd), William Buchannan and Adam Hoops of the County of Cumberland, March, 12, 1755 (op. cit. 317, 318). On April 16th. this Commission made its first report, in which it is stated, "we were very fortunate in finding a good Road all the Way, and particularly thro' the Allegheny Hills considering how mountainous that Country is. From Parnal's Nab(Parnell's Knob), or McDowel's Mill to where we stopped is about Sixty-Nine Miles" (op. cit. 368-369, 376-377). Parnell's Knob is near the present town of Loudon, Franklin County. McDowell's Mill was a few miles south of this, near the present Bridgeport. (Consult; Letters from Burd, Braddock and Morris, Col. Rec., VI, 377, 380). In June Governor Morris said, "Two Roads were ordered to be cut when they should come to Ray's Town. One to go to Will's Creek, and the other to the Crow's Foot (Turkey Foot) of the Ohoigany," He then said that the former road would not be needed, but that work on the latter road must be carried on with the greatest speed (op. cit. 396). On May 18th. John Armstrong wrote from Carlisle, to Gov. Morris, saying that work was commenced on May 6th., with only ten or fifteen men; on the 15th., 70 were at work, and that they had made 6 miles of road thirty feet wide (op. cit. 401-02). On May 31, James Burd wrote from Shippensburg, stating that on the 27th. "I was then lying at the Gap of the Sideling Hill, and begun to cut the Mountain that morning" (403). "To the Foot of the Mountain where we now lay is 19 Miles from Anthony Thompson's; but I expect before We finish the Hill the Parties ahead will be 5 or 6 Miles for-

ward. I measure the Miles with my Chain, and mark every Mile with a marking Iron" (op. cit. 404). Anthony Thompson's is mentioned in all of the distances given. Thompson's was at Cowan's Gap, about three miles northwest of the present Richmond Furnace. Governor Morris says that Mr. Peters says that he "judges that a Place called McDowell's Mill, situate upon the new Road, about twenty miles Westward of Shippensburg, is much more convenient for the magazine than Shippensburg." Peters says that he will await the Governor's "Approbiation before he (Swain begins to build or hire Store-Houses" (op. cit. 407). It was later discovered that the site where Fort Loudon was erected was a more suitable point than McDowell's Mill, as a base of supplies, so the supplies were moved from McDowell's Mill to Fort Loudon (about a mile south of the present State Road, east of the present town of Loudon). On June 16th. Gov. Morris, in a letter to General Braddock, reported that the road had reached Ray's Town (op. cit. 430-see also 425). General Braddock wrote to Morris, June 11th., "I have ordered a Party of an hundred Men as a Guard to the People working upon the new Road, which will set out this Day" (op. cit., 431). Edward Shippen wrote to Gov. Morris, from Lancaster, June 17th., "I understand Mr. Burd has cut the Road 5 Miles beyond Ray's Town, which is 90 Miles from Shippensburg" (431). Burd wrote to Gov. Morris, "From the Roads leading to the Ohio, 12th. June, 1755," "We have at present half of our Body laying at the Ford of the Juniata, which is by measure 28 Miles from Anthony Thompson's, having a good deal of digging to do down to the Ford. * * * We hope to be at Ray's Town against the middle of next week or towards the end of the week" (op. cit. 433). This Ford was at the present Juniata Crossings. On June 17th. Burd wrote from "Allogueepy's Town, 34 and a half Miles from Anthony Thompson's,' and on June 19th., from Ray's Town, concerning the arrival of Captain Hogg and his detachment of an hundred men, which Braddock had sent (op. cit. 436). On July 3rd. Gov. Morris wrote to Burd, "If I am right in this, then it shou'd seem to me that the General's Road passes thro, the great Crossings of

Ohiogany (Youghiogheny), which is but Three Miles from the Junction of the Three Branches, that form the Turkey Foot the Place where the Two Roads can best meet is at the great Crossings, and that you must open your Road so far as that" (op. cit. 452). On July 5, Burd wrote, "From the Allegheny Mountains," "We have got this far with the Road, but at present are under a very great Dilemma." He then goes on to tell of the Indians having killed "Mr. Hoops'-Man (named Arnold Vigorous)," and having captured James Smith, a brother-in-law of William Smith (op. cit. 466-467). This James Smith was captured, taken to Fort Duquesne, where he was when Braddock was defeated. His narrative is one of the most interesting and valuable documents of this period. He was but 18 years old at the time of his capture (Burd says 16). Consult; Border Life, 13-85, 1839. Col. Rec., VI. 466-67.

On June 30th, General Braddock wrote to Governor Morris "from the Camp at the last Crossing of the Yaughyaughani" (on June 28th, Braddock's army encamped at Stewart's Crossings, Connellsville, on the west side of the Youghiogheny River). Braddock says, "As I shall very soon be in want of Supplies from ye Province, I must beg you wou'd order all possible Dispatch to be made use of in finishing the new Road as far as the Crow's Foot (Turkey Foot) of the Yaughyaughani, and immediately afterwards send forward to me such Articles of Provision as shall be in your Power" (VI. 475. The army passed over the river on June 30th to the *east* side of the river (not the *west*, as Orme's Journal states), where they encamped on the "Narrows," just below Connellsville, while a road was being made over the hill on the "hog-back" (Consult; Sargent, Braddock's Expedition, 344-45). On July 17th, Burd wrote from "our Camp at the top of the Allegheny Mountains, Measured 65 Miles from A. Thompsons" (Col. Rec. VI., 484-5). Burd said in this letter, "At present I can't form any Judgement where I shall cut the General's Road, further than I know our Course leads us to the Turkey Foot, By information of Mr. Croghan when we run the Road first. Mr. Croghan assured me he wou'd be on the Road with me in order to pilott from the Place where we left off

blaizeing. Instead of that he has never been here, nor is there one Man in my Company that was ever out this Way to the Turky Foot, But the Party I send will discover the Place where we shall cut the Road and inform the General, and upon their Return I will order 'em to blaize back to me" (op. cit. 485). Burd had not heard of Braddock's defeat when he wrote this letter, but on the same day he received this news from Col. Innes, who sent a messenger from Fort Cumberland, at Will's Creek. Burd began his retreat on July 18th, going back over his road to Ray's Town, and then south to Fort Cumberland. Here he reported to Sir John St. Clair, who told him to wait until the arrival of Col. Dunbar. Upon Dunbar's arrival he was informed that the army was going to retreat to Philadelphia. Burd informed Dunbar that "if it was thought necessary that I cou'd open the Road from our Road at Ray's Town to Fort Cumberland in a Fortnight or 3 weeks at farthest (imagining that a Fort wou'd be immediately erected at that Place to shut up the other Road to save our Back Inhabitants)." But, the scared and cowardly Dunbar was too anxious to get out of all possible danger of seeing a Frenchman or an Indian to wait a day longer than absolutely necessary at Fort Cumberland. What Burd thought would be done, is what Dunbar should have done. Braddock's Road became a pathway for the Indians, who carried death and destruction into the frontiers of Pennsylvania and Virginia. Had Fort Cumberland been held by the cowardly Dunbar, the lives of hundreds would have been spared (Burd's letter to Governor Morris, Col. Rec., VI. 499-502). Governor Morris wrote to Governor Shirley, July 30th, "I do not conceive that his (Dunbar's) coming as far as Carlisle or Shippensburg will at all hinder the Forces from being in a readiness to march to Ohio this fall if it should be Judged necessary, for they will then be nigh the new Road to the Allegheny Mountains, along which an Army may March with much more ease than by the Road that Genl. Braddock took" (op. cit. 514). But, Dunbar had no intention of remaining at either Shippensburg or Carlisle, but was bent on getting to Philadelphia as soon as possible, in order that he might have the mountains between himself and all possible danger of either the French or the Indians. When the discussion, as to the route which was to be taken by the army of General Forbes, in 1758, was being discussed, this route which had been opened up by Burd was the one finally decided upon. At this time the miserable conflict between Governor Morris and the Assembly was at its height. There is no question but that this dispute between Governor Morris and Isaac Norris, and the Assembly, is one of the most pitiful, and disgusting, chapters in the history of this period (Col. Rec., VI. 624-637, etc.). In 1756, when it became necessary, for the protection of the settlements along the frontier, to erect a chain of forts, one was built at the Sugar Cabins. Governor Morris says, in a letter to Governor Sharpe, Jan. 20, 1756, in mentioning the various forts, "a fourth at the Sugar Cabins, upon the new Road, called fort Lytellton (Lyttleton); at each of these I have placed a garrison of seventy-five 'men, & ordered them to range the woods each way" (Archives, II. 556). Morris also wrote to Governor Dinwiddie, and to Col. Washington, informing them of the erection of these forts (op. cit., 560, 564). On Feb. 9, 1756, Gov. Morris, in a letter to Gov. Shirley, says, "The one stands upon the new Road opened by this Province towards the Ohio, and about twenty miles from the settlements, and I have called it Fort Lytellton, in Honour of my friend Sr. George. This fort will not only Protect the inhabitants in that part of the Province, but being upon a road that within a few miles Joyns Genl. Braddock's rout (so it was), it will prevent the march of any regulars that way into this Province, and at the same time serve as an advanced post or magazine, in case of an attempt westward" (Archives, II. 560). On Nov. 12, 1756, Col. John Armstrong writes from Carlisle, "At present we have 100 men at McDowels, Guarding and Escorting the Publick Provisions to Fort Lyttleton, and are now on their way there" (Archives, III. 51). In 1762, when C. F. Post was leading the Indians to Lancaster, he stopped at this fort. In his Journal he says, "we arriv'd at fort Littleton, & were all quartered in the fort" (Archives, IV. 95). During the Forbes expedi-

tion, 1758, Bouquet's Expedition, 1763, this fort was one of the prominent posts on the way to Fort Pitt. Consult; Frontier Forts, I. 555-558; Col. Rec., VII., 77, 445, 632; Archives, II. 556, 561, 565, 603, 752; III. 49, 51; IV. 95; for a very fine resume of the history of the road through Fort Lyttleton, The Kittochtinny Hist. Soc., VII., 152 et seq.; VI. 93 et seq.

SUSQUEHANNA. The name of a river, county, Township and a number of villages, towns, and Post Offices. Heckewelder gives the name as a corruption of Quenischachachgekhanne, "the long reach river" (a name first applied to the West Branch (See *Quenischaschaki*). He said that the name given to the North Branch was M'chewamisipu, "the river on which are extensive clear flats" (name of Wyoming, which see). The Six Nations, according to Pyrlaeus, called the river Gahonta, with same meaning. Heckewelder says that the Indians called the Susquehanna, "the great bay river" (Ind. Nations, 52). "The word Susquehanna, properly Sisquehanna, from Sisku, 'mud,' and hanne, 'a stream,' was probably at an early time of the settling of this country overheard by someone while the Indians were at the time of a flood or freshet remarking, 'Juh Achsis quehanne, which is, 'How muddy the stream is,' and therefore taken as the proper name of the river" (quoted by Beauchamp, Aboriginal Names in N. Y., 29-30). Co-hon-go-run-to, the name given by Colden, is not a name of the Susquehanna, but of the Potomac (See *Potomac*). Reichel calls it the "winding River" (Mem. Mor. Church, 84). Cusick gave the name of Ka-un-seh-wa-tau yea (Beauchamp, op. cit., 172). Morgan gave it the name of Ga-wa-no-wa-na-neh, "great island river" (Beauchamp, op. cit., 173). On De l'Isle's map of 1718 the river is called "R. des Andastes." On Herman's map, of 1670, the river is called "Sassquahana." On De l'Isle's map the Indians, inhabitating the region along this river, are called "Andastes ou Sasquehanoes." Andastes was the name which the French gave to the "Sasquesahannocks," or "Sasquesahanough" (1608). The modern form of this name is Susquehanna. Mr. Hewitt gives the meaning to Kanastoge, "at the place of the immersed pole." May it not be possible that the word from which Andaste is derived is Ka-nesta, "mud," or "clay," and that Sassqua-hana is simply the Algonkian translation of the Iroquois name? Sisku-hanna would simply be a translation of the word which was used as the name of the tribe, Kanesta, with the suffix hanna. Susquehanna would therefore be "the river of the Andastes," as noted on the map mentioned. As the Andastes, or Susquehanna, occupied this river from its headwaters to the bay this name would be a fitting one for it. Sisku is evidently simply a translation of Andaste, which was a corruption of Kanesta. The present Chemung River is called "R. de Kanestio" on Pouchot's map of 1758. This river was occupied by the Andastes(or Kanesta) before their expulsion from Carantouan by the Iroquois. The name of the river was, therefore, River of the Andastes. What the significance of Kanesta, as applied to the tribe, was, it is impossible to discover. The word Kanesta and Sisku, or Assisku, means both "mud" and "clay." Heckewelder noted that the name "muddy river," or "roily river" was not descriptive of the Susquehanna, and it is not. Is not this derivaton a solution of the meaning of Sisku as applied to this stream? The Indians who told Smith the name of the river, simply translated the Iroquois name of the tribe living upon the stream, Kanesta, by Sisku, adding Hanna, to designate the river? While the name Canestio (also Canisteo, Kanestio), is now applied only to the branch of the Susquehanna, which enters the Tioga River near Corning, N. Y., it was formerly applied by the Seneca to the Susquehanna River, to its junction with the West Branch. It is so noted on the Pouchot map of 1758, to the junction of the Chemung with the North Branch. Vaudreuil says, in 1757, "I was informed that the English had caused five hundred bateaux to be constructed at Shamoken (Shamokin), on the River Canestio" (Archives, Sec. Ser., VI. 404). And again he says, "A Seneca told me that more than one hundred men had gone with the Loups (Delaware) to the River Canestio to harass the English, who are very numerous about Shamoken, where they are really building batteaux (same ref.)." John Smith first heard of these Susquehannocks when exploring the head of Chesa-

peake Bay in 1608. He was told by the Nanticoke or Pohawtan that "They can make neere 600 able and mighty men, and are palisaded in in their Townes to defend them from the Massawomekes, their m o r t a l l enimies." He also learned that they were seated on the Susquehanna River "2 daies higher than was passable for the discoverer barge." Mr. Hewitt has identified the name of these enemies of the Susquehanna Indians, the Massawomekes, with the name M'cheuwaming, "at the great flats," which has been corrupted to Wyoming (which see). This would make the Massawomekes, of Smith, and the Scahentoarrhonons, of the Jesuit Relation of 1735, identical. The author thinks that the Scahentoarrhonons was simply another form of the name applied to the Seneca, Tsandowannes by the early writers in the Colonial Records of Pennsylvania. This name was also written Tsanandowas (Col. Rec., III. 133, 150, 273 etc.). The Massawomekes, Scahentoarrh o n o n s, Tsandowannes, Tsanandowas and the Seneca were probably the same. The historic northern village of the Andastes, or Susquehannocks, called Carantouan, was situated on the present Chemung River near the New York State line, and was directly reached from the upper branches of the river, by the Senecas, whose villages were then east of the Genesee River. The author also thinks that the Andastes were, before the war with the Iroquois, closely connected with the Seneca, and that the latter lived along the Juniata River before being driven north by the Andastes, who in turn were driven down the Susquehanna by the Seneca (See *Seneca*). Smith gives the name of six Susquehanna towns; Sasquesahanough, Quadroque, Attaock, Tesinigh, Utchowig and Cepeowig. It is probable that the first town, Sasquesahanough, was situated near the mouth of the Conewago, or at the Falls; Attaock was probably on, or near the Juniata; Quadroque, at the forks of the Susquehanna, near Northumberland; Tesinigh, on the Susquehanna, in the Wyoming Valley; Utchowig, on the West Branch, in the region of Jersey Shore, or Lock Haven, and Cepowig somewhere in the region of Gettysburg. Besides these villages, mentioned by Smith, there were a number of other villages along the upper Susquehanna, on the

Chemung Branch, which were occupied by the Susquehannas about the same time that these villages were in existence. Among these were Carantouan, Oscalui and Gahontoto. The first was situated at Spanish Hill, Bradford County, near Waverly, N. Y., the second was at the mouth of Sugar Creek, Bradford County, and the third near the mouth of Wyalusing Creek, in the same county. In 1616 Captain Hendrickson made a report of his discoveries in New Netherland, in which he says, "He also traded for and bought from the inhabitants, the Minquaes, three persons, being people belonging to this Company; which three persons were employed in the service of the Mohawks and Mahicans; giving for them' kettles, beads and merchandize" (Archives, Sec. Ser., V. 17). After the settlement of the Delaware by the Dutch and Swedes the trade with the "Minquas," as the Susquehanna Indians were called by early officials on the Delaware, was the object of the struggles between these two rival peoples. On July 19, 1655, several of the Delaware chiefs conveyed to Peter Stuyvesant a tract of land on the west shore of the Delaware, in the presence of several "Minquas" (op. cit. 266). At this time the Delaware and Susquehanna Indians were in rriendly union and it is possible that the former were subject to the latter. A Delaware chief, Mattehoon, in reply to a question concerning the ownership of the land, said, "that they were great Chiefs and Proprietors of the lands, both by ownership and by descent and by appointment of the Minquas and River Indians" (a geographic designation of the Delawares living on the river) (Archives, Sec. Ser., V. 263). The Swedes, by taking possession of the mouth of the Schuylkill, Minquas Kill, and the other streams leading westward to the creeks connecting with the Susquehanna, gained possession of this trade with the Susquehanna (Andastes, Conestoga, Minquas). The various conflicts between these rival colonies on the Delaware take up all of Volume V., Second Series, Archives of Penna., and a great part of Vol. VII.

In the Record of Upland Court (40) the name given is "Sasquehanno" (1677). While the Susquehanna (Andaste, Conestoga) belonged to the Iroquoian family, they were not members of the "League of the Iroquois,"

with whom they carried on a war which lasted for many years. This war, which had been carried on with success by the Conestoga, finally terminated in the complete subjection of the once powerful tribe. The Susquehannocks had several forts along the lower Susquehanna, where they made their final stand against their foes from the north. One of these was at the mouth of Octorara Creek. This fort figured in the Boundary Dispute between the Penns and Calverts. This fort is mentioned in the Colonial Records of 1684—"Jonas Askins heard Coll. Talbot say, that if Govr. Penn should come into Maryland, he would Seize him and his retairce (?) in their Journey to Susquehannah fort" (Col. Rec. I., 14). The depositions of various persons, concerning the situation of this fort, are given in Archives, Sec. Ser., XVI. 522-525). The other Susquehanna fort was situated opposite the place where Thomas Cresap settled, and built his fort, at Conejohela (which see). It stood below Wrightsville, and was destroyed by the Senecas in 1673-74, after which the Susquehannocks retreated to their Maryland fort, where they were defeated by the Maryland and Virginia soldiers, in 1675, when they returned to the east side of the Susquehanna, opposite Conejohela, where they built the fort at Turkey Hill, near Columbia. The author found along the shore of the river, below this point, one of the oldest types of a stone axe he has ever seen. The entire region along the river at this region, between the Conewago and Conestoga, was without doubt the region in which the Conestoga, or Susquehanna, Indians lived when carrying on the trade with the Swedes on the Delaware. Their villages then spread along the river to the mouth of Octorara Creek (See also, Archives, Sec. Ser., XVI. 710-712). The war between the Iroquois and the Susquehannas, or Conestoga, came to an official ending at the Treaty at Shackamaxon, March 13, 1677. After the defeat of the Conestoga many of them sought refuge with the Delawares, with whom they were in alliance. The subjugation of the Conestoga, no doubt, carried with it the subjugation of the Delawares (Records of Upland Court, 49). After this time the Iroquois claimed all of the lands which had been occupied by the Conestoga. It was not until much later that they set up a claim for the lands occupied by the Delawares. At a Council at Philadelphia, 1720, Civility. the Conestoga chief, said that "some of the five Nations, especially the Cayoogoes (Cayuga). had at divers times expressed a Dissatisfaction at the large Settlements made by the English on Sasquehannah, and that they seemed to claim a Property or Right to those Lands." Secretary Logan replied that the Governor of New York had bought the lands in question. and that Governor Penn had purchased the right to the lands from him. This entire subject was gone over in a letter written by Governor Keith (Col. Rec., III. 97-102). The dispute concerning the lands about Conestoga came up at various times. In 1722 a number of the chiefs of the Five Nations, with two Tuscarora, were at Philadelphia. These, in a speech, said, "We here now freely surrender to you all those Lands about Conestoga which the five Nations have claimed, and it is our desire that the same may be settled with Christians, in token whereof we give this String of Wampum" (Col. Rec., III. 201) (See also, 101, 133, 176, 183). A Deed had been given by the Conestoga for these Susquehanna lands in 1700 (Arch. Sec. Ser., XVI. 415). Governor Dongan had deeded all of the Susquehanna lands to William Penn, in 1696. Dongan stated in this Deed that these lands had been purchased or given to him by the "Sinneca Susquehanah Indians" (Archives, I. 122). At the Treaty of 1736 the Iroquois declared that these Susquehanna lands had been given to Governor Dongan in trust, and that they had in no way given up their rights to them (Archives. I. 494-498). This Deed was for all of the lands on both sides of the river to the Kittatinny Mountains, and westward "to the setting sun." In 1749 the Penns purchased all of the lands on the east side of the Susquehanna, north of this previous purchase, from the north side of the mouth of the Mahanoy, below Sunbury, to the north side of the mouth of the Lackawaxen on the Delaware (Deed and map, Archives, II. 33-37). In 1754 the Susquehanna Company purchased, at the Treaty at Albany, the tract of land beginning at the 41st degree north latitude, at ten miles east of the Susquehanna River, to the end of the 42nd degree (Archives, II. 147-158). This was the

beginning of the conflict between Connecticut and Pennsylvania, which lasted for years and cost hundreds of lives (Archives, II. 174-176; Sec. Ser., XVIII). At this same Treaty at Albany the Penns purchased all of the lands on the west side of the Susquehanna, from the Kittatinny Mountains northward to a mile above the mouth of Penn's Creek, and then northwest to the limits of the Province (Col. Rec., VI. 119-123). At this Treaty it was stated that the lands under consideration "did really belong to the Cayugas and Oneidas in Right of the Conquest of the Sasquehanna Indians" (op. cit. 117). At the Treaty of Easton, 1758, all of the lands west of the summit of the Allegheny Mountains were deeded back to the Iroquois, because of the various disputes concerning these lands (Col. Rec., VIII. 204 et seq.). At the Treaty at Fort Stanwix, 2768, all of the lands which had been deeded back to the Indians in 1758, and the lands west of the Susquehanna to Pine Creek, south of the West Branch, and south of the line to Kittanning and south of the Allegheny and Ohio Rivers, was purchased. This was the last purchase made by the Penns (Col. Rec., IX. 554-555). The land north and west of this purchase was bought from the Iroquois at Fort Stanwix in 1784, and the Triangle at Erie was purchased in 1789 (Consult a record of all of these deeds, Archives, IX. 715-724; Deed of 1789; Arch., Sec. Ser., VI. 733-4). In the various documents relating to the Susquehanna River, and the lands along it, the Seneca at no time made any claim to these lands, and yet it is frequently stated that the Seneca with other Iroquois conquered the Susquehannocks (Conestoga). In August, 1684, the Cayuga and Onondaga claimed the river and the lands (Papers Relating to the Susquehanna, 400). These tribes gave the lands to Gov. Dongan, "That Penn's people may not settle on the Susquehannah River" (op. cit. 401). These tribes stated, "Thatt we do putt the Susquehanna River above the Washinta or falls and all the rest of our land under the Great Duke of York and to nobody else" (op. cit. 402). At a Council at Albany, Sept. 26, 1683, the Cayuga and Onondaga chiefs said, "The aforesaid Land (on Susquehanna River) belongs to us, Cayuga and Onnondagos, alone; the other three Nations, vizt. the Sinnekes,

Oneydes and Maquaas have nothing to do with it" (op. cit. 396). As previously noticed the Cayuga made the claim that they owned the Susquehanna lands to William Penn (Col. Rec., III. 100). In the various disputes between the Iroquois and the Colonies of Maryland and Virginia the various purchases of these Colonies were under discussion. In 1652 Maryland bought from the Minquaas (Susquehannas) all of the land on both sides of Chesapeake Bay to the mouth of the river. The Maryland deputies at the Treaty of Lancaster claimed that Gov. Dongan sold the Susquehanna lands to William Penn in 1696, and that the Minquas (Conestoga) had confirmed this Deed in the presence of the Iroquois deputies in 1718, and that Pennsylvania had bought these lands from the Iroquois to the Kittatinny Mountains in 1736. Consequently the Iroquois had no claims against Maryland. Canassatego replied to all of these points, acknowledged the validity of these various transactions, but denied that the Iroquois had ever been paid for the lands along the Potomac (Col. Rec., IV. 709 et seq.). The Colonies of Maryland and Virginia finally made a settlement for all of these lands. After the defeat of the Susquehannas by the Iroquois, in 1675, the surviving members of the tribe were scattered. Some of them went to the Potomac, where they settled on the east bank above Piscataway Creek. Some of them returned from this place to Conestoga, near Lancaster, where they were living when they held a Treaty with William Penn in 1701 (Col. Rec., II. 15). The statement of Colden that they were removed to the Oneida country "until they lost their language" cannot be correct, as the Conestoga and Conoy which settled at Conestoga went directly there from the Potomac. The place where they settled on Conestoga Creek was probably the site of the chief town of the Susquehannocks previous to the final war with the Iroquois. Here the remnant of the once powerful tribe dwindled in numbers until in 1763 they numbered but 20. Six of these were killed by the "Paxton Boys" on the night of Dec. 14th, 1763. The remaining 14 were taken to the Workhouse at Lancaster for their own protection. On Dec. 27th fifty men rode from Paxtang to Lancaster. Rev. John Elder, the Pastor of the Presbyterian Church at Paxtang, met these men and tried to prevent them from going to Lancaster, but was not successful. They went to Lancaster, broke open the Jail in which the Conestoga were confined, and killed the last remnant of the once masterful Susquehannocks, who had been reduced to a pitiful condition, chiefly because of the unlicensed traffic in rum in their village at Conestoga (Consult; Arch. IV. 147, 148, 153, 154, 163). See Conestoga, Conejohela, Dekanoagah, Paxtang, Seneca. Owing to the various land sales along the Delaware, the Delaware began to migrate to the Susquehanna soon after the settlement of the region along the former river. After the Walking Purchase the Delawares were ordered by the Iroquois to the Susquehanna. They commenced moving to the Ohio soon after 1724. By 1755 the majority of the Indian villages south of the West Branch were deserted. The villages along the northern part of the river remained until after Sullivan's expedition of 1779, when they, too, were deserted. By that year the great majority of the Delaware and Shawnee were in the present state of Ohio. The various Indian villages are noted under their names. The various names of the Conestoga, or Susquehannock Indians, were: Andastaes, Andastiguez, Antastouais, Canastogues, Carantouais, Conestoga, Gandastogues, Minckus, Minquas, Sasquahana, Sasquesahanoughs, S a s q u e s a hannocks, Susquehannas, Susquehannah Minquays, etc. A complete list of synonyms will be found after article, Conestoga, Handbook of Amer. Ind., I. 336-337. The river is noted on the early maps as "R. des Andastes" (1718), De L' Isle; Sassquahana (1640), Herrman; Sasquesahanough (1608), Smith, and the later maps, as, Susquehanna (1749), Evans; Susquehannah (1770), Scull, (1792), Howells. The various recorded forms in the Archives and Records are simply variations of spelling the name Susquehanna, and are of no value.

SWATARA. A creek, whose source is in Lebanon County, and which enters the Susquehanna from the east at Middletown, Dauphin County. There was probably an Indian village at the mouth of this creek, but its name is not recorded. The region along the creek was settled by the Scotch-Irish from 1725-27. Jonas Davenport, the Conestoga trader, made application for 300 acres of land on the Susquehanna, at the mouth of this creek, in 1727 (Arch. Sec. Ser., XIX. 750). In the same year Roland Chambers gave a Petition to Secy. Logan, signed by 40 or 50 persons, making application for 10,000 acres of land between "Sawhatara" and Pextang, for settlement of themselves and families (op. cit. 755). From this time onward the entire valley along the creek became filled with settlers, the majority of whom were Scotch-Irish. After the breaking out of the Indian hostilities in 1755 the settlements along this creek suffered greatly at the hands of the hostile Indians (Col. Rec., VII. 303, VII. 538; VIII. 95, etc.). On account of these Indian raids, which were made through the Gap in the mountains, a number of forts were erected in this region. Among these were Manada Fort, Brown's Fort, Fort at Harper's, and Fort Swatara. The latter was erected near Swetara Gap. In the instructions to Adam Read, 1756, it is stated, "Having appointed Capt. Frederick Smith to take post with an Independent Company at the Gap where Swehatara passes the Mountains, and to station a Company at Monaday (Manada), there will be no necessity of your Continuing Longer upon Guard in that part of the Frontier" (Archives, II. 551). In 1756 Frederick Smith was appointed a Captain, and given the following instructions, "You are as soon as Possible to Proceed with the Company under your Command to the gap at Tolehaio, where Swehatara comes through the Mountain, and in some convenient place there you are to erect a Fort, of the form and dimensions herewith given you, unless you shall Judge the Staccado, already erected there, conveniently placed, in which case you will take possession of it, and make such additional works as you may think necessary to render it sufficiently strong and defenceable" (Archives, II. 552). Capt. Smith was then to leave a part of his Company here and then go to Manada Gap and erect a new fort, or make use of the old stockade. The fort at Swatara had been erected in 1754, according to a Journal (Archives, II. 161), to which no name is attached. This Journal, however, seems to be wrongly dated. It should be 1756, instead of

1754. Consult; Frontier Forts, I. 47 et seq.; See *Paxtang, Harris' Ferry, Tolihaio.*

Sawatara.—Board of Prop. (1727), Arch. Sec. Ser., XIX. 750. **Sawhatara.** —Board of Prop. (1727), Arch. Sec. Ser., XIX. 755. **Schwatara.**—LeRoy (1755), Archives, Sec. Ser., VII. 411. **Swahatawro.**—Weiser (1755), Col. Rec. VI. 657. **Swatara.** — Evans, map, 1749. **Swatara.**—Templeton (1754), Archives, II. 186. **Swataro.**—Templeton (1754), Archives, II. 186. **Swatarro.**—Lowe (1730), Archives, I. 268. **Swatawra.**—Howells, map, 1792. **Swatawro.**—Read (1756), Col. Rec. VII 303. **Sweetara.**—Weiser (1757), Archives, III. 293. **Sweet arroe.**—Butcher (1736), Col. Rec., IV. 182. **Swehatara.**—Instruc. (1756), Archives. II. 551. **Swehataro.**—Morris (1757), Col. Rec. VII. 538.

SWEGATSY, SEWGACHIE, SWEGACHEY, SWEEGOCHIE, etc. A name frequently found in the Archives and Records (Col. Rec., V. 475, 571; VI. 62, 70, 77, 80, 102, 474, etc.). A corruption of Oswegatchie, "at the very outlet," a former Iroquois village at the site of Ogdensburg, New York. The village was under the influence of the French Catholic missionaries. At the outbreak of the French and Indian War, in 1755, the Iroquois in this village took the side of the French. They also were with the British in the War of the Revolution. The name does not belong in this State.

TACONY. The name of a creek which unites with the Wingohocking to form the present Frankford Creek, which enters the Delaware from the west at Bridesburg, Philadelphia. The stream called Little Tacony enters the latter creek below Frankford. Also the name of a Township in Philadelphia, before 1682, at the mouth of Frankford Creek (Holme's map). On Hill's map of 1801-07, the name Frankford is given to the present Tacony, and to the present Frankford Creek. Tacony is given as the name of the present Little Tacony. Holme's map gives the name Francford Creek to the entire stream, including the present Tacony. Later maps give the name Frankford Creek, from the junction of the Wingohocking with the Tacony. The name is first recorded in the Patent of Gov. Francis Nicholls, dated October 25, 1667, "to the Inhabitants of Taoconinck." Caspar Fish granted his share of this land about 150 acres, to Lawrence Cock, who by deed conveyed this land to Anna (Hannah) Salter. on

Sept. 25, 1679. William Penn confirmed this by a note in his own handwriting, March 16, 1684. This land was granted to Henry Mallows, Jan. 10, 1704, by the Executors of the Will of Anna Salter (Archives, Sec. Ser., XIX. 485). The Caspar Fish, above mentioned, noted in the list or "Tydable Persons att Tacokanink," as "Casper fisck," in 1677 (Records of Upland Court, 77). On April 23, 1681, Hannah (Anna) Salter "of Toakony, Widow" conveyed her land at "Coakanake Creek To the Possion of Daniel Peage (Pegg) and his Heirs for Ever (op. cit. 445). On October 4 and 5, 1697, Jno. Tzack mortgaged to Ann Moore "all that Brick Messuage or Tenem't, and also that Tract of Land Situate at the mouth of Tacconinek Creek" (op. cit. 343). This mortgage, not being paid the land was granted to Samuel Finney, of Cheatam Hill, Lancaster County, Feb., 6 and 7, 1700. Many other interesting entries are made in the early records concerning grants of land in Tacony (See also, Archives, Third Ser., III. 311. 312, 317). In the survey to Peter Cock, of 650 acres of land called "Quissinomink," the name given to Frankford Creek is Quissinomink, and Little Tacony is called Tawacawomink. This land was surveyed Nov. 24, 1675 (Archives, Third Ser., III. 316) See *Quissinawomink*. It is difficult to find the correct form of this name. Tawacawomink seems to be the name from which Tacony has been corrupted. It may be a corruption of Tachan, "woods," with the locative ing, meaning in the woods, or "at the woods." Tauwatawique, was the Delaware for "wilderness." Or, the name may be a corrupt form of Tankhanna, "small stream." The maps of Scull (1759), (1770), and Howell's (1792) give the name Frankfort to the main stream. Holme's map (1681-84) gives the name Francford.

Quissinomink.—Holme (1675), Archives, Third Ser., III. 316. **Tacconinek.**—B. of Prop. (1702), Arch. Sec. Ser., XIX. 343. **Tackoney.**—Holme (1682), Arch. Third Ser., III. 311. **Tacony.**—Morris, map, 1848. **Tacconinok.**—Nicholls (1667), Arch. Sec. Ser., XIX. 485. **taokanink.** —Rec. Up. (1677), Record of Upland Court, 63. **Taokakink.**—Rec. Up. (1677), Record of Upland Court, 77. **Tawacawomink.**—Holme (1675), Arch. Third. Ser. III. 516. **Toaconink.**—(Tp.) Holme's map, 1681-4 **Toakony.**—Fairman (1681), Arch. Sec. Ser., XIX. 445.

TAMAQUA. A town in Schuylkill County. The name is derived from that of the stream called Tamaqua, or Little Schuylkill. Tamaque, or Tamaqua, is a corruption of Tankamochk, "little beaver," and with the the suffix, hanna, meaning "little beaver stream." The stream is referred to in 1790 as "Tamagaay or little Schuylkill" (Archives, XI. 678). See *Little Schuylkill.*

Tamagaay.—Lloyd (1790), Archives, XI. 678. **Tamaqua.**—Morris, map, 1848, also Little Schuylkill. **Tamauguay.**—Scull, map, 1770 (small map). **Tumauguay.**—Scull, map, 1770 (large map). **Little Schuylkill.**—Howells, map, 1792.

TAMARACK. The name of a P. O. in Clinton County. The name is a corruption of the Indian name of the larch tree, which seems to be a corruption of Takpeu, "damp," and hacki, "earth," or Hackmatack, "bad low lands." The term applied to the land upon which the trees grew, rather than to the tree.

TAMENEND. The name of a town in Schuylkill County, named in honor of the famous Delaware chief, Tamenend, or Tammany, the leading chief or "King" of the Delaware tribe, when William Penn made his treaty at the Shackamaxon in 1682, and from whom he purchased lands along the Delaware River. He signed the Deed of 1683 as Tammanens, for the land between Pemmapecka and Neshaminey Creeks (Archives, I. 62). His name is also given the form of Tamanen on this Deed. (See also, op. cit., 64, 65, 100, 117, 124). His mark, as recorded on these Deeds, is a rude picture of a Turtle, the tribe of which he was chief. In the Deed of 1697 he is called "King Taminy" (op. cit. 125). In 1694 he is called "Tamanee" (Col. Rec. I. 447). As the leading chief of the Unami tribe he was the leading chief, or "King," of the Delaware nation. He died before 1701, as his name does not occur in any of the transactions of the Penns with the Delawares after that time. He was succeeded by Skalitchy, who died before 1715, and was succeeded by Sassounan, or Allummapees, who died in 1747, at Shamokin (Col. Rec. II. 600; see *Shamokin*). The name Tamenend, means "the affable." The Delawares revered the memory of this famous chief. During the Revolution his admirers dubbed him a saint. The first day of May was Saint Tammany's Day, and was celebrated in Philadelphia by parades, speeches and Indian dances. This Tammany Society in Philadelphia is claimed by some as being the original of the present society of Red Men. It seems that the Sons of Tammany, in Philadelphia, was a society of Loyalist tendencies. Many similar societies were organized during the Revolution. The Tammany Society of New York, founded 1786, was at first a patriotic and charitable organization. During the first thirty years after its organization this society did a wonderful work in protecting the new Republic. During the War of 1812 it furnished three Generals and 1200 men for the army. During 1861 is furnished the Union army with the entire 42nd. N. Y. Infantry Regt., which was equipped at the expense of the society. Consult; Heckewelder, Indian Nations, 300-301, 1876; City Club of N. Y., Sec. Part, Half Moon Papers, No. 2; Del. Co. Hist. Soc., Proceedings, Vol. I., The Patron Saint of the Amer. Rev. 1902; Hist. Soc. Pa., Mag. of Hist., XXV., The Society of the Sons of St. T.; Hist. Soc. of Brown University, Papers, No. 8, The Tammany Soc. of R. I., 1877. Also any of the Encyclopaedias, under title Tammany.

TANGASCOUTACK. A creek which enters the West Branch of the Susquehanna from the south in Clinton County, at Tangas. The name may be a corruption of Tank-maskek-tuck, "small swamp creek." The various forms of the name are so corrupt that it is difficult to discover what the original form was.

Tangascootack.—Hopkins, atlas map, 1872. **Tangas.**—Present station on P. R. R. **Tangiscotac.**—State map, 1911. **Tingascogtak.** — Howell, map, 1792. **Tingascoutack.**—Scull, map, 1770 (small map). **Tingascoutack.**—Scull, map, 1770 (large map). **Tungascoatack.**—Morris, map, 1848.

TAORACKAN. The name of a place at which Ephraim Herrman, Lawrence Cock and Peter Van Brug were each granted 25 acres of land in 1681, opposite Burlington, N. J. (Records of Upland Court, 187). See *Hataorackan Creek.*

TATAMY. The name of a town in Northampton County, named in honor of Moses Fonda Tatemy (also Titamy, Totami, Tundy), a famous Delaware chief, who often acted as messenger and interpreter of the Province. He was born near Cranberry, N. J., in

the latter part of the 17th Century. He was given a tract of 300 acres of land near Stockertown, Forks Township, for his services to the Province. He was living there in 1742, when Count Zinzendorf and his party visited him. The Indian trail to the Minisinks led past Tatamy's house. The creek near his reserve was formerly called Lehietan, also Lefevre's Creek and also Tatamy's Creek. It is now called Bush Kill Creek. In 1752 William Parsons mentions this creek as "Tatamy's Creek, which bounds the Town (Easton) to the North" (Archives, II. 95, 96). When the Iroquois ordered the Delawares to remove from "the Forks," Tatamy asked that he be permitted to stay on his tract of land. The Province granted this request, provided the Iroquois would make no objection (Col. Rec. IV. 624-625). The Iroquois evidently made no objection, as Tatamy continued to live on his tract near Stockertown until his death. He was baptized by Brainerd, on July 21, 1746, when he was given the name of Moses Fonda Tatemy (Mem. Mor. Church, I. 26-27). Tatemy's son, William, was killed by an Irish boy, when on his way to the Council at Easton in 1757 (Archives, III. 209). The young man died. Heckewelder made the mistake of confusing the death of this son in his account of the life of Tatemy (Hist. Ind. Nat., 302, 337). Tatemy must have died some time during 1761, as his name does not appear after that year. Consult; Col. Rec., VIII. 132, 156, 174-5, 414, 463, 466, 491; Archives, I. 630, 641; III. 66, 209, 216, 247, 252, 341, etc.

TECHORASSI, or TEQUIRASI. The name of the tract of land below Tinicum, noted on Lindstrom's map as "Stille's land," in honor of John Stille, who was born at Tinicum in 1646, died April 24th, 1722. He was one of the original Trustees of the Swedes Church, at Wicacoa, and was buried in the church-yard of that church (Records of Upland, 78-79).

TENICUM. The name of a creek which enters the Delaware from the west in Bucks County. A corruption of Menatey, "an island," with the locative ing, or onk, signifying "at the island;" also the name of a Township, Tinicum, in the same county. See *Tinicum.* The creek in this county is noted on the early maps as follows:

Tenecum.—(Tp.) Scull, map, 1759. **Tenicum.**—Map of 1911. **Tinicum.**—Scull, map, 1759; Howell, map, 1792.

THREE SPRINGS. A prominent landmark on the Raystown Path to the Ohio, from Harris' Ferry (Harrisburg), situated at the present Three Springs, Huntingdon County. Is mentioned in the extract from Weiser's Journal to the Ohio, in 1748, "The Black Log is 8 or 10 miles South East of the Three Springs and Frank's Town lies to ye North" (Archives, II. 13). Weiser on this trip did not go by way of the Three Springs, but kept on the trail to Frankstown. In 1754 the distance is given, "From G. Croghan's to ye 3 Springs, N. 70, W. 10. 7 W. From the 3 Springs to Auchquick Gap, S. 70, W. 7, W. 5" (Archives, II. 134. In the table of distances given by John Harris, 1754, the distance from the Black Log "to the 3 Springs—10 Miles. to the sidling Hill Gap—8 Miles" (op. cit. 135). See also Colonial Records, V., 750-751; 759-763; Scull map, 1770.

TIADACHTON. See *Tyadaghton, Pine Creek, Lycoming.*

TINECUM. See *Tinicum.*

TEN MILE LICK. A landmark on the Frank's Town Path, situated near Spring Church, Armstrong County. It is mentioned in the table of distances given in 1754 by John Harris, "to the 10 mile Lick,—6 Miles, to Kiskemenette's Town on the Creek, runs into the Allegheny Rivr. 6 mils. down, (almost as large as Schuylkill),—10 Miles" (Archives, II. 136). In the table of distances given by Hugh Crawford and Andrew Montour, in 1752, one of the points mentioned is, "To the Round Holes—25 Miles" (op. cit. 133), The "10 mile Lick" is also mentioned in the extract from Weiser's Journal of 1748 (Archives, II. 12).

TEXAS. A town in Lycoming County; also a Township in Wayne County, named in honor of the state of Texas, which is a corruption of Texias, or Techan, meaning "friends," or "allies," the name given by the Hasinai to the group of tribes allied against the Apache. The name does not have any historic significance in this State. Consult; Handbook of American Indians, II. 738-740.

TIDIOUTE. The name of a creek which enters the Allegheny River from the west, near Tidioute, Warren County. The name has been given various meanings, such as "see far," "straight water," "cluster of islands," etc. The original form of the name cannot be discovered in the present corruption. The name is somewhat the same as that of the Indian village in Mass., called Titicut, which was corrupted to Titecute. This name is a corruption of Keh-teih-tuk-qut, "on the great river." The significance would not be amiss so far as Tidioute is concerned.

Tideiute.—Morris, map, 1848. **Tidioute.**—Recent maps, 1872, 1911.

TINICUM. There were two islands in the Delaware known as Matinicum, or Tinicum. One of these was the island now known as Burlington Island, the other was on the west shore of the river below the mouth of the Schuylkill. The latter was the more prominent of the two, as it was the scene of the events connected with the first settlement by the Swedes. W. R. Gerard wrongly makes Burlington Island "the seat of government of the Swedes" (Handbook American Indians, II. 754). The various names applied to these two islands are the same, hence the confusion which arises. The name is a corruption of Menatey, "an island," with the locative ing, or onk, or ung, signifying "at the island." The history of the various attempts of the Dutch and Swedes to form settlements on the Delaware are too lengthy to more than notice in this work. The various general histories, and the references given, will serve as a basis for more careful study. The various documents relating to the events connected with the settlement of the Delaware will be found in the references given in the synonomy. In 1638 the Swedes established a settlement at the site of the present Wilmington, under the direction of Peter Minuit, who had formerly been with the Dutch West India Company. He immediately built a fort and trading house at the mouth of Minquaas Creek. Both the fort and the creek were named in honor of the young Queen of Sweden, Christina. John Printz was commissioned as Governor of New Sweden, in 1642, and landed at Fort Christina Feb. 15, 1643. Printz established his seat of government on Tincium Island, where he built a fort, called Gottenburg, a mansion, and in

1646, a church. He also built a mill on Cobb's Creek and about four miles below Salem Creek he erected a fort, known as Elsinburg, thus gaining control of the western shore of the river, and the rich trade with the Minquas, Susquehannocks. In 1653 Printz returned to Sweden. He was succeeded by John Rysingh in 1653-54. The first thing that the new Governor did was to take Fort Casimir, which Stuyvesant had built near New Castle. On June 12, 1654 a Council was held with the Indians at Printz Hall, on Tinicum Island. In the spring of 1655 Governor Stuyvesant arrived on the river with an armament of seven vessels and about 600 men. On Sept. 25, 1655 the entire Swedish possessions on the river fell into the hands of the Dutch. On March 12, 1664 Charles II. granted to the Duke of York and and Albany, a tract which included the New Netherlands. Col. Richard Nicholls, with Robert Carr, Sir. George Cartwright and Samuel Maverick, with a squadron received the Dutch possessions from Stuyvesant on Sept. 8, 1664. Sir Robert Carr was sent to reduce the Dutch possessions on the Delaware, which capitulated on Oct. 1, 1664. Col. Nicholls acted as Governor until 1667, when he was succeeded by Col. Francis Lovelace. In July 1673 the Dutch, under Evertse and Benke, recaptured New York. The inhabitants of the Delaware declared their submission to Gov. Anthony Colve. The country was restored to the English in 1674, by the Treaty of Westminister, and Sir Edmund Andros was appointed Governor of the territory which had been surrendered by the Dutch, Oct. 31, 1674. On June 24, 1674, the Duke of York granted to Lord Berkley and Sir George Cartaret "the province of New Jersey." Lord Berkley sold half of his interest to John Fenwicke, in trust for Edward Byllinge, and his assigns. Byllinge conveyed his interest to William Penn, Gawen Lawrie and Nicholas Lucas, in trust for his creditors. Sir George Cartaret died in 1679, and his lands in East Jersey were sold to pay his debts. This land was bought by William Penn and eleven others, Feb. 1 and 2, 1681-82. The Duke of York made a fresh grant to these and twelve others, March 14, 1682. In 1681 Charles II. made a grant of a tract of land to William Penn, in payment of a debt of 16,000 Pounds which the British Government owed Sir William Penn, the father of William Penn, in whose honor the King named the tract Pennsylvania. Penn himself wished to call his tract New Wales, but the King insisted upon the name Pennsylvania. The King signed this Charter for Pennsylvania, March 4, 1681. In 1682 Penn published "The frame of government for the Province of Pennsylvania." He landed at Upland, in the fall of 1682, and soon after went to the region between Coaquannock and Shackamaxon, where he made various purchases from the Indians (See *Coaquannock, Shackamaxon, Minquas Creek, Schuylkill etc.*).

During all of these changes of government on the Delaware Tinicum was a most important point. The land along the western shore of the river was occupied, when first discovered, by the tribe since known as Delawares, then called River Indians, and probably some of the Minquas. or Susquehannocks, who had sought protection from the Iroquois by removing to this region. The Indians living along the river sold various tracts of land to the early Dutch and Swedish settlers. On the Schuylkill, 1656, to Arent Corson (Archives, Sec. Ser., V. 257). Mattehooren was one of the leading chiefs in these transactions. This chief, with Peminackan, Ackehoorn and Sinquees, on July 19, 1655, deeded the lands at Tinicum, which seemed to be the name of the land along the river from Minquas Creek southward, as the deed reads, "a certain portion of land named Tinnecongh, situate on the west shore of the aforesaid river, beginning at the west point of the Minquaas Kill, called in the Indian tongue Suppeckongh, unto the mouth of the bay or river called Boompjes hook, and in the Indina tongue Canaresse" (Sec. Ser., V. 266). The entire region along the western shore of the Delaware, below the mouth of the Schuylkill, was given the name which was later applied to the island itself. It was a general designation before it became a sepcial one, as was frequently the case with Indians names. The string of islands in the river, from League Island southward, gave the name Matinicum, or Tinicum, to the land along the river, near these islands. The name would therefore signify, in its broader sense, "at the islands." The island was also called Carr's Island, in honor of Sir Robert Carr (Archives. Sec. Ser., V. 603). Some writers have expressed doubt concerning the burning of the fort which Printz built upon Tinicum Island. Hudde states, in 1646, "The farthest of these is not far from Tinnekonk, which is an island, and is towards , the river side, secured by creeks and underwood; there the Governor, John Printz, keeps his residence. This is a pretty strong fort, constructed by laying very heavy hemlock, (greenen) logs the one on the other; but this fort, with all its buildings, was burnt down on the 5th. of December, 1645" (Archives, Sec. Ser., V. 110). The murder of the two "Christians" by the Indians, at "Matiniconck Island" (which is called Tinnagcong Island," in the Records of Upland Court, in reference to the same affair) evidently refers to the island at Burlington. The two men who were killed, during a drunken debauch, were Peter Veltscheerder and Christiaen Samuels (Rec. Upland, 149), who were in the employ of Peter Alrichs, and the two Indians charged with the crime were Tashiowycam and Wyannattamo (Arch. Sec. Ser., VII. 741 etc.). On account of the two names, Tinicum and Matinicum, being used for the island at Burlington, and for the island below the Schuylkill, as well as for the land along the western shore of the Delaware, below the Schuylkill, all of the various synonyms are included under this title. The context of each name will show to which of these three places the name was applied. It may be stated that as a general rule, Tinicum had reference to the region below the Schuylkill, including the island, and Matinicum referred to the present Burlington Island, but even this is a general rule, which has many exceptions. See *Matinicum.* Consult any of the general histories concerning the Swedish and Dutch settlements on the Delaware. See under title, the various place names on the Delaware River; *Coaquannock, Minquas Creek, Shackamaxon,* etc.

VanDer Donck's map of 1656, gives the name Matina Konck, as the name of the region in the present Tinicum Township, Delaware County, and the entire region as occupied by the "Sauwanoos." This name does not have reference to the tribe known as

the Shawnee, but means s i m p l y "southerners," as distinguished from the Delawares, or Algonkian tribes, living to the north of this region. The Turkey clan of the Delawares occupied the region below the Unami tribe, or clan, on the Delaware River. The name "River Indians" was the common designation of all of the Delawares living along the river. It was a geographic grouping, and not a tribal one-although the "River Indians" were all Delawares. The names of the various chiefs who were brought into contact with the first settlers are found in the references given.

Matennekonk.—Hudde (1648), Arch., Sec. Ser., V. 121. **Matina Konck.**—Van Der Donck, map, 1656. **Matineconck.**—Nicholls (1678) Arch. Sec. Ser., VII. 721. **Matinicook.** — Lovelace (1671), Arch. Sec. Ser., VII. 742. **Matiniconck.**—Nicholls (1668), op. cit., 721. **Matiniconk.**—Doc. (1671), Arch. Sec. Ser., V. 629. **Matinicom.**—Deed of 1675, same reference, 703. **Matinicum.**—Census of 1680, Arch. Sec. Ser., VII. 806. **Matinneconck.**—Hudde (1648), Arch. Sec. Ser., XVI. 237. **Matinnekonk.**—Hudde (1646), Arch. Sec. Ser., V. III. **Matoneconk Isles.**—Morris, map, 1711, Hazard's Ann., 373, 391. **Mechopinachan.**—Deed of 1649 (east side Del.) Arch. Sec. Ser., XVI. 239. **Mutiniconck.**—Doc. (1671), Arch. Sec. Ser., V. 630. **Mattinacunck.**—Tom (1673), Arch. Sec. Ser. VII. 756. **Mattinagcom Eyeland.**—Upland Court (1679), Rec. Up. Court, 141. **Mattinicom.**—Doc. (1668), Arch. Sec. Ser., XVI. 256. **Mattiniconck.**—Andros (1678), Arch. Sec. Ser., V. 739. **Mattiniconk.**—Lovelace (1671), Arch. Sec. Ser., XVI. 268. **Mattinicunk.**—Deed to Penn (1682), Archives, I. 48. **Mattinnakonk.**—Doc (1664), Arch. Sec. Ser., XVI 244. **Tamecongh.**—Deed of 1651, Arch. Sec. Ser., V. 262. **Tamicongh.**—Deed of 1651, same reference 261. **Tenecum.**—Pa. coun. (1685), Col. Rec. I, 126. **Tinicom.**—Nicholls (1672), Arch. Sec. Ser., V. 657. **Tinicum.**—LaGrange (Doc. of 1668), Arch. Sec. Ser., VII. 799. **Tinnachkonck.**—Upland Court (1681), Rec. Up. Court, 191. **Tinnackunk.**—Huygen (1663), Arch. Sec. Ser., VII. 699. **Tinnaconck.**—Tom (1673), same reference, 756. **Tinnacum.**—Census (1680), same reference, 805. **Tinnagcong.**—Upland Court (1679), Up. Court, 152. **Tinnakunck.**—Printz (1656), Arch. Sec. Ser., VII. 494. **Tinnakungk.**—VanDyck (1658), same reference, 531. **Tinnakunk.**—Beekman (1661), same reference, 671. **Tinneco.**—Beekman (1661), s a m e reference, 670. **Tinnecongh.**—Deed of 1655, op. cit., V. 266. **Tinneconhg.**—Deed of 1651, Arch. Sec Ser., V. 264. **Tinnekonck.**—Beekman (1662), op. cit., VII. 678. **Tinnekonk.**—Hudde (1648), op. cit., XVI. 237. **Tinnekoncks.**—Lindstrom, MS. map.

In the Deed of 1655, made to Peter Stuyvesant, of a "certain portion of land named Tinnecongh, situated on the west shore of the aforesaid river" (Delaware), the Deed is signed "on the land Camecouck itself," by the chief Mattehooren, who signed the Deed to Arent Corsen, for the lands on the Schuylkill River (Arch. Sec. Ser., V. 257, 267). On the map of Van Der Donck, 1656, "Kemkockes" is noted on the eastern side of the river, above the mouth of the Schuylkill.

TIOGA. The name of a river, county, township, town also the name of a former Indian village at Tioga Point, Bradford County, near Athens, the name of which should never have been changed from its historic Indian name to its meaningless present name of Athens. The name does not mean "gateway," as frequently stated. It is a corruption of De-yoh-ho-gah, "where it forks," or "at the forks." The same word, in the various Iroquois forms, is applied to the forks of various streams. The Seneca form, Diondega, was applied to "the forks" of the Ohio, at Pittsburgh. There are many variants of the same name, all having the same meaning. The Tioga River has its springs in Tioga County, flowing north to the Chemung, which it enters near Corning, New York. The name was formerly applied to the present Chemung to its junction with the North Branch at Tioga Point. It is so marked on Morris' map of 1848. On the Howell's map, 1792, it is designated as "Cayuga or Tyoga River." Evan's Map, 1755, designates the stream as "Cayuga Branch," as does also his map of 1749. Zeisberger, in his Journal of 1767 calls the stream the "Tiaogee" (MS). Pouchot's map, 1758, designates the stream as, "R. de Kanestio," which is evidently simply a variation of Andaste (See *Susquehanna*), which is a corruption of kanesta, "mud," or "clay," which has been translated into the Delaware Sisku, or Assisku, with the suffix hanna, making Susquehanna. This name was simply an Algonkian translation of the Iroquoian name Kanesta, which was corrupted by the French writers to Andaste. De l'Isle's map of 1712 gives the name "R. des Andastes" to the Susquehanna (See *Susquehanna*). Heckewelder gives Tioga as a corruption of Tiaoga, "a gate, or place of entrance." He says, "David Zeisberger, who travelled that way to Onondaga in 1750, told me

that at Tiaoga, or the Gate, Six Nation Indians were stationed for the purpose of ascertaining the character of all persons who crossed over their country, and whoever entered their territory by another way than through the Gate, or by way of the Mohawk, was suspected by them of evil purpose and treated as a spy or enemy" (Indian Names 268). Reichel says in a note, "Bishop Spangenberg, accompanied by David Zeisberger and John Shebosh, passed through the Gates of Tioga, on the 12th. of June, 1745, on the way to Onondaga. They were the first Moravians to enter the country of the Six Nations at this point of ingress." While this statement, concerning the Tioga being a "Gate" to the Iroquois country, may be correct, it does not give the correct origin of the name Tioga, nor is it true that Tioga was the southern "Gateway" to the Iroquois country. According to the statement of a number of Indians Shenango, or Chenango, was the southern "Gate-way" to the Iroquois country. The place where the Iroquois stationed guards to prevent the entrance of strangers to the Seneca country was at Passigachkunk (which see) on the present Cowanesque. According to Zeisberger's Journal of 1767 this was the point where C. F. Post was turned back, because the Iroquois would not allow him to go forward on this path which was forbidden to strangers. Zeisberger called the Cowanesque the "Tiaogee." Passigachkunk was the last town on this river. C. F. Post, John Hays, Isaac Stille and Moses Tatemy were appointed to go with Tedyuskung to the Ohio in 1760, but were turned back at Passigachkunk. Tedyuskung was allowed to go on with his Indians, but Post, Hays and the others were obliged to return (Col. Rec. VII. 491; Archives, III. 735-741). This trail up the present Chemung, down the Tioga, up the Cowanesque, across the divide to the Allegheny and then down it to the Ohio, was one of the earliest trails between the upper Susquehanna and Allegheny. It was used chiefly by the Indians during the period of hostility, 1755-1779. White men were not allowed to travel it. On account of there being no white settlements in this entire region in 1755-1760, during the period of the worst Indian raids into the settlements, the white captives were frequently taken to the villages of Tioga, and then up the river to these distant villages, from which many were returned after the hostility had ended (See *Passigachkunk*). The Indian village at the site of Athens, Bradford County, was one of the most prominent Indian villages during the period after the expulsion of the Delawares from the "Forks of the Delaware," after 1737. Many of the Delawares removed to Wyoming after the Treaty of 1744, and soon after commenced going on up the Susquehanna to Tioga Point. The village was made up of Delaware, Munsee and Mohickon, with a sprinkling of Nanticoke and Tutelo, but the two latter tribes soon moved on up to Shenango and other villages to the north. Tioga was made up chiefly of Munsee. who were hostile to the English. The friendly Delaware remained at Wyoming or Shamokin. During 1756-57 various messengers of the Province visited Tioga. In the negotations of the Province towards a peace with the Delaware, Tioga was the seat of the authority of Tedyuskung, who claimed to have been made "King" of the Delawares in 1755, by the authority of the Iroquois (Col. Rec. VII. 199). This famous chief, whose "Kingship" the Iroquois denied lived at Wyoming, but also had a home at Tioga and Passigachkunk, to which places he retired, after his raiding tours into the settlements, with his white captives (Col. Rec. VII. 242; See *Passigachkunk*). In 1756 Andrew Montour and Scarouady visited Tioga, at which time the village contained 50 cabins and 90 grown men (op. cit. 67, 68, 74, 98). In the same year Paxinosa, the Shawnee chief, was living at Tioga, when New Castle held a Council with the Indians (op. cit. 137). In the summer of 1757 two Indians, Nathaniel and Zaccheus, went to Tioga to find Tedyuskung, and were obliged to go on to Passigachkunk (op. cit. 588). In 1758 Benjamin, a friendly Indian, stated that Paxinosa and his whole family were at Tioga, and were about to remove to the Ohio (Col. Rec. VIII. 126). In 1761 some of the chiefs of the Six Nations requested that a Trading House be erected at Tioga, in order that they might be able to get goods cheaper than they could get them from General Johnson (Col. Rec. VIII. 643). Gov. Hamilton informed the Indians that he had set up two trading houses,

at Shamokin and at Pittsburgh, and could not put one at Tioga (647). In 1770 several Iroquois Indians from Tioga went to Philadelphia seeking relief, as they were in a needy condition (Col. Rec. IX. 648). During the war of the Revolution Tioga became a gathering place for the Indians and Tories. The settlement was destroyed by Col. Hartley in Sept. 1778. The Indians and Tories, under Butler, having deserted the place just before the arrival of Hartley's troops (Archives, VII. 6). On Aug. 11th. 1779 the army of General Sullivan reached Tioga, after fording the Tioga River (Chemung) just below the present Tioga Point. On the 12th. the army commenced the erection of the fort which was called Fort Sullivan. This stood in the center of the present Athens. It was about 100 yards square, with a block house at each angle. The army advanced from Tioga on Aug. 26th. Col. Shreve was left in command of the fort, with a garrison of 250 men, besides a number of invalids. The army returned to Tioga, after its expedition to the Seneca country, on Sept. 30th., leaving for Wyoming on Oct. 4th., after having demolished the fort (See Jour. Mil. Exped. Gen. Sull. 1879). A conference was held with the Indians at Tioga by Col. Timothy Pickering in Nov. 1790, and in 1791 Col. Thomas Proctor passed through on his mission to the Indians of the northwest (Arch. Sec. Ser., IV. 559 etc.). In 1787 the Boundary Commission set up the 90th., Milestone on the "'Cawwanishee Flats" (Cowanesque at the mouth of the Tioga River, on June 11th., by Andrew Ellicott and Andrew Porter. The Commission then went up the Tioga, and across the divide to the Genesee and Allegheny Rivers. At the 167 Milestone, at the crossing of Tuneungwant Creek, near Tuna, the Comuissioners were stopped by the Indians, until after the Council with the Indians (Archives, XI. 178).

Chaamonaque.—Vaudreuil (1757), Arch. Sec. Ser., VI. 404. **Diabago.**—Post (1758), quoted by Rupp, West. Penna., app. 77, (a misprint). **Diahoga.**—Hawley (1756), Col. Rec., VII. 12. **Diahogo.** —Montour (1756), the same, 67. **Iuragen.**—Bellin, map, 1755. **Taaogo.**— Ft. John Conf. (1757), N. Y. Doc. Col. Hist., VII. 260. **Ta-yo-ga.**—Morgan, League of Iro., 470. **Teaoga.**—Dearborn (1779), Jour. Sull. Exped., 66. **Teaogon.** —James (1757), quoted by Proud, Penn., II. app. 60. **Theaggen.**—Pouchot map, 1758. **Theoga.**—Vaudreuil (1757), Arch. Sec. Ser., VI. 404. **Theoge.**—the same 404. **Thyesa.**—Ellicott (1787), Archives, XI. 178. **Tiago.**—Johnson (1757), N. Y. Doc. Col. Hist., VII 279. **Tiaogos.** —Guy Park Conf. (1775), s a m e reference, VII. 560. **Tiahogan.**—Weiser (1758), Col. Rec., VIII. 120. **Tiego.**— Livermore (1779), in N. H. Hist Soc. Coll., VI. 321. **Tinogan.**—Weiser (1758), Col. Rec, VIII. 120. **Tioga.**—Scull, map, 1770. **Tioko.**—Orndt (1758), Archives, III. 350. **Tiyaoga.**—Hawley (1755), Archives, VII 49. **Toaougo.**—Horsfield (1757), Archives, III. 142 **Tohiccon.**— Evans map, 1749. **Tohicoon.**—Evans map, 1755. **Tohickon.**—Penn (1768), Col. Rec., IX. 437. **Tohikon.**—Homann Heirs map, 1756. **Toikon.**—Esnauts and Rapilly map, 1777. **Trijaoga.**—Ft. John. Conf. (1756), N. Y. Doc. Col. Hist., VII. 47. **Trizaoga.**—Hawley (1755), same reference 47. **Tyahogah.**—Bard (1758), Archives. III. 433. **Tyaoga.**—Ft. John Conf (1756). same reference. 110. **Tyoga.**—Ellicott map, 1787.

Some of the forms of the name in the Jour. of Sull. Exped. (1779), are, Teaogo, 108; Tiege, 184; Tiyuga, 125; Tyuga, 124; Tyogea, 74; Tyoga, 24 etc. Howell's map (1792), gives the name, at Tioga Point. "Lockhartsburg." Morris' map. 1848, "Athens," and "Tioga Point."

TIONA. A town in Warren County. The name is a contraction of Tionesta, (which see).

TIONESTA. The name of a river, which rises in Warren and McKean Counties, and enters the Allegheny from the east at Tionesta, Forest County; also the name of a town and township in Forest County. The name is probably a corruption of Tyonesiyo, "there it has fine banks." The same name has been corrupted to Genesee, in Potter County. David Zeisberger established a Moravian mission near the mouth of the Tionesta in 1767, at the mixed Munsee and Iroquois village of Goshgoshing (which see). There were a number of villages of the Munsee in this region (See *Hickory Town, Lawunakhannek*).

Teonista.—Morris map, 1848. **Teowenista.**—Adlum map, 1790. **Tioanesta.**— Dallas (1792), Arch. Third Ser., III. 467. **Tionesta.**—Dallas (1795), Arch Sec. Ser.. III 468. **Tyonesta.**—Howell's map, 1792. **Tyoniesta.**—Dallas (1809), Arch. Third Ser., III. 477.

TIPPECANOE. A P. O. in Fayette County. named for the Indian village on the west bank of the Wabash River, below the mouth of Tippecanoe Creek, Indiana. The name is a corruption of Kitapkwanunk, "buffalo-fish place." Gen. W. H. Harrison destroyed this village Nov. 7, 1811. The battle near this place on that day was known as the Battle of Tippecanoe, and General Harrison was called "Old Tippecanoe" because of his victory. The name has no significance of a local historical nature in this state.

TIQUAMINGY TOWN. A former Indian village, situated at the mouth of Chatham's Run, Clinton County. Noted on Scull's map, 1759.

TIOZINOSSONGACHTA. A former Indian village, at the site of Cold Spring, New York, at the mouth of Cold Spring Creek. This creek is noted on Howell's map (1792) as Inshaunshagota. Adlum's map (1790) notes the village, on the west bank of the Allegheny, and above the mouth of the creek, as Teushhanushsonggoghta. Ellicott's Boundary map, 1787, gives the form Tushanushagota. The village, at which the Friends established a mission in 1798, mentioned by Maria King as Geneseinguhta (Hist. Ceres, 26, 1896) was at the same site.

In the narrative of Mary Jemison the place is called, "Che-ua-shung-gautau" (7th. Ed., 79, 1910). In the MS. Zeisberger's Journal of 1767, he gives the form Tiozinossongatchta. He reached the village on Oct. 11th., on his way to the mouth of the Tionesta. On his return journey he reached the village on Oct. 26th. In his Journal of this date he calls it "the most central of the Seneka towns." Zeisberger passed through the village again in May 1768 on his way to the mission at Goshgoshing (which see). This village is still the home of "the old time people." Handsome Lake, the Seneca Prophet, lived at this village from 1810 to 1812 (Consult; The Code of Handsome Lake, the Seneca Prophet, 7, 12, 46, 76, 1913). On Morgan's map of 1720, the village of Deonagano is situated at this place. Another form of the name is Dyune-ga-nooh (Beauchamp, Place Names in N. Y., 63). This site has been occupied by the Seneca since about the middle of the 18th. Century. The region previous to the Seneca occupation was probably occupied by the Erie, or the Neutrals. It is possible that the Wenro spread along the river previous to 1673. Col. Proctor, in his Journal of 1791, says, "our guide conducted us in safety, at about 10 o'clock at night, to O'Beel's town, called in the Indian language, Tenachshegouchtongee, or the burnt house"

(Arch. Sec. Ser., IV. 567). O'Bail's (Cornplanter's) town was called Dionosadegi, "place of burnt houses." This village was in Warren County, Penna., near the state line (See *Cornplanter*). Proctor had evidently gotten the names of the two villages mixed.

TOBECO, TOBEES, TOBY'S CREEK. The former name of the present Clarion River, which enters the Allegheny from the east in Clarion County. Heckewelder says that the Indian name of this stream was Gawunsch-hanne, "brier-stream." It was more probably Topi-hanna, "alder stream." Toby was probably a corruption of Topi. The popular legend concerning the stream being named for a trader called Toby has no foundation in fact. The stream in Monroe County, now called Tobyhanna, has the same origin. See *Clarion River*. A branch of the Clarion River now bears the historic name, as Little Toby Creek, and Toby Creek. The trail to Venango (Franklin) crossed this creek at several places. Post followed this trail to Kuskuski in 1758.

Tobeco.—Post (1758), quoted by Hanna, I. 213, Wild. Trail. **Tobees.**—Post (1758), Archives, III. 522. **Toby's Creek.**—Evans, map, 1755; Scull, 1770; Howell, 1792; Adlum, 1790.

TOBYHANNA. The name of a creek, town and township in Monroe County. The creek rises in Monroe County and enters the Lehigh from the east near Stoddartsville, Luzerne County. The name is a corruption of Topi-hanna, "alder stream." There was an old Indian trail from Wyoming to the Minisinks, on the Delaware, which passed through Monroe County. This was one of the oldest trails in the state between the Ohio and the Delaware. The army of General Sullivan followed the course of this trail through this part of the county, from Easton, in 1779. The army encamped at "Chowder Camp," now known as Hungry Hill, in Tobyhanna Township on June 20th. On the 21st. the army passed through the Great Swamp and the Shades of Death, and encamped at "Fatigue Camp," at Barren Hill, Luzerne County, 12 miles from Wilkes-Barre.

Tobahanna.—Livermore (1779), Jour. Sull. Exped., 181. **Tobahanah.**—Norris (1779), same reference, 224. **Tobehanna.**—Campfield (1779). same reference, 53. **Tobehannah.**—Dearborn (1779), same reference, 63. **Tobehannunk.**—Fellows (1779), same reference. 86. **Tobyhanna.**—Scull map, 1770. **Tobyhannah.**—Scull map, 1759. **Toby Hannunk.**—Lodge map, 1779, No. 103 A., in Jour. Sull. Exped.

TOHICKON. A creek which enters the Delaware from the west at Point Pleasant, Bucks County. Heckewelder states that the name is a corruption of Tohickham, or Tohick-hanne, "driftwood stream." The long and troublesome dispute with Tedyuskung, the Delaware "King," concerning the lands between this creek and the Kittatinny mountains, covered the entire period when the Province was seeking to make peace with the hostile Delawares, after 1755. Tedyuskung charged the Penns with fraud. This matter came up at the Council at Easton in 1758, and again in 1761. Gov. Hamilton told this chief that these lands had been purchased before he was born (Col. Rec., VIII. 653). At the commencement of the hostility of the Delawares, Tedyuskung had been asked why his people had gone to war against the English, and he had said that it was because of the frauds which had been practiced in the various land purchases. It was shown that the land in dispute had been bought in 1686, in 1737 and again in 1749. In 1742 all of these Deeds were produced, and were acknowledged to be just and correct by the Iroquois. The Walking Purchase was the chief cause of all of the trouble at this time, and the element opposed to Gov. Hamilton were not slow to make use of Tedyuskung's charges. Consult; Col. Rec., VIII. 651, 653 etc.; Walton, Conrad Weiser, 368, 378, 380, 342, 356 etc. The various purchases made by the Penn's were all acknowledged by the Iroquois, and the Delawares were given to understand that they had nothing to do with the sale of lands. See *Lehigh, Walking Purchase, Wyoming*.

Tohiccon.—Coun. at East. (1758), Col. Rec., VIII. 204. **Tohicon.**—Evans map, 1749. **Tohickon.**—Penn (1700), quoted by Reichel, Ind. Names, 268; Evans map, 1755. **Touhickon.**—Coun. at E. (1761), Col. Rec., VIII. 651.

TOLHEO, TOLKEO, TOLEHAIO. The Indian name of Swatara Gap, Lebanon County, corrupted to "The Hole." The name may be a corruption of Poquihilleu, "broken." One of the prominent Indian trails from the Schuylkill, and from the Tulpehocken region, crossed Swatara Creek and passed through this gap in the Kittatinny mountains, and across Anthony's Wilderness to the mouth of the Mahanoy and then up the Susquehanna to Shamokin (Sunbury). The course of this trail, beyond the mountains, is shown on Evans map of 1749. It was a short cut to the West Branch, and to Shamokin. The longer path ran to Harris' Ferry (Harrisburg) and then up the river. Conrad Weiser went over this path in 1737 to Shamokin. It was also the course of Count Zinzendorf in 1742, when on his way to Shamokin (Mem. Mor. Church, 80). Spangenburg went by the same route to Shamokin, in 1745. Cammerhoff went by the longer route in 1748, but returned by this route (Penn. Mag. Hist., XXIX. 160 et seq.). During the period of Indian hostility after 1755, this pass was one of the routes followed by the Indians on their raids into the settlements along Swatara Creek. Many people were killed and captured by these bands of Indians. In October, 1755, Conrad Weiser sent 50 men to guard this pass, or gap (Col. Rec. VI. 657-58). Gov. Morris commended Weiser for this act and gave him a Colonel's Commission (op. cit., 660). In 1756 Capt. Christian Busse was ordered to go to this "Gap at Tolihaio" and erect a stockade for the protection of the settlers south of the mountains (Archives, II. 547). Gov. Morris, in a letter to Col. Washington, says that he has erected "Fort Henry at a pass through the mountains, called Tolihaio" (Archives, II. 565). This is an error. The fort was never called "Fort Henry." This fort was near Millersburg, Berks County. The fort at "The Hole" was always called Fort Swatara, or Smith's Fort, because of its erection by Captain Frederick Smith (Arch. II. 552). Fort Swatara, or the fort at "The Hole," was about a mile southwest of Inwood, Lebanon County, not far from the Gap in the Kittatinny mountains. During the period from 1755 until after the close of the Conspiracy of Pontiac, many raids were made upon settlements south of the mountains (Consult; Frontier Forts, I. 47-69). In about 1756 the Moravians established a mission, called Bethel, on Swatara Creek (Loskiel, Hist. Miss., II. 180). See *Swatara*.

Talehaio.—Morris (1756), Archives, II. 555. **Tolehaio.**—Morris (1756), Archives, II. 552. **Tolhas.**—Coun. at East. (1757), Col. Rec., VII. 706. **Tolheo.**—S. Weiser (1760), Archives, III. 713. **Tolihaio.**—Morris (1756), Archives, II. 547. **Tolkeo.**—C. Weiser (1755), Col. Rec., VI. 657. **Tullyhaes Gap.**—Elder (1755), Col. Rec., VI. 704. **Gap at Swehatara.**—Morris (1756), Archives, III. 554. **the Hole.**—Busse (1758), Archives, III. 425.

TOMBICON. Given by Heckewelder as a corruption of Tombic-hanne, "crab-apple stream." This may possibly refer to Tumbling Run, or Creek, which enters the Schuylkill at Pottsville, Schuylkill County. Tumbling Run is noted on Howell's map, 1792. The name may be a corruption of Tombicon.

TOMHICKEN. The name of a station in Luzerne County. The name may be a corruption of the Delaware name for tomahawk, Tomahikan, or a corrupt and shortened form of Tombic-hacki. The name is evidently a "made" one.

TONOLOWAY. The present name of two creeks which rise in Fulton County, and flow southward to the Potomac at Hancock, Maryland. The larger stream, which enters the river east of Hancock is called the Great Tonoloway. and the smaller stream, which enters the river at Hancock. is called Little Tonoloway. On the Pennsylvania maps the Little Tonoloway is the eastern branch of the Tonoloway. On all of the early maps, and in all of the early records the name is Conoloway, or Conolaway. The name is also applied to a mountain in Fulton County. The name is probably of Shawnee origin, and has a close relation to the name Kanawha, which is another form of Conoy. The search of Baron Graffenried for a silver mine along the Potomac in 1711 lead him to the region along the Potomac in which the Conoy, or Canawest, were living having gone there to escape the Conestoga. The Conoy probably went up the Potomac as far as Hancock, although Graffenreid estimated the place at which he found them about 50 miles above Washington. The early settlers along the Conoloway Creek told traditions of an old mine, which was one of the landmarks in the region. This "old mine" was mentioned in the earliest surveys in the region. It was there when the first white settlers entered the present Fulton County from Maryland, before 1735. The Indians complained concerning the white settlers taking up land at the Conollaways, in the Big and Little Coves, and in other places west of the Kittatinny mountains, before 1741. Various proclamations were issued by the Provincial authorities warning these settlers to leave, but they continued to remain. In 1750 a Commission was sent to the Juniata and other places to remove the settlers, and to burn their cabins. This was done on the Juniata, at Burnt Cabins and other places, but the settlers on the Big and Little Conoloway were allowed to remain, because of the dispute with Maryland, concerning the boundary line between the two governments. It was not exactly known whether these settlers were in this state, or in Maryland. As a consequence the settlers along the Conoloways were allowed to remain until the boundary line should be run, and the lands should be purchased from the Indians (Col. Rec., V. 445 et seq.; See *Burnt Cabins*). After Braddock's defeat, 1755, the entire region west of the mountains. as well as in the Cumberland Valley, suffered greatly from the raids made by the hostile Delaware and Shawnee. Benjamin Chambers wrote from "Fallow Spring" (Falling Spring), on Nov. 2, 1755, telling of the terrible raids into the Coves and along the Conoloway Creeks. These raiding parties were led by Shingas and Captain Jacobs, and were started from Kittanning on the Allegheny River. Adam Hoops, in a letter from Carlisle, said that 50 persons had been captured or killed at this time, and that the settlements at the Coves and Conoloways were burned (Col. Rec., VI. 675; Archives, II. 462, 464, 474, 757). According to a letter from Col. John Armstrong, there were about an hundred Delaware and Shawnee in these parties of Indians (Col. Rec. VI. 676). The region was frequently attacked by the hostile Indians. Many of the captives taken at this time were returned by the Indians of Ohio to Col. Bouquet in 1764. Among those returned b y "The Beaver," at the Council at Lancaster in 1762, were Elizabeth McAdam and John Lloyd, from the Little Cove, and Dorothy Shobrian from the Big Cove (Col. Rec. VIII. 728). John Martin of Great Cove requested, in 1762, the return of his wife and five children, saying that his daughter was held by the S h i n g a s (Archives, IV. 100). Among the prisoners returned to Col. Bouquet, in 1764, was a John Martin,

who may have been a son of this man. Many of the children taken from this region could not be identified. After the Treaty of Fort Stanwix, 1768, the entire region west of the mountains was rapidly filled with settlers. On Scull's map of 1759 there is a house marked "Lim's," a few miles north of the Potomac. On Howell's map, 1792, this is marked "Linn." It was on the trail leading to Licking Creek, and also on the trail to the Potomac. This evidently was a trading point, and the Linn was probably one of the early Maryland settlers on this creek. The recent state maps, and the Geological Survey maps of the U. S., are the only ones which give the name a "T," instead of a "C," in the spelling of the name. The present form is incorrect.

Canaleways.—Morris (1757), Archives, II. 575. **Canallowais.** — Armstrong (1755), Col. Rec., VI. 676. **Conolaway.** —Scull map, 1770. **Conoloway.**—Howell map, 1792; Morris map, 1848. **Conollaways.**—Petition (1750), Col. Rec., V. 453. **Conoloway.**—Scull map, 1759. **Kennalaways.**—Hoops (1755), Archives, II. 474. **Tonoloway.**—Recent maps; U. S. Geo. Survey, Hancock Quadrangle.

TOUGHKENNAMON. The name of a town in Chester County, derived from the name of a hill in New Garden Tp., same county. The name is said to mean, "Fire-brand Hill." Plitey is the Delaware word for "fire-brand." It may be a corruption of Pethakwon, "thunder," with the suffix ottin, "hill." But, the original form of the name has disappeared. Consult; Egle, Hist. Penna., 521.

TOWAMENSING. The name of one of the Townships in Philadelphia County in 1741 and also in 1762. Now a Township in Montgomery County; also the name of a Township in Carbon County. The name Towsissinck occurs in the first Deed to William Penn, in 1682. It is not recorded as Towsissimock, as stated by Heckewelder. Nor Towsissinock, as stated by Reichel. The Deed reads, "to a corner white oake, marked with the letter P, standing by the Indyan Path that Leads to an Indyan Towne called Playwickey, and near the head of a Creek called Towsissinck, And from thence westward to the Creek called Neshammonys Creek" (Archives, I. 47). This tract was below the falls at Trenton and Neshaminy Creek, and was the tract known as Pennsbury Manor (See Holme's map). Heckewelder gives the origin of the name Towsissimock, as "Dawa-simook," "the place of feeding cattle, i. e., pasture grounds. The land near the creek named in this Deed (Towsissinck) was situated at the place known by the Indians as Chiepassing, or Sepassincks (See each name under title). It is probable that the name Towsissinck is a corruption of Towin, "to ford," and "a ford," compounded with with the name for "falls" (See Chiepassing), and has the significance "the fording place at the falls." The trail crossed the Delaware near this place. Towamensing is probably a corruption of this name, and has the significance "at the fording place." William Penn, or Governor Markham, probably gave this name to the Township in Philadelphia, using the Indian name, as with the other Townships.

Toamensing.—Scull map, 1759. **Toamensong.**—Scull map, 1770.

TOWANDA. A creek the source of which is in Tioga County, and which enters the Susquehanna below the town of Towanda, Bradford County. Heckewelder gives the origin from Tawundeunk, "where we bury the dead," and says that the Nanticokes buried their dead at this place. Others give the name as a contraction of Ta-na-wun-da, "s w i f t w a t e r," or "rapids." The name however may be a corruption of the name of one of the villages of the Susquehannocks, which was situated at this place, near the mouth of the creek. The creek was one of the lines of the purchase of 1768. The name is recorded in the Deed of these lands as, Awandae (Col. Rec. IX. 554). The line crossed the Susquehanna at the mouth of this creek, and then followed its course and that of Burnet's Hills to the headwaters of Pine Creek, and then down that creek to the West Branch, and then up that stream to Cherry Tree, and from thence to Kittanning, and down the Allegheny and Ohio, to the limits of the Province. The main Indian trail up the Susquehanna ran along the eastern shore of the river. In 1763 David Zeisberger and Anthony, a convert, who had been working at the mission station of the Moravian Church at Wyalusing, spent three days at Tawandaemenk, a Munsee village, at the flats at the mouth of the creek (Life of Zeisberger, 273). During the period from the commencement of the Revolution, until Sul-

livan's expedition in 1779, this region was occupied by Delaware and Munsee who were hostile to the Americans.

Awandae.—Purchase of 1768, in Col. Rec., IX. 554. **Dewantaa.**—Weiser (1737), quoted by Hanna, I. 32. **Tawandae.**—Scull map, 1770. **Tawandee.**—Howell map, 1792. **Tawandaemenk.**—Zeisberger (1763), in DeSchweinitz, Life of Z., 273 **Towanda.**—Morris map, 1848; Tawanda, as name of creek. **Tynandaung.**—Evans map, 1749. **Towandie.**—Board of Prop. (1793), Archives, Third Ser., III. 408.

TOWSISSIMOCK. See *Towamensing.*

TSANDOWAS, TSANANDOWAS, TSANANDOWA. A name frequently applied to the Seneca, and to Wyoming. The name was applied to the place, known as Wyoming, and to the Seneca as residents of that place (See *Wyoming, Seneca*). The following references will show the use of this form of the name, and also of a few of its corruptions. As the name of a place the author has not been able to find it as referring to any other place than Wyoming.

Chanandowa.—Coun. at Phil. (1736), Col. Rec., IV. 92. **Schahaedawana.**—Treaty of 1756, Archives, II. 559. **Scha,han,do,a,na.**—Hendrick (1750), Archives. Sec. Ser., VI. 69. **Scahantowano.**—Weiser (1744). Archives, I 657. **Seahautowano.**—Weiser (1755), Archives, II. 259. **Tsanandowa.**—Coun at Phil. (1731), Col. Rec. III. 425; (1727), III. 272. **Tsanandowas.**—Chiefs at Phil. (1732), Col. Rec, III. 425, (1727, III. 435. **Tsanandowans.**—Coun. at Phil. (1733), Col. Rec.. III 425; (1727), III 512. **Tsanandowans** or **Sinickas.**—Deed of 1736. Col. Rec., VI. 124. See WYOMING. **Tsanondowaroonas** or **Sinnekaes.**—Coun. at Phil. (1721), Col Rec., III. 150.

TSCHECHSCHEQUANNUNK. See *Sheshequin.*

TUCQUAN. A town in Lancaster County. Heckewelder gives the name as a corruption of P'duc-hanna, "a winding stream." P'tuck-hanne, "a bend in a stream."

TULPEHOCKEN. The name of a creek and P. O. in Berks County. The creek rises in Berks County and enters the Schuylkill from the west opposite Reading. The name is a corruption of Tulpewi-hacki, "turtle land." In 1705 Manangy, a chief on the Schuylkill, requested Gov. Evans to give his permission to the Conoy to remove from the Susquehanna and to settle among the Schuylkill Indians at "Turpyhockin" (Col. Rec., II. 191).

This request was granted, and the Conoy removed to this place. This village is supposed to have been near Womelsdorf. Governor Evans passed through the place on his return to Philadelphia in July, 1707, from Conestoga and Paxtang (Col. Rec., II. 390). In the MS. of the Taylor Papers (Hist. Soc., Pa.) survey No. 2372, upon "Swahatawro" (Swatara), made Aug. 10, 1726, states that it is "about 8 miles northwest of the Indian settlement called Tulpehackon." The Delawares along the Schuylkill at this time were the ones which had formerly lived along the Delaware River. They gradually moved up the Schuylkill, across to the Susquehanna, and then to the Ohio. In 1723 a number of Germans from the Schohary Valley crossed to the headwaters of the Susquehanna, went down to the mouth of Swatara Creek, and then up that stream and over the divide into the Tulpehocken Valley. Weiser's father led this company. Conrad Weiser followed in 1729. The occupation of these lands, which had not been purchased from the Indians, was the cause of much trouble. Allummapees, the Delaware "King," made a complaint about this matter at the Council at Philadelphia. He said that he could hardly believe that this settlement had been made, until he saw it with his own eyes. At this time about 33 German families were living along the creek (Col. Rec., III. 319-323). Governor Gordon requested that these German settlers be allowed to occupy the land until the matter could be adjusted. Nothing was done until 1732, when the land was purchased from the Indians (Archives, I. 344-346). This purchase opened the eyes of the Iroquois as to the value of land in the Province. After this time the Delawares had little to do with the sale of land, the Iroquois claiming a right to all of their land, by right of conquest. The region was soon opened for settlement by the Deed for Settlement of the Tulpehocken Lands (Arch., I. 404-410). Conrad Weiser, on account of his knowledge of Mohawk, soon became an interpreter for the Province in its dealings with the Iroquois. He was sent on various important missions to Onondaga, Shamokin and the Ohio (Consult; Walton, Conrad Weiser; Col. Rec., IV. 640-648, 660-669; V. 348-358, 470-528; Archives, III. 32, 66, etc.). At the Council at Philadelphia in 1755, after Braddock's defeat, Scarouady reported that two messengers had come from the Ohio, who said that the Delawares on the Ohio had proclaimed war against the English. These Indians said, "When Washington was defeated We, the Delawares, were blamed as the Cause of it. We will now kill. We will not be blamed without a Cause. We make up three Parties of Delawares. One party will go against Carlisle. One down the Sasquehannah, and I myself with another party will go against Tulpohoccon to Conrad Weiser" (Col. Rec., VI. 683). The Delawares had little love for Weiser, giving him credit for having influenced the Iroquois in making the various sales of their lands along the Susquehanna. The Indian raids at Penn's Creek (which see) brought Weiser to a realization of the danger which threatened the settlement at Tulpehocken. In order to protect the settlements south of the Kittatinny Mountains, a series of forts were built along the frontiers. Weiser had charge of the erection of the forts along the frontier south of the mountains and east of the Susquehanna. Fort Swatara, Fort Henry, Fort Manada and others were erected during 1756 to protect this region (Consult; Frontier Forts, I.; See *Manada, Swatara*, etc.). During the entire period of the Indian relations with the Province, Weiser's house was a prominent center of action. Nearly all of the missionaries, messengers and traders from the Delaware and Schuylkill passed through this place on their way to the Susquehanna and Ohio. Zinzendorf, Zeisberger, Spangenberg. Cammerhoff and other prominent Moravian missionaries have left accounts of their visits to Tulpehocken in their Journals (Consult; Memorials of the Moravian Church, Reichel; History of Missions, Loskiel; Life and Times of David Zeisberger, DeSchweinitz; Cammerhoff's Journal, Mag. of Hist. and Biog. (Penna.), XXIX. 160-179; A Conrad Weiser Diary, Penn-Germania, N. S., I. 764-778 (this diary commences with a record of Weiser's birth, Nov. 2, 1696, and ends with the record of the birth of his son, Benjamin, Aug., 1744. It also contains a note concerning the death of his father, July 13, 1760, and the death of his mother, June 10, 1781. These notes were added by some one else than Conrad Weiser, as he died July 13, 1760, and his step-mother died in 1781).

Tolpohiccon.—Coun. at Phila. (1755), Col. Rec.. VI. 683. Tulphaca.—Petition of Ger. (1728), Col. Rec., III. 322. Tulpahockin.—Pa. Coun. (1728), Col. Rec., III.. 324. Tulpehackon.—Taylor Papers (1726). MS. at Hist. Soc. Pa., Survey No. 2372. Tulpehoccon.—Deed of 1733, Archives, I. 404; also Evans map. 1749. Tulpehoccen.—Orndt (1759), Col. Rec.. VIII. 406. Tulpehockens.—Scull map. 1770 (large map). Tulpenhacon.—Weiser (1755), Archives, II. 503. Tulpehockin.—Taylor Papers (1734), No. 680. Tulpihokin.—Ger. Clergy (1754), Archives, II. 186. Tulpehockon.—Scull map, 1759. Tulpohocken.—Farmer (1728), Archives, I. 218. Tulpyhocken.—Pa. Coun. (1728), Col Rec., III. 322. Tulpyhockin.—Logan (1728), Archives, I. 227. Turpyhocken.—Pa. Coun. (1707). Col. Rec., II. 390. Turpyhockin.—Pa. Coun. (1705), Col. Rec., II. 191. Tulpihocken—Orndt (1759). Col. Rec., VIII 401. Tulpahawka.—Armstrong (1768), Col. Rec., IX. 485. (Consult also; Col. Rec., XVI., 275, 277; Archives. III. 11, 426.)

TUMANARANAMING. The name of a small creek which entered the Delaware from the west at Kensington, Philadelphia. In a Deed from Robert Turner to Thomas Fairman, Sept. 12, 1689, for 21 acres of land, it is mentioned as "Tumanaramaning's Creek (i. e. the Wolf's Walk)" (Archives Sec. Ser., XIX. 187). Peter Nelson "by Right of the Duke of Yorke," was granted a tract of land "in the Fork of Tumanaromamings" (Archives, Third Ser., III. 345). This Nelson tract is noted on Reed's map of Philadelphia (1775). The run was later called Gunner's Run, in honor of Gunner Rambo who had a tract of land along it. The name is a corruption of Tumma, "a wolf," Aney. "a path," with the locative, ing, having the significance, "the place of the wolf's path." Gunner Rambo is mentioned in the Records of Upland Court. in the Census of 1677, as living at Tacony (Records of Upland, 78). Peter Rambo was one of the Justices of the Court of Upland who were sworn in on Nov. 14, 1676. Peter Rambo was one of the magistrates who welcomed Governor Stuyvesant to Tinicum in 1658. He came to the Delaware with the first company of Swedes. The various members of the Rambo family were prominent in the early history of the settlement at Shackamaxon, as well as at Upland. Gunner Rambo was living on the tract above the run, which took his name, when William Penn first went to Shackamaxon. His tract is noted on Holme's map. Consult; Watsons Annals, I. 304; Records of Upland Court, 78 etc.

Gunner's Run.—Scull map, 1759. Tumanaramanings.—Deed of 1689, Archives, Sec. Ser.. XIX. 287. Tumanaranaming.—Egle, Hist. Pa., 1019. Tumanaromamings.—Nelson's Grant (date not given), Arch. Third Ser., 345. Tumanaromanings.—Reed map, 1775.

TUNEUNGWANT. The name of a creek which rises in McKean County, and which enters the Allegheny near Carrollton, New York; also the name of a town in McKean County, which uses the contraction Tuna. In the Life of Mary Jemison (7th. Ed.) the name is given as Tu-ne-un-gwan, "an eddy, not strong" (79), and also Unawaumgwa (95). This is a mere guess, as the present name of the stream is evidently a contraction of a longer name. Ellicott's map of 1787 gives the form Tschunuangwandt, and Howell's map, 1792, Ischunuangwandt. Col. Proctor calls the place at the mouth of the creek, in 1791, Dunewangu (Arch. Sec. Ser., IV. 566). He found the ruins of Indian huts at this site.

Besides the forms noted the State map (1911) gives Tuncangwant—evidently a blunder, as no such name was ever applied to the stream. Morris' map, 1848, gives Tunungwant.

TUNKHANNA, TUNKHANNOCK. The former stream is a branch of Tobyhanna in Monroe County; the latter is the name of the stream which rises in Susquehanna County, and which enters the Susquehanna from the northeast at Tunkhannock, Wyoming County. Both names are corruptions of Tank-hanne, or Tang-hanneu, "small stream." There were a number of streams, so called by the Delawares, in various parts of the region which they occupied. Where two streams were in the same region, or where one was a tributary of the other, the smaller stream was called Tankhanne. The suffix Hannock was significant of rapidly flowing water. There was a Delaware village called Tenkhanneck at the mouth of the Tunkhannock, which was deserted in 1758 when visited by Tatemy and Hays (Archives, III. 504). Nathaniel, a Moravian convert, was baptized by Bishop Cammerhoff on May 17, 1749 (Memorials of Mor. Church, 264), while living at this village. He became an assistant to Zeisberger. The army of General Sullivan encamped on the north bank of the Tunkhannock on Aug. 3, 1779—this being the third encampment after leaving Wyoming (Wilkes-Barre).

The stream in Monroe County is recorded as follows;

Tunkhana.—Howell map, 1792. **Tunkhanna.**—Morris map, 1848.

The stream in Wyoming County is noted as follows;

Tanckhannanck.—Norris (1779), Jour. Sull Exped., 224. **Tankhanink.**—Scull map, 1770 (small). **Tankhonink.**—Scull map, 1770 (large). **Tulkhanuck.**—Nukerck (1779). Jour. Sull. Exped., 215. **Tunchannock**—Ellicott (1788), Archives. XI. 327. **Tunkaanunk.**—Shute (1779), Jour. Sull. Exped., 269. **Tunkaannock.**—Shute (1779), Jour Sull. Exped., 273. **Tunkhannak.**—Nukerck (1779), Jour. Sull. Exped., 214. **Tunkannank.**—Lodge map (1779), Jour. Sull. Exped., 103. **Tunkhannock.**—Jenkins (1779), Jour. Sull. Exped., 170. **Tunkhannuck.**—Norris (1779), Jour. Sull. Exped., 228. **Tunkhannnk.**—Grant (1779), Jour. Sull. Exped., 137. **Tunkhanock.**—Howell map, 1792.

The names of the Indian village are recorded as follows;

Tenghanoke.—Tatemy and Hays (1758), Archives, III. 507. **Tenkghanake.**—Tatemy and Hays (1758), Archives, III. 504. **Tenkhanneck.**—Reichel, in Mem. Mor. Church, 264. **Tunkhannock.**—DeSchweinitz, in Life of Zeisberger, 270.

TUPPEEKHANNA. A stream mentioned by Heckewelder as being one of the sources of Little Lehigh Creek, at Trexlertown, Lehigh County. The name means "spring stream," or "stream flowing from a spring."

TURKEY FOOT. A place frequently mentioned in the early records and journals, chiefly during the expedition of General Braddock in 1755. The Province of Pennsylvania was to build a road from Shippensburg to connect with the Braddock Road near Turkey Foot. Col. Burd had charge of the building of this road, work upon which stopped at the summit of the Allegheny Mountains, upon hearing of Braddock's defeat. This road was to be a route by which supplies were to be carried to Braddock, who wrote from Stewart's Crossing (Connellsville) on June 30th., urging the completion of the work upon this road. For the course of the road see *Sugar Cabins.* Consult; Col. Rec., VI. 301, 337, 380, 396, 452, 484, 621, 629; Archives, II. 373. In 1768, owing to the complaints of the Indians concerning the settlers occupying lands which had not been purchased from the Indians, various proclamations had been issued to the settlers at these points west of the mountain, ordering

them to remove. Finally a Commission was sent to warn these settlers to remove. In the Report made by this Commission it was stated that "eight or ten Families lived in a Place called Turkey-Foot." The names of these are given (Col. Rec., IX. 508-509). In the Census of 1785, there were 90 men living in Turkey Foot Township (Archives, X. 512). The Turkey's Foot was at the site of the present Confluence, where the three streams unite to form the Youghiogheny. It is on the line of Fayette and Somerset Counties. The present townships, Upper, and Lower Turkeyfoot, and the town of Turkey Foot, Somerset County, perpetuates this name.

Crow's Foot of the Ohiogany.—Peters (1755), Co. Rec., VI. 396. **Crow-Foot of Ohiogainy.**—Morris (1755), Col. Rec., VI. 621. **Turkey's Foot.**—Sir John St. Clair (1755), Col. Rec., VI. 301. **Turkeys foot.**—Morris (1755), Archives, II. 373. **Turkey Foot.**—Scull map, 1770; also Three Forks. **Three Forks.**—Evans map, 1755.

Gist's map of 1753 and Howell's map of 1792 also have the name Turkey Foot. On May 20, 1754 George Washington, when on his way to the Ohio, went down the Youghiogheny past Turkey Foot, about 8 miles. His plan was to send down his supplies on this stream, but this he found was not possible, because of the swift current of the stream. Consult any of the copies of Washington's Journal of 1754.

TURTLE CREEK. A creek which enters the Monongahela from the northeast above Braddock, Allegheny County. Heckewelder says that the Delawares called this stream Tulpewisipu, "turtle river." John Fraser (name frequently written Frazier), a famous Paxtang (which see) trader, who was living at a trading house at Venango (Franklin) in 1749, when the expedition of Celoron de Bienville passed through that place, was forced to leave that place in 1753, when the French army took possession of that point. Fraser's letters concerning the French occupation of that place were the first accounts received by the Province concerning this real commencement of the struggle of the French for the possession of the Ohio. Morris Turner and Ralph Kilgore, two of Fraser's servants, had been arrested by the French, when returning from the Allegheny, near Pickawillany, on

May 26, 1750, and had been sent to Canada. This was the first act of hostility of the French on the Ohio (Col. Rec., V. 480-487). On August 27, 1753, John Fraser wrote from "Forks" (of the Ohio) telling of the visit of Capt. Trent to the "forks" to view the ground upon which the fort was to be built (op. cit., 659-660). On May 25, Michael Taafe and Robert Callendar, two of John Harris' partners, when at Pine Creek, had received a letter from John Fraser, telling of the French army having reached the region near Niagara (op. cit., 614-616). Fraser was then at Venango. This news put in motion the various plans of Virginia for taking possession of the Ohio, by the erection of a fort. The attempt to build a fort on the Ohio, by Captain Trent, Washington's expedition, of 1753, and that of 1754, and Braddock's expedition in 1755, and the final capture of Fort Duquesne in 1758 by General Forbes, were the events which were the results of the news which Fraser sent from Venango. This trader had a trading house at the mouth of Turtle Creek when he was at Venango, and after his expulsion from the latter place in 1753, he went to his trading house at Turtle Creek. He was probably the first white resident of the region about the mouth of Turtle Creek. Fraser's house stood just below the mouth of this creek, at Braddock, near the fording place on the Monongahela, where Braddock's army crossed in 1755. The army marched directly past this house on July 9th, just after crossing the river. John Fraser's Trading House at Turtle Creek became one of the prominent landmarks in the great wilderness. On November 22nd, 1753, George Washington, then a youth of 23 years, and Christopher Gist, the explorer of the Ohio Company, reached Fraser's on their way to Logstown and the French forts. They again were at Fraser's house on December 30th, on their return from LeBoeuf and Venango. They remained here until Jan. 1st, 1754, waiting for horses, according to Washington's Journal. Here they met a company of 20 warriors, who were returning from the south, evidently by the trail down the Monongahela. On Dec. 31st, Washington made a visit to the mouth of the Youghiogheny to see Allaquippa, who was hurt because he had not stopped to see her on his way to Logstown. Washington and Gist left Fraser's on Jan. 1st, 1754, going over the trail to Gist's Plantations (See *Gist's*, *Jacob's Cabins*, *Venango*, etc.). Consult Darlington, Gist's Jour., 80, 86; Washington's Jour. of 1753, Western Annals, 111, 121; also in Spark's Life of Washington, etc. The company which was engaged in the building of the fort at "the forks" was commanded by Captain William Trent, with John Fraser as Lieutenant and Edward Ward as Ensign. These had received their commissions from Gov. Dinwiddie, of Virginia. When Ward surrendered this fort to Contracoeur on April 17, 1754, Trent was at Will's Creek and Fraser was at his trading house at Turtle Creek. In 1755 Braddock's army crossed the Monongahela almost directly in front of Fraser's house, and passed by it. The head of the army, led by the guides, had just reached "Fraser's Run," when the Indians were first discovered (Consult: Col. Rec., VI. 501; Sargent, Braddock's Expedition, 354). After Braddock's defeat all of the English traders were expelled from the entire region west of the mountains. In 1757 Col. Washington wrote from Fort Loudon concerning the sending out of a scouting party—from Fort Cumberland—under command of Lieut. Baker. This party, consisting of five soldiers and fifteen Cherokee Indians, returned on June 8th, bringing a French officer as a prisoner, and five scalps. Baker reported that they had killed two other officers in the party which they met "on the Head of Turtle Creek, 2 Miles from Fort Duquesne" (Col. Rec., VII. 603). The distance given is an error, or the capture took place on some other creek. Soon after the occupation of Fort Duquesne by the British, 1758, many settlers took up tracts along the course of the Braddock and Forbes roads. In 1777 Killbuck (which see) sent a warning to Col. Morgan, at Fort Pitt, concerning a proposed raid upon the settlements along this creek, probably the various branches in Westmoreland County (Archives, V. 445). Many Indian raids were made in the Bushy Run region during these years (See *Bushy Run*, *Brush Creek*, *Cock Eye's Cabin*, etc.). Consult; Frontier Forts, II. 3, et seq. Gist's map, 1753; Evan's map, 1755, and all later maps give the name Turtle Creek. Sir Peter Halkett, and his sons, and all the host of officers and men who were killed in the battle at Braddock's Fields, were later buried near the spot where they fell. Not a single marker or monument of any sort marks the site of this most historic battle, nor the graves of these men. The action took place near the present Braddock station on the P. R. R. The City of Pittsburgh, or the State of Pennsylvania, should mark this site. It is probably as sadly neglected as any spot of historic importance on the American continent.

TUSCARAWAS. A former Delaware and Wyandot village, situated on the Tuscarawas River, and just above the mouth of the Big Sandy Creek, in Ohio. It was about a quarter of a mile from the fording place on the Tuscarawas, where the Great Trail from Fort Pitt crossed that stream, on the way· to Mohickon John's Town and Sandusky. It was situated almost due west of Shinga's Town, on the Beaver River. This village was the headquarters of "King" Beaver, or Tamaque, after he left his former village at the mouth of the Beaver River. Consult; Handbook of American Indians, II. 840. The village is frequently mentioned in the Archives of this State, chiefly during the expedition of Col. Bouquet in 1764. There were three trails leading from Tuscarawas, one to the towns on the Muskingum and Sciota, the second to Sandusky and the third to Cuyahoga. Bouquet went over the first of these trails in 1764, and held his last encampment at the forks of the Muskingum, about 35 miles southwest of Tuscarawas. The inhabitants of this village had fled before Bouquet reached it. Some of the Indian chiefs met him at this place with overtures of peace, but he marched on to Muskingum, where he held a Council with the allied tribes.

TUSCARORA. The name of a creek, which enters the Juniata at Port Royal, Juniata County; of a range of mountains west of the Kittatinny range; of a valley between the Tuscarora and Kittatinny Mountains; of a village in Juniata County, and of a P. O. in Schuylkill County. These were all named in honor of the tribe which united with the Iroquois Confederation in 1713, being the last to unite with the Five Nations, as it had been called until the union of the Tuscarora made it the Six Nations. The general history of the tribe will be found in the Handbook of American Indians, and in the works of Bancroft, Parkman and other writers. The name is a corruption of Skaru-ren, "hemp gatherers." The Tuscarora belonged to the Iroquoian family, and were living in North Carolina, when first met with by the white settlers. The various wars with the settlers commenced in Sept., 1711, with the capture of Lawson, the surveyor-general of North Carolina, and Baron de Graffenried, who had gone to explore the Neuse River. They were taken to one of the villages of the Tuscarora. After the chiefs had discussed the matter for two days, it was decided to put both of the captives to death. Graffenried was finlly released, but Lawson was put to death. After various attacks upon the settlements along the Roanoke and Pamlico Sound, the South Carolina Assembly sent Col. Barnwell, with Cherokee, Catawba and Creek allies to make an attack upon the Tuscarora palisaded towns, near Newburn, North Carolina. The Tuscarora were induced to accept a treaty of peace with the settlers, but Barnwell broke this by taking some of the Indians captive, and selling them as slaves. This brought on the second Tuscarora war in the years following. Because of these wars many of the Tuscarora began to move northward. About 1713 they were living on the Potomac, and in the back parts of Virginia, and some of them may have then moved to the lower end of the Tuscarora Valley, near the Potomac. Many of the historians of the Tuscarora Valley state that the Tuscarora occupied this region, south of the Juniata, as late as 1762. This cannot be possible. It is true that Angus the Tuscarora chief, at the Council at Lancaster in 1762, said, "We should be glad to be informed of the State and Behavior of our Brethren in Tuscarora Valley, & to have some directions about the way, as we propose to make them a visit, & should be glad of a pass or recommendation, in writing, that we may be friendly received on the way and at the Valley" (Col. Rec., VIII. 722-723). The name "Tuscarora Valley" was either added to this record, or it refers to the continuation of the Tuscarora Valley beyond the Potomac. In 1762 the entire region south of the Juniata to the Potomac was filled with Scotch-Irish settlers, and there were forts at Shirleysburg, or Aughwick;

at Sugar Cabins, Fort Lyttleton, and at the southern entrance to the valley at Parnall's Knob, Fort Loudon. Besides these, there were a number of other forts towards the Potomac. There was not a spot in the entire Tuscarora Valley, in 1762, where an Indian of any tribe would dare to live. In addition, at this very same Council at Lancaster, Thomas King, an Iroquois, of the Oneida tribe, asked that a Store House be placed at Bedford, and at Cresap's, on the Potomac, as both of these places were on the "Warrior's path." At the Council at Lancaster, in 1744, Canassatego, the Iroquois, had said, to the Governor of Virginia, "There lives a Nation of Indians on the other side of your Country, the Tuscaroraes, who are our Friends, and with whom we hold Correspondence; but the Road between us and them has been stopped for some time on Account of the Misbehaviour of some of Our Warriors. We have open'd a New Road for our Warriors and they shall keep to that; but as that would be inconvenient for Messengers going to the Tuscaroraes we desire that they may go the old Road * * * * * Among these Tuscaroraes there live a few families of the Conoy Indians who are desirous to leave them and to remove to the rest of their Nation among us, and the Straight Road from them to Us lyes through the Middle of your Country. We desire you will give them a free passage through Virginia" (Col. Rec., IV. 734). This request was granted. The "New Path" is the path which is marked on Evan's map of 1749, running from Harris' Ferry, through Croghan's Gap, to the Black Log, and then southward, crossing the Potomac at Oldtown, Maryland. The "old path" ran down the Cumberland Valley and crossed the Potomac at the mouth of the Conococheague. The "Tuscarora Valley," and mountain, received its name because it was the course of the Iroquois trail to the Tuscarora country in North Carolina, and not because the Tuscarora lived in the valley. The old Tuscarora trail, which was an Iroquois trail, followed down the Tuscarora Valley, from above Harrisburg, along the western side of the Kittatinny Mountains, to the Potomac, which was crossed at Williamsport. The oldest trail was down the Cumberland Valley, from Harris' Ferry to Williamsport. This was abandoned after the valley was settled, about 1727; the

next path was down the Tuscarora Valley, and then the "New Path" cut through at Croghan's Gap, and went southward, crossing the Potomac at Cresap's, Oldtown, Md. Later the Warrior's Trail was followed from Shamokin, Sunbury, to Standing Stone, where it joined the old trail southward along the Warrior's Ridge. The "New Path" and the Warrior's Trail were practically identical south of the Black Log. The residence of the Tuscarora in the present Tuscarora Valley in this State must have been of very short duration—if they ever lived in it at all. There is not a single reference in any Journal, or upon any map, to the name of a single Tuscarora village in the Tuscarora Valley. Aughwick, which Mr. Hanna thinks may have been a Tuscarora village, was without question a Delaware village. After leaving North Carolina, the Tuscarora evidently remained for a short time in the lower end of the present Tuscarora Valley, probably with the Conoy near the mouth of the present Tonoloway Creek, near Hancock, Maryland. They then went on up to the region along the headwaters of the Susquehanna, where they were placed by the Iroquois (See *Ingaren*, *Owego*, etc.). The Tuscarora Valley was called Path Valley because of the many Indian trails which crossed it and which once ran down its entire length. The valley was settled by the Scotch-Irish before it had been purchased from the Indians. Conrad Weiser, when on his way to Logstown in 1748, mentions the attempts of the Province to keep these settlers away from these lands. He also mentions "Jacob Biat" (Pyatt), who was then there to choose a place (Archives, II. 15). "Pyatt's" became a prominent landmark on the trail to the Ohio. The place, as "Piatt's," or "Pyatt's," is noted on the Scull map of 1759, and also on Evans map of 1755. It was situated near the present Concord, P. O. In 1710 a number of Tuscarora chiefs attended a Council at Conestoga, with the chiefs from Conestoga, at which time they declared that they were "hitherto Strangers to this Place" (Col. Rec., II. 512). They also make a pathetic plea for peace and protection. At the Council at Conestoga in 1711, Governor Gookin requested that the Conestoga, as requested by Governor Penn, show friendship towards the "Palatines settled near Pequea." The Conestoga replied, "That they are extreamly well pleased with the Govrs. speech, but as they are at present in Warr with the Toscororoes and other Indians, they think that place not safe for any Christians" (Col. Rec., II. 533). In 1719 Governor Spotswood informed Governor Keith that "your Indians," meaning the Iroquois, "In the year 1712 & 1713, They were axtually in these parts assisting the Tuscarouroes, who had massacred in cold Blood some hundreds of the English and were then warring against us, and they have, at this very day, the Chief Murderers, with the greatest part of that Nation seated under their protection near Susquehanna River, whither they removed them, when they found they could no longer support them against the fforce which the English brought upon them in these parts. During the Tuscouroro War, about two hundred of your Indians set upon our Virginia Indian Traders, as they were going to the Southern Indians with a Carravan of at least eighty Horses loaded and after having killed one of our People and shot most of their Horses they made Booty of all the Goods, declaring their Reason for so doing was because They did not carry their Ammunition to the Tuscouroroes, and this Plunder was so publickly vended to the Northward, that it was no Secret to your people at Albany what a villainous part they had been acting here with your English." Various other hostile incidents are mentioned. (Col. Rec., III. 84 et seq.). The Iroquois in these trips southward to the Tuscarora region in North Carolina returned by way of the Susquehanna River, stopping at the villages of the Conoy with their prisoners. This was one of the reasons for the removal of the Conoy from the lower Susquehanna to the Juniata, and then on up the river (See *Conoy, Conejohela, Dekanoagah*). At a Council at Philadelphia in 1722, with the Conestoga and two chiefs from each of the Iroquois tribes, two others "said to be Tuscororoes" (Col. Rec., III. 201). While the Tuscarora were allied with the Iroquois, and the date of their admission to the Iroquois Confederation is fixed as early as 1713, yet it seems that they were not officially made a part of the League of the Iroquois until 1722. The region assigned to the Tuscarora, after their admission, was between the Oneidas, and the Onondagas (Archives,

Sec. Ser., VI. 154, 157). This did not mean that all of the Tuscarora were then settled in that region. Many occupied the villages along the Susquehanna (Ingaren, Owego etc.), and some still remained in North Carolina. In 1755 Governor Dobbs, of North Carolina, wrote to Governor Morris, "I Hear that the Tuskaruras, who have Joynd the Six Nations, have sent to the Tuskaruras here for 30 men to Joyn them next Spring, and that they are Sasquehanning them to have them ready" (Archives, II. 537). The request of Augus, before mentioned, in 1762, for permission to visit his brethren in the "Tuscarora Valley" evidently refers to North Carolina, and not this state, for the reasons mentioned. In the request of Kinderuntie, the head warrior of the Seneca, at the Council at Lancaster in 1762, for permission to use the "old War path from Shamokin, which lies along the Foot of the Allegheny Hills," the reference is to the Warrior's Path, from Shamokin along the eastern side of Warrior's Mountain, to the crossing of the Potomac at Old Town, Maryland (Col. Rec., VIII. 769). This was not the Tuscarora Trail down the Tuscarora Valley, from the Juniata to the mouth of the Conococheague. The Tuscarora villages along the upper Susquehanna were destroyed during Sullivan's expedition in 1779. Consult; Jour. Mil. Exped. Gen. Sull., 1779. After their admission to the Iroquois Confederation the Tuscarora attended the various Councils held with the Province, but they did not share in the gifts for the various land sales, as they were not allied with the Iroquois when the conquests of the tribes living in the region claimed by the Iroquois, took place. During the Revolution the Tuscarora and the Oneida, as tribes, took the side of the Americans. In 1775 a number of Tuscarora, Nanticoke and Conoy, visited Philadelphia, on a friendly visit. They stated that they were very poor and in great need of clothing. These Indians were then living on the upper Susquehanna (Col. Rec., X. 238). The Tuscarora were friendly to the white settlers in this state from the time of their first entrance to it. In Grant's defeat, in Pittsburgh, in 1758, the Tuscaroras were commended because of their assistance to that ill-fated body of English troops (Archives, III. 547).

In the following list of synonyms

only those found in the Archives and maps of this state are given. A complete list of the various names of the tribe will be found in the Handbook of American Indians, under title. The creek in Juniata County is noted on Scull's map 1770. The creek in Wyoming County is noted on Scull's map as Tuscaroge (1770), and on Howell's map (1792), as Tuscarora. The Mountain range, south of the Juniata, is noted on Evans' map (1749), as Tuscarora Hills; on Scull's map (1770), as Tuscarora Mountains, and on Scull's map (1759), as Tuscarora. The valley is noted on Scull's map (1759), as Path Valley, as it also is on Scull's map of 1770.

Tuscarora Creek.—B. of Prop. (1766). Arch. Third Ser., I. 115. **Tuscarora Path.**—Swaine (1755), Col. Rec., VI. 473. **Tuscarora Path Valley.**—Coun. at East. (1761), Col. Rec., VIII. 650. **Tuscarora path.**—Weiser (1748), Archives, II. 15. **Toskerrora Valey.**—Croghan (1754), Archives, II. 218. **Tuscarora Valley.**—Peters (1755), Col. Rec., VI. 767. **Tuscaroro.**—Potter (1755), Col. Rec., VI. 674. **Tuskarora.**—Patterson (1756), Archives, II 218. **Tuskerrora Valley.**—Croghan (1754), Archives, II. 173. **Tuscarora Mountain.**—Peters (1755), Col Rec., VI. 378. **Tuscarrora Hill.**—Cookson (1749), Archives, II. 43. **Tuscarrora mountains.**—Cookson (1749), Archives, II. 42.

The following names of the Tuscarora Indians are recorded in the state documents;

Toscororoes.—Gookin (1711), Col. Rec., II 533. **Tuscaroraes.**—Coun. at Lan. (1744), Col. Rec, IV. 734. **Tuscaroroes.** —Coun. at Cones (1710), Col. Rec., II. 511. **Tuscarouroes.**—Spotswood (1719), Col. Rec., III. 84 **Tuscororoes.**—Pa. Coun. (1722), Col. Rec III. 201. **Tuskarorows.**—Lowe (1730), Archives, I. 268. **Tuskaruras.**—Dobbs (1755), Archives, II. 537.

TUTELO TOWN. A former Indian village, mentioned in the examination of Samuel Clifford, an escaped Indian captive, as situated "about forty miles above Diahoga" (Tioga), in Archives, III. 44. The Tutelo formerly lived in Virginia and North Carolina. They were of the Siouan family. They were first mentioned by John Smith in 1609, as Monacan. They then occupied the upper James and Rappahannock Rivers. The Northern Indians carried on a war of extermination against the Tutelo, Saponi and other Siouan tribes of the south. In 1722 the Iroquois made peace with them. Many of them removed to the region of Shamokin, where some were living in 1745, during the visits of Brainerd, the Presbyterian missionary. They later moved on up the Susquehanna to the Conoy and Nanticoke villages of Chenango, Owego, etc. The reference is probably to one of these villages. The tribe is now extinct, the last full-blood having died in 1871. Consult; Mooney, Siouan Tribes of the East, 1894.

TWIGHTWEES. The common English name for the tribe called Miamis by the French. It is frequently referred to in the records of this state, although there were no Miami, or Twightwee, villages in it. The name is a corruption of Twahtwah, the cry of the crane. Weiser approaches this form in his name of Towick-Towicks (Archives, II. 9). When they first came in contact with the traders from Pennsylvania, they were living in the Miami and Wabash region. The visit of Conrad Weiser to Logstown in 1748 was the cause of the Twightwees desire to form an alliance with the English. The trade of the Miami had been entirely in the hands of the French. In the Memoir of 1718, it is stated, "The Miamis are sixty leagues from Lake Erie, and number 400, all well formed men, and well tatooed; the women are numerous. * * * The women are well clothed, but the men use scarcely any covering and are tatooed all over the body" (Archives, Sec. Ser., VI. 56). The lack of clothing was the cause of the name "Naked Indians," which was applied to the Twightwees (Col. Rec., III. 330). The Twightwees, according to the letter of Ann LeTort, had gone to Conestoga in 1703 and "cut off two families of neighbor Indians at Conestoga" (Col. Rec., II. 121). The first official relation of the Twightwees with the Province was due in a great measure to Weiser's visit to Logstown, but before that time the traders of Pennsylvania had been going westward to the Miami to trade. James LeTort, Hugh Crawford, Edmund Cartlidge and other traders from the Susquehanna had been carrying on a trade with the Indians of Ohio and Indiana long before Weiser went to Logstown in 1748. Morris Turner and Ralph Kilgore, John Fraser's partners (See *Turtle Creek, Venango*) had been captured by the Indian allies of the French traders on Mad Creek, near Pickawillany, in May 1750 (Col. Rec., V. 482). These traders had been engaged in the Indian trade west of the Ohio for several years before that time. The Iroquois had made peace with the Miami, or Twightwee, about 1721. After that time the Twightwees became dissatisfied with the prices paid to them by the French traders, and were anxious for the English traders to go among them. In June 1748 the Provincial Council was informed by a letter from Logstown, that the Twightwees, who had left the French influence, were anxious to form an alliance with the English, and that with this end in view, some of their chiefs were on their way to hold a Council at Lancaster. Weiser and Montour were called before the Provincial Council to give some information concerning the Shawnee chiefs who had sent this information, and concerning the Twightwees. Weiser was just about ready to make this trip to the Ohio when this information was given. Montour was sent on ahead to meet the Twightwee chiefs and to try to persuade them to go to Philadelphia. Montour met them, but could not persuade them to change their plans, so four Commissioners were appointed to meet with them at Lancaster. This alliance of the English with the Miami was of very great influence (Col. Rec., V. 290, 299-300, 307-318, 433-434). In July 1750, Hugh Crawford sent a message from the Twightwees to Gov. Hamilton, telling of the attempts being made by the French to win them back (op. cit. 437-438). Gov. Hamilton sent a reply to this message (op. cit., 450-451). When Christopher Gist was on his tour of exploration in 1750 he went through several of the Twightwees towns along the Miami River. While at the Twightwee Town, or Pickawillany Town, about two and a half miles north of the present Piqua, Andrew Montour delivered the message from the English. While here Gist viewed the fort which the Miamis had built. This fort was built by the Twightwees, and not by the French, or the traders, as was once thought. Little Turtle, the Miami chief, so informed General Wayne, at the Treaty of Greenville, Aug. 1795. Gist met a number of the Pennsylvania traders on this trip, among whom was Hugh Crawford (Consult; Darlington, Gist's Journals, 47-55, 123-127). In 1751 Andrew Montour and George Croghan were commissioned by Gov. Hamilton to distribute the pres-

ents to the various western Indians at Logstown (Col. Rec., V. 518-522). The Twightwees were especially mentioned in the messages to these Indians. Croghan and Montour reached Logstown on May 18th. Joncaire, the French officer, was then there, and held a Council with the Indians. Croghan delivered the messages from Governor Hamilton, and held a Treaty with the Iroquois, Delaware, Shawnee, Wyandot and Twightwee (Consult; Croghan's Journal, Col. Rec., V. 530-540). The killing of 30 Twightwee warriors by the French; led to the application to Governor Hamilton by the Shawnee, for help in their fight against the French. Governor Hamilton realizing that he could do nothing with his Assembly, which was made up of Quakers, wrote to Governor Clinton, telling him that he could nothing to assist his Indian allies (op. cit., 575). The Twightwees killed 15 Frenchmen, which a c t brought a large force of French against them. They then appealed to Pennsylvania and Virginia for assistance. Then it was that Pennsylvania and Virginia commenced to realize that the entire t r a d e o f t h e Ohio was threatened. The letter of John Fraser, the trader at Venango, telling of the preparations which the French were making near Lake Erie for the actual entry into the Ohio, led to the various efforts of Virginia, through the Ohio Company, to take possession of the Ohio River (See *Venango, Turtle Creek, Allegheny, Ohio, Logstown* etc. Consult; Colonial Records, V. 617, 633, 667, etc.). In December, 1754, after Washington's defeat, Scarouady, at a Council at Philadelphia, said, "The Delawares, Shawonese, Owendats (Wyandot), and Twightwees are our Allies; we expect they are in full Friendship with us; you may depend on the Truth of what I say, they are our fast Friends" (Col. Rec., VI. 195). When the French occupied the Ohio in 1753 many of the Twightwees went over to them, along with the Delaware and Shawnee and helped to defeat Braddock in 1755. They were at the Council which General Stanwix and George Croghan held at Fort Pitt in October 1759 (Col. Rec., VIII. 429-435). A number of the chiefs were present at the Council at Lancaster in 1762 (op. cit., 723-774). During the war of the Revolution the Twightwees were allied with the hostile Delaware, Shawnee and Wyandot.

The Twightwee, or Miami, made a number of treaties with the United States at various times after the Treaty at Greenville, Ohio, with General Anthony Wayne in Aug., 1795. Consult; Hanna, Wilderness Trail, II. 257 et seq.; Hassler, Old Westmoreland, 33, 83-84; Bancroft, Hist. of U. S., II. 92, 155, 364-365; III. 41-41; Handbook of Amer. Ind., I. 852-855. The name of this tribe as recorded in the Archives and Colonial Records, of this state, is nearly always given the English form of Twightwee, or its various corruptions. The French name, Miami, is only used in the recorded documents of French writers. The following are the forms recorded;

Towicktowicks.—Weiser (1748), Archives, II. 8. **Towick-Towicks.**—the same, 9. **Towittois.**—LeTort (1703), Col. Rec., II. 121. **Twechtwese.**—(or naked Indians, call'd by the French Miamies) 1728, Col. Rec., III. 330. **Tweuchtwese.**—Coun. at Phil. (1721), Col Rec., II. 132. **Twichtwees.**—Weiser (1748), Archives, II 11. **Twicktwees.**—the same. **Twightwees.**—Palmer (1748), Col Rec., V. 299 **Twigtwees**—Coun. at Phil. 1748), same reference, 289. **Miamis.**—DuChesneau, (1681), Arch.. Sec. Ser., VI. 7, 8, etc.

TWO LICK CREEK. A branch of Black Lick Creek, in Indiana County. On Scull's map of 1770, the name Two Lick was applied to the main stream, which is now called Black Lick, which enters the Conemaugh from the north below Blairsville. The Indian name of the stream was Nischa-honi, "two licks." It is possible that the present name of the main stream, Black Lick, was due to a mistake in writing, or hearing, the Indian name. Neska, "black," and Nischa, "two," are so similar in sound, and in form, that Nischa could have easily been mistaken for Neska, hence the name "Black Lick," instead of "Two Lick," which is the oldest recorded name of the stream. It is mentioned as one of the points on the table of distances given by John Harris in 1754, as "to P. Shaver's Sleeping place, at two large licks,—12 Miles" (Archives, II. 136). The "Shawana Cabins," which was 12 miles from this point, was situated on Crooked Creek, according to Scull's map (1770), and not on Two Lick Creek, as stated by Mr. Hanna. "Tohoguses Cabbins" is simply the Iroquois name for "Shawnee Cabins" (which see). There may have been another place called Shawnee Cabins on the south branch of Two Lick Creek, near the present

Cookport. The Two Licks are possibly to be identified with the ones mentioned at the mouth of Ramsey's Run. Howell's map (1792) gives the name Black Lick, to the creek now known by that name, and Two Lick Creek, as a branch of this stream.

TYADAGHTON, TIADAGHTON etc. The name of the present Pine Creek, Lycoming County. Its head springs are in Potter and Tioga Counties. There was much dispute concerning the exact stream which the Indians meant by this name in the purchase at Fort Stanwix. At first it was thought to mean the present Lycoming Creek, and the line of the purchase was so indicated on the map. The statement on the Historical Map of Penna. (1875), that Lycoming Creek was the "Legal boundary of the Purchase of Nov. 5th., 1768," is not correct. It was explained by the Iroquois that they understood the name Tiadaghton to refer to the stream known as Pine Creek (Col. Rec., IX. 554; Archives, X. 357). The name "Limping Messenger," which Spangenberg gives to Lycoming Creek, may be a translation of the name of Pine Creek. See *Pine Creek.*

UMBELICAMENCE. The name of a former Indian village, mentioned in the Patent of the 5,000 acres which were granted to Major Jasper Farmer, on the Schuylkill River. This tract was immediately above Gulielma Maria Penn's Manor of Springfield, between the Wissahickon and the Schuylkill. Major Jasper Farmer agreed with William Penn in 1682, for the purchase of this tract. On his way over Farmer died, leaving a widow and three sons, Jasper, Richard and Edward. In Jan. 1683-84, Jasper the son, applied for this tract of land, in behalf of his father, his brother Richard and himself. It was a part of the "Lands called by the Indians Umbelicamence." No survey of this tract was made. "But it is alleged that William Penn with his own hands marked a Tree, for a Beginning near the Indian Town Umbelicamence." Jasper died and left his share to his wife, Catherine, who afterwards married one Billup. Richard also died, leaving Edward as the sole survivor of the Farmer family. On Feb. 7, 1689, Thomas Holme was authorized to survey for Edward Farmer 3750 acres, and for Catherine Farmer (then Billup) 1250 acres. The survey for

Edward commenced at the tree marked by the Proprietary (Archives, Third Ser., I. 196-197). The tract for Catherine Farmer (now Billup) was granted to her Feb. 12, 1690 (Arch. Sec. Ser., XIX. 33). In 1702 the tract is mentioned, after the death of Catherine, when Thomas Farmer, "her heir," asks for a resurvey. The land is stated to be "near the White Marsh on Schuylkill" (op. cit., 197). This tract is again mentioned in 1704, when Thomas Fairman makes his claim of a shortage in the one fourth of this tract, which he claimed (op. cit., 433). The Indian village, which gave this tract its point of commencement, must have been on the Schuylkill or the Wissahickon, probably the latter, in White Marsh Township, Montgomery County. The name is probably a corruption of Ulakanahemunschi, "an elm tree." Schauweminschi, is "red beech tree"; Tanikaniminschi, "white beech tree"; Ulakanaheminschi, "elm tree."

Umbelicamence.—Patent of 1683 (quoted 1767), Archives, Third Ser., I. 197.
Umbilicamenca.—Patent of 1683 (quoted 1704), Archives, Sec. Ser., XIX. 433.

UNADILLA. A former Indian village at the mouth of Unadilla Creek, on both sides of the Susquehanna. The village, which had been evacuated, was destroyed by Col. William Butler in the fall of 1778. The troops had marched down the west side of the Susquehanna, which was crossed at this point, and then crossed again just below the mouth of Unadilla Creek (See map and letter of Capt. William Gray, Archives, Sec. Ser., XV. 289-292). General Clinton's Brigade encamped here on August 12, 1779, when on its way to join the army of General Sullivan at Tioga Point, for the expedition up the Susquehanna. The various villages in this region had been occupied by the Tuscarora.

Unadilla.—Campfield (1779), Jour. Sull. Exped., 55. **Unedelly.**—VanHovenburgh (1779), op. cit., 277. **Unendilla.**—Gray (1778), Arch. Sec. Ser., XV. 291. **Unindilla.**—Beatty (1779), Jour. Sull. Exped., 23.

VENANGO. The former name of the present French Creek, which enters the Allegheny from the northwest in Venango County; also the name of a former Indian village, and prominent trading point, at the mouth of this creek, at the site of Franklin. The name is perpetuated in the name of the county through which this creek ran, and in which the village

was situated. The name is a corruption of the Indian name Onenge, "a mink." This name is given by Zeisberger and DeSchweinitz. It is also given by Loskiel, "Onenge or Venango" (Hist. Miss., III. 35). Loskiel got his information from Zeisberger (Hist. N. Amer. Ind., 42; also, DeSchweinitz, Life of Zeis., 358). The name, as commonly used by the Delawares, was Winingus, "a mink," which was the form from which nearly all of the corruptions, as Winingo, were derived. The French name of the stream was Riviere aux Boeufs, or Riviere au Boeuf, "Buffalo River." It is so noted on Bonnecamp's map (1749). The first mention of the river by this name is in the "Memoir" of Sabrevios de Bleury, of 1718, in which he says, "This Ohio, or Beautiful River, rises 30 leagues south of the Seneca nation. Beyond Fort des Sables on Lake Ontario and near the River aux boeufs is a river that flows into this Beautiful river" (Arch. Sec. Ser., VI. 50). M. de St. Pierre, the Commander of the fort to which Washington went in 1753, dates his reply to Gov. Dinwiddie's letter, which Washington delivered, "From the Fort on the River au Boeuf" (same ref. 165-166). On Gist's map of this mission of 1753 the creek is marked French Creek. Washington calls the creek by this name in his Journal of 1753 (Western Annals, 113). Evans' map of 1755 gives the name as "Frenchy Cr. or Toranadachkoa." The name French Creek was first used by Washington, probably because he did not know the Indian, or the French name of the stream, and was given by him because the French had taken possession of it. According to the Deposition of Stephen Coffen (1754), there was an Indian village at the mouth of this creek called Ganagarah'hare "on the Banks of Belle Riviere, where the River O Boeff empties into it" (Arch. Sec. Ser., VI. 184). Washington says in his Journal of 1753, "This is an old Indian town, situated at the mouth of French Creek, on Ohio; it lies north, about sixty miles from the Logstown, but more than seventy the way we were obliged to go" (Western Annals, 113). On Aug. 3, 1749 Celoron de Bienville, who had descended the Conewango and Allegheny from Lake Chautauqua stopped at the village, which then consisted of 9 or 10 cabins. All of the Indians, save six Iroquois, had taken to the woods, as had also John Fraser, the English trader, who had a trading house and a blacksmith shop at the place. Celoron does not mention Fraser by name, but simply refers to him as "an English merchant." Fraser remained at this place until 1753, when he was driven away by the French. Edward Shippen, in sending Fraser's letter to Governor Hamilton, says, "Weningo is the name of an Indian Town on Ohio where Mr Fraser has had a Gunsmith's Shop for many Years; it is situate eighty Miles up the said River beyond the Log's Town, and Casewago (Cussewago) is Twenty Miles above Weningo." Fraser had said that the French were building a fort "at a Place called Caseoago up French Creek." This was an error. The fort was erected at Waterford, at the head of French Creek, and was known as Fort Le Boeuf. Many writers have fallen into the error of following Fraser's statement. No French fort was ever erected at Cussewago (Col. Rec., V. 659-661). When Washington and Gist reached Venango in 1753 the French flag was flying from the house from which Fraser had been driven. Washington found Captain Joncaire in command. Washington and Gist remained at Venango from Dec. 4th., until the 11th., when they set out for Fort Le Boeuf. They reached Venango, on their return, on the 22nd. and left for Virginia on the 23rd. (Consult; Washington's Jour. of 1753, Western Annals, 113-118; Darlington, Gist, 81-84). The expedition of Celoron de Bienville in 1749, and his report of the rebellion of the Twightwees, under La Demoiselle (called Old Britain, by the English), led the French authorities in Canada to take active steps for the holding of the Ohio Valley (Archives, Sec. Ser., VI. 130, 160 et seq.). Celoron's expedition also aroused the Colonies of Pennsylvania and Virginia, and the latter through the efforts of Gov. Dinwiddie and the Ohio Company, took the initiative in the attempt to hold the trade on the Ohio, by building the fort at "the forks" (See *Pittsburgh, Shannopin's Town*). Early in Jan. 1753 the French force left Quebec, landing at Presqu' Isle in May. The fort known as Fort la Presqu' Isle was built immediately, being finished in June. This post was garrisoned by about 100 men, and the army moved on to the headwaters of French Creek, where the second fort, called Fort le Boeuf, was built, near the site of the present Waterford,

Erie County. Owing to the lateness of the season, the building of the third fort at the mouth of French Creek, was postponed until spring. The point was however held by Captain Chalbert de Joncaire, who expelled the English traders—John Fraser among them (Arch. Sec. Ser., VI. 161). These actions of the French aroused the Indians on the Ohio, who through the Half King, Tanachharrison, warned the French officers to withdraw from the region (Col. Rec., V. 623, 630, 635, 658-660, 665-686, 731-735; Washington's Jour. of 1753; Gist's Jour. 1753). The French Fort at Venango, at the mouth of French Creek, was finished in the spring of 1754, and was called Fort Machault, but was always given the title "French fort at Venango," by the English. During the French occupation of the Ohio, this fort was a base of supplies. After the desertion of Fort Duquesne, Nov. 25, 1758, Venango became a rallying place for all of the Indians hostile to the English. In the summer of 1759 there were about 1,000 Indians of various tribes gathered about the mouth of French Creek. Col. Hugh Mercer, wrote from Fort Pitt, Jan. 8, 1759, telling of the gathering of a great force at Venango, for the purpose of making an attempt to re-capture the former place (Col. Rec., VIII. 292). During the summer of 1759 the French abandoned all of their forts in northwestern Pennsylvania. The British then built a fort at the mouth of French Creek, in the summer of 1760, which was called Fort Venango. A small garrison, under Lieut. Gordon, was placed at this point. In the early summer of 1763, during the Conspiracy of Pontiac, or Pontiac's War, as it should be called, the entire garrison was blotted out by the hostile Indians. Not a soul escaped (Col. Rec., VIII. 394-396; IX. 35; Conspiracy of Pontiac, Parkman, II. 18-25, 1901). Lieut. Gordon was put to death by torture, and the fort was burned to the ground. At the close of the War of the Revolution, owing to the various Indian raids from the Seneca country, the United States erected a fort at Venango, in the spring of 1787, which was called Fort Franklin (See Frontier Forts, II. 585-608). In 1794 Major Ebenezer Denny, with a detachment of troops, went from Pittsburgh to Fort Franklin, for the purpose of protecting the Commissioners at Presqu' Isle and LeBoeuf, and also to cut off the Iroquois from being of any assistance to the western Indians, against which General Wayne was getting ready an expedition. He reached Fort Franklin on June 12th., and found it "in a wretched state of defense. The men in the fort, about twenty, almost all invalids and unable to make any repairs" (Denny's Jour., in Mem. Hist. Soc. Pa., VII. 387). There were various trails leading to Venango, from Erie, from the Beaver River, from Fort Pitt and from the Susquehanna. The trail from the Beaver ran east from the mouth of the Mahoning, near the former village of Kuskuski. This trail was followed by Washington and Gist in 1753, and by C. F. Post, from Venango to Kuskuski, in 1758. The trail up the Allegheny was followed by Zeisberger in 1769 from the Moravian village below Kuskuski, to the village on the Allegheny, at Lawunakhanneck. He passed the ruins of Fort Venango on this trip. He says, "The fort was entirely consumed. A short distance from it stood a saw mill. This the Indians spared, probably with the intention of using it, but not understanding its machinery it has been neglected and fallen to pieces. On the bank above Onenge we found a cannon of curious w o r k m a n s h i p, brought that far by the savages from the fort. Had we discovered it on our way down we would have taken it to Fort Pitt" (Zeisberger's Jour., Life and Times of Zeisberger, 358). There was another trail from the Shenango River near the present Sharpsville, and another branch left this Shenango trail at the "Big Bend," near the former village of Pymatuning. These trails connected the Mahoning, Muskingum and other trails in Ohio, with the upper Allegheny, and also with the village at the mouth of Beaver River. Hutchin's map of 1764 outlines the course of these trails. The land trail from Fort Pitt ran almost directly north from the Ohio, opposite the mouth of Saw Mill Run. This trail was used in the passage of troops and supplies to Fort Venango and Fort Franklin. This trail is mentioned by General Irvine in 1785 (Archives, XI. 514, 518). A branch of this trail ran west along Slippery Rock Creek and the Conoquenessing to the Beaver River—this being the trail from Kuskuski to Venango. The trail from the Susquehanna followed the course of the Kittanning Trail to

Canoe Place, now Cherry Tree Indiana County, and about four miles beyond this point the Venango Path left the Kittanning Path, near Cookport, Indiana County. From here the Venango Path ran northward across the Little Mahoning, near the mouth of Ross Run; then to the forks of the Mahoning, and on across the present Red Bank, Clarion and Sandy Creeks to the Allegheny River, which was crossed just below the mouth of French Creek. This trail was used by the traders from Frankstown and the various points along the Susquehanna. It was also, in part, the trail from Shamokin (Sunbury), and the West Branch Valley. The latter trail was followed by C. F. Post, from Shamokin, in 1758, and also by Ettwein in 1772. It is frequently mentioned in the Journals of the Moravian missionaries. This Chinklaclamoose Path led through the present Clearfield, striking the Venango Path, from Cherry Tree, near the forks of the Mahoning, west of Punxsutawney. One of the oldest trails between the Allegheny, Susquehanna and Delaware ran to the headwaters of the Allegheny, at Port Allegany, and crossed the divide to the West Branch. With a portage of about 18 miles over this divide, an Indian could go in a canoe from Chesapeake Bay to the Gulf of Mexico. The author has been over the entire course of this "water trail." Another trail went on up the Allegheny to its headwaters, near Coudersport, Potter County, and then over the divide to the waters of the Genesee, and on to the Cowanesque, Tioga Chemung and Susquehanna. This last trail was followed by Zeisberger in 1767, when on his way to the mouth of the Tionesta. See *Cowanesque, Passigachkunk, Shamokin, Allegheny, Ohio, Kittanning, Frankstown, Raystown, Juniata* etc.

Beef or **French Creek.**—Nuremburg map, 1756. **French Creek.** — Washington (1753), Jour., in Western Annals, 113. **French Cr.**—Gist (1753), map, in Dar. Gist's Jour. **Onenge.**—Zeisberger (1769), in DeSchweinitz, Life of Zeis, 358. **Oninge.**—Homann Heirs map, 1756. **Oningo.**—Esnauts and Rapilly map, 1777. **River aux boeufs.**—Bleury (1718), Arch. Sec Ser., VI. 49. **Riviere aux Boeufs.**—Pidon (1754), Archives, II 124. **R. Aux Boeufs.**—Bonnecamp map, 1749. **River au Boeuf.**—Duquesne (1753), Arch. Sec. Ser., VI. 161 **Venanga.**—Lattre map, 1784. **Venango.**—Washington (1753), Western Annals, 113. **Veningo.**—Shirley (1755), N. Y. Doc. Col. Hist., VI 957. **Vinango.**—Nuremberg map, 1756. **Viningo.**—Gist map,

1753. **Wenango.**—Evans map, 1755. **Weningo.**—Shippen (1753), Col. Rec., V. 660. **Weningo Town.**—Peters (1754), Col. Rec., V. 759. **Fort Franklin.**—Howell map, 1792. **Fort Machault.**—Duquesne (1756), Arch Sec. Ser., VI. 253 **Fort Mackhault.**—Vaudreuil (1757), Arch. Sec. Ser., VI. 406. **Fort of Venango.**—Pa Coun. (1789), Col. Rec., XVI. 161. **Machault.**—Fevre (1758), Archives, III. 363 **F. Machault.**—Pouchot map, 1758

The village mentioned in the Deposition of Stephen Coffen is recorded as follows ;

Ganagarahhare.—Coffen (1754), Col. Rec., VI. 9. **Ganagarah'hare.**—Coffen (1754), Arch. Sec. Ser., VI. 186.

On Bonnecamp's map of 1749, this village is noted as "Village du Loups" (Village of Delawares). See *Cussewago, Conewango*. The name given by Coffen, may be a corruption of Gannagare'hare, "a great pole, on the end of it." What this had reference to—if such is the origin of the name—is hard to make out. Just below the mouth of French Creek, on the Allegheny River, about 6 miles below Franklin, is a large rock covered with inscriptions. This rock has always been know as "Indian God Rock," or "the Indian God." The various carvings are evidently intended to commemorate various triumphs. A female figure is that of a captive. As the pathway of the Iroquois ran past this rock for many years before the settlement of the Ohio, the inscriptions, no doubt, have reference to the wars with the western or southern Indians. Many of the captives of the Miamis and Illinois were brought back by this route.

WALKING PURCHASE. T h e name given to the purchase of the lands, in the Forks of the Delaware, deeded to William Penn by the Indians, August 28, 1686, the line of which was run in Sept. 1737, in a day and half walk, in accordance with the conditions of the deed. The Deed for the lands in this Purchase is contained in Archives, I. 541-543. The Deposition of Nicholas Scull, concerning the walk, is found in Colonial Records, VII. 400. James Yeates and Edward Marshall, together with some Indians, started on this walk on the morning of Sept. 19, 1737, from Wrightstown, going in a northerly course, along the old Durham Road to Durham Creek, and from there in a westerly direction, and at about 2 o'clock they forded the Lehigh about

half a mile below Bethlehem, and from thence in a northwest course through the present Bethlehem, and passed on through the northeast angle of Hanover Township, into Allen Township, and stopped at sunset at the site of Howell's Mill, on the Hockendauqua, where they passed the night of the 19th. of Sept. This was the site of an old Indian village, at which Tishekunk lived. The next morning the walkers continued the "walk," crossing the mountains near the Lehigh Water Gap, and finishing the walk, after having covered about 60 or 65 miles. From the point where this walk was finished a line was drawn, parallel to the line of the previous purchase of 1749, to near the mouth of the Lackawaxen. This purchase contained about 1,200 square miles, including in its limits the upper part of the present Bucks County, ninetenths of Northampton County, a large part of Carbon County, and about a fourth of Monroe and Pike Counties This land included the greater part of the Minisinks, the habitat of the Munsee clan of the Delawares. This purchase was one of the chief causes of the alienation of the Delawares, and was the basis of the charge of "fraud," which Tedyuskung brought against the Province, and which was the cause of much discussion between the Governor and the Assembly. It came up at every Indian Council until its final settlement in 1758. The Delawares denied the right of the Iroquois to any of the lands on the Delaware River, and also denied that the Iroquois had any right to say what disposition the Delawares should make of these lands. The Delawares refused to leave the lands which were included in this purchase. At the Treaty at Philadelphia in 1742 Canassatego, in one of the most stinging speeches which was ever delivered at an Indian Council, demanded that the Delawares remove at once to Wyoming or Shamokin, and to forever let all "Land Affairs" alone (Col. Rec., IV. 578-580). The Iroquois, at this Council, came into the place which had been previously occupied by the Delawares, in dealing with the Penns. The Delawares retreated to Wyoming and to the Ohio, burning with indignation because of the wrong which had been done them. The Munsee became bitter foes of the English from that time onward. This land sale was the chief cause of the hostility of the

Delaware and Shawnee, which later drenched the Province in blood. The charge of "fraud" in the Walking Purchase was brought up by Tedyuskung at the Treaty at Easton in 1756, at which time a Committee was appointed to investigate the entire matter. This Committee made a report in 1758, in which all of the Indian land sales were discussed (Col. Rec., VIII. 246-261). In 1762 Tedyuskung went to Philadelphia and was told that if he would withdraw this charge of fraud, in the Walking Purchase, that 400 Pounds would be at his disposal. He made a public acknowledgement which suited the Governor, Hamilton, and was paid the 400 Pounds (Col. Rec., VIII. 708). But, the "Walking Purchase" had cost the Province the alienation of the great body of the Delawares during the entire period of hostility after the defeat of Braddock, 1755. Consult; Walton, Conrad Weiser, II. 59, 65 etc.; Col. Rec., VII. 324; VIII. 246, 661, 740, 751; Archives, III. 86, 244-248, 576, 666; IV. 85-86; Egle. Hist. Penna., 966, 987.

WALLENPAUPACK. A branch of Lackawaxin Creek, between Pike and Wayne Counties. The name is a corruption of Walinkpapeek, "deep, still water," or "a deep spring." An old Indian trail from the Minisinks crossed this creek near the junction of the two branches, running on to Lackawanna River, and down that stream to the Susquehanna.

Waullenpaupack.—Morris map, 1848. **Walenpapeck.** — Howell's map, 1792. **Wallenpanpack.** — Scull's map, 1770. **Wallinpapeck.**—Stewart (1775), Archives, IV. 691.

WALLPACK. There was an Indian village, noted on Evans' map of 1755 as Wallpack, situated near the present Stillwater, N. J. The present name is a translation of the Indian name, which is a corruption of Walinkpapeek, from Woa-lac, "a hole," Tuppeek, "a pool," hence, a "turn-hole," or "eddy." There was a ferry across the Delaware, just below the Walpack Bend, which is noted on Scull's map of 1770. At this point an Indian trail crossed the river leading to the Minisinks in New Jersey. The ferry was about 15 miles above DePui's, or DuPui, who lived about 3 miles above the Delaware Water Gap. The place is mentioned in the early records.

Wallpack.—Dupui (1758), Archives, III. 424. **Walpack Perry.**—Scull map, 1770.

Wolpack.—Williamson (1762), Archives, IV. 84.

WAMPUM. The name of a town in Lawrence County. The name is a contraction of Wampumpeak, "a string"(of shell beads). These shell beads became a medium of exchange between the Indians. The black wampum was more valuable than the white, the former being valued at about twice the latter. Wampum was also used in a ceremonial way. Messages of war and peace were sent by belts of wampum, the colors of which were significant. Each declaration, in a formal "speech," was impressed by the presentation of a string of wampum, or a number of strings. At treaties large belts, with various figures woven into various designs, were presented. The use of wampum at an Indian Council can be studied in the record of any of the Councils with the Indians in the Colonial Records or Archives. Consult, as an example, Col. Rec., V. 665-685, in the report of the Treaty at Carlisle in 1753. Consult; Handbook of Amer. Ind. II. 904 et seq.; Memoirs Hist. Soc. Pa., VI. 205 et seq., concerning the Belt of Wampum, given to William Penn by the Indians in 1682. The present town of Wampum is near the site of the former Moravian village on the Beaver River. See *Languntouteneunk.*

WANAMIE. The name of a P. O. in Luzerne County. A corruption of Unami, the name of the Turtle tribe of the Delawares. The name is sometimes recorded in this form. Archives, III. 415.

WANNETA. A P. O. in Erie County. Possibly a corruption of Juniata, which see.

WAPPASUNING. The name of a creek in Bradford County, which enters the Susquehanna near Nichols, Tioga County, N. Y. The name is a corruption of Wapachsinnink, "place of white stones." The Delaware name for silver was Woap-ach-sin, "white stone." A Post-Office in Bradford County has a corruption of the name, as Wapaseming.

Wappasuning. — Howell's map, 1792. **Wapposening.**—Present state map, 1911, 1912. **Wepasening.**—Morris map, 1848.

WAPWALLOPEN. The name of a creek which enters the Susquehanna from the east at Wapwallopen, Luzerne County. The Little Wapwallopen enters a few miles above.

The name is a corruption of Woaphallack-pink, "white hemp place," or "where the white hemp g r o w s." Reichel says that the Indians, Gottlieb and Mary, two Moravian converts from this creek, wrote the name Wambhallobank (Indian Names, 270). These converts were baptized at Bethlehem in 1745. They were then living on this creek. Evans' map of 1755 gives an Indian village above the mouth of this creek called Opolopona, which is probably a corruption of the name. Scull's map of 1759 notes an "Old Indian Town" just above the mouth of the creek, on the west side of the Susquehanna, and his map of 1770 notes this as "Old Town." It was at the point where the trail from the Great Island (Lock Haven) intersected the trail up the western side of the Susquehanna, leading to Wyoming. Another trail to Wyoming ran up the Wapwallopen to its head, through Wapwallopen Valley, and crossed to Wyoming. The trail to the Great Island was a branch of the "Warriors Path," from Wyoming to the Susquehanna, crossing the trails leading to Shamokin. It was a short cut to the West Branch, the Bald Eagle Valley, the Juniata and to the "Warriors Path" leading across the Potomac, at Oldtown, Md.

Opolopona.—Evans map. 1755. **Wambhallobank.**—Reichel. Ind. Names, 270. **Wapwallopen.** — Morris map, 1848. **Whopehawly.**—Scull map, 1759; Howell's map, 1792. **Whopehowly.**—Scull map, 1770.

WARRIORS RIDGE, WARRIORS RUN, WARRIORS TRAIL, WARRIORS MARK etc.

The Warriors Ridge, or Great Warrior Ridge, is cut by the Juniata above Huntingdon, running southwest to the Potomac, above Oldtown, Md. The mountain receives its name because the Warriors Trail, from Shamokin to Virginia and the Carolinas ran along the valley at its eastern side. This great trail had various northern branches, running to the various parts of the Iroquois country in New York. The chief branch ran from Wyoming down the Susquehanna, on the western shore, to Shamokin, where various branches which led to the Bald Eagle Valley, and along the foot of the mountains on the western shore, to the Juniata, where these branches united at Huntingdon. Another path from Wyoming cut overland from above Wapwallopen Creek, near the mouth of Shickshinny Creek,

to near the present Watsontown, Northumberland County, and then on up the West Branch to the Big Island (Lock Haven), and then up the Bald Eagle Valley to Milesburg, and then up Spring Creek and across to Huntingdon. There were various branches of the trail from Shamokin to the Juniata region, one of which intersected the Juniata Path near the present Mifflintown. Another trail from the upper Susquehanna ran along the eastern shore of the river to Harris' Ferry (Harrisburg), where it crossed the river and ran down the Cumberland Valley to Croghan's Gap (Sterritt's), where it cut through the Kittatinny mountains, running on to the Black Log, where it joined the path leading to Bloody Run, where it struck the main Warriors Path from Huntingdon to the Potomac. An older branch of the Warriors trail ran down the Susquehanna, from S h a m o k i n, crossed the river at Harrisburg, and then went down the Cumberland Valley to the mouth of the Conococheague, where it crossed the Potomac. Another later trail ran down the Tuscarora Valley, crossing the Potomac at the same point. These trails united in the north at Shamokin or the Great Island. From the latter place the trail ran up the West Branch to Emporium and then over the divide to the waters of the Allegheny, and on to the Seneca country. Another branch ran up Pine Creek and over the divide to the Genesee, and another branch ran up Lycoming Creek to its headwaters and then across to the Tioga, or to the Susquehanna, via the Sheshequin route. From Wyoming the trails branched to the Delaware region and to the present Chemung River, as well as up the North Branch. Huntingdon, or Standing Stone, was a meeting place for many of the trails from the Iroquois country. From this point the Warriors Path crossed the Juniata and followed, in the main, the present course of the Huntingdon and Broad Top Mountain R. R. to Everett, Bedford County, and then went southward along the foot of Warriors Mountain to Oldtown, Md., where it crossed the Potomac, near where Col. Cresap had his trading house. At the Council at Lancaster in 1762, Governor Hamilton requested the Iroquois, when going on their war trails to the south, to go "by the Old War path from Shamokin, which lies along the Foot of the Allegheny Hills & which is the nearest Way they can go to the Enemies Country" (Col. Rec. VIII. 769)'. This was the trail through Everett and Oldtown. All of these trails were war paths, and not trading trails. There were other trails which were called Warriors Trails, but the above mentioned were the trails so designated by the Indians themselves. The Catawba Trail (See *Catawba*) across Westmoreland and Fayette Counties, and the trail up the Monongahela were used as war paths, as were others in various parts of the state. The Great Warrior Trail, however, was the one running along Warriors Mountain, from Huntingdon to Oldtown, and on south. These trails were used by the Iroquois in their war expeditions against the southern Indians, with whom the Iroquois had been at war "since the world began," according to the statement of an Iroquois chief (See *Catawba, Cherokee, Shamokin, Standing Stone, Wyoming, Bald Eagle, Big Island, Pine Creek, Lycoming* etc. Consult; Scull map, 1759, 1770; Evans map, 1749, 1755.

WARRIORS RUN. A small creek which enters the West Branch at Watsontown, Northumberland County. The Warriors Path from Wyoming reached the West Branch, on its course to the Great Island, near the mouth of Warriors Run. Shikellamy, the Iroquois deputy, lived for a time near the intersection of these trails (from Wyoming and Shamokin) below the present Milton. In 1745 Bishop Spangenberg and Conrad Weiser passed up the trail from Shamokin, on their way to Onondaga, stopping for the night on June 7th. at "Warriors Camp," at the mouth of Warriors Run. The region was settled soon after the purchase of 1768. During the hostility of 1778-79 many Indian raids were made into the entire West Branch region. Fort Freeland was built on Warriors Run, about 4 miles from Watsontown, in the fall of 1778. It was a stockade about the house of Jacob Freeland. This fort was destroyed by the Indians, under Hiokatoo, the Seneca chief who had married Mary Jemison, the "White Woman of the Genesee," and a company of soldiers under Capt. McDonald, on July 29, 1779. This force consisted of about 300. The fort was defended by but 21 men, who finally surrendered, on condition

that the women and children be allowed to go to Sunbury. After the surrender of the fort Captain Hawkins Boone and Captain Samuel Daugherty arrived with a force of 30 men. Not knowing that the fort had been taken they made a rush across Warriors Run. and at the first fire of the enemy both Captain Boone and Captain Daugherty were killed, with nearly half of their men. According to the statement in the Narrative of Mary Jemison, 14 of the men were killed (Consult; Frontier Forts, I. 381-385; Archives, XII. 362-366; Meginness, Otzinachson, 248-255; Narrative of the Life of Mary Jemison, 7th. Ed., 189). Opposite the mouth of Warriors Run, at the mouth of White Deer Creek, Fort Menninger was erected in the spring of 1778. This was abandoned during the "Big Runaway" during the summer of 1778. The fort was burned by the Indians July 8, 1779. It was occupied after this time by various detachments of troops (Consult; Frontier Forts, I. 392). Soon after the Warriors Run valley was settled the dispute of Pennsylvania and Connecticut was at its height. Thomas Ball wrote from Sunbury, Sept. 26, 1775, to Joseph Shippen, telling him of the arrival of "a Party of Connecticut intruders, supposed to be a detachment from Colonel Butler's Regiment, consisting as nearly as can be conjectured, of 300 men, arrived last Saturday night at Freeland's Mill, on the Warriours Run, about 13 Miles distance from this Town." In the Deposition of Peter Smith, Oct. 5, 1775, he states, "that on the evening of Monday, the twenty-fifth of September last, this Deponent went to the house of Garrett Freeland, of the Warrior's Run, and there saw a number of men from Wyoming on Guard in a School house who pressed him much to join with them, and acquainted him that they were come to enforce the Connecticut Laws, and Settle the Vacant Land" (Archives, IV. 661, 662, 665-666). This attempt of the Connecticut settlers to take possession of the West Branch Valley was the cause of much trouble, and there is no doubt but that it was the chief cause of the Indian raids into the valley during the years which followed. The Connecticut Dispute was the most costly dispute, in lives and money, which the Province ever had during its history. (Consult; Archives, IV. 669-678, 687-691; Archives,

Sec. Ser., XVIII, entire vol.). At a meeting of the Susquehanna Company, as the Connecticut Company was called, at Hartford, Conn., April 22, 1773, the various Connecticut towns on the West Branch were named. These were New Weathersfield, Yalestown, Bethlehem, Judea, Charlestown and New Simsburg (Archives, Sec. Ser., XVIII. 86-87). Governor Hoyt, in his "Syllabus of the Controversy between Connecticut and Pennsylvania," says, "It involved the lives of hundreds, was the ruin of thousands, and cost the state millons. It wore out one entire generation" (Frontier Forts, I. 424).

Warriors Run.—Scull map, 1770. **Warrior's Run.**—Sluman (1775), Archives, IV. 661. **Warriours Run.**—Ball (1775), Archives, IV. 662.

WARRIORS MARK. The name of a station in Huntingdon County.

WARRIORS RIDGE. A station in Huntingdon County, near the gap through the Warriors Mountain, or Ridge.

WATER STREET. The name of a prominent landmark on the Frankstown Trail, from Huntingdon to Frankstown. The mountain gap is so narrow at this point, that the traders were obliged to travel through the water of the Juniata, hence the name. The trail from Standing Stone crossed the river between Alexandria and Petersburg, and then ran on through Water Street. Water Street Creek enters the Juniata east of the village of Water Street. Consult; Archives, II. 136; XI. 684.

WAUKESHA. The name of a town in Clearfield County, named after the city in Wisconsin. A corruption of Wagosh, or Wauk-tsha, "fox." The Delaware word for the gray fox is Woakus.

WAWA. The name of a P. O. in Delaware County. May be a corruption of some Indian word. Has no meaning whatever in this form.

WAWASET. The name of a P. O. in Chester County. Same as above.

WECHQUETANK. A corruption of Wekquitank, the name of a species of willow, according to Heckewelder, which grew near the village of that name on Head's Creek, Monroe County. Head's Creek, or Hoeth's Creek, is a branch of the present Big Creek, for-

merly Poco Poco, or Poca Poca, creek, which enters the Lehigh at Weissport Carbon County (See *Pohopoco*). In April 1760 Gottlieb Senseman with thirty Indians from Bethlehem, who had formerly been at Gnadenheutten, established the mission at Wechquetank. Bernard A. Grube had charge of this mission, which prospered greatly. It was visited by Bishop Spangenberg and David Zeisberger at various times. This mission flourished until the breaking out of the Indian hostility in 1763, during the Pontiac War. The feeling against all Indians was so strong among the settlers that the Christian Indians at the various mission villages were constantly threatened, not only by the white settlers, but also by the hostile Indians. A number of strange Indians from the Ohio region visited Wechquetank, Nain and Bethlehem. In August a comapny of soldiers, under Captain Wetterhold, killed an Indian woman named Zippora, as she was sleeping in a barn. This act made the settlers uneasy, fearing that the Indians would avenge the death of this woman. Various threatening messages were sent to Wechquetank. On October 8th. an Indian raid upon the Irish settlement near Bethlehem, in which several were killed. As a consequence of this act, and because of the constant threats of the settlers in the region, Wechquetank was deserted on October 11, 1763. The Indians were obliged to leave their houses, fields, harvests and the greater part of their cattle behind them. They went to Nazareth. On Nov. 6th. an order reached Nazareth, from Philadelphia, commanding all of the Indians from Nain and Wechquetank to go to Philadelphia, for their own safety. The Indians left Nazareth on Nov. 8th., going to Bethlehem where they were joined by the Indians from Nain. They reached the barracks in Philadelphia on Nov. 11th. Wechquetank was burned by the white settlers, and an attempt was made to set fire to Bethlehem on the night of Nov. 18th. On the 20th. of March 1765 the Moravian set out from Philadelphia for Nain On April 3rd. they left this place, passing through Bethlehem, on their way to Wyalusing, which was reached on May 9th. (See *Wyalusing;* Consult; Loskiel, Hist. Miss., II. 193-234; DeSchweinitz, Life of Zeisberger, 277-278). Fort Allen, at the site of Gnadenheutten, was built in Jan. 1756, at the site of the present Weissport, and Fort N o r r i s was built in Feb. 1756, near the present Kresgeville.

Wechquetank (Consult; Frontier Forts, I. 184-236). **Wechquetank.**—Loskiel (1794), Hist. Miss., II. 193. **Wequetano.** —Reichel, in Mem. Mor. Church, 38.

WELAGAMIKA. A c c o r d i n g t o Heckewelder this was the name of the Nazareth tract, when the Moravians first went there in 1740. It is a corruption of Wehlick, "best," and Hacki, "land," and signifies "rich soil."

WEST CONSHOHOCKEN. T h e name of a town in Montgomery County. See *Conshohocken.*

WEST MOSHANNON. A town in Clearfield County. See *Moshannon.*

WHEELING. The name of a creek which forms a part of the boundary between Washington and Greene Counties, and which enters the Ohio from the east at Wheeling, W. Va. The name is derived from Wihl, "a head," with the locative, ing, "place of a head." Heckewelder says that the Indians said that they had decapitated a prisoner, and placed his head upon a pole, hence the name. The name was probably applied to the site of the present city of Wheeling, which was a meeting place for the Indians, as it was near the intersection of a number of trails. Several Indian trails crossed from the Ohio from the mouth of Wheeling, Fish, Grave and other creeks along the river, to various points on the Monongahela. One of the forks of the South Fork of Wheeling Creek, and one of the forks of Fish Creek, was called Warrior Fork, because of the trails to the Monongahela. The trail from Wheeling to Fort Pitt ran across the Warrior Fork of Wheeling Creek, through Washington, and then down Chartiers Creek, and cut across the Saw Mill Run, and down that stream to the gap in Coal Hill, and on up to Fort Pitt. The branch from Fish Creek crossed to the head of Dunkards Creek and then on to the Monongahela, where it joined the Catawba Trail. Both of these trails had various branches leading to various points on the Monongahela. The trail through Washington branched near that place, one fork leading to Fort Pitt and the other to the head of Mingo Creek and down it to the present Monongahela, another branch running directly to the site of Redstone Old Fort (Brownsville), and then on to the Potomac, by way of Nemacolin's Trail. All of these trails were used by the hostile Delaware and Shawnee during the period after these tribes were driven beyond the Ohio. The region through which they passed was under the jurisdiction of the Virginia Courts, during the Boundary Dispute, and during 1773-1782 they were the paths followed by the hostile parties of Indians into the settlements along Chartiers Creek, and throughout the present Washington and Greene Counties. Nearly all of the expeditions into the Indian Country, beyond the Ohio, during this period, were made up of the adherents of the Virginia Courts, and were conducted by the officers holding commissions from the Colony of Virginia. The various expeditions during "Dunmore's War" were all undertaken by the Virginia adherents. This war began in the spring of 1774, when the Virginia Boundary Dispute was at its height. Dr. John Connolly, as the representative of Lord Dunmore, the Royal Governor of Virginia, had taken possession of Fort Pitt, and named it Fort Dunmore. In June 1774 he had advised the building of a fort at Wheeling, for the protection of the frontier settlements and as a base of supplies for the expeditions into the region beyond the Ohio. Lord Dunmore approved of this plan on June 20th. (Archives, IV. 522, 539). Early in July Major Angus McDonald assembled the troops at Wheeling and erected the fort, which was called Fort Fincastle, in honor of Lord Dunmore, one of whose titles was Viscount Fincastle. The work upon this fort was directed by Ebenezer Zane and John Caldwell. The fort was enlarged in 1777 and called Fort Henry, in honor of Patrick Henry. Lord Dunmore arrived at Wheeling on Sept. 30, 1774, with 1200 men for his expedition against the Indians. Returning in Nov., after this expedition, he left a garrison of 25 men at this point. These were discharged in June, 1775, (Consult; History of Fayette County, Ellis, 66 et seq.; History of Washington County, Crumrine, under title, Dunmore; Archives, IV. and V., under titles Dunmore, Connolly; Western Annals, 217-259; Doddridge's Notes, 171 (1912 Ed.); Archives of West Virginia, 231 et seq., Third Report;

Old Westmoreland, Hassler under title, Connolly and Dunmore). Fort Henry was the scene of two Indian attacks of great moment, that of 1777 and that of 1782 (Consult; Western Annals, 257-261; Old Westmoreland, 184). Gibson's Gunpowder Plot (1777), Hand's Squaw Campaign (1777), Brodhead's Expedition to Coshocton (1781), General Clarke's Expedition (1781), Lochry's Expedition (1781), and various other events during the period made Fort Henry the scene of many thrilling events (Consult; Old Westmoreland, Doddridge's Notes, Wither's Chronicles of Border Warfare, Border Life, etc., under titles, Fort Henry, Wheeling, Clarke, etc.

There were several frontier forts and block-houses in this State near the various trails leading from Wheeling. Among these were Beeman's Block House, on Beeman's Run, on the North Fork of Wheeling Creek; Ryerson's Block House, on the war path from the Ohio to the Monongahela, at the junction of the north and south forks of Dunkard Branch of Wheeling Creek; Jackson's Fort, near Waynesburg, and others within the present counties of Washington and Greene (Consult; Frontier Forts, II. 425, 442, 437, etc.; Crumrine's History of Washington County, under titles). During the period of Indian hostility the entire southwestern part of Pennsylvania suffered greatly from the raids of the Indians. The most unfortunate expedition of Col. Wm. Crawford to Sandusky, after the brutal expedition of Col. Williamson against the Christian Indians at Gnadenhuetten, in 1782, added some very dark pages to the history of this historic region along the Ohio (Consult; Old Westmoreland, 155-161, 162-169; Archives, Sec. Ser., XIV. 690-727; Butterfield, Hist. Account of Exped. against Sandusky, 1873; DeSchweinitz, Life of Zeisberger, 537-557, etc.; See *Gnadenhuetten.* Black's Cabin, where the first courts of the Virginia county of Ohio were held, was situated 11 miles northeast of Wheeling, on the north fork of Short Creek. This court was removed to Wheeling in 1797 (Consult; Annals of Carnegie Museum, III. 7, 78 et seq.; The Old Virginia Court House at Augusta Town. Crumrine, 31-32). This Cabin was at the town of West Liberty. The court was first held at this place in Black's Cabin, Jan. 6, 1777. The entire period of the Boundary Dispute and the Indian hostility made these two southwestern counties of this State the scene of bitter conflict, not only between the settlers and the Indians, but also between the adherents of the two rival Colonies.

Weeling.—Evans map, 1755. **Weiling.**—Smith (1775), Archives, IV. 632. **Whaling.**—Mackay (1774), Archives, IV. 517. **Wheelin.**—Dunmore (1774), Archives, IV. 522. **Wheeling.**—St. Clair (1774), Archives, IV. 519.

WHITE DEER. The name of a creek which enters the West Branch opposite Watsontown, at White Deer, Union County; also the name of the present Township through which it flows. The name is a translation of Woap'tuchanne, "white-deer stream." Woap, or Wapsu, "white," Achtu, "deer," Hanne, "stream." Peter Smith took up land at the mouth of this creek in 1772. Later his widow erected a mill at this place in 1775. The mill was burned by the Indians July 8, 1779, when one man was killed. In May, 1779, John Semple and his wife were killed near this place (Archives. VII. 574). There were other Indian raids into this valley at various times during 1778-79.

White Deer.—Scull map, 1770.

WHITE DEER HOLE. The name of a creek which enters the West Branch just above the former stream, in Union County. Scull's map of 1759 gives the name "White Flint Creek," with the Indian name as "Opaghtanoten." This is probably a corruption of Woap-achtu-woalhen, "white-deerdigs a hole," having the significance, "where the white deer digs." In 1789, Caleb Farley built a grist-mill on this creek.

Opaghtanoten. — Scull map, 1759. **Opauchtooalin.**—Map of West Penna., 1755, in Dar. Gist's Jour. **White Deer hole.**—Scull, 1770. **White Deer Hole.**—Howell map, 1792. **White Flint.**—Scull map, 1759. **White Hole.**—Hopkins Atlas, 1872.

WICCACO. The Indian name of the region which was just south of the old City of Philadelphia, now included in the city, north of Hollander Creek and along the Delaware. According to Watson, from information given him, the name signified "pleasant place." This was evidently a guess. The name is probably a corruption of Wiquajeu, "the head of a creek," or Wiquiechink, at the end, or point." The Indian village called Wequiaquenske (Egle's Hist. Pa. 1077), which the author of the history of Philadelphia, Thompson Wescott, says "the site of which is not known," was probably situated at the mouth of Hollander Creek, or along its upper waters. Wiquek, is "head of a creek." The village name, Wequiaquenske, may be compounded of Wiquek, "head of a creek," Kuwe, "pine tree," with the corrupt suffix ske, signifying "the place of pine trees at the head of the creek." Some of the earlier forms of the name, as Wickegkoo, very closely approach the correct form of Wiquajeu, "the head of a creek." The Swens, or Swensons, were granted a Patent to the Wiccaco tract, between Hollanders Creek and the Delaware, in 1664. In 1676, Oele Swenson, or Olle Swen, was sworn in as one of the Justices of the Court at Upland, by order of Gov. Andros (Records of Upland Court, 35-36). In the Census of the various settlements along the Delaware in 1673, Swen Swansa, Olla Swansa and Andrew Swansa are given as living at "Witka Coo" (Archives, Sec. Ser., VII. 806). On Holme's map of the Province of Penna., "And Swanson, Swen Swanson and Wolla Swanson" are given as the owners of the land at Wiccaco. This land was at the head of a creek, which was a branch of Hollander Creek. In 1701 the tract of the Swanson family was mentioned as having been granted by a Patent from William Penn (date not given) (Archives, Sec. Ser., XIX. 265). In 1691 "Wolla" Swenson granted a part of these lands to James Thomas (op. cit. 420). In 1669 a Block House was built at Wiccaco. In 1675 the Court at New Castle directed the Magistrates to "cause a church to be built at Wickegkoo" (Haz. Ann., 417). In 1679 complaint was made that the church property at Wiccaco and Tinicum was out of repair. Orders were issued to the Wardens of these churches to see that the members attended to the repairs needed, upon pain of a fine of fifty guilders" for each offense of neglect (Rec. Up. Court, 152-153). In 1700 a brick church was erected, to replace the old log church. This church, known as the "Old Swedes Church," is still standing. In 1737 Richard Renshaw was granted permission to run a ferry from Wiccaco to Gloucester (Arch. Third Ser. I. 99).

Weccoco.—B. of Prop. (1719), Archives, Sec. Ser., XIX. 696. **wicaco.**—Upland Court (1679), Rec. Up. Court, 152. **Wicacoe.**—Census (1673), Arch. Sec. Ser., VII. 805. **Wicaqueke.**—Tom (1673), Arch. Sec. Ser., VII. 756. **Wiccaco.**—Holmes map, 1681-3. **Wickaco.**—B. of Prop. (1719), Arch Sec. Ser., XIX. 664. **Wickakee.**—Tom (1671), Arch. Sec. Ser., V. 639. **Wickakoe.**—B. of Prop. (1701), op. cit., XIX. 265 **Wickegkoo.**—Rec of N. C. (1675), quoted Rec. Upland Court, 152. **Witka Coo.**—Census (1673), Arch. Sec. Ser., VII. 806.

WICONISCO. The name of a creek which enters the Susquehanna from the east at Millersburg, Dauphin County; the name of a P. O. in the same county. The name is a corruption of Wikenkniskeu, "muddy house," or "muddy camp"—from Wik, or Wiquoam, "a house," and Nisk-as-sisku, "muddy." Shippen had a trading house at the mouth of this creek. Bishop Cammerhoff crossed this creek, at its mouth, and stopped at a house (Jan. 12, 1748), where his host informed him "that on the west bank of the river opposite to his house, began the great path to the Allegheny country, estimated to be three or four hundred miles distant" (Cammerhoff's Jour., in Penna. Mag. Hist., XXIX. 167). This path was one of the branches of the trail leading from the Susquehanna to the Juniata, and then on to Frankstown. It struck the Juniata at "Ohesson," at the mouth of Kishacoquillas Creek, near the present Lewistown. There were several branches of the Juniata Path to various points on the Susquehanna. One crossed the river at Sunbury and ran to Mifflintown. The path from McKees' trading house, near the mouth of Mahantango Creek, ran to Thompsontown, on the Juniata. These paths all connected with the trail to Shamokin, and to Harris' Ferry. There were a number of trading houses at various points along the Susquehanna, below the present Sunbury. Among these were the houses of Thomas McKee, Welsh, Shippen, English, Reed, Armstrong, Williams, Barbers, Harris, etc. During the summer of 1778 the inhabitants from the Wiconisco Valley fled because of the various raids along the Kittatinny Mountains. Among the early settlers in the valley was Andrew Lycan, after whom the valley is named

(Lykens Valley). His house was attacked by the Indians March 7, 1756.

Berry's Creek.—Scull map, 1759. **Wiconesco.**—Galbraith (1778), Archives, IV. 642. **Wisconisco.**—Cammerhoff (1748), Pa. Mag. Hist., XXIX. 167. **Wikinisky.**—Adlum map, 1790. **Wikinisky.**—Howell map, 1792. **Wikisnisky.**—Scull map, 1770.

WILLAWANNA. The name of a town on the Susquehanna River, in Bradford County; formerly the name of an Indian village of which Egohohowen, or Egobund, was the chief. This Munsee chief had married a daughter of French Margaret, named Esther, who became the most infamous of the Montours, and was known as Queen Esther, or the "Fiend of Wyoming." The name of the village, Wilawane, is a corruption of Wilawan —from Wil, "a head"—having the significance of "headgear," or "horns." It is the Delaware translation of the Iroquois Chemung, which has the same significance. During the period of Indian hostility the chief of the Munsee, Egohohowen, carried many white prisoners to this village from various places along the frontiers (Col. Rec., VIII. 152, 159, 196, 209, 435; Archives, III. 506, 740; IV. 90). The village was situated near the present Willawanna, Bradford County. From the reading of Zeisberger's Journals of the northern side of the Chemung, near 1767-68 it would seem to have been on the northern side of the Chemung, near the present Chemung. When Zeisberger passed through the village on Nov. 3, 1767, on his return from the mission on the Allegheny, he found all of the Indians away hunting "except the chief Egohund, who asked me many questions about Goschgoschunk" (MS. of Zeis. Jour., 1767). After leaving this village Zeisberger went on to Sheshequin, where he could not cross the river on account of the high water. This statement would indicate that he had been on the south side of the stream, up to that point, and that Wilawane was at the site of the present town of that name.

Wilawane. — DeSchweinitz, Life of Zeis., 324. **Willewane.** — Zeisberger (1767), MS. Jour., at Bethlehem. **Wilawana.**—Name of P. O., official name. **Willawanna.**—Present name, map, 1912.

WILLS CREEK. The name of a creek which rises in Bedford and Somerset Counties and flows southward to the Potomac at Cumberland, Md. Also Wills Mountain, which is the name of the ridge which runs southward from Bedford to Cumberland, Md. Both were named in honor of an Indian named Will, who lived near the site of Cumberland, before 1755 (See Loudermilk's Hist. Cumb., Md.). The mouth of Wills Creek became famous as the site of Fort Cumberland, which was the starting point of Braddock's expedition in 1755. Previous to the various events which took place at this point, for the possession of the Ohio, the region had been occupied by the Shawnee. These had gradually moved to the Susquehanna and to the Ohio about 1698. On Mayo's map of 1737 all of the old Shawnee towns along the Potomac are marked "Shanno Indian Fields, deserted." The Shawnee had moved to this region from South Carolina and had then removed to the Susquehanna and Ohio, before their final reunion in Ohio after 1760. The beautiful valley of the Potomac from Will's Creek to Oldtown was deserted before the coming of the various white settlers and traders. The Shawnee town at the mouth of Will's Creek was known as Caiuctecuc, or Cucuchetuc. The creek was also known by this name. The Indian named Will remained after these Shawnee had withdrawn from the region. He is said to have lived on the creek, on the west side of Will's Mountain, about three miles from the mouth of the creek. One of the surveys of the land here by Col. Thomas Cresap was designated as "Wills Town." Loudermilk says that the Indian after whom the town, mountain and creek were named, lived here for many years, and that he left several children, who married white settlers. The Ohio Company built a Store House at the mouth of Wills Creek in 1749-50. In 1750 Christopher Gist was authorized to explore the region along the Ohio for this Company. On this trip he set out from Old Town, going by the Warriors Path to Everett, and then over the trail to the Ohio. In 1751 Gist was commissioned "to look out & observe the nearest & most convenient Road You can find from the Company's Store at Will's Creek to a Landing at Mohongeyela" (Dar. Gist, 67).

Gist set out on this trip on Nov. 4, 1751, from the Company's Store at Will's Creek, on the south bank of the

Potomac, opposite the present Cumberland. He passed through the Gap in the mountains 4 miles west of Cumberland, going over the trail to the mouth of Redstone Creek, which later became known as Nemacolin's Trail. Gist returned to Will's Creek on March 29, 1752. In 1752 and 1753 Gist, Cresap and Nemacolin blazed and opened this road from the mouth of Will's Creek to the mouth of Redstone Creek, where the Ohio Company later built another Store House (See *Redstone*). On Nov. 14, 1753, "Major George Washington came to my house at Will's Creek, and delivered me a letter from the council in Virginia, requesting me to attend him up to the commandant of the French fort on the Ohio River" (Dar. Gist, 80). Washington and Gist set out on this mission from Will's Creek on Nov. 15th, going over the trail to Gist's Plantation, at Mount Braddock, and then over the Catawba Trail to the Ohio (See *Shannopin's Town, Logstown, Venango, Turtle Creek*). They returned to Will's Creek on Jan. 6, 1754 (Consult; Gist's Jour., and Washington's Jour. of 1753, in Dar. Gist, and in Western Annals, etc.). Washington returned from this expedition to Williamsburg and made his report to Gov. Dinwiddie. It was immediately determined to get ready for an expedition to drive the French from the Ohio. Ward having surrendered the fort which the Ohio Company was building to the French army which had descended the Allegheny. Col. Joshua Fry was put in command of this expedition. He died on May 31, and was succeeded by Washington, in command of the troops for the expedition. Washington was at Will's Creek on April 23, having heard at Old Town of the capture of Ward's fort on the Ohio. A Council of War was held at Will's Creek, at which it was decided to advance as far as the mouth of Redstone Creek, and there wait for "fresh orders." Washington reached the Little Meadows on May 9th, and encamped at the Little Crossings (Castleman River), where he remained until the 12th. On the 18th the little force reached the Great Crossings, at Somerfield, where it remained for several days. Washington went down the Youghiogheny to Turkey Foot, which was reached on the 20th. He examined the region, which, he said, "we found very con-venient to build a fort." He returned to the Great Crossings, after his trip below Turkey Foot, and advanced towards the Great Meadows, which was reached on the 24th. On the 27th Christopher Gist arrived from his plantation, at Mount Braddock, telling of the visit of a detachment of about 50 French soldiers having been at his plantation the day before. On the 27th news came from the Half King, Tanachharrison, who was encamped about 6 miles away at the Great Rock, that he had discovered a party of French in a secluded ravine. Washington at once set out with all of his troops, save forty men (most of the accounts state that he took forty men with him—this is an error). He reached the camp of the Half King. and then pressed on through the night to the spot. where on the morning he discovered the detachment commanded by M. de Jummonville. In the fight which followed Jummonville was killed. This was the first actual bloodshed in the war which "set the world on fire" for seven years. Washington returned to the Great Meadows, where a fortification which was later called Fort Necessity was erected. On the 16th of June Washington advanced towards Redstone Creek. In cutting and making the road thirteen days were spent in reaching Gist's Plantation. which was reached on the 29th of June. Capt. Lewis had been sent ahead to open the road from Gist's to Redstone. When Washington reached Gist's he received the information that a large French force was advancing up the Monongahela. At a Council of War it was decided to throw up intrenchments at Gist's. and there await the coming of the French army. Messengers were sent out recalling Capt. Lewis from Redstone, and Capt. Polson, who was out scouting, and also to Capt. Mackay, at the Great Meadows, to march to Gists. When all of these officers had reached Gist's, with their troops, another Council of War was held and it was decided to retreat at once to Will's Creek. This was immediately done, the army reaching the Great Meadows on July 1st. The fort, or intrenchment, was strengthened, and named Fort Necessity. This fort stood just below the present National Pike, at Mount Washington, in a valley on the table-land beyond the summit of Laurel Ridge. Washington was criticised by the

Half King, and by many later writers, as to the situation of this fort. There is hardly a spot in the entire region more unfitted for a fort site. The French army, under M. Coulon de Villers, reached Gist's on July 2nd, and had intended returning to Fort Duquesne, when a deserter from Washington's force was captured and told of the situation of Washington's little army at Fort Necessity (See *Gist's, Redstone*). At sunrise some of the French army had reached Fort Necessity, on July 3rd. After a fight during the greater part of the day, Washington finally surrendered on the night of July 3rd, and on the morning of July 4th Washington commenced his retreat to Will's Creek (Consult; Lowdermilk, Hist. Cumb., 41-82; Olden Time, II. 191-210; Sparks, Life of Wash., II. 1-67; Colonial Records, VI. 28, 51, 181; Archives, Sec. Ser., VI. 168, 170). Fort Cumberland was built at Will's Creek during the winter of 1754-55, under the direction of Col. James Innes. This fort was the starting point of the Braddock expedition against Fort Duquesne. The detachment, under Major Chapman, left Fort Cumberland on May 30th. On June 7th the 44th Regt., under Sir Peter Halket, left the fort, with General Braddock following. Lieut. Col. Burton followed on the 8th, with the Independent Companies, followed by Colonel Dunbar, with the 48th Regt. on the 10th. Braddock's army marched over the road which Washington had cut the year before to Gist's Plantation, and then went northward across the Catawba Trail to Stewart's Crossings (Connellsville), through Mount Pleasant, to the mouth of Turtle Creek, where on July 9th the expedition ended in "Braddock's defeat," and the total ruin of his army (Consult; Sargent, Hist. Brad. Exped., 1855; Lowdermilk, Hist. Cumb., 95-195; Parkman, Conspiracy of Pontiac. I. 108-120; Parkman, Montcalm and Wolfe, I. 194-242; any general history of the U. S.; Colonial Records. VI. 303, 307, 321, 331, 365, 317, etc.; Archives, III. 203, 258, 261, 285, etc.—see Index, under title, Braddock). The author has been over the course of the Braddock Road, which is well outlined in Sargent's history and well pictured in the series of Postal Cards published by John K. Lacock, Amity, Pa., and which will be accurately defined in the history of this expedition being written by Mr. Lacock. After Braddock's defeat and death, Col. Dunbar retreated to Will's Creek, and then to Winchester, and from thence up the Cumberland Valley to Shippensburg, and on to Philadelphia (Kittochtinny Hist. Soc. Pub., I. 1898; Archives of W. Va., Third Rep., 1910-1911—the latter ref. has a good map of Braddock's Road from Williamsport, at the mouth of the Conococheague, to Fort Cumberland). After Dunbar's cowardly retreat from Fort Cumberland the entire frontier of Pennsylvania and Virginia was overrun by hostile Indians, who reached the settlements over the road which had been opened to the Ohio. It is difficult to trace the origin of the Indian name of Will's Creek. The suffix, tuck, is the common suffix used to designate a "creek." What the first part of this name was corrupted from is impossible to tell. The author has been able to find only the following forms, which are all corruptions of the name recorded on Fry and Jefferson's map of 1755. Darlington says that Fry and Jefferson's map of 1751 gives the name as Caicutuck (Dar. Gist's Jour., 137). This may be so, but the name as given on Fry and Jefferson's map of 1755 is "Caicuctuck, or Wills Creek." The form used by Lowdermilk, in his History of Cumberland, Md., is "Caiuctucuc." Sargent, in Braddock's Exped., uses the form "Cucucbetuc" (195).

Will's Creek.—Gist (1751), in Dar. Gist Jour., 68; Evans map, 1755 etc.

WINGOHOCKING. The name of the south branch of Frankford Creek, which enters that stream at the junction with Tacony to form the creek now known as Frankford Creek. Heckewelder gives the name as a corruption of Wingehacking, "a favorite spot for planting." Wingan, "sweet"; Hacki, "earth," with the locative, ing. The compound more probably signifies "place of sweet earth," which was, of course, "good for planting." This creek was the boundary of the boundary of the "Liberties." The lands of Griffith Jones and John Moon were on the opposite side of the creek. The creek is marked, without a name, on Holme's map. It is shown on Reed's map, with its present name.

Wiggohocking.—Bound. of Liberties (1777), Arch. Third Ser., III. 312, 317.
Wingohocking.—Reed's map, 1777.

WISSAHICKON. A creek which rises in Montgomery County and flows southward to the Schuylkill, which it enters at Wissahickon, Philadelphia. Heckewelder gives this as a corruption of Wisameckhan, "cat-fish stream." In 1677, John Mattson, Swen Lom and Lace Dalbo were granted a tract of 300 acres "att ye place Called wiessahitkonk on ye westsyde up in ye Schuyl Kill" (Records of Upland Court, 62). The creek was afterwards called Whitpaine Creek, in honor of Richard Whitpaine, who owned several tracts of land at the head of this creek. The creek was later called by its old Indian name.

Whitpaine Creek.—Holme's map, 1681-3. **Wiessahitkonk.**—Rec. Up. (1677), Records of Up. Court, 62. **Wissahickon.**—Scull map, 1759.

WISSINOMING. Heckewelder says that this creek was the "Tacony, or North branch of Frankford Creek" This is an error. The Indian name of Frankford Creek, or the north branch of it on some early maps, was Quessinawomink (which see). Wissinoming may be a corruption of this name. The name, however, is now applied to the small creek which enters the Delaware just above the mouth of Frankford Creek, at Wissinoming. Heckewelder gives this name as a corruption of Wischanemunk, "where we were frightened."

WOLF CREEK. The name of a creek which rises in Mercer County and which flows south to Slippery Rock Creek, which it enters in Butler County; also a Township in the former county. The creek was called by the Delawares, Tummeink, "place of wolves." Tummaa, or Timmeu, "a wolf," with the locative, ing. After the destruction of the Erie by the Iroquois the entire region south of Lake Erie became infested with great packs of wolves.

Wolf Creek.—Morris map, 1848.

WOPSONONOCK. The name of a station in Blair County. The name is not a historic one. It is probably a compound, made up of Woapeu, "white," with some other word of Indian origin, and the suffix, ock, "country," or "land." Woapasum-ock would be "white sunshine land." Woap-achsin-ock would be "white stone land," etc.

WYALUSING. The name of a former Indian village, belonging to the Munsee tribe, situated about two miles below the present Wyalusing, on the east side of the Susquehanna, opposite the mouth of Sugar Run. David Craft said that the present mouth of Wyalusing Creek is now about a mile above where it was at the time of the establishment of the Moravian Mission at this place by Zeisberger. The name is a corruption of M'chwihillusink, "the place of the old man," or, as Heckewelder translates it, 'the dwelling place of the hoary veteran," so called from an ancient warrior who lived near. The name is always written in the various Moravian records Machiwihilusing. After the establishment of the Moravian mission at this place in 1763, it was called Friedenshuetten, "Tents of Peace." This site was occupied by the Susquehanna, Conestoga, at an early date by the village called Gohontoto, which is mentioned by Bishop Cammerhoff, who visited the place in 1750. He says, "Here, they tell me, was in early times an Indian town, traces of which are still noticeable, e. g., corn-pits, etc., inhabited by a distinct nation (neither Aquinoschioni, i. e., Iroquois, nor Delawares), who spoke a peculiar language and were called Tehotitachsae; against these the Five Nations warred, and rooted them out. The Cayugas for a time held a number of them, but the nation and their language are now exterminated and extinct" (Camm. Jour., 1750, quoted in Jour. Mil. Exped. Gen. Sull., 124). The tribe mentioned was the Tutelo. In 1752 Papunhank, a Munsee chief, settled at this place with 20 families. This chief frequently visited Philadelphia, and made great pretensions as a religious teacher (Col. Rec., VIII. 484, 488, 490, 499, 586, 634, 648; IX. 45, 66, 77, 85, 94, 135; Archives, III. 507, 744; IV. 90, 138; DeSchweinitz, Life of Zeis., 267, 271-72, 289, 324-335). Through the teaching of Papunhank the Munsee in the village were aroused to a great interest in religion. They sent to Bethlehem for a teacher. Zeisberger and Anthony, a Delaware, at once responded to this call. They left Wechquetank (which see) on the 16th of May, going northward to the trail from the Minisinks to Wyoming. They had a most difficult journey through the tangled wilderness. They stopped at Wyoming, where Zeisberger visited the Connecticut settlers at the mouth of Mill Creek. On May 23, 1663, they reached Wyalusing. Here Zeisberger preached to large congregations until the 26th, when they returned to Bethlehem, with a request from the Indians that a regular mission be established in the village. Zeisberger was appointed to this mission, and returned in June, with Nathaniel, a brother of Anthony, from Tunkhannock. Zeisberger's work at Wyalusing was very successful. On the 26th of June, Papunhank was baptized, at a most solemn assembly of the whole town. On the 30th of June Zeisberger was recalled to Bethlehem, because of the various Indian massacres during the Conspiracy of Pontiac. Then came the various events of the Conspiracy of Pontiac; the battle of Bushy Run, the massacre of the Conestoga, etc., which made the removal of all of the Christian Indians to Philadelphia necessary, for their own safety. After the close of this period of hostility the Christian Indians left Philadelphia on the 12th of March, 1765, for Wyalusing. They went by way of the previous villages of Nain, where a farewell service was held on April 3rd, and visited the deserted village of Wechquetank, where they spent the Holy Week. On April 11th they started on the trail northward over Monroe County, through the Great Swamp, reaching the Susquehanna ten miles above Wyoming, and reaching Wyalusing on May 9th. This mission prospered greatly. In the summer of 1765 an embassy was sent to Togahaju, the Cayuga chief, who had oversight of the land in this region, asking permission to build a town at Wyalusing. This request was refused, but the Christian Indians were invited to settle at the head of Cayuga Lake. The delegates promised to lay this decision before the mission at Wyalusing, and report when the corn was ripe. This they neglected to do. Togahaju then sent a message to Wyalusing informing the inhabitants of Friedenshuetten of this neglect. Zeisberger then went at once to the Cayuga Town, where he laid the entire matter before the Council, which finally granted the request, and gave them a grant of land along the river at Wyalusing, "as far as a man can walk in two days." A town was laid out, and given the name by which the mission was known, Friedenshuetten,

"Tents of Peace." The village contained 29 houses and 13 huts, on one street, in the center of which was the chapel, opposite which was the Mission House. The town was a model in every way. In Sept. Zeisberger was recalled, and Schmick was placed at Friedenshuetten as resident missionary. A report that the Onondaga Council had declared that the grant of land made by Togahaju was void, made it necessary for Zeisberger to make a trip to Onondaga with Senseman. After various trips to see the Cayuga chief, the Iroquois finally declared that the grant made by Togahaju was valid, and approved, "The Aquanoschioni have a fire at Friedenshuetten; let their Christian cousins, and the teachers of their Christian cousins, guard it well" (Life of Zeis., 307-319). In 1767 Zeisberger visited the Allegheny River, accompanied by Anthony and Papunhank, going by way of the Chemung, Tioga, Cowanesque and Allegheny to the mouth of the Tionesta, near which was Goshgoshing (which see). After his return from this trip Zeisberger remained at Christiansbrunn. Early in May, 1768, Zeisberger returned to the Allegheny, accompanied by a number of the Christian Indians from Friedenshuetten. He selected a site for a mission house, near the town of Goshgoshing (See also *Lawunakhanneck*). This mission was abandoned April 17, 1770, the Indains going to the Beaver River, where they established the mission of Friedensstadt, "City of Peace" (See *Friedensstadt*, or *Languntouteneunk*). As the land on the Susquehanna, which included the village of Wyalusing, or Friedenshuetten, had been sold by the Iroquois to the Penns, at the Treaty of Fort Stanwix, in 1768, and as the war between the Connecticut settlers and the Pennamites was troubling the entire region, it was decided to remove the entire settlement to the Beaver River. The entire village of Christian Indians set out from Wyalusing on June 11, 1772, going in two parties, under Ettwein and Roth, to the Big Island, one by land and the other by water. These numbered 204 persons (Consult; DeSchweinitz, Life of Zeisberger, 368-372; Loskiel, Hist. Miss., II. 191, 203, 231-234; III. 1-77; Reichel, Mem. Mor. Church, 37; Heckewelder, Ind. Nations, 83, 196; Hanna, Wild. Trail, I. 214-216). During the Revolution Wyalusing and

Sheshequin became meeting places for the hostile Indans and the Tories. On Sept. 28, 1778, Col. Hartley marched from Sheshequin, which he destroyed, and encamped that night at Wyalusing, from which the Indians had fled just before his arrival. On the 29th Hartley's detachment was attacked by the Indians, near this village; the Indians were defeated, leaving 10 dead on the field (Archives, VII. 5-9). On August 5-7, 1779, the army of General Sullivan encamped at the site of the Indian village, not a single remnant of which then remained. Consult: Col. Rec., VIII. 493-4, 634, 648, 667, 670. 709, 770; IX. 45, 66, 77, 86, 94, 97, 425, 436; Archives, III. 736-41; IV. 60, 125, 127, 138, 451; VI. 773; VII. 7; X. 266; Archives, Sec. Ser., II. 633; Jour. Mil. Exped. Gen. Sull., 5, 39, etc.

Friedenshuetten.—Loskiel (1794), Hist. Miss., III. 1. **Machachlosung.**—Post (1760), Archives, III. 743. **Machelusing.** —Letter (1764). Archives, III. 170. **Machochlaung.**—Post (1760). Archives, III. 744. **Machochloschung.**—Post (1760), Archives, III 744. **Machwihilusing**—Loskiel (1794), Hist. Miss., II. 191. **Mahackloosing.**—Proud, Penna., II. 320. **Makahelousink.**—Tedy. (1761), Col. Rec., III. 636. **Makehalousing, Papounan's House.** —Tedy. (1761), Col. Rec, III 635. **M'chwihillusink.**—Heckewelder, in Trans. Am. Phil. Soc., N. S., IV. 362. **M'chwihilusing.** — Heckewelder, Ind. Names (Reichel, Ed.), 271. **Michalloasen.**—Pa. Coun (1760), Col. Rec., VIII. 492. **Monmuchloosen.**—Pa. Coun. (1760), Archives, III. 743. **Papounan's Town.** —Hamilton (1761), Col. Rec., VIII. 648. **Waghaloosen.**—Pa. Coun (1760), Col. Rec., VIII. 492. **Wealusing.**—Grant (1779), Mil. Exped. Gen. Sull., 138. **Wealuskingtown.**—Machin (1779), Mil. Exped. Gen Sull., 194. **Wialosing.**—Ger. Flats Conf. (1770), in N. Y. Doc. Col Hist., VIII. 243. **Wialusing.**—Grant (1779), Jour Mil. Exped. Gen. Sull., 138. **Wighaloosen.**—Penn (1768), Col. Rec., IX. 425, 436. **Wighalosscon.**—Pa. Coun. (1760), Col. Rec., VIII. 492. **Wighalousin.**—Hamilton (1761), Col. Rec., VIII. 648. **Wildlucit.**—Fellows (1779), Jour. Mil. Exped. Gen. Sull., 86. **Wyalousing.**—Petition to Penn (1764), Col. Rec., IX. 139. **Wyalucey.**—Roberts (1779), Jour. Mil. Exped. Gen. Sull., 242. **Wyalucing.**—Barton (1779). Jour. Mil Exped. Gen. Sull., 5. **Wyalusing.**—Hartley (1778), Archives, VII. 7. **Wyalusing Town.**—Scull map, 1770. **Wybusing.**—Campfield (1779), Jour. Mil. Exped. Gen. Sull., 53. **Wyeluting.** —Livermore (1779), Jour. Mil. Exped. Gen. Sull., 183. **Wylucing.**—Gookin (1779, Jour. Mil. Exped. Gen. Sull., 104. **Wylusink.**—Blake (1779), Jour. Mil. Exped. Gen. Sull., 39. **Wylutanunk.** —Grant (1779), Jour. Mil. Exped. Gen. Sull., 108. **Wyolusing.** — Dearborn (1779), Jour. Mil. Exped. Gen. Sull., 69.

The creek is noted on Howell's map, 1792, as Wyalusing Creek.

WYNOLA. The name of a small lake in Wyoming County. The name is of recent origin, or so badly corrupted that its derivation cannot be discovered. On Morris' map of 1848 this lake is called "Beiches Pond," and on the Hopkins map of 1872 it is called "Crooked Pond."

WYNOOSKA. The name of a village in Pike County. There was an Indian village on the Hudson River called Winooskeek. There is a river and a village in Vermont, called Winooski, which is said to mean "beautiful river." This, however, is doubtful. Winui, or winne, signifies "pleasant."

WYOMING. The name of a county, a valley and a former Indian village. The name is a corruption of M'cheuomi, or M'cheuwami, having the significance of "great flats." Heckewelder says that the North Branch of the Susquehanna was called M'cheuweami-sipu, "the river of the extensive flats." He said that the Iroquois called it Gahonta, a word of like significance. The Iroquois name Skehandowana, or Schandowana, was frequently used by Conrad Weiser, in referring to the Wyoming Valley. Tsanandowa, and Tsanandowana, was also a Seneca form of the name (See *Tsanandowa*). All of these names have the same significance of "large flats," or "great meadows," and were first applied to the region now known as the Wyoming Valley, rather than to a particular village in it. The locative of M'cheuwami would be M'cheuoming or M'cheuwaming, meaning "at the great flats." Hewitt says that the animate plural of this word would be M'cheuomek, which was probably the name which was corrupted by John Smith to Massawomecke, who were the mortal enemies of the Susquehannocks. mentioned by him in 1608. This would identify the Massawomecks of Smith, and the Scahentoarrhonons of the Jesuit Relation for 1635, as being the same. The Massawomecks and the Scahentoarrhonons were the "people of the great flats." The name Scahantowano was the name given to Wyoming at the Treaty at Lancaster in 1744 (Archives, I. 657). The author is of the opinion that the Seneca were the occupants of these "great flats" before their occupation of the region in New York. Or, that the Massa-

womecks, of Smith; the Scahentoarrhonons, of the Jesuit Relation; the
Tsanandowas, of the early Colonial
Records, and the Seneca of later history, were all of the same Iroquoian
tribe. These inhabitants of "the great
flats" were destroyed by the Iroquois
in 1652. They were probably a remnant of the Seneca which had remained behind on the Juniata (later
going to Wyoming) at the time of the
eastern migration of the Delaware
and Iroquois (See *Juniata, Seneca,
Allegheny, Delaware*). The Massawomecks, or Scahentoarrhonons, had
probably driven the Susquehannocks
southward from the upper Susquehanna, before the final conflict between
the Seneca of New York with the
Carantouannais, who probably crossed
from Carantouan to the West Branch
valley, after the destruction of their
village in the wars with the Iroquois
(See *Carantouan*). The first mention
of Wyoming in the Archives of this
State is perhaps that of 1712, in which,
at a Council at Philadelphia, the
Indians present a number of gifts
from the Five Nations; "The first was
from that Town our Indians call
Mechatenawgha, or Sennecaes, being
the Tsanondouans, & consisted of six
Beavers, &—drest skins" (Col. Rec.,
II. 557). If this name refers to
M'cheuwami, which seems certain,
then the Seneca were living at Wyoming in 1712. The first settlement, of
historic record, was made by the
Shawnee and Minisinks, who were
driven from the Forks of the Delaware
after 1742. Nutimus, with a number
of his followers, settled near the present Wilkes-Barre, and Kakowatchky.
the Shawnee "King," from the Forks
of the Delaware, settled at Shawnee
Flats, at the present Plymouth, in
1728. This chief and his clan remained
here until about 1743, when he removed to Logstown, on the Ohio (Col.
Rec., III. 309, 330, 507). This chief
remained true to the English. even
after many of the Shawnee had gone
over to the French influence, under
the leadership of Peter Chartier (Col.
Rec., IV. 643; V. 311, 314, 531; VI.
155, 160). After the departure of this
Shawnee "King" to the Ohio, Paxinosa
(See *Paxinous*) became the leading
chief at Wyoming. Paxinosa was at
Wyoming when Count Zinzendorf visited the Shawnee, in 1742 (Consult;
Mem. Mor. Church, X. 67, 109. 327,
332; Loskiel, Hist. Miss., II. 32, 80,

181). When Zinzendorf visited Wyoming in 1742 it was occupied chiefly by
Shawnee. In 1751 the Nanticoke had
a village at the lower end of the valley, on the east side of the river, near
the present Nanticoke (which see).
When Mack, the Moravian missionary,
visited Wyoming in 1744, there were
but 6 or 7 cabins in the town. The
sites of these various villages are
shown on the maps of the Manors of
Stoke and Sunbury (Arch. Third Ser.,
IV. Nos. 66 and 67). At the Treaty
at Albany in 1754, when the Iroquois
sold the lands drained by the Juniata
to the Penns, they reserved the lands
at Wyoming as a hunting ground, and
as a place of refuge from the French
(Col. Rec., VI. 119). John Shikellamy,
son of Shikellamy, was appointed to
look after these lands. At the Council
at Easton, in 1757, Tedyuskung. the
Delaware "King," asked that these
lands at Wyoming be so fixed "that it
shall not be lawful for us or our children ever to sell, or for you or any
of your children ever to buy" (Col.
Rec., VII. 678). When it was discovered that this land had been sold at
the Treaty at Albany by the Mohawk
to Lydius, the agent of the Connecticut Company, Conrad Weiser declared
that this sale was fraudulent, and that
unless the settlement of this region
was prevented, and the Deed declared
null and void, an Indian war would
result. The attempt of Connecticut to
take possession of this region resulted
in the long dispute between the Penns
and the Susquehanna Company, and
was the direct cause of the so-called
"Massacre of Wyoming," which was
nothing less, or more, than the final
attempt of the Indians to drive the
white settlers from lands which had
not been purchased from them. In
1755 the Mohawk refused to accept the
second payment for these lands. In
July of the same year came Braddock's
defeat, and then came the vengeance
of the Indians who had been cheated
in 1737 and again in 1754. As the
clouds began to gather over the valley
of Wyoming, Paxinosa, the friendly
Shawnee chief, removed to Tioga, and
then to the Ohio, in 1758. Tedyuskung
removed to Tioga in the early part of
the summer of 1756. Loskiel says that
in 1756 Wyoming was entirely deserted (Hist. Miss. 181). After the
Council of 1757 the Penns offered to
pass a law granting to Tedyuskung,
and his tribe, the Wyoming lands. as

a perpetual possession. But, this was not done, chiefly because the lands had not then been bought from the Iroquois. Tedyuskung made various requests for a fort at Wyoming, for teachers, for ministers, saying, "You must consider that I have a soul as well as another" (Col. Rec., VIII. 47). Tedyuskung had removed to Wyoming in the spring of 1758. At the Treaty at Easton, 1758, he again presented his request for a permanent grant of the Wyoming lands, and charged the Mohawks with having fraudulently sold these lands. Tedyuskung had to pay with his life for the statements he made at this Council. The Province was anxious to make peace with the Delaware and Shawne, as the expedition of Gen. Forbes was getting ready for its attempt to take possession of the Ohio. Thompson and Post were sent on a mission to Wyoming, but were warned by Tedyuskung from doing so, as the woods were filled with bands of hostile Indians (Archives, III. 412-422). In the spring of 1763 a number of Connecticut families settled at Wyoming (Archives, IV. 105). This foolish attempt at settlement, in existing conditions, led to an attack by the Indians, in which 20 of the settlers were killed (op. cit., 127). Again, in 1769, another party of settlers entered the valley, and commenced the erection of Fort Durkee, at Wilkes-Barre (Frontier Forts, I. 425). The Pennsylvania authorities erected Fort Wyoming in 1771, for the reduction of the former fort. Mill Creek Fort was erected in 1772; Forty Fort, in 1770 (Consult; Frontier Forts, I. 423-466). The hostility during the French and Indian War, the Conspiracy of Pontiac, the fraudulent purchase of 1754, the attempt of Connecticut settlers to take possession of this land which the Indians regarded as their one place of refuge, the War of the Pennamites, the War of the Revolution, the hostility of the Iroquois—all these events made the attempt of the Connecticut settlers to take possession of the Wyoming Valley the most utterly foolhardy thing which was ever attempted in American history. The "massacre of Wyoming" was, under existing conditions, a foregone conclusion. While the cruelty of the event is without excuse, yet, the Indians had given warnings from 1763, as had every Indian authority in the Province. The Indians had appealed to every Council

from the very first attempt at settlement, to drive these "squatters" out, but, if the Province was powerless to drive out the "squatters" from the Juniata Valley, from the Great and Little Coves, from the West Branch, it was utterly unable to cope with the determined attempt of colonists from another Colony to settle on Indian lands. Every effort had been made by the Indians to settle the matter in a peaceful way. Every effort had been made by the Provincial authorities to enforce her decrees of removal, from the time of the first settlement of the Connecticut colonists at Cushietunk (which see) in 1761. All of these efforts had failed. Then the Indian did the inevitable. He did exactly what men have always done, and as they always will do, when their possessions are taken against their will, and after all appeals to law or equity have failed, then comes the inevitable appeal to the last Court of Red Man and White Man, the bloody Court of Arms. The "massacre of Wyoming," cruel and bloody as it was, has been repeated again and again, not by Indians, but by civilized men of every race. The "Battle of Wounded Knee," in which United States troops slaughtered harmless Indian women and children with the death-dealing machine guns, was without a shadow of the excuse which the Indians had for the "Massacre of Wyoming." The one was committed as an act of revenge, upon harmless women and children, by the army of a Christian nation; the other was an act of vengeance for broken promises, and committed only after every other appeal had failed. Both were brutal, but one can be justified—if any appeal to arms can be justified—while the other, in the light of calm reason, was without even the shadow of an excuse. In June of 1778, when the settlers became aware of the fact that a large force of Indians and Tories was approaching, under Maj. John Butler, they sought refuge in the various forts about Wyoming. The majority gathered at Forty Fort. Butler's army consisted of about 1,100 men. Of these about 200 were British, 200 Tories, and about 700 Indians, chiefly Seneca and Cayuga. They descended the Susquehanna to a point a few miles above Wyoming, where they landed. On July 1st the army encamped above Wyoming, at the head of the valley. On July 2nd the army marched to Forty Fort, and demanded its surrender. This was refused. The entire number of men in the fort was less than 400 men, chiefly old men and boys. On July 3rd this small force marched out to attack the enemy. Then followed the defeat, and the fearful massacre (Consult; Parkman, Conspiracy of Pontiac, II. 109 (first massacre) ; Frontier Forts, I. 438 et seq.; Egle, Hist. Penna., 898-906 ; Archives, VI. 626, 629, 631, etc.; various publications of the Wyoming Hist. Soc., 1895, etc.; Miner, Hist. Wyoming; Harvey, Hist. Wyoming Valley; Archives, Sec. Ser., XVIII (Connecticut Dispute—entire vol.). After the massacre of Wyoming the entire frontier was subject to Indian raids. In the fall of 1778 Col. Thomas Hartley went on an expedition up the Susquehanna to Sheshequin, Tioga, and other points along the river, returning by way of Wyoming, after a fight with the Indians near Wyalusing (Archives, VII. 5-9). In order to drive the Indians back upon the British for subsistence, and to take away the base of supplies in the Indian country along the lakes of New York, Washington decided to send an expedition up the Susquehanna to destroy the Indian villages and cornfields in that region, and to send another expedition up the Allegheny to destroy the villages in the Seneca country. Gen. John Sullivan had command of the former expedition, and Col. Daniel Brodhead of the latter. These two expeditions were to unite in the Genesee region, but the success of both forces made such a union unnecessary. Sullivan's army reached Wyoming on June 14th, where it remained until the 31st of July, awaiting supplies. The place at that time was filled with the widows and orphans of those who had been killed in the massacre the year before. The army reached Wyoming, on its return from the expedition, on Oct. 7th, and left for Easton on Oct. 10th (Consult; Jour. Mil. Exped. Gen. Sullivan). Various Indian trails passed through Wyoming, from the Iroquois country to the Carolinas, and between the Susquehanna and the Delaware and the Ohio. One of the oldest trails between the Delaware and the Susquehanna was that which went from Wyoming to the Delaware Water Gap. This trail is shown on the Manor of Stoke map, and also on the maps which are found in the Journals of Sullivan's expedition. There was also a trail up the Susquehanna to the mouth of the Lackawanna, and then up that stream to its head, and then across to the mouth of Calkin's Creek, at the site of the former settlement of Cushitunk, now Cochecton. The trail from this point on the Delaware, by way of Little Meadows, across Moosic Mountain to Capoose Mountain, and on to Wyoming, was the course followed by the Connecticut settlers to Wyoming. It was the first wagon road from the Hudson and Delaware to the Susquehanna. The trail from Wyoming to the Delaware Water Gap forked, one branch running on to the "Forks" at Easton. The main trail up the river, from Shamokin, ran along the western side of the river to the Shawnee Town, at Plymouth, and on up to Sheshequin. Another trail ran across to the head of the Wapwallopen Valley, and then down it to the Susquehanna, where it crossed to the western shore, joining the Shamokin Trail, down the river, or went by way of the Warrior's Trail to the Great Island. The trail up the Susquehanna, from Wyoming, along the eastern shore of the river, was that followed by the army of General Sullivan in 1779. The Trail to the Great Island, by way of Shamokin, was one of the first trails to the Ohio. This was perhaps the course of Arnold Viele in 1694, as it was the course of Post in 1758. It ran up the West Branch to the Great Island, where it crossed and ran up the Bald Eagle to Marsh Creek, and then up that stream, over the divide to Clearfield and on to the Allegheny, by several branches, one going to Kittanning, and another to Venango (Franklin). The Trail up the Bald Eagle Valley cut through the mountain at Milesburg and ran on to Standing Stone, and there joined the Warriors Path to the Potomac, at Old Town. All of these main trails had many branches, running to various points on the main trails leading east and west (See *Big Island, Frankstown, Raystown, Shamokin, Standing Stone, Juniata, Kittanning, Venango,* etc.; Consult; Scull's map, 1759; Howell's map, 1792; Morris' map, 1848, and the maps of the Manor of Stoke and Sunbury, previously mentioned). The Journals of Post, Weiser, Hays and others are also full of information as to the courses of these trails (Archives, III. 412, 520, 735; Col. Rec., VIII. 142;

also Zinzendorf, Mem. Mor. Church, I.). In the following list of synonyms Tsanandowana, and its various forms, is omitted, as these are given under title *Tsanandowa*, which see.

Mahaniahy.—Thomas (1742), Col. Rec., IV. 572. **Mahaniay.**—Pa. Coun. (1742), Col. Rec., IV. 570. (These two ref. may refer simply to the creek, now known as Mahanoy.) **Maughwawame.**—Day, Penn., 431, 1843. **M'chenomi.**—Heckewelder, in Trans. Amer. Philos. Soc., N. S. IV. 361. **M'chenwami.**—Heckewelder, in Indian Names, 272. **M'chwauwaumi.**—Day, in op. Cit. **Mechatenawgha.**—Pa. Coun. (1712), Col. Rec., II. 557. **Mechayomy.**—Pa. Coun. (1732), Col. Rec., III. 451. **Meehayomy.**—Pa. Coun. (1728), Col. Rec., III. 326. **Meheahoaming.**—Cartlidge (1732), Archives, I. 329. **Scahantowano.**—Coun. at Lan. (1744), Archives, I. 657. **Schahandowa.**—Coun. at Mt. John. (1755), Archives, Sec. Ser., VI. 293. **Schahacdawana.**—Treaty (1756), Archives, II. 559. **Seahantowano.**—Weiser (1755), Archives, II. 259. **Skehandowana.**—Zinzendorf (1742), Mem. Mor. Church, I. 86. **Chanandowa.**—Pa. Coun. (1727), Col. Rec. IV. 92. **Tsanandowa.**—Pa. Coun., Col. Rec., III. 273. **Waioming.**—Zeisberger (1755), Archives, II. 459. **Waiomink.**—Day, Penn., 432. **Wajomick.**—Loskiel (1794), in Rupp, West Penna., App. 358; Loskiel, Hist. Miss., II. 32. **Wajomik.**—Drake, Ind. Chron., 184. **Waughwauwame.**—Drake, Tecumseh, 13, 1852. **Wawamie.**—Day, Penn., 432. **Wayomick.** — Horsfield (1755), Archives, II. 492. **Wayoming.**—Horsfield (1755), Archives, II. 491. **Weoming.**—Machin (1779), Jour. Mil. Exped. Gen. Sullivan, 194. **Weyoming.**—Hardenburgh (1779), Jour. Mil. Exped. Gen. Sullivan, 123. **Wioming.**—Evans map, 1749. **Wiomink.**—Peters (1757), Archives, III. 288. **Woyumoth.**—Allummapees (1743), Col. Rec. IV. 643. **Wyaming.**—La Tour, map 1782, Col. Rec., IV. **Wyomin.**—Canassatego (1742), 580. **Wyoming.**—Johnson (1756), in R. I. Col. Rec., V. 529. **Wyomink.**—Stanwix (1757), Archives, III. 301. **Wyomish.**—Hess (1756, Archives III. 56.

WYMISSING. The name of a creek which enters the Schuylkill from the south, opposite Reading, Berks County. Now called Wyamissing. The origin is not known.

Wyamissing.—Present name. **Wyassing.** Howell map, 1792. **Wymissing.**—Scull map, 1759, 1770; Morris map, 1848.

WYSOX. A creek which enters the Susquehanna from the north in Bradford County, near Wysox. The army of Gen. Sullivan crossed this creek about half a mile from its mouth on July 9th, 1779. According to Day (Hist. Penna., 137), there was a tribe of this name which had a battle with the Indians at the mouth of Towanda Creek. There is no record of any such

a conflict, nor is there any reference to a tribe of this name. The older name of the stream is Wysaukin, which Heckewelder says is a corruption of Wisachgimi, "place of grapes." The Delaware name for grapes was Wi-sach-gim, and for rum, Wi-sachgank. The name may be a corruption of the same word which has been corrupted to Wissahickon, which means, according to Heckewelder, "cat-fish stream." But, both of these words may be corruptions of Wissu-hacki, "rich land," or "fat land." The name may be a corruption of Assisku-hacki, "muddy country." The name is so corrupted that it is mere guesswork to try to figure out its origin. The name given by Rogers, as a translation— possibly—in his Journal (Sull. Exped., 259), as Weesauking, or "Rush Meadow Creek," may be a corruption of Schingaskunk, "a bog meadow," or Sikunikan, "rushes," with the locative, ing, meaning "place of rushes." Almost any such combination of words might be made from some of the many corruptions of the real name.

Meshokin.—Roberts (1779), Jour. Mil. Exped. Gen. Sullivan, 242. **Waysocking.**—VanHovenburgh (1779), Jour. Mil. Exped. Gen. Sull., 282. **Weesaucking.**—Campfield (1779), Jour. Mil. Exped. Gen. Sull., 54. **Weesauking, or Rush Meadow Creek.**—Rogers (1779), Jour. Mil. Exped. Gen. Sull., 259. **Wesauking.**—Fellows (1779), Jour. Mil. Exped. Gen. Sull., 86. **Wesawking.**—Dearborn (1779), Jour. Mil. Exped. Gen. Sull., 69. **Wesocking.**—Adlum map, 1790. **Whissanking.**—Nukerck (1779), op. cit., 220. **Wishooken.**—Pownall map, 1776. **Wissahin.**—Grant (1779), op. cit., 138. **Wysaukin** (1779), Beatty, Arch. Sec. Ser., XV. 250. **Wissawkin.**—Lodge map, 1779, No. 103 B. in op. cit. **Wysawkin.**—Howell map, 1792. **Wysox.**—Recent maps.

WYWAMIC. The name of a mountain in Monroe County. The origin of the name is not known. It may be a corruption of Wiquey, "birch bark," and Komac, or Comac, "place." Consult; Egle, Hist. Pa., 947.

YELLOW BREECHES CREEK. A creek which enters the Susquehanna from the west at New Cumberland, on line of Cumberland and York Counties. See *Callapatscink.*

YOROONWAGO. A former Seneca village situated on the upper Allegheny River, near the present Corydon, Warren County. It was one of the villages destroyed by Col. Brodhead in 1779, on his expedition up the Allegheny.

Brodhead says in his letter to Washington, "At the upper Seneca Towns we found a painted image or War post, clothed in Dog skin, & John Montour told me this Town was called Yoghroonwago, besides this we found seven other Towns, consiting in the whole of one hundred and thirty Houses, some of which were large enough for the accommodation of three or four Indian families. The Troops remained on the ground three whole days destroying the Towns & Corn Fields. I never saw finer Corn altho' it was planted much thicker than common with our Farmers." The amount of corn destroyed covered about 500 acres. In Brodhead's letter to General Sullivan he says "Yahrungwago is about forty miles on this side Jenesseo" (Archives, XII. 156, 165; Jour. Mil. Exped. Gen. Sullivan, 308). This village was in the region of the Cornplanter Reservation, and was no doubt the town which is noted on Ellicott's map as Tushhanushhagota. The village is wrongly placed on the Historical Map of Penn. (1875), as it was above, and not below, Conewango. See *Cornplanter.*

Yahrungwago.—Brodhead (1779), Archives, XII. 166. **Yoghroonwago.**—Brodhead (1779), Archives, XII. 156. **Yoghwonwaga.**—Albach, in Western Annals, 304. **Yoroonwago.**—Hist. map of Penna., 1875 (wrongly situated).

YOUGHIOGHENY. The name of a river which enters the Monongahela from the south at McKeesport, Allegheny County. The three tributaries which form this stream rise in Maryland, West Virginia and Pennsylvania. The union of the three main branches is at Confluence, formerly Turkey Foot (which see), on the boundary of Fayette and Somerset Counties. Darlington gives the derivation of the name as Yough, "four," and Hanne, "streams." Heckewelder gives it as a corruption of Juh-wiah-hanne, "a stream flowing in a contrary direction." This could be literally translated as "circuitous stream," or "winding stream." The latter derivation is correct, and is a correct descriptive name. The Delaware for "four" is not Yough, but Newo. The Shawnee is Nevaa, or Neaway. Darlington says that the stream is marked on Mayo's map of 1737 as "Spring heads of Yokyo-gane, a small branch of the Monongahela." In the Mayo map of 1737, which the author has seen, this river

is not noted at all. The "Spring Head," noted, is that of the Savage River, and not the Youghiogheny. On Gists' map of 1753 it is noted as Yaugh Yaugh gone, and in his Journal of 1751 it is mentioned as Yaughaughgaine (Dar. Gist, 68). On Fry and Jefferson's map, 1755, it is noted as Yawyawganey. On Lewis Evans' map of 1755 it is noted as Yoxhio Geni. The river and its name, which afforded a wide scope of orthographic effort for the writers of the period, first came into prominence after the organization of the Ohio Company and the tours of Christopher Gist, 1749-1753. After that time Washington's expedition of 1754, Braddock's expedition of 1755, the Boundary Dispute with Virginia, the Whisky Insurrection of 1794, and various other historic events, made the Youghiogheny region occupy a prominent place in the history of the times. These various events are mentioned under other titles (See *Redstone, Will's Creek, Sugar Cabins, Turtle Creek, Logstown, Venango,* etc.). Christopher Gist explored this region in 1751-52, when on his mission to the Ohio (Consult; Darlington, Gist's Journals). He evidently selected the site for his plantation at the present Mount Braddock, Fayette County, while on this trip, and commenced his improvement of it in the spring of 1753. He then built some houses and started the first actual settlement west of the mountains, within the Ohio Valley. John Fraser and other traders had built trading houses before this time, at Venango, Turtle Creek, Redstone and other places, but Gist's Plantation was the first actual settlement in all of the region beyond the mountains. That Gist had a settlement here in the winter of 1753 is shown both by his own and Washington's Journal of 1753. Washington says in his Journal, of 1753, "According to the best observation I could make, Mr. Gist's new settlement (which we passed by) bears almost west northwest seventy miles from Will's Creek." On his return from this trip he reached Gist's on Jan. 1st, 1754, where he bought a horse and saddle (Consult; Olden Time, I. 12-26; Rupp, West. Penna., apx. 34-50; any other account of Washington's trip of 1753). About the same time that Gist built his houses at Mount Braddock, William Stewart, who was acquainted with Gist, settled at the place which afterwards was known as "Stewart's Crossings," at the site of the present Connellsville. The William Stewart who took the deposition in 1786 (Ellis, Hist. Fayette County, 57) may have been a son of "Henry Steward," who accompanied Washington and Gist to Venango in 1753. Both father and son settled at the place known as "Stewart's Crossings," which was at the point where the Catawba Trail crossed the Youghiogheny River, running down Robinson's Run (Opossum Run), across the river to the mouth of Mounts Creek, and then over the Narrows at Connellsville. "Stewart's" is noted on Evans' map of 1755. It is almost certain that Stewart's cabin was situated at the place where Col. William Crawford settled in 1766, as the spring near Crawford's house would be the natural place for such a cabin site, and Crawford would most probably build his house at the improvement which Stewart had made. The recent great fill made at this place by the Western Maryland R. R. has destroyed completely the topography of the place, covering the region in which Crawford's house stood, and changing the former course of the Robinson Run. After Washingtons' defeat at Fort Necessity, July 3, 1754, all of the settlers in the region returned to Will's Creek. Coulon de Villers, the French commander, destroyed all of the settlements in the region upon his return to Fort Duquesne. In Washington's expedition, 1754, and in Braddock's expedition, 1755, the various crossings of the Youghiogheny are mentioned. The "Little Crossings" was the fording place on the Castleman branch, near Grantsville, Md. The "Great Crossings" was near Somerfield, Penna. "Stewart's Crossings" was at the lower end of Connellsville. The last crossing was at the place where Braddock wrote, on June 30th, 1755, to Governor Morris, dating his letter "from the Camp at the last Crossing of the Yaughyaughani" (Col. Rec., VI. 475). Washington in 1754 had encamped at the "Great Crossings" for several days, in order that he might examine the stream, with a view of transporting his supplies by water. He went to "Turkey Foot" (which see), at Confluence, which he said was "a convenient place to build a fort," and went on down the river about 10 miles, finally giving up the idea of

trying to make use of the stream, on account of its rapid current, rocks and narrow channel (Consult; Gist's Jour., 1751-2, 1753; Washington's Jour., 1753-1754; See *Turkey Foot*). Braddock's army reached the "Little Crossings" on June 19, 1755, and encamped on the west side of the stream (Sargent, Brad. Exped., 337-338). On the 24th it crossed the river at the "Great Crossings" and marched on to the camp at the east side of the Great Meadows, about 4 miles east of Farmington. On June 27th the army passed Gist's Plantation, where it encamped. On the 28th the march was to "Stewart's Crossings," where the army encamped on the west (not east, as stated by Orme) side of the Youghiogheny. The course of Braddock's Road from Fort Cumberland had been over the road which had been opened by the Ohio Company, and which was the course of Washington in 1754, to Gist's Plantation. From this point Braddock went north over the Catawba Trail, over a road which had never been opened. From Gist's to the Monongahela the entire road had to be cut by Braddock's troops. The river was crossed on June 30th and the army encamped about a mile from the river, below the present Connellsville, on the "Narrows" (Consult; Sargent, Braddock's Expedition; Centen. Hist. of Bor. of Connellsville, 20 et seq., 1906; Ellis, Hist. Fayette County, 40 et seq.; Hulbert, Hist. Highways, IV.; Lowdermilk, Hist. Cum., Md., 95-135). A cut on the hill-side just above the river is still visible. This marks the only spot where Braddock's Road can still be traced at "Stewart's Crossings." The mouth of Mounts Creek is now much lower down the river than it formerly was, and the various R. R. and highway cuts have changed the topography greatly within the last few years. After the capture of Fort Duquesne, in 1758, settlers soon commenced to take up lands in the region which was reached by the Braddock Road. The most of these were from Virginia and Maryland. As the land in the region had not been purchased from the Indians the Penns sought to remove these "squatters." But conditions were the same here as elsewhere in the Province. The settlers refused to remove, after many complaints from the Iroquois, who claimed jurisdiction of the region. The years 1765-66 marked the great influx of settlers. Previous to that time the number of settlers along the river was not great. The great majority of the settlers took up land at Redstone, Gist's, Turkey Foot and Stewart's Crossings. Gov. Penn issued a Proclamation in 1765 forbidding settlers to take up lands in the region which had not been purchased, but the settlers paid no attention to it. In 1765 King George issued a letter instructing Gov. John Penn to see that the "Royal Proclamation" of 1763 concerning the removal of all those "who have irregularly seated themselves on Lands to the Westward of the Allegheny Mountains, immediately evacuate those Settlements" be carried out (Col. Rec., IX. 321). George Croghan wrote from Fort Pitt, May 26, 1766, "But if some effectual measures are not speedily taken to remove those People settled on Red Stone Creek * * * and the Governors pursue Vigorous measures to deter the Frontier Inhabitants from Murthering Indians which pass to and from War against their natural Enemies, the Consequences may be dreadful, & We involved in all the Calamitys of another general War" (op. cit. 322-323). Joseph Fox, the Speaker of the Assembly, said in a message to the Governor, "But as we apprehend many of those rash people have gone from Virginia, between which province and this the Boundary has not been exactly ascertained, nor is it distinctly known on which side of the supposed Boundary those people are seated, & as that Province will be alike involved in the fatal Consequences of such a manifest Breach of Faith, with the Indians, We beg leave to recommend it to your Honour"—to see that the Governor of Virginia take steps to remove these settlers (op. cit. 324-325). This was done, and the Governor of Virginia issued a Proclamation. Gov. John Penn issued a Proclamation in Sept., 1766 (op. cit. 327-328). Much was done by both of the colonies to drive these settlers away from the Indian lands, but nothing came of it. The settlers would come back, even after having been driven out. In Feb., 1768, Gov. Penn issued another Proclamation, warning these "squatters" to leave on penalty of "Death without Benefit of Clergy," and a Commission, consisting of Rev. John Steel, John Allison, Christopher Lemies and Capt. James Potter, was appointed to go to these settlements and warn the people to leave (op. cit. 480-483). This Commission, visited these settlements at Redstone, Stewart's Crossings, Great Crossings, Turkey Foot and Gist's and made a report (op. cit. 506-510). Meetings were held with the settlers at Gist's and at Redstone. The Proclamation was read, the people warned— but continued to stay. In the list of names given in this report many names of persons who were living in the region are not given. Among these are Col. William Crawford, Richard Gist, William Cromwell, Hugh Stevenson, etc. These men did not obey the call to meet the Commission at Gist's, or Redstone. At the Council at Fort Pitt in April and May, 1768, the entire question concerning these settlers was discussed, and it was decided to send a commission, with a number of the Indian chiefs, to the various points to warn the settlers to leave. When the time came the Indians were unwilling to go on the mission, and when asked for a reason, Kiasutha (Guyasuta) said that all of the Indians were unwilling to go "to carry a Message from us to the White People, ordering them to remove from our Lands. They say they would not chuse to incur the ill Will of those People; for, if they should now be removed, they will hereafter return to their Settlements when the English have purchased the Country from us, And we shall be very unhappy, if, by our Conduct towards them at this Time, we shall give them reason to dislike us, and treat us in an unkind Manner, when they again become our Neighbors" (op. cit. 342). It seems strange that these very people, whom the Indians did not wish to offend by driving them from these lands, from which they had been ordered by the Proclamation of the King, Governor, Assembly, should be the most bitter foes of the Indians in the years which followed. The very people who were permitted to stay by the Indians, when the Governors of both Colonies were ordering them to leave, made up the majority of the active leaders in the expeditions into the Indian country beyond the Ohio, in later years. The Treaty of Fort Stanwix, in the summer of 1768, opened these lands for the occupation of the white settlers—who had taken possession of them long before they were bought. The Boundary Dispute with Virginia was the next event to keep this region in the "lime-light." Virginia claimed the entire region south of the Kiskiminetas. A large majority of the settlers along the Youghiogheny and Monongahela were from Virginia, and as a consequence the Virginia side of the controversy was well supported in the region. The early settlers of the Shenandoah Valley had gone there from the Cumberland Valley, and from central Pennsylvania. These were the people who came over the Braddock Road into the region along the Youghiogheny and Monongahela. They were mostly Scotch-Irish, and Presbyterian. The German element took up the land in the Glades in Somerset County, or along the region of Dunkard Creek. In the conflict between the two rival colonies the chief actors on both sides were of the same stock. The entire region claimed by Virginia was called the District of West Augusta. This District was divided into three counties in Oct., 1776. These counties were Ohio, Yohogania and Monongalia. The Youghiogheny region was in the second county, Yohogania. Edward Ward, William Crawford, Dorsey Pentecost, William Harrison, Zachariah Connell and others—31 in all—were commissioned as Justices of this new county, which held its Courts at Andrew Heath's, near the present West Elizabeth (Consult; Annals of Carnegie Museum, I. 525 et seq.; III. 6 et seq.; Crumrine, The Old Virginia Court House at Augusta Town, 1905; Hist. Connellsville, 5-64, 1906; Ellis, Hist. Fayette County, 114-128; Archives, Third Ser., III. 483-572; Hassler, Old Westmoreland, 5-10; Old Redstone, 304 et seq.; Archives, IV. 435, 479, 481, 483, 522, 546, etc.; VII. 133, 467; VIII. 713; IX. 4, 193, 233, 300, 343, 374, 402, 438, etc.). Washington visited the home of Col. William Crawford at "Stewart's Crossings" in 1770, when on his way to the Ohio, spending several days with him. He also visited his own lands at Perryopolis (Consult; Washington's Journal of 1770, Olden Time, I. 416-432). The Seventh Virginia Regt. was raised chiefly through the efforts of Col. Crawford; his recruiting station being at his home. The West Augusta Regt., or the Thirteenth Virginia, was also recruited along the Youghiogheny and Monongahela. Crawford was appointed Colonel of the Seventh in 1776. Col. Crawford went on the ill-fated expedition to Sandusky in 1782, when he was captured and put to death at the

stake (Consult; Archives, Sec. Ser., XIV. 708-725; Border Wars, 131-149; Doddrodges Notes, 206 et seq., 1912; Albach, West. Annals, 227-381; Heckewelder, Ind. Nations, 133, 284-285; DeSchweinitz, Life of Zeisberger, 567-572). In 1784 Dr. John Ewing, when on his way to finish the survey of Mason and Dixon's Line, stopped at Stewarts Crossings to visit Mrs. Crawford. He says, "Dined at Mrs. Crawford's the widow of Coll. Crawford, who was murdered by the Indians, and after dinner proceeded to Beson's Tavern." * * * "At half a mile from Mrs. Crawford's there is a most beautiful cascade in Harrison's Run where the water falls perpendicularly over a broad Limestone Rock about 20 feet" (Archives, Sixth Ser., XIV. 11). This is the falls now known as "Robinson's Falls," on Robinson's Run—the correct name of which was, no doubt, Harrison's Run—Benjamin Harrison and William Harrison were two of the Justices of the Court of West Augusta. Sarah Crawford, the eldest daughter of Col. Crawford, was married to William Harrison, who perished in the Sandusky expedition. Harrison lived near Crawford, whose house stood near the run, which should be either Opossum Run, or Harrison's Run. The various other places along the Youghiogheny are noted under various titles. Dunmore's War, 1774; the Revolution, the Whisky Insurrection are also noted under other titles (See *Redstone, Sewickley, Jacob's Cabin, Turtle Creek*, etc.).

Ohiogainy.—Morris (1755), Col. Rec., VI. 621. **Ohiogane.**—Traders map, 1753. **Ohiogany.**—Pa. Coun. (1755), Col. Rec., VI. 396. **Yaughaughgaine.**—Gist (1751), Dar. Gist Jour., 68. **Yaughyaugani.**—Braddock (1755), Col. Rec., VI. 398. **Yaugyaughani.**—Braddock (1755), Col. Rec., VI. 475. **Yaugh Yaugh gone.**—Gist map, 1753. **Yawyawganey.**—Fry and Jefferson map, 1755. **Yogh-yo-gaine.**—Croghan (1751), Col Rec., V. 531. **Yohiogain.**—Map West. Penna. and Va., 1755 (?)—must be later, in Dar. Gist. **Yohiogani.**—Morris (1755), Col. Rec., VI. 629. **Youch.**—Scott (1781), Archives, IX. 440. **Youghhagainni.** — Marshall (1781), Archives, IX. 343. **Yougheagany.**—St. Clair (1755), Col. Rec, VI. 300. **Yougheogenny.**—Steel (1768), Col. Rec., IX. 507. **Youhiagany.**—Gist (1753), in Dar. Gist Jour., 80. **Youghiogany.**—Scull map, 1770. **Youghiogeny.** Pa. Coun. (1768), Col Rec., IX. 481. **Youghiogheny.** — Morris map, 1848. **Yoxhiogeni.**—Dagworthy (1757), Col. Rec., VII. 633. **Yoxhio Geni.**—Orme (1755), Sargent, Hist. Brad Exped., 336; Evans map, 1755 The County, of the Virginia jurisdiction. **Yogagania.**—

Brodhead (1779), Archives, XII. 169.
Yohogania.—Harrison (1784), Archives,
X. 602. **Younghagonia.**—Brodhead (1779),
Archives, X. 176.

YOUNG WOMANS CREEK. A
creek which enters the West Branch
of the Susquehanna from the north,
in Clinton County. The Indian name
of the stream was Mianquaunk, or
Maunquay (which see). The name
may be a corruption of Minqua—for
Conestoga—which tribe formerly occupied this part of the West Branch.
The name, however, may be a corruption of which the present name is a
translation. The suffix, qua or quay,
is the usual female designation in compound words, as in Ochqueu, "a
woman"; Ochquechum, "female of
beasts"; Ochquehelleu, "female of
birds," etc. There was a village at
the mouth of this creek called Young
Womans Town. The name on the Scull
map for the creek is Maunquay (1759).
On Scull's map (1770) the name is
Mianquaunk, which was probably the
name of the village. See *Maunquay.*

ZINACHSON. See *Otzinachson,
Shamokin.* The name is a contraction
of the former, a name of the West
Branch. Weiser in 1754 says that the
Delawares from the Ohio were going
to settle upon the "Big Island upon
Zinacksy River" (Col. Rec., VI. 37).

APPENDIX A

VILLAGES IN NEW YORK, DESTROYED BY GEN. SULLIVAN'S ARMY, DURING 1779.

The following villages were destroyed by Sullivan's army in 1779, in addition to those mentioned in the body of this Handbook. As these are within the state of New York, but associated with the expedition of Gen. Sullivan, they are given in this appendix.

APPLETOWN. Also called Condawhaw, a former village on the east side of Seneca Lake, at the site of the present North Hector. Sullivan's army encamped here on Sept. 4, 1779. The village was burning when the army reached the place.

ADJUTA. Also Kanaghsaws and Yoxsaw, a village situated about one mile north of Conesus Center. It consisted of 18 houses. Between the village and the lake there were extensive corn fields. It was from this place that Lieut. Boyd and a detachment of 19 men were sent on a scouting expedition, which resulted in the capture of Boyd and the death of all but two of his men. Consult; Journals of General Sullivan's Expedition, 131. The army passed through this place on Sept. 13th, 1779.

CANADASAGA. A former Seneca village, situated about one and a half miles west of Geneva. It was a large and important village, and was frequently called "Seneca Castle." Sir William Johnson erected a stockade fort at this place in 1756. In 1779 it was composed of about 60 houses, surrounded by extensive fruit orchards. It was destroyed Sept. 9th, 1779. The name signifies, "at the new town."

CHEMUNG. Sullivan's army encamped here on August 28th, 1779. See note in the body of this book.

CHENUSSIO. A former village at the junction of Canaseraga Creek with the Genesee River. This town was not in existence at the time of Sullivan's expedition. This was the town which Lieut. Boyd was sent to examine with his scouting party. General Sullivan being confused by the maps which he had, which placed the great Seneca village at this location on the east side of the river with the large village on the west side of the river. See *Genesee.*

CHOHARO. A former Cayuga village at the foot of Cayuga Lake. Was the same as the St. Stephen of the Jesuit Relations. It was destroyed by the detachment under Col. Butler, Sept. 20, 1779. The name is said to signify, "the place of rushes."

CONDAWHAW. Same as Appletown, at site of North Hector. The name Ken-daw-ya is said by Gallatin to signify "prairie."

CONIHUNTO. An Indian village about 14 miles below Unadilla, on the Susquehanna River, on an island near Afton. It was destroyed by Butler in 1778. Clinton's Brigade passed through the place Aug. 13, 1779.

COREORGONEL. Also He-ho-risskanadia. A Cayuga village on the west side of Cayuga Inlet, two miles south of Ithaca. It was destroyed by Sullivan's army, Sept. 24, 1779. It then contained 25 houses. This village had been occupied by a remnant of the Catawba, according to Gen. J. S. Clark. This is an error, as the Tutelo (of the same family as the Catawba) were placed here by the Iroquois.

CHONODOTE. A former village at the site of Aurora. Also called Peach Town because of the immense peach orchards about the place. It consisted of 14 houses when it was destroyed Sept. 24, 1779.

CAYUGA CASTLE. A former village of 15 houses, at the site of Springport, Cayuga County. Destroyed Sept. 22nd, 1779.

CAYUGA, UPPER. A former village near Ledyard, Cayuga County, contained 14 houses, destroyed the same date as the above.

CAYUGA, EAST or OLD TOWN. A village of 13 houses situated at the southeast part of Springport. Destroyed Sept. 22, 1779.

GATHTSEGWAROHARE. A former village on the east side of Canaseraga Creek, about two miles above its confluence with the Genesee River. Lieut. Boyd and his detachment reached this village on Sept. 13th, and found it abandoned. He sent two men back to report to Gen. Sullivan. As Sullivan's army approached the village that evening it was fired upon by the Indians, who then retreated. The army then destroyed the immense corn fields about the village on Sept. 14th. It contained 25 houses. The name signifies "spear laid up."

Gen. Clark says that the Squakie tribe which occupied this region was a remnant of the Erie, who were destroyed by the Iroquois. See op. cit. 132.

GEWAUGA. Same as Cayuga Castle, mentioned before, or near the site of Union Springs.

HONEOYE. An Indian village at the foot of the lake of the same name, about half a mile east of the outlet. It contained about 20 houses. One of the houses was occupied by Capt. Cummunings and about 50 men, who were left here on Sept. 12th, when the army advanced. Consult; op. cit., 31, 130. The name is said to signify "finger lying," or "there it lies." See article in body of book.

KENDAIA. An Indian village situated on the eastern shore of Seneca Lake, in the present town of Romulus, about half a mile from the lake. The army of Gen. Sullivan encamped here on Sept. 5, 1779. Nearly all of the Journals of the expedition mention the wonderful Indian tombs in the place. It was aso called Appletown.

KANANDAIGUA. A former Seneca village situated in the western part of the present Canandaigua. It contained 23 houses, and was surrounded by corn fields and orchards, when it was destroyed by Sullivan's army, Sept 10th, 1779. The name Ga-nun-da-gwa signifies "place selected for a village."

KANAWLOHALLA. A former Seneca village at the site of Elmira. Destroyed by Sullivan's army August 31, 1779. The name signifies "a head fastened to the end of an object," or "head on a pole."

MAMACATING or **MAMACOTTING.** A former village at the site of Wurtzboro. Said to have been named in honor of an Indian chief. A blockhouse was built at this place during the Revolution. Gen. Clinton's Brigade passed through the place on May 6th, 1779, on its way to join Sullivan's army at Tioga. Another significance of the name is given as "dividing the waters."

SHAWHIANGTO. A former Tuscarora village at the site of Windsor, Broome County. This was one of the villages in which the Tuscarora were placed by the Iroquois in 1712. It contained about 12 houses, when it was destroyed by Clinton's Brigade, August 17th, 1779.

SKOI-YASE. A former Cayuga village at the site of Waterloo. Destroyed Sept. 8th, 1779.

SKANNAYUTENATE. A former village at the present village of Canoga, on the north bank of Canoga creek. Said to have been the birth-place of Sagoyewatha, or Red Jacket, the famous Seneca orator. The village was destroyed by Col. Dearborn's detachment of Sullivan's army, Sept. 21st, 1779. The name is said to signify, "on the other side of the lake."

SWAHYAWANAH. A former village situated in the northeast of the present town of Romulus, Seneca County, near the shore of the lake. Was burned by a detachment of Sullivan's army Sept. 22nd, 1779. It then consisted of three houses and some corn fields.

The various Journals of the expedition of Gen. John Sullivan give many variations of these names. Consult; Journals of the Military Expedition of Major General John Sullivan, 1878; Archives of Penna., Second Series, XV. 221-293, 1890; Journal of Lieut. Col. Adam Hubley, Jr., 1779 (Dr. J. W. Jordan, Ed.) 1909. The other villages destroyed by the army of General Sullivan are found in the body of this book, under title. These villages were; Newtychanning, Old Chemung, New Chemung, Ingaren, Otsiningo (Shenango), Chugnutt, Owegy, Mauckatawangum, and a few smaller villages. The other points mentioned in the line of march are; Great Swamp, Shadow of Death, Wyoming, Sheshequin, Lackawanna, Tioga, and all of the creeks along the course of the march from the Delaware to the Susquehanna, and up the river to the various Indian villages. See these under title.

APPENDIX B

PREHISTORIC WORKS IN PENNSYLVANIA.

There are scattered throughout Pennsylvania various remains of prehistoric works, which were erected by the aboriginal inhabitants of the region. These consist of mounds, burial grounds, single graves, petroglyphs, or rock carvings, kitchen midden, workshop refuse heaps, caches of flint implements and other relics of a past occupancy of the region, before the coming of the Europeans. The term prehistoric has reference to the period before the actual commencement of the period of written history. This period of written history commenced in 1608, with the tour of exploration of Capt. John Smith up the Susquehanna River. Previous to that year the history of Pennsylvania is merely traditionary. The tradition of the eastward migration of the Lenape and Iroquois, given by Heckewelder (See *Allegheny*), which is founded, not only upon the records of the Delawares, as contained in the Walam Olum, but also upon recent scientific examination of the history of the Cherokee and other tribes, is the starting point of even the traditional history of the human occupancy of the Ohio region, and of the later occupancy of the Delaware River by the people found there when the continent was first occupied by the Europeans.

The length of time which man has lived upon the American continent, has been a fertile theme for the writers of many fanciful, as well as fantastic books and articles. Many problems arise in the attempt to solve this problem. As all of the people living on the continent were without any system of writing, they left no record whatever of their development, much less of their origin. As a consequence, the only evidences which can possibly be used, are those which can be furnished by archaeology and ethnology. When the continent was first discovered by the Europeans, the race living upon it had such marked characteristics as to make it a separate race, differing in every respect from the races of the Old World. This fact alone would imply a period of long separation from the parent stock, from which it sprang.

But, not only was this a fact, but it was also a fact that the various tribes then living upon the continent, had been in existence for so long a period that their manners, customs, religion and language had become as entirely separated from each other as were those of the European and the Indian race.

During the early years of the investigation concerning the origin of the American Indian, there were many people who made attempts to prove that the American Indian was derived from one of the European races. This theory is now held by no American ethnologist. Later investigation has shown that the history of man on the American continent is about the same as the history of man on any of the continents of the Eastern Hemisphere.

The vast accumulations of shell heaps, and a careful study of the differences of the shells found in these heaps; the various mounds, with the succession of forest trees which have grown upon them; the finding of skeletons, flint implements and other relics of man, in various gravel and sand strata, are all evidences of a long period of human occupancy. But, none of these carry us back more than 3,000 years, at the very limit. Not a single relic of man has yet been found in any of the Glacial deposits. One single bone has been found in the Glacial gravel—and it is not known whether it is that of a man or an animal. The mounds, shell heaps, kitchen midden and other remains furnish evidence of a period of long occupancy, but as to the length of that period, or from where the people came, nothing whatever can be authoritatively said.

The dispersion of the various linguistic groups would seem to indicate that the point of dispersion, or the cradle of the Indian race, was on the northwestern part of the continent, on the Pacific coast. The similiarity between the Esquimaux and the Tartar, or Mongolian races, might give some ground of plausibility to the theory that the Indians are descendants of these peoples of Asia, who crossed to North America in the region of Alaska.

But, even this theory is confronted with many difficulties, as there is not the slightest resemblance in language, customs or religion of the Tartar, or Mongolian, and the American Indian. Manners and customs change, so does religion, but the roots of a language do not change.

Many utter fallacies once had a very wide-spread following, even among scholars. Among these may be mentioned, the one that the Indians are the lost tribes of Israel. Neither a student of the Bible, or a student of Ethnology could give any credance to such a thoroughly unfounded supposition. This theory was advanced by Father Duran in 1585, and was later advanced by other writers, among whom were Thomas Thorowgood, who in 1652 published a work called Digitus Dei, in which he presented various arguments to support this theory. Later writers obtained their arguments from this book. The theory is presented every now and then in the articles which are published in various popular works. The theory is hard to kill, even if it does not have the shadow of an argument upon which to base itself. In the first place the American continent was occupied long before the Tribe of Israel were "lost," and in the second place there is absolutely no racial characteristics in common between the Jew and the Indian. The resemblance in religious rite and ceremony between these of the Jew and the Indian, are found among all primitive races on the face of the earth, and rest upon physical or physiological phenomena entirely.

Other writers have attempted to prove the Greek, Chinese, Phoenician, Welsh and Irish origin of the Indians. All such arguments are based upon similarity in manners, customs, traditions, myths and arts which belong alike to all of the races of men during their primitive state. The traditions of all primitive people, living in the realm of Nature, are the same. The sun, moon, stars, the wind, thunder, lightning, tempest, the ebb and flow of the tide—all of the natural phenomena are found as the basis of the myths and traditions of all races, Jew, Greek, Roman, Assyrian, Egyptian, and American Indian, and prove nothing whatever, save the childhood of every race.

The Indian language bears no resemblance whatever to the Hebrew, Egyptian, Phoenician, Celtic, or any other language. It is a language in itself, and is not only distinct from other languages, but, as has been stated before, it contains languages which are entirely distinct from each other. Of the 56 linguistic groups, north of Mexico, no two have languages which are alike. There is just as much difference in any two of these languages as there is between English and Chinese. The vocabulary, the grammar, and even the unchanging roots of words, bear no relation whatever to each other. Just as long a time was necessary to produce the difference between the language of the Catawba and the Iroquois as was needed to produce the difference between the English and Japanese, and this condition existed when the continent was first discovered.

The other popular fallacy, which dies hard, is that concerning a race of prehistoric mound builders, which occupied the continent previous to its occupancy by the historic Indian. Many books and articles have been written concerning these "Mound Builders," of a far greater culture than that of the American Indian. Every argument advanced to prove the existence of this race, falls to the ground, when given careful scientific examination. There never has been found in any mound, grave, shell heap, or any other work of the past on the American continent, any article of war, hunting or household use, which was not used by the Indians living in the region in which the mound, grave, or other remains, of the past stood. In fact many of the articles which were brought by the Europeans, such as coins, steel-knives; etc., have been found in many of the mounds and graves, ascribed to these "Mound Builders." Nor has a single evidence of any higher state of culture ever been found in any of these remains. The flint implements, pottery, and other articles found in these mounds, were the same as those used by the Indians which inhabited the region when the first white explorers and settlers came into it. Not only is that a fact, but it is also a fact that, as stated by DeSoto and others, that many of these mounds were made, and in use, by the Indians, after the continent was discovered. The mounds in the Gulf states, and in the Natchez country, were in use by the Indians when DeSoto passed through the region in 1540. The Cherokee and Shawnee were mound builders within historic times, and these were probably the builders of the various earthworks along the Ohio, and in western Pennsylvania. The ancestors of the Cherokee, the Alligewi, or Talligewi, of the upper Ohio, probably built many of the mounds along the Monongahela, Youghiogheny and Ohio as they retreated southward before the Iroquois. Many of these mounds were built 200 or 300 years before the region was visited by the Europeans, but none of them show a much earlier date of erection—even when the statements of the first explorers in the region are given the greatest latitude of age, as evidenced by trees of from 200 to 300 years of age standing on their summits.

All of the facts in the case are on the side of the comparatively recent origin of all of these remains in Pennsylvania. It may be safely said, in view of these facts, that the ancestors of the Indians built all of the mounds in the entire region north of Mexico. There is not a single scientific fact in support of any other theory.

The fallacy in regard to the nomadic habits of the Indian has been noticed in the introduction to this book. The Indian was not nomadic. He occupied his tribal habitat for generations, and it may safely be said that the ancestors—perhaps many generations distant— of the Indians living in any particular region, as a traditional habitat at the time of the discovery of the continent, were the builders of the mounds, graves and other prehistoric works found in that region.

A list of the various Indian remains found in Pennsylvania, follows: This list is, no doubt, very incomplete, but it will serve as a guide for more extended investigation. Many of the items have been taken from the "Catalogue of Prehistoric Works," by Cyrus Thomas, and published by the Bureau of Ethnology, 1891, as Bulletin Number 12. Consult: Handbook of American Indians, articles on Archaeology, Antiquity, Mound Builders, Shell Heaps; The Problem of the Ohio Mounds, Cyrus Thomas, 1889; The Circular, Square, and Octagonal Earthworks of Ohio, Thomas, 1889, etc. The author will be obliged for any information concerning any Indian works, of any sort, which may not be contained in this list, which is arranged according to counties, for the sake of easy reference. Many of the following are found in the list given by Cyrus Thomas in the Catalogue of

Prehistoric Works, before mentioned, pages 189-193.

ADAMS COUNTY. The site of an early Indian settlement, near Gettysburg. May possibly be the site of one of the Susquehannock (Conestoga) villages mentioned by John Smith, in 1608. See Smithsonian Report, 1879, p. 446.

ALLEGHENY COUNTY. A large burial mound at the site of McKees Rocks, below Pittsburgh, overlooking the Ohio River. This mound was investigated by the Carnegie Museum of Pittsburgh. A number of skeletons, in stone graves, and a great quantity of flint arrow-heads, shells, beads and other articles were removed. These are now in the Carnegie Museum. The mound was evidently a burial mound, and not a fortification. It was mentioned by many of the early travellers down the Ohio River. Coll. Mass. Hist. Soc., III. 23, 1794. Thomas Ashe, Travels, 21-22, 1808; Pittsburgh Times, May 15, 1886, etc.

Semi-circular mound, stone mound, and stone graves, near Bridgeville.

Stone Mounds, near Thompson Station, and also on the opposite side of the Monongahela River. These, and various other mounds, were found along the Monongahela River at various points. Some of them were noted on the early maps as "Indian Forts."

It is stated, as a tradition, that the hill, now known as Grant's Hill, on which the Allegheny Court House now stands, in Pittsburgh, was formerly the site of an Indian burial place. The author can find no authority for this tradition.

ARMSTRONG COUNTY. There was a large mound at Manorville, between Kittanning and Ford City from which many skeletons have been removed. J. W. King, of Kittanning, has made a study of this mound.

BEAVER COUNTY. Mounds near Beaver Falls and mounds at the mouth of Beaver River. Mentioned by Gerard Fowke.

Petroglyphs on the bed-rock of the Ohio River, near the mouth of Little Beaver Creek, at Smith's Ferry. These "Picture Rocks" were exposed a few years ago, during low water. They are now covered by the slack-water of the dam. They extend across the river to Georgetown. Representations of eagles, turtles, deer and various other birds and animals cover the rocks in the bed of the river. The author has a number of photographs of these carvings. An Indian trail crossed the Ohio at this point, cutting overland to Wheeling and to the mouth of Yellow Creek. The inscriptions are possibly records of hunting and fishing expeditions; autographs of chiefs, etc. They are perhaps, the most extensive petroglyphs in the state. Illustrations of a few of these pictures are printed in Hanna, Wilderness Trail, Vol. 1.

BRADFORD COUNTY. Large burial ground on the Murray farm, opposite Tioga Point. This site was examined by the Susquehanna Archaeological Expedition in June, 1916. Many skeletons were found. This was probably an Andaste burial site. Dr. Warren K. Moorehead was Director of this expedition. See Second Reports of Pa. Historical Commission, 116-143, 1918.

BUCKS COUNTY. Some small mounds, which are said to have been Indian graves, in Hilltown Township, mentioned in Doylestown Democrat, Sept. 29, 1885.

A number of ancient remains, supposed to be sites of Indian villages, on the Delaware in Durham Township. Many relics have been found at this site. Place known as "Durham Cave," in which petrified bones were found. See Smithsonian Report, 1883, 872-876.

BUTLER COUNTY. Stone piles, and old trail, near Harrisville. Smithsonian Report, 1879, 446.

CAMERON COUNTY. A former Indian burial place, near the mouth of Sterling Run. About 17 skeletons were found at this place in 1873 by Mr. Earle. See Egle, History of Pennsylvania, 483. These skeletons were covered with about 30 inches of shale and clay, and had evidently been covered by the deposit of clay and soil by natural deposit, rather than by artificial means.

CHESTER COUNTY. Indian graves, near West Chester. Smithsonian Report, 1879, 446. Indian burial ground, on West Branch of Brandywine, or Minquaas Creek. Examined by E. A. Barber. See American Naturalist, Vol. XIII. 294-296, 1879.

CLINTON COUNTY. Various burial grounds have been found in this county at different points on the West Branch, and it tributaries. The largest of these was situated at the site of the present Lock Haven, where many skeletons were unearthed when the workmen were digging the old canal. These ancient burial grounds were also found along Quinn's Run, and below the mouth of the Bald Eagle Creek, at McElhatten and at various points along Pine Creek. The entire West Branch, in the present Cameron, Clinton, Lycoming and Northumberland Counties was probably occupied by the Wenro and the Susquehanna (Andastes, Conestoga) before these tribes were driven from the region by the Iroquois. Many flint and stone implements have been found along the river, and on its various tributaries. See Meginness, Otzinachson, 27 et seq.

CRAWFORD COUNTY. Numerous mounds about Pymatuning swamp, in the region of Linesville. Hutchins mentions these in his Description of 1764. See also Smithsonian Report, 1879, 446. The place marked "Delaware Grove," on Morris map of 1848, should be "Delaware Graves," according to Hutchins map.

Ancient inclosure, or fort, on French Creek, about 4 miles from Meadeville. See Warden's Research, 48.

Mounds about Geneva.

Mounds about Centreville.

CUMBERLAND COUNTY. An Indian Cave, on the Conodoguinet, near Carlisle. The cave is said to have contained human bones. The author has examined this cave, the bottom of which is covered with a deep deposit of mud. If the Indians of the state ever made use of any sort of a rock-shelter, this cave would surely be used. No extensive examination of the cave has ever been made. See Day, Hist. Coll. of Penna., 270-271.

ERIE COUNTY. A mound beyond Shannon's Crossing on the E. & P. R. R.

A mound 10 miles north of Union and 2 miles west of Wattsburgh.

FAYETTE COUNTY. There were a number of mounds and burial grounds in various parts of this county. Redstone Old Fort, at Brownsville, was perhaps the most noted of these. Thomas Ashe visited it in 1806, and left an account of his observations, which are not in accordance with the observations of the early settlers in the region. According to his account it was a pentagon, which inclosed about

13 acres, in the middle of which stood a mound 30 feet high. The mound was later the site of Fort Burd (See Article on *Redstone*). Consult; Ellis, Hist. Fayette County, 18; Veech, Monongahela of Old. Judge Veech accepted the view that these earthworks were made by "a race more intelligent, or of a people of different habits of life" than were the Indians. Which theory has long since been exploded. These mounds were probably erected by the Shawnee, or the Cherokee, previous to their southern migration. There were a number of them at various points along the Monongahela and Youghiogheny Rivers (Consult; Ellis, Hist. Fayette County, 16-19; Veech, Monongahela of Old). Several of these "Indian Forts" were noted on Scull's map of 1770. One was situated at the present Belle Vernon, another on the Youghiogheny, opposite Broadford, another on the ridge south of Perryopolis, another opposite the present Dawson, near the mouth of Dickerson Run, and another on Mounts Creek, above Irishman's Run and at various other places in the present bounds of Fayette County. Various graves have been found at many points along the Catawba Trail (See *Catawba*) which ran through this region, and on the summit of the Laurel Hill, near where the "Mud Pike" crosses, a burial ground existed, from which many relics have been taken. The author has examined several of these so-called "Indian mounds" and found that the formation was due to entirely natural causes, and were not made by man, as the rock strata a few feet below the surface was entirely undisturbed. One such "mound" exists at the summit of the mountains, above the Youghiogheny River, near Fort Hill. This formation is due entirely to erosion. It was no doubt used by the Indians, as an observation place, but it was not built by them. The graves which are found along the Catawba Trail were probably made by the Iroquois, as they returned from their expeditions to the south. The wounded warriors were probably buried near the place where they died. Similar graves are found along nearly all of the Iroquois trails across the state. Consult the works cited.

FOREST COUNTY. Mounds near East Hickory. Burial ground below mouth of the West Hickory creek. Burying Ground, mentioned by Gen. W. B. Irvine, in 1785, as about 13

miles above Hickory Bottom, "from a tradition they have that some extraordinary man was buried there many hundreds of years ago" (Archives, XI. 517).

FRANKLIN COUNTY. A former Indian burial ground occupied the site of the present grounds near the Falling Springs Presbyterian Church, Chambersburg. This, evidently belonged to the Delaware and Shawnee, and was visited by the Indians after the settlement of the Cumberland Valley by the Scotch-Irish. It is said that the Indians came to the place until 1834 to visit the graves of their ancestors (Consult; Publications of the Kittochtinny Hist. Soc., I. 6-7, 1900).

FULTON COUNTY. A former Indian burial ground on Scrub Ridge Mountain, about 7 miles southwest of McConnellsburg.

GREENE COUNTY. A mound about 2 miles above the mouth of the creek, opposite Millsborough, Washington County; also mounds and graves at various places in the region of Waynesburg. Many relics have been found in this region, which was on the trail between the Ohio and Monongahela.

INDIANA COUNTY. A mound at the junction of Black Lick Creek and the Conemaugh River. Mentioned by Warden, Recherch, (1854), p. 18. The various salt springs in this county were also used in the making of salt.

LANCASTER COUNTY. This county contains many remains of the early Indian occupation. Probably of the Susquehannocks (Conestoga), who occupied the region until their final overthrow by the Iroquois in 1675. The "Picture Rocks," below the mouth of Conestoga Creek, are perhaps the most famous of these remains (Consult; Hanna, Wilderness Trail, I. 61, 62, 65). The two forts of the Susquehannocks were also situated near the present Washington Borough and Wrightsville. Many relics have been found in this entire region. The various creeks, running into the Susquehanna also contained, along their shores, various burial places, caches, etc. The entire region from the headwaters of the Susquehanna to the mouth of Octoraro Creek, contains evidences of this early Susquehannock, or Conestoga, occupation.

LAWRENCE COUNTY. A mound at the site of the present New Castle, and on the Mahoning River, at the sites of the Kuskuskies. See Smithsonian Report, 1871, 406-407; 1877, 306-307.

LUZERNE COUNTY. Mound at Nanticoke, where the dead were buried. Smithsonian Report, 1881, 686.

Mound near Wilkes-Barre, said to have been erected by the Delawares over the dead of the "Grasshopper War." Annals of Binghampton, 1840, 173.

LYCOMING COUNTY. Fortification near mouth of Pine Creek, with burial ground near. Day, Hist. Coll. Penna., 1843, 44-45; Warden, Recherch, 18; Meginness, Otzinachson, 28.

Also burial ground below Williamsport, near Halls Station. See Meginness, Otzinachson, 28.

Also mound on Muncy Creek; another opposite mouth of the Lycoming Creek, at mouth of Loyalsock and other places along the Susquehanna. These are noted on Scull's and Evan's maps as "Conestoga Indian F." These works were all made by the Susquehannocks, or Conestoga.

MIFFLIN COUNTY. Burial mound near the junction of Kishacoquillas Creek and the Juniata River, near Lewistown. Smithsonian Report, 1879, 446.

MONROE COUNTY. Indian grave near Delaware Water Gap. Amer. Nat., XIII. 297.

NORTHAMPTON COUNTY. A stone inclosure, near Danielsville.

Village site, near Cherryville. See Amer. Antiq., Vol. IX. No. 9, 311-312.

NORTHUMBERLAND COUNTY. An ancient burial ground at the site of Sunbury, where stood the former village of Shamokin. Many graves have been found at the upper end of the former Indian village, opposite the end of the island. The Iroquois Deputy, Shikellamy, was buried in this old grave-yard. Many relics have been dug up at this place, near the site of old Fort Augusta.

A stone mound 30 feet in diameter and 8 feet high, near Milton. See Warden, Recherch, 1834, 18.

TIOGA COUNTY. Ancient stone pyramids on the Tioga River, at the New York line, mentioned by David Zeisberger in 1767. See *Tioga.*

VENANGO COUNTY. "Indian God Rock," on the bank of the Allegheny River, 6 miles below Franklin. A boulder about 22 feet in length and 14 feet in breadth, containing various carvings. Consult; Egle, Hist. Penna., 1120-1121; Day, Hist. Coll. Penna., 638-639.

Indian graves near Franklin and Cooperstown.

Cave, in which various relics have been found, opposite Oleopolis. Consult; Hist. Mag., 2nd. Ser., II. 178 (1887).

WARREN COUNTY. Stone heap opposite Tidioute, on Allegheny River. Has been examined. Human bones found under it.

Inclosure on the west side of Brokenstraw Creek, about 3 miles up the creek from Pittsfield.

Group of mounds near Irvineton, in one of which pure silver was found. Science, Vol. V., 419-420, 1885.

WASHINGTON COUNTY. Mound at Monongahela.

Three stone graves, below Monongahela.

Six stone mounds, opposite Belle Vernon.

Two burial places on Pigeon Creek, about 5 miles from Monongahela.

Mound on a ridge near Cross Creek, which contained a stone wall.

Three mounds near Shireoaks.

Stone mound near Lock No. 4.

Stone mound, opposite Coal Bluff.

WESTMORELAND COUNTY. Stone graves, opposite Monongahela.

Mound in Wheatfield Township. Day, Hist. Coll. Pa., 680.

Burial ground, about 15 miles from Mt. Pleasant, in which dead were buried under piles of stones. Smithsonian Report, 1881, 681.

This catalogue is by no means complete. The author has given only the remains which he has examined, or of which he has a record. There are, no doubt, many more in the state, which are not given in this list. The author requests information concerning any such works, of which the reader has positive knowledge.

Many of the works, given in this list, have been entirely obliterated by the growth of towns and cities, and by the cuts made by railroads and state highways, within the past twenty years. A list of all such works should have been made many years ago.

The site known as "Spanish Hill" in Bradford County, opposite Waverly,

New York, was probably the site of the palisaded town of the Susquehannocks, called Carantouan (which see). At the site of Roulette, Potter County, there was probably a store-house, used for corn. This was probably built by the Indians previous to Sullivan's expedition up the Susquehanna and Brodhead's expedition up the Allegheny, in 1779. It was burnt in some manner before the first settlers came into the region. The number of caches, or storage places, for flint implements and other stone instruments, are so numerous that they cannot be listed. These are found along the trails, at village sites, in graves and along streams. In some of these caches along the mountain trails, as many as a peck of flint arrow-heads were deposited by the warriors or hunters, for future use. The warrior, or hunter, never returned to get this supply, which some farmer boy may now plow up in a new clearing. The author has often thought, as he has picked up these beautiful arrow-points, along the old trails through the mountains of Pennsylvania, of what a tale these little "flints" might tell—if they could talk. There may be "sermons in stones," but these little relics of the distant past are as silent as are the lips of the warriors who once sent them on their mission of death.

NAMES HAVING AN INDIAN ORIGIN

The following list of names, having an Indian origin, are now used as names of cities, villages and stations.

Some of them are historic, while others are not identified in any way with the history of the state.

Agawam ....Clearfield County
Alfarata ....Huntingdon County
Alfarata ....Mifflin County
Algonquin Junct. .....Luzerne County
Aliquippa ....Beaver County
Allegheny Junct. ....Butler County
Allegheny Landing ....Berks County
Allegheny Mines ......Butler County
Alleghenyville ....Berks County
Allegrippus ....Blair County
Alliquippa ....Bedford County
Analomink ....Monroe County
Aquashicola ....Carbon County
Aquetong ....Bucks County
Aramingo ....Montgomery County
Aughwick ....Huntingdon County
Aughwick Mills ...Huntingdon County
Awwa Junct. (?) ....Lawrence County
Bald Eagle ....Blair County
Baldeagle ....York County
Bald Eagle Junct. .....Clinton County
Beaver ....Beaver County
Black Hawk ....Beaver County
Black Lick ....Indiana County
Black Log ....Huntingdon County
Brandt ....Susquehanna County
Cacoosing ....Berks County
Callapoose ....Wayne County
Calumet ....Westmoreland County
Canyock (?) ....Cambria County
Capouse Breaker .Lackawanna County
Castanea ....Clinton County
Catasaqua ....Lehigh County
Catawissa ....Columbia County
Catawissa Bridge ....Columbia County
Catawissa Junct. ....Columbia County
Cayuga ....Lackawanna County
Chautauqua ....Lebanon County
Chemung ....Lycoming County
Chickies ....Lancaster County
Chicora ....Butler County
Chillisquaque .Northumberland County
Chippewa ....Lycoming County
Chulasky (?) .Northumberland County
Cinnaminson .....Philadelphia County
Cocalico ....Lancaster County
Cocolamus ....Juniata County
Codorus ....Lancaster County
Codorus ....York County
Codorus Mills ....York County
Conashaugh ....Pike County
Conemaugh ....Cambria County
Conemaugh Furnace ....
..........Westmoreland County
Conestoga ....Chester County
Conestoga ....Lancaster County

Conestoga Station ..Lancaster County
Conewago ....Dauphin County
Conewago ....York County
Conneaut Lake ......Crawford County
Conneaut Center ....Crawford County
Conneaut Junct. ....Erie County
Conneautville ....Crawford County
Conneaut Station ...Crawford County
Conococheague Junct. Franklin County
Conoquenessing ....Butler County
Conoy ....Lancaster County
Conshohocken ....Montgomery County
Coplay ....Lehigh County
Cornplanter ....Warren County
Cowanesque ....Tioga County
Cowanshannoc .....Armstrong County
Cush Creek ....Indiana County
Cush Creek Junct. ...Clearfield County
Cush Cushion ....Indiana County
Daguscahonda ....Elk County
Dagus Mines ....Elk County
Dagus Crossing ....Elk County
Dahoga ....Elk County
East Conemaugh .....Cambria County
East Conshohocken Montgomery County
East Mahanoy ....Schuylkill County
East Mauch Chunk ....Carbon County
East Manayunk ..Montgomery County
East Nanticoke ......Luzerne County
East Texas ....Lehigh County
East Towanda ......Bradford County
Equinunk ....Wayne County
Erie ....Erie County
Erie Junct. ....Jefferson County
Frankstown ....Blair County
Ganoga Lake ....Sullivan County
Gawango ....Warren County
Genesee ....Potter County
Genesee Fork ....Potter County
Genesee Springs ......Potter County
Glen Onoko ....Carbon County
Guyasuta ....Allegheny County
Haleeka ....Lycoming County
Hiawatha ....Wayne County
Hoboken ....Allegheny County
Hocking Junct. ......Somerset County
Hocking Mines ......Somerset County
Hokendauqua ....Lehigh County
Hokendauqua Junct. ..Lehigh County
Holicong ....Bucks County
Honeoye ....Potter County
Indiana ....Indiana County
Indiana Junct. ......Jefferson County
Indian Creek ....Fayette County
Indiancreek ....McKean County
Indian Head ....Fayette County

Indianland ......Northampton County
Indian Lane ....Centre County
Indian Orchard ....Wayne County
Indian Ridge ....Schuylkill County
Indian Run ....Elk County
Indianrun ....Mercer County
Indian Springs ....Bedford County
Iroquois ....Perry County
Jack's Creek ....Mifflin County
Jack's Mountain ......Adams County
Jacobs Creek ...Westmoreland County
Juneau ....Indiana County
Juniata ....Blair County
Juniata ....Fayette County
Juniata Bridge ....Perry County
Juniata Furnace ....Perry County
Juniata Mines ....Centre County
Juniataville ....Fayette County
Keewaydin ....Clearfield County
Kingsessing ......Philadelphia County
Kinzua ....Warren County
Kinzua Bridge ....McKean County
Kinzua Viaduct ......McKean County
Kishacoquillas ....Mifflin County
Kishacoquillas Valley Junct. .....
...................Mifflin County
Kiskiminetas Junct. ....
...........Westmoreland County
Kissimmee ....Snyder County
Kittanning ....Armstrong County
Kittanning Point ....Blair County
Kittatinny ....Carbon County
Klondike ....Jefferson County
Klondike ....Mercer County
Kushequa ....McKean County
Lackawanna .....Lackawanna County
Lackawaxen ....Pike County
Lake Yinola ....Wyoming County
Letort ....Lancaster County
Lamoka ....Bradford County
Lehigh ....Lackawanna County
Lehigh ....Monroe County
Lehigh Furnace ....Lehigh County
Lehigh Gap ....Carbon County
Lehigh Tannery ......Carbon County
Lehighton ....Carbon County
Lehigh Valley ....Lehigh County
Lenape ....Armstrong County
Lenape ....Chester County
Lenni ....Delaware County
Lenni Mills ....Delaware County
Lingohocken ....Bucks County
Little Oley ....Berks County
Little Toby ....Clearfield County
Lower Catasaqua ......Lehigh County
Lower Coplay ....Lehigh County
Lower Lehighton ......Carbon County
Lower Saucon ...Northampton County
Loyalhanna ....Westmoreland County
Loyalsock ....Lycoming County
Loyalsock Junct. .....Sullivan County
Loyalsock Station ...Lycoming County
Lycippus ....Westmoreland County
Lycoming ....Lycoming County

Macungie ....Lehigh County
Mahanoy .....Northumberland County
Mahanoy ....Perry County
Mahanoy City ......Schuylkill County
Mahanoy Junct. ....Schuylkill County
Mahanoy Plane ....Schuylkill County
Mahantango ....Dauphin County
Mahantango ....Juniata County
Mahoning ....Armstrong County
Mahoning ....Carbon County
Mahoningtown ......Lawrence County
Maiden Creek ....Berks County
Manatawney ....Berks County
Manatawney Station ....Berks County
Manayunk ....Philadelphia County
Manhattan ....Tioga County
Manito ....Westmoreland County
Marcus Hook ....Delaware County
Masthope ....Pike County
Mattewana ....Mifflin County
Mauch Chunk ....Carbon County
Maxatawney ....Berks County
Mehoopany ....Wyoming County
Mehoopany Station ..Wyoming County
Mengwe ....Lycoming County
Meshoppen ....Wyoming County
Milwaukee ......Lackawanna County
Mingo ....Montgomery County
Mingoville ....Centre County
Minnequa ....Bradford County
Minooka ....Lackawanna County
Minooka Junct. ...Lackawanna County
Minqua ....Lancaster County
Minsi ....Monroe County
Mocanaqua ....Luzerne County
Mokoma ....Sullivan County
Mohawk ....Crawford County
Monocacy ....Berks County
Monocacy Station ......Berks County
Monongahela .....Washington County
Monongahela Furnace ....
...............Allegheny County
Monongahela Junct. ..Allegheny County
Montour Junct. .....Allegheny County
Montour Junct. ....Perry County
Montoursville ....Lycoming County
Moosic ....Lackawanna County
Mooween (?) ....Indiana County
Moravia ....Lawrence County
Moravia Station ....Lawrence County
Moselem ....Berks County
Moselem Springs ....Berks County
Moshannon ....Centre County
Moshannon ....Clearfield County
Mount Pocono ....Monroe County
Muncy ....Lycoming County
Muncy Station ......Lycoming County
Muncy Valley ....Sullivan County
Naginey ....Mifflin County
Nanticoke ....Luzerne County
Nantmeal Valley ......Chester County
Nauvoo ....Tioga County
Navarro (?) ......Washington County
Nayaug ....Lackawanna County

Nebraska ....Forest County
Nekoda ....Perry County
Nescopec ....Luzerne County
Nescopeck ....Luzerne County
Nescopeck Pass ....Luzerne County
Neshamminy ....Bucks County
Neshamminy Falls .....Bucks County
Neshamminy Station ....Bucks County
Neshannock ....Mercer County
Neshannock Falls ...Lawrence County
Nesquehoning ....Carbon County
Nesquehoning Junct. ...Carbon County
Neversink ....Berks County
New Buffalo ....Perry County
New Mahoning ....Carbon County
New Texas ....Allegheny County
New Texas ....Lehigh County
Niagra ....Wayne County
Niantic ....Montgomery County
Nippenose ....Lycoming County
Nippenose Park .....Lycoming County
Nittany ....Centre County
Nockamixon ....Bucks County
Norconk ....Bradford County
North Bangor ...Northampton County
North Buffalo ......Armstrong County
New Codorus ....York County
New Coplay ....Lehigh County
North Manayunk .Philadelphia County
North Mehoopany ...Wyoming County
North Sewickley .....Beaver County
North Towanda ......Bradford County
Noxen ....Wyoming County
Nuangola (?) ......Luzerne County
Nuangola Station .....Luzerne County
Octorara ....Lancaster County
Ogontz ....Montgomery County
Ogontz School ...Montgomery County
Ohiopyle ....Fayette County
Ohioville ....Beaver County
Okeson (?) ....Juniata County
Okete ....York County
Okiola ....Delaware County
Okome ....Lycoming County
Oley ....Berks County
Oneida ....Schuylkill County
Oneida Junct. ....Luzerne County
Ono ....Lebanon County
Onondaga ....Jefferson County
Ontelaunee ....Berks County
Oregon ....Lancaster County
Oregon Hill ....Lycoming County
Osceola ....Tioga County
Osceola ....Clearfield County
Osceola Junct. ....Centre County
Osceola Mills ....Clearfield County
Osceolatown ....Clearfield County
Ottawa ....Montour County
Owasse ....Tioga County
Palanka ....Washington County
Passayunk ....Philadelphia County
Paupac ....Pike County
Paxinos ......Northumberland County
Paxinosa ....Northampton County

Paxtang ....Dauphin County
Paxton ....Dauphin County
Paxtoma ....Dauphin County
Pennypack ....Philadelphia County
Penobscot ....Luzerne County
Pequea ....Lancaster County
Pequea Creek ......Lancaster County
Pequea Station .....Lancaster County
Perkasie ....Bucks County
Perkiomen Junct. .....Chester County
Perkiomenville ...Montgomery County
Picture Rocks ....Chester County
Pocahontas ....Somerset County
Pocono ....Monroe County
Pocono Lake ....Monroe County
Pocono Manor ....Monroe County
Pocono Pines ....Monroe County
Pocono Summit ....Monroe County
Pocopson ....Chester County
Poponoming ....Monroe County
Port Allegany ....McKean County
Port Indian .....Montgomery County
Puckerty ....Jefferson County
Punxsutawney ......Jefferson County
Pymatuning ....Mercer County
Quakake ....Carbon County
Quakake ....Schuylkill County
Quemahoning ....Somerset County
Quemahoning Junct. .Somerset County
Rappahannock ......Schuylkill County
Saco (?) ....Bradford County
Saco ....Lackawanna County
Sagamore ....Armstrong County
Saginaw ....York County
Salunga ....Lancaster County
Sanatoga ....Montgomery County
Sancanac ....Chester County
Santee ....Northampton County
Saucon ....Lehigh County
Saucona Lake ....Lehigh County
Scahonda ....Elk County
Sciota ....Monroe County
Sciotavale ....Bradford County
Sciota ....Centre County
Secane ....Delaware County
Seneca ....Venango County
Sensenig ....Lancaster County
Sewickley ....Allegheny County
Sewickleyville ......Allegheny County
Shackamaxon ....Philadelphia County
Shamokin ....Northumberland County
Shamokin Dam ....Snyder County
Shannopin ....Beaver County
Shawanese ....Luzerne County
Shawmut ....Clearfield County
Shawnee ....Mifflin County
Shawnee on Delaware .Monroe County
Shehawken ....Wayne County
Shelocta ....Indiana County
Shenandoah ....Schuylkill County
Shenandoah Junct. ..Schuylkill County
Shenango ....Lawrence County
Shenango ....Mercer County
Sheshequin ....Bradford County

Shickshinny ....Luzerne County	Tuscarora ....Schuylkill County
Shingiss ....Washington County	Unamis ....Somerset County
Shohola ....Pike County	Upper Lehigh ....Luzerne County
Shohola Falls ....Pike County	Upper Lehigh Junct. ..Luzerne County
Sinnamahoning ......Cameron County	Mauch Chunk ....Carbon County
Siousca (?) ....Clinton County	Utah ....Indiana County
Sitka ....Fayette County	Utahville ....Clearfield County
Skippack ....Montgomery County	Venango ....Crawford County
South Erie ....Erie County	Venango ....Venango County
Standing Stone ......Bradford County	Wago ....York County
Starrucca ....Wayne County	Wago Junct. ....York County
Starrucca Station Susquehanna County	Wahneta ....Perry County
Suscon ....Luzerne County	Wampum ....Lawrence County
Susquehanna ....Lancaster County	Wanamie ....Luzerne County
Susquehanna ....Susquehanna County	Wanda ....Fayette County
Susquehanna Bridge .Clearfield County	Wandin ....Indiana County
Susquehanna Junct. ...Indiana County	Wanguam ....Wayne County
Swatara ....Schuylkill County	Wanneta ....Erie County
Swatara Gap ....Lebanon County	Wapasening ....Bradford County
Swatara Junct. ....Schuylkill County	Wapwallopen ....Luzerne County
Swatara Station .....Dauphin County	Warrior Run ....Luzerne County
Swenoda ....Montour County	Warrior Run .Northumberland County
Tacony ....Philadelphia County	Warrior Ridge ....Huntingdon County
Tamenend ....Schuylkill County	Warrior Mark ....Huntingdon County
Tamaqua ....Schuylkill County	Waukesha ....Clearfield County
Tamarac ....Crawford County	Wawa (?) ....Delaware County
Tamarack ....Clinton County	Wawset ....Chester County
Tampico ....Susquehanna County	Wesauking ....Bradford County
Tangas ....Clinton County	Wesco (?) ....Washington County
Tanguy ....Chester County	West Bangor ....Northampton County
Tanoma ....Indiana County	West Bangor ....York County
Tatamy ....Northampton County	West Bangor Junct. ....
Tecumseh Tannery ...Bedford County	.............Northampton County
Tedyuskung ....Pike County	Westcolang ....Pike County
Tiadaghton ....Tioga County	West Conshocken .Montgomery County
Tidioute ....Warren County	West Coplay ....Lehigh County
Tinicum ....Bucks County	West Indiana ....Indiana County
Tioga ....Philadelphia County	West Kittanning ...Armstrong County
Tioga ....Tioga County	West Manayunk ..Montgomery County
Tioga Junct. ....Tioga County	West Monocacy ....Berks County
Tiona ....Warren County	West Moshannon ....Clearfield County
Tionesta ....Forest County	West Nanticoke ......Luzerne County
Tionesta Station ......Forest County	West Wyoming ......Luzerne County
Tionesta Tannery ....Warren County	West Yough ....Fayette County
Tionesta Valley Junct. ....Elk County	Wheeling Junct. ....Allegheny County
Tippecanoe ....Fayette County	Wiconisco ....Dauphin County
Toboyne ....Perry County	Wilawana ....Bradford County
Tobyhanna ....Monroe County	Wingohocking ....Philadelphia County
Toby Mines ....Elk County	Wissahickon .....Philadelphia County
Tohickon ....Bucks County	Wissinoming .....Philadelphia County
Tomhickon ....Luzerne County	Wopsononock ....Blair County
Toughkenamon ....Chester County	Wyalusing ....Bradford County
Towanda ....Bradford County	Wyola ....Delaware County
Towanda Junct. .....Bradford County	Wyoming ....Luzerne County
Tucquan ....Lancaster County	Wyomissing ....Berks County
Tulpehocken ....Berks County	Wyomissing Junct. .....Berks County
Tulpehocken .....Philadelphia County	Wysox ....Bradford County
Tuna ....McKean County	Yohoghany .....Westmoreland County
Tuna Creek ....McKean County	Yough ....Fayette County
Tunkhannock ....Wyoming County	Yough Slope ....Westmoreland County
Tuscarora ....Juniata County	Yukon ....Westmoreland County

Many of the above names would hardly be recognized as being of Indian origin because of the change from the forms they once had.

Salunga is a part of the name Chiquesalunga; Toby is a corruption of a part of the name, Topi-hanna; Coplay is a corruption of Copeechan; Dagus is a part of the name Daguscahonda; Yough is a part of the name Youghioghenny, and so on through the list. Some of the names included in this list may not be of Indian origin at all, but they have been made up of Indian sounds. All of the historic names are found in the body of this work. There are about 10,200 Place Names in Pennsylvania (not including the names of streams), of this number about 480 are Indian names, historic and otherwise. Many of the names of historic places are not used in the state at present. It would be well to use these names, for new villages and other places, rather than to adopt names, such as Texas and Utah, which have no association whatever with the state. Some of the historic place names, such as Shamokin, Shannopin, Tioga etc., have been given to places which are far away from the place to which they belong, while the place to which the name does belong has been given a name which has no historical or even American significance whatever.

The following Counties have Indian names;

Allegheny, Erie, Indiana, Juniata, Lackawanna, Lehigh, Lycoming, Montour, Susquehanna, Tioga and Venango. Beaver should possibly be added, as its name is a translation of the Indian name, Tamaque, or Amochk, meaning "beaver."

The following Townships, arranged accordingly to Counties, have names of Indian origin;

Allegheny County—Chartiers, Indiana, Ohio, Sewickley, Killbuck.
Adams County—Conewago.
Armstrong County—Cowanshannock, Kiskiminetas, Kittanning, Mahoning.
Beaver County—Chippewa, New Sewickley, North Sewickley, Ohio, Big Beaver.
Bedford County—Juniata.
Berks County—Maxatawney, Otelaunee, Tulpehocken, Upper Tulpehocken, Oley.
Blair County—Allegheny, Frankstown, Juniata, Logan.
Bradford County—Sheshequin, Standing Stone, Towanda, North Towanda, Tuscarora, Wyalusing, Wysox.
Bucks County—Nockamixon, Perkasie, Tinicum.
Butler County—Allegheny, Conoquenessing, Venango.
Cambria County—Allegheny, Black Lick, Conemaugh, East Conemaugh, Susquehanna.
Carbon County—Mauch Chunk, Lehigh, Lower Towamensing, Mahoning Towamensing.
Cameron County—(none).
Centre County—(none).
Chester County—Nantmeal, Pocopson.

Clarion County—Toby.
Clearfield County—(none).
Clinton County—Bald Eagle, Logan (?).
Columbia County—Catawissa, Montour, Roaring Creek.
Crawford County—Conneaut, Cussewago, Shenango, Venango.
Cumberland County—(none).
Dauphin County—Conewago, Lower Paxton, Lower Swatara, Middle Paxton, Susquehanna, Swatara, Upper Paxton, Wiconisco.
Delaware County—Tinicum.
Elk County—(none).
Erie County—Conneaut, Venango.
Fayette County—(none).
Forest County—Hickory, Tionesta.
Franklin County—(none).
Fulton County—(none).
Greene County—Monongahela.
Huntingdon County—Juniata, Logan (?), Oneida, North Warriors Mark, South Warriorsmark.
Indiana County—Canoe, Conemaugh, Mahoning.
Jefferson County—(none).
Juniata County—Susquehanna, Tuscarora.
Lackawanna County—Lackawanna, Lehigh.

Lancaster County—East Cocalico, West Cocalico, Conestoga, Conoy, Pequea.

Lawrence County—Mahoning, Neshannock, Shenango, Big Beaver, Little Beaver, North Beaver.

Lebanon County—Swatara.

Lehigh County—Lower Macungie, Upper Macungie, Upper Saucon.

Luzerne County—Nescopeck.

Lycoming County—Loyalsock, Lycoming, Muncy Creek, Nippenose, Old Lycoming, Susquehanna.

McKean County—(none).

Mercer County—Delaware, East Lackawannock, Lackawannock, Pymatuning, Shenango.

Mifflin County—(none).

Monroe County—Pocono, Tobyhanna, Tunkhannock.

Montgomery County—Perkiomen, Skippack, Towamencing.

Montour County—Mahoning.

Northampton County—Lehigh, Upper Saucon.

Northumberland County—Chillisquaque, Little Mahanoy, Lower Mahanoy, Shamokin, Upper Mahanoy, Delaware.

Perry County—Juniata, Toboyne, Tuscarora.

Philadelphia County—(formerly had Kingsess, Manatawney, Perkiomen, Skippack, Passyunk, Moyamensing, Towamensing, Wayamensing. The City now includes all of these).

Pike County—Lackawaxen, Shohola, Delaware.

Potter County—Allegany, Genesee, Oswayo.

Schyulkill County—Mahanoy, Mahantongo, West Mahanoy.

Snyder County—(none).

Somerset County—Allegheny, Conemaugh, Quemahoning.

Sullivan County—(none).

Susquehanna County—Apolacon, Choconut.

Tioga County—Tioga.

Union County—(none).

Venango County—Allegheny, Cornplanter.

Warren County—Conewango, Kinzua, Brokenstraw.

Washington County—Chartiers, Peters, Cross Creek.

Wayne County—Lehigh, Oregon, Paupack, Texas.

Westmoreland County—Allegheny, Loyalhanna, Sewickley.

Wyoming County—Mehoopany, Meshoppen, Noxen (?), Tunkhannock.

York County—Codorus, Conewago, North Codorus.

Many of the above counties formerly contained Townships having Indian names. These have disappeared because of the growth in population of the Township, which has developed into a City. Many of these names, however, have been retained in the names of the Postal Districts, or sub-stations, in the city of which they have become a part. A few of the above names are translations of the Indian names. The list of Boroughs, villages, and stations will be found in the list which follows. All names of rivers and creeks will be found in the body of the work.

HISTORICAL NOTES

Historical Notes are given under the following Titles;

Actagouche
Adeeky, See Kittanning
Adjouquay
Allaquippa
Allegheny
Allequippas
Analomink
Antietam
Aploacon
Aquago, See Owego
Aquanshicola
Aquetong
Aramingo

Arronemink
Assarughney
Assunepachla
Aughwick
Bald Eagle
Beaver
Beaver Dams
Beech Creek
Big Island
Big Lick
Black Legs Creek
Black Lick, See Nesquehoning
Black Log.

Bloody Run
Brandt
Brokenstraw Creek
Brushy Creek
Buckaloons
Buffalo Creek
Burnt Cabins
Callapouse, See Capouse
Callapatscink
Calumet
Canadohta
Canaserage
Candowsa
Canoe Place
Capouse
Carantouan
Carkoen Creek
Carkoen's Hook
Cashietunk, See Coshecton
Catasaqua
Catawba
Catawissa
Catfish Camp
Chartiers Creek
Chartiers Town
Chemung
Chenastry, See Otzinachson
Chenango, See Shenango
Cherokee
Chester Creek
Chinkanning
Chicora
Chickasaw
Chiepassing
Chillisquaque
Chinklaclamoose
Chiquesalunga
Choconut, See Chugnut
Chowatin
Choctaw
Chugnut
Clarion
Clearfield Creek
Clistowakin
Coaquannock
Cocalico
Cocolamus
Cock Eye's Cabin
Cocoosing
Codorus
Cohocksink
Conejohela
Conemaugh
Conestoga
Conewango
Conewago
Conewanta
Conewingo
Conneaut
Conococheague
Conodogwinet
Conolloways
Cononodaw
Conoquenessing
Conoy

Conshohocken
Copeechan
Cornplanter
Coshecton
Cove Spring
Cowanesque
Cowanshannock
Crooked Creek
Cross Creek
Crum Creek
Cussewago
Daguscahonda
Dahoga, See Tioga
Dekanoagah
Delaware
Delaware, Falls of
Delaware, Forks of
Delaware Water Gap
Delaware, Indians
Deundaga, See Pittsburgh
Diahoga, See Tioga
Duck Creek, See Quin Quingua
Dunewangua, See Tuneungwant
Dunning's Sleeping Place
East Mauch Chunk, See Mauch Chunk
Easton, See Lehigh
East Texas, See Texas
Elk Creek
Endless Mountains, See Kittatinny
Edmund's Swamp
Equinunk
Erie
Fishing Creek
Frankstown
French Creek
French Margaret's
Friedenshuetten, See Wyalusing
Friedensstadt, See Languntouteneunk
Ganagarahhare
Ganoga Lake
Gawango
Genesee
Genossa
Glasswanoge
Gnadenhuetten
Gnahay
Guyasuta, See Cornplanter
Goshgoshink
Garagaroharre
Great Island, See Big Island
Harris' Ferry
Hart's Log
Hataorackan Creek
Hiawatha
Hickory Town
Hockendauqua
Hocking Junction
Hog's Town, See Goshgoshink
Honeoye
Hoopany Creek
Indian
Inomoy
Ingaren
Iroquois
Jack's Narrows

Jacobs Creek
Jacobs Cabins
Jenuchsedaga
Juniata
Kankanken, See Carkoen's
Keewaudin
Kickenapaulings
Killbuck
King Beaver's Town
Kingsessing
Kinzua
Kishacoquillas
Kiskiminetas
Kittanning
Kittatinny
Kushequa
Kushkushdatening
Kuskuski
Lacomick Creek
Lackawanna
Lackawannock
Lackawaxen
Lamoco
Lamoka
Languntouteneunk
Lawunakhannek
Lehigh
Lehighton
Lenape
Lenni Mills
Lepos Peters Town
Lequepees
Le Tort's Spring
Lick Run.
Little Beaver
Little Conemaugh
Little Moshannon
Little Schuylkill
Logan's Valley
Logstown
Long Island
Loyalhanna
Loyalsock
Lycamahoning
Lycippus
Lycoming
Macungy
Maghinquechahocking
Maguck
Mahackensink
Mahoning
Mahanoy
Mahontango
Makerisk Kitton
Makoomihay
Malson
Manahan
Manaitin
Manatawny
Manayunk
Mancatawangum
Manhattan
Marcus Hook
Masgeek-hanne

Matinicum
Mattawana
Mauch Chunk
Maunquay
Maxatawny
Mecheek-menatey
Meech-hanne
Meggeckesjouw
Mehoopany
Meniologameka
Meshoppen
Miantonomah
Milwaukee
Mingo Bottom
Mingo Town
Minisink
Minnequa
Minooka
Minquas Creek
Mitchell's Sleeping Place
Mohocamac
Mohocks Branch
Mohulbucteetam
Mokoma
Moncanaqua
Monocasy
Monockonock
Monody
Monongahela
Monseytown
Montour
Moosic
Moravia
Moselem
Moshannon
Muckinipattus
Mowhewamick
Moyamensing
Muncy
Munsee
Murdering Town
Muscanetcunk
Naaman's Creek
Nanticoke
Nayaug
Nekoda
Nemacolin's Trail
Nescopec
Neshaminy
Neshannock
Nesquehoning
Neversink
Newtown
Newtychanning
Niantic
Nippenose
Nittabakonck
Nittany
Nockamixon
Nolamattink
North Mehoopany
North Sewickley
North Towanda
Octorara

Oghquagy
Ogontz
Ohesson
Ohiopyle
Ohio
Okehocking
Okome
Old Town
Oley
Oneida
Onoko, Glen
Onondaga
Ontelaunee
Opessa's Town
Onontejo
Oquaga
Orechton's Island
Oscalui
Osceola
Osewingo, See Shenango
Oskohary
Ostonwakin
Oswayo
Otsiningy, See Shenango
Ottawa
Otzinachson
Ouaquago, See Owego
Owego
Paghahacking
Paint Creek
Pahkehoma
Panawakee
Passigachkunk
Passyunk
Panpack
Paxinous
Paxtang, See Paxton
Paxton
Pechoquealing
Pennypack
Penn's Creek
Penobscot
Pequea
Perkiomen
Peter's Creek
Pine Creek
Pittsburgh
Playwicky
Plum Creek
Poakopohkunk
Pocahontas
Pochapuchkung
Pocono
Pocopson
Pohopco
Poketo
Popacton
Popometang
Poponoming
Poquessing
Portage Creek
Port Allegany
Potomac
Punxsutawney

Pymatuning
Quakake
Queen Esther's Town
Que, Isle of,
Quemahoning
Quenischaschacki
Queonemysing
Quissinawomink
Quilutimack
Quing Quingus
Quitapahilla
Raccoon Creek
Raystown
Redstone
Sagamore
Saginaw
Sakhauwotung
Salt Lick
Salt Lick Town
Sandy Lick Creek
Sankinack
Salunga
Saucon
Sawcunk, See Shingas T.
Schantowano, See Wyoming
Schuylkill
Sciota
Secane
Seekaughkunt
Senangelstown
Seneca
Sepassincks
Serechen
Sewickley
Shades of Death
Shadow of Death
Shackamaxon
Shallyschohking
Shamokin
Shannopin's Town
Shawmut
Shawnee
Shawnee Cabins
Shawnee Flats
Shaver's Sleeping Place
Shehawken
Shelocta
Shenandoah
Shenango
Sheoquaga
Sheshequin
Shickshinny
Shikellamy's Town
Shingas Old Town
Shohola
Shohokin
Sinnemahoning
Skehandowana
Skippack
Slippery Rock
Snake Town
Standing Stone
Starucca
Stillwater Creek
Stony Creek

Sugar Cabins
Susquehanna
Swatara
Swegatsy
Tacony
Tamaqua
Tamarack
Tamenend
Tangascoutack
Taorackan
Tatamy
Techorassi
Tenicum
Three Springs
Ten Mile Run
Texas
Tidioute
Tinicum
Tioga
Tiona
Tionesta
Tippecanoe
Tiquamingy Town
Tiozinossogachta
Tobeco
Tobyhanna
Tohickon
Tolheo
Tombicon
Tomihicken
Tonoloway
Toughkenamon
Towamensing
Towanda
Tsanandowa
Tucquan
Tulpehocken
Tumanaranaming
Tuneungwant
Tunkhanna
Tunkhannock
Tuppehanna
Turkey Foot
Turtle Creek
Tuscarawas
Tuscarora
Tutelo Town
Twightwees

Two Lick Creek
Tyadaghton
Umbelicamence
Unadilla
Venango
Wallenpaupack
Wallpack
Wampum
Wanamie
Wanneta
Wappasuning
Wapwallopen
Warriors Ridge
Warriors Run
Warriors Trail
Water Street
Waukesha
Wawa
Wawaset
Wechquetank
Welagamika
West Conshohocken
West Moshannon
Wheeling
White Deer
White Deer Hole
Wiccaco
Wiconisco
Willawanna
Will's Creek
Wingohocking
Wissahickon
Wissinoming
Wolf Creek
Wopsononock
Wyalusing
Wynola
Wynooska
Wyoming
Wymissing
Wysox
Wywamick
Yellow Breeches Creek
Yoroonwago
Youghiogheny
Young Woman's Creek
Zinachson

BIBLIOGRAPHY

It is impossible to give a complete list of all of the authorities used, as many of these were records of various County Courts, documents in various Historical Societies, magazine articles, letters, information received from persons at many places along the old trails, and many other sources of information. When possible these sources are mentioned under the various articles. The chief authorities used were the Colonial Records and Archives of Pennsylvania, and the various Journals of the early explorers and travellers through this state. The early maps, a list of which follows, were constantly used, not only when writing the articles, but also on the tramps over the Indian trails, and early traders paths.

The dates of publication of the Colonial Records and Archives, from which quotations are made, are as follows:

Colonial Records—Vols. I. II. III., 1852; IV. V. VI. VII., 1851; VIII. IX. X. XI., 1852; XII. XIII. XIV. XV. XVI., 1853. Archives, First Series; I. II., 1852; III. to VIII., 1853; IX. X., 1854; XI., 1855; XII., 1856.

Archives, Second Series—Vol. 1., 1874; II., 1876; III., 1875; IV., 1876; V., 1890; VI., 1877; VII., 1878; VIII., 1896; IX., 1895; X., 1896; XI., 1895; XII., 1896; XIII., 1896; XIV., 1888; XV., 1893; XVI., 1890; XVII., 1892; XVIII., 1893; XIX., 1893.

Archives, Third Series—I. II., 1894; III., 1896; IV., 1894; V. to X., 1896; XI. to XX., 1897; XXI., 1898; XXII., 1897; XXIII. to XXV., 1897; XXVI., 1899—besides four Index Vols.

Fifth Series—Vols. I. to VIII., 1906.

Sixth Series—Vols. I. to XVI., 1906-1907.

Frontier Forts of Pennsylvania—Vols. I. II., 1896.

References are made to the following works:

Albach, J. R., Western Annals, Pittsburgh, 1858.

Albert, G. D., History of Westmoreland County, 1882.

American Historical Association, Report, Part. 2, 1905 (Bibliography).

Beauchamp, W. M., Aboriginal Place Names in New York, 1907.

Boucher, J. N., History of Westmoreland County, 1906.

Boucher, J. N., History of Century and a Half of Pittsburgh, 1908.

Brackenridge, H. M., History of Whiskey Insurrection, 1859.

Brodhead, L. W., Delaware Water Gap, 1870.

Bureau of American Ethnology, various Reports and Bulletins.

Burk, J. D., History of Virginia, 1804-1816.

Butterfield, C. W., Historical Account of the Exped. against Sandusky, 1873.

Butterfield, C. W., History of the Girtys, Cincinnati, 1890.

Cammerhoff, Bishop, Journal of 1748, in Penna. Magazine Hist. and Biog., XXIX., 160, 1905.

Carnegie Museum, Annals of Vols. I. III.

Centennial History of Connellsville, (a number of Editors), 1906.

Chapman, T. J., The French in the Ohio Valley, 1887.

Contributions to American History, Memorials Hist. Soc. Penna., VI., 1858.

Cort, Cyrus, Col. Henry Bouquet, and his Campaigns of 1763-64. 1883.

Craig, N. B., History of Pittsburgh, 1851.

Crumrine, Boyd, History of Washington County, 1882.

Crumrine, Boyd, History of the Old Virginia Court at Augusta Town, 1905.

Darlington, W. M., Gist's Journals, 1893.

Darlington, Mary C., Fort Pitt and Letters from the Frontier, 1892.

Day, Sherman, Historical Collections of Penna., 1843.

Denny, Ebenezer, Journal of, in Memorials of Hist. Soc. Penna., VIII., 1860.

DeSchweinitz, Edmund, Life and Times of David Zeisberger, 1870.

Doddridges Notes, (Ritenour Ed.), 1912.

Drake, S. G., Biography and Hist. of Indians of North America, 1834.

Drake, S. G., Aboriginal Races of North America, 1848.

Dunn, J. P., True Indian Stories, 1908.

Ellis, Franklin, History of Fayette County, 1882.

Egle, Wm. H., History of Pennsylvania, 1883.

Findley, Wm. History of the Insurrection of 1794, 1796.

Fiske, John, New France and New England, 1902.

Ford, W. C., Writings of Washington, 1889-1893.

Frost, John, Border Wars of the West, 1854.

Handbook of American Indians, Parts 1 and 2, 1907-1910.

Hamilton Library Association, Carlisle, various publications.

Hanna, C. A., Wilderness Trail, Vols. I and II., 1911.

Hassler, E. W., Old Westmoreland, 1900.

Hazard, Ebenezer, Historical Collections, 1792-1794.

Heckewelder, John, Narrative of the Missions of the U. B. Church, 1820.

Heckewelder, John, Indian Nations of Penna., Memorials of Hist. Soc. Penna., XII. 1876.

Heckewelder, John, Names which the Lenni-Lennape etc., 1872.

Hemminger, J. D., Old Roads of Cumberland County, Carlisle, 1909.

Hennepin, Louis, A New Discovery of a Vast Country, etc., Chicago, 1903.

Historical and Scientific Sketches of Michigan, 1834.

Houghton, Frederick, The Seneca Nation from 1655 to 1687, Buffalo, 1912.

Hulbert, Archer B., Historic Highways, Vol. 2., 1902.

Indian Affairs, Reports of Commissioner of, 1849-1912.

Jenkins, H. M., Pennsylvania, Colonial and Federal, 3 Vols., 1905.

Jordan, John W., The Journal of Lieut. Col Adam Hubley, 1909.

Killikenny, S. H., History of Pittsburgh, 1906.

Kittochtinny Historical Society, Vols. I to VII., 1898-1912.

Loskiel G. H., History of the Missions of the U. B. etc., London, 1794.

Lowdermilk, W. H., History of Cumberland, Maryland, 1878.

Meginness, J. F., Otzinachson, a History of the West Branch, 1856.

Memoirs of the Hist. Soc. Penna., I. to XIV., 1826-1895.

Miner, C. P., History of Wyoming, 1845.

Mooney, James, The Siouan Tribes of the East, Washington, 1894.

McCauley, J. H., History of Franklin County, 1878.

McKnight, Charles, Captain Jack, the Scout, 1873.

New York, Documents relating to Colonial History, I. to XV., 1853-1887.

Newton, J. H., History of Venango County, 1879.

Olden Time, N. B. Craig, 2 Vols., 1846.

Parke, Judge J. E., Historical Gleanings, Boston, 1886.

Parker, A. C., The Code of Handsome Lake, 1913.

Parkman, Francis, Conspiracy of Pontiac, 1895.

Parkman, Francis, Montcalm a n d Wolfe, 1897-1898.

Patterson, A. W., History of the Backwoods, 1843.

Pilling, J. C., Bibliography of the Iroquoian Language, Washington, 1888.

Pilling, J. C., Bibliography of the Algonquian Language, Washington, 1891.

Pritts, J., Border Life, 1839.

Records of Upland Court, Memorials of Hist. Soc. Penna., VII., 1860.

Reichel, W. C., Memorials of the Moravian Church, Vol. I., 1870.

Rupp, I. D., History of Western Penna., 1846.

Sargent, Winthrop, Hist. Braddock's Expedition, Mem. Hist. Soc. Penna., V. 1855.

Searight, T. B., The Old Pike (Cumberland, or National), 1894.

Sparks, Jared, Writings of Washington, 1834-1837.

Smith, William, Historical Account of Bouquet's Exped., 1764, 1868.

Smith, Joseph, Old Redstone, 1854.

Smithsonian Institution, various Reports-mentioned under article.

Sullivan, Gen. John., The Journals of the Military Exped. of 1887.

Thomas, Cyrus, Work on Mound Exploration, Washington, 1887.

Thomas, Cyrus, The Circular, Square and Octagonal Earthworks of Ohio, 1889.

Thomas, Cyrus, Catalogue of Prehistoric Works, Washington, 1891.

Thomas, Cyrus, Problem of the Ohio Mounds, Washington, 1889.

Thwaites, R. G., Early Western Travels, 1748-1846, I.-XXXII., 1904-1907.

Thwaites, R. G., Jesuit Relations, I.-LXXIII., 1896-1901.

Tioga County Historical Society, Wellsboro, various publications.

Tooker, W. W., The Indian Place Names on Long Island, 1911.

VanVoorhis, J. S., The Old and New Monongahela, 1893.

Veech, James, Monongahela of Old, 1858-1892.

Virginia Historical Soc. Collections, N. S., I.-XI., 1882-1892.

Waddell, Jos. A., Annals of Augusta County, Virginia, Richmond, 1886.

Walton, J. S., Conrad Weiser and the Indian Policy of Col. Penna., 1900.

Watson, J. F., Annals of Philadelphia, 2 Vols., 1850.

West Virginia, Reports of the Dept. of Archives and Hist., 3 Vols. 1906-1911.

Wyoming Commemorative Association, various publications, 1882-1903.

Wyoming Hist. and Geological Society, Various publications, 1895 etc.

Zeisberger, David, History of the Indians of North America, 1910.

Zeisberger, David, Journals of 1767 and 1768, MS. copy from original.

The following maps have been used, and are referred to in the various articles:

Adlum, Pennsylvania, 1790.

Bellin, Louisiana, 1744.

Bonnecamp, Ohio River, 1749.

Coronelli, Lake Region, 1689.

Crevcoeur, Beaver, Muskingum, 1787.

DeAbbeville (Sanson), America, 1656.

De Lisle, Louisiana, 1718.

DeWitt, Susquehanna River, 1790.

Ellicott, Bound. Survey, 1786.

Esnaut and Rapilly, U. S., 1777.

Evans, Penna., Ohio, etc., 1749, 1755, 1775.

Filson, Kentucky, 1784.

Franquelin, Ohio Valley, 1684.

Fry and Jefferson, Penna., etc., 1755.

Gist, West Penna., 1753.

Guy Johnson, New York etc., 1771.

Hennepin, Louisiana, 1687.

Herrmann, Maryland, 1670.

Hill, Philadelphia, 1801-07.

Historical Map of Penna., 1875.

Holme, Penna., 1681-03.

Homann Herrs, 1756.

Howell, Penna., 1792.

Hutchins, Ohio, Penna., etc., 1764.

Jacobsz, America, 1621.

Lindström's Geographia Americae, Amandus Johnson, 1925.

Lodge, Susquehanna, 1779.

Manor Maps, Archives, 3rd. Ser., IV.

Mayo, Potomac, 1737.

Morris, Penna., 1848.

Pouchot, Penna., etc., 1758.

Pownall, Penna., etc., 1776.

Reed, Philadelphia, 1777.

Scull, Penna., 1759.

Scull, Penna., 1770.

Taylor Survey Maps, MS. Hist. Soc. Pa.

Van Der Donck, New Neth., 1656.

Van Keulen, New France, 1720.

Vaugondy, America, 1778.

West. Penna., and Virginia, 1756.

U. S. Geological Survey Maps.

Pennsylvania Geological Survey maps.

Recent state maps, published by the Dept. of Internal Affairs.

Also many of the Warrantee Survey maps, maps of the "Donation Lands" etc.